RICHES AND RENUNCIATION

OXFORD STUDIES IN SOCIAL AND CULTURAL ANTHROPOLOGY

Oxford Studies in Social and Cultural Anthropology represents the work of authors, new and established, which will set the criteria of excellence in ethnographic description and innovation in analysis. The series serves as an essential source of information about the world and the discipline.

OTHER TITLES IN THE SERIES

Organizing Jainism in India and England
Marcus Banks

Society and Exchange in Nias
Andrew Beatty

Global Migrants, Local Lives: Travel and Transformation in Rural Bangladesh
Katy Gardner

Contested Hierarchies: A Collaborative Ethnography of Caste in the
Kathmandu Valley, Nepal
David N. Gellner and Declan Quigley

The Culture of Coincidence: Accident and Absolute Liability in Huli
Laurence Goldman

The Female Bridegroom: A Comparative Study of Life-Crisis
Rituals in South India and Sri Lanka
Anthony Good

Of Mixed Blood: Kinship and History in Peruvian Amazonia
Peter Gow

Exchange in Oceania: A Graph Theoretic Analysis
Per Hage and Frank Harary

The Archetypal Actions of Ritual: A Theory of Ritual Illustrated by
the Jain Rite of Worship
Caroline Humphrey and James Laidlaw

The People of the Alas Valley: A Study of an Ethnic Group of Northern Sumatra
Akifumi Iwabuchi

Nuer Prophets: A History of Prophecy from the Upper Nile
in the Nineteenth and Twentieth Centuries
Douglas H. Johnson

Knowledge and Secrecy in an Aboriginal Religion: Yolngu of North-East Arnhem Land
Ian Keen

The Interpretation of Caste
Declan Quigley

The Arabesk Debate: Music and Musicians in Modern Turkey
Martin Stokes

Inside the Cult: Religious Innovation and Transmission
in Papua New Guinea
Harvey Whitehouse

RICHES
AND
RENUNCIATION

RELIGION, ECONOMY, AND
SOCIETY AMONG THE JAINS

JAMES LAIDLAW

CLARENDON PRESS · OXFORD
1995

Oxford University Press, Walton Street, Oxford OX2 6DP

Oxford New York
Athens Auckland Bangkok Bombay
Calcutta Cape Town Dar es Salaam Delhi
Florence Hong Kong Istanbul Karachi
Kuala Lumpur Madras Madrid Melbourne
Mexico City Nairobi Paris Singapore
Taipei Tokyo Toronto
and associated companies in
Berlin Ibadan

Oxford is a trade mark of Oxford University Press

Published in the United States
by Oxford University Press Inc., New York

British Library Cataloguing in Publication Data
Data available

Library of Congress Cataloging in Publication Data

Laidlaw, James.
Riches and renunciation: religion, economy, and society among the Jains/James Laidlaw.
—(Oxford studies in social and cultural anthropology)
Includes bibliographical references.
1. Jainism—India—Jaipur. 2. Jainism—Social aspects. 3. Jaipur (India)—Religious life
and customs. I. Title II. Series.
BL1325.9.J34L35 1995   294.4'0954'4—dc20   95-20277
ISBN 0–19–828031–9
ISBN 0–19–828042–4 (Pbk)

1 3 5 7 9 10 8 6 4 2

Typeset by Best-set Typesetter Ltd., Hong Kong
Printed in Great Britain
on acid-free paper by
Biddles Ltd., Guildford and King's Lynn

ACKNOWLEDGEMENTS

I SHOULD like to thank all those who helped me during the fieldwork on which this book is based, which was conducted in north-west India, mostly in the city of Jaipur, between 1984 and 1990. Kavita Srivastava was a source of moral guidance, practical support, and intellectual stimulation during all this time. She and her family always made me welcome, and I am deeply indebted to them all. Kamal Dagga was an unfailing source of help, companionship, and good humour. Sunita Meharchandani, as Sunita Jain, discussed with me almost every puzzle about Jainism I came across in the later years of fieldwork, and for her interest and her help I am extremely grateful.

I should like to be able to thank all the people I met during those years who helped me in learning about Jainism, but of course there are many whose names I never knew. A collective thanks seems in order to a religious community which has been, as a whole, extraordinarily open and helpful. The following people were especially kind and generous with their time and knowledge in various aspects of my work: the late Pravartini Sajjan Shri ji Maharaj Sahab, Gani Shri Mani Prabh Sagar ji Maharaj Sahab, Sadhvi Priyadarshana Shri ji Maharaj Sahab, Dr Narendra Bhanavat, Dr Hukamchand Bharilla, Mr and Mrs P. L. Dagga, Mr and Mrs H. Dhaddha, Mr S. L. Gandhi, Ravinder Jain, Prem Chand Jain, Mr and Mrs S. C. Jain, Anju Dhaddha Mishra, Sanjeev Mishra, Shri Dhanroopmal Nagori, the late Mrs Phophalia, Mrs Saceti, Dr K. C. Sogani, Meenu Srivastava, Dr (Mrs) Pawan Surana, the late Shri Rajroop-ji Tank, and Mr D. C. Tank. Both Shri Jyoti Kumar Kothari and Shri Rajendra Kumar Shrimal spent many hours teaching me about Jainism. I hope they are not now too dismayed.

I am grateful to the Jain Vishva Bharati and the University of Rajasthan, both of which granted me affiliation during fieldwork; and to Professor N. K. Singhi, of the Department of Sociology at the University, for his insights into Jain society. Professor and Mrs T. K. N. Unnithan were kind and supportive during all my stays in Jaipur, and I am extremely grateful to them. I wish that it were still possible to thank in person the late Dr K. M. Mathur, who gave me a home in Jaipur for many years.

In Cambridge, my greatest academic debt is to Carrie Humphrey, who, as teacher, colleague, collaborator, and friend, has been my model all along of how to be an anthropologist. She has been prevailed upon to comment on all parts of this book, in all the stages of its long development. As has Peter Allen. His help, encouragement, and moral support have been, quite simply, conditions *sine qua non* for the completion of the work. The following people have read all or parts of one or more of the many versions the book has gone through, and I am grateful for their comments, corrections, and criticisms: Alan Babb, Marcus Banks, Chris Bayly, Barbara Bodenhorn, Pascal Boyer, Michael Carrithers, John Cort, Richard Davies, Paul Dundas, Catharine Edwards, Chris Fuller, Diego Gambetta, Leo Howe, Tanya Luhrmann, Hamish Park, Jonathan Parry, Josephine Reynell, Roger Smedley, Vinay Srivastava, Paul Taylor, and Giles Tillotson. Thanks also are due, for academic guidance and advice, to Stephen Hugh-Jones, Alan Macfarlane, K. R. Norman, and John D. Smith.

Much of the early research for this book was conducted with the financial support of the Economic and Social Research Council. I have also benefited from grants from the Nuffield Foundation, the Richards Fund, and the Smuts Memorial Fund.

King's College Cambridge has given me not only generous financial support, but also an extraordinarily stimulating environment in which to learn and work, and a home. Like many people at King's, I am indebted to Tony Tanner, for warning me of the dangers of the Penelope Syndrome, and insisting that I get the thing finished.

CONTENTS

List of Plates and Figures　　　　　　　　　　　　　　ix
List of Maps　　　　　　　　　　　　　　　　　　　　x

1. Introduction　　　　　　　　　　　　　　　　　　1

　　PART I. STANCES, RELATIONSHIPS, EVALUATIONS
2. The Mystery of the Visible　　　　　　　　　　　　25
3. Aspects of Organization　　　　　　　　　　　　　48
4. A Theology of Interdiction　　　　　　　　　　　　65

　　PART II. VARIOUS AND PARTICULAR LOCATIONS
5. Social Dimensions of Jain Identity　　　　　　　　　83
6. City, Locality, and Leadership　　　　　　　　　　120

　　PART III. FORMS OF RENOUNCING SELF
7. The Ascetic Imperative　　　　　　　　　　　　　151
8. Schemes, Regimes, and Religious Retirement　　　　173
9. Acts Which Are Not　　　　　　　　　　　　　　190
10. Fasting: Scorched Earth and Fertile Soil　　　　　　216
11. Embodied Ontologies　　　　　　　　　　　　　230
12. Paryushan: Austerity and Increase in Counterpoint　275

　　PART IV. MATTERS FOR NEGOTIATION
13. The Values and Perils of Exchange　　　　　　　　289
14. The Gift That Doesn't Really Happen　　　　　　　302
15. Magnificent Parsimony　　　　　　　　　　　　324

　　PART V. RICHES AND REDEMPTION
16. Family Enterprise and Religious Community　　　　349
17. Diwali: Renunciation Humanized and Riches Redeemed　364
18. Conclusion　　　　　　　　　　　　　　　　　388

Glossary　　　　　　　　　　　　　　　　　　　395
References　　　　　　　　　　　　　　　　　　399
Index　　　　　　　　　　　　　　　　　　　　427

LIST OF PLATES AND FIGURES

Plates

I.	Khartar Gacch nuns with a layman	2
II.	A *samosaran* painting	32
III.	A Jain layman bathing a Jina statue	45
IV.	A *siddha-cakra puja*	46
V.	Jain nuns blessing a fasting woman	57
VI and VII.	Idols of Jain protector deities	66–7
VIII.	Jain temples at Palitana	96
IX and X.	Street scenes in Jaipur	128–9
XI.	The late Shriman Amarcand-ji Nahar	234
XII.	A Shvetambar Jina idol	246
XIII.	A Guru Dev idol	260
XIV.	The late *pravartini* Vicakshan Shri-ji and a disciple	264
XV.	An idol of Vicakshan Shri-ji	265
XVI–XVIII.	Nuns on their alms-round in Jaipur	310–11
XIX–XXII.	Diwali in Jaipur	366–7

Figures

1.	*Siddha-cakra yantra*	222
2.	Rice pattern used in temple-worship and at sermons	268

LIST OF MAPS

1. Western India   86
2. Jaipur City   121

1

Introduction

JAIN renouncers are men and women who have left their families and given away all their material possessions to lead a wandering life of asceticism and religious teaching. There are several different Jain traditions, and the rules which renouncers follow vary between them, but in all cases the life they prescribe is one of justly famed severity.

Jain renouncers all go barefoot, they do not bathe, and they do not shave or cut their hair, so in some traditions the men have beards, but it is common practice twice each year to pull out the hair from both the head and face by hand; and on many of the older men only wispy white remnants of a beard remain. All Jain renouncers carry a special broom with which to brush insects from their way without harming them. They lead a celibate and itinerant life, travelling in small, single-sex groups, and making their way on foot between towns and villages, teaching the importance of non-attachment and non-violence, and encouraging others to follow their example in fasting and other ascetic practices. The ideal, and in some cases the actual culmination of the renouncer's life, is a fast to death.

From whichever tradition they come, Jain monks and nuns make an arresting sight. The monks in the Digambar (or 'sky-clad') tradition go completely naked; in some groups of the Shvetambar (or 'white-clad') tradition, who all wear only simple white robes, neither monks nor nuns are ever to be seen without masks strapped to their faces to cover the mouth and nose. These practices are ways of realizing two of the most insistent concerns of all Jain renouncers: *aparigraha*, or having no attachments, especially personal property; and *ahimsa*, avoiding causing harm to even the tiniest living thing. The face-masks prevent insects from being accidentally swallowed, and minimize the harm which the renouncer's hot breath will cause to unseen life-forms in the air.

Thus a vivid image of a religious ideal—an exemplary ascetic life of world-renunciation, non-attachment, and non-violence—is inscribed on Jain renouncers' bodies and legible wherever they are present. And Jain teaching makes clear that this image is the central ideal of the religion.

PLATE I. Khartar Gacch nuns with a layman. This photograph was taken in the Dadabari in Jaipur. A young layman is receiving religious instruction from a senior nun. She is consulting a Sanskrit text while two of her disciples look on.

The goal of the renouncer's austere way of life is a condition which the Jains call *moksh*, the final liberation of the soul from earthly and embodied existence. Each living thing has a soul whose innate qualities are insight, knowledge, energy, and bliss. Unimpeded, the soul would rise to the summit of the universe, there to subsist forever in tranquil enjoyment of these qualities, as a pure and perfect consciousness. But from beginningless time each soul has been obliged repeatedly to live and die in countless embodied forms: as a human being; an animal; a plant; a tiny unseen creature which lives only for an instant in air, fire, earth, or water; as an inhabitant of one of many terrible hells; or as one of many classes of deity in an elaborate hierarchy of heavens. These gods certainly enjoy pleasure, but this universe of circulating souls is overwhelmingly characterized by pain, sickness, wickedness, loss, and want, and even their pleasure is transitory. Like all other forms of life the gods will soon go through the agonies of death, then those of birth, and resume their life of suffering in another body.

The cycle of death and rebirth is called *samsar*, and the force which keeps it in motion is *karma*. The word *karma* means 'action' and also the unseen 'traces' of action. The idea that these traces affect what happens to the agent in the future according to a broadly ethical logic—if you do good *karma* your *karma* will bring you good results—is ubiquitous in Indic religious traditions, but the general idea takes many forms.[1] Jain teachers are unique, I think, in claiming unequivocally that *karma* is a kind of matter, and therefore something which conforms to mechanical laws of cause and effect.[2] Each action by a living thing causes particles of *karma* matter to adhere to its soul. They obscure its true qualities so that it suffers anger, pride, delusion, and greed. This leads it to initiate still further actions, attract still further *karma*, and so still further perpetuate its suffering.

The rules which govern a renouncer's life interrupt this vicious cycle. By disciplined ascetic practice and carefully abstaining from any sinful action, he or she may progressively extricate the soul from entanglement with *karma*. Even after a life-time of harsh asceticism it is impossible actually to achieve this goal, but almost everything Jain renouncers do— each of the austerities prescribed in their monastic rule—is conceived as a step towards reaching it. It will take many, many lives, and it is not until the last particle falls away, and the last of its bodies dies, that the soul will achieve this religion's highest goal.

The defining figures in Jainism are thus not those hedonistic deities, but the ascetic renouncers. It is renouncers, both living and dead, who are the central objects of religious veneration. Incomparably the greatest of these are the twenty-four fabled renouncers of the distant past, the Jinas—the word means 'Conquerors'—who each in their own time discovered how finally to escape the cycle of death and rebirth, and by teaching this to others founded an order of Jain renouncers and so re-established, for the age in which they each lived, the Jain religion. The Jinas have all attained *moksh*, so they are forever removed entirely from human affairs—not a real presence but a divine absence.

What kind of life is founded on the pursuit of an impossible goal? What kind of religion is focused on such a quest?

This book is a study of how Jainism is practised in north-west India. The focus is on two Shvetambar Jain traditions, the Khartar Gacch and

---

[1] Keyes and Daniel, *Karma*; O'Flaherty, *Karma and Rebirth*; Pappu, *Dimensions of Karma*. The expression 'Indic religion' is used in this book in recognition of the densely overlapping symbolism, and thematic similarities in doctrine, which link Jainism, Buddhism, and the diverse traditions known as 'Hinduism.' Although Islam is not in this sense very 'Indic', I do not mean to imply that it is not an 'Indian religion'.

[2] See Jaini, 'Karma and Rebirth'; Reichenbach, *Law of Karma*, ch. 6.

Tapa Gacch, and most especially on the families who are followers of these traditions in the main Jain districts of Jaipur city. As is generally the case among the Jains, these families are on the whole active and dedicated followers of the religion. This is especially so during periods when there are renouncers living among them, but even at other times the social mores of the community and the everyday lives of its members are shaped in profound ways by Jain religious values. The daily rites in local temples are well attended and local public events are almost all religious. Like the renouncers, members of Jain families engage in ascetic exercises and in periodic fasting.

But this does not mean that lay Jain communities come to resemble renouncer orders. Nothing in the latter's strict regime would prepare one for the celebration and enthusiasm which attend Jain religious ceremonies, for the colour and opulence of their collective life, for their wealth, for their frank and cheerful pride in that wealth, or for the manifold ways it is linked with asceticism. Like most Jain communities, the Khartar Gacch and Tapa Gacch Jains of Jaipur are generally affluent, and their collective religious life is presided over by members of the most successful business families—in this case, for the most part, wealthy merchants who dominate the city's emerald-trading market, which is one of the largest in the world. It would be going too far to say that it is always the richest lay Jains who have the reputation for being the most religious; but it would only be going too far. In any case it is clear that the Jain religion provides for these families a medium in which to celebrate their worldly success, and to express and affirm the continuity of both family and local community. Yet the doctrine of the religion, as expressed by local teachers and by Jain renouncers themselves, is a soteriology—a project and a set of prescriptions for how to bring one's life to an end.

This book is about how it is possible to live by that ideal. In this respect it joins a number of recent attempts to deepen our understanding of the role renunciation plays in Indian religious life. How does renunciation comport with more worldly ethical values such as auspiciousness, purity, and domesticity?[3] What are the competing understandings and evalu-

---

[3] Das, *Structure and Cognition*; Khare, *Hearth and Home*; Madan, *Non-Renunciation*; Marglin, *Wives of the God-King*; and the essays collected by Carman and Marglin, *Purity and Auspiciousness*, have all illustrated the subtlety and importance of non-renunciatory values in Hinduism; while Gold, *Fruitful Journeys*, has shown how, in pilgrimage, renunciation does play a part in ordinary Hindu life. On this see also Daniel, *Fluid Signs*. Studies which stress non-renunciatory aspects of Buddhism include Southwold, *Buddhism in Life*; Ortner, *Sherpas Through Their Rituals*.

ations of renunciation in the Indic world?[4] How and by whom are ascetic ideals invoked in political conflict and status competition?[5] The Jain case poses a question of particular force, which I shall try to answer in this book. How is it possible to live by impossibly strict ascetic values?

While I shall describe in general terms how renouncers themselves are organized to do this, I shall not be concerned with whether or not, or in what ways, the reality of renouncers' spiritual life corresponds to the inscribed meaning of their life and practice. My interest is in the social and cultural form of the religion as a whole, and this means I shall be concerned for the most part with lay Jains: those people, several thousand times more numerous than the renouncers themselves, who retain homes and families, but for whom the centre of their religious life is the veneration and emulation of these living ascetics, and the worship—perhaps in the form of temple idols[6]—of the Jinas and other great renouncers of the past.

And if I seek to answer this question principally with respect to lay Jains this is not because I think that it is problematic only for them. This has been the implicit assumption of much of the anthropology of Indic religions—including some of the very best works on Hinduism and Buddhism—which has substantially been phrased as an attempt to explain the relation between a body of dedicated ascetics and their mass following of worldly householders: whether the religion of the laity conforms to ancient doctrine, and whether or not the lay followers domesticate the religion and distort the project of the renouncers. There are two main reasons why I prefer to try to understand Jainism by asking how it is possible anyway to live by Jain ascetic values.

---

[4] Among those who have offered alternatives to Dumont's model ('World Renunciation') of opposition and dialogue between renouncer and man-in-the-world, are Bradford, 'Indian Renouncer'; Burghart, ('Hierarchical Models'); ('Renunciation'); Das (*Structure and Cognition*); Denton ('Varieties of Female Asceticism'); Gellner (*Monk, Householder and Priest*); Heesterman, ('Householder and Wanderer'); (*Inner Conflict of Tradition*); Olivelle, (*Renunciation in Hinduism*); and Tambiah, ('The Renouncer').

[5] See Khare's analysis (*Untouchable as Himself*) of renouncers as ideological innovators and political leaders among Untouchables in Lucknow. See also Alter, 'Celibacy and Nationalism'; Ortner, *High Religion*; Tambiah, *Buddhism Betrayed?*.

[6] Here, and generally throughout, I use the word 'idol' to translate *murti*. Caroline Humphrey and I have explained in *Archetypal Actions* (ch. 2, n. 1) why we prefer this word (which English-speaking Jains I knew in Jaipur all used) to the now conventional academic euphemism, 'image'. I hope it will be clear that absolutely no disapprobation of any kind is intended. Indeed, my discomfort with the euphemism derives in part from the deference it shows to the iconoclast.

First, with the 'domestication' question, conceptual space becomes divided into a slot for a historically original set of teachings on the one hand, and a generalized notion of the religion of 'the masses' (a conception derived from Max Weber and more distantly from David Hume) on the other. Both these terms are problematic.

The historiography of Christianity has made plain to us that there are profound difficulties and incoherences in any attempt to recover 'the historical Jesus', and these are at least as problematic in a Buddhist, Hindu, or Jain context.[7] Jain tradition holds that its most important scriptures have all been lost, and that those which survive were first written down, imperfectly, nearly a thousand years after the events they describe.[8] But this problem is more than an empirical one. It is not so much that the slot for original doctrine cannot be filled reliably, but that by regarding the content of the religion as fixed at the start, everything else—that is to say, religious history—becomes by definition a matter either of deviation or return. As Gombrich puts it, writing of Theravada Buddhism, 'the point of interest is not just what the Buddha said, but what his hearers have heard'.[9]

Equally problematic is the idea that the presence of a laity is itself explanatory of religious change. The Weberian habit of assigning religious ideas, practices, and styles to one or more social class is only a slightly more sophisticated version of Hume's intuition that 'the religion of the vulgar' is always and everywhere the same. As Peter Brown has persuasively argued, the monolithic and unchanging characterization of 'popular religion' which this kind of thinking implies is a serious obstacle to understanding, as it misinterprets real discontinuities in ideas and practice as merely further forms of the same old superstitions.[10] It encourages the question, which is, ultimately, either theological or vacuous: are these people really Buddhist, Jain, or whatever? There are, to be sure,

---

[7] See Bultmann, *History of Synoptic Tradition*; *New Testament and Mythology*. Interesting discussions of parallels between New Testament scholarship and the search for a historical Buddha include Almond, *British Discovery of Buddhism*; Pye, *Cardinal Meaning*; Southwold, *Buddhism in Life*. Carrithers (*The Buddha*) tackles these problems by proceeding, in some respects, in the opposite direction, presenting a life of the Buddha which is a vehicle for the teachings which have come to be central to the tradition.

[8] See excellent discussions of Jain scripture, and of how complex the application of the notion of scripture is in Jainism, by Cort ('Svetambar Jain Scripture'), Dundas (*The Jains*, ch. 3), and Folkert (*Scripture and Community*).

[9] Gombrich, *Theravada Buddhism*, 21.

[10] Brown, *Cult of Saints*, ch. 1.

several important questions which arise from the fact that what is, on the face of it, such an unpromising candidate, came to be a mass religion with a large and varied following, and there are questions too about how the tradition has changed over time. But these are all properly historical questions about how certain ideas have caught on in certain social milieux,[11] and it does not seem helpful to try to pose them as a sociological question about the relation between essentialized entities ('the *sangh*' and 'the laity'; 'renouncers' and 'followers').

The second, and to my mind more important problem with the conventional question, is that it turns on a notion of *conformity* with precepts and therefore on a radically inadequate conception of what the relation between values and practice ever could be. Better, I think, to begin with Nietzsche's insistence that an ascetic life is anyway a self-contradiction: 'We stand before a discord that *wants* to be discordant, that *enjoys* itself in this suffering and even grows more self-confident and triumphant the more its own presupposition, its physiological capacity for life, *decreases*.'[12] Where ideals are unrealizable, and where incommensurable values are in conflict—and I take it that this at least is always to some degree the case—then living in the light of an ideal must always be something more subtle and complex than merely conforming to it.

How then, is it possible to live by impossible ideals? The advantage of addressing this question to Jainism is that the problem is so very graphic there. The demands of Jain asceticism have a pretty good claim to be the most uncompromising of any enduring historical tradition: the most aggressively impractical set of injunctions which any large number of diverse families and communities has ever tried to live by. They have done so, albeit in a turbulent history of change, schism, and occasionally recriminatory 'reform', for well over two millennia. This directs our attention to the fact that yawning gaps between hope and reality are not necessarily dysfunctions of social organization, or deviations from religious systems. The fact that lay Jains make up what is—in thoroughly worldly material terms—one of the most conspicuously successful communities in India, only makes more striking and visible a question which must also arise in the case of renouncers themselves.

---

[11] Examples of studies which do address these historical questions (though necessarily, for the most part, only for recent history) include Carrithers, 'Modern Ascetics'; *Forest Monks*; Gombrich and Obeyesekere, *Buddhism Transformed*; Van der Veer, 'Taming the Ascetic'.

[12] Nietzsche, *Genealogy of Morals*, 553–4.

Matters of Doctrine

The aim of the book, as must now be clear, is interpretive: to describe a form of life in a way which makes an initially puzzling state of affairs comprehensible, or, in the Comaroffs' apt phrase, to contextualize the curious.[13] But there are, I think, three main concerns running through the book which might properly be called theoretical, and these I shall introduce in turn, in this and the next two sections. The first is motivated by scepticism about the practice of explaining social life with reference to underlying systems of ideas, whether this be 'doctrine', as this term is used in anthropological and other studies of religion; or the related notion of 'culture' (or 'mentality'), as this is used more generally in anthropological and historical studies. Both 'doctrine' and 'culture', used in these ways, are ontological fictions—more fantastic, in general, the more they are invoked to explain—and not less so for the fact that they are regularly composed by people about themselves as well as by anthropologists writing about others. To show, in analysis, that whole domains of a people's thought and practice are deducible from a few presuppositions and principles was once thought to be an obvious explanatory virtue. If one considers, on the other hand, that the form and extent of cultural coherence may in fact be variable, then it becomes clear that to achieve coherence in analysis may be systematically distorting. This thought leads to a desire for greater naturalism in social analysis: explaining conduct in terms of ideas, interests, or whatever, which individuals can be shown actually to possess, rather than inventing entities (a conceptual scheme, world-view, mentality, or ideology) and having to suppose a level for these to exist in. Several otherwise disparate lines of thought in current social theory come together in attempting to conduct analysis with a degree of what Pascal Boyer refers to as 'ontological modesty'.[14] Fredrik Barth's recent writings, which include an attempt to reformulate how individual interest, intention, and choice connect with what we call 'culture', is one I find especially sympathetic, but there are many other current projects. While I shall not be attempting to develop any of these lines of thought as such here, I shall draw, rather opportunistically, on insights from them all.

This concern colours how one looks at religious doctrine. It is an obvious point, but one with great consequences for ethnographic writing, that people generally do not learn their religion by proceeding, so to speak, from the logical ground up—premises first and entailments later.

---

[13] Comaroff and Comaroff, *Ethnography and the Historical Imagination*, 4.

[14] Boyer, 'Cognitive Aspects', 11.

Nor do they recapitulate the history of their religion, learning original doctrines in their infancy, and the symbolic elaborations and theological niceties of great clerics and saints in the years of their own maturity. It would be odd to suppose that the religion people practise in adult life somehow comes to be organized conceptually in either of these two ways—to be either logically or historically tidy. The most inescapable elements of a religion—the poles to which practitioners' thoughts turn in a crisis, and the images they dwell upon in worship—are rarely those which would be regarded by religious authorities as the most fundamental axioms or postulates. Nor is religious practice best understood as the acting out of a theory. People learn religious practices. They can have various experiences of them and various responses to them. They might or might not form or learn meanings for them, commentaries on them, or theories about them, and some of these might be validated as doctrine. But it would be a mistake to regard such theories as historically or logically antecedent to practice, or to assume that the theories themselves must all be self-consistent. Attempts to make them so, whether they are the great scholastic exercises of famed religious teachers or *ad hoc* exegeses of daily rituals given by ordinary lay people, are part of the process of production of religious doctrine—theology—and as such they are a subject of anthropological inquiry. But they are only a part of the subject, because much religious practice takes place in the absence of a theory to explain it; and even where such theories are formulated, it would be a mistake to assume that they underlie experience or practice, or that people's religious lives are in any sense based upon them. As Wittgenstein reminded us, we can fear the gods without believing in them.[15] I shall be concerned throughout to decompose the notion of 'doctrine' and to focus instead on the representations which are actually observable in practice and which, as Barth notes, need be, and frequently are no more than 'knowledge in handy bits'.[16]

When I speak, as I shall, of Jainism it will not be to refer to an ideological or cultural system, even an ideal-typical one, but to a socio-historical phenomenon—what Carrithers has aptly referred to as an 'enduring historical stream'.[17] There are continuities, but also change and flow, so that while one can talk validly of the same stream at different times, one can't expect, stepping into it, that it will be the same. My description will focus on practices and representations (material, not supposedly 'collective'

---

[15] Wittgenstein, *Remarks on Frazer*, 8. See also Wittgenstein, *Lectures and Conversations*; Phillips, *Religion Without Explanation*, ch. 3.

[16] Barth, *Balinese Worlds*, 320.   [17] Carrithers, 'Jainism and Buddhism'.

mental representations), and on the diverse ways they are understood. In taking this approach I am not supposing that there are no conventions, premisses, representations, or values which are shared and publicly embraced, but only that we should not presume that those there are cohere in a consistent system. Indeed, in a complex civilization, with millennia of concerted cultural production behind it, and part now of a nation-state, with mass education, mass travel, and global mass communications, it should be obvious that there are too many to form a single system, or to be understood by everyone in the same shared way. In Chapter 2 I shall introduce the most important imaginative reference-points in Jainism—doctrines, images, narratives, and explicit theoretical schemes—and rather than attempting to accomplish consistency by assigning single translations to them, or logical relations between them, I shall try to convey something of the disparate meanings and values they evoke.

Questions of Authenticity

I remarked above that asking whether Jains are really Jains is a theological question. This reminds us that, while it not appropriate, for the reasons I have rehearsed, as a starting-point for anthropological description, it is always available to Jains themselves, and as is the case in Buddhism, asking some form of this question has been a recurrent and insistent part of the tradition.[18] It is something which contact with recent historicist Christianity (especially evangelical Protestantism), and also with various Western 'alternative' enthusiasms for Indian religions, has done much to strengthen and renew.[19]

But perhaps there is another way out. Why not simply invert the terms of the question, and declare popular practice, rather than doctrine, to be the authentic 'real Jainism'? This kind of approach has been recently and rather prominently suggested by Martin Southwold, in his study of a village in Sri Lanka, entitled *Buddhism in Life*. Southwold opens his book with a ringing opposition between ideal Buddhism ('what they, or others, say they ought to do and think') and actual Buddhism ('the Buddhism of observable reality'). The latter, as seen especially in the ethical intuitions of Sri Lankan villagers, is, he claims, 'real Buddhism'. Religious authorities, monks and lay teachers alike, whether they are speaking of the example of the Buddha, the content of scripture, the teachings of tra-

---

[18] Gellner, 'Anthropology of Buddhism'.
[19] Carrithers, *Forest Monks*; Gombrich and Obeyesekere, *Buddhism Transformed*.

dition, or the forms of monastic discipline, where they criticize some practice or belief which they believe to be 'un-Buddhist', are all dismissed as not part of real Buddhism at all. But Southwold's distinction between saying and doing misses the target, I think. What his villagers say they ought to do and think, is part of what they do, observably, do and think. Their thinking and saying it is plainly part of what they do. And one of the things they think and say is that certain other people do, properly as they see it, tell them what to think and do. However much it may offend Southwold's sensibilities, notions of religious authority are central facts about a religious tradition—in life as much as in texts. It is as misleading simply to wish them away as it is impertinent to declare them unreal. Southwold is led to this position by his attempt to adjudicate on questions of religious authenticity. It is as far as the anthropologist should go, at least as anthropologist, to describe the processes of adjudication that are at work. In Buddhism (as in Jainism) there is no reason to suppose that religious authority is new, so dismissing those who claim it with the stigma of Western influence really misses the point. And even if particular forms of authority are new, they can scarcely be removed by an anthropologist's terminological fiat. How far back would they have to go to count as 'Buddhist'?

One way in which Jains are Jains, is by questioning whether or not they are: by thinking about what it takes to be a Jain and who is a good Jain, about which practices are virtuous, which dubious, and which sinful. Religious traditions have distinctive ways of doing this. In Chapter 3, which introduces the social organization of Jain religious tradition, I shall say a bit about the forms of religious authority there are, and in Chapter 4 I shall try to describe how questioning their own religiosity is a routine and intrinsic part of the religious sensibilities of the Jains I knew in Jaipur. So if citing doctrine to question the integrity—even the possibility—of Jain religious life would be a poor framework for an interpretation of the religion, it is, none the less, an inescapable part of it. Both the questioning itself, and the understanding of religion from which it springs, are explicitly and forcefully stated by those very lay followers who appear to be thrown into such a poor light by them. They fast, perform ascetic rites, and worship the great saints of the past, but they also know and readily state that their worldly attachments are lethal snares which will keep them in the world of rebirth. It would be possible to try to make a seamless totality of Jain religious life, to combine the ascetic with the opulent in a composite picture where the contrast between the values of ascetic renunciation and the lives led by wealthy lay Jains would seem less stark.

But this would be a mistake. The contrast is stark, and Jains themselves insist upon it.

The most damaging effect of posing judgemental questions of authenticity is that it leads one either to miss, or to be analytically intolerant of, moral conflict and complexity. This is no less true of populist than it is of élitist judgements. Southwold knew two village monks whom he liked and respected. They broke both the letter and the spirit of the monastic rules on celibacy. So Southwold declares that these rules, and indeed the whole corpus to which they belong, is not authentically Buddhist. These people are good, so they must be good in all respects and from all points of view, and any renegade point of view must be condemned and dismissed. The thought that to be a good Buddhist might involve relinquishing some other virtues is not considered by Southwold. And nor does he notice that this thought is expressed by, and troubling to, Buddhists themselves. It is obvious in an ethics of renunciation, if it is obvious anywhere, that not all ethical values are compossible, and that religion is not ever all there is to ethics. Some of the parts of yourself which you give up will have been admirable and valued in other ways.

Ethical Distinctions

To understand Jainism is to understand how people can live by, without in an obvious sense conforming to, ethical and religious values; and how they can live by contradictory and conflicting values. To understand this kind of ethical and cultural complexity, it is necessary to keep it in focus, which means not reducing or explaining away any of the elements which are in play. The temptation, succumbed to all too often in the anthropology of religion and especially where other-worldly values are concerned, is to explain aspects of people's religious life which they may think are central and irreducible, by deriving them from something else, such as economic or political interest. I do not mean, of course, to deny that there are connections to be drawn, indeed it will be one of my main preoccupations to try to do this, but we should not expect this to make matters simpler.[20]

[20] It is interesting that moral philosophers make such little use of anthropology, although one might expect that a post-Wittgensteinian concern with the uses of moral concepts might have turned moral philosophy in an ethnographic direction. This has indeed been the case, but interest has focused almost exclusively on the imaginatively reconstructed ethics of Classical Greece (e.g. Nussbaum, *Fragility of Goodness*; Williams, *Shame and Necessity*; see also MacIntyre, *After Virtue*; Putnam, *Reason, Truth and History*). And when Derek Parfit, in an appendix to *Reasons and Persons* (502–3), briefly considers Buddhist conceptions of the

In order to locate, as precisely as possible, the kind of ethical complexities we shall be dealing with, I want to introduce three distinctions between kinds of ethical thinking and practice. Their purpose, it should be emphasized, is not to set up formal comparisons between Jainism and other ethical traditions, but to enable us to register the variety of ethical thinking which Jain religious life includes. They are broad distinctions, they cross-cut each other, and I shall not be using them to provide technical or analytical terms, but they do, I think, helpfully chart out the terrain we shall be covering.

The first distinction is between moral judgements whose authority rests on custom, convention, or law, and those which are grounded in a view of the nature of things. In some form or another this distinction is of course an exceedingly venerable one in Western moral philosophy, but I owe the formulation I use here to an interesting discussion by Stuart Hampshire.[21] Hampshire points to the profound difference in the form, and not just the content, of these two kinds of moral claims. The latter presupposes notions of human nature and the human predicament, so that the claims and standards invoked have ideally universal application. Claims which appeal to a notion of justice, Hampshire suggests, generally take this universalizing form. Such claims are always true, if they are true, of all people everywhere. The characteristic argument for these nature-based moral claims is, Hampshire notes, a 'stripping down procedure' in which contingent and variable factors are seen through. This procedure, 'removes a supposed overlay, or dressing, of local custom, of distinctive cultural factors, and removes the moral idiosyncrasies of individuals, which have their local explanations and temporal causes'.[22] Moral claims which are, by contrast, based on convention, have no such requirements of convergence and universality, and the characteristic ways of justifying them are different too. Certain virtues and ideals are justified, when challenged, with reference to the particular way of life they belong to, and just because they are and have been an integral part of it. To be committed to such ideals it is not necessary to think that they are universal, that they are required by human reason, or dictated by human nature. But they are not less binding, and certainly they are not less central to one's moral life, for that.

person, he does so by looking only at a study of textual sources (albeit a rich and subtle one), and not at all at ethnographic accounts (Collins, *Selfless Persons*). This general neglect must, at least partly, be anthropology's fault, and I think that an overly deterministic conception of culture, and a deafness to ethical conflict and complexity, go some way to explaining it.

[21] Hampshire, *Morality and Conflict*, esp. chs. 6 and 7.   [22] Ibid. 129.

Hampshire sums up as follows: 'There are two kinds of moral claim—those that, when challenged are referred to universal needs of human beings and to their reasonable calculations, which should be the same everywhere, and hence to the stripping down argument: and those that, when challenged, are referred only to the description of a desired and respected way of life, in which these moral claims have been an element essential within that life.'[23] He remarks that there are good reasons to expect that most people have been, and always will be ready to acknowledge both kinds of moral claim, but it is also true that in different cultural settings, and different historical periods, the relative status and persuasiveness of these different kinds of claim varies considerably. For instance, the respectability of cultural relativism notwithstanding (it is respectable as a universal value), the educated classes of North Atlantic countries have probably never found arguments which appeal to their own local traditions for moral justification less compelling than they do today, and if you want to be persuasive with such people, you will do better to talk universally, in terms of 'rights'. By contrast, for instance, Norbert Elias describes how in seventeenth-century France '*économie*', while it was a virtue for the bourgeoisie, was explicitly recognized as a vice if exhibited by a member of the nobility, and the latter's virtue of prodigality was equally a moral weakness in the former. The claims these virtues had on those who were committed to them derived from the place they had in their way of life, and not from a universalizing argument that would have made them equally compelling for all.[24]

For the Jains of Jaipur many centrally important moral values—caste duties, family loyalties, business responsibilities—are framed in ways which are self-consciously particularistic. The idea that virtues and duties are profoundly different for different classes of person (the idea of *jati-dharma*), different sexes (*purush-* and *stri-dharma*), and different individuals (*swa-dharma*), is explicitly recognized, and these are notions which are widely recognized throughout the Indic world. T. N. Madan's evocative description of the particularistic ethics of Kashmiri Pandits, though it differs, as of course it would, in particulars, nicely captures the kind of convention-based ethics which are central to Jains' way of life. Madan describes the notion of routine duties—*nityakarma*, 'the chores and rites of daily life properly performed'—and how these belong to particular, historically and culturally located, Pandit ways of life. This includes the honest and dutiful performance of one's work, provision for one's family, and matters such as cleanliness and politeness. Everyone knows that these

---

[23] Ibid. 138.   [24] Elias, *The Court Society*, 67 and *passim*.

vary between castes, classes, and religious groups, and of course they are differentiated by gender, age, and kinship; and they are justified, as Madan notes, on the grounds that 'This is our way of life'.[25]

This distinction gives us the following questions. Are claims for the value of Jain ascetic renunciation typically couched as issuing from nature or from convention? Does Jain doctrine, as it is formulated and taught by religious authorities, describe the human predicament (and indeed that of all sentient beings), formulate universal values (such as non-violence), and prescribe universal moral rules? Or does Jain teaching set out a very specific soteriological project, a way of life which could only ever be pursued by one small group as distinguished from others, in particular cultural and institutional settings? Now, as I said, the point is to understand the variety and complexity of Jain ethical life, so it should come as no surprise that the answer to both these questions is 'yes'. While I used a contrast between Western talk about rights and the flexible and contextual applications of *dharma* to help set up the distinction, it should immediately be said that Jainism (and, I fully expect, any other slice of Indian life one cared to look at) includes ethical thinking in both these modes.[26] Understanding the tradition requires that we register how and in what ways they are combined. When are Jain teachings framed as nature-based moral arguments, and when as elements in a way of life? To put a slightly different, and perhaps a more anthropologically familiar question: are apparently universal values and virtues in practice associated with, or appropriated by, persons in only certain social positions?

A second distinction between kinds of ethical thinking has been coined by Michael Carrithers, in a response to Mauss's classic paper on the

[25] Madan, 'Ideology of Householder', 108. By Madan's account, the Pandits do not share quite the ethical predicament of Jains, because a general and profound scepticism about renouncers and renunciation is associated with a rather more unequivocal commitment to what he calls 'the ideology of the householder' than I think is common among Jains.

[26] I am aware, of course, of a set of arguments to the effect that a distinction between metaphysical orders of nature and law is foundational in 'Western culture' (Schneider, *American Kinship*) and not made at all in 'South Asian culture'. This is the idea that the 'South Asian mind' is committed to a doctrine of 'biological substantivism' according to which all moral matters are underwritten by, indeed indistinguishable from, biological nature. While this doctrine, propounded most eloquently by Marriott 'Hindu Transactions' and Marriott and Inden 'Ethnosociology of Caste', was influential for a while, it has been extensively criticized in recent years, and I cannot see how it could illuminate the ethnography I present here. See Appadurai, 'Homo Hierarchicus?'; Béteille, 'Race, Caste and Gender'; and Parry, 'End of the Body', who all argue persuasively that the contrast between an undifferentiated 'West' and an equally homogenized 'South Asia' is overdrawn, and see also Keesing, 'Conventional Metaphors', for just one discussion, not focused on this case, of the mistakes in interpretive practice which such an approach depends upon.

concept of the person.[27] In that paper, Mauss traced the genealogy of the modern self, from the finite series of roles (*personnages*) which people filled in the ritual and dance of early society (his models for this are drawn from the Pueblos, the American North-West, and Australia), to the individual in modern democratic society as the site of moral, political, and metaphysical value. Mauss begins his paper by conceding that all humans everywhere have a sense of 'self' (*moi*), of their spiritual and physical individuality, but his subject, he insists, is the socially constructed concepts they have formed of this. The turning-point in his story is Roman law, where for the first time the person (*persona*) as an individual being separate from social roles became the bearer of rights and duties.

Carrithers points out that when Mauss set aside the sense of self from his discussion, he left out of the picture a whole realm of cultural and intellectual history.[28] Mauss's paper gives us a history of a conception of the individual human as a social being, a member of a significant and ordered collectivity. But there is also another kind of conception, which Carrithers distinguishes from the former as a *moi*, as opposed to a *personne* theory. A *moi* theory is one which conceives the individuality of the human being in a cosmic (physical and/or spiritual) as opposed to a social context, and is therefore a conception of the individual as a spiritual and moral agent, rather than as the subject of a political or social order. And Carrithers notes that if, as Mauss claimed, Roman law constituted a decisive step in abstract thinking about the *personne*, then the India which produced Buddhism made a similar contribution to thinking about the *moi*.[29]

Carrithers notes that *moi* theories have been formulated in, for example, German Romanticism, Stoicism, Theravada Buddhism, and Protestant Christianity, and he suggests that the appeal of Theravada Buddhism for nineteenth-century German Romantics (documented wonderfully in Schwab's *The Oriental Renaissance*) shows that even widely different theories can answer similar sets of preoccupations in satisfying ways, to people in radically different social and political settings.

These *moi*-oriented moral systems are substantially different from the sort of collectively organised and collectively impressed representations which Mauss derives from his ideal type of primitive society. For they have begun, not from an image of man in the primeval ritual dance, but from images of human beings alone:

---

[27] Mauss, 'Category of the Human Mind'.

[28] That Mauss recognized that the 'sense of self' could have a history, is strongly suggested by his roughly contemporaneous essay, 'Body Techniques'.

[29] Carrithers, 'Alternative History of Self', 253.

communing with nature for the German Romantics, acting against his own intrinsic human nature for the Stoics, meditating in the forest for Theravada Buddhists, struggling in one's room in prayer for Protestant Christians. These certainly have their own social history. They have certainly produced Dionysian cults of subjection to the collective as well as the Apollonian moral constraint they overtly prescribe. They by no means lead us to reject the collectively conceived legal and political history of the *personne* which Mauss desiderates. But they do have their own development, their own logic, and their own relative autonomy.[30]

When Jain doctrine is formulated as a nature-based universal theory, as in the teachings of many Jain philosophers and theologians, it is as a *moi*-oriented moral system. In this it is different, for instance, from liberal political theory as expressed in talk of human rights, which in Carrithers's terms is a *personne*-theory. That is to say, Carrithers's distinction picks out for us the persistently central subject-matter of Jain philosophical thinking, the kind of moral theory it has developed. The Jain tradition emerged in the same place and time as Buddhism, and was indeed one of early Buddhism's closest interlocutors in what Carrithers rightly refers to as 'one of the most creative periods of thought in human history'.[31] Through all its internal schisms, and in dialogue and debate with their Buddhist, Hindu, Sikh, Muslim, Christian, and Secularist counterparts, thinkers in the Jain tradition have been centrally concerned to develop and explore a distinctive vision of the predicament of the individual human soul, alone in an impersonal cosmic system of cause and effect, and burdened with the consequences of its former actions. But do Jain religious symbols, concepts, narratives, and values, also serve in thinking about the *personne*? Do they form, if not perhaps a distinctive and original theory of this kind, elements none the less in people's thinking about their place in social collectivities? Jain doctrine certainly does not look like a social theory, and, as with Buddhism, it is probably true to say that it was not formulated to be such, but as we shall see in Parts II, IV, and V below, one can find in contemporary Jainism conceptions of what it is to be a member of a caste, a profession, a state, a family, and of course a religious community, which are built out of elements of their *moi*-theory.

So far I have been using the terms 'ethics' and 'morality' interchangeably, but the third distinction I wish to introduce is to identify differences between them. Bernard Williams, in *Ethics and the Limits of Philosophy*, argues that morality should be seen as a particular development of the

---

[30] Ibid. 248.

[31] On the social context in which Buddhism and Jainism emerged, see Carrithers, *The Buddha*; Gombrich, *Theravada Buddhism*; and Thapar, *Ancient Indian Social History*.

ethical, the latter being defined very broadly as answers to the question, 'How should one live?' In morality, the idea of social expectation is developed rather more than that of individual character; but the peculiarity of this particular variety of ethical thinking is the idea that to act morally is to choose to act in conformity with a special sort of obligation. Thus morality recognizes only one kind of ethical consideration, abstracting the exercise of the will, in choosing between good and evil, from all other considerations. Morality is, as Williams says, a 'peculiar institution': a remarkably narrow conception of ethical life, but one that has become dominant in modern Western culture. There are different versions of morality—it is not just one theory—but they have in common the idea of moral *obligations* as a unique kind of requirement we can find ourselves under (thus we get the notion of the moral as opposed to self-interest, of the 'moral point of view' as one among many) and the idea of the moral decision, which involves only the question of whether we conform to the obligation or not, and therefore only the will. The question, when someone acts badly, therefore becomes whether or not they acted voluntarily, for only if they did is the characteristic reaction of morality—blame— appropriate.

When we ask whether someone acted voluntarily, we are asking, roughly, whether he really acted, whether he knew what he was doing, and whether he intended this or that aspect of what happened. This practice takes the agent together with his character, and does not raise questions about his freedom to have chosen some other character. The blame system, most of the time, closely concentrates on the conditions of the particular act; and it is able to do this because it does not operate on its own. It is surrounded by other practices of encouragement and discouragement, acceptance and rejection, which work on desire and character to shape them into the requirements and possibilities of ethical life. Morality neglects this surrounding and sees only that focused, particularized judgement.[32]

Michel Foucault also developed a distinction between ethics and morality. The formulation is not the same as Williams's, and their projects and language are so intricately different that I doubt it would be useful (and certainly not here) to work out the relation between them in an analytical way. But both of them explore—and both call them 'ethics' and look to classical Greece to understand them—the possibilities of choosing, and working to develop 'some other character', as a remedy to what they perceive as the peculiar deficiencies of modern morals in the West. And Foucault also developed an analysis of the practices, which Williams refers to here, that shape desire and character.

---

[32] Williams, *Ethics and Philosophy*, 194.

Foucault described his later work, the uncompleted 'History of Sexuality', as a genealogy of ethics. Within the whole field of human life which we think of loosely as morals, he distinguished the formulated rules or 'moral codes', which people are required to follow, from individuals' behaviour in relation to those rules (how they variously respect, obey, disregard, or resist them), and also distinguished both of these from what he calls 'ethics': 'the kind of relationship you ought to have with yourself'.[33] A relationship with the self, for Foucault, 'is not simply "self-awareness" but self-formation as an "ethical subject," a process in which the individual delimits that part of himself that will form the object of his moral practice, defines his position relative to the precept he will follow, and decides on a certain mode of being that will serve as his moral goal. And this requires him to act upon himself, to monitor, test, improve, and transform himself.'[34] This last aspect includes 'asceticism', a term which, like the Greek *askesis*, Foucault used in a broad sense of self-forming activity, 'a training of oneself by oneself'.[35] He argued that while moral codes remained remarkably constant in the transition from pagan to Christian morals, the ethics, or 'forms of subjectivation' changed markedly. Thus his history of morals in that period is essentially a history of 'the way in which individuals are urged to constitute themselves as subjects of moral conduct'.

Morals, in the broad sense, is always comprised of codes and also modes of subjectivation, but these two elements are elaborated and developed to different degrees in different places and different times, so Foucault distinguishes broadly between 'code-oriented' and 'ethics-oriented' moralities. Whereas in the former, moral rules are elaborately specified, and socially established and enforced (not always successfully, to be sure), the latter involve restrictions, disciplines, exercises, and so forth, which the individual accepts, in order to be and to become a certain kind of person. It is this general feature, rather than a specific content such as 'self-denial', which makes moralities 'ascetic' in Foucault's terms.

Now, different as they are, these two ways of locating the ethical both prompt a severe reflection on the way anthropology has generally written about morals, for it has remained confined by the neo-Kantian legacy bequeathed to it by Durkheim, with his concern with the constraint of the 'moral law', and has persisted in writing about moral matters using almost exclusively juridical language.[36] The forms of ethical self-fashioning

---

[33] Foucault, 'Genealogy of Ethics', 352; *History of Sexuality*, ii. 25–6.

[34] Foucault, *History of Sexuality*, ii. 28.   [35] Foucault, 'Genealogy of Ethics', 364.

[36] See discussion by Pocock, 'Ethnography of Morals'; Wolfram, 'Anthropology and Morality'.

which both Foucault and Williams point to, and the consequences these have for the way the self is organized, have remained largely unexplored.

Does Jainism appear as a set of socially sanctioned rules which one is required to obey, or as an ethics, a range of techniques of the self which you exercise in order to be and become a Jain? Once again, the answer to this question is, 'both'. For those living in a Jain community there are certainly socially sanctioned moral codes which have a Jain content, and where one may speak of conformity, as a narrow matter of more or less voluntary moral choice. But actually much more centrally, I think, Jainism is an ethics: or rather, it is principally as an ethics that Jain asceticism appears in lay life.

One of the interesting things about Foucault's notion of modes of subjectivation, is that it enables us to go beyond the observation that there are culturally variable 'concepts of the person', to look at the ways in which, in 'self-forming activity', persons are made as the kinds of subjects they are, in social practice.[37] This brings into focus the possibility that because the kind of subject one becomes is a matter of how one is positioned, with respect to present or postulated others, in different social practices, one might not be a stably coherent 'self' at all, but rather 'distributed', so to say, between the different kind of subject one is in different situations. All of this is to say that if selves are not given but made—if, as Judith Butler puts it, 'the "doer" is variably constructed in and through the deed'[38]—then they are generally made piece-meal, here and there, from shreds and patches, in dialogue with various alters, and the result is fragmentary rather than seamless. This gives us the notion of a self which may be divided against itself, an assemblage of possibly conflicting 'subject positions'. This book begins by describing the different sorts of subject Jains might variously be in different sorts of religious discourse and practice. Thus in the three chapters of Part I, I shall describe, respectively, stances *vis-à-vis* the Jina, relationships with renouncers, and evaluations of oneself in relation to doctrinal ideals and standards. From all this it will be apparent that there is a fairly extensive repertoire of ways of being Jain. And the point is that more or less all lay Jains are committed, more or less, to all of them. The simple idea that Jains worship deceased renouncers and emulate those who are living implies a range of different religious subject positions: different kinds of religious self which one ought to—but cannot all at the same time—be. The self that Jainism proposes for its followers to make of themselves is

[37] See discussion by Fraser, *Unruly Practices*.
[38] Bulter, *Gender Trouble*, 142.

fragmented and incomplete, torn between conflicting ideals and focused ultimately on an impossible one. And more than this, as we shall see in Chapter 4, it furnishes them with powerful devices whereby, with ideals and exemplars of heroic asceticism always imaginatively before them, one of those selves is called upon to accuse and indict the others. This is what it is to live by conflicting and impossible ideals.

If it is the case that this agonistic fragmentation of the self is posited in religious practice, which we can think of, narrowly, as being a matter of who and how one is in relation to the Jinas and to ascetic renouncers, then I shall suggest that the conflicts between these different ways of being Jain are resolved, in so far as they are, in a wider domain of sociality. This will not be, for anthropologists, a surprising or radical claim. For Jain renouncers, every single thing they do is both enabled and regulated by monastic rules and forms of interpersonal monastic authority. By definition, the forms of social practice—the ways of going on—which bring the conflicting ideals they live by into relation with each other are all 'religious' (although in fact, as we shall see, this does not mean that they are only religious). For the laity, a religious life requires for its completion—by 'completion' I mean here wholeness as distinct from termination—parts of life which are locally defined as altogether external to religion.

This book begins from the observation that people may hold values which are in irreducible conflict, and that logical consistency in what we casually identify as a culture, is not something which is necessarily there to be found. It takes work to create, reproduce, and maintain it, and it is always partial. In so far as people manage, in particular cultural traditions and particular local communities, to create lives which are ethically and intellectually coherent, they are not just inheriting a ready-made, complete, and integrated package, but sustaining and reproducing the achievement of culture. Jainism can be made to look like the ordered execution of a single doctrinal programme, and as is the case perhaps in all cultural traditions, some of its greatest minds have always wished to make it so; but looking at Jainism as an enduring form of life, one is struck by a different achievement. It seems to provide its followers with ideas, institutions, relationships, and practices—a set of ways of going on—which together make conflicting values compossible, and impossible ideals compelling. This is a considerable achievement, and one that calls for elucidation. At this point the anthropologist takes over from the theologian.

PART I

Stances, Relationships, Evaluations

2

The Mystery of the Visible

It is only shallow people who do not judge by appearances. The true mystery of the world is the visible, not the invisible.

Oscar Wilde

IN this chapter I shall attempt to provide an introduction to religious thought in Shvetambar Jainism, by describing the images, narratives, and schemes which I referred to in Chapter 1 as the tradition's central imaginative reference-points. The question we shall have in mind is; where does the Jain subject find him or herself placed with respect to these images and schemes?

In the Introduction I urged that we should not assume some hidden order or level, unconsciously shared, where apparently contradictory beliefs cohere—an underlying world-view. What we know that people do share is, so to speak, on the surface: practices, representations, signs, and utterances, which are enacted, seen, and heard. Thus Jains may share a set of emblematic statements about what 'we Jains' believe, statements such as 'everything depends upon *karma*', which are bold and general enough to allow a number of different commentaries and nuanced understandings. They also share much that is not necessarily propositional in form at all. This includes practices, such as fasting; and bodily movements, including postures and gestures deployed in ritual, which they may have learned as children, and can perform without really having to think about them at all. And there is visual imagery—a medium of religious thought which has been very controversial in Jainism, as it has in many other religious traditions.[1]

There are, of course, many modes and media in which Jains learn, exchange, and discuss religious ideas. I want to draw special attention at the start to two of these, because we shall meet versions of them time and again, and because Jain religious and moral discourse, from renouncers' sermons to relatively informal conversation, typically switches repeatedly between them. These are narrative and tabulation: they attempt to encap-

[1] In this chapter I shall consider one of the most potent symbolic images in Jain tradition, representations of the Jina preaching; and I shall return to the matter for a more extended discussion of temple idols in ch. 11. (See also Humphrey and Laidlaw, *Archetypal Actions*.)

sulate religious principles and values in, respectively, a story and an analytical list or scheme. Both, of course, are always open to different interpretations according to how and by whom they are used, and in fact individuals often present their own interpretation of Jainism by using a story to illustrate an item on a list, and by using a list to pick out the point of a story.[2]

Jainism is Impossible

Let us take, as a starting-point, Jain doctrine concerning *karma*. Now, the Jain philosophical literature about *karma*—on just how this material substance interacts with the immaterial soul, the effects to which different kinds of action give rise, the many types and sub-types of *karma*—all this forms a vast body of writing which shows subtle variations and changes over time. However, almost every day I was in Jaipur, someone would sum up for me the basic thrust of what they took Jain teaching on the subject to be:

Everything depends upon *karma*. If you do good actions, you will get a good result. If you sin, you must suffer that too. That is all. Nothing to be done.

If I have to suffer because of my *karma*, no one can help me and nothing can change that.

As Jains we know we are alone in this world. Only by our own actions can we gain help. Only by cleansing our own souls.

The way to cleanse the soul is to refrain from all worldly activity, to renounce material possessions, to practise non-violence after the manner of Jain renouncers, and to fast. In order to hear this view of the kernel of Jain teaching there is no need to go to renouncers, or to particularly scholarly lay people. It is common knowledge among all even remotely religious Jains. In scores of popular stories the hero or heroine proves his or her religious insight and correctness by rejecting all other explanations of some state of affairs in the world. It may seem, for instance, that witchcraft is the cause of this or that misfortune, but the fact that the witchcraft happened, the fact that it worked, and the fact that its effects were thus and so, can only be explained in terms of *karma*. And the standard idiom in which these stories signal religious enlightenment, or conversion to Jainism, is for the protagonist to realize and declare that, 'everything depends upon *karma*'. When great Jain saints intervene in

---

[2] See also Carrithers, *Why Humans Have Cultures*, ch. 6.

these stories, it is to reveal to people the events of their previous lives and how these events explain what has happened in this life. Thus they convince people that 'everything depends upon *karma*', and so attract new followers to the religion.

During fieldwork in Jaipur, whenever I met someone for the first time and explained that I had come to learn about Jainism, some version of the view that everything depends upon *karma* was frequently the first and most important thing they thought I ought to know. They gave no indication of regarding it as an unwelcome doctrine which they would rather forget about, or an esoteric part of their religion which applies only to renouncers. For although its message is a stringent one, it is a part of Jainism of which its followers are self-consciously proud.

Jainism is the most difficult religion. In fact it is impossible. We get no help from any gods, or from anyone. We just have to cleanse our souls. Other religions are easy, but they are not very ambitious. In all other religions when you are in difficulty you can pray to God for help, and maybe God comes down to help. But Jainism is not a religion of coming down. In Jainism it is we who must go up. We have only to help ourselves. In Jainism we are supposed to become God. That is the only thing.

So the vision of Jainism as requiring each individual to engage in severe asceticism for the sake of their own salvation occupies a prominent and not unwelcome place in lay Jains' self-descriptions. This is not to say that there is a single conceptual scheme or theory which all Jains share, even about the subject of *karma*. If all action causes *karma* to attach to the soul, does this not include the actions which are designed to remove it: ascetic practices such as fasting, confession rites, and so on? Does the intention with which an action is performed, and not just its physical effects, affect its moral quality and its *karmik* effect on the soul? As we shall see below (Chapter 9) there is no unanimity about the answers to these questions in Jain tradition. Forceful and vivid assertions of quite contrasting views have authoritative religious status and religious practice is understood in the light of different interpretations.

While talk of cleansing one's soul implies that all *karma* is bad (and therefore that all action is sinful), Jains routinely talk about 'good *karma*', equating this sometimes with good luck (*saubhagya*), sometimes with 'auspiciousness' (*shubh*), but most often with *punya*, which is 'merit' or the results of ethically good actions. This might be any of a whole range of good actions, although the paradigm of an act of *punya* is to make a generous gift (see Chapters 13 and 16). The idea that in some sort of internal account-book one can balance sinful actions (*pap*) with acts of merit has been reported from other communities where thinking in terms of *karma* is prevalent, and the idea of doing something virtuous to make up for something of which one is guilty is of course much more widespread than that. Because the Jain imagery of *karma* is so materialist, the thought that it is quantifiable has a certain plausibility. On important religious occasions the Jains organize parades with didactic bill-boards and *tableaux vivants*. One of the favourites is a huge balance, with a child sitting on each of the two pans. One child (usually a boy) is dressed in white and sits on the higher of the two pans, representing merit (*punya*); the other (usually a girl), sitting in the lower pan, is dressed in red and represents sin (*pap*).[3] Such thinking allows for the possibility, widely reported from the Buddhist world, that lay people might see their religion in terms of gaining 'good *karma*' so as to ensure a 'good rebirth'—to be wealthy, or a god.

But while the conceptual distinction between gaining good *karma* and removing all *karma* is clear enough, there is no correspondingly clear distinction between the practices which might cause these internal processes. The workings of *karmik* cause and effect are unknowable, except to those with supernatural insight. Thus what appears from the outside to be two instances of the same act will have different effects, depending on the *karma* already present in those who perform them, and the mental attitude (*bhav*) with which they are performed. To make a donation is more likely to bring merit, and so luck and good fortune, but in so far as it is motivated by non-attachment to material possessions (*aparigraha*), or mercy (*day*) and non-violence (*ahimsa*), it might also effect the purification of the soul. Conversely, ascetic practices such as fasting or confession are most naturally thought of as removing *karma*. All asceticism is described as 'heat' (*tap*, *tapas*) and as burning *karma* off the soul. But even in the case of the most pious monk, only distant future events will reveal whether he has succeeded in destroying his *karma*s or only in gaining more merit. As the hagiographies of Jain saints illustrate, at any time before ultimate enlightenment the results of religious acts are the same: a good rebirth. And as we shall see below (Chapter 10), this uncertainty is in some ways welcome.

So no exercise of accounting and trade-off could be either comprehen-

---

[3] It may seem odd that sin should be weightier than merit, and thus appear to be worth more, but we should remember that the pure soul is light and that it is weighed down by *karma*: more so by sin than by merit.

sive or certain. While Jains often talk of a sinful act as a debt which must
be repaid, they also maintain that some debts must be paid in kind. This
idea furnishes Jain didactics with some of its most lurid material. Children's books in particular are full of examples of frightening retribution
which follows this logic. One tale tells of a man sentenced by a king to be
skinned alive. A Jain monk reveals the real reason for his fate: in his
previous life he was on the whole a good man, but one day he took
particular pleasure in peeling a mango with great care, so that the skin
came off in one piece. The soul of that mango was reborn as the king who
was now sentencing him to a similar fate. If in this or an earlier life you
have committed a sin of some kind, especially an act of cruel or even
careless violence, then sooner or later, you can never know when, you will
have to pay for it in an appropriate way. Quite how that will be, you
similarly cannot know. As this popular story indicates, the turns that
karmik causality can take are unpredictable.

There was a king who had two wives. The first wife had no children and one day
the second wife gave birth to a son. The first wife was jealous, and wanted to kill
the child. But the second wife was very trusting and one day when the baby was
only two months old she left him with the queen. The queen was making chapatis
at the time and so she took a very hot chapati and placed it on the baby's head. The
baby died instantly and the queen took the chapati away so no one would know
what had happened. The mother returned and saw the baby had died. She wept
bitterly, but there was nothing she could do.

After ninety-nine further births, the queen was born as a man named
Gajsukumal who became a *muni* (a Jain monk) and was very pious and finally
attained *moksh*. But he had to face the *karma* of that long-ago action. The baby was
reborn as a man named Sambal, and when Sambal saw Gajsukumal the hatred
from before came back to him. The *muni* was in standing meditation. Sambal filled
a small stove with burning coal and put it on the *muni*'s head.

Gajsukumal felt no bad thoughts for the person doing this. He thought, 'In a
previous birth I must have done this to someone, because everything depends
upon *karma*'. So he attained *moksh*.

When Jains engage in ascetic practices such as fasting, they can understand these actions in terms of gaining merit, and luck and good fortune
for the future, or as small but definite steps towards final release, and both
ways of seeing things can be assimilated to the general truth that everything depends upon *karma*.

When someone says that 'everything depends upon *karma*', they are
never saying anything contentious. The claim is sometimes difficult to

believe, and it isn't always clear exactly what it means, but it is always incontrovertibly true.[4] As a style of reasoning, invoking *karma* thus has a terrific range (literally anything can be, and indeed ought to be explained by it), but it has very limited force. To say that this man is rich because he made a generous donation in a previous life is to make a substantive point about which actions are good, and to recommend those actions. This sort of thing one hears a lot, but of course, such reasoning is always very limited: there are actually no data about people's former lives, so the conclusions are generally trite (although the imagery, as we saw, can be arresting). You could make the point about generosity in one of a whole range of other ways, and doing so in terms of *karma* adds nothing at all to your point about generosity. And you would use *karmik* explanation in exactly the same way—and Jain teachers do this too—if your point were to recommend thrift. *Karma* then is not a theory about how things in the world are caused, but an idiom in which many, mutually incompatible hypotheses can be readily and authoritatively expressed.[5] Much more specific is the claim—actually more salient in everyday life than use of the idiom to explain particular events, and always in any case appended to those explanations whenever they are made—that somehow or other absolutely everything is caused by *karma*, and that it is meet and right to say so. Just because everything depends upon *karma*, anything said in these terms about particular states of affairs in the world is always less to the point than the general conception of the human predicament which the very act of choosing that style of reasoning evokes, for it calls forth the image of each soul locked in its own unique fate, which is fixed by its previous actions, labouring for release through ascetic practice. Asserting or accepting that everything depends upon *karma* is to take a particular stance with respect to oneself, and with respect also to exemplars such as the Jinas: the stance of the individual 'striver' (*shramana/shramani*) and ascetic (*tapasi/tapasvi*). From this stance a Jain is one who tries, however imperfectly, to emulate the heroic asceticism of the Jinas. Laity and present-day renouncers alike, from this perspective, are striving after this

---

[4] Something similar may be the case in many Hindu contexts, and would explain why, as Sharma ('Theodicy', 358) remarks, while *karma* may not be the first explanation a person might offer for misfortune, 'it is generally the last that he will abandon'.

[5] That this can be the case in Hinduism too is illustrated by Wadley and Derr's presentation (in 'Eating Sins') of the explanations people in Karimpur offered for a fire which destroyed several houses in the village. Much of the village reached a consensus, over time, that the fire was the merited punishment for sins committed by the Brahmins, and in support of this conclusion *karma* was invoked, but in doing so people used a wide range of quite contrasting reasonings.

impossibly exacting ascetic ideal. However, it is also true that the Jinas, the twenty-four great sages who have founded and refounded the order of Jain renouncers, are complex figures who are more than simply the apotheosis of severe asceticism.

Gentle Conquest

The following passage envisages the founding of the Jain religion. It comes from the work of the great twelfth-century Shvetambar renouncer Hemacandra Suri. An adviser to kings, logician, grammarian, theologian, and epic poet, Hemacandra has had an enormous impact on Shvetambar Jainism. If he did not devise them, many of the ideas, formulae, and images around which Jain religious thought and ritual turn gained prominence through his writings.[6] The picture this passage paints is not found in early Jainism,[7] so a historicist view of 'Jain doctrine' would not include it, but it has achieved a place in art and ritual comparable to that of the crucifixion in Roman Christianity (Plate II).

In common with other Indic traditions, Jain teachers have held that the universe has been created and destroyed over and over again in vastly long world-ages. In his *Trishashti-shalaka-purusha-caritra*, Hemacandra tells the history of the present world-age through the lives of its sixty-three most illustrious persons.[8] The first is Rishabh Dev, or Adinath, the First Lord, which is to say the first Jina. The word *jina* means conqueror, and the Jinas are those who have conquered their own desires and passions, and so escaped the cycle of death and rebirth. 'Jain', a secondary formation from 'Jina', means 'pertaining to the conqueror'.

Rishabh was the first king, but he renounced his kingdom to become a wandering holy man. In this mythological view, therefore, kingship and Jain asceticism share a common origin. We will see that they remain linked, in various ways, in contemporary Jainism. Hemacandra describes how, as a result of his penances and his blameless conduct, Rishabh

---

[6] See Tawney, *Prabandhacintamani*, for Acarya Merutunga's mythological history of Jainism in western India, concerned in large part with Hemacandra. See also Buhler, *Life of Hemacandracarya*; Sharma, 'Hemacandra'; and Dundas, *The Jains*, 115–17. As Williams (*Jaina Yoga*, 11) remarks, 'There is scarcely a branch of literature or science as then known to which he did not contribute, and his influence both on his contemporaries and on the whole subsequent history of Svetambara Jainism and through Asadhara to some extent even on the Digambaras can scarcely be overestimated.'

[7] The first full description of the *samosaran* as it is envisaged today seems to date from the 5th c. AD. See Dundas, *The Jains*, 30–1, 175.

[8] On this important genre of 'Universal History', see Cort, 'Jaina Puranas'.

PLATE II. A *samosaran* painting. This painting is from Rajasthan (dated AD 1800), and shows the Jina sitting at the centre of the assembly hall constructed by the gods for his sermon. It also shows how he is seen by those who have gathered there: because the gods have made replicas of him, he appears to be facing in four directions at once, so all those present feel he is looking at them. Attendants fan him and play drums. Jain monks and nuns, and lay men and women, have gathered, along with deities of various kinds and all manner of birds and animals. In the outer ring are the vehicles and entourages of the kings and gods.

purifies his soul so that he attains omniscience (*keval gyan*). Rishabh Dev now will certainly attain salvation or release (*moksh*) when his present life comes to an end. But instead of proceeding straight to liberation he remains on earth to preach, and so, by founding the Jain religion, he helps countless others to attain the same goal. Hemacandra describes how the

gods construct a great assembly-hall—*samavasarana* or, more colloquially, *samosaran*—from which he delivers his sermon.[9]

Then the thrones of all the Indras (kings of gods) shook . . . the bells in the
heavens rang . . . [All the Indras] came there with troops of gods making great
haste as if from desire to be the first.

Then the Vayukumaras (wind gods) themselves, purged of pride, cleaned the
surface of the earth one *yojana* (eight miles). The Meghakumaras (cloud gods)
sprinkled the earth with fragrant water . . . The Vyantaras (gods of the intermedi-
ate realm) covered the surface of the earth with shining mosaics of gold and
jewels . . . In the four directions they created arches of jewels, rubies, and
gold . . . Then the Vimanpatis (lords of heavens) made the uppermost rampart of
jewels . . . In the middle part, moreover, the Jyotishpatis (lords of light) made
a wall of gold, as if the light of their own bodies had been collected
together . . . Outside of that, a wall of silver was made by the Bhavanapatis (lower
gods) . . . In each rampart four ornamental gateways were made . . . In the midst
[was] a *caitya* tree made by the Vyantaras, rising for three *kosh* (a *kosh* is two
miles) . . . Beneath it, they made a platform with manifold jewels; on it they made
a dais of incomparable gems. In the centre of it [facing] the east, they made next
a jewelled lion-throne with a foot-stool . . . Above it were made three white umbrellas like three distinct signs of the Master's lordship over the three worlds . . .

Then the Lord of the World entered . . . [He] sat on the lion-throne, facing the
east, like the sun on the eastern mountain, for the destruction of the darkness of
the confusion of the world. At once the Vyantara women made three images of the
Blessed One placed on jewelled thrones in the other directions . . . Then behind
his body appeared the Lord's halo, compared with which the sun-disc was like a
fire-fly.

The structure is at once an imperial audience hall, festooned with traditional Indian regalia, and a symbolic portrayal of the whole cosmos,
centred on the Jina. The three miraculous replicas of him complete the
symmetry, so that he is oriented at once to the four cardinal directions,
and as the whole world gathers around him, the people and animals are rearranged into classes according to their distance from a centre which is
both royal and religious. Hemacandra describes the positions allotted to
men and women, to Jain monks and nuns, to all classes of spirit and deity,
and even to the animals who gather to listen: 'there was no restraint, and
no dissension at all; even between enemies there was no mutual jealousy or

[9] Johnson (*Trishashti-shalaka-purusha-caritra*, i. 188–94). I have abstracted these passages
from what is there a very lengthy description, changed the spellings to conform with the
system used in the rest of this book, and added in parentheses some explanatory notes. For
other sources and descriptions, see Caillat and Kumar, *Jain Cosmology*; Shah, *Studies in
Jaina Art*, 85; Bhandarkar, 'Jaina Iconography'.

fear.' The equation here between a temporal ruler (a *cakravartin*, lord of the four quarters) and the spiritual sovereign (who is lord of the three worlds—the heavens, earths, and hells) is perhaps a surprising one in a religion which is famous, if for anything, for its emphasis on non-violence. In fact, imagery of warfare and martial valour runs right through Jainism: asceticism as a battle to overcome spiritual enemies, enlightenment as final conquest, and omniscience as unchallenged rule.[10]

So the Jina is not just an exemplar of renunciation, but also the focus of a conception of the cosmos. While his teaching is that one should renounce and leave the world, he does not leave the world unchanged, and the image of the *samosaran* is the image of a world re-oriented around this central figure who is, at once, teacher, king, ascetic, god, and God.

Redemptive Sound and Vision

Countless souls have become perfected (*siddha*) and achieved release, but only those who preach from a *samosaran* and establish the religion as a social fact are called Tirthankars, or ford-builders. *Tirtha* means 'crossing-place', and is used widely in Indian religious traditions to talk about salvation. Certain rivers and bathing places, as well as sacred cities, temples, and mountain-tops, are known as *tirtha*s, places where deities appear on earth or where the passage out of the world of suffering is comparatively easy.[11] In Jain imagery, the religious community of monks, nuns, lay men, and lay women is a four-fold *tirtha*, a crossing established at the *samosaran*, and the Jinas are therefore builders of that crossing—Tirthankars.

One pair of words used for lay Jain men and women—*shravak* and *shravika*—means 'listener', for a religious life may be figured as listening at a *samosaran*, and renouncers' sermons are always a partial re-creation of this (Chapter 11). And as the point in the story about replica idols of the Jina emphasizes, the listener also sees the Jina, and the idea which is found throughout the Indian religious world of visual interaction with a deity or saint as itself a redemptive experience,[12] is fully exploited in Jain worship.

---

[10] See Babb, 'Monks and Miracles'; 'Great Choice'; Dundas, 'Digambar Jain Warrior'. I shall return to this subject below (chs. 5 and 7), but it is well to say now that Jain emphasis on non-violence does not necessarily imply any hostility to warfare or to those who prosecute it. All the Tirthankars were born of Kshatriya (royal and hence military) families, and were reared and educated to be soldiers. See also Tambiah, *World Conqueror*, on symbolic equivalence and practical symbiosis between kings and monks in Theravada Buddhism.

[11] Eck, 'India's Tirthas'; Fuller, *Camphor Flame*, 207–10.

[12] Babb, 'Glancing'; Eck, *Darsan*.

This idea of Jainism as an assembly of listeners, and therefore of the lay Jain as a member of an elaborately structured and differentiated, and holistically imagined community, contrasts notably with the atomistic idea of the striver—the individual soul passing countless lives locked in its own entanglement with *karma*, and responsible individually for its own salvation. It is a vivid image of religious community,[13] and an image too of salvation and quasi-magical redemption, because the sight and sound of the Tirthankar preaching are enough to enable some virtuous souls to proceed straight to liberation.[14]

But it stops short of being a vision of universal salvation. To my knowledge, no Jain teacher has ever held out the hope of universal release from death and rebirth, or reinterpreted escape from the world in utopian terms, as the perfection or redemption of the world. The countless unseen living things which live and die in the elements include some which are destined never to attain release,[15] and the gods and animals who attend the *samosaran* are unable to do so during their current lives because *moksh* is only possible from a human birth. The Tirthankar constructs a crossing-place, or, to use another important Jain image, lays out a path towards release (*moksh-marg*); but except for the lucky few, it is still for the individual to take that path and make his or her way along it. The inequalities between persons are never entirely effaced or transcended, even by the imagery of Jains as assembled worshippers and listeners.

Other Times, Other Places, Other Persons

Accounts which describe Jainism as 'atheistic', because the Jinas are mortal humans and yet the highest beings it conceives, are very misleading. There is an important element in the Jain understanding of the Tirthankar which sees him as a human being: a striver who by hard work achieved spiritual perfection. The idea that lay Jains today should also strive in this way is a very important one, and it relies upon this thought— the thought expressed by the man who said, 'We are supposed to become God.' But this must be set beside a quite different conception of the Tirthankar as a central part of the natural history of the cosmos.

Twenty-four Tirthankars appear on earth during each world-age. These immensely long cycles of time, in which the moral and physical condition of the world in turn degenerates and improves, have been

---

[13] Carrithers and Humphrey, *Assembly of Listeners*.

[14] See, for an example, Humphrey and Laidlaw, *Archetypal Actions*, 215–16.

[15] See Jaini, 'Bhavyatva and Abhavyatva'.

divided both by Jain writers and their Hindu counterparts into stages. The schemes are different, though, because while Hindu writers have envisaged slow deteriorations, followed by divine intervention to destroy the world and then create it anew, the Jains describe an entirely regular, entirely natural and mechanical process of gradual decline followed by gradual improvement—a massive sinusoidal curve in which symmetrical upward (*utsarpini*) and downward (*avasarpini*) world-ages follow smoothly from each other—a process which belongs to the same law-governed universe in which the mechanical effects of *karma* take place. Ours is a downward age. Each age has six stages. The first Tirthankar, and so Jainism, only appears towards the end of the third stage of decline, because until then the world is so felicitously constructed that no one wants to attain release. The remaining twenty-three Tirthankars are born during the fourth stage. Physical and moral decline go together, so according to some accounts Rishabh lived for 8,400,000 years,[16] but Shitalnath, the tenth Jina, for only 100,000. Parshvanath, the twenty-third, lived for 100 years and Mahavir, the last and an elder contemporary of the Buddha, for seventy-two. Less than a century after the death of Mahavir, the world entered its fifth declining stage, and since then release has been impossible. As in many religions, the possibility of salvation is thus denied for the here and now. We only have an imperfect or incomplete form of the true religion. (It is in this light, I believe, that we should see the claims made by all Jain traditions that the 'true scriptures' have been lost). The complete version is located, in the Jain case, both in another time and another place.[17]

It is often assumed, perhaps because in so many ways Jain doctrine resembles that of the Theravada Buddhists, that Jains believe, or at any rate Jain orthodoxy holds, that only renouncers can achieve enlightenment and release. This does appear to be the position which Digambar teachers have taken, but Shvetambar tradition is clear that certain householders have attained *moksh* and everyone I knew in Jaipur, lay Jains and renouncers alike, was agreed that this is so.[18] The stories of some of the lay persons who have done so, such as Rishabh's elder son Bharat and his mother Maru Devi, are well-known.

---

[16] This is a sort of all-purpose very large number (like saying 'zillions').

[17] In Theravada Buddhism there is a rather more radical distancing. It is generally held that only monks and nuns have attained *nirvana* in the past, and that no one can do so now. Southwold (*Buddhism in Life*, 205) reports that Buddhist villagers in Sri Lanka, in the 1970s, told him that *nirvana* is not possible within four births.

[18] The *Uttaradhyayana Sutra* (Jacobi, *Jaina Sutras*, ii. 210–11) classifies the souls which have achieved liberation as follows: 'those of women, men, hermaphrodites, of orthodox, heterodox, and householders.'

One day, as he was dressing, Bharat looked in the mirror. He noticed that a ring had fallen from one of his fingers. How different, how ugly, and how vulnerable the finger looked without its jewelled adornment. At once Bharat was overcome by the realization that without false ornament and disguise, all life is impermanent and subject to decay. Thinking this, the memory of his previous lives came back to him. He immediately attained omniscience.[19]

There are not many such fortunate people, but the list seems open-ended. A Khartar Gacch nun explained to me,

Anand Shravak, who lived in Mahavir's time, he attained *moksh* . . . No, actually he didn't.[20] He went to the twelfth heaven to become a god. Maru Devi, she went to *moksh* and so did Prithvi Chandra. Eh? Oh, he was a king and was in his coronation, and he thought, 'I am going to sit on my throne, but when will I sit on the throne of my own soul', and when he was thinking that he attained omniscience. Then there is Suna Sagar. He was sitting in his marriage ceremony. The priest was saying *mantra*s and suddenly said 'be careful' to his assistant. He was giving him some instruction or other. But Suna Sagar thought, 'Yes, I should be careful for my soul. I should not marry.' So he got omniscience.

So why is Jainism impossible? I began to ask the nun about a Jain layman who died only recently, and who is claimed by his admirers to have attained *moksh*.

No. Shrimad Rajcandra did not, but Devcand-ji did.[21] Not here, in another place, in Mahavideha. The Tirthankar Simandhar Swami is there. So we can go to *moksh* if we work to make preparation [i.e. if we work to be reborn there], and for this it is necessary to do good *karma*. Many people now are saying that Sajjan Shri-ji [the speaker's own guru, a renouncer] has gone there . . . Certainly, householders can attain *moksh*. Of course, these days it is not possible to get *moksh* from this place, for householders or even for us; but previously it was possible also for householders.

Shvetambar tradition holds out hope of rebirth in a place called Mahavideha: one of several mysterious and unreachable 'continents'. A Tirthankar, Simandhar Swami, is currently preaching there and release is

---

[19] There is evidence that Shvetambar renouncers, perhaps unsurprisingly, have occasionally played down the possibility of lay persons achieving liberation. Hemacandra, for instance, in his account of the Bharat story (*Trishashti-shalaka-purusha-caritra*, i. 376–8) equivocates, implying that Bharat became, *de facto*, a self-initiated renouncer because he removed his ornaments and attained enlightenment. But so far as popular belief, and renouncers' teachings today are concerned, Bharat is unanimously regarded as having achieved release as a layman.

[20] See below (ch. 8).

[21] On Shrimad Rajcandra, see below (ch. 10). Devcand-ji is a famous 18th-c. renouncer-saint.

therefore possible.[22] So the pattern of cosmic time which distinguishes conditions which are too favourable to worldly felicity to call for renunciation, from those which are too degenerate to allow for it, and which locates the world we live in between these two extremes, also has a spatial variant. We live in the *karma-bhumi*, the realm of action, where striving towards liberation is possible. There are other 'continents' where, as in the heavens, only enjoyment is to be found, so progress towards salvation is impossible. And in Mahavideha, as here in times past, a Jina makes liberation possible. Thus the image of redemptive listening is kept imaginatively alive, and Jain saints often report having visited Mahavideha in their dreams, or having had visions in which they saw that certain holy people have gone there, and are now sitting for the Jina's sermon. There are even temples in India where idols of Simandhar Swami are worshipped.

Perfect Selves and Others

It should already be clear that a very important element of what it is to be a Jain, whether you are a householder or a renouncer, is to see yourself as an 'other' of the Jina. Now as this figure is richly and variously imagined, this can be done in several ways.

Like every other living thing a Tirthankar has been born countless times before, but his or her final life, although there are individual embellishments, proceeds as the inevitable unfolding of the same fixed pattern. The five crucial events in the life of each Tirthankar, which are called the five beneficent (literally 'welfare-producing') moments or *panc kalyanak*, are conception (*garbha* or *cyavana*), birth (*janam*), renunciation (*diksha*), omniscience (*keval-gyan*), and liberation (*moksh*). The life of each Jina, because it consists of these five stages, is itself a sacred symbolic structure. While the moment of omniscience, represented in the *samosaran*, is the principal focus of attention and worship, all five are frequently superimposed or combined with each other in both art and ritual. Each is the focus of some kind of ritual action, and each is a possible reference-point for some form of specifically Jain identity.

Several of the twenty-four Tirthankars remain, so far as most ordinary Jains are concerned, almost undifferentiated, just one of a list of names. Others have been given full and colourful life-stories, and some have been incorporated into pan-Indian epic and mythic tales. For instance,

---

[22] For discussion of Simandhar Swami, see Dundas, *The Jains*, 230–1.

Neminath, the twenty-second Tirthankar, has been incorporated into the Krishna legends.[23] Such stories have been used by Jain teachers to comment on the moral worth of various Hindu deities and heroes, to adapt popular epics and folktales for Jain didactic purposes, and to incorporate various aspects of Hinduism into Jain teaching in a suitably orthodox way. The five-stage sacred biography allows Jains to 'think with' the Tirthankars in these ways without their exemplary status being reduced to that of merely human, or even merely mythical, individuals.

I shall now give a brief account of the five beneficent moments. In doing so, I shall follow the biography of the last Tirthankar, Mahavir, in a Shvetambar text called the *Kalpa Sutra*.[24] I choose this text because, as we shall see in Chapter 12, sermons based on it and rituals employing it are at the heart of some of the most important events in the Jain religious year. So the story is very well-known, and it is this 'performance version', including the rites and ceremonies where it is enacted, that I shall use to tell the story. My concern will be both to fill out the biography which the five-stage schema evokes, and also to point, as the story unfolds, to the broad kinds of religious stance which lay Jains can occupy in relation to the Tirthankar's changing guises.[25]

The first moment is when the Tirthankar descends from the heaven where he has spent his previous life, and enters the womb of a queen, who is lying half-asleep in her chamber. As the saviour-to-be enters her body, she has the first of fourteen visions.

Then [she] saw in her first dream a fine, enormous elephant, possessing all lucky marks, with strong thighs and four mighty tusks; who was whiter than an empty great cloud, or a heap of pearls, or the ocean of milk, or the moon-beams, or spray of water, or the silver mountain; whose temples were perfumed with fragrant musk-fluid, which attracted the bees; equalling in dimension the best elephant of the king of the gods; uttering a fine deep sound like the thunder of a big and large rain-cloud.[26]

This is followed by thirteen equally superlative dreams: of a bull, a lion,

[23] Burgess, 'Satrunjaya Mahatmyam', 288–302.

[24] See the text and translation edited by Vinay Sagar, *Kalpa Sutra*, the translation by Jacobi, *Jaina Sutras*, i, and discussion in Cort, 'Svetambar Jain Scripture', and Dundas, *The Jains*, ch. 3. The Shvetambar miniature-painting tradition in western India was built mostly around illustration of the *Kalpa Sutra*. See Brown, *Catalogue of Miniature Paintings*; Coomaraswamy, *Catalogue of Indian Collections*; Doshi, *Jain Painting*; Kramrisch, 'Jaina Painting'.

[25] The idea of looking at how actors situate themselves with respect to cultural schemas is adapted from Ortner, *High Religion*.

[26] Jacobi, *Jaina Sutras*, i. 231; Vinay Sagar, *Kalpa Sutra*, 63–5.

the goddess Shri or Lakshmi (goddess of wealth and well-being), a gar-land of flowers, the moon, the sun, a banner, an overflowing urn, a lotus pond, a sea, a celestial palace, a heap of jewels, and a flame. (The mother of the Buddha is said to have had these same fourteen dreams when his soul entered her body.) When an astrologer is consulted about the meaning of the dreams, it is revealed that the queen will soon give birth to a child who will be, 'The lord of a realm with a large and extensive army and train of waggons, a universal emperor (*cakravartin*) or a Jina, the lord of the three worlds, the universal emperor of the law (*dharma*—religion)'.[27] 'Mahavir' means 'great hero', and in his story the identifi-cation of Jina and temporal ruler is particularly emphatic. His soul de-scended first into the womb of a Brahmin woman, but was removed on the orders of Indra, king of the gods, and placed in that of the Kshatriya woman on the grounds that, 'It never has happened, nor does it happen, nor will it happen, that Jinas, emperors, [or other great heroes], in the past, present, or future, should be born in low families, mean families, degraded families, poor families, indigent families, beggar families, or brahmanical families.'[28]

The next beneficent moment is birth. Ever since Mahavir entered his mother's womb, the wealth of the kingdom has been increasing, so his parents name him Vardhaman, 'he who augments'. When these events are re-enacted, as at the installation of a new temple idol, the most sought-after ritual roles include those of the Jina's father and mother, for which people dress in their finest clothes and jewellery, put on crowns and other regalia, and are carried in processions in a palanquin. The mother's four-teen visions are basically a catalogue of things which in Indic culture in general are regarded as auspicious (*shubh or mangal*). It is conventional to talk of them as symbols of auspiciousness, but this implies that they indicate or refer to something else, some definite unseen quality—'auspi-ciousness'. However, it is probably better to talk about 'auspicious sym-bols': to leave open the question of whether and when this is the case, to indicate that their being auspicious is partly a matter of context and use, and to help us bear in mind that frequently these symbols do not stand for anything apart from themselves. They are, on one level, a sensual evo-cation of good fortune, especially when put together in this fashion; and often in ritual, too, things which are said for the purpose to be auspicious, such as flowers, sweets, certain kinds of leaves, fruits, and so on, are literally heaped up to stand for the unspecific good fortune that it is hoped

---

[27] Jacobi, *Jaina Sutras*, 247; Vinay Sagar, *Kalpa Sutra*, 125.
[28] Jacobi, *Jaina Sutras*, 225; Vinay Sagar, *Kalpa Sutra*, 33.

the ritual will bring (Chapters 12 and 17). But none of these things refers to anything in particular, or has a meaning which is different from that of any of the others. And rather than postulating an unseen metaphysical referent it is better, following Sperber,[29] to note the range of ideas and associations they evoke—worldly happiness, good health, peace, material plenty, sensual enjoyment, fertility, and natural increase and growth—and then to note that all of these are necessarily *given up* in Jain asceticism. But, as is the case here, those around the great renouncer, and particularly his kinsmen and consociates, benefit in worldly terms from his auspicious presence in the world.

In that night in which the venerable ascetic Mahavir was born, many demons in Vaishramana's[30] service belonging to the animal world, rained down on the palace of King Siddhartha [Mahavir's father] one great shower of silver, gold, diamonds, clothes, ornaments, leaves, flowers, fruits, seeds, garlands, perfumes, sandal, powder, and riches.[31]

The Jina is thus portrayed as auspicious, as giving rise to things and processes which bring welfare (*kalyan*), increase (*barkat*), and profit (*labh*), although they are the antithesis of his message and his project.

The third great moment is renunciation. Unlike the Buddha, who discovered his vocation when he happened on an old man, a sick man, and a corpse, the Tirthankar always knows what his destiny is. Before he is even born Mahavir decides when his renunciation will be. In order to spare his mother discomfort, he has been lying perfectly still in her womb, and she begins to suspect that he has died. Knowing that she is distressed (he is already clairvoyant) he kicks gently to reassure her. Struck by how deeply distraught she is, Mahavir resolves not to renounce the world until his parents have died and gone, as he already knows they will, to be gods.[32] By the time they die he is 30 years old, married, and has fathered a daughter. Shortly afterwards he is awakened to his destiny, as all Tirthankars are, by a host of gods who come to urge him not to delay any longer. These particular gods—Laukantika gods—have a special interest in the matter, as they are all destined to achieve liberation as Jain renouncers in their next life, and obviously they cannot do this until Jainism

---

[29] Sperber, *Rethinking Symbolism*. Keesing ('Conventional Metaphors') argues persuasively for great caution in attributing metaphysical beliefs and ontological commitments on the basis of what might only be metaphorical and figurative language.

[30] Vaishramana is another name for Kubera, king of the *yaksha*s (tree-spirits), and the pot-bellied money-bags of Indian mythology. See also ch. 17.

[31] Jacobi, *Jaina Sutras*, i. 251–2. Vinay Sagar, *Kalpa Sutra*, 143–5.

[32] Jacobi, *Jaina Sutras*, 250; Vinay Sagar, *Kalpa Sutra*, 137–9.

is established by the Tirthankar. Mahavir leaves his family and renounces all his possessions.

> He left his silver, he left his gold, he left his riches, corn, majesty, and kingdom; his army, grain, treasure, storehouse, town, seraglio, and subjects; he quitted and rejected his real, valuable property, such as riches, gold, precious stones, jewels, pearls, conches, stones, corals, rubies &c; he distributed presents through proper persons, he distributed presents to indigent persons.[33]

This distribution of wealth is known as the *varshi dan* (year-gift) because so vast is his treasury that it takes a whole year to give it all away. Once again, then, the Jina brings material benefit to others, although this time in a different way. Having already been the unintentional cause of great wealth and good fortune before his birth, now the Tirthankar's embarkation on his religious quest consists of intentionally distributing all his material possessions. Great stress is placed on how much has been renounced. The more you have, the more heroic it is to renounce it. This time it is his subjects who benefit, as he exchanges temporal for other-worldly imperium.

He then leaves his city in a great procession. Under a tree, he removes his clothes and ornaments and with his own hands plucks out his hair in five handfuls. He fasts for two-and-a-half days, puts on a renouncer's robe, and sets out alone for the homeless wandering life of an ascetic striver. He fasts, meditates, neglects his body, and undergoes great hardship. He loses his robe, so wanders naked, and accepts alms in his bare hands. He is worshipped by some villagers, who anoint his body with sweet oils. This brings swarms of insects who bite and sting him. He is attacked by other villagers who are offended by his nakedness, or whose greetings he does not acknowledge because he is deep in meditation. He is set upon by animals and by demons seeking to divert him from his path. But in the thirteenth year of his wandering, squatting in the heat of the sun, having taken no food or water for two-and-a-half days, he achieves complete enlightenment, the fourth beneficent moment (*keval gyan*). 'He knew and saw all conditions of the world, of gods, men, and demons: whence they come, whither they go, whether they are born as men or animals or become gods or hell-beings, the ideas, the thoughts of their minds, the food, doings, desires, the open and secret deeds of all the living beings in the whole world.'[34]

This brings us back to the point at which the destiny of the Tirthankar,

---

[33] Jacobi, *Jaina Sutras*, 257; Vinay Sagar, *Kalpa Sutra*, 163–5.
[34] Jacobi, *Jaina Sutras*, i. 263–4; Vinay Sagar, *Kalpa Sutra*, 187.

which is to be not just a sage or renouncer but also a teacher and saviour, is fulfilled. The *Kalpa Sutra* says nothing at all about the time between his omniscience and his death, except to list the places where he spent the rainy season. In general, Jain tradition is very reticent about representing the omniscient Jina as doing anything other than sitting in the *samosaran*. At this stage in his life, biography is completely eclipsed and he becomes purely a sacred symbol. In manuscript illustrations and in modern religious painting, so far as I am aware, he is shown only in the same two bodily postures in which he is represented in temple idols: sitting to preach and standing bolt upright in ascetic penance, so burning away the last residual *karma* from his soul. The four kinds of *karma* which remain after he has attained omniscience are those which make up a particular person or self.

1. *nam karma*—'name', this is identity in a general sense including gender, size, shape, and station in society;
2. *gotra karma*—family or lineage;
3. *vedniya karma*—that which produces feelings of happiness and sadness;
4. *ayu karma*—that which determines the duration of one's life.

Finally, as these drop away, the Tirthankar's soul is disburdened of its personhood and becomes a pure, abstract soul.

Neither rough nor soft; neither heavy nor light; neither cold nor hot; neither harsh nor smooth; he is without body, without resurrection, without contact (of matter), he is not feminine nor masculine nor neuter; he perceives, he knows, but there is no analogy (whereby to know the nature of the liberated soul); its essence is without form; there is no condition of the unconditioned. There is no sound, no colour, no smell, no taste, no touch—nothing of that kind.[35]

Thus, according to the *Acaranga Sutra*, is the fifth *kalyanak*, *moksh*. When the last particles of *karma* have gone, he dies. His soul ascends to the summit of the universe.

Mahavir is regarded by contemporary scholarship as a historical figure and the other Jinas, with the possible exception of Parshvanath, as mythical, but as we saw above they are all integrated in Jain religious thought into a single scheme which smoothly overrides that distinction, and locates their lives in a cosmological framework fixed by ineluctable laws. The life of each Tirthankar, and his or her preaching from the *samosaran*, is no chance event. They are not just people who happened to achieve

---

[35] Jacobi, *Jaina Sutras*, i. 52. See also the *Kalpa Sutra* (trans. Jacobi, 264–5).

salvation, but an integral and supremely important part of the order of things. Moreover, from this point of view the unique divinity of the Tirthankar consists in the almost complete absence of anything we would call individual or personal identity.

The paradigmatic and schematic quality of the Tirthankar's life is emphasized by the symbolic parallel between the *samosaran* and the events which follow his birth. If the *samosaran* is, as I suggested above, Jainism's crucifixion, then this is its Magi story. Here is Hemacandra again, this time on the birth of Rishabh Dev.

> At that time the thrones of the Indras, though immovable as mountain peaks, trembled like hearts from confusion. Shakra (king of all the Indras) . . . instructed his general of infantry . . . 'Summon all gods for his birth-bath' . . .
>
> Some from devotion to the *arhat*, like deer windwards; some drawn by Shakra's command, like iron by a magnet; some made to move by their wives, like aquatic monsters by the river floods . . . the gods came by means of shining cars . . .
>
> Shakra made himself five-fold; then there were five Shakras. Suitable devotion to the Master cannot be made by people with one body. Of these, one Sankrandana came forward, bowed, and said reverently, 'O Blessed One, allow me', and with auspicious devotion, took the Lord of the World . . . flew through the air . . . surrounded by gods filling the sky . . . [and] reached Mt. Meru.[36]

Throughout the Indic world Mount Meru is known as the *axis mundi*, joining heaven and earth. It is here that the gods take the infant Jina to bathe him. Every morning in Jain temples this is re-enacted in a ritual known as *snatra puja*, or 'bath-worship'. For this rite, a metal idol of the Jina is placed on a three-tiered silver platform in the centre of the temple, and this, which is said for other purposes to represent the *samosaran*, now becomes Mount Meru.

Although the Tirthankar who figures in this story is a baby, born as a prince in a royal household and not yet even a renouncer, he is represented by means of the same statue of an omniscient saint seated in meditation that represents the preacher in the *samosaran*. The myth and the rite involve another superimposition, because the bathing which takes place is both washing a new-born baby to clean away the pollution of childbirth, and *abhishek*, the anointing of a king. This superimposition of different stages in the Tirthankar's life is seen also in the way larger stone and marble Shvetambar idols are dressed in crowns and royal ornaments for worship, and indeed many elaborate, collective rites involve worship, simultaneously or in turn, of all five beneficent moments in the Jina's life.

---

[36] Johnson, *Trishashti-shalaka-purusha-caritra*, i. 108–22. Again, the passage given here is abstracted from a lengthy description.

PLATE III. A Jain layman bathing a Jina statue. Playing the part of Indra, king of the gods, a Jain layman bathes a Jina statue which here represents the newly born prince, brought by the gods to Mt. Meru. This re-enactment of the mythic events took place during rites for the installation of a new temple idol. (Photograph by Caroline Humphrey.)

When a new statue is consecrated in a Jain temple these events are acted out in a lengthy ritual which takes several days, the *panc kalyanak mahapujan* ('great worship of the five beneficent moments'). In this rite, in the *snatra puja*, and in many other contexts, lay Jains play the parts of these gods and goddesses, the Indras and Indranis (Plates III and IV). The Indras construct, as we have seen, the *samosaran* for the Tirthankar, and they worship him with a lustral bath. They are also portrayed furnishing Mahavir with his renouncer's robe, and in some accounts, with much of the riches he gives away in *varshi dan*. When the Tirthankars are troubled by demons and other enemies, these deities step in with magical power to protect them, although of course they do not really need protection.

We have seen already several ways in which lay Jain identity might be thought about, and we shall see each of these, in the chapters which follow, realized in everyday religious practice. He or she might be an ascetic striver, labouring like the renouncer to follow the Jina's example and free the soul of *karma*; or a listener, either attending a renouncer's sermon or worshipping a Jina idol, and like those attending the *samosaran* (on which both sermon and temple are modelled) hoping for miraculous redemption. Or, like Mahavir's parents, lay Jains might cast themselves as

PLATE IV. *A siddha-cakra puja.* A Jain layman, playing the part of Indra, holds an offering on a small tray, before adding it to the array of grains, fruits, and sweets of various colours laid out on the table before him. A small metal idol of a Jina is sitting in a *samosaran* on the left. Some Jain nuns are sitting watching in the background. Another man (foreground right) is dabbing a *siddha-cakra yantra* with sandalwood paste. This was a large collective *puja* in a temple in Jaipur, and several hundred people are looking on.

fortunate kinsmen, as the lay community takes quasi-familial pride in 'its' renouncers. Another stance is that of subject, and recipient of largesse from a magical renouncer-king. This possibility is most fully developed in the cults of renouncer-saints who have lived since the time of Mahavir, from the latter's own disciple Gautam Swami (Chapter 17) to the celebrated Khartar Gacch saints, the Dada Guru Devs (Chapters 3 and 5). Yet another possible stance, which lay Jains are particularly encouraged to adopt in temple ritual, is to imagine the self as being already like the omniscient Tirthankar—scarcely a self at all, but an abstract soul stripped of all qualities except the Jina's own infinite perfections.[37] To these conceptions of lay religious identity we must now add one more, one of which we shall see versions and variations throughout this book, because he or she might also be a royal god: a worshipper, but unlike the listener at the *samosaran*, also a patron and protector.

[37] For more on this mirroring, and in certain respects perhaps narcissistic aspect of ritual worship, see Humphrey and Laidlaw, *Archetypal Actions*, ch. 11.

3

Aspects of Organization

THE previous chapter introduced Shvetambar Jainism by looking at its most salient symbols and schemas. This chapter sketches the social organization of the practices which generate and transmit them, and identifies some of the relationships on which religious life is built.

Founders and Reformers

The major division within Jainism today—that between the Shvetambars and Digambars—was firmly established by the fifth century; and according to Jain tradition this was not the first but the eighth major schism to have occurred within the fold. Further schisms have occurred with impressive regularity, and new groups continue to appear, so that today there is quite a range of contending traditions practising and preaching subtly different versions of Jainism.[1]

The lay community we are concerned with in this book includes followers of two spiritual lineages of Jain renouncers, the Tapa Gacch and the Khartar Gacch. Both are Shvetambar, so there are both male and female renouncers among them (among the Digambars, women may not progress beyond the status of novices) and, as the name implies, renouncers of both sexes dress only in plain white robes. The Tapa Gacch and Khartar Gacch are both known as Mandir Margis (those of the temple path), and as Murti Pujaks (those who worship idols), because unlike some other Shvetambars—the Sthanakvasis and the Terapanthis—lay followers of these traditions build and worship in elaborate temples dedicated to the Jinas. Other Mandir Margi traditions include the Anchal Gacch and the Paican Gacch, but these have no significant followings in Jaipur.

Temple worship has probably always been controversial in Shvetambar Jainism, and there is a fairly continuous tradition of organized opposition

---

[1] An excellent general account of Jain sectarian history is given in Dundas, *The Jains*. On the Digambars, see also Carrithers, 'Naked Ascetics'; 'Jainism and Buddhism'; Jaini *Jaina Path*; on the Shvetambars, see also Cort, 'Svetambar Mendicant'; Dundas, 'Tenth Wonder'; Humphrey and Laidlaw, *Archetypal Actions*, ch. 2.

which goes back at least to the fifteenth century, when the Gujarati layman Lonka Shah claimed to have discovered in ancient texts that the practice was illegitimate. He founded a new sect, the Lonka Gacch, from which the Sthanakvasis and Terapanthis of today are descended. These traditions are influential, although they have fewer followers than the Mandir Margi traditions. The Terapanth especially is skilful at projecting itself as a modern movement, and as representative of Jainism as a whole in national and international religious fora. So the Mandir Margi schools, such as the Tapa Gacch and Khartar Gacch, maintain their practice of temple worship against the opposition from these traditions, as a deliberate and sustained choice. The renouncers, although they are restricted by their monastic vows in the role they may play in temple ritual (see Chapter 11), are none the less vociferous in providing, in print and in their sermons, powerful intellectual justifications for the practice, and replies to the arguments of rival schools.

Two rival Jain traditions require a brief introduction here. The Shvetambar Terapanth was founded in the eighteenth century in western Rajasthan, by a disillusioned Sthanakvasi renouncer who is now known to his followers as Acarya Bhikshu. Like the tradition he came from, Bhikshu was opposed to the worship of temple idols, but he also objected to the way Sthanakvasi renouncers lived in halls built specially for their use, and prescribed instead that his disciples should sleep in the homes of lay followers.[2] He had some distinctive teachings about non-violence, and the relation of Jainism to social ethics, which will be discussed below (Chapters 7 and 14). And the Terapanth has come to have a distinctive organization too. Whereas in all other Shvetambar traditions renouncers live under the authority of their own guru, and small travelling groups have day-to-day autonomy from the most senior renouncers (*acaryas*) of the tradition, the Terapanth is a single, tightly-run sect, in which all renouncers are answerable to a single *acarya*. The present leader, Acarya Tulsi, has been particularly effective in using the modern mass-media to raise the public profile of this sect in India.

The Kanji Swami Panth, though formally Digambar, pursues a vigorous proselytizing campaign whose targets include Shvetambars and also non-Jains. Although it does give formal recognition to Digambar monks,

---

[2] In practice, today, the wealthy lay followers who own the houses where Terapanthi renouncers lodge usually live in another, nearby house. For a study of the Terapanth, informed by psychoanalytic theory, and based on fieldwork at the village of Ladnun in Rajasthan, which is the main Terapanthi headquarters, see Goonasekara, 'Renunciation and Monasticism'.

this sect does not have renouncers of its own and is led instead by lay pandits, who give lectures and conduct study sessions to promote its views. It was founded in the mid-1930s by a Shvetambar monk from southern Gujarat, who switched allegiance, declaring himself a Digambar layman.[3] It is now influential in Jaipur through its alliance with a local Digambar group there, the followers of the eighteenth-century Jaipur layman, Pandit Todarmal. Like Kanji Swami (and like Banarsidas, another lay reformer of a century before him[4]) Todarmal was influenced by the mystical doctrines attributed to the second-century Digambar saint Kunda Kunda. This movement does not oppose temple ritual—its followers worship in Digambar temples—but its teachers concentrate on the dissemination of the Kanji Swami version of Jainism, which differs distinctly from that taught by the Mandir Margi traditions (see Chapter 9). This they do in Jaipur from a well-organized, entirely lay organization running an extensive publishing and teaching programme in Todarmal's name.

The Khartar Gacch and the Tapa Gacch, both much older traditions than either of these, were also born in controversy. The emergence of the Khartar Gacch can be traced to the eleventh century. At this time, under the patronage of kings ruling the area that now comprises Saurashtra, northern Gujarat, and southern Rajasthan, Shvetambar Jainism achieved its greatest cultural prominence, and debates about correct monastic practice were at the same time high matters of state. One of the main points at issue was whether renouncers should journey from place to place or whether they could live permanently in temples (*caityas*) or monasteries (*maths*). The Khartars opposed the so-called *caitya-vasis*, or temple-dwellers, and argued that laxity in this area led to attachment to material possessions, and so to disregard for other rules on non-violence and receiving alms. In 1024, it is said, king Durlabha arranged a public debate at Anahillawara Patan (in Gujarat), between the itinerant renouncer Jineshvar Suri, and Sura, a prominent temple-dwelling monk. Not only did Jineshvar defeat his opponent, but the king bestowed on him the epithet 'Khartar'—sharp-witted and fierce—and from this the present order takes its name.[5]

One of the distinctive features of the Khartar Gacch is worship of four leading renouncers who lived between the eleventh and the early seventeenth centuries, and who are now regarded as the patriarchs of that

---

[3] See Dundas, *The Jains*, 227–32, for the best account available in English.

[4] See Humphrey and Laidlaw, *Archetypal Actions*, chs. 2 and 9; Lath, *Ardhakathanaka*.

[5] Dundas, 'Tenth Wonder', 182–3; Klatt, 'Extracts', 245–6; Schubring, *Doctrine of the Jainas*, 63–5.

tradition. They are known collectively as the Dada Guru Devs—*dada* means paternal grandfather, *guru* means religious teacher, and *dev* means deity.[6] In addition to securing the *gacch*'s dominance over the *caitya-vasi*s, these saints saved its followers from Muslim persecutors, Hindu rivals, robbers, evil demons, and natural disasters. They also converted not only many individuals, but whole castes to Jainism, and indeed they are seen as having virtually refounded Shvetambar Jain society in Rajasthan (Chapter 5). Following a widespread South-Asian tradition, the Guru Devs have been worshipped for centuries—probably more or less since their deaths—in the form of footprint shrines, and in recent decades also as anthropomorphic statues (see Plate XIII). Worshippers continue to report that these saints appear before them in times of crisis and afford magical help and protection in a host of everyday ways. Indeed, the cult of the Guru Devs is burgeoning: their shrines are crowded on Mondays, full-moon days, and on certain days there are busy evening and even all-night singing vigils. New shrines and temples continue to appear, and new miracles are reported all the time.

Founded two centuries after the Khartar Gacch, the Tapa Gacch also traces its origins to a leading monk who revolted against what he saw as the lax practices of his age. Jagaccandra Suri left the Vata Gacch (which no longer exists) and he and his followers became established as a new sect when king Jaitrasimha of Chitor, in southern Rajasthan, was impressed by his austerities (*tap*), and named the new movement accordingly. The most celebrated renouncer in subsequent Tapa Gacch history is Hiravijay Suri, a contemporary of Jin Chandra Suri, the fourth Khartar Gacch Guru Dev, and like him linked in various hagiographical stories with the Mughal Emperor Akbar.[7] His statues, like those of the Guru Devs in the Khartar Gacch, are worshipped in Tapa Gacch temples, but he is not credited with the same magical powers, and therefore plays a more low-key role in the tradition's cultic practice.[8]

---

[6] The four Guru Devs are: Jin Datt Suri (AD 1075–154), Manidhari Jin Chandra Suri (1140–66), Jin Kushal Suri (1280–1332), and Jin Chandra Suri (1538–1613). Dates according to local sources in Jaipur. See also Babb, 'Monks and Miracles'; 'Great Choice'; Humphrey and Laidlaw, *Archetypal Actions*; Laidlaw, 'Profit, Salvation, and Profitable Saints'.

[7] See Findly, 'Jahangir's Vow of Non-Violence'; Smith, 'Jain Teachers of Akbar'.

[8] John E. Cort's doctoral dissertation, 'Liberation and Wellbeing' contains an excellent and detailed study of the present-day Tapa Gacch, based on extensive fieldwork in northern Gujarat. The picture he presents of lay Shvetambar Jainism in that area, although it is set out in rather different terms, is broadly compatible, I think, with the account developed here. See also Dundas, *The Jains*, 123–4.

Shvetambar Jainism came to be dominated by the new 'reformist' orders, but the so-called lax practices they identified persisted. Within both the Tapa Gacch and the Khartar Gacch the descendants of the *caitya-vasi*s, who came to be called *yati*s, remained powerful religious leaders, maintaining close links with the ruling Rajput and Muslim courts, control of considerable property, and large lay followings. Until earlier this century they were the main religious leaders of local Jain communities, who also acted as caste bards and genealogists to lay Jain communities,[9] but there has been a revival in the number, importance, and prestige of propertyless, itinerant renouncers, and *yati*s have found it increasingly difficult to attract new recruits.[10] This revival was spearheaded in the Tapa Gacch, but its effects are to be seen now in all the Shvetambar traditions. While the number of *sadhu*s and *sadhvi*s in the *gacch*s has risen, from probably a few dozen in the mid-nineteenth century to something approaching six thousand today, the *yati*s are reduced to only a handful.

*Yati*s are, in theory at any rate, celibate, but unlike renouncers they own property, they cut their hair and shave, they wear shoes, and they may travel on buses and trains. In Jaipur, and in other parts of Rajasthan (they are rarer in Gujarat and among the Tapa Gacch), they act as paid ritual specialists, helping at large temple rituals and selling tantric and magico-medical services. Because of this, they are increasingly seen not as authoritative religious leaders, but as higher-ranking *pujari*s. The latter are ritual specialists, typically Brahmins, who help worshippers through rites they do not know, but they also grind sandalwood paste for use in the temple, ring the bell at prescribed points in time, clear away offerings, clean the temple after worship is over, and generally perform the tasks of temple servants. *Yati*s still retain an association with renouncers which *pujari*s do not have, and some of them are, as individuals, highly respected. But the institution has been decisively undermined. In a development which parallels, in many ways, the shift in control of Hindu temples from hereditary priests to lay trusts, what was formerly *yati*s' property has mostly been claimed by the lay Jain organizations which administer temples and religious funds. In terms both of numbers and religious authority, they are now overshadowed by the *sadhu*s and, more especially, by the *sadhvi*s.

In 1990 there were just twenty Khartar Gacch monks and 189 nuns.

[9] Granoff, 'Religious Biography'.
[10] For more on *yati*s see Burgess, *Temples of Satrunjaya*, 6–7; 'Papers on Satrunjaya—VII'; Cort, 'Svetambar Mendicant'.

Since the Tapa Gacch revival in the mid-nineteenth century, its re-nouncers have remained very much more numerous than all the other *gacch*s put together—they are roughly five-sixths of the total. But Tapa Gacch renouncers are heavily concentrated in Gujarat and visits to Jaipur are not very frequent. The Khartar Gacch has a larger lay following in Jaipur, and over the last couple of decades there has rarely been a time when no Khartar Gacch renouncers have been in the city. So it is Khartar Gacch renouncers who tend to be the focus of religious attention among all Mandir Margi Jains in Jaipur. Within the Tapa Gacch, during this century, there have arisen two schismatic movements, which are now controversially recognized in Gujarat as separate sects, the Vimal Gacch and the Tristuti Gacch.[11] But the Jaipur laity, because it has such limited contact with Tapa Gacch renouncers, takes little part in the disputes involved here, and when a group of Tristuti Gacch *sadhu*s visited the city, they were housed in the Tapa Gacch temple and treated like any other Tapa Gacch renouncers, in spite of the *sadhu*s' own attempts to interest people in their claim to separate recognition.

Renouncers and Householders

Shvetambar *gacch*s are organized as spiritual lineages, descent being traced from guru to disciple. A young renouncer is under the authority of her guru, who takes charge of her training, education, and discipline. She must formally receive her guru's permission for everything she does, and normally lives and travels with her.[12] Each travelling group is called a family (*parivar*), a tribe or company (*gana*), or a circle or association (*mandal*). Authority is exercised by its most senior member (*ganin* if the group is male, *ganini* if female), and through this leader each is connected by pupilary descent to other such travelling groups. When a renouncer acquires disciples of her own she may travel with them as a separate group, and only then will she live more or less permanently apart from her own guru. Attracting disciples raises the status of a renouncer, and gives her relative autonomy within the *gacch* structure.

For most of the year, renouncers live at one place for only a few days or at most a few weeks at a time and they cover long distances in the course of the year. Their journeying is called *vihar*, a word used in other Indian

[11] Cort, 'Svetambar Mendicant', 658–63.

[12] Because the vast majority of Shvetambar renouncers today, including many of the most respected, are women (and because using 'he or she' can become cumbersome), I shall in general, and other things being equal, refer to renouncers with feminine pronouns.

religious traditions for a monastery. By keeping on the move in this way, they remain independent of any particular lay community, thus realizing their ideal of being without a home. In practice, some renouncers do tend to remain within their own favourite areas, and as they become too old to move around the most senior renouncers tend to travel within an increasingly small area, keeping a few of their younger followers with them. The late Khartar Gacch *acarya* Kanti Sagar Suri spent a lot of his time in western Rajasthan, near the famous temple of Nakora-ji, and two recent *pravartini*s, Vicakshan Shri-ji and Sajjan Shri-ji, spent their last years in Jaipur.

During the monsoon season in India, swarms of insects enjoy a brief reign over the whole country. It would be impossible to be sure of not stepping on any, and thus committing *himsa*, so travelling is suspended and Jain renouncers, like those of many other Indic ascetic traditions, observe a four-month rains retreat (called Caturmas or Caumasi) between mid-July and mid-November,[13] when they stay in one place, in extended and close contact with a particular lay community. Caturmas is the time when Jain families are likely to engage most in ascetic rites and fasting, and this is done under the leadership and guidance of any renouncers who are resident in the community (Chapter 12).

There is close contact between Jain renouncers and the laity of towns and villages they pass through. They are welcomed by a procession which escorts them to their lodgings, and thereafter they receive visits from lay Jains wishing to receive blessings and take vows for fasts and other ascetic practices (Chapters 9 and 10). The renouncers are usually expected to provide daily sermons too (Chapter 11). They must receive all their food as alms from the kitchens of lay households. The family does not have to be Jain, but the food must be strictly vegetarian and conform to many rules and restrictions as to how it is prepared and the conditions under which it is given (Chapters 14 and 15).

Below (Chapter 6) I shall discuss the social organization of local religious communities, and the extent to which they depend on patronage and leadership of particular individuals and families (see also Chapters 8, 15, and 16); but it is worth noting now that the presence of particular renouncers in a locality can have a direct effect on both religious consciousness and the intensity of religious practice. The arrival of a group of well-known, charismatic renouncers can bring local Jains together as Jains, and encourages them to attend sermons, take up regular temple

---

[13] The lunar months of Shravan (Savan), Bhadra (Bhadom), Ashvin (Kvar), and Karttik.

worship, and even make permanent changes in dietary practice in response to their teaching and example. This community-building by renouncers, which can be seen as a routine recapitulation of the mytho-historical founding of Jain sects and castes (see Chapter 5) by saint-ascetics, is especially marked among the Digambars, because there are so very few of them,[14] but it is observable among Shvetambars too. Jaini has suggested that the itinerancy of Jain renouncers, and the need which their alms-collecting places on them for day-to-day interaction with the laity, explains the greater resilience which Jainism has shown in India, and why even in the relative absence of royal patronage it did not die out there, as did Buddhism.[15]

Larger local Jain communities maintain buildings called *upashraya*s, often attached to temples, for renouncers to lodge in. A Jain *upashraya* is a very particular kind of public space. Lay Jains expect open access to their renouncers, and for large portions of the day they meet in what one might call 'open session'. People come, sit for some time, perhaps speaking, perhaps not, and go when they choose. The renouncer carries on a conversation with a collective interlocutor, the members of which come and go, without, in general, any perceptible change in the flow of talk. But although the arrangements at a meeting of this sort, and the tone of the proceedings, suggest something between an audience chamber and a *salon*, the setting and the trappings speak by contrast of severe asceticism. *Upashraya*s are often grand and expensive buildings, but they tend, in contrast to the sumptuously decorated and incense-heavy temples, to be empty, echoing halls with stone or marble floors, whitewashed walls, hardly any furniture, and, for decoration, only stern portraits of deceased renouncers.

Apart from the sparse furniture found in *upashraya*s, renouncers must carry everything they need—all their clothes, books, and personal effects—from place to place as they travel. Most of what they have is prescribed: white cotton clothes, and a light woollen blanket; a staff (*dand*); a cloth to hold before the mouth when speaking (*muh-patti*); two brushes (*ogha*s) for sweeping the ground before sitting down and while walking; a set of wooden bowls (*patra*s), in which to receive alms; and a rosary (*mala*) for prayer and meditation. The most personal things they have are religious books, pictures of famous Jain saints, pens, notebooks, and a clock. Even these they are said not to own. Lay families donate them

---

[14] Carrithers, 'Bahubali Affair'; 'Naked Ascetics'.
[15] Jaini, 'Disappearance of Buddhism'.

to the order, and individual renouncers have use of them with their guru's permission, although in practice lay families do occasionally make gifts to individual renouncers.

Women and Men

Shvetambar tradition holds that female renouncers have always outnumbered the men,[16] and unlike in several other South Asian religious traditions they are neither marginalized,[17] nor systematically redefined as male (although see Chapter 11).[18] Shvetambars maintain that the nineteenth Tirthankar, Mallinath, was a woman (the Digambars disagree). By far the majority of Shvetambars who take on full renunciation these days are women, so the decline of the *yatis* (who all seem to have been men) has contributed to a decisive shift this century in the gender composition of religious authority in Shvetambar Jainism. This has gone farthest in the Khartar Gacch, where not only are female renouncers vastly in the majority, but they also include among them the tradition's most charismatic and influential religious leaders.

There is still in theory a categorical subordination of all female to all male renouncers. As Cort points out, the system essentially consists of male spiritual lineages, with nuns organized into lines which are conceived as adjuncts to those of monks.[19] But on the other hand, as seen from within each *gacch*, the nuns are organized into a parallel system, with travelling groups combining and dividing without reference to the groups in which monks are organized, and with pupilary descent being traced through leading nuns. The female equivalent of an *acarya*, a *pravartini*, should, if asked, submit the itineraries of the travelling groups under her authority for the approval of an *acarya*. And in theory, I was often told, even the most senior female renouncer would greet even the most junior male renouncer deferentially, if they were to meet. But on the other hand this rule was told to me as something odd and interesting, perhaps even a bit funny. And in practice, groups of nuns and monks operate separately and independently. They hardly ever meet. The salient fact, I think, is

---

[16] The *Kalpa Sutra* (Jacobi, *Jaina Sutras*, i. 284) tells us that Rishabh, the first Jina, led a Jain community of 84,000 monks, 300,000 nuns, 305,000 laymen, and 554,000 lay women. See also Burgess, 'Satrunjaya Mahatmyam', 303.

[17] Ojha, 'Feminine Asceticism'; Van der Veer, 'Power of Detachment'. But see also Denton, 'Varieties of Female Asceticism'.

[18] Srivastava, 'On Women and Renunciation'; White, 'Mother Guru'.

[19] Cort, 'Shvetambar Mendicant', 662.

PLATE V. Jain nuns blessing a fasting woman. During the Jain festival of Paryushan (Chapter 12) a young Jain woman is engaged on a long fast. Each morning of the fast, she comes to take a vow before Jain nuns and receives a blessing. Perfumed sandalwood powder (*vasakshep*) is sprinkled on her head and the nun recites a prayer for protection and success.

that women are easily the majority among the living exemplars of Jain asceticism, and the figures of religious status and authority. Shvetambar nuns are also religious teachers, administering vows to lay people who undertake fasts, giving blessings, taking leading parts in collective worship, and giving sermons to assemblies of lay men and women (see Plate V).[20]

[20] In the Tapa Gacch, it is said, female renouncers do not give sermons, although they do so regularly in all the other Shvetambar traditions. There were scarcely ever Tapa Gacch nuns in Jaipur while I was there, so I have no idea how rigorously this rule is followed (there must be scope for crossing the boundary between teaching in small groups, which is supposed to be allowed, and a sermon). And as no one I spoke to commented in any detail on the rule, I have no notion of what the reason for it might be. Cort ('Liberation and Wellbeing', 307–8) reports that he was unable to find a precise reason for the ban in Patan (see also Cort, 'Shvetambar Mendicant', 557; Shântâ, *La Voie Jaina*, 418). Cort indicates

This does not translate into anything resembling sexual equality in lay Jain families, where patterns of authority, in terms of both age and sex, generally resemble those in non-Jain Hindu households of similar caste and class. Babb's study of the Brahma Kumari movement, which he argues is an indigenous form of Indian feminism, illustrates the potential of renunciation to transform gender relations.[21] But Shvetambar Jainism does not, as the Brahma Kumaris do, reject the common imagery which represents women as the paradigm temptation, trapping men in worldly life. It is true that female renouncers in the Shvetambar tradition are not really implicated in this. Their renunciation of worldly life is as complete as that of their male colleagues. And as Josephine Reynell's research has amply demonstrated, lay Jain women not only predominate in almost all domains of religious practice, but they are also the principal agents of its transmission and reproduction.[22] Whether as renouncers, or among the laity, women in this tradition are, in Babb's terms, 'soteriological agents'. But only for renouncers can this agency be exercised with any degree of autonomy from men. And as we shall see, religious life for lay Jains is intimately part of the politics of marriage and family life.

So gender patterning will be a theme in much that follows. In Greek ethics, as described by Foucault, the central virtues were unambiguously gendered male: 'Self-mastery was a way of being a man with respect to oneself . . . in the full meaning of the word, moderation was a man's virtue.'[23] We shall see below (Chapter 11) that central Jain virtues are much more ambiguously gendered. If Foucault is right, the Greeks developed, 'an ethics for men: an ethics thought, written, and taught by men, and addressed to men—free men, obviously'.[24] Not so its Jain counterpart: not only because women are renouncers and therefore religious and ethical teachers, and not only because lay ascetic practice is dominated—and not only numerically—by women, but because lay Jainism is in the end a project for families, as well as for individuals. Religious practice also changes with age, and ethical completeness is a family's collective, if not always or necessarily a happily co-operative, project and

---

that people described it to him as a matter of 'customary practice', which suggests that they too were struck by the fact that no doctrinal justification seems to be current. I can report, however, that the Tapa Gacch community in Jaipur, on at least one occasion, invited Khartar Gacch nuns to their temple to give sermons, which suggests it is not a rule enforced by the laity.

[21] Babb, *Redemptive Encounters*, 139–55.
[22] Reynell, 'Women and Jain Community'.
[23] Foucault, *History of Sexuality*, ii. 82–3.   [24] Ibid. 22.

achievement. Some common patterns of male and female religious conduct only fully make sense, as we shall see, if they are a complement to the other.

Discipleship and Devotion

The following verse in Prakrit is the liturgical formula which comes most readily to the lips of lay Jains. It is called the *nokar mantra* (or *namaskara mantra*). Every Jain knows it by heart, some people ensure that it is the first thing they say each day, and most others at least begin their morning prayers with it.

namo arihantanam	I bow before the Arihants/Tirthankars
namo siddhanam	I bow before the perfected and liberated souls (*siddha*s)
namo ayariyanam	I bow before the leaders of the ascetic order (*acarya*s)
namo uvajjhayanam	I bow before the ascetic religious teachers (*upadhyaya*s)
namo loe savva-sahunam	I bow before all the renouncers (*sadhu*s) in the world.
eso panca namokkaro	This five-fold salutation,
savva-pavappanasano	Which destroys all sin,
mamgalanam ca savvesim	Is pre-eminent as the most auspicious
padhamam havai mangalam	Of all auspicious things.

The *nokar mantra* is the principal means by which devout Jains summarily express their affiliation to the religion. Most collective *puja*s begin with it, as do sermons by renouncers. It is recited during meditation and fasting, and it is the prayer which people use most as an incantation to repeat with a rosary. Another name it is known by is the *panc-parmeshthi mantra*—the *mantra* of the five highest divinities. But we should note that the formula of five 'divinities', which is a standard one used over and over again in Jain religious discourse, is in fact a list of ranks of renouncers, and it is important to bear in mind that however prominent gods of more or less supernatural aspect are in Jain religious life, it is consistently and exclusively renouncers who are worshipped as God. The thought that an invocation of these prophets of harsh asceticism is an auspicious thing is at first sight strikingly counter-intuitive. But as we saw in Chapter 2, this-worldly felicity is represented in Jain religious symbolism as in various ways the product of asceticism. And as we shall see in Chapter 4, and then repeatedly as the book proceeds, Jain religious discourse has frequent recourse to counter-intuitive claims, of which this idea may serve as illustration: renouncers and the Jinas, as exemplary ascetics and world-renouncers, stand not at the opposite moral pole from enjoyment of worldly good fortune and bounty, but are in fact its highest form.

The list of ranks of renouncers in the *nokar mantra*—the five 'highest divinities'—clearly suggests a continuity between the Jinas and living renouncers of today. The latter are not of course the same as the Jinas, but they are believed to be connected to Lord Mahavir by direct spiritual descent (most *gacch*s trace their pupilary succession back to Sudharman Swami, one of Mahavir's own disciples). Renouncers are not all equally strict, ascetic, and knowledgeable, but as this *mantra* implies, they are all treated formally as categorically sacred persons. As we shall see below, pious lay Jains take life-long vows from renouncers which bind them to religious conduct (Chapter 8), and they embark on fasts and other ascetic practices by taking vows before them (Chapters 9 and 10). In these respects lay Jains are the religious pupils or disciples, *shishya*s or *cela*s, of renouncers. This is a relation in which, as the *nokar mantra* implies, every Jain lay person necessarily stands to every Jain renouncer.

However, India's religious vocabulary allows the guru another possible partner, distinguishable from the disciple: the devotee. Their relationship is such a powerful and pervasive one in the Indian religious context that it is no surprise to find it as an ideal and an aspiration among Jains. For the devotee, or *bhakt*, a guru is not so much a teacher, still less a bureaucratic superior, as a direct and unmediated manifestation of the divine. A devotee's meeting with his or her guru is a 'redemptive encounter', a source of grace and infallible religious guidance and a fount of worldly prosperity and success.

The paradigm in the Jain tradition of the *sadhu* as benevolent, grace-dispensing guru is Gautam Swami, one of Mahavir's own disciples, who from the beginning of the Christian era began emerging in Jain literature as a distinctive character, more human and approachable, and at the same time more conventionally 'god-like' than the splendidly austere Tirthankars (see Chapter 17). Temple images of Gautam Swami are known from the thirteenth century, and from the same time too there are ritual texts referring to the miraculous help his worshippers hoped to receive from him.[25] The Dada Guru Devs have come to be seen in a similar way, and as in contemporary Hinduism, there are even Jain renouncers who are more or less deified during their lifetimes.

[25] See Dundas, *The Jains*, 33–4.

One of the more colourful Hindu instances of this, the cult surrounding Sathya Sai Baba, has been beautifully described by L. A. Babb.[26] And Peter Van der Veer's account of Ramanandi ascetics at Ayodhya illustrates how a whole religious movement can be structured around guru–*bhakt* relationships. As Van der Veer remarks, the guru-follower relationship is the only organizational structure of any importance in this tradition.

Every sadhu may go and roam throughout India, teaching, with certain limits, his own religious message; and great value is put on that freedom of the sadhu. Moreover, any sadhu can be chosen by any layman as his guru. For lay disciples the person of the guru is of primal importance, not the doctrinal orthodoxy of his teaching. The guru–disciple relation is a personal one, which gives a great span of freedom in doctrinal and practical matters.[27]

In this context, discipleship and devotion do not seem to be distinguished. Van der Veer describes how a *sadhu* acquires followers in essentially the same way from among other *sadhus* and from among the laity. This reflects the fact that the boundary between being a renouncer and being a householder is not very firm among the Ramanandis, many of whose renouncers (the so-called *rasik* devotionalists) have homes and even spouses.

Although, in the Jain case, such guru–devotee relations do not structure renouncer orders as a whole, they do coexist alongside the essentially institutional and hierarchical relations between gurus and disciples. Obviously the former can be the basis for much larger though more diffuse followings. Babb describes how the nationwide Sai Baba movement is held together by the devotion of followers who believe they have been chosen personally by a guru they have in fact never met. There are a few Jain renouncers who attract followings of this kind. As in the Hindu cases, it is the perceived and reputed personal qualities of the renouncer, and not the content of their teaching, that is the focus of attention.

A striking recent example was the renouncer Shanti Vijay Suri-ji (1889–1943).[28] Shanti Vijay became famous for the minor feats of magic he performed, such as knowing people's names and thoughts on sight, and being in two places at once, but mostly he was famous as a very strict, distant hermit, a meditation-master, and a mystic. He spent his later years living alone in a cave near the top of Mount Abu in Rajasthan, which, in addition to being an important Jain temple site, is a traditional retreat for

[26] Babb, *Redemptive Encounters*, 159–201. See also Swallow, 'Ashes and Powers'.

[27] Van der Veer, *Gods on Earth*, 75–6. See also Van der Veer, 'Taming the Ascetic'; Burghart, 'Wandering Ascetics'.

[28] He never became an *acarya* in a Jain order, but his devotees confer on him the *acarya*'s title, *suri*, and I have followed them in this here.

Hindu ascetics. In some respects he ceased to be a Jain monk at all, for he stopped travelling from place to place, lived alone, stopped performing the regular ascetic rites of Jain monastic life, stopped delivering formal sermons on Jain doctrine, and rather than going on the prescribed alms round he received food from devotees who came to visit him in his cave. Shanti Vijay's following, like the diffuse groups of distant devotees of celebrated Hindu gurus, cut across the normal lines of sect affiliation, and he indeed declared himself to be a member of no specific Jain order.[29] This is an extreme version of a tendency which, in a much more attenuated form, is routine in Jainism, and in that form qualifies and supplements the institutionalized loyalty and discipleship of lay Jains to all renouncers.

Until he ended his life with a fast in April 1991, Acarya Hastimal-ji Maharaj Sahab was one of the most senior renouncers in the Sthanakvasi tradition. He was known as a very learned man, author of several works of Jain history, but it was not for this reason that he attracted so many devotees, including many who are not themselves Sthanakvasis. I met Jains who believed that he appeared to them in dreams and, although he belonged to a tradition which rejects the use of images in worship, his devotees often kept pictures of him in their houses and prayed before them. I first heard of him in the mid-1980s from the Singhis, a Sthanakvasi family I knew in Jaipur. It was a stressful time for them. Mr Singhi had been unwell and they were embroiled in a legal battle with some tenants. One day Mrs Singhi announced that she was planning a trip to Jodhpur because she had so much tension at this time, and so many difficult decisions to make, that she felt she had to see her guru. She showed me a picture of him, which she had hanging in her room, and explained how the day before, when she had called out loud to it for help, she had felt that he was replying to her, telling her to come and see him. 'Of course,' she said, 'he will not tell me what to do, but if I go to meet him I will know.' She pointed to the photograph: 'If you look at those eyes, see how spiritual and powerful they are, and if you see him really you will just know that he has real spiritual power (*adhyatmik shakti*). In the past he has performed many miracles. He is close to being God [i.e. a Tirthankar].'

Like Mrs Singhi, many people believed that the blessing of this *acarya* would bring benefit to them. When I met him in 1990, he was spending Caturmas in Pali, not far from Jodhpur, and several thousand people had come to meet him there. He was staying at a large meeting-hall (like an

---

[29] Shanti Vijay Suri was not born into the Jain community. He was a Raika, a member of a semi-nomadic pastoral people. He was initiated, as a child, into the Tapa Gacch, but the only two renouncers he initiated (both nuns) joined the Khartar Gacch.

upashraya, but referred to in this sect as a *sthanak*), perched above one of the narrow lanes in the heart of the old town. There were banners hanging across the alleyways and crowds of people queuing all the way down the stairs and out into the street. I arrived in the evening so the crowd consisted only of men: the *acarya* interpreted very strictly the rules on avoiding members of the opposite sex, and granted audience to women only between eight and ten-thirty in the mornings and between two and four in the afternoon. The room was in darkness when I got there, because he allowed no artificial light (and indeed no electricity) near him. The *acarya* had many disciples, and a number of the younger monks could be glimpsed across the large hall, talking quietly in twos and threes or sitting alone in prayer.

Relations between such celebrated gurus and the great majority of their devotees are an intriguing combination of intimacy and distance. The tone in which many people speak of their relationship to 'my guru' is reminiscent of the spurious familiarity with which British people often speak of members of the royal family. Although Mrs Singhi told me, 'He knows me very well', she had probably never spent more than a few minutes actually in conversation with her guru, and cannot have seen him more than once every two or three years. The *acarya* was on a wooden dais surrounded by a large silent crowd. Many were just sitting watching but a steady stream managed to stumble out of the confusion on the darkened stairs, to come up and pay their respects. The man in the centre of all this was very small and frail. He either could not or would not speak out loud, and talked through a young renouncer who stood at his side and relayed the guru's whispered words. This disciple also had another job to do. It is generally believed that this *acarya*'s blessings are conveyed with particular effectiveness to those who touch his right toe (a belief which is also ubiquitous in Hindu devotional traditions and reflected directly in the Guru Dev cult—indeed Hastimal's close followers referred to him as 'Guru Dev'), and although his feet are normally concealed in the folds of his robes, occasionally he does allow this. But every so often a particularly enthusiastic devotee will make an unauthorized lunge for the master's feet, and his disciple must be on hand to protect him from such predations.

The apparent paradox which surrounds guru–*bhakt* relations in Jainism, and the reason they remain in general firmly subordinate to sect-based institutionalized followings, is that the closer a lay Jain actually comes to having a recognized devotee-relationship with a particular renouncer, the closer, that is, the relationship to his or her guru comes to the ideal, the more likely both parties are to deny that it exists. Even Jains who would travel hundreds of miles to meet a particular renouncer, before embarking on a new business venture or arranging a marriage, who were received cordially, and perhaps even taken into private conclave with their guru, will be equivocal if asked who their guru is. 'All Jain renouncers are my guru', they will say, 'all *sadhu*s who have taken the five vows [i.e. been initiated into the Jain order].' 'They are all following Jain *dharma* and we believe in them all.' 'We do reverence to all Jain *sadhus*—they are like Mahavir Swami and we do *bhakti* to them all.' The reason for this is that while everyone desires them, close personal ties between Jain renouncers and lay Jains are 'not allowed' in Jainism, because renouncers have given up all personal attachments. For lay Jains to criticize renouncers or differentiate between them on the basis of their individual qualities is similarly not allowed, because their renunciation, being in the manner laid down by the Tirthankars, is axiomatically exemplary. Thus religious devotion can be seen from another perspective as positively irreligious—as attempts to circumvent the truth that everything depends upon *karma*. And, as if to lock the situation in paradox, to take just this stance, to declare that particular devotion is sinful, and to criticize their devotees in these terms, is the kind of evidence of strictness and insight for which devotees most admire their gurus.

4

A Theology of Interdiction

Whenever a philosopher says something is 'really real' you can be really sure that what he says is 'really real' isn't real, really.

G. E. Moore

IN Jain temples, in addition to idols of the Tirthankars and other great Jain saints of the past such as the Guru Devs, there are several other kinds of sacred representations. There are usually a few of the many named gods and goddesses who are devotees and protectors of the Tirthankars, known respectively as *yaksha*s and *yakshi*s (also as *shasan dev*s and *shasan devi*s). Like those of many of the high gods in the Hindu pantheon, these are anthropomorphic statues, sometimes with animal heads and many arms. The goddesses, especially, are popular figures in Jain temples. Today the most commonly found, in the form of small statues which, like those in Vaishnava Hindu temples, are dressed in gowns of sequinned and gilded cloth, are the patronesses respectively of the first and twenty-third Jinas, the goddesses Cakeshvari and Padmavati. In addition there are the *bhairu*s, said to be a form of Shiva and depicted as armed, moustachioed warriors. Then there are the *bhumiya*s or 'lords of the soil', and *kshetrapal*s or 'guardians of the place', both represented as almost featureless blobs covered in vermilion and silver foil, but usually with eyes and the sugges-tion of facial features. All these kinds of deities—*yaksha*s, *bhairu*s, *bhumiya*s, and *kshetrapal*s—are worshipped by non-Jains in the region too, in roadside shrines throughout the countryside and in grand Hindu temples. They are said to perform miracles—marvels (*camatkar*) or proofs (*parcya*) of their divinity. They guard Jain temples, and inflict illness and misfortune on those who show disrespect to the religion. Lay Jains pray and make vows to them to obtain worldly success and for their help in destroying enemies (Plates VI and VII).

This raises a question, which is familiar from the anthropology of Hinduism and Buddhism, of how propitiation of these miracle-working deities fits with beliefs about *karma*.[1] In these cases too, *karma* exists alongside other possible kinds of explanation of otherwise unexplained

---

[1] See Babb, 'Destiny and Responsibility'; Fuller, *Camphor Flame*, 245–52; Gombrich, *Precept and Practice*, ch. 5; Kolenda, 'Religious Anxiety and Hindu Fate'; Obeyesekere,

PLATES VI AND VII. IDOLS OF JAIN PROTECTOR DEITIES.

PLATE VI. Kshetrapal, who guards particular places, especially temple compounds. This one is in the Dadabari temple in Jaipur.

PLATE VII. Ghantakarn, a martial deity said to be linked to the Hindu god,
Hanuman. His vehicle, a lion, sits at his feet. He is carrying a bow and arrow;
he also has a club, a weight, a sword, and a shield; and he is surrounded by
bells and magical diagrams. For worship, a silver crown has been placed on his
head, various parts of his body have been daubed with sandalwood paste, and
he has been decorated with flowers.

events: notably 'fate' (though just how far this can actually be distinguished from *karma* seems variable), angry or malevolent deities, ghosts, and witchcraft. To some authors, partly because Weber encouraged us to see the doctrine of *karma* as a uniquely complete theodicy,[2] these beliefs have appeared to contradict and therefore to be in competition with *karma*. This problem has been countered with the observation that, partly because of the different palliatives or remedies that follow from these different explanations, they tend to be invoked in different contexts. The problem seems to me a false one because, as I argued in Chapter 2, *karma* is not really a theory at all. But the Jain insistence that everything *ought* to be explained in terms of *karma* reminds us that ideas can be brought into competition by other forces than those of logical entailment. People who appeal to *karma* in one context and witchcraft in another are after all reflective persons, capable of remembering what they have said and done from one context to another. Even if, as we anthropologists have at length reassured ourselves, there is no question of irrationality in appealing to these different frames of reference to explain different aspects of the way the world is, we ought still to remember that rationality is not the only virtue which people might be concerned to exhibit. Babb, writing of Hinduism, has pointed out that the insufficiencies of *karmik* imagery as therapy and consolation—its tendency both to imply that misfortune might really be your own fault and to be rather unspecific about what your fault might have been—have another side. *Karma* imagery rather powerfully suggests an ethical content for all one's actions, and suggests also consequential moral links between them. Therefore, as Babb rightly observes, 'to apply the karmic frame of reference to life's problems is to relate them to a higher order of moral responsibility'.[3] When my Jain friends cited *karma*, with evident pride and approval, as the kernel of Jain teaching they had, I think, some such thought in mind. Perhaps discussion of *karma* as theodicy is too much dominated by questions of which explanation is likely to appeal at the time to those actually suffering misfortune.[4] If moral thinking, and reflection on the causes of suffering, consisted only of isolated *ad hoc* attempts to comfort oneself with the best possible self-justification, then no doubt *karma* would play an insignifi-

---

'Theodicy, Sin and Salvation'; Sharma, 'Theodicy and the Doctrine of Karma'; Spiro, *Buddhism and Society*, 155–9.

[2] Weber, 'Social Psychology of World Religions'; *Economy and Society*, 523–6; *Religion of India*, 121–2.

[3] Babb, 'Destiny and Responsibility', 178.

[4] Wadley and Derr ('Eating Sins') provide an interesting corrective.

cant part in it. But this is not so, and any explanation of one's own misfortune, if it is to take root in public discourse, must survive in the sometimes frosty climate of other people's perceptions and reflections. It must survive, too, beside explanations for equally surprising good fortune, and for cases where suffering is generally seen as merited. And just because they are propagated by those who have been fortunate, some of these explanations are likely to be hardier.

The coexistence of a strong commitment to the idea of *karma* as the proper way to explain events, and belief in supernatural agencies who intervene miraculously in human affairs, does present a problem, but it is not a problem which can be solved by asking how they can be made logically consistent. In the Jain case at least, what makes them compossible is a widespread sense that one of them is not allowed, together with routine and well-established practices for recognizing and declaring that this is so.

Miracles Are Not Allowed

This is how Hemacandra continues his account, which I began to relate in Chapter 2, of how the gods all gathered from around the world, under the direction of Indra, to bathe, anoint, and worship the infant Jina.

They created water pots a *yojana* (eight miles) high, gold, silver, made of jewels, gold and silver, gold and jewels . . . [They] took water from the ocean of milk . . . At the *tirtha*s [sacred places] . . . they took water, lotuses, etc. . . . After mixing together the fragrant substances and water, they went quickly to Mt. Meru.

The Indra of Acyuta began to bathe the Lord of the World, bending the pitcher a little, as if it were his own head. Then the gods beat loudly drums that made the mountains of the gods reverberate . . . Some blew conches loudly . . . The streams of water falling from these pitchers with *yojana*-wide mouths looked like cascades from mouths of mountain-caves . . . As soon as the Lord's bath-water fell on the ground, with devotion it was seized by some . . . 'Where, pray, will we obtain that again?' With this thought, some gods put the water on their heads like men in a desert. Some gods with eagerness sprinkled their bodies again and again, like elephants suffering from summer heat. Advancing quickly on the plateaux of Mt. Meru, the water formed a thousand rivers on all sides.

The gods anoint themselves with the water which flows off the baby's body. The reader familiar with the ethnography of South Asian religion will be struck by a remarkable piece of restraint—they do not drink it. To do so, to ingest some normally impure form of bodily substance, is a standard way in which worshippers receive blessings from sacred persons and sacred images. The water in which a sacred object has been bathed is called *prakshal* (and in some traditions *nirmalya*) and Jains too drink *prakshal* in certain circumstances. But they do not generally drink that in which an idol of a Tirthankar has been bathed. This is not because they do not think it will have beneficial effects, but rather—and this is why I say 'generally'—because it is, as people say, not allowed.

Snatra puja, a ritual re-enactment of the Jina's birth-bath, is performed every day in Jain temples and many of those who perform the rite will afterwards take a little of the water and milk mixture which is used, and dab some on their foreheads or their eye-lids. Some people will refer to the bathing myth as the reason they do this, or to another well-known story (that of Mena Sundari, see Chapter 10); others say simply that it is the blessing (*ashirvad*) of the Jina, or that it 'destroys evil and gives protection'. Some people take the *prakshal* away with them, and others come to the temple to collect some of it, even if they have not taken part in the rite. At home, people quietly admit, they do sometimes drink the *prakshal*, and give a little to anyone who is ill, although they know they ought not to.

One of the reasons the water from this daily ritual is thought to have especially strong curative powers is that a *yantra* is bathed and worshipped along with the Tirthankar statue. *Yantra*s are geometric designs, many with distinct tantric elements, which are either painted on paper or cloth or inscribed on metal. They are used in temple worship, as a focus for prayer and concentration, and some are associated with particular religious fasts. Use of *yantra*s is not a marginal, or even just a lay practice.[5] The brushes which renouncers use to sweep away insects before sitting down have lengths of cotton cloth wrapped round the handles, and these have *yantra*s painted on them. But although their use is widespread, it is not unproblematic. One day I was talking with a senior Khartar Gacch

---

[5] Jaini (*Jaina Path*, 254) consigns the use of *yantra*s to a rather evasive footnote: 'Only a few . . . are still used for rituals of propitiation. These rituals were supervised by advanced laymen (yatis, ksullakas, bhattarakas, etc.) and were kept strictly within the discipline enjoined by the sravakacaras. Mendicants [renouncers] could not take part in the ceremonies, but they could chant the mantras. Lacking the basic ingredients of the tantric cult—fusion of the mundane and the supermundane—such practices seem to have had little effect upon the development of Jainism.' The shift in tense is symptomatic. And *yati*s are not laymen, but a class of renouncer. The passage elides the fact that renouncers take just the same part in rites involving *yantra*s as they do in those without them. *Yantra*s occur in almost every corner of Jain religious practice, including important ascetic practices presided over by renouncers (ch. 10).

nun about *yantra*s. She was explaining the designs of some of them, and telling me how powerful they are.

There are so many *yantra*s you can use in *puja* (worship) or for *mala* [as a rosary, to count recitation of prayers]. There is Rishi Mandal, Bhaktamar Yantra, and Siddha Cakra Yantra, like this . . . They can be used as medicine too. Oh yes, you can tie it round your neck [in an amulet] or you can drink the *prakshal* of the *yantra* [the water in which it has been bathed]. But the *prakshal* of the Jina, this cannot be drunk. But the *prakshal* of Guru Dev, this can be drunk. We people [Jains] also don't use *tulsi* (sweet basil), as the Vaishnavas [Hindus] do in the water we use to bathe them. Actually, true Jains don't believe (*nahim mante*) in any of these things. *Puja* is only for getting rid of our *karma*s. We don't believe in miracles (*camatkar*), only in *karma*.

The nun here distinguishes the Guru Devs, from whom one might expect miraculous intervention and help, from the Tirthankars, who are forever removed from human affairs, and she does this by saying that while you may drink the water in which a Guru Dev idol has been bathed, you should not drink the Tirthankar's *prakshal*. A similar distinction was made by many people I spoke to, such as the man who said, 'We sit before Guru Dev and do *bhakt* (devotion) and we say, "Oh Guru Dev, I want forgiveness"; but we cannot ask this from the Tirthankar. He has gone to *moksh*.'

But then the nun takes a different position. Actually, she says, we Jains do not believe in miracles, only in *karma*—everything depends upon *karma*. This thought was undoubtedly prompted by her incidental reference to Hindu practice. But it is a thought she might have expressed at any time. Now in saying that we—true Jains—do not believe in miracles or *yantra*s or 'all these things', she is not necessarily saying that they do not happen. The word she uses, '*manana*', is used to say that one believes in a deity, follows a practice, obeys a rule, or accepts something as right or proper.[6] You can use these things, and look, they do work (ours work as well as anyone else's). But what true Jains accept is that everything depends upon *karma*. Magical help, in other words, is available, but not really allowed.

These days, the most popular of the Jain miracle-working deities in Rajasthan is one of the *bhairu*s, Nakora Bhairu-ji, who guards a large Khartar Gacch temple complex near the village of Nakora in western

---

[6] Gold ('Spirit Possession') gives some good examples of how this last usage can be performative, thus: 'he is a distant cousin but we accept him as a son'; 'the prayer here mentions offerings of cloth, but we give this string and accept it as clothing' or 'when we give this pure well-water to a dying man it is accepted as Ganges water'.

Rajasthan.[7] The main idol in this temple is a statue of the twenty-third Tirthankar, Parshvanath. Long ago, the story goes, the idol was housed in a temple in Gujarat, but Muslim invaders sacked it and Jains managed only just in time to flee with the idol. When they reached Nakora, the cart on which the idol was sitting would move no further, no matter how many horses or elephants were set to shift it. Thus the idol had chosen the site, and chosen as its protector the *bhairu* who lives in that place. Nakora-ji is one of several magical temple complexes in Rajasthan and Gujarat, mostly in remote rural areas, where the idol has either chosen the site in this way, or been found underground as a result of some magical sign.[8] Nakora-ji has become the most popular of these among the Shvetambar Jain community in Jaipur—their popularity waxes and wanes with their reputation for working miracles—and almost every office and shop there displays a photograph of him. Many of the big Jain business families in Jaipur list this temple complex as a part-owner of the family firm. Each year, in return for the help the *bhairu* gives them in their business dealings, they make a payment to the temple funds.

In the past, Jain authors have written lengthy cosmological treatises which attempt to provide an orderly framework for all the various deities, spirits, and other supernatural powers. But this is not an area of inquiry to which Jain intellectuals are devoting much energy at present. (This may have something to do with the prestige of 'Western science', and indeed developing the claim that Jainism is compatible with, or even a part of science, is perhaps the most intense area of intellectual productivity today). If any of these comprehensive cosmologies ever enjoyed widespread understanding and acceptance, none seems to do so now. They are ignored in the sermons and didactic writings of renouncers and lay literati alike. No one would be thought of as an expert on Jainism because they had mastered this knowledge. The result is that while these deities continue to play a very prominent part in religious life, they occupy a rather hazy, and, I suspect, rapidly disintegrating domain in Jain culture.[9] The following, abstracted from my field-notes, can perhaps illustrate what I mean.

---

[7] Among the Tapa Gacch the most popular deities appear to be Manibhadra Vir, a fierce deity with a hog's head and four arms, who rides an elephant and grants miracles, especially when worshipped with fire (*hawan*); and Ghantakarn, who is also found in Khartar Gacch temples (Plate VII). His cult centre is at Mahudi, in northern Gujarat.

[8] See Humphrey, 'Fairs and Miracles'.

[9] See Endicott, *Batek Negrito Religion*, for a discussion of how the names, actions, and images of deities can be unstably connected in people's conceptions and accounts.

When I arrive for my regular interview with Saceti-ji I find about ten of his friends, all distinguished elderly men, lounging on a big mattress in the spacious first-floor room, drinking tea. Saceti-ji has brought his friends along so they can see him teaching me about Jainism, so he has me sit beside him on the mattress and calls for the first of my questions. I ask a couple of rather technical questions about *karma*. He expounds easily and his friends nod sagely. Then, I comment on the picture on the wall of Nakora Bhairu-ji and begin to ask about him. Before long we are into a splendid free-for-all argument. How many *bhairu*s are there? 'Just one,' says one of the old men, 'Nakora Bhairu-ji, at this temple near Balotra. The idol in the Jaipur temple is of the same *bhairu*.' 'No, No!', says someone else, '*Bhairu* is a caste, there are so many of them—one in every village. But the one at the Nakora temple is the top, he is the *chaudhary* (headman).' 'Nakora is really like Indra', says another man, 'He is chief among gods and protects the Jain religion. There are sixty-four Indras, and like this there are many *bhairu*s.' 'Rubbish', says someone else . . .

It is probably already the case that there is no fact of the matter, which could be derived from contemporary Jain culture, about the questions these men were debating.

But it would be a mistake to assume that relative lack of conceptual integration implies that these deities are moribund—they are not less respected for being more mysterious. If the realm they exist in is hazy, they are vivid enough. When a friend of mine in Jaipur told me that her marriage had been arranged, she said, 'This means I now have two visits to make'. One of these visits was to Nakora-ji. The year before she had visited the temple and prayed to the *bhairu* that she should get married. Now she must go back, as she promised, and worship there. The other trip she had to make was to a place not far from Jaipur called Malpura, where there is a shrine to the Dada Gurus, on the spot where the third Dada, Jin Kushal Suri-ji, has been known to appear before worshippers and is frequently reported as granting boons and performing miracles. My friend had made a pledge (*bolna*) before this idol that she would not eat a certain kind of sweet of which she is particularly fond until her marriage had been arranged, and now she would return to the temple and give thanks, before eating that sweet again.[10] Another family I know had a less happy experience. They went on a visit to Nakora-ji, and one of the sons of the family, who is something of a religious sceptic, broke a very important rule. Sweets which have been offered at the *bhairu* shrine (but not those which have been offered to the Jina Parshvanath) are distributed as

[10] For similar kinds of pledge among Hindus in Rajasthan, see Atal, 'Cult of Bheru', 145; Gold, *Fruitful Journeys*, 142–9; Mayer, *Caste and Kinship*, 188–93.

prasad, or blessing. Eating the *prasad*, like drinking *prakshal*, is thought to be beneficial. But you must not take these sweets away. Only those who actually come to the shrine should receive its benefits. But the young man took some of the sweets away and shortly afterwards his mother died in a traffic accident. The family is convinced that the *bhairu* brought this about.

What does one say about these miracles worked by powerful and sometimes vengeful deities in return for devotion, offerings, and pledges, in the context of the clear avowals of belief in a rule-governed, determinist, ethical universe which I described above? The usual way for anthropologists to deal with a situation of this sort is to try to fit these apparently conflicting sets of practices and contradictory sets of beliefs into a single causal theory: to engage in theology and the formation of doctrine on their informants' behalf. The Jains themselves do provide help, if one wanted to do this kind of thing. For instance, when I asked how it is that gods perform their miracles, I was often told that they have *shakti* (power). Now at first I was pleased by this because I knew that an admirable study of village Hinduism had been organized around just this notion.[11] But on reflection, it is hard not to see an element of tautology in this reply. I had asked how gods perform miracles, and had been told that they have the power to perform miracles: a polite way of being told I had asked a stupid question. It would have been easy enough to take this reply, as anthropologists have done in other circumstances, as a quasi-scientific conjecture about a special substance which gods are in possession of, but in fact there is no evidence for this.[12] I could discern no theory about how this power worked, and I suppose it would scarcely be miraculous power if one could. When I asked how the Dada Guru Devs performed miracles, some people said they had spiritual power (*adhyatmik shakti*), others said it was because they were celibate. Celibacy, especially in men (see Chapter 11), is said to produce heat in the body, and this can be turned to magical power.[13] But these people would often add that because they were Jain saints, and Jainism is a religion of non-violence, this heat is a cool heat. Others said that it isn't the Guru Devs who perform the miracles at all— they don't have that sort of power. And they found this easy to explain:

---

[11] Wadley, *Shakti*.

[12] For a parallel case see Boyer, 'Causal Thinking'; Needham, 'Skulls and Causality'; Rosaldo, *Knowledge and Passion*.

[13] This theme is widespread among South Asian religious traditions. See O'Flaherty, *Siva*, and for an excellent discussion of the origins of such ideas in the poetics of Vedic sacrificial language, see Kaelber, 'Tapas and Purification'.

the Guru Devs have helpers, *bhairu*s and other spirits, who have the power to perform miracles!

There are a few people who are sceptical about the miracles which others report.

Really these miracles are just the work of people's own confidence. We say that this road goes to Sanganer, but of course the road doesn't go anywhere. We go along the road. Similarly the Guru Dev does not actually help, but faith in him makes people stronger.

In general, however, it is taken for granted that miracles can happen, but this does not make them unproblematic. One woman said,

The Tirthankars don't do miracles. It is a sin to ask because we are supposed to become like them. The Dada Guru Devs can do miracles and people ask them for favours. They did not go to *moksh*. Now they are in heaven. All that I have asked from Guru Dev I have got. It all depends on your faith (*shraddha*). Actually we are not supposed to ask him, but we live in this world and have many problems, so we have to ask. Last year I lost a very expensive earring, and I prayed to Dada-ji every day and after a whole month it turned up again.

Torn between wanting to impress me with the Guru Dev's power to grant favours, and the injunction to pursue *karmik* self-help through ascetic practice, she does not look for a causal explanation of miracles that will reconcile them logically with *karma*, but cites instead her own ethical imperfection and attachment as the reason she should want supernatural help. On one occasion I asked a particularly acute young businessman if he had ever been to Nakora-ji. He laughed a bit and said simply, 'Miracles are not allowed in Jainism.'

When I asked people how it could be that these miracles can happen, when 'everything depends upon *karma*', their answers almost always suggested an ethical reconciliation for particular cases rather than anything that could count as a concern with a general causal explanation.

Jain *sadhu*s only do *camatkar* to save the Jain religion (*dharma*), though they don't believe in them.[14]

It is the good thoughts and concentration that is the important thing. If you go to Bhagwan (he means a Jina statue in a temple) feeling that you have done some bad

[14] It is interesting, by the way, that perhaps the most approved motive for the Guru Devs' miracles is to attract new followers to Jainism: exactly the sort of motive of which Christian teachers have been concerned to excuse Christ. He, they insist, acted only out of compassion for the suffering of those He helped. For the Guru Devs, as renouncers, this emotion—or 'passion'—would be inappropriate, unless it takes the form of inducing others to renounce too.

thing, and you feel very sorry, only then magical gods (*camatkari devta*s) will help you.

*Sadhu*s can only do *camatkar* if they have been doing good work. It is like business—you only get the reward of your work.

In Jaipur everyone performs Guru Dev *puja*, for weddings and all other auspicious (*mangal*) occasions, but in Calcutta they do a different *puja*, *sattar-bhedi puja* (worship using seventy different offerings, performed to the Jinas). Why? [Laughs] Oh! In Jaipur people prefer to perform *puja* to Guru Dev, because they can help us. But their *camatkar* are only for good things. They work only because of faith (*vishvas*), and they are only for the benefit of everyone. If any devotee (*bhakt*) is in trouble he is saved only because of faith. There are no miracles (*camatkar*) in Jain philosophy (or 'in the Jain view'—*darshan*).

Many bad people can do miracles, in Hindu *dharma* there are many examples, but this is not the case in Jainism. In Jainism the power for miracles will only work for good deeds.

One young man gave a slightly different account. Appealing to the quantifiability of *karma*, he suggests, though a bit uncertainly, that deities might reduce the effect of past deeds.

If you do good, you will get good, and if you do bad then some bad will come to you. It all depends on your own soul. But a *camatkari devta* can help, if they see that you are very devoted. So if it is in your *karma* that you should have a car accident, then you will definitely have one, definitely. Nothing can change that. But the *devta*s may be able to save you from dying in the crash. But we do not really know.

The powers of Jain saints and protector gods to perform miracles are not in any sense secret, and the rites and forms of worship in which they are invoked are grand, public, and well-advertised affairs. But whenever I set out to ask questions and investigate these things in detail, I could be sure of meeting resistance and reluctance from people in a way that I otherwise never did. People would say dismissively that none of this is interesting, that we don't have any of that in Jainism, that you should not be spending your time on such things, and so on. I, of course, was not put off. Miracles and magic are eminently anthropological subjects which I felt I ought to know about, so I did my best to lure people into talking about them. But the most intelligent of my informants, those who understood best the nature of my work, would duck and weave or gently but firmly steer me onto something else.

Usually this was done with great patience and good humour, but once or twice I made people cross. Early in fieldwork I came across a sung prayer called the *Guru iktisa*. A woman gave me a pamphlet which had this printed in it, and many people, I soon learned, would sing it regularly on their visits to Guru Dev shrines. It first praises the Guru Devs in colourful hyperbole for all the miracles they have performed and then asks that they help the worshipper in similar ways: a standard praise-song format used in popular religion throughout South Asia.[15] A few days later I was with a rather stern Jain man who was telling me all about *karma*. This reminded me of the prayer, so I said I'd like to ask him about it and started to rummage in my bag for the pamphlet, but he became suddenly rather tetchy. 'There's no need,' he said. 'There is nothing to explain. It is very easy and simple, you can understand it well enough without me.' It took me some time to realize that the most interesting thing about such cat-and-mouse chases was not the quarry, which was usually unremarkable: miracles, magical practices, divination, and spirit possession similar to dozens of other cases in the literature. The interesting thing is the form the chases took, and only when that is understood can the place of these magical practices in Jain religious life be seen in the correct light. This man did not deny the truth or efficacy of anything in the prayer. But he was not prepared to talk about it in the same breath as the intricacies of *karma*. He had been telling me about the central and most elevated part of his religion, and I had suddenly asked about something utterly common-place and straightforward. The difference between *karma* and miracles which he wanted to maintain was not one between things which are true or possible and things which are not, but between things which are and are not valuable.

The reason that I was being nudged and gently obstructed in these ways was this. I was meeting a whole set of ways of ranking and distinguishing aspects of religious belief and practice (as more and less 'allowed'), and an insistent and punctilious readiness of people to apply these distinctions to themselves. As with the relationship between gurus and devotees (Chapter 3), these practices of interdiction and correction are a central part of what it is self-consciously to be a Jain.

A Question of Reality

When people told me that what they did and believed was not allowed, or was not really Jainism, they used a number of different vocabularies and rhetorical moves, in ways which picked out different aspects of religion

---

[15] Babb ('Great Choice', 29) points out that this prayer is modelled on a popular song in praise of the Hindu deity, Hanuman.

for high and low evaluation. For instance, one can distinguish between following strict rules (*khara niyam*) and loose (*shital*) practice. Or, to take another example, some things are described as 'true' (*sac* or *sahi*) Jainism and others as 'really part of Hindu religion'. The latter might well include certain strict practices. On other occasions the relevant distinction is between the 'religious' (*dharmik*) and the 'worldly' (*laukik*), or the 'spiritual' (*adhyatmik*) and the 'conventional' (*vyavaharik*), and these oppositions can often be used to criticize strict ascetic practice, which can be seen in both cases as an instance of the latter term.

Perhaps the most important such distinction is that between *drayva* and *bhav*. These terms have roots in philosophical and scholarly analysis, where they can be used to distinguish 'substance' from 'essence' or 'material' from 'form',[16] but they have been absorbed into everyday Jain (and indeed Hindu) religious and ethical discourse, to distinguish lower and higher forms of an action. Thus, to use an example we shall meet again, one kind of good action is *abhay-dan*, the gift of non-fear. The ordinary or *dravya* form of this act is to save a person or an animal from death, injury, or pain. But the essential, the 'really real' form of *abhay-dan* is to preach the Jain religion. This will not actually save the person's life. Indeed, the effect of the teaching may be that they engage in a fast to death. But *bhav abhay-dan* is a gift of non-fear because anyone who has become convinced that everything depends upon *karma*, and is striving for omniscience and release, knows not to fear death. Now, Jain renouncers will generally say that whereas the gross form of *abhay-dan* is an act of merit, and is likely to bring good *karma*, the real form actually destroys *karma*. But again, it is impossible to know, and the same action can have completely different consequences depending on the mental attitude—and this too can be referred to as 'the *bhav*'—with which it is performed.

In the epigraph at the head of this chapter, G. E. Moore is speaking up for common sense: when philosophers insist that an abstraction (such as 'Spirit') is 'really real', this is because it isn't real at all. Moore's attitude would not find favour among religious Jains, but they would recognize very easily, I think, the terms in which he states his preference. In a whole range of religious and ethical domains, their religion enjoins them to turn away from, and renounce, aspects of the world which, according to the prevailing culture in which they live, are both practical and desirable. They should renounce their families, their homes, their dependants, their businesses, their caste; even though they have moral duties to all of these.

[16] Alsdorf, 'Niksepa'; Bhatt, *Canonical Niksepa*; Dixit, *Jaina Ontology*.

They should renounce sources of worldly help, such as prayers to powerful deities and the curative powers of magic. Even diving in to save the
drowning child, they are told, is a superficial, limited, and worldly form of
a higher virtue. But the lower form is not simply false or imaginary. It is
real enough, but seen from a lower viewpoint. Jainism includes and indeed
embraces both symbols and practices which can be seen from more than
one viewpoint—the Dada Gurus are ascetic renouncers as well as magical
gods—but it also involves, as a set of dispositions which are widely
dispersed among both renouncers and the lay population, ways of evaluating and ranking those viewpoints.

The problem Jains have with miracles is not whether or not they are
possible in causal and mechanical terms. That would be a stupid question
to ask about miracles, but if you really want one, some kind of account can
always be devised to reconcile them to a causal theory. The problem is that
they are not allowed. They are, in Moore's terms, 'real really': the way
that common knowledge, common sense, and common experience all
suggest that things must be.[17] But they are not 'really real', they do not
figure in the understanding of the way things are which informs ascetic
renunciation. From the latter point of view they should be renounced,
along with other worldly things, even if all one does is acknowledge and
assert this, without necessarily giving them up in practice. The interdiction does the necessary work, even if you don't always follow it.

It does its work by re-problematizing in a distinctively Jain way. The
fact that the Dada Guru Devs are at the same time Jain renouncers and
also miracle-working deities makes them attractive objects of devotion and
worship. In place of the polarity between the Jina, embodiment of all the
highest values, and the *bhairu* who is merely his servant and follower, here
we have a single figure who combines ascetic values and worldly felicity.
You can pray to the Guru Dev and praise his strict life of other-worldly
wandering, and at the same time ask his help in worldly affairs. Like
Wittgenstein's duck-rabbit drawing, the Guru Devs can be read two ways,
as ascetics and as beneficent deities.[18] Perhaps riches and renunciation
aren't so far apart after all. But things are not so easy. 'Yes the Guru Devs
can grant miracles, but of course we should not ask.' The apparent solution is only a suspension, and the components separate out. Thus Jin
Kushal Suri-ji, the third Guru Dev and the one with vastly the greatest

[17] I am aware that Moore would have been horrified to see himself associated with this
particular thought about what the 'real' includes; but this is the penalty, I suppose, for
coining a memorable phrase.

[18] Wittgenstein, *Philosophical Investigations*, 194.

reputation for miracles, has for this very reason acquired a pair of companions. He is regularly represented in wall-paintings and in books as flanked by two figures, and these are *bhairu-ji*s—a dark-skinned and a light-skinned or Kala and Ghora Bhairu-ji. They are the same kind of deities as the one who performs miracles at Nakora-ji and it is they, even moderately reflective worshippers will say, who perform the Guru Dev's miracles. Because he is a Jain saint the Guru Dev can't really be getting people through their exams, getting them a job, finding their earrings, bringing them a son, and improving their business prospects. The miracles are 'really' done by the *bhairu-ji*s.

As I have said, just which actions, beliefs, or values are identified as *bhav* and *dravya* varies according to circumstance, according to who is speaking and for what purpose. But the widespread use of this distinction as a way of ranking religious practices, or the aspects of the self which engage in these practices, lends Jain ethical and religious discourse its distinctive tone of uncensorious censure. Jains I knew were constantly drawing my attention to their failure to practice what they called 'real Jainism', or pointing out in ironical amusement how the popularity of the Guru Devs was because of worldly desires, and so on. But real Jainism, as they also said, is impossible. One way to express how it is that devout Jains live with and by their impossible ideals, is that it is a matter of situating themselves, and of constantly re-negotiating their position, between the real really and the really real.

PART II

Various and Particular Locations

5

Social Dimensions of Jain Identity

JUST outside the city wall in Jaipur is a Muslim neighbourhood. It is immediately apparent as such: people dress differently, the shop signs are in Urdu, and, more important from the Jain point of view, there are several butchers' shops and the road is often partially blocked by sheep. Often I had cause to go through this area with a Jain friend, usually on a rickshaw, and whoever it was would mark the passage in some way or other: by putting a handkerchief to their nose, or by remarking on the impending fate of the animals. On one occasion my companion, a devoutly religious young man, suddenly asked the driver to stop and scurried over towards one of the shops. I waited, perplexed. After a few minutes he returned, climbed in, and told the driver to go on. Obviously pleased with himself, he waited for me to ask what he had been doing and then explained that today was a Hindu religious holiday, one of a number of days in the year when the government requires butchers' shops to remain closed. He had spotted one that looked open, and had gone to check. 'They pull their shutters almost down, hoping no one will notice,' he said. 'Tomorrow I shall report them.' I congratulated him on his vigilance and he offered to give me a list of the days on which this ban operated, so that I could do the same. I must have looked horrified, for he added, 'Yes, I suppose you're right. The police would never listen to you.'

Indological studies of Jainism have tended to concentrate on its unique soteriology, and sociological studies which have dealt with the Jains have tended to describe them simply as part of the 'business community'. Religion as a source of social identity has tended to fall through the middle. Max Weber, in his brief discussion of Jainism, did attempt to hold both religious and economic factors in view,[1] but partly because the sources he had available were so unreliable, what he has to say is misleading in almost all its major points. The most damaging mistake he makes, however, is to assume that the Jains are a bounded, and therefore easily identified social group, and to take this group's persistence through time

---

[1] Weber, *Religion of India*, 193–204.

as unproblematic, so that questions may be asked in the abstract about the effects of their holding such-and-such a doctrine.

The Jains are not a cultural island, but are, rather, constituted socially and imagined culturally in relation to other sections of Indian society. And here, 'in relation to' often means 'against'. Islam provides only the most persistently hostile opposition. In this chapter I shall sketch the main reference-points of Jain social identity, and these are, for the most part, contrastive. This is, I suspect, a general feature of complex cultural settings, where, as Ulf Hannerz has remarked, people's cultural outlook includes a perspective on other people's perspectives.[2] Nor, one must immediately add, are Jains united among themselves, and I shall also describe divisions of caste and sect. The picture is complex, because the reference-points are subtly overlapping and the internal divisions are cross-cutting. The problem is therefore similar to that which Fredrik Barth found in Bali: 'the connections we are trying to conceptualize are linkages without determinate edges, in a body without a surface for a boundary.'[3]

Jains in India

Almost everywhere they live, Jains are a minority. At a little over three million, they make up less than a half of one per cent of the population of India.[4] They are to be found in very small numbers in all parts of the country, but are concentrated in three large home territories. Jains living elsewhere tend to think of themselves as coming originally from one of these areas, and often look there for marriage partners.

The first of these regions is in the Deccan, where the greatest concentration of Digambars lives. There are, it seems, whole districts in this region where the majority of Jains are farmers, and where Jain farmers make up the majority of the population.[5] The second area, and the one we are directly concerned with, is a wide band stretching across north-

---

[2] Hannerz, *Cultural Complexity*, ch. 3.   [3] Barth, *Balinese Worlds*, 4.

[4] In 1981, when the latest available Government of India census was taken, there were 3,206,038 Jains in India, of a total population of 665,287,849. The Jain population exceeds 1% of the total in only four states: Rajasthan (1.82%), Maharasthra (1.496%), Gujarat (1.37%), and the Union Territory of Delhi (1.19%). The censuses may underestimate the total number of Jains in India, because some Jain families enter 'Hindu' as their religion and in the past entered 'Jain' as their caste. See Mahias, *Délivrance et convivialité*, 13–14.

[5] Carrithers, 'Foundations of Community', 261–2.

western India, encompassing the cities of Delhi and Bombay, the states of Rajasthan and Gujarat, and the contiguous areas of the Punjab, Haryana, and Madhya Pradesh. This is where the main concentration of Shvetambars is to be found, although even here the population is unevenly spread. Certain villages and small towns are predominantly Jain, but no whole District has a Jain population which exceeds 7 per cent of the total.[6] The third block of Jain concentration, this time once again Digambar, covers Delhi, the eastern parts of Rajasthan, and the neighbouring parts of Madhya Pradesh, so it overlaps with the eastern end of the Shvetambar block. But as I shall explain below, the Shvetambars and Digambars are to a quite remarkable degree socially separated, so although eastern Rajasthan, including Jaipur, is an area with substantial numbers from both traditions, we can take the Shvetambar distribution as a separate one.

These regions, though vague and unnamed, are nevertheless contexts which are at least as relevant as formal political entities for locating local Jain communities. At first sight the states of Gujarat and Rajasthan seem like rather different places: politically separate since the fifteenth century, and apparently divided linguistically.[7] In fact, although it is possible to identify several characteristic local cultural features, for most people who live there the idea of Rajasthan does not seem to be a particularly powerful focus of identity. Smaller areas, often corresponding to pre-Independence states, are perhaps more generally salient for the majority of the population.[8] But for Shvetambar Jains the relevant point to make is that they are not contained by any of these local identities. The whole north-

---

[6] According to the 1981 census Kutch, in Gujarat, is the district with the highest proportion of Jains (6.72%), followed by Jalor (5.2%) and Pali (4.6%), both in Rajasthan.

[7] The linguistic division is, however, rather artificial, and not much of a problem for the Jains. As elsewhere in India, the educated middle classes of both states sustain their social and economic position with a command of English and Hindi. The vernaculars of the uneducated of the region still show something of a continuum, with people even quite far on either side of the political boundary able to understand each other. The emergence of Gujarati as a distinct written language can be dated to the early decades of this century (Mahatma Gandhi making a significant contribution), and the idea that all Rajasthan speaks Hindi is a legal fiction. The different dialects within the state, which are identified to some considerable extent with former princely domains, have not received political support since Independence, despite the fact that at the western and southern extremities of the state the vernacular is really quite far from standard Hindi, and in the latter case very similar to Gujarati. Hindi, as taught in government schools, is as foreign to much of Rajasthan as it is to anywhere in Gujarat.

[8] Lodrick, 'Rajasthan as a Region'.

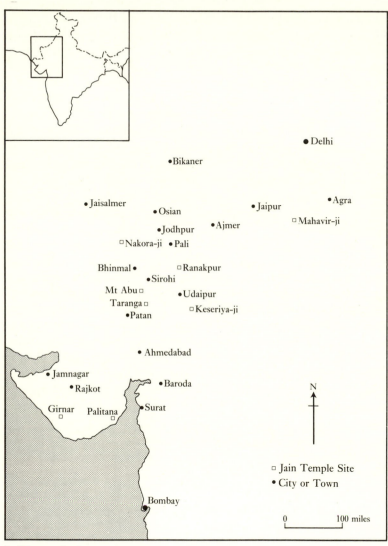

1. Western India.

western region is for them a single arena of social, economic, and religious life, linked by a single sacred geography (Map 1). As traders, financiers, and brokers it is their business and their *forte* to be constantly making and renewing social ties, which frequently combine kinship, commercial, and religious strands, right across the region.

A Merchant Laity

Jainism drew its first supporters from among urban peoples, largely traders and merchants—from the same milieux, in fact, as did Buddhism. The social homogeneity of the lay Jain community in subsequent millennia has sometimes been exaggerated,[9] but the extent to which Shvetambar Jainism especially has remained a religion of the commercial élite is by any standards remarkable. Such references as there are to lay Jains in the Shvetambar canon simply presume that those who are not kings will be wealthy merchants. And in the seventh century, when the first texts specifically directed at the laity began to appear, they were, as Jaini notes, 'clearly oriented towards the situation of a merchant community'.[10] Secular as well as religious sources indicate the substantial presence of Jains in trade. The merchant layman was not just a religious topos (although he certainly was that). A creditable history of inland trade in western India during the first centuries of this millennium has been pieced together almost entirely from Jain sources.[11] In the vast world of Indian Ocean trade, it is clear that Jains were prominent among the communities of Indian merchants who linked inland agriculture and manufacturing, through the port-cities of western India, to the Persian Gulf and the Red Sea, and from there to Europe, and also to east Africa, South-East Asia, China, and Japan.[12] This trade was funded substantially by the indigenous Indian banking system, in which Jains were prominent.[13] And the highly sophisticated merchant capitalism which developed especially from the sixteenth century in India—largely independently, it would seem, of the

[9] Nevaskar, *Capitalists Without Capitalism*; Stevenson, *Heart of Jainism; Modern Jainism*; and Weber, *Religion of India*, all write as if Jains were all and only business people.

[10] Jaini, *Jaina Path*, 178.

[11] Jain, *Trade and Traders*.

[12] Chaudhuri, *Trade and Civilization; Asia Before Europe*; Curtin, *Cross-Cultural Trade*; Das Gupta, 'Indian Merchants'; Gopal, *Commerce and Crafts*; Pearson, *Merchants and Rulers*. The world of Indian Ocean trade in the 12th c. is brilliantly evoked by Ghosh in *In an Antique Land*.

[13] Bhargava, *Indigenous Banking*; Habib, 'Usury'; 'Bills of Exchange'; Jain, *Indigenous Banking*.

development of that in Europe[14]—was an enterprise in which Jains played a very substantial part.[15]

In western India today, almost everyone who wants to refer to Jains will do so using the word 'Baniya'. It is worth dwelling a little on this word (also 'Vaniya' in Gujarat and 'Voniya' in southern Rajasthan—all from *vanij*, the Sanskrit for merchant). It is a general term for traders, money-lenders, merchants, and financiers; it is also used, in something like the way 'Brahmin', 'Kisan', or 'Harijan' may be used, as a generic name for a number of castes, all of which are in this case traditionally associated with trade: Shrimals, Oswals, Paliwals, Porwals, Khandelwals, Agarwals, and others. A large number, though by no means all the members of these castes are in fact traders, but the word is used of them all, regardless of their profession, because it is 'the Baniya way' to be a trader, to think and behave like a trader, whatever he or she actually does for a living. Reciprocally, all Jain and Hindu traders can also be referred to as Baniyas, even if not from one of these Baniya castes.[16] (Muslims, even those who are merchants, are not Baniyas). In all these senses, Baniya is exactly synonymous with 'Mahajan'.[17]

Thus a range of Jain and Hindu people are grouped together under these terms, by the overlapping criteria of caste and occupation, birth and conduct. Both words suggest what merchant people are like and can be used to attribute certain qualities to any person. In fact, they carry whole clusters of connotations of physique, clothing, mannerisms, diet, speech, morals, and temperament. The particular connotations of the two terms are different, and the choice between them, though it seems to vary in precise implication from place to place, is always an eloquent one. While 'Mahajan' means literally 'great person', and is unambiguously honorific, 'Baniya' is often at least in part derogatory. Christine Cottam Ellis reports that both Jain and Hindu traders in the Rajasthani market town which she calls 'Mandi' prefer to be known as Mahajans.[18] In Jaipur, I heard Baniya used much more as a generic self-description. Perhaps, in this more

---

[14] Fuller, 'Misconceiving the Grain Heap'; Perlin, 'Proto-Industrialization'; Rudner, *Caste and Capitalism*.

[15] Bayly, *Rulers, Townsmen and Bazaars*; *Indian Society*; Das Gupta, *Decline of Surat*; Haynes, *Rhetoric and Ritual*; Subrahmanyam and Bayly, 'Portfolio Capitalists'.

[16] In 'Tezibazar' some castes such as *teli* and *bhuj*, whose members are all engaged in trade, are regarded as Baniya (Fox, *Zamindar to Ballot Box*, 39–40). The same castes would not be termed Baniya elsewhere, where their members are not merchants.

[17] The word 'Mahajan' can also be used to refer to a merchants' guild. This is a common usage in Gujarat and in Central India, although not in Rajasthan.

[18] Cottam Ellis, 'Jain Merchant Castes', 84.

socially differentiated and culturally sophisticated setting, Mahajan is just too grandiloquent to be entirely unironic. It sounds too servile when used as a form of address,[19] and too arrogant if used of oneself. It is used only referentially, of the distinguished head of a wealthy business house, especially if he is very traditional in dress and manners. The preferred honorific for such a merchant is to address him as a *seth* (from *shreshthin*— the Sanskrit for chief). But all *seth*s are Baniyas.[20]

'It's Rajputs That We Are Not'

Jainism began in eastern India, in the area that is now Bihar. Movement of Jains westward into Rajasthan and Gujarat probably began very early (via Mathura, which became a major Jain centre around the beginning of the Christian era). But Shvetambar Jains today invoke a different origin. They are not migrants from the east, but converts, whose origins are in Rajasthan. And although they are now Baniyas, their forebears were Rajputs, members of the dominant warrior and landowning caste. This is a striking lineage for Jains to claim: from hunters and warriors to vegetarian traders; from extravagant aristocrats for whom the provision of wine and women are a necessary part of good hospitality, to frugal merchants and money-lenders for whom even tea is a slightly dubious stimulant. Today, the cultural contrast and political competition between Jain Baniyas and Hindu Rajput élites is one of the most striking social facts about western India, and it remains to be seen whether the recent rise of Hindu fundamentalism will reverse the dominance the Baniyas have on balance enjoyed since Independence or effect a reconciliation or a new alliance between them. But notwithstanding, and perhaps in some way

---

[19] See also Fox, *Zamindar to Ballot Box*, 46.

[20] The proportion of Rajasthani or Gujarati Baniyas who are Jains is very difficult to estimate. The censuses have rarely provided information on either the occupational distribution of religious groups, or the religious composition of occupational categories. Since 1941 they have given no figures for caste. For Rajasthan the last detailed surveys are to be found in the *Rajputana Gazetteers* of 1908–9, edited by Erskine. They do not cover Jaipur, but for most of the region they provide figures for both religion and caste. According to these sources, Jains comprised 53% of Baniyas/Mahajans in Ajmer-Merwara, 68% in Mewar, and 21% in Jaisalmer. Erskine, in the Jodhpur section of the Gazetteer, estimated that nearly four-fifths of the Mahajans there were Jain. These figures are very old, and in any case it is of limited value to try to quantify what is in fact a shifting distinction which matters much more in some places than in others. As we shall see, the extent to which Jains are socially distinct from other Baniyas in particular local communities varies according to local demographic circumstances and depends on commercial and political contingencies.

underlying, this antipathy, these stories of Jains' Rajput origins recall and combine two mythological archetypes both of which link the religion and royalty. As 'kings who might have been',[21] these Rajput converts resemble the Tirthankars, who, as we saw in Chapter 2, also renounced a royal inheritance for a life of non-violence, exchanging temporal for spiritual valour. And as royalty who support and patronize renouncers, they resemble the Indras and other royal gods of Jain mythology, who worship, support, and patronize the Tirthankars. The caste origin myths which tell of this Rajput ancestry therefore transpose the idea of the lay Jain as a renouncer's kingly worshipper and patron from the eternal cosmic realm of the Tirthankars to a more proximate time and place, so that it becomes an important element in the social identity of Jains in western India today.

The origin myths in each case come in several versions, although always located in one of just a few paradigmatic mytho-historical times: 'around the time of Mahavir', 'the time the Muslims came', or 'the time of Akbar'. The names of the castes are mostly derived from the towns where the stories take place. Thus the Oswals come from Osian, the Porwals and Shrimals come from the old city of Shrimal, now called Bhinmal,[22] and the Paliwals are from Pali (Map 1). There is a large corpus of stories in circulation. Some explain the emergence of a particular caste, others tell of a schism producing two castes, or of the origins of individual lineages within these castes. Different versions assign higher status to different castes, by tracing their descent to Rajput nobles as opposed to mere commoners. But the main elements of the stories are remarkably constant. They all involve a celebrated Jain renouncer—the Guru Devs are very prominent in Khartar Gacch versions of these stories—who comes to the town during a time of crisis. Perhaps there is famine, Muslim invaders are attacking temples, a demon is molesting the townspeople, or the king's son is dying from a snake-bite. The Jain saint performs miracles which end the crisis, and having thus gained their undivided attention, preaches to the king and his subjects to convince them to become Jains.

In most of these stories, the converts promptly lay down their weapons and take to trade, but the stories also make clear that this was not a withdrawal from affairs of state. And as if to have things all possible ways, Jain tradition also tells of great Jain generals and ministers who serve their

---

[21] This phrase is borrowed from Babb's excellent analyses of this literature ('Monks and Miracles'; 'Great Choice'. See also Granoff, 'Religious Biography and Clan History'; 'Jain Biographies'.

[22] Some versions give the place of origin of the Porwals as Patan, in northern Gujarat.

country and their king, in battle or through brilliant statecraft. In fact, Jain versions of this region's history are full of Jain and Hindu Rajput pairings: either Jain renouncers and the kings whose gurus they were (such as Hemacandra and Kumarapala), or Jain ministers (one of the famous examples is Vimal Shah, to whom a temple on Mount Abu is attributed), who advised and financed their rulers. One story tells how Rana Pratap of Mewar, revered as the Rajput king most determined to resist the Mughal Emperor Akbar, was able to recover from a crushing military defeat only because his Jain minister Bhama Shah advanced enough of his own money for a new army to be raised. Another tells how the great Jain temple at Ranakpur was built on land granted by Rana Kumbha to a faithful Jain minister. Some lineages among the Oswals, collectively known as *mutsaddi*s, continue to use quasi-royal names, such as Singhvi, and some have had enduring connections with Rajput courts, at Jodhpur, Udaipur, and Sirohi. The Bhandaris, an Oswal lineage, say they are descended from the Chauhan Rajput rulers of Ajmer who were converted to Jainism, and so brought into the Oswal fold, by the tenth-century Jain saint Yasobhadra Suri, but also that they continued to provide ministers, treasurers, and generals to the Maharajas of Jodhpur.[23] In the past, these lineages tended to marry among themselves, but never became truly separate from the rest of the caste, because, as we shall see, merchant finance and statecraft were closely tied and mutually dependent. Merchant families arranged and provided credit for Maharajas and nobles, and often became involved in revenue administration in the course of ensuring repayment. This pattern of traders being linked to particular Rajput landowners and lords, in relationships which could be tense and distant, but were generally of mutual benefit, has been common right across the region.[24]

When a non-Hindu or low-status group in India starts claiming Rajput descent, this is often seen as evidence that they are succumbing to (or benefiting from) Hinduization,[25] and there are well-documented cases of this kind.[26] But for the Jains it seems that an assertion that they once were Rajputs, while it certainly includes them in the Hindu world in the widest

---

[23] Tank, *Jaina Historical Studies*, 17–21.

[24] Chakravarti, *Contradiction and Change*, 45–53; Haynes, 'From Avoidance to Confrontation'; Rudolph and Rudolph, *Essays on Rajputana*, esp. 157–8; Spodek, 'Rulers and Merchants'; Tod, *Travels*, 52–3.

[25] Kulke, 'Weber's Study of Hinduization'.

[26] Carstairs, 'Village in Rajasthan'; *Death of a Witch*; Munshi, 'Tribal Absorption'; Sinha, 'State Formation and Rajput Myth'.

sense, and does so in a suitably senior position, is much more an assertion of a specific sort of distinctiveness, with specifically Jain religious content which might be quite lost on outsiders.

A Merchant Diaspora

There are small communities of Shvetambar Jains in all parts of India. Almost all these people trace their origins more or less directly to north-western India and ultimately to the desert area of western Rajasthan once known as Marwar. Modern South Asia has been profoundly influenced by these migrations, and the social character of Jainism has been greatly shaped by them. We have already seen that Jain castes are named after places of origin, so that their mobile and migratory past is part of popular historical consciousness. It is impossible to say when business families from Marwar first started moving to Gujarat, but almost all Gujarati trading peoples now claim to be of Marwari origin. There are enough specific family histories to give some content to the general impression,[27] and these Gujaratis, together with migrants coming directly from Marwar, contributed heavily to the great expansions of the Bombay business community in the late nineteenth century and between the two World Wars.[28] Jains from Rajasthan started to arrive in eastern India in the late sixteenth century, along with the Rajput chiefs who conquered the area for the Mughal empire.[29] The Marwari 'great firms' which grew up there in the eighteenth and early nineteenth centuries were followed by substantial Marwari migrations of the late nineteenth century. The larger of these 'great firms' had offices in both Calcutta and Bombay, and business portfolios which included opium trading, banking, gold wholesaling, wool export, and insurance. Many of the businessmen who went on in the twentieth century to lay the foundations of Indian manufacturing industry began as clerks, brokers, and agents in these firms.[30]

Entrepreneurial migration by Jains from this region has not been confined to India. The Indian Ocean trade had taken Gujarati Baniyas, including Jains, to East Africa and to the port cities of the Persian Gulf,

[27] Mehta, *Indian Merchants*; Tripathi, *Dynamics of a Tradition*; Tripathi and Mehta, *Business Houses*.

[28] Gordon, *Businessmen and Politics*, 40–55, 69–78; Tindall, *City of Gold*.

[29] Gopal, 'Jainas in Bihar'; 'Jain Merchants in Eastern India'.

[30] Kessinger, 'Regional Economy'; Rungta, *Rise of Business Corporations*; Sharma, 'The Marwaris'; Timberg, *The Marwaris*; 'North Indian Firm'.

since at least the fifteenth century. In the last two decades of the nine-teenth century both Shrimal and Oswal Shvetambars left Gujarat in very considerable numbers for East Africa, where as part of a larger South Asian community they became involved both in business and in govern-ment administration. They prospered sufficiently to organize famine re-lief back in their home districts in India, and to send funds to build several new Jain temples there. Since the late 1960s and early 1970s, when most of these people were forced to leave East Africa, they have established new Jain communities, which new families continue to join directly from India, in England and North America.[31]

Religious links between India and these diaspora communities are being forged in various ways. Jain renouncers have traditionally been prohibited from travelling in vehicles, but the leader of the Shvetambar Terapanth has introduced a new class of renouncer within his fold (called *saman/samani*) and these renouncers are exempt from this and a few other rules, so that foreign travel is possible for them. And one Sthanakvasi monk, Sushil Muni, decided for himself that these rules are no longer relevant to the modern world, and undertook proselytizing vists to Jain communities in north America. Although his followers, in formal terms, are few, his innovations met with guarded approval from Jains I knew in Jaipur, and people followed his travels in the media with some interest. But generally, Jain communities overseas have had to reproduce Jain religious culture without the presence of renouncers, and a priority for many of them has been the establishment of a temple, with an idol which has been consecrated in India by a Jain *acarya*. Printed publications, formal religious classes, collective performance of ascetic rites (see Part III) in Jain 'community centres', and, increasingly, the use of video re-cordings of sermons and rituals performed in India, also play their part.

When it was capital of British India, Calcutta was an important centre of Marwari Jains, who had gone there in search of business opportunities in the shadow of imperial power. Today, with the capital in New Delhi and the port of Calcutta in terminal decline, the attraction which this city has for such people is much reduced and both the numbers and the influence of its Jain community are waning. Some Jains from Calcutta have returned to western India, but others have looked further: to the hinterland of Bengal, the hill areas around Darjeeling, or to the still more

---

[31] Banks, *Organizing Jainism*, ch. 5; Chaudhuri, *Trade and Civilisation*; Curtin, *Cross-Cultural Trade*, 137–48.

remote areas of the north-eastern states. They must be doing well, as recent press reports suggest that local separatist and terrorist movements are partly directed against them.

Elusive Boundaries

Generally, Jain Baniyas have conformed to, and indeed over time contributed substantially to shaping, the moral world of Hindus of their class and region. For instance, while the Jain doctrine and practice of *ahimsa* (non-violence) is certainly distinctive (Chapter 7), it has developed in close dialogue with Hinduism.[32] The prevalence of vegetarianism among the Hindu merchant peoples of the region is probably attributable to Jain influence;[33] and deep philosophical differences between Jainism and any conceivable brand of Hinduism have not prevented this. But neither did such differences prevent St Thomas Christians on the Malabar coast from being fully incorporated into the higher reaches of the local hierarchy, and from acting as patrons of local Hindu temples, before campaigning on their behalf by British Christian missionaries established them as separate from Hinduism, so that they forfeited both their internal community cohesion and their elevated position in local society.[34] The Jains were perhaps fortunate not to attract much sympathetic interest from the British during the colonial period.[35] They remain distinct from, but at the same time subtly integrated with, their Hindu Baniya counterparts.

Many Hindu festivals also have a religious significance for Jains, and while the ceremonies which are performed inside the respective temples may differ, the public, social celebrations often merge. Diwali, perhaps the major festival for both Jain and Hindu Baniyas, is a case in point. The religious significance of this holiday is completely different in the two religions (see Chapter 17), but in Jaipur as in many towns throughout the region, Jain and Hindu merchants together pay for the main bazaars to be decorated for the occasion. Often the Jains are, to the outside eye, quite indistinguishable from Hindu Baniyas. At the spring festival of Vasant Panchami, like Hindus, Jain women will wear new, bright yellow and orange saris to welcome the new season. At Holi, like Hindus, Jain youths cover each other with coloured water and powders. And Jains attend

---

[32] Tähtinsen, *Ahimsa*.

[33] See Williams, *New Face of Hinduism*; see also Dumont, *Homo Hierarchicus*, 148–51.

[34] Bayly, *Saints, Goddesses and Kings*, 249–53.

[35] This point comes out particularly clearly if the Jains are compared to the Parsis. On the latter, see Luhrmann, 'The Good Parsi'.

public Hindu celebrations such as Dashehra, Gangaur, and Ganesh Caturthi (see Chapter 12). There are Jains among the regular visitors to the most popular local Vaishnava temples in and around Jaipur: the Ganesh-ji temple at Moti Doongri, the Govind Dev temple in the City Palace, and the Sila Devi temple in the old palace at Amber. A Jain funeral procession looks and sounds exactly like a Hindu one (indeed, death ritual is 'contracted out' to Hindu culture). You have to listen quite hard to catch that when the people in the procession are chanting that the name of God is Truth, the name they say is 'Arihant' rather than Lord Ram, and if a Hindu *sadhu* joins the procession, bellowing the more usual Hindu cry, no one ever seems perturbed. Even in localities where Jains are numerous enough to form a recognizable group within the wider category of Baniyas, they are culturally very close to the Hindus of their class and caste.

They are close, however, in rather a specific way. While it is common for Jains to take an active part in the main calendrical Hindu religious festivals, even when there is no Jain religious content to them, the reverse only rarely occurs (some exceptions will be discussed below). This points to one of the reasons why it is so difficult to identify boundaries to the Jain community. The image of a bounded entity—a part of a greater whole— is in fact a misleading one. Jain cultural distinctiveness does not rest on rituals or practices in which people are marked as different and counted in or out, which is to say that it is not constituted by symbolized boundaries. What seems to make the difference, rather, is a distinctive way of being indistinct. By this I mean to point to a range of practices and relationships through which Jains *participate* in Hindu public culture in India, and do so as Jains, but which have the effect, for them, of producing and repro- ducing a sense of cultural distinctness. Thus separateness is maintained in part through acts of inclusion. This means that it makes no sense to think of the Jain community as a part of Indian society. It is, rather, a way of being within it. It means too that its boundaries have the curious quality of a two-way mirror: the Jains can see that they are there, and can see out; while those on the other side can easily be misled into thinking that there is nothing inside to see. So they are not boundaries which the Jains are in any sense contained within. Their community, close and intimate as it may be in some places, is quite unlike a ghetto. Early in *The Portrait of a Lady*, Henry James has Isabel Archer describe the 'aristocratic situation' of Madame Merle: 'That's the supreme good fortune: to be in a better position for appreciating people than they are for appreciating you', and one can see that the sort of boundaries the Jains maintain, in creating

PLATE VIII. Jain temples at Palitana. Palitana, also called Shatrunjaya ('Defeat of Enemies') is one of several important Jain pilgrimage places on mountain tops in Western India. Worshippers come from all over the country to the many rest-houses at the foot of the mountain. In the very early morning they begin the long climb, barefoot, to the fortified city of temples at the top. (The elderly, the infirm, or the lazy, can be carried in palanquins.)

and reproducing asymmetries of intelligibility, are also a form of social dominance.

All the most magnificent Jain temples are far from urban centres, out in the countryside where no one else has reason to go, or at the inaccessible tops of mountains such as Abu, Taranga, Palitana, and Girnar (Plate VIII). In Jaipur, as in all the towns of the region, Jain temples tend to be tucked away behind shops, and unlike Hindu temples, with their prominent *shikhar* spires, they look from the outside more or less like ordinary houses. Inside, they are extremely lavish: richly painted and covered in gold leaf, with hundreds of marble idols, canopies of rich brocades, and in some cases solid silver doors across the entrance to the sanctum. But on certain occasions, in a way which I think is characteristic of the Jains' management of their boundaries, they can be transformed into blaring advertisements of Jain wealth, as fund-raising ceremonies are broadcast to the whole surrounding neighbourhood through bellowing public-address systems, and on other occasions the Jains issue forth from these temples, carrying one of their idols in a great silver palanquin, and parade their religious concerns on didactic billboards and floats.[36]

In Jaipur, Jain religious events are by and large attended only by Jains, but in smaller towns and villages, when Jain wealth can create events of unequalled splendour, and where the arrival of any saint or holy man is more of an event, this is not the case. There, when Jain renouncers are present, they attract the attention of the whole population. In the autumn of 1990, I travelled through the Pali, Jalor, and Barmer districts of western Rajasthan to meet some groups of Jain renouncers who were spending their four-month annual retreat there. I reached a small village which I shall call 'Mohangarh', and which I knew in advance to have a substantial Jain population: about 350 households out of a total of 1000. But the Jains who actually lived there permanently turned out to be only the elderly of those families, their children having gone to start new businesses elsewhere, mostly in Bangalore and other parts of southern India. Being thus depleted in numbers had not lessened the Jains' prominence in the village. As far as I could tell every single Jain house had recently been rebuilt, by the same contractor to virtually identical designs. Although most of them were empty for much of the year, these were large, two-storey buildings which entirely filled their modest plots and dwarfed the non-Jain cottages between.

Until the turn of this century, although always subject to drought, this area was quite prosperous, with considerable through trade between north India and the Indus basin and large periodic fairs selling camels, horses, and cattle. There are some extraordinarily fine merchants' houses in nearby Jaisalmer, dating from the first years of the nineteenth century, which testify to spectacular wealth. But when the railway through the Punjab was opened, connecting north India directly to Sindh, this trade more or less ceased. Writing in the first decade of this century, Erskine recalled how caravans had previously passed constantly through Jaisalmer, and observed that in only a few years trade decreased to almost nothing, and the population plummeted.[37] This fuelled the migrations of

---

[36] Banks, *Organizing Jainism*, 195, comments that religious events among Jains in Leicester, England, are all confined inside the Jain Centre there, which I take to be an index of the contrast between the social dominance of Jains in western India and their place in British society. One can see analogies too in the sphere of mythology, where Jains have incorporated a selected range of Hindu deities and heroes into their pantheon but also managed, as Jaini ('Rsabha as an Avatara') has shown, to beat off Vaishnava attempts to co-opt the Jina Rishabh as a form of their paramount God, Vishnu.

[37] Erskine, *Western Rajputana States*, 27.

Jains from the region which continued through the 1920s and 1930s. Since Partition and the closing of the border the area has become even more peripheral, and the effect has been that almost the whole Jain population has gone to make its money elsewhere. They have not severed the connection with the area entirely though, and they send money home to extend and embellish their houses, as did earlier generations of migrants from northern Rajasthan.[38] Some elderly members of the community have remained in Mohangarh, or returned to enjoy a peaceful retirement. In addition, people come back regularly for religious occasions and for family rites of passage, especially marriages. The local (Oswal) caste committee in Mohangarh still imposes rules regulating expenditure at marriage in a way that is impossible these days in a city such as Jaipur. There are limits to the number of musicians who may be employed and the kind of food that may be provided, so the costs of holding the ceremony are kept much lower than they would be in Bangalore. This is not an isolated example. The neighbouring and rather larger town, 'Shivra', was similar, as many of the towns and villages right across this area seemed to be, though I had less time to investigate. Henri Stern describes a village he calls 'R', near Jodhpur, where a similar situation prevails, although in that case the Jain population had been smaller than in Mohangarh and Shivra, and migrated mostly to Bombay.[39]

At the time I went to Mohangarh three Shvetambar monks were spending the rains retreat there, and the place had rather a festive air. A major Jain festival, Paryushan, had been celebrated just a few weeks before, and some of those who had come back for this had yet to return to the south. In addition, there was a steady stream of Jain visitors from neighbouring towns and villages, who came for two or three days to attend sermons and ask for blessings from the renouncers. I met a man and his son who had come because the boy was due to sit examinations, a woman who had come to vow to fast as a celebration of her recovery from illness, and several families who just wanted to pay their respects to a Jain renouncer. These people, like me, were billeted in empty houses, and invited to people's homes to bathe and take breakfast, and for meals to the *bhojan shala* (dining-hall maintained by the religious community). The co-ordination of these arrangements was undertaken by the senior monk, who asked solicitously after our comfort and quietly gave the impression of being in charge of the whole village.

A big contribution to the sense of occasion was made by the local non-

---

[38] Cooper, 'Painted Walls of Churu'.   [39] Stern, 'Secteur economique'.

Jain population of the village and from various settlements nearby. They came to all the sermons, cramming the back of the hall and joining in with a couple of songs they had learned during the preceding three months. I met a group of about a dozen Raika women (the Raikas are a community of semi-nomadic pastoralists) who were working nearby on a road-building scheme, funded by the government as famine relief. The contractor was a Jain Baniya, but they were working directly under a Raika foreman. The reason they had come to Mohangarh, they said, was to see the holy man. They had heard about the Baniya saint, but had very little idea about the content of Jain religion. Most of the sermons were delivered in the same very Sanskritized Hindi as in Jaipur, so these people must have had little idea of their content. But the sermons included stories in more accessible language and the main practical theme the renouncers were trying to get across—vegetarianism—was clearly having an impact.

In Shivra, where a group of nuns was staying, the effect of this kind of influence was clear. I attended a sermon, in a hall filled with Jains, Hindu Baniyas, and villagers from the local area. The subject was spiritual insight (*samyak-darshan*) and the sermon was a combination of technical disquisition and tirade: metaphysical distinctions between levels of insight, and warnings that none of us could achieve even the lowest level if we did not mend our ways. It was the time of *naupad oli-ji*, a twice-yearly Jain fast, and at the end of her sermon the nun called out for everyone who was going to fast that day to stand up to take their vow. Almost half the hall stood up. As she recited the short Prakrit text in a loud, clear, authoritative voice these people stood with their heads bowed and their hands folded in prayer. The women, in this rather conservative place, had the ends of their saris hanging down, completely covering their faces. The renouncer afterwards told me proudly how several of the non-Jains in the village had embarked on Jain fasts, and others had given up eating onions and garlic while the renouncers were in the village, so that they would be able to offer their food as alms to Jain renouncers.

As it is presented for external consumption, Jainism is more or less a campaign for vegetarianism. If Jain renouncers find themselves with any influence on people, it is this that they first seek to effect. Lay Jain organizations also set up travelling exhibitions to persuade people both of the nutritional benefits of a vegetarian diet and of the terrible *karmik* penalties of eating meat. A painted board, popular in Jain processions, shows a man happily roasting a goat for his supper and then on the next board he is shown in hell being tormented with fire by demons. Another favourite theme is the suffering in store for those who overload pack animals or maltreat stray dogs, and much Jain charitable expenditure goes on homes and hospitals for stray or sick animals.

Jain monks and nuns are regularly recruited from outside the lay Jain population, often as young adolescents attracted to a charismatic guru. Vinay Srivastava records how several people from among the Raikas have become renouncers in one or other of the Shvetambar *gacch*s. He writes, 'The Raikas take immense pride in saying that their renouncers were so great that they became the deities of the Baniyas, and this otherwise "miserly caste" even today spends millions of rupees in keeping their names alive.' Shanti Vijay Suri (the unorthodox renouncer mentioned in Chapter 3) is the most celebrated of these. Raikas in Sadri (south-central Rajasthan) tell of how he used to berate their parents and grandparents for selling the lambs they reared, telling them that they would share the sin with the butchers when the animals came to be slaughtered.[40] These people are entirely dependent on the income from sale of the lambs, and could not seriously contemplate following the saint's injunctions, so one might expect them to object when one of their number, recruited to the religion of a dominant community, then takes to attacking their means of livelihood, but this strictness only served to increased his prestige, and remains, along with his other patrons' wealth, an important element in the continuing veneration of this saint.

In Chapter 4, I mentioned the distinctive hinterland temple complexes which Jains have built in Rajasthan and Gujarat, where a Tirthankar statue and a guardian deity between them perform a variety of miracles for Jain devotees. There, I discussed the religious and ethical complexities in Jainism which the existence of these sites points to. They are also another point of religious contact with non-Jains, again involving a very qualified and selective presentation of the religion to outsiders. Almost all Jain temples are open to non-Jains, and high-caste Hindus will happily go in.[41] Lower-caste Hindus and Adivasis (so-called 'tribals') on the other hand, would not normally enter a building which they would see as reserved for Baniyas. Thus generally, Tirthankar idols are much less accessible than renouncers to the non-Jain rural population. But these special magical

[40] Srivastava, 'On Renunciation', 20–1.

[41] The Shvetambar temples at Dilwara, on Mount Abu, are regular features on the sight-seeing itineraries of Hindus. Mount Abu is a Rajasthan hill station, a popular place for upper-middle-class families wishing to escape the summer heat, and for honeymoon couples. Gujarat is a 'dry' state and so Abu, which is just over the border, is a popular weekend destination for affluent young couples from Ahmedabad.

statues are made accessible to particular local groups, in specified ways, for a short time each year.[42]

Each of these temples hosts a regular fair, which attracts the low-caste and Adivasi villagers from some considerable distance around, and which plays a significant part in the local economy. A Hindi booklet published by the management committee of the Mahavir-ji temple (eastern Rajasthan) proudly announces that the fair proves the unity of traditional, national, and spiritual perspectives, because not only Jains but all peoples participate in a Jain religious ceremony which also has government sponsorship. It lists Minas, Gujars, Jats, Ahirs, 'and even leather workers', as participants.[43] According to Jain tradition the fairs at Nakora-ji (western Rajasthan) began in 1907–8, in order to fulfil a vision which a Jain astrologer-*yati* received of crowds of pilgrims all arriving at the site together.[44] Interestingly, this is around the time when the economic fortunes of this desert area were otherwise declining, and it could be that the fairs are a more or less conscious attempt at regional planning. The fairs, at which most of the traders are Jains, are a focus for major exchanges of agricultural and urban manufactured goods. They attract considerable funds to pay for the upkeep of the temples, and are used by local Jain traders and money-lenders to establish and renew debt and clientage relationships with local farmers and tribals. In all these ways the economic dominance of Jains in the local economy is reproduced and extended, as is their pivotal position in linking substantial rural populations to sources of credit and commodities in the urban centres.

Each fair is arranged to coincide with the most important ritual event in the year, a procession (*rath yatra*) in which the miraculous idol is taken in a chariot from the Jain temple to the place where it came to rest or was found underground. At various stages the local villagers play a central part, pushing the cart on its journey and accompanying the idol back into the main temple at the end. The myths associated with the founding of the temple explain why the participation of the local people is required.

The statue is found underground by a local low-caste farmer. He installs it in a humble shrine where local people begin worshipping. A rich Jain merchant learns of the idol, realizes it is Jain, and arranges to have a splendid new temple built for it. As the idol is loaded on a cart to be taken away, the poor farmer asks, 'Are you

---

[42] The following account draws freely on Caroline Humphrey's paper on these temple sites ('Fairs and Miracles') supplemented by my own observations at Mahavir-ji, Nakora-ji, Padampura, and Keseriya-ji. Further descriptions of the fair at Mahavir-ji are given by Erdman (*Patrons and Performers*, 59–63) and Kakar (*Shamans, Mystics and Doctors*).

[43] Jain, *Shri Mahavir-ji*.   [44] Maniprabh Sagar, *Nakora tirth ka itihas*, 39.

going to desert the poor people for the rich people? Do you prefer almonds and rich dried fruits to our humble drop of milk?' When the time comes to leave, however, the cart cannot be moved; no matter how hard the bullocks are urged or how many people help to push. The merchant prays for an explanation, and the god replies, 'Until [the man who found the statue] pushes the wheel and sees me off without complaint, I will not budge.' Thus assured of the god's affection, the man touches the wheel and the cart moves off towards the idol's new home.[45]

As Caroline Humphrey has shown, the pattern of religious participation in the ceremonies which accompany the fair allows the villagers into the sacred site and access to the magical power of the statues, but on strictly limited terms.[46] They may enter only on certain days, and they may see (*darshan lena*) the idol, but not touch it or perform worship (*puja*) as the Jains do. As is the case with Harijan participation in many village festivals in south India, and in an exact reversal of the Jains' own participation in Hindu life, the inclusion of the lower-status people in the rite serves precisely to portray the extent of their social subordination.[47] The procession redraws the distinction between the humble site where the statue was found and the gleaming marble temple it now stands in, between the 'lower castes' and the Jains.

Perhaps the most striking thing about the way the Jains run these fairs is that while they make positive efforts to encourage local participation, they make no attempt at all to encourage the villagers to share their specifically Jain ideas about the meaning or religious importance of what is done. The point in this story when the merchant prays to 'the idol' and receives a reply from 'the god', touches on some extremely knotty, and incessantly debated points. The idol is of a Tirthankar. He could not grant miracles and certainly would not wish to for he is permanently removed from worldly affairs. Would he, as a soul free from all attachments, be likely to show particular attachment to this peasant farmer? Certain idols might be miraculous, because of the renouncer who consecrated them, or gods who protect them, or whatever, but the God who is embodied in them (the Jina) is not the god (*bhairu* or *kshetrapal*) who performs mir-

---

[45] The theme of cows dropping milk to reveal hidden idols underground is found throughout the subcontinent. For Hindu versions in Gujarat see Pocock, *Mind, Body and Wealth*, 84. For Hindu south India, see Eichinger Ferro-Luzzi, *The Self-Milking Cow*, and Shulman, *Tamil Temple Myths*, 93–110; and for Muslim appropriation of these same themes, see Bayly, *Saints, Goddesses and Kings*, 120–1.

[46] Humphrey, 'Fairs and Miracles', 207–10, 216–25.

[47] Fuller, *Camphor Flame*, 131–9.

acles. As I discussed in Chapter 4, debate about these unresolved issues is a central part of Jains' understanding of the religion. The villagers, by contrast, are not participants in these discussions. They do not even call the statues by Jain names. They use their own names for the deities, and sing devotional songs which have nothing to do with the Tirthankar represented or with any aspect of Jainism. The Jains are content to leave these people to their own ideas about the statue, commenting wryly on how 'ignorant' and 'simple' they are, and noting with distaste their disregard for the etiquette of Jain worship. Thus while the fairs enable deeper penetration of hinterland markets by Jain traders, and establish points of contact between Jains and local people, they do not diminish the distance between them. And while they open up Jain religious sites to include non-Jains, what they include them in is certainly not Jainism.

Caste Stereotypes and Religious Antipathies

Baniyas in general and Jains in particular have held, on the whole, a secure and elevated social position in western India. This has probably been most true in parts of Gujarat, where under Muslim and British rule Baniyas were indisputably at the top of the indigenous social hierarchy,[48] but even in Rajasthan they have generally derived social prestige and power both from their wealth and from their association with the Rajput aristocracy. On the other hand, in the folklore of the region, Baniyas appear by turns as figures of fun, and as objects of distrust and dislike. As one Rajasthani proverb advises, 'The mango, the lemon, and the Baniya—they only yield when they are pressed hard by the neck'.[49] Jains will casually and jokingly cite the fact that 'We are Baniyas', to explain a frugal family practice, or the fact they went to work on a Sunday. But the same word is used by non-Baniyas, with venom rather than humour, to suggest a greedy, grasping, cowardly, and effeminate man; and his sly, surly, and almost invariably fat wife. The conviction that they are all miserly (*kanjus*) is given its most lurid expression in the epithet, 'fly-suckers' (*makki-jus*). The idea is that rather than waste it, they will suck the food from the body of a fly which has fallen in their bowl. In view of the Jains' vegetarianism and scrupulous concern for insect life, this is a particularly wounding image. So in close

---

[48] As Cort notes ('Jains, Caste, and Hierarchy'), citing Pocock's *Kanbi and Patidar*, when the economic position of Gujarati Patels improved dramatically in the mid-nineteenth century, the manners and customs they emulated in order to turn economic into social success were neither Rajput nor Brahmin, but Baniya.

[49] Ahuja, *Folklore of Rajasthan*, 114.

parallel to the way the word Jew has from time to time been used in Europe, it is possible to call someone a Baniya.

The comparison with Jews in Europe—however fleeting, and one would not wish to pursue it very far—reminds us that the Jains are, after all, a religious minority in Brahmanical Hindu civilization, and they have not been immune from religious persecution.[50] Jains are both the paradigmatic Baniyas and also, because they are heterodox, potentially outsiders. They have frequently responded to threatening militancy among Hindus by merging, at least to the outside eye, with their Hindu caste-fellows.[51] These days Jain identification with the broader Baniya category extends to playing with political fire. In recent years the Bharatiya Janata Party (BJP) has gained considerable support in Jaipur and there have been violent Hindu–Muslim clashes in the city. The party is popular among Jains, and at least one of the richest Jain merchants in the city is known as a generous contributor to its funds. A Jain was one of the BJP Members of Parliament who went on a fast in the summer of 1990 to protest against government policy. The BJP, together with the associated organizations, the RSS (Rashtriya Swayamsevak Sangh) and VHP (Vishva Hindu Parishad), are often described as 'Hindu fundamentalist', but so far none shows any sign of interpreting the Hindu identity it represents in a scripturalist or doctrinal way that would exclude Jains, and some Jains are active and full participants precisely because they are socially part of one of the interest-groups it represents most fervently: the urban, upper-caste, increasingly entrepreneurial middle-class.

Muslims, even middle-class Muslim merchants, are not Baniyas, and being themselves followers of a minority religion does not much dispose Jains to take the Muslims' part in the increasingly incendiary communal tensions which have affected north India. Islam occupies a prominent place in Shvetambar mytho-history in this region. According to the received view, all ruined temples were destroyed by Muslims, and all broken idols which turn up underground were desecrated by them.

---

[50] Obeyesekere, *Pattini*, 516–23; Thapar, *Cultural Transaction*, 15–22; 'Imagined Communities', 219–20. Generally, Jains were treated just as well or badly as Hindus by Muslim rulers. Occasionally, naked Digambar statues have excited special outrage. The Emperor Babur, for instance, describes in his memoirs (see Beveridge, *Babur-Nama*, 611–12) how he was so shocked at the sight of the colossal Digambar statues at Gwalior that he ordered their genitals to be chiselled off. As to whether the Emperor took offence simply at the visibility of the penises (Unlikely perhaps, given what he tells us elsewhere in the same text), or at the fact that those on Jina statues are rendered with such long foreskins as to seem almost assertively uncircumcised, one can only guess.

[51] See Banks, *Organizing Jainism*, 27–8; Jaini, *Jaina Path*, 288–304.

Celebrated Jain saints are remembered for their ability to confound Muslim teachers and to avert the danger of Muslim persecution. Long and often bitter episodes of hostility between Jains and especially Shaivite Hindus, although recorded in medieval Jain literature, are largely ignored today.[52] In the Jaipur gem trade, the vast majority of the labourers employed by Jain merchants are Muslims, and contact with them is routine. But in the Jain world these people are socially invisible and inaudible. The labourers are poor and therefore not smartly dressed, but though they are evidently scrubbed and respectable, their employers casually remark in their presence that of course Muslims do not wash properly. Some people even affect to believe that the ritual ablutions performed at a mosque are the only washing Muslims do. Others firmly maintain that the reason Muslims do not eat pork is that the pig, 'the most dirty animal', is sacred in their religion. This attitude is not just an expression of class. There are Jains in Jaipur who are poor, and for all the opulence and even ostentation of Jain religious celebrations these people are not excluded. One Jain man I knew quite well does exactly the same work, cutting and polishing stones, as the Muslim craftsmen (he was the only one I knew). He and his family participated fully in local community events and I never saw them treated with anything other than courtesy.

How are lay Jains seen by their client groups in rural areas? The picture seems variable and changeable, which perhaps explains the trouble the Jains go to with those fairs. Vinay Srivastava describes generally good relations between Jains and Raikas. The Raikas distinguish the merely miserly (*kanjus*) Jain money-lenders from the local Rajput landowners who are 'oppressive' (*zalim*). When the Raikas used to go out with their herds for months at a time, they left their wives and children to work as domestic servants for Jain Baniyas, and even today pay a fee for the privilege of depositing their savings with them.[53] Migrating Jain families take Raika boys as domestic servants or employ them in their new businesses. And Jains are the only source of money for the feasts the Raikas hold on the death of a member of their family, which are their main collective social events.[54]

As is the case throughout the region, almost everyone is in debt to the Baniyas, and as studies of rural credit have shown, the general practice tends to be debt farming, whereby the money-lender holds the villagers in permanent debt, securing a reliable income and a perpetual client. The

---

[52] There are exceptions, including a few stories associated with the Guru Devs.
[53] Srivastava, 'On Renunciation', 18.   [54] Srivastava, personal communication.

relationship hovers between paternalism and naked exploitation. In times
of drought the villagers become directly and absolutely dependent on the
money-lender, and the money-lender, to preserve his future income,
generally advances just enough credit to keep the villagers alive.[55] Money-
lenders are, naturally, secretive about their business transactions, but in
1983 Howard Jones was able to study the account-books of some of the
Digambar Jain shopkeepers and money-lenders in a village in Dungarpur,
in south-east Rajasthan. He found that these small firms (general goods
stores, cloth retailers, and the like) had extensive credit networks: they
sold goods on credit, mostly to high-caste villagers; and they practised
pawn-broking, overwhelmingly with the Bhil tribals who live in scattered
settlements around the village. The Hindu villagers were reluctant to use
this demeaning (and expensive) way of raising cash, but the Bhils frequently had to, and accepted on-the-spot cash for their gold and silver
jewellery, often for immediate consumption needs.[56]

It is no surprise, if this is as typical as anecdotal evidence suggests, that
in times of drought and famine, the relationship can occasionally become
explosive. In the summer of 1985, in the region of Sirohi in southern
Rajasthan (not far from where Jones had worked), there were a number of
violent attacks on Jain renouncers by lower-caste Hindu villagers. This
was a year of severe drought in Rajasthan, and the attackers believed the
renouncers were performing rituals and chanting magical spells to prevent
the rains from coming. These 'Baniya priests', they thought, were working on behalf of the merchants and money-lenders among their followers
to ensure that the price of grain would remain high and that poor villagers
would be dragged ever further into debt. The accusations were not original. Quanungo, citing a seventeenth-century Rajasthani source, writes,
'Nainsi tells us in his *Khyat* how the Baniyas of Kelakot in Cutch-
Bhujnagar, threatened with ruin on account of four years' successive rain-
fall and bumper crops in that dry region, had recourse to a *vartiya* (tantric
wizard) to lock up rains and create famine in the land!'[57] A. K. Forbes, in
1856, tells another story of this kind from Gujarat,[58] and Malcolm Dar-

---

[55] See Michie, 'Baniyas'. Parry (*Caste and Kinship*, 323) comments that in rural Kangra
the money-lender is often seen as a public benefactor. Cheesman ('Omnipresent Bania',
462), writing of nineteenth-century Sindh, summarizes the Baniyas' method thus: 'The
bania, without whose finance cultivation could hardly have continued at all, prospered at the
expense of the agrarian population, simultaneously keeping agriculturalists alive and impov-
erishing them.'

[56] Jones, 'Jain Shopkeepers'.   [57] Quanungo, *Studies in Rajput History*, 58.
[58] Forbes, *Ras Mala*, i. 299.

ling, writing in 1925 of Jain money-lenders in the Punjab, informs us coolly, 'It is characteristic of the Bania that in times of scarcity his superstitions are as much directed to prevent a fall of rain as the cultivator's are to secure it.'[59] And H. A. Rose, to whom Darling refers, describes how, 'Banias sometimes keep off rain by giving an unwed girl some oil which she pours on the ground.'[60]

The immediate inspiration for the 1985 attackers was almost certainly the doctrines of one Anoop Das. Since at least the 1880s, the Bhils of the Udaipur region had been in intermittent revolt against the government of the Mewar State and its Rajput aristocracy, over land rights and levels of taxation, especially the hated system of forced labour known as *begar*. In 1917 the Girahias of neighbouring Sirohi State began a series of similar protests which continued through the 1920s when they were led, ironically enough, by Motilal Tejawat, an Oswal. Another Adivasi and lower-caste leader, the poet and song-writer Anoop Das, was probably also of high-caste origin (sources disagree about whether he was Brahmin or Rajput). He gave the movements a messianic turn with the creation of the Anoop Mandal, a puritanical religious and political organization which, like similar Devi-cult movements in Gujarat,[61] held out the combined hope of political independence, economic uplift, and social and moral regeneration. To prosecute this, the orientation of these movements changed during the inter-war period, with attacks now directed at the Baniyas: merchants who sold the people alcohol and money-lenders who lent them the money to buy it, and then held them in debt-bondage.[62] The Anoop Mandal opposed the Independence movement in Rajasthan (which, such as it was, was led by urban Baniyas in most of the former princely states)[63] and continues today to regard the Rajasthan Government as the agent of the Baniyas.

Anoop Das seems to have given his movement a specifically anti-Jain ideology, and although support for the Anoop Mandal does seem fairly localized,[64] the 1985 attacks were a continuation of a series of actions over the preceding decades, including attempted economic boycott.[65] In his

[59] Darling, *Punjab Peasant*, 177.   [60] Rose, *Glossary of the Punjab*, i. 132–3.

[61] Hardiman, *Coming of Devi*; 'Bhils and Shahukars'. These movements were directed largely against Parsi traders.

[62] Ram, *Agrarian Movements*, 75–101; Sarkar, *Modern India*; Sharma, *Peasant Movements*.

[63] Chaudhry, *Rajasthan*; Kamal and Stern, 'Jaipur's Freedom Struggle'; Sisson, *Congress Party in Rajasthan*; Stern, *Cat and the Lion*.

[64] Vinay Srivastava tells me that it has no support in nearby Sadri.

[65] Singhi, 'Jains in a Rajasthan Town', 156–9.

songs and other writings, Anoop Das played up religious differences between Hindus and Jains, to portray the latter as exploiting outsiders. His posthumously published *Jagat Hitkarni* draws attention to the honoured place given in Jain mythology to Ravana, the villain of Hindu versions of the *Ramayana* epic.[66] He claimed too that Jains practised magic to stop the rain, their spells being disguised in the cryptic and in any case certainly evil scribblings of their account-books.[67]

A Fitfully Imagined Community

Jains, and indeed for the most part all Baniyas, tend to be perceived from outside as a homogeneous block. In fact they are divided along caste as well as religious lines, although which lines make for effective divisions—caste, sub-caste, religion, sect, region, business, or just wealth—is variable and changeable. I have already mentioned the major religious sects and schools into which the Jains are divided, and the fact that they are also divided by caste. Now the irony that a religion of peace and non-violence should be riven internally by so many divisions—and they are often hostile—is not lost on Jains themselves. Before going on to look at caste and sect divisions, a few words should be said about the affectionately held, but only fitfully acted upon ambition to unite all Jains on the basis of shared religion.

In September 1990 the Shvetambar Jains in Jaipur held a *goth*, a vast feast to which any Shvetambar Jain in the city could come. The point of this event was to affirm a united social and religious community. Everyone was expected to make a donation beforehand, but this could be as much or as little as one liked. As is usually the case with such events, a handful of wealthy merchants had made handsome donations at the outset, so there was no concern about whether the *goth* would cover its costs, and even families I knew to be very short of money were there. It was, in a distinctively Jain way, sumptuous. There are not very many kinds of food which escape religious censure in Jainism, yet which can be made into a feast. The one which serves best, and was used on this occasion, is a traditional Rajasthani dish, *dal bhati*. This consists of balls of maize and millet flour, some sweet, some savoury, some stuffed with almonds, raisins, and

---

[66] In Jain tradition Ravana is extolled as a great devotee of the Tirthankars, and although he is a villain in the Jain versions of the Rama story, he is rather a heroic villain (a bit like Milton's Satan). For surveys of the many Jain versions of the Rama epic, see Bhayani, 'Narrative of Rama'; Jaini, 'Jaina Puranas'; Narasimhachar, 'Jaina Ramayanas'.

[67] Unnithan, 'Constructing Difference', 242–56.

cashew-nuts, all cooked in temporary ovens made from cow-dung and served with thick lentil sauces. It is simple food, and the way to make it more luxurious is simple too: it is made with, cooked in, dipped in, and otherwise made the occasion for consuming, the greatest possible quantity of ghee (clarified butter). I went along with a family of friends. The daughter was of marriageable age, and everyone who mattered would be there, so we went in our smartest outfits. Huge marquees had been erected on the playing-fields of a Jain-sponsored school. In the first courtyard there were bookstalls for each of the main religious traditions within Shvetambar Jainism: the Terapanth, the Sthanakvasi, the Khartar Gacch, and the Tapa Gacch. The second court had bright coloured lights, music, and four decorated canopies under which rows of tables were laid out for the meal. Teams of volunteers filed past spooning out food, always giving more than one asked for. The four tents had names so the organizers could announce where spaces were free. One could choose between Diamond, Ruby, Emerald, and Sapphire.

This *goth* was the occasion for much excitement and pride. In the weeks before it took place, almost everyone I met told me about it. They were pleased at the prospect, and keen that I should witness it. As one man, a leader of the Tapa Gacch, said to me, 'We are the same caste (*jati*), the same community (*samaj*). We have their sisters with us, and we send our sisters to them. But they will not come in our temples, and we will not go into their buildings. But this is a beginning.' In so far, then, as the point of this event was an affirmation of social unity, it was telling, for although there is a large Digambar Jain population in Jaipur (indeed there are rather more Digambars than Shvetambars) this was a Shvetambar event, with no Digambars present.

Relations between Digambar and Shvetambar Jains are generally far from cordial: both social contact and intermarriage are rare, and throughout the region there is sporadic violent conflict over the ownership of disputed temples.[68] Religious leaders from time to time call for unity between the two traditions, and a few self-consciously modern organizations draw members from both. Once a year both Digambars and Shvetambars parade together through the streets of many cities, including

---

[68] At the last count, Digambar and Shvetambar Jains were in dispute over 134 pilgrimage sites throughout the country. Many of these disputes are of great antiquity, but as rich Shvetambars from Rajasthan and Gujarat move in greater numbers into south-central India, which has in the past been a Digambar stronghold, new disputes are arising. For an analysis of one such dispute, in which the Shvetambars aligned themselves with Maratha Hindu politicians against Digambars, see Carrithers, 'Bahubali Affair'.

Jaipur, to celebrate the birthday of Lord Mahavir.[69] But this only serves to display the depth of the social division between them, for the tidy rows of uniformed school children are there to represent separate schools and the didactic floats and placards are provided by separate organizations. Scholars of religion are wont to say that the differences in religious belief and practice between Digambars and Shvetambars are trivial;[70] but the texture of any religious event, and even the appearance of any religious building, is profoundly different in the two traditions.

The extent of the social separation of Digambars and Shvetambars is shown most clearly in the fact that all main castes which have Jain members also include substantial numbers who are Vaishnava Hindus, but that the Jain members of these castes are in each case from only one of the two Jain traditions. So there are Hindus and Digambar Jains among the Agarwals and Khandelwals, and among Oswals, Shrimals, Paliwals, and Porwals there are Hindus and Shvetambar Jains. Marriage between Hindus and Jains is possible in most of these castes, although it is rare.[71] On the Digambar side, in Jaipur, Jain and Hindu Agarwals appear to marry quite regularly, although Khandelwals do not, and there are reports of similar patterns elsewhere.[72] And on the Shvetambar side, marriage between Hindus and Jains among the Oswals, while not common, is widely reported in the literature and certainly happens in Jaipur today without causing any fuss.[73] The Shrimals in Jaipur all seem to be Jain, and I never heard of a marriage between a Jaipur Shrimal family and Hindu Shrimals from elsewhere, but in other parts of the region, where Jain and

[69] This is Mahavir Jayanti, the only national holiday with an exclusively Jain significance. It is celebrated on the 13th day of the brightening half (i.e. two days before full-moon) of the lunar month of Chait (March–April).

[70] Cort ('Models of the Jains'; 'Svetambara Mendicant') and Folkert (*Scripture and Community*) rightly identify this as one of several misleading clichés which have been endlessly repeated in Western scholarship on Jainism.

[71] Confusingly, there are some Brahmins who have the same caste names as Jain and Hindu Baniyas. Marriage is not possible between Jains and these people. On Brahmin Shrimals, see Erskine, *Western Rajputana States*, 85; Lath, *Ardhakathanaka*, 106; Stern, 'Secteur economique', 149. The existence of Brahmin Khandelwals is reported by Crooke, *North-Western Provinces*, iii. 225 and Erskine, *Western Rajputana States*. For the case in Gujarat, see Das, *Structure and Cognition*, 11–12.

[72] Agarwal, 'Diksa Ceremony'; Cottam, 'Merchant Castes'; Hazelhurst, 'Caste and Merchant Communities', 290.

[73] Jain 'Anthropological Study of Jainism', 88) reports cases of Dasa Shrimal Jains in Bombay marrying Dasa Shrimal Hindus, as well as marriage between Dasa Oswal and Porwal Jains. Axelrod ('Social and Demographic Comparison', 145) reports a similar situation in Bombay in the early 1970s.

Hindu Shrimals live together, such marriages are reported.[74] Yet marriage between Digambars and Shvetambars is much less common. If these religious traditions are similar, the effect is repulsion, as with magnets of the same pole.

A Qualified Commitment to Caste

In so far as there is a caste system, the Jains, one might say, are in it but not of it. Innumerable Jains told me that 'we Jains do not believe in caste', and knew that in saying this they had the authority of scripture behind them. The Shvetambar canon contains several passages explicitly dis-avowing the notion that spiritual worth and religious purity are inherited along with caste status at birth, an opinion which has been repeated time without number by Jain teachers through the ages. While Jains are organ-ized into castes, marry within caste, and observe various caste-based restrictions and practices, all this has generally been regarded as an aspect of their conformity to the social norms of Hindu society, rather than as having any religious importance.[75] At the same time there is no evidence that a comprehensive rejection of caste restrictions has ever been a serious possibility among Jains.

Jainism's being anti-caste has for the most part been a matter of re-pudiating the supposed intrinsic religious superiority and purity of Brah-mins. The story which we encountered in Chapter 2, of Indra transferring the embryo of Mahavir from a Brahmin to a Kshatriya mother, indicates the kind of contemptuous mockery of Brahmin claims in which Jain literature abounds, and off-hand rebuttals of those same claims are easy to elicit in conversation from lay Jains today. I spent a little time studying

---

[74] Cort, 'Jains, Caste, and Hierarchy'.

[75] See Jaini, *Jaina Path*, 289–91, which discusses the mythological charter for the caste system by the 9th-century Digambar teacher, Jinasena. The *varna*s, which are instituted by Rishabh and Bharat, are conceived not as part of the cosmic order but as a political solution to lawlessness and disorder. The priestly caste is not created first, as in theistic Hindu accounts, but last, and on the basis not of birth but of adherence to Jain ethical rules. Hemacandra's Shvetambar version (Johnson, *Trishashti-shalaka-purusha-caritra*, i. 155, 343–6) likewise focuses on social order and on conduct. Before he renounces, Rishabh creates four divisions of men, Ugras (guardsmen), Bhogas (ministers), Rajayanyas (Lord's companions), and the people, who were the Kshatriyas. Bharat arranges daily alms for pious laymen who spend their time in religious study. But it becomes necessary to test those who ask for alms. Genuine laymen can recite a litany which Bharat has taught them and which ends with 'Do not kill'—'*mahana*'. So they become known as 'Brahmanas'. Hemacandra also declares the Vedas to be corrupt versions of texts by these learned pious Jains.

funerary rites among the Jains. Twelve days after a cremation an orthodox Hindu family will call a group of Brahmins to their home and offer them a meal. When I asked a Jain friend if his people did this too, he replied impishly, 'They might be Brahmins, but actually any beggars will do'.

The canonical *Uttaradhyayana Sutra* tells the story of Harikesha, a Jain renouncer of low birth, who approaches a Brahmin sacrificial enclosure. Seeing the sage's coarse features and ragged appearance, the priests shout abuse at him and try to send him away. A *yaksha* in a nearby tree has compassion for Harikesha. Making his own body invisible, the *yaksha* answers on the saint's behalf, requesting alms from the Brahmins. When they refuse he invokes the image of a virtuous sage as a fertile field: to give him alms is to plant seed which will lead in time to a harvest of merit and good fortune. The Brahmins reply, 'All the world knows that we are (as it were) the field on which gifts sown grow up as merit; Brahmins of pure birth and knowledge are the blessed fields.' When the *yaksha* replies in turn that their conduct is not pure, because they are full of anger and pride, and because they kill, lie, steal, and own property, they call on a gang of youths to attack Harikesha.

Now a beautiful princess named Bhadra appears on the scene. She tells how her father made a gift of her to this monk, but that he did not even think impure thoughts about her, let alone touch her. On hearing this, more *yaksha*s come to protect the sage and attack his assailants. The Brahmins, seeing they are defeated, fall down before Harikesha. They beg him to show mercy and to share his wisdom with them. He explains that real sacrifice is not performed with fire, ladle, and fuel, but with good conduct and penance. Asked how, without bathing, it is possible to remain pure, he replies, 'The Law is my pond, celibacy my holy bathing place, which is not turbid, and throughout clean for the soul; there I make ablutions; pure, clean, and thoroughly cooled I get rid of hatred (or impurity).'[76]

Elsewhere in the same text another Jain sage is refused alms by Brahmin priests, although this time the Jain too is of Brahmin birth. He discourses to the priests on what it is to be a true Brahmin. As the 'true sacrifice' is not an external but an internal renunciation, Brahminhood is a matter of purity, but purity of thought and conduct, rather than birth. Most especially, as in the earlier episode, the idea of a true Brahmin is used to extol the virtues of chastity.

[76] Jacobi, *Jaina Sutras*, ii. 50–6. This episode exactly parallels the Buddhist story of Matanga (Jataka no. 497). See also below (ch. 11).

He who is called by the people a Brahmin and is worshipped like fire (is no true Brahmin). But him we call a true Brahmin, whom the wise point out as such. He who has no worldly attachment after entering the order, who does not repent of having become a monk, and who takes delight in the noble words, him we call a Brahmin. He who is exempt from love, hatred, and fear, (and who shines forth) like burnished gold, purified in fire, him we call a Brahmin. . . . He who does not carnally love divine, human or animal beings, in thoughts, words or acts, him we call a Brahmin. . . . One becomes a Shramana by equanimity, a Brahmin by chastity, a Muni by knowledge, and a Tapas by penance. By one's actions one becomes a Brahmin, or a Kshatriya, or a Vaishya, or a Shudra.[77]

If this is a rejection of caste, it is both complex and qualified. We should note first that nothing is said about the justice or otherwise of hierarchical distinctions between lay persons. Implicitly, these are left in place. The issue is the bearing birth has on one's spiritual quest, and more particularly on the spiritual quest of those who have renounced their place in lay society, whatever that might have been. The text makes the twofold point that a high birth does not, as Brahmins believe, guarantee spiritual excellence, and that neither does a low birth prevent it. And it is precisely the notion that a Brahmin is indeed pure and spiritually excellent that is used in order to make these points. The rhetoric is effective, but it scarely constitutes a rejection of caste distinction as such; any more than the suggestion that a real gentleman can be known by his manners and accomplishments, rather than merely by his pedigree, constitutes a repudiation of class.

Where there are few lay Jains, renouncers tend to have problems in obtaining permitted food. A senior Shvetambar Terapanthi nun once explained to me how they cope with this problem when they go to the Punjab, in terms which reveal just how ambivalent the rejection of caste in Jainism can be.

We don't take onions, and we always tell people that they shouldn't too; but so long as it has been prepared separately, we will take food from people who do normally eat onions. Of course, we can't take from Scheduled Castes or from Muslims. In villages, we take from Rajputs, Jats, Gujars. These people are Kshatriyas, so they are pure (*shuddh*). Some of them come and take a vow not to take non-vegetarian food any more, and we prefer to go and take from them . . . In the cities there are always Jains, so we never need to take from anyone else.

As Mahias found among Digambars in Delhi,[78] in Jaipur many Shvetambars affirm that all their castes—Oswals, Shrimals, Porwals,

---

[77] Jacobi, *Jaina Sutras*, ii. 136–41.   [78] Mahias, *Délivrance et convivialité*, 42.

Paliwals—are of equal status. But I also found plenty of people to argue for the superiority of their own caste.

One sort of caste distinction—that between Bisa (twenty) and Dasa (ten) sub-castes—does seem plainly hierarchical. In many parts of the region some or all of the Jain castes are divided into two separate groups between which there is no intermarriage,[79] and this is also true of non-Jain Baniyas.[80] In these cases they are effectively separate castes, but unlike the difference between, say, Oswal and Shrimal, where a status difference is not always implied, and certainly not always agreed upon, Bisas are always regarded as superior to Dasas, the latter's inferiority being explained by their supposed descent from illegitimate children, mixed marriages, or the commensually promiscuous.[81] In Jaipur the idea of such a status distinction is well-understood, and it is well known that people elsewhere are socially divided by it, but everyone claims to be Bisas.[82] So there, the distinction does not pick out stable social categories or caste groups, but it is used in an *ad hoc* way (sometimes expressed as *bare sath* and *chote sath*— the big ones and the small ones) to pass judgements on the relative social status of particular families. In a somewhat similar way, in other places too, differences in social status which are not in any direct sense caste-based are expressed in caste terms using this distinction. Thus in Sirohi, in southern Rajasthan, the distinction between Bisa and Dasa Oswals corresponds to one of profession: between officials in the service of the state and those involved in private enterprise and trade (the ranking of these being despite the fact that the businessmen are richer).[83] And in Jamnagar some members of the urban Oswal caste, the Jamnagari Oswals, claim that they are Bisa in contradistinction to the other group of Oswals in the town, those whose forebears arrived from the rural hinterland, and who are usually known as Halari Visa Oswals. Here the claim is in effect that because they are socially superior, that makes them the Bisas and makes the Halari Visa Oswals the Dasas: 'You might have been Bisa (Visa) where you were before, but here, next to us, you are Dasa.'[84]

---

[79] Agarwal, 'Patterns of Jati'; Banks, *Organizing Jainism*, 52; Cort, 'Liberation and Well-being', 135–45; Cottam Ellis, 'Jain Merchant Castes'; Mahias, *Déliverance et convivialité*, 58. Sangave ('Reform Movements', 233–4) indicates that there is hypermagous marriage between Dasa and Bisa Digambars. Russell (*Tribes and Castes*, 120) mentions Dasas becoming Bisas as a result of 'upward mobility'.

[80] Dumont, *Homo Hierarchicus*, 121; Sangave, *Jaina Community*, 76–85; Shah, 'Division and Hierarchy', 7).

[81] Banks, *Organizing Jainism*, 51; Sangave, *Jaina Community*, 85–7.

[82] Stern ('Secteur economique', 146) reports a similar situation in 'R'.

[83] Singhi, 'Jains in a Rajasthan Town', 140–1.   [84] Banks, *Organizing Jainism*, 52.

I have been told, variously, that Jainism should not observe caste distinctions, that it does not really have them, that caste prejudice was important in the past but is not so now, and that the existence of castes among Jains is a recent Hindu influence which was unknown in the distant past. These days, ambivalence about the legitimacy of caste distinctions—and denyng their existence, especially to outsiders—hardly makes Jains unique in middle-class, urban India.[85] But it is generally agreed, and this does pick out Jains from many Hindus of similar caste and class, that in so far as caste is legitimate, this is as a worldly institution which is firmly subordinate to religious values.[86]

There is a difference, on the one hand, between caste division among Jains, which has this limited moral force (and which, as we shall see, is certainly not rigid) and the yawning gap in status, wealth, and power which exists between Jains as Baniyas and their various servants, workers, and debtors, a gap which is frequently articulated in terms of caste, even when the people on the other end of the distinction are Muslims (who may be members of no caste) or poor Brahmins (whose caste status is supposed to be high). It is true that some Sthanakvasi *acarya*s have made efforts to convert non-Baniyas to Jainism, and there are small non-Baniya Jain communities here and there.[87] But generally, while non-Jain recruits are welcomed as renouncers (except in the Shvetambar Terapanth), access to the property, power, and prestige of lay Jain communities is not so readily extended.[88] And the continuous theme in Jain renouncers' teachings, that caste is not a religious matter in the sense that it does not define the soul's capacity to achieve liberation, has only rarely and recently been converted into a social or political message. This element, then, of Dumont's vision of renunciation in India, although characteristically exaggerated, does effectively counter a tempting misreading of the rejection of caste in renouncer traditions: 'Only Westerners could mistakenly suppose that

[85] Béteille, 'Caste and Family'; Bharati, 'Denial of Caste'.

[86] Lath ('Somadeva Suri', 27) finds this reasoning in the writings of the 10th-c. Digambar Somadeva Suri, who justifies caste as part of the worldly (*laukika*) but not the supraworldly (*paralaukika*) moral order: a distinction which is, as Lath notes, 'quite alien to the Hindu law books'.

[87] Both Banks (*Organizing Jainism*, 110) and Cort ('Liberation and Wellbeing', 137–9) report small Sthanakvasi followings among lower castes: Bhavsars and Khatris in Jamnagar, Bhavsars and Ramis in Patan. In both cases the adoption of Jainism seems to be going along with upward occupational mobility.

[88] Mehta ('Community, Consciousness, and Identity', 106) reports that in the early 1980s, when a Sthanakvasi monk in a village near Chitor converted some Khatiks to Jainism, they were excluded from the lay Sangh.

some sects of renouncers would have tried to change the social order.'[89] Lines of caste show considerable fluidity among Jains, but this is always within the parameters set by their Baniya identity, and, as I mentioned above, hardly ever involves crossing the boundary between Digambars and Shvetambars.

So it is not that Jains are flexible about caste, but rather that they are flexible about just what counts in particular cases as being of the same caste. In Jaipur, there is a preference for marriage within the Oswal or Shrimal castes. No stigma attaches to a marriage between the two, although conceptually the distinction remains perfectly clear. But many people will say that because of this they are not really separate castes any more. In considering potential marriage partners, caste is one of a range of complicated, cross-cutting lines of identity and division: kinship, status, class, religious affiliation, locality, profession, which can be set off one against another, and none of which are all-or-nothing matters.

Entangled Divisions

It is very difficult indeed to separate caste division among Jains from division along lines of religious affiliation. Either caste or sect can become the basis for endogamy. Either can be, from time to time, the most salient criterion people use in deciding who is and who is not the same 'kind' (*jati*) as themselves. The word *jati*, ordinarily translated as 'caste', is used as readily to specify religious affiliation as it is to distinguish Oswal from Shrimal, or Baniya from Brahmin. Such and such a religious practice, I would often be told, is done by all Jains, 'but also other *jatis*'. To the question, 'What is your *jati*?', both 'Jain' and 'Shvetambar *Jain*', as well as 'Oswal' or 'Shrimal', are perfectly legitimate answers. *Jain* caste origin myths, as we saw above, are stories of *religious* conversion, from which manners and social mores, and so caste status, follow. The same myths also invoke class background to explain the rankings of different Jain castes.

This entanglement of caste, class, and religion can also be seen in the story of Baniya settlement in Bengal. I mentioned above how Jain migration from Rajasthan began in the late sixteenth century with Mughal conquest of the region. During the seventeenth century trading communities of Jains settled in both Awadh and Bengal, and there was a

---

[89] Dumont, 'Modified View', 95.

community of Jain Oswals in Murshidabad by the beginning of the eighteenth century.[90] In manners and style of dress, these traders and financiers had adapted themselves to their Muslim-dominated milieu, and spoke Bengali, but they none the less built many fine Jain temples. There seems to have been a distinct business community defined in religious terms.[91]

Marwari immigration in the nineteenth century began with the extension of well-established 'great firms' into new areas. The first Marwari Baniyas to settle in the city of Calcutta were Shrimal jewellers. The East India Company's city was by now the imperial capital of north India, and these wealthy court jewellers and financiers extended their businesses there, from the increasingly subsidiary capitals of Patna, Delhi, and Lucknow. Although mostly Shrimal Jains, the community which grew there was of mixed caste origin, and referred to itself as 'Johri Sath', emphasizing occupational, at the expense of caste and religious identity. Meanwhile, some of the prominent Murshidabad families, like that of the celebrated Jagat Seth, changed their religious affiliation from Jain to Hindu, as they drifted into the dominant business and land-owning community of Bengal, which was Vaishnava Hindu.[92]

After the railway links from the Gangetic plain were opened in the middle of the nineteenth century, the character of migration changed. No longer in whole lineages, but in single households from different parts of Rajasthan, Jain and Hindu Baniyas migrated in larger numbers.[93] These families were for the most part neither especially wealthy nor well connected. They retained strong links with Rajasthan, and continued to draw marriage partners from there. Seen as new immigrants—still 'Marwaris'—they were distinguished from their more established predecessors. While the Oswals of Murshidabad would not marry these Marwari Oswals, whether Jain or Hindu, they did increasingly intermarry with the jewellers of Calcutta, although they were Shrimals, so the group they formed over time reconstituted endogamous caste along lines of religion and class.[94]

In parts of Uttar Pradesh and Madhya Pradesh, there are Digambar Jains called Parvadas. This is said to be a caste, and like other Baniya castes traces its origin to Rajasthan. It is fairly rigorously endogamous, but

[90] Little, *House of Jagatseth.*   [91] Jain, 'Jain Oswal', 394.

[92] Bayly, *Rulers, Townsmen and Bazaars*, 390.

[93] Timberg, *The Marwaris*; Sharma, 'Marwaris', 200–2.

[94] Jain, 'Jain Oswal', 396.

its real distinctiveness, and its separation from the other Digambars of the area, rests on the fact that all its members, and more or less only its members, are followers of the Digambar Taranapanth.[95] So in this case, religious affiliation is straightforwardly aligned with caste in that locality. But generally the situation is much more complex.

A local caste might be split into groups affiliated to different religious traditions. This might or might not, over time, lead the caste to split in terms of marriage. A single religious tradition might be represented in each locality by two temple communities belonging to different castes. Such division in the laity, if it is reflected across a wide area, might lead in time to a split in a renouncer lineage, as renouncers have to decide which caste's patronage to accept. There might be an organization based on religious affiliation which embraces members from more than one caste, and this might encourage intermarriage, and so lead to the fusion of previously separate castes. This last, I would guess, has all but happened in Jaipur between Shrimals and Oswals in the Khartar Gacch.

When a Khartar Gacch Shrimal friend was telling me once about a religious ceremony he thought I should go to, he mentioned that it would take place in what he called, 'the Shrimal temple'. In the conversation which followed, I began by asking if there was an Oswal temple in Jaipur.

No. Shrimal is part of Oswal. They are not really *jati*s, just groups that come from a particular area. Oswals and Shrimals marry each other.

And Porwals?

No, we do not marry Porwals. There is some difference in customs, but no difference between Shrimals and Oswals.

What about Khartar Gacch and Tapa Gacch *jati*s and Digambars and Shvetambars?

Between Tapa Gacch and Khartar Gacch there is no problem of marriage. No, it is different with Digambar–Shvetambar. Digamber–Shvetambar are different *jati*s, and I don't know about what *jati*s there are in the Digambars. We don't really know those people.

So the only distinction he was unhappy to express in terms of *jati* (caste) was that between Oswals and Shrimals, which is universally referred to in the literature as a caste distinction.

---

[95] See Jain, 'Anthropological Study of Jainism', for a description of a community of Parvadas.

This chapter has dealt, in general terms, with the dimensions and dynamics of Jain social identity: how Jain distinctiveness, where it is, is variously conceived and enacted. Against this background, I shall proceed in the next chapter to look in more detail at how things are in Jaipur.

6

City, Locality, and Leadership

THE Jain population in Jaipur is not in any straightforward sense representative of others in the region. It is quite large, and even by Jain
standards it is rich. In terms of Jain religious composition, Jaipur is also
unusual. It is one of very few centres where the whole gamut of sectarian
opinion, Digambar and Shvetambar, is represented in one place. Most
local Jain communities are more homogeneous, both in social and religious terms. Yet it would not be quite right either to see Jaipur as a
microcosm of the Jain population of India as a whole. The Jain population
in the city is large and diverse, but here the Digambars are more numerous than the Shvetambars (they are the minority India-wide), in a region
in which the Shvetambars generally predominate, and the dominant
Shvetambar presence in the city is an extremely conservative business
community, whose majority religious allegiance is to one of the smallest
renouncer lineages. So Jaipur is a special case. Before going on to describe
the Shvetambar community there, it would be helpful to say something
about the kind of special place it is.

An Exemplary Centre

Since 1949 Jaipur city has been capital of the state of Rajasthan (Map 2).
Before Independence, and the incorporation of the princely states into the
new Union, it was the capital of Jaipur State, which was also called by an
older name, Dhundhar. Although Jaipur had been, successively, a
feudatory of the Mughal, Maratha, and British empires, it had been ruled
directly by Rajput Maharajas of the Kacchawaha clan, who claim to have
controlled the area since the beginning of the eleventh century, and their
descendants remain colourful if not always very constructive public
figures in local politics today.[1] I have mentioned that the idea of a Rajput
ancestry is an important aspect of Jain identity. The imagery of this

---

[1] Certain members of the former royal family still like to make grand princely gestures
and, not quite reconciled perhaps to the changes since Independence, do not always remember to check that they still own a piece of land before magnificently donating it to a worthy
cause.

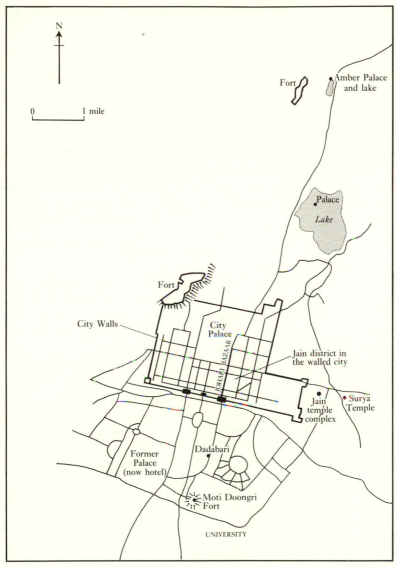

2. Jaipur City.

Rajput ancestry is certainly vivid: moustachioed princes endlessly on tiger hunts, saffron-clad warriors in towering desert fortresses, magical statues being rescued from Muslim iconoclasts, and widowed princesses falling in grief and devotion on their husband's funeral pyres. The myth has had a long history of re-invention. It was already the location of a past Golden Age when Mughal armies first entered the region in the sixteenth century and it was given a glamorous, if deeply frivolous embodiment in the princely protectorates of the British Raj. The building of Jaipur stood at the apogee of one other, more serious but also fleeting, resurrection of the myth.

Along each of the main streets in Jaipur's walled city, the façades are all pink, and fashioned in the same distinctively precious style: filigree arrangements of slender fluted columns, dainty cusped arches, and onion domes arranged on top of painted blocks with tiny shuttered windows, broad eaves, projecting balconies, and low-relief detailing picked out in white. The landmarks are generally royal or religious. A vast site at the centre of the city is occupied by the royal palace, whose perimeter walls are punctuated by gateway arches, long lattice screens, a tall watch-tower, and the famous Hawa Mahal, or Palace of the Winds: a bizarre croquembouche of domed windows. Religious buildings are more or less everywhere, although only the Hindu ones are obvious. A temple to Surya, the Sun, looks all the way across the city from a hill-top a little beyond the eastern wall. In addition to scores of grander temples, on raised courtyards behind the street façades, there are hundreds of smaller shrines, one on almost every corner, and several in the middle of the road, obliging traffic to divide and flow around them.

The most enjoyable, as well as the most gloriously deceptive way to arrive in Jaipur is by bus from Delhi, but it must be on a Sunday. No matter which day you choose, most of the drive is very dreary, through mile after mile of the dry, flat, and featureless north-Indian plain. On weekdays the bus takes the modern by-pass round the eastern edge of the city, through shanty towns and neat government housing estates. It then turns to the west through the southern suburbs, and by this circuitous route arrives finally, in an area to the west of the walled city full of cheap hotels, second-hand tyre sellers, and mechanics' workshops, at an over-crowded bus station. On a Sunday, however, although the bus drops its passengers at the same grim terminus, it does so at the end of an impressively exotic drive, which begins a few miles to the north of Jaipur, at Amber.

Amber, forerunner of Jaipur as the Kacchawaha capital is, though now substantially in ruins, still a perfect realization of 'romantic rajput splendour'. It is dominated by a vast fortress on a high ridge. Below is a beautiful fortified palace, perched on a cliff and reflected in a small lake. Crammed in the valley around are a host of temples and mosques, all dilapidated but mostly still in use, and a number of grand town houses, many now broken up into smaller dwellings. On all sides are low but dramatically jagged hills, of which every ridge and peak is topped with a rampart, a turret, or a fort. The bus squeezes into the valley through a narrow gateway, drives below the palace, and on to Jaipur past five miles of romantic exotica: more fortifications, then down from the hills past a temple and a splendid little palace in the middle of a lake, past rows of royal cenotaphs, and finally through a great painted gateway in the city wall.

The unwary visitor consulting a second-rate guidebook will learn that Jaipur is a 'heavily fortified', 'ancient capital' of which the 'impregnable walls' and all the principal buildings are made from pink sandstone.[2] But this gleaming citadel of the oriental potentate is a thin illusion. Like all its principal buildings, the walls and gates of the city are not stone at all, but rubble, rendered in plaster and painted pink. By 1727, when the city was founded and these 'fortifications' built, even the real thing was militarily redundant. Similarities in decorative style between Amber and Jaipur mask a firm discontinuity in planning and design, for the latter is on an almost entirely regular grid pattern, having been conceived and built to a single plan in only ten years.[3] And while Amber was genuinely a fortress city, and the new city has the superficial appearance of one, Jaipur was built as part of a state-building policy based essentially on attracting and encouraging commerce and trade.

The ruler who built Jaipur, and after whom it is named, was Maharaja Sawai Jai Singh II. When his reign began, in 1700, he was, like other local rulers in the high Mughal empire, a subordinate landlord, graded and ranked according to the quality of service he provided to the Emperor. After Aurangzeb's death, in a fratricidal contest for the Mughal throne, he backed the losing candidate, and the victor, Bahadur Shah, deprived him of his capital and most of his lands. But in 1708, with the imperial armies

---

[2] An example, picked more or less at random, is the much-used *India: A Travel Survival Kit* (374).

[3] Tillotson (*Rajput Palaces*, 169–74) shows that the plan of the city is based on a diagram (*mandala*) from a Hindu treatise on architecture.

tied down elsewhere, and with the help of the rulers of Jodhpur and Udaipur, he was able to recapture Amber.[4] The episode was symptomatic: the Great Mughal no longer had the power to enforce a change of ruler in one of his close client states. In the decades that followed, as the empire by degrees collapsed, Jaipur, like several other former Mughal provinces,[5] emerged from the debris enriched, enlarged, and for the first time since the advent of Mughal power in India, politically independent. Jai Singh not only created a new city, he also re-formed his kingdom into a new kind of state.[6]

From the relatively small and fragmented set of lands he inherited, Jai Singh was able to put together a large, cohesive state (the largest it would ever be); and from being no more than *primus inter pares* among his clansmen, he was able to assert decisive sovereignty. These achievements resulted hardly at all from force of arms, but from quiet political manœuvering. In a time of political uncertainty, but agricultural boom and flourishing trade,[7] Jai Singh secured rights on large tracts of Mughal land both from the Emperor himself and from Muslim courtiers and Rajput nobles who had until then held the land directly under the Emperor. Thus neighbouring and previously independent kings, nobles, and landowners were redefined as feudatories of the new state.[8] Newly cohesive and newly independent states were emerging in other parts of the empire too, such as Hyderabad, Awadh, and Bengal. As Bayly comments, such rulers, 'moved from the status of "refractory" bucolic zamindars as they had been under the Mughals to the dignity of a raja and maharaja'.[9]

The new capital was both a celebration of success, and a successful bid to consolidate the state; it created an ostentatiously prosperous and fashionable trading centre which would attract the revenue needed to sustain the new regime. New states across India at this time were looking to trade, often associated with pilgrimage, to provide revenue for the raja with which, among other things, he could pay a professional army and so further decrease his dependence on forces supplied by prebendal clients.

---

[4] Roy, *History of Jaipur City*, 3–6; Sarkar, *History of Jaipur*, 161–2.

[5] Bayly, *Indian Society*, ch. 1; Cohn, 'Political Systems'; Peabody, 'Whose Turban?', 734.

[6] Stern, *Cat and the Lion*, 9–10.

[7] See Hasan *et al.*, 'Pattern of Agricultural Production'; Singh, 'Nature and Incidence of Taxes'.

[8] Gupta, *Agrarian System*; Sarkar, *History of Jaipur*, 218–20; Singh, *State, Landlords and Peasants*; Stern, *Cat and the Lion*. See also Wills *et al.*, *A Collection of Reports*, for the research which first brought much of this to light.

[9] Bayly, *Rulers, Townsmen and Bazaars*, 11–12.

Although much of the building of the city was left to private enterprise, the state laid out the main streets and set down regulations for the buildings which were to front them. The city as a whole was to hang on the skeleton of the main bazaars, and one of the glories of the design was that the shops along these thoroughfares were lined with continuous columned arcades.[10] This detail, and indeed the whole project—its panache, its grand and aristocratic style but commercial rationale—reminds one of what Nash was later to do, on a more limited scale, in London. Even the attitude to building materials was the same: Jaipur's pink wash achieved, cheaply and quickly, a satisfying unity in long variegated street façades, and served as a passable imitation of the more sumptuous red sandstone which the Mughals had used, more sparingly, in Delhi, Agra, Lahore, and Fatehpur Sikri. The building of Jaipur re-invented and adapted an old Rajput tradition of focusing state patronage on a capital and royal palace. This of course is in striking contrast to the kingdoms of southern India, created around sponsorship of vast temple complexes. If Jaipur was to be a new realm, drawing explicitly on the idioms of pre-Mughal kingship, and if the city and palace were to be an exemplary centre, this kingdom nevertheless differed profoundly from the Negara, for the latter finally collapsed when infected by its port cities with the spirit of commerce. Jaipur, by contrast, was built to incorporate it.[11]

The Kingdom of Merchants

Merchants and traders played a part in almost every stage of the revenue system of the new state. Recent research on Jaipur land and tax records suggests a particularly deep penetration of the state into local markets, with more than half the annual revenue being collected in kind by state officials and sold to grain merchants who were then free to take advantage of seasonal fluctuations to sell the grain to their best advantage. As Bajekal notes, 'Given that the amil (revenue official) was invariably a member of the commercial community and was allowed a limited discretionary authority, the disposal of the in-kind revenue provided an inherent scope for manipulation.'[12] Even when revenue was collected in cash, local merchants were involved in remitting money to the city by means of credit notes which were cashed by the city's bankers. When, as was usually the

[10] Tillotson, *Rajput Palaces*, 174–5.

[11] See Geertz, *Negara*. On the palace as temple and as 'exemplary center' of the kingdom (109–16); and on the port-city as the unwitting precursor of colonial subjugation (92–7).

[12] Bajekal, 'State and Rural Grain Market', 103.

case, the state needed cash urgently, revenue could be demanded in advance of the harvest, in which case local money-lenders lent to cultivators against anticipated crop yield. The same trading communities, dominated by Jains, combined the roles of revenue collectors (*amil*s), village record keepers (*patwari*s), money-lenders, traders, and urban bankers.[13] Max Weber's supposition that religious doctrines excluded Jain merchants from 'typical oriental participation in "political capitalism" (accumulation of wealth by officials, tax farmers, state purveyors)',[14] seems not to have been well-founded.

Merchants were attracted to Jaipur from all over north India: by its increased importance as a trading centre, by its state-centred market in luxury goods, and by the promise of tax concessions and building subsidies from the Maharaja.[15] Thus the city quickly became established as a major commercial centre, and only twelve years after the foundation ceremony, it was already known as a centre for jewellery manufacture and for banking.[16] When Delhi was sacked by the Persians in 1739 and then again, in 1761, by an alliance of Afghans and Marathas, further traders arrived as refugees. As the century progressed the decline of Mughal power accelerated. In its wake, new social groups as well as new successor states gained prominence and power. In the cities of Rajasthan and Gujarat, where Mughal bureaucracy had never been well established, new associations of urban merchants were able to negotiate directly with the local rajas, and secure charters of rights to freedom from state interference.[17]

In 1764 the Digambar Jains in Jaipur organized a great *puja* and sent out a circular letter inviting Jains from other cities, such as Agra and Delhi. Roy quotes from the letter a passage which, as he remarks, shows all the

[13] Gupta, *Agrarian System*; Sharma, 'Indigenous Banking'; 'Vyaparis and Mahajans'; Singh, *State, Landlord and Peasant*, ch. 9.

[14] Weber, *Religion of India*, 200.

[15] Gupta, 'Migration of Traders', 278, 317–18; Roy, *History of Jaipur City*, 57; Sarkar, *History of Jaipur*, 207. On rulers in Gujarat 'courting' traders at this time, see Haynes, 'From Avoidance to Confrontation'.

[16] Amber, like most Rajput courts, had always provided patronage for jewellers and gem traders, especially in its more prosperous times. One of Jai Singh's predecessors, Raja Man Singh II, had been Akbar's governor of the north-west frontier and Bhargava (*Indigenous Banking*, 215) records that he had brought jewellers from Multan back to Amber. See also Roy, *History of Jaipur City*, 89.

[17] Bayly, *Rulers, Townsmen and Bazaars*, 174–6; Bhargava, *Indigenous Banking*, 213–14; Gillion, *Ahmedabad*, 30–5.

smug satisfaction of a business community with a firm grip on the administration; but also, perhaps, the nervous overstatement of a community which knows it needs to keep things that way.

In this city you would not find wine sellers, butchers and prostitutes. Also killing of animals is prohibited. The Raja's name is Madhav Singh. In this kingdom you would not find sinful activities which are prohibited by the Raja. And there are many Jains resident here. All important courtiers are Jains. And all the merchants are Jains. Though there are others too, but they are in a minority, not in a majority. Six, seven or eight or ten thousand Jain merchants have their residencies here. In no other town would you find so many Jains.[18]

Jaipur has not always been prosperous. In the later years of the century the state was subject to repeated raids by Maratha armies, and constant demands for tribute. Inclusion under the British umbrella, in the first years of the nineteenth century, only saw the ransom bill rise, and until 1840 (when the demands were reduced) the state remained in permanent debt to its bankers.[19] However, although Jains (a Digambar faction) only actually controlled the government openly for a short and rather inglorious period, the merchant community has never had to cope with conditions which were much less favourable than those described in this letter. They remained, until the 1930s, the pivot of the state finance system.

During the minority of Maharaja Sawai Ram Singh (1838–59), British officials began reforming the land-tenure system, and would have excluded the local commercial classes from their extremely profitable position as intermediary between the state and agrarian society, but on his assumption of full powers the Maharaja reversed the process. The British Agency was not able to introduce its preferred *ryotwari* system, in which the state taxed cultivators directly, until well into the 1920s.[20] Jaipur merchants established a regional monopoly in dealings in precious stones and metals, subtly integrated with informal banking, which later developed into the international emerald trade of today.[21] They led the local branch of the Independence movement, and stepped neatly into govern-

---

[18] Roy, *History of Jaipur City*, 56–7.

[19] Stern, *Cat and the Lion*, 92–3.   [20] Ibid. 162–9.

[21] The development of the gem market first emerges in official sources in the reports of the Political Agent in Jaipur for the years 1869–71 (Bradford, *Jeypore Reports*). He explains that Jaipur was the money market for the region, provided it with precious metals and precious stones; and describes it as 'a sort of Lombard street to Rajputana' (May 1870, p. 85). See also Baylay, 'Gazeteer of Jaipur', 150; Roy, *History of Jaipur City*, 85–9; Stern, *Cat and the Lion*, 160–4.

PLATES IX AND X. STREET SCENES IN JAIPUR.

PLATE IX. The Johari Bazaar in the early morning.

ment after the creation of the state of Rajasthan.[22] Little wonder that throughout its history Jaipur has been, and still is, popularly known as 'Baniya Raj'—the kingdom of merchants.

The Johari Bazaar

The Johari Bazaar, or Jewellery Market, is one of several broad and elegant thoroughfares which divide the city of Jaipur into rectangular districts. These roads, together with the tight grids of narrow alleyways which connect them, are almost always teeming with people and clogged with traffic. The busiest and palpably the most important of these, the Johari Bazaar is the centre of the Jaipur gem business (see Plates IX and X).

At first sight the nature of this business seems obvious. There are lots of comfortable show-rooms selling elaborate jewellery in gold, silver, and precious stones, smaller shops selling cheaper versions of the same thing, and others specializing in the more folksy silver handicrafts sold to tourists. But none of this is the real gem business. Employing far more people,

---

[22] Chaudhry, *Rajasthan*; Kamal and Stern, 'Jaipur's Freedom Struggle'; Plunkett, *Weaving the Web of Power*; Sisson, *Congress Party in Rajasthan*.

PLATE X. One of the lanes off the Johari Bazaar in the Shvetambar Jain district.

infinitely more profitably, is a market which co-ordinates the import, processing, trading, and export of large consignments of emeralds. Jaipur's emerald market is, in terms of the quantity of material it handles, the largest in the world, but it is almost entirely hidden from public view, in the alleyways off the Bazaar, many of which are accessible only on foot or by bicycle. And even here, close up, the gem market is almost impossible to detect, since it all takes place in rooms in people's houses. The city has a number of specialist shopping districts, but this area just has the usual mix of neighbourhood shops: grocers, chemists, sari shops, tailors, cobblers, paan sellers, and sweet-makers, with their huge vats of boiling milk perched on the front ledge of the shop. The names of the shops tell you that many are run by Jains—Adinath Medicals, Mahavir Traders— but apart from that there is little to mark the area out.

From the roof of one of the buildings, if you look across the lane and through a neighbour's window, you might see a couple of emerald traders: a stately middle-aged man dressed in folds of white cotton, and his son, probably in Western clothes, sitting on a mattress in the middle of the room, examining a pile of emeralds with an eye-glass and tweezers. A few of the more successful merchants have modernized the rooms they conduct their business from, with new marble floors, big glass windows to replace the old barred and shuttered ones, and in some cases even air-conditioning. But even these remain tucked away, embedded in domestic space. The buildings along the alleyways are large *havelis*: houses built on three or four floors around one or more courtyards, and accessible only through narrow gateways between the shops. So, to meet that merchant and his son, you might have to enter through an unmarked passage from the street into the courtyard of a private house, go across the court to the far corner, climb the narrowest, winding, unlit staircase, walk along a balcony on the first floor past a woman sifting rice, to the entrance to another staircase in the opposite corner of the courtyard, and then climb to the next floor.

The area is hot, noisy, and overcrowded, and the water supply intermittent, but rents are very high. For those who work in the gem market it is a distinct advantage to live here because this is a face-to-face business in which deals are concluded on the spot. A youngster starting out in business must be as near as possible to potential deals, so if he is not from an already established Jaipur gem family (as most people are), he will be obliged to live in a tiny, windowless room in the depths of some grand *haveli*. Some of the more wealthy local families now have comfortable villas in the suburbs, but although several schemes have been proposed for moving the emerald market out there too, none has yet succeeded, so they also tend to retain their city-centre *haveli*s.

A substantial community of Shvetambar Jains, probably about a thousand families, lives, works, shops, and worships in this small area. They own the great majority of the *haveli*s in the Johari Bazaar area and they also dominate the emerald trade. The area has the greatest concentration of Jains in the city, and is the centre of Shvetambar religious life. Within a few dozen yards of each other are five Shvetambar temples and a score of other religious buildings: offices, libraries, meeting-halls, and renouncers' lodgings. Jains who live in and around this area certainly think of it as their district. The faces in the shops, on the street corners, and in the temples soon became familiar to me, and by the end of my last period of fieldwork I found, like those who lived there, that it was rare for me to walk from one building to another without meeting someone I knew. In many ways, it felt like a village: or at least, beginning as one inevitably did from an anthropology of South Asia overwhelmingly dominated by village studies, I found myself thinking of it as one. But of course it is not. And the descriptive holism involved in imagining this kind of unit of analysis—the continental analogue, no doubt, of Malinowski's South Sea Island—would be inappropriate too.[23]

The interweaving of residence, business, and religion puts a definite Jain stamp on the district, but as so often with urban space, theirs is not the only stamp. The Johari Bazaar area is socially mixed, with a substantial sprinkling of non-Jain merchants also active in the gem market, and with rich merchants and their non-Jain servants, tenants, and tradesmen all living on top of each other. There is no Jain monopoly on property ownership in the district, and no corporation or authority regulating sales, and while Jains are a higher proportion of the population here than elsewhere in the city, their preponderance is not total, nor is its extent clearly bounded. In so far as there is a Jain district, it is at best a matter of degree, and shades off into other districts with different distinctive but similarly qualified identities.

Although an urban neighbourhood such as this is full of people one knows by sight and even to talk to, any interaction tends to be one-dimensional, and rarely strays from its scripted course. Even people who buy regularly from the same shop do not necessarily know more than the name and caste of the shopkeeper. In relations with their own tenants, Jain

[23] See Appadurai, 'Is Homo Hierarchicus?'; Strathern, 'Parts and Wholes'; Thornton, 'Rhetoric of Holism'.

families take an interest in the school careers of the children and so on, but their neighbours' tenants may be just names and faces. Unlike in a village, and despite the familiarity and apparent intimacy of the area, people who live here still deal routinely in the streets, at stalls and shops, and even in religious fora such as temples and meeting-halls, with people they do not know and whom they identify and assess according to their dress, speech, and bearing, matching them to impersonal social stereotypes.[24]

In so far, also, as the term 'village' has connotations of a settled and relatively stable community, it is inappropriate here. The Jains in this district appear very 'traditional' indeed. Almost all families are involved in the gem business, women observe quite strict purdah in many families, a high degree of social conformity is expected, gossip is rife, and sexual mores are strict. But none of this means that people are deeply rooted to place, or parochial in outlook, or that there is a community which is in any sense closed. Although people are conscious that Jains have been present since the founding of Jaipur city, and it is easy to find a family which will claim to have been there since then, on closer inspection it becomes clear that a large number of people, including many of the most venerable village elder types, are first or second generation immigrants. They have come from all parts of Rajasthan, from Delhi, and from Gujarat. And although most marriages are between Jaipur families, they are also regularly arranged with others in villages and towns throughout north-western India, and among the rich, even further afield. Many Jaipur families have one of their sons now established in some other important business centre such as Bombay, Ahmedabad, or Bangalore. Even some of the most apparently 'traditional' people are widely travelled, and the gem business takes its more successful operators on regular trips to the United States, Europe, and the Far East. So swiftly changing is the Jain population—and, in this city of mushrooming suburbs, so increasingly dispersed—that in the mid-1980s a directory was compiled of all the Shvetambar families, to announce and reconfirm the community's sense of itself, and to help people in their search for suitable marriage partners.[25] For reasons I shall discuss below, we should assent to Jain residents' own claim that they form a definite community in this place, but we should note too that they—and especially some individuals among them—need to work to make it so.

---

[24] For some perceptive remarks on 'the myth of personalized, face-to-face contact in the traditional city' and on how she learned how far it can be from reality, even while it is affirmed by local residents, see Kumar, *Friends, Brothers, and Informants*.

[25] Shrishrimal, *Jaypur dayrektri*; *Jaypur purak suci*.

The Dadabari Temple

My second fictive village was outside the walled city. About a mile south of the city gate on the otherwise flat plain is a single rocky hill—the Moti Doongar, or Pearl Hill. On top is rather a romantic-looking fortress, a Hindu temple is set in the rock beneath, and lying somewhat to its north is a large Shvetambar Jain temple complex, the Moti Doongri Dadabari, consisting of a pleasant walled garden, with offices, kitchens, a *bhojan-shala*, an *upashraya*, and a temple. Its centrepiece is a shrine to the four Dada Guru Devs, which attracts visitors from many Jain traditions, including those which officially reject the veneration of idols. Outside the Johari Bazaar, Jains in Jaipur are rather widely dispersed, but the Dadabari has become the nucleus of a small Shvetambar settlement.

In the late nineteenth century, when the Dadabari was built, Moti Doongri Road was the main highway south from Jaipur city, and along it were scattered the court residencies of some of the most important Rajput nobles. From outside, the Dadabari looks rather like one of these, except that now it is by far the best maintained. The others have fallen into decay (as, to some extent, has the Rajput aristocracy which built them), or have been converted into hotels and primary schools. The city has now expanded to engulf this area entirely, with new main roads superseding the old one. To the north-west of the Dadabari is the huge government hospital and the university medical college; to the east, an area settled by Digambar Jains who fled from the Punjab in 1947; to the south-east, a largely Sikh district; to the south, the university; and to the south-west a former royal palace, now the city's most expensive tourist hotel. Around the Dadabari there are shops, and even some light industry, but mostly spacious bungalows, some of which are very luxurious indeed. As in the Johari Bazaar, virtually all the Jains are in the gem trade. There are a few professionals and academics, but in general this area is too expensive for anyone other than those in business.

In the same deceptive way that the Johari Bazaar looks 'traditional', this area looks rather 'modern', with the layout of a cantonment suburb, lots of smart modern cars, craft shops, fast-food restaurants, and bungalows being refaced in the latest New Delhi fashion. Overall, more of the women who live here work than do those in the walled city, but for the great majority who do not, life is more constrained and isolated, because they are more or less confined to the house and receive fewer visitors. Although the Jains who live here have neighbours from other religions and castes, I saw almost no evidence of anything more than the barest and most superficial contact. And to sustain the comfortable bungalows set in gardens with neat lawns and flower-beds, Jain families here employ far more servants than those in the walled city, and almost all have a whole family lodged in little huts or an annexe at the back of the house. Finally, because of the attraction of the Dadabari temple, which is run by Shrimals of the Khartar Gacch, the caste and sect composition of the Jain community here is actually more homogeneous than in the Johari Bazaar area.

Fieldwork in Jaipur

For most of my fieldwork I lived near the Dadabari, in a set of rooms in the house of a university professor; not a Jain, but a Kayasth. On my first fieldwork visit, in 1983, I had stayed in a Jain household as a paying guest, living close to the family and eating all my meals with them. This worked well in many ways. I didn't feel lonely in the inevitable empty moments when my other contacts were still sparse, and I could gossip with my 'auntie' and still feel that I was working. In 1985 I returned to Jaipur on a collaborative project with Caroline Humphrey and Marcus Banks, and we stayed at the University. In 1986, when I returned alone, I again arranged to stay with the same Jain family. I moved out after a couple of months, in search partly of more privacy, but mostly of more flexibility, fixed mealtimes having turned out to be an intolerable constraint on my work. I wanted to live near the Dadabari and was fortunate enough to find Dr Mathur, who liked having foreign tenants and offered me rooms at a rent so low that even a British graduate student could afford them. So I moved into his spruce white-washed bungalow in a quiet sidestreet, and this became my home in Jaipur, off and on, for several years. There were only two sources of noise: a Hindu man, whom I never saw but who lived over the wall outside my bedroom and would come down to the bottom of his garden at dawn to chant his morning prayers; and a gentle drumming in the afternoons from the school for classical Indian dance next door.

I never for a moment contemplated converting to Jainism, but I was greatly drawn to the oddly tranquil industriousness of Jain temples. Morning worship is particularly beautiful, and I often began the day with a visit to a temple. Sometimes, cycling up Moti Doongri Road, I would stop at the Dadabari, and sometimes go straight to one of temples in the city, depending on whom I was to meet later on. From before dawn each morning, people arrive to perform *puja*, dressed in fresh, clean cotton and carrying offerings of flowers, fruits, and sweets. They much prefer to walk to the temple and those who live close enough begin their devotions with prayers and songs as they pick their way through the dirt and rubbish on the road. Most people come alone, but some others meet up at a fixed time each morning to perform *puja* together. Still others come for a shorter time, to pay their respects, say short prayers, and spend a quiet few minutes before getting on with their day. This is what I would often do. It was a good way to keep up contacts, as one often ran into people and ended by chatting outside or drifting off to have tea together. It was also a good way to meet new people, whom curiosity would drive to polite enquiries or questioning looks. Even when nothing else came of it, there was always the ritual itself to watch, and it was a pleasant way to start the day before going off to see the first of my regular interlocutors.

Anthropologists often talk rather loosely about how one goes about 'fitting in' and being 'accepted' among the people one works with, and some even talk about being accepted, 'as one of them'. In Jaipur, there was no social entity which was organic enough to encourage thoughts of incorporation. No one, not even a Jain, is just 'accepted' *tout simple*. You are always accepted as something in particular. If I were to be accepted it would have to be with particular families and particular people. Of course, I did appear at religious events in the company of respected local figures, and could often enough be seen in conversation with renouncers, and both these probably gave my presence a certain legitimacy. But my work relied crucially on families opening themselves to me in ways which occur only on a one-by-one basis. I have spent a total of about nineteen months working in Jaipur, in six separate visits spread over seven years. A few informants survived from the very beginning to the very end, but there was a slow turnover as some people got bored with silly questions, or relations turned a bit sour, and right up to my last days someone new would introduce themselves to me in a temple or be introduced by a friend.

When I came for my first visit to Jaipur to study Jainism I was young (still an undergraduate and not yet 20), and people's reactions to me were conditioned by this. I had a terror of being drawn into a ruinous business deal involving thousands of pounds worth of emeralds—young Jain businessmen can be especially lean and hungry on the export front—so I cultivated an ostentatious lack of interest in gem trading, at the expense, I suspect, of seeming even more naïve than I was. I did try to fit in but, largely for budgetary reasons, my ways of doing so clustered round the frugal and unsophisticated. I rode a bicycle, dressed mostly in white cotton, and drank the tap-water with what turned out to be regrettable alacrity. Many people assumed I was going to become a Jain renouncer or at least go back and convert people to Jainism at home. My denials carried little weight. When I failed to explain satisfactorily what had brought me precisely to Jaipur to do precisely this research, the suspicion that I had probably been a Jain in a previous life became, for many, an apparently unshakeable conviction.

Behind the crowded street scenes, where sheer numbers give an impression of frenetic activity, the pace of life and work in the Johari Bazaar is really rather relaxed. I was never short of people who had time to sit and talk. For a long time in the middle of my fieldwork I hardly arranged interviews at all. I could set off in the morning confident that between dropping in on friends, meeting people in the street, running into someone at someone else's shop, and popping into one of the temples to see who was there or to talk with renouncers, I would be occupied until late in the evening. I was a young man, living on my own, with (unthinkably) no woman to look after me, so I was inexorably incorporated into three Jain households in the Johari Bazaar (and one non-Jain household outside of it): places where I was expected to turn up whenever I liked, and where if too long passed without my coming for a meal, someone would be sent to look for me and check that I hadn't fallen ill again.

I think in many respects my fieldwork was probably rather easy. I can remember just one person who was actively unwelcoming and thought my presence intrusive (I may have suppressed a few). Generally, most people felt it was high time their religion was better known in the West and were delighted to be helpful. Even my always halting Hindi was enough to convince them I was serious. (Indeed, more than once when I was travelling elsewhere in India I gained access to a closed Jain temple on the basis of little more than a clear recitation of the *nokar mantra*.)

I was preceded in Jaipur by Caroline Humphrey, who had worked there briefly in 1982 and had actually found what I came to think of as my Dadabari; and also by Josephine Reynell, who was finishing her research among Jain women there when I first arrived in 1983. This was a great advantage for me. Josephine introduced me to some of the first Jains I met in Jaipur, and the tact and sensitivity of both my predecessors meant that I was entering a community where people already thought well of anthropologists. (I also had the added, if slightly more embarrassing advantage, that a few of the men thought Josephine's focus on women was in urgent need of redress.)

The seclusion of women might have been a major problem, but early on I discovered that having a female companion from a local Jain family was almost always enough to enable me to speak with the women of even the most conservative Jain household (my limited experience with Rajputs was somewhat tougher). Over the years several people helped me on a more or less regular basis: helping me find my way around and accompanying me to interview new people; inviting me to join them on trips to various towns, villages, and pilgrimage places; going through tape recordings of renouncers' sermons or interviews with me; or just coming along, for company, to lengthy rituals or meetings.[26] From time to time I was able to pay someone for regular help, although I rarely used formal question schedules in interview, never used questionnaires, and never sent assistants to collect information without me. And much of the most useful help I received—often involving hours of work and regular meetings—was given with spontaneous generosity and often, it seemed to me, because people were genuinely interested in the questions I was asking. Perhaps the greatest advantage I had is that so many Jains are both proud of their religion, and conscious of its distinctiveness within the broader Indian religious scene. Many, many times, if I happened to be alone in a temple or at a big religious gathering, someone I had never met before would appear at my shoulder and begin courteously to explain, 'There are two kinds of Jainism, Digambar and Shvetambar . . .'

There were of course complications, and the most pressing of these was precisely the dispersed, unbounded, elusive nature of the object I had come to study. Not far from the Dadabari is a small colony of mud-built houses. Although I never really got much closer than to cycle past, from the road it has a respectable pastoral look. Early in the morning, as smartly dressed Jains are making their way to the temple, the people who live here are bathing under taps by the side of the road, making tea in the open spaces between their houses, and tending to the buffalo whose milk and dung they sell. This scene served for me, especially in low moments when I didn't seem to be making progress, as an emblem of how much easier, I imagined, fieldwork would be in a village—the paradigm, preferred even over a caste, of the anthropological object in India. There, one could count up all the people and make sure one had got them all, whereas I was

---

[26] Like Gold (*Fruitful Journeys*, 21), I found that especially for a first meeting with someone in their home or office, taking along a friend or assistant ('or a blurred composite of the two') generally made things easier (see also Kumar, *Friends, Brothers, and Informants*, ch. 15). Their explanations of what I was up to usually satisfied more quickly than my own; the interviewee could place my friend, and thus in a vicarious way me; language was less likely to be a barrier, and three-way conversations were generally more interesting and less like interviews. Most of my regular companions and assistants were women, and this meant that I could meet Jain women, even comparatively secluded women, fairly freely.

dealing with overlapping and open-ended categories of people and it just did not make sense to try to count them up. There, so much of life would take place in clearly identified open spaces, and would bear some legible relationship to the whole; whereas in Jaipur, it is scattered across the whole city and tucked away in shuttered houses, and refused ever to be convincingly detached from people's disparate situations and projects. The people I knew did routinely talk about an object which I might write about—the 'community' of Murti-Pujak Shvetambar Jains—but I could never get it in focus. In time I became convinced (reassured?) that this was not just a matter of my short-sightedness.

A Property-Owning Plutocracy

Just what is implied in speaking, as I have been, of a local Jain community? This is not a straightforward matter.[27] Where there may be said, as in this case, to be a Jain community (or *samaj*), this is an always emergent local product of a confluence of different interests and identities. The community centred on the Johari Bazaar in Jaipur has no formal boundaries, no necessary and sufficient criteria of membership, and no name. Distinctions between families in terms of caste, kinship, class, occupation, residence, and religious affiliation are all in play, but they cut across each other, and none serves directly to constitute a local community, to create a grounded sense of there being a collectivity to which one might in some sense belong. What does so serve, I think, are two sets of processes: patronage of communally owned religious buildings, and participation in the events they house.

All religious property, such as temples and *upashrayas*, is assigned or affiliated to a renouncer tradition: to one of the Murti Pujak *gacch*s, the Terapanthis, or the Sthanakvasis. Some even have a more narrow affiliation, such as to one of the sub-lineages within the Tapa Gacch or a particular Sthanakvasi *acarya*. But this is not church property. Renouncers do not hold or control it, and unlike the monks in much of Buddhist Asia, who derive income from land attached to temples and monasteries, they control no income either. The property is actually

---

[27] As this book is going to the printers, I have come across Mattison Mines's new book *Public Faces, Private Voices*. This work describes the Beeri Chettiar community in central Madras and offers an analysis of the relation between individuality and community which, although it is expressed in rather different terms, is in harmony with that developed here for Jains in Jaipur. I have added a few references to Mines's work, but it is not possible at this late stage to rework the presentation of my own material in the light of it.

owned by lay people, either individually or, more usually, through some kind of association or corporation, usually called a Sangh or Sabha ('society' or 'assembly'). These lay organizations, in contrast to the renouncer lineages with whom the buildings are associated, are not defined simply on sectarian lines.

Probably the largest Jain building in the Johari Bazaar area is the main Tapa Gacch temple, which houses most of the *gacch*'s activities in the city. It contains not only a temple but also an assembly-hall (*dharma shala*), kitchens, *bhojan-shala*, *upashraya*, a library, a religious school, and a shop where special religious equipment (*upakar*) can be bought, either for use in ritual, or to present as a gift to renouncers.[28] The whole complex is owned and run by the Shvetambar Jain Tapa Gacch Sangh.[29] As with the other such organizations I shall mention, although people who call themselves Tapa Gacch Jains can be found in many parts of the city, membership of the Sangh, and still more use of the temple, is heavily concentrated among those who live in the Johari Bazaar area.

The main Khartar Gacch temple, the Panchayati Mandir, is owned and run by the Jaipur Khartar Gacch Sangh.[30] This organization also owns two large buildings which face each other across an alleyway not far away. Shiv-ji Ram Bhawan is a *dharma shala*, used for large religious gatherings. The *bhojan-shala* and kitchens can also be rented privately for secular events, such as weddings. Vicakshan Bhawan is an *upashraya*, with a preaching hall on the ground floor. Next to the temple is a second *upashraya*, so both monks and nuns can be accommodated at the same time, in separate buildings.[31]

[28] The kitchen here is used to give women from poorer Jain families an opportunity to make some money in a private, religious, and thus respectable context, by making pastries and preserves which are then sold to local Jains.

[29] This organization claims about 450 household heads (probably about 2,000 people) as members. All the members of the management committee are Oswals. It also runs a small temple nearby, which belongs to a rich Oswal family who now live outside Jaipur.

[30] The Khartar Gacch Sangh had a register of 1,472 voting members (adult men and women) in 1985. Of those, 1,045 lived in the walled city (1,017 men, 28 women) and 427 outside (386 men, 41 women). These figures indicate that in most cases heads of households join on behalf of their families. The women who join in their own right are in some cases just very religiously active, and in others those who participate in some of the charitable and social activities organized by the Sangh. There was one place reserved for a woman on the management committee of eleven. In addition to the property in the walled city, mentioned here, the Sangh owns a largely disused temple in Amber, a large temple complex to the east of the city, and is in the process of building new temples in some of the fast-growing outer suburbs of Jaipur.

[31] Directly behind the Vicakshan Bhawan is another Khartar Gacch *upashraya*. This one

Just a little way from the Panchayati Mandir is another Khartar Gacch temple, but this does not belong to the Khartar Gacch Sangh. Together with an *upashraya* next door, it is owned and run by the local committee of the Shrimal caste, the Shrimal Sabha.[32] It is not unusual for Jain religious property to be owned by local caste groups, indeed in parts of Gujarat almost all religious property is owned according to caste.[33] In Jaipur, among the Shvetambars, only the Shrimal caste holds religious property. The Khartar Gacch Sangh is dominated numerically by Oswals, but there are Shrimals on the committee, and many Shrimals are members of both associations. The Tapa Gacch too is dominated by Oswals, but members of other Jain castes are not excluded.[34]

Now, although it seems to be a matter of caste, many Shrimals prefer to express the relationship between the Shrimal Sabha and the Khartar Gacch Sangh in religious terms. The Shrimal temple was once the seat of a lineage of *yati*s, and in a hall on the ground floor there is the throne (*gadi*) of Rang Suri-ji, the leading *yati* who established that tradition. Like most *yati* lineages, this one has now died out, and this may well have been the occasion for the building passing to the caste association, but the *gadi* is preserved. The Shrimals continue to venerate the *yati* tradition, and explain their semi-detached relation to the Khartar Gacch Sangh with reference to this difference in religious practice.

The Shrimal Sabha also owns the Moti Doongri Dadabari, and so the Jain 'village' around there is predominantly Shrimal. But it should be emphasized that Oswals are not in the least discouraged from attending these Shrimal-owned temples, and those who live near the Dadabari are happy to attend regularly, making small financial contributions through the offerings they make during worship. Indeed, although the ownership of the Dadabari is on this narrow caste basis, it is probably the single religious centre in Jaipur which draws regular visitors from the widest circle of Jains. Especially on Mondays and full-moon days there is a steady stream of visitors from the Tapa Gacch and Khartar Gacch, from the

is not used by itinerant renouncers, but as a permanent home for two of the few remaining *yati*s of the Khartar Gacch. There is another *yati* in Jaipur with a reputation for tantric powers and knowledge of *mantra*s (magical words) and *yantra*s (magical diagrams).

[32] The Shrimal Sabha has 166 members (household heads), and is run by a committee of fifteen.

[33] Banks, *Organizing Jainism*, ch. 4.

[34] There are apparently both Paliwal and Khandelwal families who are members. This is slightly surprising as Khandelwal Jains usually follow the Digambar tradition, but these are isolated cases.

normally non-idolatrous Sthanakvasi and Terapanth, and even the odd
Digambar. In fact, Jains do not seem to feel much constrained in which
temples they may visit. Among Shvetambars in Jaipur, many people go
regularly to the one which happens to be nearest to where they live,
regardless of its official caste or sect affiliation, and attend big ceremonies
in any of them, if they know or are related to its sponsor, or just if they feel
like going. In 1990, during the rains, there were several Khartar Gacch
nuns in Jaipur and no renouncers from the Tapa Gacch, so a couple of the
Khartar Gacch nuns went over to the Tapa Gacch *upashraya* to preside
over their annual celebrations. Such co-operation would, I think, be impossible, were not the two sects part locally of the same socially grounded
religious community.

So in close proximity, sharing the same district, and sustained by the
same gem business, there are three religious organizations whose constitu-
encies—both those who pay for and those who take part in their activities—overlap. The Tapa Gacch Sangh is dominated by Oswals, the same
caste which predominates in the Khartar Gacch Sangh. While these two
sects are thus united by caste, the Khartar Gacch is itself partly divided
along caste lines, by the presence of the Shrimal Sabha. For a handful of
rich Shrimals leadership of the Sabha is a source of prestige. Characteristically, those same élite merchants who head the Shrimal Sabha are
careful to promote their reputation also in the Oswal-dominated forum of
the Khartar Gacch Sangh by turning up to make donations at its main
fund-raising events, as well as those of the Shrimal Sabha. The most
important of these events is a celebration of the birth of Lord Mahavir
which is held during the rainy season (see Chapters 12 and 16). The
centripetal force of this event is illustrated by the fact that it also draws to
it some members of the same Oswal and Shrimal castes who have married
into Jain traditions which do not practise temple worship, and so do not
hold their own celebrations.

I have mentioned patronage and participation. This points immediately
to the fact that the community we are concerned with is distinctly unequal, in two different sorts of ways. It is unequal first because participation admits of degrees: a family can participate more or less fully in the
collective activities which are housed in these buildings. Any particular
family is not simply a member of the community or not; it is more or less
near its centres, and the community exists in so far as families cluster
around these centres. To some degree they do this in straightforward
spatial terms, by buying or renting houses as near as possible to the
buildings concerned, but this in itself is not essential. When I speak of

clustering I mean to refer to a social process which can take different forms. In addition to residence, other factors which are involved in being near the centre are participation in the gem market, and also active religious participation, caste identity, kinship links to others who are more centrally placed, and wealth.

Spatial clustering is undoubtedly important, and all the more striking because residential property in the main Jain centres in Jaipur is among the most expensive in the city. It is true that local religious trusts maintain medical and educational facilities in these places, and this should remind us that a family's willingness to go to the trouble and expense of living close to the religious centre, being not different in kind to the way families in England incur costs in order to live near a good school, is a perfectly unsurprising form of social investment. But it would be a big mistake to ignore the more directly religious imperatives involved. It should become clear as we proceed that Jainism calls on its lay followers to engage in a range of religious practices which more or less require proximity to a temple and *upashraya*. This is especially a factor for women, whose freedom to move around the city on their own is quite restricted. Living near an *upashraya* can give people regular contact with renouncers, and increases greatly their opportunities to offer them alms (see Part IV). So in order to be a good lay Jain, it helps to be near the centre of a Jain religious community.

The community is unequal, secondly, because patronage—really large-scale financial contribution—is open only to a few families and makes their relation to the community different in kind. The heads of these families I shall refer to as 'notables'—local terms include *seth* and Mahajan (Chapter 5), *bare log* (big people), and *punyashali* (Chapter 16). The term 'notable', which derives from Weber,[35] has already been used in studies of the politics of Indian towns in the colonial period,[36] but a further reason for using it derives from a comparison drawn from much farther afield. Paul Veyne's description of euergetism in Hellenistic Greece brings out admirably some of the political features of patronage which I think are also important in Jain communities.[37] The essentials of the system, which continued in different forms into Republican and Imperial Rome, are outlined in the following paragraphs.

Among the rich of Hellenistic Greek cities there were those who contributed on a huge scale to public funds. They put up temples and other

---

[35] Weber, *Economy and Society*, i. 289–91; ii. 948–52.
[36] Bayly, 'Local Control'; Haynes, *Rhetoric and Ritual*.
[37] Veyne, *Bread and Circuses*, chs. 1 and 2; see also Elster, *Political Psychology*, 35–69.

public buildings, funded public entertainments at the circus and the arena, and provided banquets and other public pleasures. These notables competed for public office, making vast donations to embellish the city as they did so, although public office brought with it only the expectation that they would go on to make still more, and similarly magnificent, donations.

The same is true of the rich Jain merchants who sit on temple management committees and are patrons of the community. Almost no religious ceremony of any importance passes without a call for donations. They are an ever-present (as well as being in practical terms essential) aspect of Jain religious life. Control of local lay organizations lies in the hands of small management committees which are usually formally elected, but are in practice composed entirely of those members of the local élite who make the biggest donations to them. They are almost invariably elected unopposed, and continue to pay what Veyne calls 'the price of honour' by making similar donations thereafter. Indeed, when donations are called for, everyone present looks immediately to the members of these committees.

The distinctive thing about Hellenestic notables' donations was that they were made to the city, and so to the citizens as such, rather than to the poor. They were not 'charity' (and Veyne carefully distinguishes them from later Christian practice), but acts of public patronage. In the Jain case there are certainly funds and organizations which may properly be called charitable, and which are supported by wealthy donors.[38] But much more emphasis, and much more money, is put into the provision of collective and public goods by these lay organizations.[39] Some of these

---

[38] Haynes ('From Tribute to Philanthropy') convincingly demonstrates, for the merchants of Surat, that munificent support for philanthropic causes during the colonial period should be seen as part of this local élite's accommodation to British rule, and as an extension and adaptation of tribute-giving practices of pre-colonial and early colonial times. In the same way Jain patronage these days of famine-relief projects and the famous 'Jaipur Foot' project (a series of hospitals dedicated to the rehabilitation of amputees which began as a Jain initiative in Jaipur, but is now largely government-funded) is addressed to the state and to national public opinion. See Sangave, *Jaina Community*, 312 ff., for a general survey of Jain charitable activities. Cort ('Two Ideals', 399–411) shows how prominent religious gifts are in the authorized biographies of wealthy Jain merchants in Gujarat. Other studies of the merchant practices which I describe here as euergetism include Bayly, 'Indian Merchants'; Lewandowski, 'Merchants and Kingship'; Mayer, 'Public Service and Individual Merit'; Mines, *Public Faces, Private Voices*; Rudner, 'Religious Gifting and Inland Commerce'.

[39] The following institutions in Jaipur were established, or are supported in whole or in part, by members of the Jain community: three undergraduate colleges, five schools, seven libraries, seven publishers (publishing religious books which are distributed free or at very

public goods, such as educational institutions and medical dispensaries, are open to non-Jains, but even these are located in Jain residential areas, organized with Jain needs in mind, and have their Jain affiliation clearly advertised. And the bulk of the euergetism which gem merchants in Jaipur engage in provides for collective Jain religious life: maintaining temples and other buildings, providing religious feasts, and financing religious ceremonies.

I have already described the main religious buildings in Jaipur, and the uses to which they are put. Let us look briefly at the feasts. The most common form of religious feast is that which follows a fast (called a *parana*), but feasts are also held after regular *pujas*, at various points in the calendar, and for a host of other reasons. The distinction which is relevant here is between two kinds of feast, *pritibhoj* and *swamivatsal*. *Pritibhoj* ('meal of affection') is held by a family to celebrate a marriage, the birth of a child, a recovery from illness, or any other good fortune which the family has enjoyed, and this might include the successful completion of a fast by a family member. As the name implies, the guests are chosen personally by the hosts. But who is invited and who is not, and who accepts invitations from whom, are for that reason matters of social, financial, and caste status as well as kinship and friendship. So the feasts are firmly embedded in complex social relations and reciprocities, and they are ways of forging, expressing, renewing, or repudiating social ties and obligations. *Swamivatsal* is different. This is an occasion for all and only Jains, and therefore to provide this is to give a public good to Jains as Jains. Whereas *priti* means love and affection between equals ('brotherly love'), *vatsal* (a very important notion in Vaishnavite Hinduism) connotes tenderness and nurturing care, especially towards an offspring. *Swamivatsal* is a feast to which every Jain is free to come. No invitations as such are sent. The event is advertised, and anyone who counts themselves a Jain may join. Unlike attendance at a *pritibhoj*, your right to come does not depend on there being people who want to please you. Even if you are of no social consequence at all, you can still belong to the religious community.

low cost), six religious journals, two hospitals (one very large and only partly charitable, the other a specialist centre for the rehabilitation of amputees), three clinics, two charitable medical dispensaries, and two animal hospitals. Lodrick (*Sacred Cows, Sacred Places*) points out that while a number of Hindu (Vaishnava) religious traditions support hospitals for sick cows (*goshalas*), hospitals and homes for a whole range of animals, from stray dogs, through birds and rats to bugs and beetles, are peculiarly Jain.

A *swamivatsal* is funded through donations. Sometimes this is done by several people together sponsoring a feast, but often just one wealthy merchant agrees to make a *tithi* donation for the day of the event. *Tithi* simply means 'lunar day' and giving *tithi* means sponsoring all the religious festivities that day—this might include all the offerings in a grand *puja*, and paying the ritual specialists and musicians, as well as providing a feast.[40] In Jaipur these are held several times each year, regularly at ceremonies to commemorate the founding of certain temples and invariably they are held at irregular events such as initiating a renouncer, consecrating an idol, founding a temple, or opening a public building. In 1986, when an idol of a recently deceased nun was consecrated in a temple just outside Jaipur, tens of thousands of people came from all over India to festivities which lasted for a full five days. The notables of the Jaipur community provided *swamivatsal* meals for all who wished to take them, as well as accommodation for all the visitors, for the whole of this celebration.

The identity of the donor of a *tithi* is almost always announced, and as a statement of benevolent provision to the whole religious community it is hard to improve upon. The famous description by Fustel de Coulanges, in *The Ancient City*, of the urban social bond as accomplished in a 'holy communion meal', could scarcely have a better instantiation. So although it is appropriate to speak of patronage of religious buildings and institutions, the relations which these donations sustain are not patron–client ties. The gifts are public benefactions, the provision by individuals of essentially collective goods, and in the Jain case what they do is help to create and sustain a distinct public realm—a community. Here the Jain case differs somewhat from that described by Veyne. For if the Greek notables, as he says, found that 'local government was there for the taking', so that they were compelled to pick it up or else lose prestige,[41] Jain notables are engaged in a more creative undertaking, carving out, through their munificence, the social domain over which they preside. This is perhaps most clearly evident in Jaipur at present in the way the leaders of the sect organizations are helping found temples in some of the new residential areas, outside the old city walls, which are to be, like the Dadabari, the nucleii of new satellites of the Johari Bazaar community.

---

[40] Lodrick (*Sacred Cows*, 92) mentions this as a specifically Jain way of funding animal homes, and the form of the donation is the same. The donor agrees to provide money to pay for the food of the animals in the home on the same day or days each year.

[41] Veyne, *Bread and Circuses*, 123.

But the motivation is the same. In both cases the notables are, more than anything else, pleasing themselves: giving expression to their sense of social superiority in conspicuous magnificence.

And the result is the same too: a sphere of local autonomy—in one case the city, in the other the religious community—which is not the locus of real political power (in both cases firmly subordinate to the state), and not the place where class interests, if this were the notables' business, could be defended.[42] This point is important because it helps us keep the phenomenon in perspective, and so to see how extraordinary it is.

The Jains of Jaipur sustain what is by any standards a lavish public life, with fine public buildings, opulent rituals, and sumptuous feasts, almost entirely from voluntary donations. As with the clustering I spoke of in relation to religious participation, there is a sense in which public religious giving can be seen as a social investment strategy. It advertises the wealth of a rich merchant family in a morally approved way, and so augments its standing in the community. And as I shall explain in Chapter 16, notions of moral, social, and business standing are intimately inter-connected. But this does not really make the magnificent support of religious institutions any less extravagant, and in particular it does not explain it. As Veyne comments, euergetism 'reflected a class psychology without serving class interests'.[43] To understand their generosity, it would be as much a mistake to look for a functional explanation to demonstrate that they are really acting in narrow self-interest, as it would to think we had explained anything by piously indicating a religious motivation. Euergetism is not actually necessary for rich merchants with a successful business, and there are a few who, as their co-religionists see it, do not play their part. What euergetism is necessary for is honour or reputation (*izzat, nam*), being regarded as leader of the community, one of the 'big men' (*bare log*), a *seth*. And it is this I think which motivates it. If we remember how important kingly and lordly patronage is to images of the lay Jain—the Indra and Indrani who worship and support the Tirthankars; the converted Rajputs who follow Jain saints—we can glimpse how the status that is acquired here can also be a religious one.

The local Jain community is not then a supra-organic entity, which exists somehow over and above the individual (still less is the latter absent from the scene). Instead it is quite substantially produced and reproduced through the agency of named and celebrated individuals.[44] Nor is local

---

[42] Veyne, *Bread and Circuses*, 154.   [43] Ibid. 148.

[44] In this connection compare Khare, *Untouchable as Himself*; Mines and Gourishankar, 'Leadership and Individuality'; Mines, *Public Faces, Private Voices*.

Jain community something which exists within boundaries, but is rather a set of processes and practices which cluster around the ownership, management, funding, and use of property. It is intrinsically, and at its very foundation, unequal; and it is at best what Barth has called a 'disordered, open system'.[45] The community is a religious one, in that it is formed and reproduced around religious institutions, and in that sense it shows how the Jain religion, for all that it is focused on renunciation of family, caste, and social identity, can take a very specific social form and define, to a significant degree, a substantial social milieu.[46]

Carrithers and Humphrey, in their programmatic essay 'Jains as a Community', insist that it is a mistake to try to reduce Jain social identity to caste. They note that Jainism shows 'integrative resources' which go well beyond, and could not be explained in terms of, bounded endogamous groups. They rightly remark that seeing Jain social organization simply as a matter of caste could not explain the many supra-local manifestations of Jain identity, cohesiveness, and, on occasions, political efficacy.[47] And Romila Thapar's examination of the dimensions of local and supra-local identity in Indian history suggests that Shramanic movements, such as Buddhism and Jainism, have repeatedly brought people together for concerted political and economic action on a wider scale than have those identities we now call 'Hindu'.[48] I have suggested that both the cultural and the organizational constitutions of local Jain communities are founded on open-ended and expansive processes. They include, but are certainly not reducible to, matters of caste. Seen this way, it seems less of a mystery that there should be manifestations of community at the regional and national level—such that one can speak at least occasionally of

---

[45] Barth, 'Towards Greater Naturalism'.

[46] It is clear, as I mentioned above, that the extent to which Jains form distinct local communities at all varies with time and place, and there is evidence that how they are constituted may vary slightly too. Banks's ethnography (*Organizing Jainism*, pt. 1; and personal communication) suggests that in Jamnagar collective events are more commonly supported by donations collected by caste committees from large numbers of caste members, and much less by *tithi* donations by a single family than is the case in Jaipur. In Jamnagar there are simply far fewer families who are rich enough to practise euergetism, and it is also the case (and, perhaps, as a result) that Jains there are much more deeply divided along caste lines. It may be that in other communities which are smaller and poorer than Jaipur the distinction between patronage and participation is similarly less clear-cut, and that euergetism is less a matter simply of wealth. Feuchtwang describes a similar difference between the patronage of local temples in rich and poor areas on Taiwan (*Imperial Metaphor*, 142–3).

[47] Carrithers and Humphrey, 'Jains as a Community', 9–12.

[48] Thapar, 'Imagined Communities'.

the Jain community. This capacity, though realized, to be sure, through national organizations, the mass media, political parties, and the state, is grounded in the characteristics of local Jain communities as open, unsystematic, and manifestly the product of ongoing action and choice. Jains' routine experience of religious community is not only that it might be imagined, but also that it may be conjured up.

PART III

Forms of
Renouncing Self

7

The Ascetic Imperative

THE chapters which follow cover two main themes. They deal with the ways in which the asceticism of Jain renouncers is incorporated into lay religious life; and the ways in which the spiritual virtues of renunciation are displayed and made available in sacred representations. The connection between these themes is the way the human body in Jainism is made an instrument of religious action and a medium of religious thought. So the subject of this part of the book is the constitution of the religious self in Jainism. What does one do, to make oneself a Jain self?

The short answer to this, and the place we must begin, is asceticism, by which I mean a regime of self-imposed but at the same time authoritatively prescribed and ordered bodily disciplines. This is the way persons make themselves Jains, or fashion the Jain-ness of themselves. For renouncers, of course, this takes place within the framework of the order—a 'total institution' where their whole daily routine is ordered, and where they are subject to monastic authority. So the question arises: to what extent, and in what ways, does this institutionalized, professionally religious life inform the lives of those who do not directly participate in it, but who are, none the less, Jains? Lay Jains too may undergo a form of this institutionalized life for limited periods of time, but in practice very few of them do so, and those only very rarely. Nor would it answer our question to say that 'monasticism' as a set of values or a world-view is generalized through, or permeates, Jain society. We need to say how and for whom.

These chapters view Jain asceticism not as a code of rules and prohibitions, but as a set of projects—forms of religious self-fashioning—and they proceed by examining the social practices through which they are pursued. In this perspective, asceticism embraces a range of modes of working on, and re-forming, the self. In this chapter I shall examine the most universal and routine manifestations of lay Jain asceticism, in the observation of non-violence and in dietary regulation, and then, in Chapter 8, I shall look at the most complete packages of ordered monastic discipline, which just a few lay Jains very occasionally undertake.

Between these two extremes lie disciplinary rites known as *samayik* and *pratikraman* (Chapter 9), and elaborate scripted fasts (Chapter 10). They are all performed occasionally by nearly everyone, but with frequencies which vary radically between individuals, between men and women, and between different stages in the same person's life-cycle. They are none the less the centrepiece of the analysis because, as I shall be trying to show, these bodily practices develop the aptitudes and dispositions—and thereby induce the experiences—which centrally are what it is to be religious in a Jain context. They accomplish what Talal Asad, writing of Christian monasticism, has called the proper organization of the soul.[1] And it is in this profound self-ordering that Jainism as an ascetic project— the development of ascetic persons—is carried most deeply into lay life. I shall try to show how these ascetic practices work on a particular conception of the relation between the body and inner state. In Peircean terms (which, I hasten to add, I shall use only informally[2]), this conception is an indexical one: a relation between outside and inside which is at the same time signification and causation. The body is used as a tool, or a weapon, in the ascetic project of improving the condition of the soul, and the effects of this are indicated in turn by the body's aptitude in performance of these rites.[3]

If this makes these ascetic disciplines a locus for what Foucault has called a 'regime of truth', I shall be concerned to show that the 'sovereignty' this regime enjoys is very far from total. The 'meaning' of these practices is crucially untamed. Fasting in particular allows the simultaneous pursuit of both renunciatory and worldly ends. And I shall go on (in Chapter 11) to sketch two further versions, also embodied in Jain religious practice, of what Charles Taylor has called, 'the moral topography of the self'.[4] The first, a radical dualism which enjoins the destruction of the body, turns out, curiously, to be largely the preserve of those opposed to the rigours of monastic renunciation. It is, in a way, the dark side of Jain mysticism. The other, where the body is seen as iconic representation of the excellences of the perfect soul, is most clearly expressed in idol worship.

[1] Asad, *Genealogies of Religion*, 138.

[2] See Peirce, *Collected Papers*, ii, esp. §§ 230–307. Beyond the well-known triad of icon, index, and symbol, I shall not be attempting to develop or to follow a formal typology. For an interesting ethnography which does, see Daniel, *Fluid Signs*.

[3] The conception, as Peirce would have expected, is actually triadic, with notions of body, soul, and mind in play. See also Parkin, 'Reason, Emotion, and Power'.

[4] Taylor, 'Moral Topography'; *Sources of the Self*, 111–99. Appadurai ('Topographies of the Self'), apparently independently, uses a very similar notion.

Ahimsa: An Ethic of Quarantine

Jainism uses a number of different images to talk about asceticism and spiritual progress, all of which envisage cumulative steps towards the attainment of a goal, or progressive cultivation and development. Thus the ascetic can be described as advancing on a long and difficult path towards enlightenment; as learning by degrees the watchfulness necessary to restrain attachment and emotion; as progressively scrubbing every speck of *karma* from the soul; as training the will and the body to bear the ordeal of a fast to death; and, perhaps most of all, as engaged in a fierce struggle to repel and destroy the enemies of the soul.

The most routine and pervasive way in which this ascetic renunciation enters the lives of lay Jains is in their diet. To say that Jains are strictly vegetarian hardly begins to convey either the rigour and severity of the rules which some Jains put themselves under or the centrality of such practices to Jain religious life. Moreover, it misses the most important fact about Jain rules about food, which is that there is no single set of rules. In addition to occasional fasting and absolute abstention from a range of forbidden foods, the diet of pious lay Jains is moulded in a number of ways by religious considerations. Almost everything about food is problematic. Some people pride themselves on setting a numerical limit to the types of foods they will eat (and this means everything that passes their lips, including toothpaste). Some refuse all seasoning, so that eating becomes a form of austerity. In detail, the regimes which different families and individuals put themselves under vary considerably, with many families making only the occasional gesture towards austerities which for others are routine. And the same person will adopt very different regimes as their place in the family changes. However, these regimes are all more or less strict versions of the same thing: that is, different points on a continuum which begins from the basic avoidance of a few forbidden foods, strives towards an ideal which seems to recede as you approach it, and which turns out in the end to be a fast to death. That is to say, these various forms of asceticism are not expressions of the same logical principle, or deductions from the same precept, still less applications of a legislated code, but varyingly imperfect realizations of the same aesthetic and moral ideal. To understand how this is the case, we need to look closely at the element of Jain religious practice which is most well known, and probably also most misunderstood: *ahimsa*.

One noted Jain scholar remarks that *ahimsa* is, '*the* virtue: all other restraints are simply elaborations of this central one'.[5] While there are Jain savants who propose other ways of assigning priority to Jain precepts and practices,[6] this is a claim that would command considerable agreement among Jains. The catch-phrase '*ahimsa paramo dharmah*' (non-violence is the highest duty or religion) is both a rallying cry and a badge of identity. The word *ahimsa*, which is well-known outside India through the influence of Mahatma Gandhi, is conventionally translated into English as 'non-violence'. Learned Jains often dispute this translation, claiming that such a negative expression misses the fact that it acts as a positive injunction in every facet of life. This objection has considerable force, and although when I translate *ahimsa* it will be as 'non-violence', I shall also add my own reasons why Jain non-violence should not be confused with any of the medley of pacifism, animal welfare, Nonconformist Christianity, and New Age enthusiasms which that expression is apt to call to mind.

Perhaps my most vivid memory from my first trip to Jaipur is the day of the first heavy monsoon rain. It was mid-morning and I was sitting looking down into the Johari Bazaar from the house of one of the city's most prominent gem merchants. The streets outside were awash, and were running so deep that scooter engines were flooded and refusing to start. I was learning about Jain philosophy from Vijay-ji, a young man who was, by common consent, the local lay expert on the subject. The scene outside prompted him to raise the subject of non-violence.

You see only rain outside, and people rushing to get to work. But Jain religion sees much more than that. Today there is much *himsa* (violence) being done. Jain renouncers will have to fast. If they were to go out now they would kill many creatures [Jain renouncers have to go out to collect alms for each meal], so they will not have anything to eat.

He went on to explain how Jainism is very precise, how it goes into the very greatest detail. Jain philosophy sees violence in a rainy day because fresh water is full of tiny creatures, and it is important not to harm even these.

Jains have always believed in tiny, invisible creatures. Western science has only

---

[5] Jaini, *Jaina Path*, 167.

[6] Teachers of the Digambar Kanji Swami movement, for instance, argue that 'non-attachment' (*akincanya* or *aparigraha*) is the central virtue, from which all others derive. A Khartar Gacch lay teacher I knew, who gives classes on Jain philosophy at religious camps, argued for renunciation (*tyag*). A renouncer I asked said asceticism (*tapas*) is the most important principle.

recently discovered these. But Jainism has known about them all along. They knew them in the time of Acarya Hemacandra and King Kumarapala. This was a long time ago, perhaps the tenth century. The king was going to war, and the *acarya* taught him about non-violence. All the arrows in the king's army were disinfected so that they would not harm air-beings when they flew through the air. In Jainism you must be very thorough.

I asked another Jain layman about war. Surely 'non-violent' Jains should not be soldiers?

No, Jain religion does not say you should be a coward. Jains are heroes. Religion first teaches you about duty. So if it is part of your duty to go to the front in war, you should do that. It is different for renouncers, but laymen should do that duty. There were always Jain warriors, and they were very religious. Jain warriors used always to stop when the time came for *samayik* (a meditational exercise performed by many Jains at the same time every morning), and perform their *samayik* on horseback.

When learned Jains assert that *ahimsa* is not the same as what we mean by non-violence, they are surely right.

Looking out of the window, my friend referred me to the fact that Jain renouncers may not touch fresh water, and they drink water only if it has been recently boiled. When on a fast, lay people adopt the same practice. Anyone you ask about this will give the same explanation: in even a small glass of fresh water (*kacca pani*—literally raw or uncooked water), there are millions upon millions of tiny creatures, and in drinking this water you would kill them all. Boiled water is free of such creatures, so drinking boiled water is non-violence. This is a puzzling explanation. The creatures still die. Killing them, indeed, is the point of boiling the water. So why is this thought to be better? There are two lines of argument to follow. One goes through the division of labour: the person who boils the water and so does the killing may not be the person who drinks it. This indeed is routinely the case, as renouncers never boil water themselves. They are forbidden to use fire with just the same severity as they are forbidden to use unboiled water, and their water is boiled in advance by lay people, who may or may not be Jains. This suggests that the virtue of drinking boiled water depends on the sin involved being taken on by someone else. But this is not the whole story. I shall return to these transactional issues below (Chapter 14), but for the moment let us follow a different line of argument.

Only a few lay people drink boiled water regularly, but to do so is a necessary part of many commonly performed fasts, and at such times, unlike renouncers, they are supposed to boil their own. The water is boiled at home, usually by the most senior woman, and this in no way diminishes the virtue or effectiveness of her fast. Why should this be? Almost always, when I tried to raise this kind of question with Jain friends, they had very little to say on the matter. They always thought the virtue of drinking boiled water obvious, and more to the point, it is a religious virtue to see that it is obvious.

Let us look at some more of the forms *ahimsa* takes, to see what people think a rigorous application of the principle involves. Although they do not take a full bath, renouncers do occasionally wash themselves, using damp cloths soaked in small quantities of boiled water. They never take a bath in what one nun described to me as 'the modern way'. Her recommended method was as follows.

You should take very little water in a pot and use that. The water should be collected in the pot again and thrown at a place where there is no danger of killing life-forms (*jiv*s). Soap should not be used. We believe that if water is kept in a pot, 'bacteria' will start forming, so the water should be spilled somewhere, like sand, where it will dry. If anything like soap is mixed in the water the growth of bacteria will increase.

So to increase the growth of creatures violates 'non-violence'. From before sunset until well after sunrise, renouncers are supposed not to go outside. If they do, they should place a woollen cloth over their head. The explanation, given me by a senior renouncer, is as follows.

During these periods millions of the very tiniest creatures (*tras apakay* and *suksham apakay*) fall out of the sky towards the earth. They would fall on us and die. In any case they will die in fifteen minutes, but if we put a cloth on our heads they will be absorbed instantly.

One of the classes of prohibited food is *zamikand*—plants which grow underground. This class of foods is not avoided by Vaishnava Hindus, even those who are generally speaking as strictly vegetarian as the Jains. The category includes all roots, bulbs, and tubers (the leaves of these plants are not prohibited, though of course not all are edible anyway). Anyone, if asked, can give one or more of a cluster of reasons for this (even if they themselves do not observe the prohibition).

1. The earth is full of tiny *jiv*s, and millions of these are killed when these plants are pulled up.
2. They are bursting with life (they sprout spontaneously even if not planted).

3. They contain an infinite number of *jiv*s (even a tiny part of the root, if planted, will grow).
4. They have a bad effect on you, heating the blood and inflaming the passions.

The last explanation, which is not unique to *zamikand*, is felt particularly to apply to onions and garlic, but I have heard it said also of the potato. In particular, the belief that onions and garlic have aphrodisiac properties is widespread beyond Jainism, and many pious Hindus avoid them too. Jains tend to explain this property as a consequence of the others: a food which is full of life-forms is bound to have this bad effect. Turmeric and ginger are root plants, but many of those who avoid *zamikand* will eat the dry powdered spices made from these roots. The reason people invariably give for this is that in this form they cannot grow again. What makes fresh root plants inedible then is that they are still capable of germinating and growing. In reducing them to a powdered form (which again is, after all, to 'kill' them) they become edible.

Now, it is important to realize that the practice of *ahimsa* is closely tied to a way of seeing the world, an element of what Jains call the right view (*samyak darshan*). The rules make sense in terms of this view, and following the rules is supposed to lead one to see things the right way. When Vinay-ji looked out of the window and said that he saw violence out there in the rain, he was reporting a spiritual accomplishment of his. Similarly, one nun I interviewed about her reasons for becoming a renouncer said that the decision came one morning when she walked into the kitchen. There was a cockroach in the middle of the floor, 'And I just looked at it and suddenly I thought, "Why should I stay in this world where there is just suffering and death and rebirth?".' Vinay-ji was saying that in the rain he could see *samsar*, he could see that life in this world consists of millions and millions of souls constantly being born, suffering, committing violence, and dying: a constant cycle in which each soul does this countless numbers of times. The monsoon rain shows us something of what the world is really like. With the rains, all kinds of swarms of insects come briefly into existence. They are everywhere and it is impossible not to kill some. They live for a while and they die. And Jainism teaches that even though we cannot see it, this is happening all the time on an even smaller scale in water, air, fire, and soil. Although our lives last a little longer, they are just the same, and they are part of this awful, endless cycle. Next time we might be one of these insects, or a fire body, which is born and dies again, doubtless in unspeakable agony, in an instant.

It would be a mistake to try to derive all the practices which are regarded by Jains as applications of non-violence from a single underlying theory. There are inevitably points of incongruity and even contradiction. Moreover, as I have indicated, almost any aspect of life can be seen in terms of non-violence, almost any practice criticized in terms of it. What I think makes all these concerns and criticisms instances of the same phenomenon—why it seems to Jains to make sense to say that the same principle is being applied in each case—is that they are all ways of dealing with, and so in turn ways of constructing and realizing, a practical understanding of the world as being populated in this horrifying way with innumerable unseen forms of life.

A great deal of the discipline which renouncers live under makes sense in the light of this vision. They must learn to sleep lightly, and not to move in their sleep. If they do, they should perform a penance. Whenever they sit down, they should lightly sweep the floor to remove any creatures that are there. They should always move slowly, and never wave their arms about, for the air is full of creatures who are killed whenever one moves, and one should try to minimize this. For the same reason they should talk as little as possible, and always in a soft voice.

Samyak darshan is, among other things, seeing human life in the same light as the teeming of life in fresh water. So part of the virtue in boiling water is just that it involves acknowledging this vision and applying it in an everyday practice. It is part of coming to see the life you lead, in all its mundane detail, in this essentially religious way. But this does not yet tell us why it is more non-violent to kill these creatures by boiling the water than it is to kill them by drinking it. Why does it not seem to matter that the creatures die anyway?

Few lay Jains drink boiled water regularly. To prepare it is time-consuming and inconvenient, the fuel used is costly, and almost everyone is agreed that boiled water tastes awful. As a second best, all water used in Jain households is filtered. This is done by placing a piece of muslin over the end of all the taps in the house so that any creatures over a certain size will be trapped in it and die there. No one regards this as a very adequate way of dealing with the teeming infestations the water is held to contain. Many *jiv*s will get through, and renouncers may not drink water which has only been filtered. But every single Jain household I have been in does have these filters in place. It is a token. Such second-best practices are indispensible to the anthropologist, because in a case such as this, where the point of the first-rate version is so deeply and implicitly felt that it is difficult to get people to articulate it, they give a suggestion about what the point of that better version is felt to be. And obviously the point of filtering, as a version of boiling, is that it is effective in so far as it keeps some of these millions of tiny creatures out of the water one drinks. 'Non-violence' involves, as a very considerable element, the avoidance of life. The creatures in the boiled water have died, as they would have done anyway. The point is that for the short period, before they begin to appear again, it becomes possible to drink water that is free of life.

The terrifying vision which practising *ahimsa* develops of swarming, teeming life is characterized as much by reproduction and growth as it is by death. Indeed, what this vision does is to emphasize that these are all part of the same process. The diverse practices called *ahimsa* are united not by an argument or as means to any particular desired outcome, but by an aesthetic sensibility. Each of them makes sense as a way of avoiding contact, especially bodily contact, with life-forms, and as people learn these practices, and they become second nature, the sensibility they develop is actually a horror of this omnipresent fertility and fecundity. It is an ethic of quarantine. One cannot stop the constant cycle of death and rebirth. All one can do is temporarily keep it at bay, and this is what boiling water or covering one's head with a blanket does. These practices, which are central pillars of non-violence in Jainism, function neither to minimize deaths, nor, in the normal sense, to save life.

Universal Sympathy

I do not mean to suggest that Jains do not feel affection for animals, or pity at the sight of suffering. There is absolutely no question about this. They do. More to the point, assiduous practice of *ahimsa* and careful thought about Jain teachings also develop such sentiments. But this happens in a very particular way. The peculiar tenor of the aesthetic sensibility which Jains call *ahimsa* can perhaps be illustrated by the following incident. I was waiting for a friend to return from work, sitting chatting with his wife. His mother was there, and so too was his sister-in-law who was nursing a baby. The television was playing in the corner but no one was paying any attention until a documentary programme about fish-farming began. The film showed no harm being inflicted on any of the fish, although the reason they were being farmed was I suppose easy enough to deduce. All we saw was frame after frame of lots and lots of fish: small ones, then larger ones, and finally, fully grown fish, all swimming about in very large numbers in rather small tanks. We saw them being poured from one tank to another as they got bigger, and here the screen was entirely filled with the swarming, wriggling creatures. Although we saw absolutely no violence and there was no suggestion at all that the fish were in any discomfort, this film caused a minor crisis. My friend's mother was riveted to the screen, in horrified fascination. She made us all watch, and the younger women joined her in her mounting distress. They kept up a litany of exclamations, 'Oh! Look, look. Oh! What is it. Look . . . What will happen now? Look!' As the fish got bigger and teemed more vigorously, the older woman took the baby in her lap and hugged it. At the climax of her distress, the litany became a magical incantation as she took to repeating, 'Oh Bhagwan! Oh Bhagwan!', and finally, 'Oh Ram, Ram, Ram, Ram, Ram, Ram'.[7] Now I am sure that it was not any anticipated events, such as the death or consumption of the fish, that caused this reaction. What was on the screen in front of us was, in itself, horrifying: just as the nun I mentioned above saw suffering and death when she stumbled on a cockroach, and just as Vijay-ji saw it in the rain. Amplified and vividly portrayed, it was exactly what all the filtering and boiling of water, all the powdering of ginger and the abhorrence of fermentation are designed to keep pious Jains away from. It was *samsar*.

Jaini makes the following observation on renouncers' practice of 'non-violence'.

It has sometimes been suggested that Jaina holy men are overly preoccupied with beings of a lower order, to the detriment of their concern for higher animals or with humankind. But this criticism fails to take into account the fact that a mendicant has *already*, as part of his lay vows, established a pattern of absolutely nonharmful behavior towards the more highly evolved creatures; his attention to the well-being of the ekendriya [single-sensed creatures] and element bodies by no means excludes this prior commitment, but rather carries it to its widest possible extent. Indeed, Jainas consider their practice of ahimsa unique in the universality of its application.[8]

There are several things to say about this passage. The first is incidental to the argument at present, but will be important in the next chapter, so I shall just mention it in passing, and this is that almost no Jain renouncers do actually take the lay vows before they join the order. Also, the lay vows are, as we shall see, concerned almost as insistently with insects and unseen creatures as the renouncers' vows are. But the points of interest

---

[7] This *mantra* is of course not a specifically Jain one, but here, as in many things, popular Jain religious practice includes a lot of Vaishnava Hindu themes. What probably lay behind her employing this one is the idea that the name of Lord Ram has a particularly powerful protective force.

[8] Jaini, *Jaina Path*, 242.

here are, first of all, the nature of the misperception of Jain ethics which Jaini here sets out to rebut, and secondly, an aspect of Jain ethics which his rebuttal points up. First, the misperception. From the extraordinary care which Jain renouncers put into applying *ahimsa* to insects, and the fact that Jain teachings on such issues as warfare, law, state authority, and so on are not especially remarkable, it might be supposed that Jain teachers have been more or less indifferent to the sufferings of people and higher animals. Some observers of Jainism have indeed suggested this.[9] Jaini is right to point out that this is not so, and to counter the suggestion that the attention focused on insects is somehow at the expense of humankind. There are enough famine-relief projects, hospitals, and medical dispensaries funded and run by Jains to show—even to those who do not know Jains personally—that this is mistaken. But the way Jaini goes about making his point hardly closes the gap between *ahisma* and the moral sensibility he anticipates in most of his readership, whom he surely rightly expects will find the Jain precept puzzling and unfamiliar. The picture we are presented with is one in which 'absolutely nonharmful behavior' towards human beings is a quality which a person can relatively easily develop to perfection. The problems which beset human relations—conflicting values and loyalties, greed, injustice, prejudice, misunderstanding—are not the most difficult obstacles to the realization of non-violence. The more difficult challenge, requiring all the rigours of renunciation, is to extend that behaviour, and the sentiments that motivate it, from persons to microbes.

A prominent theme in Jain teaching is that one's own soul is interchangeable with that of any other being. Thus a common way for renouncers to teach about *ahimsa* is as follows: '*ahim*' means 'I'; '*sa*' means 'he'.[10] The essence of *ahimsa* is realizing that 'I' am the same as 'he' is, that all living beings are equal. They all have a soul just like ours, and so we should not harm them. Each of the innumerable living beings in the world possesses a soul (*jiv, atma*, or *jivatma*) which, in essence, is the same as a human soul and thus ultimately capable of perfection and release. The souls of the highest god or the richest king and those of microscopic beings are interchangeable.

[9] Thus Stevenson (*Heart of Jainism*, 295) writes, 'When animals and insects are killed that a Jaina may have light to study, material for clothing, shoes to wear, bread to eat, water with which to wash, or air to breathe, it seems to him that the sin of murder has been committed (for the Jaina have not yet learnt clearly to distinguish between human and animal life).'

[10] Obviously this exegesis is not intended to be in the normal sense etymological.

It is comparatively easy to imagine this in the case of another person; more difficult with 'beings of a lower order'. To develop the *ahimsa* sensibility is to overcome this difficulty. Thus even those Jain traditions which sanction and practise charitable giving to the poor, and maintain animal refuges (and, as we shall see, not all approve unequivocally), all see these expressions of non-violence as unambiguously lower and cruder forms of the virtue. So in advancing beyond the forms of non-violence practised by the ordinary Jain, the saint does not develop a deeper sympathy, or a more complex understanding, or more vivid empathy with other beings; what he or she does, as Jaini says, is to extend the same insight to more implausible objects. Indeed, he or she feels no attachment, no special or interested sympathy for any persons or creatures at all. What non-violence means in interaction between people is something which is so straightforward, so unilateral, that it can be extended to beings with only one sense.[11]

And the vigilant observation of non-violence leads beyond good actions, such as charity, to non-action. Each and every action might harm these beings and cause one's own soul to accumulate harmful *karma*, so all worldly activity is strictly incompatible with the full realization of *ahimsa*. So the person who manages to achieve 'the universality of its application' will undertake a controlled, ritualized fast to death. This is known as *samadhi maran* (and among the Digambars, *sallekhana*). It is not just a distantly imagined ideal but is practised occasionally by both renouncers and devout members of the laity.[12] A more thoroughly anti-humanist doctrine is difficult to imagine.

[11] Jain vegetarianism thus has a very different basis from the arguments for 'animal rights' which enjoy some popularity in the Anglo-Saxon world at present. Proponents of these views argue that it is a prejudice, 'speciesism', which prevents us from treating (at least some) animals on an equal moral footing with ourselves. (At least some) animals, the argument goes, have rights to life, liberty, and the pursuit of happiness, just as persons do. There is a set of objections to this (Williams, *Ethics and Philosophy*, 118–19) which takes the form of pointing out that our relations to animals are irreducibly unlike our relations to each other, for animals cannot share our understanding of ourselves in such a way as to make them participants as well as objects of our deliberations. So the only question to ask is how we should treat them. So 'speciesism' is not a prejudice but an accurate portrayal of what our moral relation to animals must necessarily be. While animal rights campaigners want us to treat (at least some) animals as if they were human moral agents, Jain non-violence seems to avoid these objections by implying that the relevant moral responsibilities to other humans are, ideally, straightforward enough to be extended without remainder to all other life-forms. But the move is hardly likely to be congenial to most Western 'animal rights' activists.

[12] Jains have been much concerned that Western observers should not confuse this practice with suicide. It should be undertaken only with the permission of one's religious preceptor, it is slow and controlled, and very definitely not a gesture of despair.

Representations of the Jina's preaching (*samosaran*) always include the image of a range of animals, including predators and prey, sitting peacefully together, and one of the standard themes in hagiographies of Jain saints is that a similar thing occurred at their sermons. It would be possible to take the image of the 'lion and the lamb' (and these are quite often the animals used) as a redemptive vision of how Jain teaching transforms the world it enters. In a sense it is, but only in a very limited sense. As I mentioned in Chapter 2, Jainism has hardly any place at all for a vision of the world made good. Yes, the influence of Jain teaching, and especially the presence of great Jain saints, makes people and animals behave well, but this is not so that a permanent just order may be established. It is so that each of those people and creatures may experience a change of vision, and embark on their own journey to escape the world. There was a time, in a distant golden age, when the world was naturally peaceful and harmonious. But just for this reason, this was a time when religious action and progress towards enlightenment were impossible. In these days, the days of religion, to pursue non-violence is to work against the way the world is, and against the way the world we actually live in ever could be.

There are, of course, dozens of stories, especially about the Tirthankars, of spirits, people, or animals being persuaded or inspired to renounce violence by the teaching or the stoic example of devout Jains. In one of his previous lives, Lord Mahavir is a lion. He is just about to pounce upon and devour a deer, when some Jain monks come by. Suddenly the lion's mind is filled with knowledge of his former lives (*jati smaran gyan*). He remembers not only the beginningless series of births and deaths he has been through and all the suffering that life in the world really entails, but also that having heard of the Jain religion, he already knows the way to escape this. This is a turning-point for Mahavir, his first experience of *samyak darshan* (the right view), and he now embarks on the path which although it lasts for several more lives, takes him directly to final liberation. As a carnivore there is only one way to begin on this path, so he immediately undertakes a fast to death. This story is echoed by one which takes place in his final life, after he has renounced the world and is wandering from place to place, practising penance and meditation (see also p. 253). He is bitten by a snake, but instead of turning on the creature he speaks to it gently, appealing to it to give up violence. Amazed at this man's reaction, and soothed and won over by his words, the snake repents, returns to its cave, and starves to death. Now, it seems very odd indeed that this is an image of blessing: of the beneficent presence of a saint leading another onto the road to righteousness. But that is what it is.

The reformist and self-consciously modernizing Shvetambar order, the Terapanth, construes *ahimsa* in its own distinctive way. Terapanthi teachers have argued that the Jain principle of *ahimsa* is a principle of non-action: all active intervention in the world is motivated by attachment and desire and is the cause of sin. These pronouncements have been extremely controversial. It is a common practice, especially among the Sthanakvasis, for wealthy lay people to pay butchers not to slaughter animals on Jain holy days, and wherever the Jains have acquired sufficient political power, they have pushed for state bans on animal slaughter on as many days as they can. These practices (often called 'mercy'—*daya*) are, Terapanth leaders have argued, very risky; and if presented as specifically Jain religious acts, they are so misleading as to be positively harmful. Allegedly, the founder of the Terapanth, Acarya Bhikshu, used this example to explain the case.[13] 'Suppose a cat is chasing a rat. Is it *ahimsa* to save the rat? No, it is not *ahimsa* to hurt one and protect the other. If the cat is starved and the rat is saved, this only shifts the misfortune.' The Terapanthis have argued that if you do intervene in this way, you can bring terrible consequences on yourself. Now you will be responsible for all the sins the rat goes on to commit, for had you left well alone, none of them would have occurred. This has often been understood in other Jain traditions simply as an argument against mercy and non-violence. When I met the present leader of the Terapanth, Acarya Tulsi, and put to him the views of my Mandir Margi friends, he countered thus.

Mercy can only be done when the opponent's heart is changed. When we save someone by force, or by some wrong means, or by tempting, then we do not consider it spiritual (*adhyatmik*) mercy. It can be from a worldly point of view (*laukik drishtikon*), but not from the spiritual. Suppose we save a rat by beating the cat who is chasing him, that is not pure *daya*. Suppose some person is killing some creature and we give him money, that is not pure *daya*. Until the heart of the killer is changed, it cannot be considered pure *daya*. Changing a violent man to a non-violent man—that is *daya*.

Opponents object that this doctrine means in practice that the only way to prevent suffering is to convert oppressors to Jainism, which, whatever else it is, is unlikely to work in time. So one ends up standing back and watching things happen. The only kind of intervention allowed is sermonizing. But the Terapanthis can point out that all Jain traditions

---

[13] It may be that this example originated as a Sthanakvasi caricature of the Terapanthi position, but it has been so successful that religious teachers on all sides now use it, and give to it their different interpretations and commentaries.

accept this as the only possible course of action for renouncers. If other traditions allow householders to take apparently more direct and effective action, they are merely bowing to confused thinking and sentimentality. To let householders believe that such action is religious, when it is in fact submitting to passion, and so binds one's soul with more *karma*, is cruelly misleading. The Terapanth has not said that charity or other conventional forms of *daya* are wrong, just that they are not real Jainism, although this has meant in practice that its followers have largely given up these things. Instead, they make donations directly to the national sect organization.

So to return, finally, to that boiled water: I hope we can now see that the popular Jain confidence that this is obviously the way to pursue non-violence is not so puzzling as it at first sight seemed. First of all, it renders the water temporarily inert by arresting for a while the processes of birth and death within it. As with drying turmeric and ginger, this makes it fit to be consumed. Secondly, it does so at a distance. Although the creatures die and although you are still the agent of their death, just as with filtering this does enable you to avoid bodily contact with the creatures, to keep that teeming world of birth and death at bay. So the question of whether or not these tiny creatures die is beside the point. They will die anyway. The thinking behind the practice is not consequentialist, in the sense that the object is not to reduce the number of deaths that occur. Against the background of the Jain view of how suffering and death permeate the whole of existence, and are governed by the great cosmic causality of *karma*, this would indeed be a trivial and insignificant gesture. But if Jain ethics on this point is non-consequentialist, it is so in a singular way. The reason why most readers of this book are not consequentialists is that for each of them there are some people whose happiness and suffering are peculiarly their concern, some states of affairs which are peculiarly their responsibility.[14] They cannot weigh the desirability of all states of affairs in the world equally, because some have a morally more significant re-lation to their life and their identity than do others. This is not what makes a difference in the Jain case. Indeed, the Jain position relies on an argu-ment for seeing all living things as morally equivalent, which goes well beyond what any Western ethical scheme has proposed. The difference between the deaths of water-beings by boiling and by being drunk inheres in the kind of action by which they are killed. Boiling water and then drinking it differs from drinking unboiled water in that in the latter case the killing is an action you do with your body, and in Jain religious

[14] Williams, 'Persons, Character and Morality'.

practice, as will become clear as this part of the book proceeds, bodily action occupies a special place. The essential background to understanding its special place is to see that *ahimsa*, which is arguably the centrepiece of Jain ethics, is a response to a religiously informed perception of the world as already inhabited. In so far as it cultivates that perception of the world, Jain religious practice involves avoiding living things.

'Tasteless as Mouthfuls of Sand'

Let us see how this works out in dietary practice, which is actually the way young Jains learn about *ahimsa*, the way they come to think about their distinctiveness as Jains, and the most routine medium through which that distinctiveness is made part of the self.

As I mentioned above, lay Jains are not united by adherence to a single set of rules which distinguish them all, collectively, from those of other faiths. The rules which do have a measure of social compulsion behind them—basic vegetarianism—are common to many other groups in the region. And the prohibition which most signally distinguishes Jains from vegetarian Hindu Baniyas—that on eating all root vegetables—is not particularly widely or consistently observed. As in many other domains, what is distinctively Jain is not a set of practices which they all share, but techniques by which they may distinguish themselves, and therefore an idiom in which they are ranked and divided.

Now I should say, before going any further, that Jains, like anybody else, have whole sets of views about what foods are good for you, and like most people who live in places where starvation due to poverty is visible on the streets, many among them subscribe implicitly to the idea that to be plump is a sign of good health, good spirits, happiness, and wealth. Outside a few fashionable circles, you can still judge the affluence of people on the streets of an Indian city reasonably accurately if you assume a rough correlation with physical bulk. The Jains, as we have seen, are a notably affluent community and no exception to this rule. But against this background, substantial as it is, Jain religious discourse about food is pretty well all about limiting, omitting, and abstaining.

Some of these restrictions are universal, and their meaning and application straightforward. Meat, fish, eggs, alcohol, and honey are all reviled, and anyone brought up as a pious Jain comes to regard consuming any of them as categorically and self-evidently wicked. So intense is the revulsion at the idea of eating meat that it is commonly referred to simply as *abhaksh*, 'not to be eaten'. Of course, it is well known that outside the Jain community and among 'other castes' people do eat meat. But although, in what is generally a tolerant religious community which is well-travelled and well-informed about other cultures, I have spoken with very many Jains about this, none of them has ever seen these facts as pointing to a real disagreement. It is simply never countenanced that there might be good and pious people who doubt that eating meat is wrong, or who assert in good faith that it is right. If people in other religions and other communities eat meat, this must be because they are cruel, stupid, or, most likely, just weak and self-indulgent. Time and again I have been assured that Jesus and Muhammad prohibited meat and alcohol. And I do not think I have heard a Jain deny, as many Western vegetarians do, that a diet including meat is more enjoyable than one without. Indeed, almost everyone seemed confident that all the foods prohibited by their religion are tremendously tempting. Thus although meat is referred to as *abhaksh*, there is a clear recognition that others do eat forbidden foods, and therefore that they are definitely food. Indeed, in this respect basic Jain distinctiveness is constructed as a collective resistance to temptation.

But as renouncers constantly reiterate, living without meat, alcohol, and honey is only the essential minimum of decent human conduct. As one renouncer said, 'Meat-eaters have the shape of humans, but they are not really human.' Conforming to a set of minimum requirements scarcely constitutes religious practice, which requires that you advance beyond this. The impact of this message is plain to see in lay Jain communities. Even an average Jain family will either always go without, or will on certain chosen days forego the use of onions, garlic, butter,[15] aubergines or other squashes, potatoes or other root vegetables, or modern manufactured foods.

In avoiding these foods, lay families are selectively adopting restrictions which are all compulsory for renouncers. Although the precise content of the rules varies between sects and lineages, there is in each case a set of very well-known rules to which any renouncer is expected by her followers and required by her guru to adhere. Because they receive all their food directly from the hands of their lay followers, it would be difficult for renouncers discreetly to bend these rules, and all lay people have to learn

---

[15] Butter, along with meat, alcohol, and honey, is listed in many Jain texts as one of the foods most to be avoided, the *maha-vighai*. But in my experience butter is not regarded with the same horror as the others, and the prohibition against it is not absolute. Even very pious lay people will eat fresh butter which has been made at home, but they think that life-forms grow in it very quickly, so they will not keep it for long and they will not buy commercially produced butter.

them if they want to offer acceptable food. In the Khartar Gacch, no renouncers eat green or leafy vegetables during the four months of the rainy season, nor do they ever take food or water at night. During the rains, it is said, there are so many insects around that any green vegetables you ate would be bound to contain some. At night, if you eat in the dark you will be unable to check that insects have not fallen in your food, and if you use artificial light, that will only attract them. Only very strict laypeople give up green vegetables for the whole of the rains, or abstain consistently from eating after dark. But most families do follow these rules from time to time. There are two days in each lunar fortnight, the eighth (*athai*) and the fourteenth (*caudas*), which are regarded as particularly auspicious for religious activities, so people follow these kinds of rules more then than at other times. And there are various religious festivals (*parv*) during the year, which also call for a fast, a restricted diet, or some other gesture towards greater austerity. And however poor by these standards their everyday practice may be, for eight days during the rainy season, in a festival called Paryushan, and especially on the last day, Samvatsari, all Jain families adopt some extra dietary restriction.

The women in many families do not eat at night, even if their husbands do, and in general women are much more strict about dietary practice than men are. Each family, and to some considerable extent each individual, sets rules for themselves and then varies them according to circumstance throughout the year. The range of practice which results is, one must emphasize, considerable. But they all do this within a framework set by renouncers' practice, and the discourse about food within which they make their choices is shot through with ascetic values. But this does not mean that matters are in the least straightforward, and apart from vegetarianism, which is more or less axiomatic, almost nothing is certain enough to be left unsaid. Indeed, questions of what may be eaten, when, and how are pervasive themes in religious discourse. Deciding which dietary rules to follow is the most salient way in which lay families decide how strict they will be, and observing which rules others follow is a convenient way of assessing other families. 'She has given up salt', or, 'He even eats potatoes', are short-hand summaries of where people stand on a well-understood and subtly calibrated scale.

Renouncers' sermons are full of warnings about the millions of lives which are destroyed if one eats potatoes, marrows, aubergines, ice, leavened bread, or packaged food; full of calls to give up pickles and spices, which are not necessary to sustain the body and only exist to please the senses; and of suggestions to limit the intake of sugar, salt, oil, ghee, curd, and even milk. This last list, which is called the six *vighai*, is especially revealing.[16] Milk, curd, and ghee are staple elements of most Jains' diet. They are regarded as healthy, and relatively free of life-forms so that the sin involved in consuming them is not great. In fact, it is something of a status symbol to insist that all one's food is cooked in ghee, or to claim that one falls ill if another cooking medium is used. Yet most groups of renouncers make a point of arranging each day for one of their number to consume no *vighai*. Pious lay Jains take vows to renounce, say, salt on Mondays, ghee on the eighth day of each fortnight, or anything cooked in oil during religious festivals. Some fasts, held at particular times of year, require total abstinence from all the *vighai*. Religious books and pamphlets often contain lists of prohibited foods and the *vighai* always appear on these. But like many rules in Jainism, the injunction not to eat these foods is not really a rule at all. Unlike the prohibition on meat, the idea that a Jain should not take milk, for instance, is more of a signpost towards higher virtues than a fence around unspeakable vice, and these virtues, it is accepted, are practically unattainable. Thus even essential, staple, and admittedly barely violent foods are prohibited. The prohibition is at once notional (no one enforces it or blames you for not observing it consistently, and hardly anyone even strives to do so) yet at the same time its recognition, and intermittent experience of what it would be to fulfil it, are inserted routinely into everyday life.

The rules which prohibit potatoes and eating after sunset are followed more by lay women than by men, and more by the old than by the young. A young man draws no serious censure if he includes potatoes in his diet, but in later life this would be more likely to attract disapproving comment, especially if he were to take on a generally religious persona. On the other hand chilli, which everyone agrees should be avoided, is a regular and prominent part of almost everyone's diet, and while both tea and paan should in theory be avoided too, pretty well everyone is addicted to the first, and many men are to the second. But nevertheless, to be religious necessarily involves the sense that one ought to strive towards the most exacting ideals. Most lay families restrict their diet more than normal during religious festivals, and some do so on certain days each month. Many young Jain men (the standard for a woman is more strict) will eat onions outside the home, but not on fast days or religious festivals, and think it impious to attend a temple or come into the presence of a

---

[16] Banks (*Organizing Jainism*, 92) and Mahias (*Délivrance*, 249) give slightly different (and differing) lists.

renouncer having done so. Whatever level an individual sets his or her normal dietary practice at, all religious events during the year (with the exception of Diwali, to be discussed in Chapter 17) call for, and are met with, some small act of further renunciation. Thus the sense of pervasive asceticism which lay Jainism exudes comes not from uniform adherence to a set of socially enforced rules, still less from any sense that its followers live lives of consistent or imposed privation, but rather from the fact that because everyone must make a whole series of decisions for themselves, and adjust their diet continuously for a range of religious reasons, it is always a subject of conscious reflection and practical reasoning.

If you ask a Jain to explain why a particular food is to be avoided, he or she is likely to say that it is a matter of *ahimsa*. The same person might also point to the effect the food will have on you: heating the blood, inflaming the passions, inducing slothfulness, or causing illness. Generally, discourse about food mingles these two concerns closely. Beliefs about the effects of different foods on body temperature and humours, although they vary quite a lot in detail, use similar idioms and exemplify similar concerns throughout the subcontinent.[17] But the religious connotations of food are one of the most striking differences between the Jains and their caste-fellow Hindus. Both Jains and Vallabhacharya (or Pushti Marg) Hindus make offerings of sweets in temples, the former before idols of the Jinas, the latter before Lord Krishna. But while Vallabhas speak of their pleasure in nurturing the deity, of the devotion expressed in giving him delicious food to eat, and receive these sweets back as Krishna's grace (*pushti*), Jains are very clear that the Jina does not actually receive the offerings they make, and they generally say that when they place sweets before the Jinas they express their desire or intention to give up all pleasure in eating, or all delicious food, or all food, or all pleasure of any kind. For this reason, they say, they never receive back any of the food renounced. While the Jains are enjoined to give up anything which awakens the senses or excites the passions, Pushti Marg worship proceeds, as Bennett says, 'by utilizing all the things in this world considered precious or pleasing to the senses in the service of the deity'.[18]

---

[17] I have in mind contextually variable classifications of foods as more or less 'hot' and 'cold' (which is to do with the effect the food has on the person, rather than its temperature: ice-cream, notoriously, is a 'hot' food), and as being *sattvik*, *rajsik*, and *tamsik*: broadly, foods which have respectively a calming and elevating, an exciting and aphrodisiac, and an enervating and corrupting effect. See Beck, 'Colour and Heat'; Daniel, *Fluid Signs*, ch. 5.

[18] Bennett, 'In Nanda Baba's House', 182. See also Pocock, *Mind, Body and Wealth*, and Williams, *New Face of Hinduism*, ch. 4 on the related Satsang tradition.

We can see Jainism's own view of how tough it is in the *Antakriddashah Sutra*, eighth *Anga* of the Shvetambar canon. It is the time of the twenty-second Tirthankar, Neminath, and prince Goyama, having heard the saviour preach, has decided to enter the Jain order immediately. His parents try first to dissuade him, and then to persuade him at least to delay. It is not that they consider Jainism unworthy, indeed it is precisely its virtues against which they warn the young man.

The Niggantha (Jain) doctrine is true, sublime, absolute, perfect, rational, pure; it cuts out arrows; it is a path of success, a path of salvation, a path of issue, a path of extinction, a path void of all grief. It is single in its view, as a snake; single of edge, like a razor; as barley-corns of iron to chew; tasteless as mouthfuls of sand.

They explain further, by outlining the rules which govern the renouncer's alms-round.

To Niggantha friars, child, it is not allowed to eat or drink fare prepared after their coming, nor specially prepared fare, nor purchased fare, nor fare specially set aside, nor specially cooked, nor famine-food [food prepared during conditions of famine], nor rain-food [prepared during heavy rain], nor forest-food, nor food of sickness, nor fare of roots, of bulbs, of fruits, of seeds, or of green vegetables.[19]

Goyama renounces, joins the order, and practises the asceticism of which he has been warned.

So by this noble, abundant, zealous, earnest, happy, blissful, lucky, auspicious, splendid, lofty, magnificent, excelling, exalted, stately mortification Friar Goyama became withered, wizened, fleshless; he became a mere frame of bone and skin; he grew so that his bones rattled, emaciated, overspread with veins. . . . and like a fire confined within a heap of ashes he shone mightily with glow, with lustre, and with splendour of glowing lustre.

In time he declares, 'I will wait without eagerness for death by wasting away in starvation.'[20]

The understanding which informs Jain *ahimsa* means that even the most everyday rules about food point, however hesitantly, in this direction. It is not in the least that all lay Jains are expected to perform this kind of fast. On the contrary, for all but the most religious it would be considered a vanity and a sin. But every single day lay Jains adjust their conduct in ways which respond to the same religious vision as that which led Goyama to his decision.

Lay Jains accept rules of basic human decency, but the ethics of their religious life look out towards ideals of severe renunciation which are very

---

[19] Barnett, *Antagada-dasao*, 42–3.   [20] Ibid. 57–8.

far indeed from that starting-point. It is oriented by a vivid, if also uniquely bleak, vision of life, and an aesthetic of discipline, withdrawal, and avoidance, informed by that vision. The attitude to the regulation of food, in which there are not so much religious rules but open-ended injunctions which it would be almost impossible ever to fulfil, illustrates this well, and indeed it is itself a central plank of Jain religious asceticism. The ideal is, essentially and necessarily, impossible.

8

Schemes, Regimes, and Religious Retirement

JAIN tradition provides a set of five vows which a lay person may adopt. These are the five *anuvrat*s, or 'lesser restraints'. They are homonomous with, but in application quite distinct from, the five *mahavrat*s, or 'great restraints', which all Jain renouncers take as the final and in theory irreversible stage of their initiation. Both sets of vows, then, are:

1. non-violence (*ahimsa*)
2. not stealing (*asteya* or *acorya*)
3. not telling lies (*amrisa*, *ajhuth*, or *satya*)
4. sexual continence (*brahmacarya* or *amaithun*)
5. non-attachment (*aparigraha*).

It looks at first sight as if this formula neatly links lay ethics to renunciation and gives a straightforward answer to the question of how the impossibility of Jain ascetic ideals is accommodated in practice. Lay Jains are enjoined to observe lesser versions of renouncers' vows. So lay religiosity is plainly specified as a paler version of what renouncers do. In his book, *The Jaina Path of Purification*, Jaini interprets these lay vows, and indeed lay religiosity in general, in just this way. For those who cannot proceed straight to renunciation, there is a 'lower path' parallel to that which the renouncer walks. Thus, 'the vows of the layman are really just a modified, relatively weak version of the *real* Jaina vows'.[1] Jaini also draws another scheme from Jain texts, a ladder of fourteen levels of spiritual advance, or *gunasthana*s. He interprets the lower levels as corresponding to the lay path, so that the lay vows are also lower rungs of the same ladder as that which the renouncer climbs. By adopting the lay vows, and following them ever more rigorously, a layman eventually reaches a stage where, 'he is ready for the exalted practices of the mendicant path, a path which may at last carry his soul to the brink of liberation'.[2] This enables Jaini to integrate Jain doctrine into a single, coherent scheme around the metaphor of the 'path of purification', even if in joining his two principal

---

[1] Jaini, *Jaina Path*, 160, emphasis in the original.   [2] Ibid. 185.

metaphors he creates a somewhat dizzying geometry. But the overall impression this gives of lay Jainism is misleading, at least for the Shvetambars. Even a student of Indic religion as experienced and sophisticated as S. J. Tambiah has inferred from it that, 'especially among the Svetambar community, monkhood is often seen as a culmination of the householder's life'.[3] This is not the case.

The *anuvrat*s neither provide a summary of lay religion in Jainism, nor are they in practice a preparation for renunciation. The number of people who take the lay vows is vanishingly small, and for none of those who do is it a preparation for life as a renouncer. It is instead a form of retirement in lay life, a rather specific sort of resting-place. It is, moreover, a privileged one. Rather more women than men take these vows, and the privileges which doing so brings differ somewhat in the two cases. But regardless of sex, it remains true that the small number of people who take these vows includes, typically, some of the most wealthy in a local community; and far from it being in any way a severance of social ties, for almost all of them it signals the adoption of a rather active role in the social life of the community.

Training for Retirement

As a set of ethical precepts, the five *anuvrat*s are obviously so general that pretty well anyone could subscribe to them, but just for this reason they are not much of a basis, on their own, for a code of religious ethics. You could no more deduce the distinctive character of Jainism as a practical religion, or anticipate its variations, from these five precepts, than you could see the ethics of the Society of Jesus and the Salvation Army written on Moses' tablets. For renouncers, embracing the five *mahavrat*s involves much more than they explicitly state. Indeed, it involves no less than the complete extinction of their former lay identity, their caste, their family, their profession, and (except for some male Sthanakvasis) their name; and their incorporation into the total institution of a Jain monastic order.

For lay people, too, the five vows in themselves are incomplete. A further seven, which do not mirror any adopted by renouncers, are added; and it is these which impose specific obligations. The way for lay people to adopt the full set of twelve restraints—the *baravrat*s—is to take vows

---

[3] Tambiah, 'Renouncer', 307. Digambar renouncers do seem more commonly to be initiated at a relatively advanced age. See Carrithers, 'Naked Ascetics'; see also Cort, 'Shvetambar Mendicant', 653.

before a leading renouncer, in a big public ceremony which is held (in the temple-going traditions) in the presence of an idol of one of the Tirthankars. Those who do this are accorded the title *shravak* or *grihasth sadhak* (although these titles are not much used in practice). There is no absolute requirement that one should adopt all twelve restraints, but most of the very few people who take any, take them all.

Renouncers who administer the vows give a small pamphlet to each potential *shravak*. In these pamphlets each of the twelve restraints is interpreted by means of a series of specific vows (*pratigyas* or *saugandhs*), each of which is for life. There is a certain amount of choice. Throughout the text, there are lists of several possible versions of the vows, each more exacting than the last; and at several places, where the number of times a given duty should be performed or the limit on certain activities is set, the text leaves a blank space for different values to be inserted. Before the ceremony the prospective *shravak* or *shravika* discusses with his or her garu which vows, limits, and values to set. There are several sections of exceptions (*agar*), for circumstances in which a general injunction need not apply. As we shall see, even in these texts, and broken down into specific vows, the five *anuvrat*s remain fairly general. It is the seven supplementary vows which give them a specific and distinctively Jain content, and which effectively shape everyday conduct. So the apparent symmetry of the five vows taken by renouncers and lay people soon breaks down on closer inspection.

The twelve restraints could in theory be construed so leniently that every lay Jain could formally adopt them. In this way they could indeed serve as the lower rungs of a ladder leading through formal renunciation and on towards enlightenment. This is not what happens. Instead, a few lay people attend a strict religious camp after which, if they acquit themselves reasonably well, they are allowed to take the *baravrat*s. The vows thus function as a privilege signalling already achieved religious status, and neither the ascetic nature of the test nor the ascetic content of the vows themselves prevents this from being at the same time an elevated social status. There are a few people, basically poor widows, for whom the restraints give virtuous form and meaning to privations they bear out of necessity. But for most of those who adopt the twelve restraints it is a privilege, an expression of financial and familial security, of success achieved and secured. The test they must go through before earning this religious imprimatur to social success is a residential camp organized from time to time by senior renouncers, called *updhan*.

At an *updhan* lay Jains live under a strict religious discipline, with the sexes rigorously segregated.[4] With the important and, as we shall see in Chapter 14, emblematic exception of the way they acquire their food, those who take part in *updhan* must conduct themselves in ways normally prescribed for renouncers. The normal practice is to attend three such camps for periods of fifty-one, thirty-five, and twenty-eight days respectively. During the camps, lay people must remain silent unless addressed by the presiding renouncer. They get up early, live in spartan surroundings without any modern conveniences, and eat only one light meal each alternate day. They perform long ascetic rituals and regular temple worship, and attend religious lectures and classes. The rites they have to perform, involving meditational concentration, recitation of prayers, and confession, are modelled on those which make up the routine monastic discipline of renouncers. Any infractions of the many and pedantic regulations require still more such rites and periods of fasting, to be performed in the months which follow the camp. The renouncer who imposes them will call these requirements penances (*prayshcitt*), but the candidates, understandably, tend much more readily to speak of punishments (*dand*).

Buddhism makes much more extensive use than does Jainism of devices which blur or allow temporary crossings of the distinction between householder and renouncer. In some parts of the Buddhist world, it is common practice for young boys in rural areas to take temporary initiation into the Buddhist order, often for as little as a single rains retreat, so that a period spent as a monk functions as an extended life-cycle ritual. As Tambiah shows, this practice effects an integration of monastic life into the householder's life-cycle parallel to that achieved in the Brahmanical *ashram* scheme.[5] It also restructures the polarity of householder and renouncer

---

[4] An *updhan* is always sponsored by a wealthy lay person, who usually takes part, He or she thus practises renunciation and also encourages and enables others to do so. An example is an *updhan* held in Malpura, near Jaipur, in 1990. This was sponsored by a wealthy Jain man from Tonk, who took part. He paid for all the expenses, food, special clothes, and so on, so that those who wished to take part could do so without paying anything. One woman I knew in Jaipur, who took part, would probably not have been able to do so if she had had to pay herself. 102 people from all over Rajasthan took part, of whom 85 were women (rather more had planned to attend, but rioting in Jaipur dissuaded many from going). An event such as this is a major occasion for rich lay Jains to make donations for the glorification of the religion (*prabhavana*). So about fifty lay Jains (most of whom were not participants) made gifts of cooking utensils, commemorative coins, photographs, and so on, to the participants. At the end of this event, 51 people took at least some of the *baravrats*.

[5] See Tambiah, *Buddhism and the Spirit Cults*, 268; see also Keyes, 'Ambiguous Gender'.

into a system of inter-generational reciprocity: all men, at different stages in their lives, both pay for and benefit from the maintenance of monasteries and the education they provide. In urban contexts this has meant that renunciation can operate as an avenue to social mobility, with monks receiving education from the *sangha* and returning to lay life with better economic prospects than when they left it.[6]

Temporary initiation for youths, of the kind which has been widespread in Buddhism, seems never to have been popular among Jains, who have tended to regard membership of the order as absolutely and unconditionally for life. The institution of the *updhan*, which is certainly a recent revival if not a recent invention in Jainism, is built on a different model (one which Buddhism also has available in the form of temporary adoption of the eight precepts). In the *samayik* rite, as we shall see (Chapter 9), a lay Jain is said to become like a renouncer for something less than an hour, and in an ancient practice called *paushadh*, he or she spends the whole day in an *upashraya*, devoting the time exclusively to religious activities. The *updhan* is like *paushadh*, extended over a longer period. There is no suggestion that the participants really become renouncers. Rather they experience what real Jainism is like as a preparatory training to taking up the lay status of *shravaks*.

In parts of the Buddhist world, in recent decades, the practice of temporary initiation for the young has been superseded by the propagation among the laity of meditation, hitherto reserved only for monks. Gombrich and Obeyesekere describe this as, 'the greatest single change to have come over Buddhism in Sri Lanka (and indeed in the other Theravadin countries) since the Second World War'.[7] Urban lay Buddhists no longer take as their model the disciplined orthodox monk, working patiently for enlightenment in some distant future rebirth, but instead the charismatic hermits of the recently revitalized tradition of forest monks, whose advanced meditation is thought to bring them miraculous powers and even liberation in the here and now.[8] Tambiah describes how urban monasteries in Thailand which are affiliated to the forest hermitages have begun to hold residential courses for lay people who become 'temporary monks' to learn the meditation techniques developed by forest saints. But he adds that the trend is in general away from

For similar temporary initiation in Nepali Mahayana Buddhism, see Gellner 'Monastic Initiation'.

[6] Bunnag, *Buddhist Monk*, 42–50.
[7] Gombrich and Obeyesekere, *Buddhism Transformed*, 237.
[8] Carrithers, *Forest Monks*; Tambiah, *Saints of the Forest*.

such schemes based on the traditional model of the monk, towards day classes which local lay residents can attend as part of their routine devotions. In Sri Lanka, numerous meditation centres are part of a growing movement of lay meditation which is bypassing the traditional *sangha* altogether and promoting the attainment of higher states of consciousness which draw more directly on Hindu devotional idioms than on anything in the tradition of Buddhist meditation.[9]

In the Jain *updhan*, by contrast, the emphasis is overwhelmingly on monastic discipline, and on the authority of renouncers. Lay participants learn long and complex rites of confession; they learn the rationale behind Jain food restrictions and how to practise *ahimsa* ever more strictly; they learn the correct way to perform full worship of Jina idols and veneration of living renouncers. In the meditation centre in the Buddhist monastery at Chiengmai, which Tambiah describes, pupils report daily to the abbot on their progress, but for the most part they practise meditation alone in their own rooms. As the course progresses they actually abandon the normal monk's routines, such as going on alms-rounds or conducting rituals.[10] The emphasis in the Jain practice goes the opposite way: participants are expected to progress in their participation in collective rituals which are performed under close surveillance and instruction. The abbot of the Thai monastery explained to Tambiah that he forbids his pupils to read books during the course, because someone who is dedicated to practising meditation in solitude does not need the theoretical knowledge of books. In the Jain *updhan* participants are expected to memorize lists of terms from Jain philosophy and texts to recite in rituals, and they sit a written exam on all this at the end of the camp.

Updhan is thus not integrated into lay life, as meditation practice now increasingly is in the Buddhist world. It is a rite of passage. It is undergone almost exclusively by middle-aged or elderly lay Jains, and so occupies a quite different place in the life-cycle from Buddhist temporary initiation. Far from being the first stage of a separate religious career, or an educational opportunity in youth, it marks entry into an optional final stage of lay life.

The Twelve Restraints

An important part of the *updhan* is for the guru and lay disciple to agree on the specific limits and requirements to be set for the vows they will

---

[9] Gombrich, 'Monastery to Meditation Centre'; Gombrich and Obeyesekere, *Buddhism Transformed*, especially chs. 8, 10, and 13.

[10] Tambiah, *Saints of the Forest*, 173–4.

take. Obviously each individual is expected to reach for the most
ambitious targets they think they can manage; but on the other hand, as
the renouncers are very careful to warn, these vows are irreversible.
Circumstances change, you become older and weaker, so you must be
careful that you will be able to maintain whatever standard you set. The
pamphlets used are produced by local temple committees and vary in
details, but only slightly. I shall describe that used in Jaipur by the
Khartar Gacch.

1. *Ahimsa.* They vow not to harm any helpless creature. There are
exceptions in respect of doing work, putting medicine on wounds, and
cleaning the house. It is further required that only strained water will be
used in the house.

2. *Asteya.* There are four vows under the restraint on theft. It is taken
for granted that they will not actually steal anything, so the first vow is not
to borrow anything without the permission of the owner, if stealing it
would be a crime. A list of exceptions makes clear that this wording is
intended to allow a joke, such as hiding something belonging to a member
of your own family. The other three vows forbid adulteration of commodities for sale, cheating in the weighing of goods for sale, and buying or
handling stolen goods.

3. *Satya.* Vows listed under the restraint on lying, in addition to deceitful untruth and dishonest business conduct, prohibit speaking or writing to cause hurt or offence.

4. *Brahmacarya.* Under the restraint of sexual continence, a compulsory vow prescribes marital fidelity, and there are further optional vows
never to engage in sexual intercourse after a particular time in the evening,
on certain days in the month, or at any time.

5. *Aparigraha.* The non-attachment restraint requires that they set a
limit to the total capital value of their property. They vow that all they
earn in excess of that will be given for religious purposes.

Even when broken down into more specific vows, the *anuvrat*s remain
rather bloodless. There are only two important choices to make: the limit
set on property and the level of sexual restraint. About the former, even
renouncers are quite frank that people should not set this too low; they
must not put their children's inheritance at risk. So generally people set
the limit way beyond their most optimistic expectations, and in practice
the *aparigraha vrat* is taken as an injunction to make generous religious
gifts, rather than to dispose of property, or to stop earning it.
Unsurprisingly, this vow is often a target for those who see formal vows
and statuses, such as the *baravrat*s, as a veil for religious hypocrisy. The

limits set on sexual conduct must be agreed between spouses. In practice, this means that before a renouncer administers the vow to a woman, she will obtain the husband's permission. This is potentially the most constraining commitment in the *anuvrat*s, because the most precise. In an absolutely characteristic inversion of Hindu mores, Jains are enjoined especially to avoid sexual intercourse on the most auspicious days of the month—the eighth and fourteenth days of each lunar fortnight. Hindus are advised, *per contra*, that because these days are auspicious, conception is likely to produce a son, so that it becomes almost a religious duty for a married couple to have intercourse on those days.[11]

The remaining seven *vrat*s include rules and restrictions which are much more specific than those in the five *anuvrat*s.

6. *disha pariman*. People set a limit to how far they may travel from their home.

7. *bhogopabhog pariman*. This fixes limits to the number of ornaments, soaps, perfumes, and foods they can use. People vow to give up some luxuries, to limit how often they use others, and thus fix limits to how they may enjoy their wealth without having actually to reduce it.

8. *anarth dand tyag*. This prohibits 'unnecessary or excessive violence', so gives some more precise rules for *ahimsa*. It prohibits either participating in, or encouraging anyone else in, occupations involving violence, and specifically mentions farming because of the earth-bodies which are destroyed by digging and ploughing. It instructs that pots of liquid should never be left uncovered and calls for restraint or total abstention from card games, theatre, cinema, and gambling.

9. *samayik*. This is an ascetic exercise involving prayer and concentration. People vow to perform it daily. Included here too is a vow to perform a rite of confession (*pratikraman*) a certain number of times a year. (On both *samayik* and *pratikraman*, see Chapter 8.)

10. *deshavkashik vrat*. At first sight this looks straightforward: one vows to set a limit on the area one moves around in. But in fact this vow is complex and far reaching. We shall return to it in a moment.

11. *paushadh*. The vow is to perform this exercise, which has been mentioned briefly above, at least once a year.

12. *atithi samvibhag*. People vow to be hospitable to unexpected guests. This includes (and indeed principally concerns) presenting alms to Jain renouncers, so there are vows to ensure that the food they prepare at home is suitable for renouncers. Under this heading there are also vows to say a

---

[11] Das, 'Body Symbolism'; Parry, 'End of the Body'.

short prayer before eating, and to make gifts of food to the needy, and money to charitable causes. Like those under *bhogopabhog*, these provisions give more specific content to the *aparigraha anuvrat*.

Jaini glosses the *deshavkashik vrat* as follows:

One elects to remain within an area even narrower than that called for by the digvrata. This restraint is necessarily temporary, lasting no more than a day or two. During that time the aspirant does not go beyond his 'normal surroundings,'—his dwelling place, the temple, the fasting hall, or the confines of the village. He is also encouraged (though not required) to cut down on as many worldly activities as possible, particularly those that originate beyond the spacial and temporal limits of the vrata.[12]

This anodyne formula has come to be interpreted in ways which mean that more than any other of the twelve restraints, it sets the tone for the life of a *shravak*. Whatever the thought behind its original formulation, this restraint has become the focus for that powerful coupling of austerity and *ahimsa* which gives Jain religiosity its relentless precision and force. Limiting the area of one's activities means approaching by degrees the state of non-action. It means subjecting oneself and all one's activities to examination and restraint in the light of the violence inevitably caused.

In the pamphlets, there are two sub-headings for the *deshavkashik vrat*. The first, curiously tucked away under this rather unimportant looking heading, is provision for fasting, a religious activity which plays an extremely important part in lay Jain religious life (see Chapter 10). There are six kinds of fast laid down, and each *shravak* chooses how many of each to perform during the year. The second element is a list of fourteen vows called the 'fourteen disciplines' (*caudah niyam*). This is a list of fourteen different ways in which one's action can be made less sinful by limiting its scope: by reining in and limiting its necessarily sinful impact upon the world. Here is the list. It is not a very coherent one, but perhaps its very and-another-thing tone serves to indicate its purpose well enough. The glosses given are derived from conversations I had with lay Jains who have taken the vows.

---

[12] Jaini, *Jaina Path*, 180. We should notice in passing that this, or the *disha pariman vrat*, or some combination of the two, misled Max Weber in his attempt to understand why Jainism failed to develop modern capitalism. He seems to have thought that lay Jains lived permanently under the minute authority of renouncers, who forbade travelling except with specific and limited permission. Instead, as we see, these vows are rare, voluntary, and not motivated, as Weber thought, by an extreme form of 'the familar Hindu suspicion of change of place' (*Religion of India*, 197). See also *Protestant Ethic*, 191.

1. *sacitt*—avoiding all seeds (until they are made into flour).
2. *dravya*—limiting the number of substances one eats or puts in one's mouth.
3. *vighai*—avoiding sugar, salt, oil, ghee, curd, and milk.
4. *upanah*—limiting the number of shoes and socks one puts on during the year.
5. *tambol*—avoiding all stimulants and digestives such as paan, betel nut, and cardamom.
6. *vastra*—limiting the number of clothes one wears, both at any one time and throughout the year.
7. *kusum*—avoiding the use of anything scented such as perfume or flowers.
8. *vahan*—limiting the number of vehicles one uses.
9. *shayan*—limiting the items of furniture one uses.[13]
10. *vilepan*—avoiding or limiting all creams, powders, and oils which are applied to the body.
11. *brahmacarya*—avoiding sexual relations and also joking and flirtation.
12. *disha*—limiting travel in each of the four directions and also in elevation.
13. *snan*—limiting the number of times one bathes, and the water one uses to do so.
14. *bhatt*—limiting the amount (as distinct from variety) of food one eats.

The main requirement for observing these disciplines is keeping check-lists: of the different kinds of foods one eats, the number of times one does without salt or oil, the number of clothes one wears, and so on. We will encounter the element of self-surveillance again, and we should also note, for future reference, how the provisions on this list overlap with other *baravrat*s. This apparently unsystematic aspect of the formulation is seen by those who take them as evidence for how thorough they are. They point out that some religious practices, such as sexual continence and fasting, are interpreted and recommended from more than one point of view. The manuals I consulted went to the trouble of emphasizing that eating at night, adding salt to food, and making pickle are proscribed by the fourteen disciplines as well as under the *bhogopabhog* and other *vrat*s, as is having anything to do with mining, brick-making, cutting down

---

[13] This means, for instance, setting a limit to the number of mattresses or chairs one will sit on in a day. When one reaches the limit, one must stand or sit on the bare floor.

trees, digging, selling alcohol, branding animals, burning forests, or emptying ponds.

In sum, it is clear that the *anuvrat*s, being ethical desiderata of such generality that almost anyone might profess allegiance to them, are converted in the *baravrat*s into a prescription for a form of life which is distinctively and specifically Jain. This is done through a whole armoury of ascetic practices, mostly ritualized, which include rites of confession and concentration, penances, fasting (and a near infinity of specific modulations and restrictions on diet), and a formal scheme for monitoring daily activity. It is through these techniques of self-training, which are also widely adopted by lay Jains who have not formally taken the *baravrat*s, that the asceticism of Jain renunciation enters the lives of lay Jains.

Religious Retirement

Becoming a *shravak* has come to be the capstone of a particular élite style of life: a leisured, dignified semi-retirement which combines neatly with social precedence. Without exception, the people I have met or heard of who have taken the *baravrat*s have reached the age when their children have grown up and married. The vows would intrude heavily on the normal business of earning a living or running a home. More to the point, they are considered respectable only for those who have already fulfilled their responsibilities. I have never heard of a case where they were a prelude to full renunciation. Indeed, the people I knew who had taken these vows generally seemed content with things as they were.

Mrs Golecha is a widow who lives with her two married sons and their wives and small children in a large, comfortable villa near the Moti Doongri Dadabari. She is rather an animated woman: open, enthusiastic, and friendly, with a matter-of-fact, occasionally rather curt manner, who speaks confidently and quickly. She was almost always to be seen at big religious events such as collective *puja*s and parades, was often in the *upashraya*s chatting with renouncers, and unlike younger married women, seemed free to make visits to friends and relatives at will. She regularly joined in various collective fasts, for which groups of women gather and spend the day together in an *upashraya*, and depending on the kind of fast it is (see Chapter 10), perhaps having a meal together too.[14] I had talked

---

[14] For an excellent discussion of the social club aspects of women's religious practice, see Reynell, 'Honour, Nurture and Festivity', ch. 5.

with her several times at the Dadabari, where she had told me that she had taken the *baravrat*s and invited me to her house to see how she performed the *pratikraman* rite (see Chapter 9). I arrived with a friend, Sushila, and we were shown first to a big upstairs living room, where we sat to have tea on one of the sofas. Mrs Golecha pulled up a coffee table instead, and sat on that, explaining proudly that she limits the number of soft cushions she sits on. After a few minutes chatting about other things she returned to this theme. She gestured towards a large double bed at the other end of the room, which turned out to belong to one of her sons and his wife. 'I never sit on that', she said, and looking at me added, 'For at least an hour after you have gone, I will not sit on the sofa either.' Making what seemed at the time a puzzling connection, she went on to explain that now, having taken the *baravrat*s, she does what she likes. 'I don't cook for other people any more, I don't eat food left over from the day before, I won't eat spicy food.' When she is fasting (which is every other day), she said, 'No one can make any demands on me.' 'I used to do what others liked, but no more.' She took us to the room set aside for her daily rites, with a shrine and a little pile of religious books. I asked Mrs Golecha how, given the time she spent in religious activities, her life differed from that of renouncers. 'Well,' she said, 'they have to eat from wooden bowls, whereas I can use the utensils I want. They can't wear coloured clothes, only white ones.[15] They can't eat what they want, whereas I can even cook for myself if I want to.'

One *shravak* I knew in Jaipur, whom I shall call Mr Kothari, was particularly helpful in discussing in detail the terms of his vows, and how following them had affected his day-to-day life. He is, I think, quite typical of men who take the twelve restraints, and I shall use his case to bring out what seem to me the most important points.

Mr Kothari is a man in late middle-age. A corpulent, good-natured man, he is an extremely wealthy jeweller, with grown-up married sons who have taken over his business (although he does still dabble). Two of his brothers also run successful gem-trading businesses in Jaipur, and other branches of the family provide him with contacts in Delhi, Bombay, and elsewhere. None of this considerable patrimony will be interfered with by his adoption of the twelve restraints, and it will all pass as normal to his children. Mr Kothari does not consider himself a particularly strict or ascetic person. He emphasizes that his wife, who has also taken the

---

[15] In some Jaipur Jain families Mrs Golecha, as a widow, might have been constrained to wear only white, but she evidently wore what she liked.

*baravrat*s, is much better at fasting than he is. He talked easily of all the faults he collected during his last *updhan* and of his difficulty with some of the restrictions he is under. He enjoys playing cards, and has set the limit of the number of games he can play in a month at what he admits is an embarrassingly high level. But he sees the *baravrat*s as a framework which will enable him to work harder and harder 'on the purification of my soul', and he has committed himself to a large number of fasts and ascetic rites. But his 'religious work' also includes more public duties.

Because Mr Kothari has passed on the running of the family firm to his sons, he has plenty of time to attend public religious events. As with Mrs Golecha, his vows formalize and extend the privileges of seniority in a large and successful family. Such people are the most regular participants at *puja*s and other religious ceremonies. They often spend whole mornings in the *upashraya* listening to renouncers' sermons. Their sons, who must go to work, and their daughters, who must do or at least supervise housework and the preparation of lunch, come for a short period, but they mostly leave by about ten o'clock. There are far fewer such men than women, so their participation is especially important in events where only men may take part. The most important example of this is the procession which carries a body to the cremation ground, and which usually takes place within hours of death. Far from being a renunciation of worldly activity, adopting the *baravrat*s has meant that Mr Kothari is now free to fulfil all his familial and social duties.

His wife, as he says, is more strict than he is. She performs *pratikraman* every day, and she fasts more frequently and for longer. But there is absolutely no danger of her becoming a renouncer either. Now that her sons are married, and her daughters-in-law take responsibility for the housework, she is free to enjoy the privilege of having time to devote to religious activities. Lay fasting, as we shall see below (Chapters 10 and 12), while certainly informed by ascetic renunciation, also involves ample affirmation of the worldly values of good health and good fortune, marriage, and the family. Before marriage, many young women undertake quite gruelling fasts, and success in these is taken as sign of their virtue, a sign that they will make a good wife. The young women themselves say that they hope the merit from the fast will secure for them a good husband. Mrs Kothari is one of many elderly Jain women who sustain levels of fasting and performance of ascetic rites which rival or surpass those of renouncers themselves. But the way these fasts are celebrated marks them off firmly from those which renouncers do. The honour her fast brings to the family is celebrated in a procession through the local streets, for which she dresses in her finest clothes and jewellery. For her husband, this is also a good occasion to fulfil the *aparigraha* (non-possession) and *atithi samvibhag* (hospitality) vows. He will almost certainly distribute sweets or coconuts among the crowd, make gifts of cooking utensils or clothes to others who have performed the same fast, and might well arrange a feast to which neighbours, business colleagues, friends, and other members of the religious community are invited. He might announce a gift to a religious fund, a temple, or a charity. And some forms of fasting are actually regulated forms of eating, and this can be done collectively, in events which are quite convivial.

All the substantial building work which Jain communities undertake, and the considerable collective temple worship and feasting they organize, is paid for by individual donors. Another of the privileges which comes with the semi-retirement enjoyed by *shravak*s, is taking a full part in organizing these activities, usually by sitting on one or more of the temple management or trust committees. The potential advantages of managing the money you have donated for tax-free religious and charitable purposes are obvious enough to be passed over without extended comment. There are other aspects I would rather draw attention to here. During the time I have been visiting Jaipur, the Khartar Gacch alone has undertaken a number of major building projects: three temples in outlying parts of the city, two large marble memorial halls for recently deceased renouncers, a hostel for people from outside Jaipur coming to visit sick relatives in hospital (this was aborted), and the renovation and extension of the main meeting and function hall. In all these projects a series of practical problems were constantly cropping up: a contractor was not using the mix of cement he said he would, electricity could not be installed until an official had been bribed, and so on. Although renouncers were keen to promote these projects and took a close interest in their progress, they could take no direct part in sorting out problems such as these. Taking the *baravrat*s signals of a layman that he has the time and the religious commitment to take them on. Mr Kothari was in fact principal treasurer for one of these projects and one of an easily recognizable élite who preside over the religious community's public life. When we were going through the details of his *baravrat* vows together and came to the provisions of his *satya* (truth) restraint, I noticed what seemed like rather a flagrant exception. According to his sheet, he was allowed to tell 'harmless' untruths in business. As he hardly ever did business anymore, this seemed odd and I quizzed him about it. 'Well,' he said, 'it's impossible to do business and really tell the truth. No-one will pay you thirty thousand rupees if you tell them you paid twenty, and I might want to do some business now and then. Besides, for religious work we have to deal with the government, for permits and licenses, and who can deal with the government without telling lies?' One can understand why he and his guru preferred to write 'business' as the exception here, rather than 'building Jain temples'.

The Limits of Lay Renunciation

Adopting the *baravrats* is not preparation for a renouncer's life, but an eminently social role. The vows are limited, then, not only by who is able to adopt them, but also in the place they occupy in the life of those who can and do. These limits to the lay vows can be seen in their textual charter, which is a very ancient and distinguished one: the tenth *Anga* of the Shvetambar canon, the *Upasakadasha Sutra* or *Uvasaga Dasao*.[16]

This text tells the story of ten virtuous laymen of the time of Mahavir, of the vows they took, the difficulties they overcame in abiding by them, and the heavenly abodes in which they were, as a consequence, reborn. The first chapter, which provides a template for all the others, tells of the first man to take the twelve restraints, Anand Shravak. After hearing a sermon by Mahavir, Anand declares he is convinced by Jain doctrine, but that he is unable to become a monk. The issues of psychology and motivation, of just what is involved in being convinced, and yet not moved to renounce, are left completely unexamined; but as the story goes on, it becomes clear that whatever the reason is, it does not prevent Anand from engaging in fierce asceticism. A substantial proportion of the text, however, consists of lists of property and possessions. Anand's immense wealth and business interests are first enumerated and he later proceeds to specify the limited but still substantial property he will keep, together with all the types of perfumes and oils, foods, drinks, clothes, and other goods he will continue to use.

K. R. Norman has suggested that the lists of specific restrictions may be later additions to a text in which the main point was, originally, that Anand was declaring allegiance exclusively to Jain renouncers and teachers, and that the text therefore represents a pragmatic recognition of the fact that the religion could not survive without lay followers.[17] The main point, for our purposes, is that comprehensive as the rules and restrictions in the text as we now have it are, the formula fails in two ways.

---

[16] Hoernle, *Uvasagadasao*.   [17] Norman, 'Role of the Layman', 35.

Although his wife has followed him in accepting the vows, Anand declares after some time that he has been unable properly to abide by the rules while still living with his family. He puts his son in charge of his household, declares that no one may consult him about the affairs of the world, leaves his home, and establishes himself permanently in a fasting-house. Thereafter, through prolonged fasting, he makes great spiritual progress and becomes 'withered, emaciated and reduced to a skeleton'. So although his vows are presented as a template for lay religious life, Anand has, in practical terms, ceased to be a layman. He no longer maintains a household, so he can no longer fulfil some of the vows he took before Mahavir. Significantly, he can no longer provide food, shelter, and support for Jain renouncers (which, if Norman is correct, was the point of the scheme in the first place). The Jain ascetic imperative prevails over pragmatic considerations of religious sociology.

After leaving his family and his home and moving permanently into a fasting-house, Anand Shravak finally makes a vow to fast to death.

> Truly, through these ascetic exercises I have become reduced to a skeleton; yet there is still in me effort, work, strength, vigour, manly power and energy of faith; therefore . . . it is better for me, tomorrow . . . after sunrise to devote myself to determined self-mortification by the last mortal emaciation, renouncing all food and drink and patiently waiting for my end.[18]

The text informs us that Anand is reborn in a high heaven, but given that he is fortunate enough to have been born when a Jina is on the earth, and given the rigours of asceticism he has gone through, it is interesting that the Jain authors (renouncers) withheld liberation from him. The examples in Shvetambar tradition of householders who have gained *moksh*, such as those I mentioned in Chapter 2, had to work a lot less hard than this to achieve a greater—indeed the ultimate—end. So the formula fails to achieve for Anand either the continuation of his life as a householder or the most, in terms of spiritual achievement, that was possible from the lay estate. As we shall see below (Chapter 17), Jain mytho-history provides examples of lay people who have combined asceticism much more successfully with the life of a householder.

The *anuvrat* formula, then, is both more and less then the neat reconciliation of lay and monastic ethics which it appears at first sight to be. It is more because, as it is filled out in practice in the twelve restraints, it defines a prominent and important role—indeed, if we follow the arguments of Part II, a constitutive one—in Jain communities. It is less,

---

[18] Hoernle, *Uvasagadasao*, 47.

because it is specialized, both in the sense that only the already privileged, in general, adopt that role, and in the further sense that doing so shapes a rather limited period in even their lives. Most strikingly, it does not, as Jaini suggests, lead people towards monastic renunciation, even in a case such as that of Anand Shravak where it does lead them out of their household. None the less, in this chapter we have met, albeit briefly, the range of practices through which ascetic renunciation is integrated into lay Jain life, for the impressive ascetic armoury laid out in the pamphlets for the twelve restraints—fasts, confessions, rites of meditation, and the habits of control and self-surveillance set out in the fourteen disciplines—are adopted very widely in Jain communities outside the framework of life-long vows. To understand lay Jainism is to understand the effects and import of these practices, the varieties of meanings that are attributed to them, and the contexts and patterns—of which the twelve restraints, to conclude, is only one—in which they are practised.

9

Acts Which Are Not

IN the previous chapter I described how and why the adoption of the five *anuvrat* vows plays such a limited role in Jain religious life. I tried to specify just what that place is, and why the vows' being limited to a very few people is central to their meaning and import. The simple fact that so few people take them has of course been noticed by authors who nevertheless offer these vows as a summary of lay Jainism. Thus Jaini observes,

While theoretically set down for all laymen, [they] tend to constitute an ideal path followed only by a highly select few. Certainly the ethical codes which underlie these disciplines strongly influence the outlook of the community at large, but it is a rare individual who actually *vows* to accept the restraints or perform the holy activities described there.

This is all true, especially if one interprets 'select' appropriately. But the comment also runs together two distinctions which I think it would be helpful to separate. First, there is the distinction between general moral rules and specific ethical and religious practices. As Jaini rightly says, even if very few people take these vows, the principles of non-violence, truth, respect for property, chastity, and non-possessiveness are respected throughout Jain communities. But that does not get us very far, and does not tell us how and when these principles are enacted. Secondly, there is a distinction between religious observance that is casual or haphazard and that which is bound by vows. In the Jain context we must be extremely careful about a distinction of this sort. Jaini implies here that for all those who do not take the *anuvrats*, lay Jainism should be seen as an essentially voluntary affair, not covered by vows. Thus he continues,

For most Jainas, practice of their faith centers upon a diverse group of daily rituals and periodic ceremonies. Many of these may be equivalent in substance to aspects of the 'ideal' lay path, but they differ significantly in that no compulsion attaches to them; unbound by any vow, the layman performs such activities only if and when he desires to.[1]

---

[1] Jaini, *Jaina Path*, 188. Norman ('Role of the Layman', 37) echoes this view.

Similarly, Cort writes, 'The religious ascetic life of the Jain layperson consists not of binding, obligatory behavior governed by vows, but of voluntary behavior governed by individual decision.'[2] As a point about the variability of individual religious practice, this is fair enough. It derives from the fact that lay Jain asceticism is an ethics, much more than it is a moral code, and we shall be detained time and again below while I set out the range of options that lay Jains have to choose from in fulfilling particular religious duties. But the opposition between binding vows and voluntary decision is a misleading one. Whenever lay Jains engage in any serious religious practice they are bound by a vow. Indeed, it is only by taking a vow that they count as performing those actions at all.

Vows and Intentions: The Building Blocks of Ascetic Practice

Vows such as those for the *anuvrat*s which bind one in perpetuity are called *pratigya* or *saugandh*. But there is a different kind of vow, the *paccakkhan*, which is a formal and binding but temporary vow. Each of the specific practices, including fasting, of which Jain asceticism is composed requires a *paccakkhan* to bring it into being. While it is true that lay Jains decide for themselves which of these vows to take, and in that sense their asceticism is voluntary, it is equally true that ascetic conduct unbound by any vow is not ascetic conduct at all. All my informants were clear that fasting, confession, or whatever, without the *paccakkhan*, just would not work. It would not be *tapasya*: it would not clean the soul.

Why should it be that ascetic action must take place under a vow? To begin to answer this, we need to look at a few of the things Jain teachers have had to say about how the thoughts or intentions behind an action bear on the effect it will have, through the operations of *karma*, on the soul. It would be a mistake to look for a single Jain view on this question. There is no single view expressed either in ancient sacred texts or in religious debate and practice today. The best one can do is indicate the terrain which Jain teachers have charted out, and around which contemporary asceticism tends to move.

The canonical *Sutrakritanga Sutra* sets out Jain arguments against a number of other Indian religious schools, including the Buddhists who were known to stress that the intention behind an action determines its *karmik* effect.[3] The image of life and death which, as we saw, motivates

---

[2] Cort, 'Liberation and Wellbeing', 260.

[3] Interestingly, Gombrich (*Precept and Practice*, ch. 6) reported in the early 1970s that the moral intuitions of Buddhist villagers in Sri Lanka were dominated by an ethic of intention.

and haunts the Jain pursuit of non-violence, is set out vividly here. In all its wandering through high and low forms of life, a soul commits sin and accumulates *karma*. This is unavoidable. 'There is sin without sinful thoughts.' Even sustaining life involves sin. The text has this to say about trees.

These living beings feed on the liquid substance of these particles of earth, the origin of various things; these beings consume earth-bodies, water-bodies, fire-bodies, wind-bodies, bodies of plants; they deprive of life the bodies of manifold movable and immovable beings; the destroyed bodies which have been consumed before, or absorbed by the rind, (are) digested and assimilated (by them).[4]

This view, which implies that merely sustaining life involves sin, is pressed home as the text then describes how every embodied soul (creepers, grasses, water-borne plants, human beings, aquatic animals with five senses, quadrupeds with five senses, reptiles, terrestrial animals walking on their arms, aerial animals, parasites, vermin, and even precious stones) commits *himsa*. They are all, it says, 'born in bodies, grown in bodies, feeding on bodies, experience their *karma*, are actuated by it, have their form and duration of life determined by it', so they are caught in the cycle of sin and death that is *samsar*.

Some Jain teachers have argued, against the apparently fatalistic consequences of such a view, that the *karma* caused by actions which are also religious duties comes to fruition instantaneously and so has no lasting deleterious effect on the soul.[5] Jains I knew in Jaipur preferred a quantitative solution: the amount of *karma* which results from religious ritual is less than the amount it removes, although this is only guaranteed if it is performed correctly and with absolute care. In these ways religious practice can be thought of as consisting of forms of action which are also non-actions; that one can act to undo the consequences of previous action, without thereby committing further sin. It is a precarious thought which can lead in several directions. How does one perform a religious action as a 'non-action'?

The Kanji Swami Panth, taking one possible line, is equivocal about the value of any outward bodily actions, including the whole apparatus of Jain asceticism on which formal renunciation rests. Thus a typical sermon I attended by one of its pandits was entirely taken up with a discussion of *pratikraman*, a formalized confession ritual. The pandit distinguished the worldly or conventional view (*vyavahara nay*) of *pratikraman*, as a good action which has a good effect on the soul; from the definite (*nishcay*) or

---

⁴ Jacobi, *Jaina Sutras*, ii. 389.   ⁵ See Dundas, *The Jains*, 85, 139–40.

pure (*shuddh*) perspective on the same action; which would see that, as an action, it actually causes *karma* and so cannot really help one achieve enlightenment. So *pratikraman* itself should be renounced. There are two ways of not performing *pratikraman*, the pandit told his audience, two forms of *a-pratikraman*, although they might look the same to those with only the worldly view. One is that of the irreligious man, whose failure to perform *pratikraman* ties him to further *karma* and perpetuates his suffering. The other is that of the enlightened man who transcends action—transcends, as in this case, the outer form of *pratikraman*—to enact *a-pratikraman*, which means he actually does nothing. This form of not-acting, the pandit concluded, is what Jains should aim at. It is this that will really free the soul of *karma*.[6] The only way to avoid harmful action and attain pure inaction is through contemplation of the soul.

The different lines of thinking on this question are by no means tidily contained by sectarian divisions,[7] but in the Murti Pujak traditions a more usual way of construing religious action as non-action is to concentrate on correct and disciplined performance, so that all *unnecessary* physical movement is minimized. In addition—or rather, as we shall see, as an extension of this—the discipline involved in preventing unnecessary physical movement also keeps the mind in check. The fact that physical action does involve sin, even if there is no evil intention, does not mean that the intention is irrelevant. The sixth-century Jain saint Jinabhadra writes,

There will not be injury simply because the world is crowded with souls. It is the intention that ultimately matters. From the real point of view, a man does not become a killer only because he has killed or because the world is crowded with souls, or remain innocent only because he has not killed physically . . . Even if a person does not actually kill, he becomes a killer if he has the intention to kill; while a doctor has to cause pain but is still non-injuring and injuring because his intention is pure . . . For it is the intention which is the deciding factor, not the external act, which is inconclusive. From the real point of view, it is the evil intention which is *himsa* whether it materializes into an evil act of injuring or not.

[6] One should add that this trick is played in turn on every aspect of conventional doctrine and practice: so the next class might well consider how, from the pure view, the soul is not really bound to *karma* at all. Judging from the conduct of these classes, which are vigorous question and answer sessions in which all those present join in and anyone displaying signs of being stuck in the conventional standpoint is roundly refuted from all sides, people soon get the hang of the technique.

[7] I attended some classes held by the Kanji Swami Panth in Jaipur because there were members of the Khartar Gacch who were influenced by their ideas and causing something of a stir by airing them at Khartar Gacch gatherings.

There can be non-violence even when an external act of violence has been committed and violence even when it has not been committed.[8]

Jinabhadra's view is hardly comforting; for he both accepts the vision of the world as already inhabited by life-forms which will be harmed by every physical action, and also insists that intention to act can constitute sin, even if none of these creatures are in fact killed. Not all action is sinful and binds the soul to further suffering, he says, but any action might be, even a careless thought.

One line of argument, which Jainism shares with much Hindu thinking (such as the *Bhagavad Gita*), is that if an action is performed in a state of mental detachment—without desire (*nishkam*)—then sin may not result. The *Uttaradhyayana Sutra* has the following explanation for how *karmik* matter affects the soul.

There is glue (as it were) in pleasure: those who are not given to pleasure, are not soiled by it; those who love pleasures, must wander about in the *samsar*; those who do not, will be liberated. If you take two clods of clay, one wet, the other dry, and fling them against the wall, the wet one will stick to it. Thus foolish men, who love pleasure, will be fastened (to *karma*), but the passionless will not, even as the dry clod of clay (does not stick to the wall).[9]

But this does not mean that sin only attaches to actions which are pleasurable. There is a famous Jain story of a very devout layman who spent all his time in study and performing pious works. He was poor, and in the evening he read his books by the light from his neighbour's window. When he died he was reborn in hell, because his attachment to his study had meant that he forgot to ask his neighbour's permission before making use of his light.[10] This carelessness, even though in pursuit of religion, was a sin, as it broke his vow of not taking what has not been freely given (*asteya*). Even apparently virtuous actions, and innocent intentions, must be subjected to scrutiny lest they lead to unintended sin.

In the sections which follow I shall describe the main forms of ascetic practice which lay Jains engage in, and discuss what people in Jaipur had to say about the mental states with which they should, properly, be

---

[8] Quoted by Malvania, 'Theory and Practice of Non-Violence', 39–40, and Dundas, *The Jains*, 139–40.

[9] Jacobi, *Jaina Sutras*, ii. 141.

[10] Incidentally, it is worth noting that the idiom in which Buddhists commonly explain the idea of sharing merit through rejoicing in the merit gained by others (*anumodan*) is that one can benefit from another's good deed without detracting from their merit, just as many people can benefit from the light of a lamp. It is difficult not to read the Jain story as a repudiation of that view.

performed. In this way we will find answers not only to the question of how action that is also non-action is possible—how one can act to untie *karma* from the soul—but also to the equally pressing question for lay religiosity of how non-action can also be action—how the renouncer's asceticism might be integrated in a helpful way into lay life, to earn religious merit and promote worldly good fortune.

'*Real Jainism*'

Shvetambar tradition lays down six 'necessary duties' which renouncers should perform each day: the *avashyaka*s. Lay Jains are enjoined to perform them as often as they can.

1. *samayik*—attaining mental tranquillity by excluding all worldly thoughts.
2. *caubis-stavan*—veneration, by reciting their names, of the twenty-four Jinas.
3. *vandan*—veneration of renouncers and/or one's guru.
4. *pratikraman*—'casting off', or repenting of sin.
5. *kaussagg*—'abandoning the body', that is, the physical austerity of holding one's body motionless.
6. *paccakkhan*—a vow to perform an austerity of some kind, paradigmatically a fast.

While conceptually, as general intentions or as hoped-for results, these six duties are fairly clearly distinguishable, they are each actually performed by engaging in one or more specific rituals, and in these rituals the six duties are mutually interdependent and intertwined in ways which are, at first sight, quite bewilderingly complex.[11]

The six *avashyaka*s are common to all Shvetambar traditions, and unlike temple ritual, they are considered to be valid religious actions for both lay Jains and renouncers in all these traditions. The source for the scheme is a canonical text called the *Avashyaka Sutra*. The text itself is

---

[11] To get a clear picture of how people actually perform these six duties, based only on the texts, would I think be impossible. In the course of his generally clear discussion of Sanskrit *shravakacar*s, Williams (*Jaina Yoga*) has cause to note that the *vandan* is 'associated with' a number of other rites, including *pratikraman* (202), that performing *samayik* 'includes' *pratikraman* and *vandan* (133), that *pratikraman* 'forms a prelude' to the *caitya-vandan* (203), that *caitya-vandan* 'comprises elements' of the *samayik*, *caubis-stavan*, and *vandan* (187), and that the *paccakkhan* is 'linked with' the *vandan* (207). When he comes to consider *kaussagg*, Williams observes, perhaps in desperation, that despite its status in the literature as a separate *avashyaka*, 'it is, in reality, an adjunct to other rites' (213).

lost, or rather survives only embedded in a versified Prakrit commentary known as the *Avashyaka Niryukti*.[12] As this commentary 'really consists for the most part of lists of catchwords without any syntactic link between them',[13] it has in turn become the centre of a vast literature of further commentaries and illustrative narratives from which many of the most popular Jain religious stories are derived.[14] The core of what survives are six short passages for recitation in rites which fulfil, respectively, each of the six duties. Prominent renouncers today produce their own manuals on the six duties: texts which draw, via those produced by their own teachers, on the ancient texts, commentaries, and commentaries on commentaries, and to which they add their own advice about preparations one should make before performing the rites, postures to be adopted, and gestures to be employed. There are many available versions of these 'performance texts', and the rites are performed slightly differently in each Shvetambar sect and school.[15]

The short pieces of text that correspond to each duty in the original *sutra* are used today in a variety of ritual contexts. Two or more of the six passages occur frequently in the same rituals, shuffled and repeated in various combinations, together with other texts: songs, prayers, chants, magical formulas, and lists; and the rituals they are used in vary from relatively short and informal individual devotions to collective rites of great length and complexity. To make things even more confusing, the long rites in which one or more of the *avashyaka* texts are recited, themselves bear the names of one or more of the *avashyaka*s. So, for example, the short texts for *caubis-stavan* and *vandan*, as well as that for *samayik*, are recited during a rite which is known as the *samayik*. There are several *pratikraman*s, as well as at least one of each of the other *avashyaka*s, during the rite called *pratikraman*.

The simplest way to explain the situation is to distinguish whole rituals from distinct ritualized acts of which they are composed. A ritual is an event or social practice which is composed for the most part of a series of ritualized acts. So for instance the Jain *puja* (temple worship) might

---

[12] For further discussion see Alsdorf ('Jaina Exegetical Literature'), Bruhn ('Avashyaka Studies'). See also Winternitz (*History of Indian Literature*, ii. 413) and Jaini (*Jaina Path*, 48).

[13] Balbir, 'Stories from Avashyaka Commentaries', 70.

[14] See ibid. and Balbir, 'Monkey and Weaver Bird'; Bruhn, 'Repetition'; Mette, 'Tales of the Namaskara-Vyakhya'.

[15] The description I shall give below is of Khartar Gacch practice. Shântâ (*Voie Jaina*) gives some information on these rites among Sthanakvasi *sadhvi*s.

include, in addition to washing the idol, waving lamps and incense, and making a series of offerings, the performance of one or more of the *avashyaka* ritual acts, such as *caubis-stavan*.[16]

In contemporary lay ascetic practice there are four rituals which are composed, wholly or partly, of these ritual acts, and it is by performing these that lay Jains fulfil, if they do, their 'necessary duties'. One is *vandan*, the formal greeting performed whenever a lay Jain comes into the presence of a renouncer.[17] A full *vandan* is in many ways like the worship of temple idols (see Chapter 11), but versions of it are part of three main ascetic practices of Jainism, the *samayik, pratikraman*, and fasting.

I discussed in Chapters 2 and 4 how the unseen effects of religious action can be conceptualized in different ways, particularly around the ambiguity between acquiring good *karma* and removing any *karma*. In so far as lay Jains see themselves as *shramana*s or strivers—as distinct, say, from appreciative sponsors—it is the latter image they will tend to use, although, as we shall see, the ambiguity never fully disappears. Conceived this way, *samayik, pratikraman*, and fasting are all forms of ascetic 'burning' (*tap, tapas*), which removes *karma* from the soul. When devout Jains, even Mandir Margis, say that *puja* is not 'real Jainism', that it is for merit (*punya*) rather than for religion (*dharma*), or that it is borrowed from Hinduism, at least part of what they are pointing to is that it is not built up, as these rites are, principally of *avashyaka* acts. In the Mandir Margi traditions, most people perform temple worship more often than they do any other religious practice, and it is central to their religious sensibilities. But it is an equally important fact about their religious sensibility that they regard those rites as in a sense inferior to these three. So it is worth considering in some detail each of these forms of Real Jainism.

1. *Samayik*—a period of forty-eight minutes spent sitting quietly reciting certain texts (including the *Samayik Sutra*) and telling a rosary. Mostly this is performed in the morning. Many people

---

[16] In each of these minimal ritual acts, recitation of the text is usually accompanied by certain bodily postures and movements. To perform *caubis-stavan*, you crouch, sitting on your right ankle with your left knee raised straight in front of you, and recite a prayer which includes the names of the twenty-four Tirthankars (called the *Logass Sutra*). To perform *paccakkhan*, you stand with your legs together, but leaning slightly forwards, with hands clasped, rather as in Christian prayer, but held high and close against the chest.

[17] It varies, depending on the status of the renouncer and the formality of the occasion, from being a respectful bow and salutation to a series of full prostrations while reciting a longish Prakrit text. In its full form the *vandan* ritual includes the *pratikraman* ritual act. See Williams, *Jaina Yoga*, 199–200.

perform it alone, or in single-sex groups with other members of their household, but others go to an *upashraya* to perform it in larger groups.

2. *Pratikraman*—a rite of confession and repentance, which includes all six *avashyaka* ritual acts and takes anything from one to four hours to complete. Renouncers perform it twice each day. All lay Jains perform it at least once a year, but hardly any ever perform it more than once a day.

3. *Tapasya*—a fast or other ascetic practice. It involves making a *paccakkhan* (temporary vow), usually before a renouncer or a Jina idol.

The canonical list of six duties therefore resolves itself, when one looks from schemes and models to practices, into these three ascetic 'weapons', which we shall look at in detail in the remainder of this and in the next chapter.

Samayik—*Attaining Equipoise*

The most natural way to describe *samayik* is as a period of quiet meditation and prayer, but a few words need to be said so that this is not misunderstood. In common with other Indic religious traditions, medieval Jain texts refer to an elaborate set of techniques: a ladder of increasingly pure forms of meditation which in theory a Jain saint must pass through as he or she approaches omniscience.[18] In addition, some Jain authors have adopted language and concepts from tantric yoga,[19] shorn, of course, of their 'left-hand' and sexual aspects. Indeed, Jainism has made quite substantial contributions to tantric art and iconography. The tantric idea of projecting deities into parts of the worshipper's body (*nyas*) is used widely in Jain temple ritual, as are tantric diagrams (*mandalas*, *yantras*) as a focus for worship. However, while tantric language and imagery have been incorporated into popular ritual, the more esoteric flights of tantrism have had no discernible impact on Jainism's staid and puritanical codes of conduct. The ethereal forms of meditation which are said to lead to final liberation may never have been of more than theoretical importance, adopted in imitation of Shaivite mystical Hinduism,[20] and are considered by most Jain traditions today (the exception is the Kanji Swami Panth) to

---

[18] Jaini, *Jaina Path*, 251–8; Tatia, *Jain Philosophy*.

[19] Eliade, *Yoga*, ch. 6; Tatia, *Jain Philosophy*, 282–90.

[20] Dundas, *The Jains*, 143–6.

be well beyond the conceivable ambitions of any living being. Jains have concentrated instead on the development of detailed rituals which employ combinations of physical movements and recitation of texts to act upon the mind in ways which will then be reflected in conduct. Thus meditation (*dhyan*) in Jainism tends not to mean the encouragement of anything very imaginative.

I had a couple of friends in Jaipur with pronounced spiritual leanings, interested in exploring meditation. Finding little in Jain tradition to answer that interest, they were attending classes in Vipassana meditation run by a Buddhist group in a Hindu *ashram* in Jaipur.[21] In recent years the Shvetambar Terapanth has been promoting what it calls a revival of ancient Jain meditation, *preksha dhyan*. It will be interesting to see how successful this is. To date, it has had no real impact on the Mandir Margi schools.

Among the latter, *dhyan* ('meditation') is always incorporated into a more encompassing frame of ritual, and consists of the repeated performance of formal mental exercises. Sometimes this is reciting a text out loud but most often it is repeating a *mantra*. The virtue of reciting these *mantra*s is that they contain and concentrate one's thoughts, and the explicit concern which Jain teachers have in the context of meditation is not to encourage elaborate feats of visualization, but to teach how to control and rein in the mind. Mental activity must be controlled and limited, for just like the motions of the body, it is action (*karma*). This Jain monk compares the self to a state, defended from its enemies (the desires which lead to sin) by a standing army.

All the inner guards should be posted only in those inward regions where there is the definite possibility of enemy attacks. And that inner vulnerable boundary is our 'Mind'. The check-posts must be erected in the mind, where the evil desires of sins are waiting in the bush with their strategy against us. If once these armies of sins go strong in the regions of our mind and capture it, if they rush on into the area of our body, then there is sure defeat and ruin.[22]

In this context, the mind (*man*) is seen as a sense-organ of the body, like taste or touch, a medium where desire arises. Here is one Jain intellectual on the virtues of controlling one's thoughts.

While the material constituent of mind has permanence, the modes which are responsible for the mental processes are ever changing, making mind the most

---

[21] On the development of this form of meditation and its growing popularity among the Buddhist laity in Sri Lanka, see Gombrich and Obeyesekere, *Buddhism Transformed*.

[22] Chandrashekhar Vijay-ji, *Call for Vigilance*, 283.

restless of all the sense organs. It is this restlessness of mind which may lead one to perdition, and to save oneself from it, the first thing one is required to do is to establish a complete control over mind, to delimit the zone over which it moves and to reduce it steadily till the zone totally disappears. Left to itself, mind penetrates and trespasses into any part of the universe with a speed that is faster than the speed of light. . . . Mind is a good servant but a bad master. It is mind that helps one to attain higher consciousness. It is like a ladder. But if it be given free play, it is the most potent instrument of self-annihilation.[23]

Even the transports of the imagination, this author suggests, are equivalent to careless and uncontrolled movements of the body, and imagined sins lead as surely to perdition as executed ones.

These views of meditation are reflected in the *samayik* ritual. In form, it is quite simple. Celebrants place a small woollen mat on the ground for an 'hour' (*ghanta* or *muhuratt*), which in this as in all Jain ritual contexts means forty-eight minutes. During this time they sit still, reciting prayers, religious songs, *mantra*s, and other religious texts. Men usually wear a cotton *dhoti* for *samayik*, rather than Western clothes, but this is not necessary, and women mostly wear a normal sari. It is considered desirable to have a *carwala* (a brush which is similar to the *ogha* carried by renouncers), and to use this to sweep the ground and mat before sitting down, but again this is not essential. In a large family the women may all perform *samayik* together first thing in the morning, spending the time either in silence or singing in unison. At any renouncer's sermon, there will be a number of people sitting on woollen mats, telling rosaries, performing *samayik* while listening to the sermon. Especially for pious elderly women, the ritual is an absolutely fixed part of their daily routine. I remember once when I was travelling by train with a family, the mother sat on her bunk telling her rosary silently, her lips just moving and her sari hanging over her eyes, as the whole train was getting up, shouting for tea, having breakfast, changing clothes, and plying backwards and forwards to the lavatory.

Samayik always includes a vow to abstain from harmful actions. To fulfil this, one must refrain from all bodily movement, one must not speak to or recognize anyone else, and one must not think any worldly thoughts—they must be crowded out by meditation. This can be done in many ways. Some people recite a full *Samayik Sutra*, which will be a compilation of texts put together by a renouncer and published and distributed by a lay Jain organization. Mostly these contain texts for the

---

[23] Lalwani, *Sramana Bhagavana Mahavira*, 95.

other *avashyaka* ritual acts, together with prayers and songs.[24] Some people memorize one of these texts, but it is considered quite acceptable to read it. Still others content themselves with reciting a few prayers they know by heart, or just the *nokar-mantra*, over and over again.

The best way to bring out the question of mental states in this ritual is to contrast it with temple worship, *puja*. Just as in the case of *puja*, and in the case of all religious actions in Jainism, more or less everyone will say that in addition to getting the actions correct, you should have *bhav* (on *bhav* and *dravya*, see Chapter 4). In *puja*, Jain teachers recommend a range of meanings that worshippers should rehearse, either as they perform physical acts and make offerings, or during a period of contemplation and prayer after the offerings are made. Thus each act or offering either states a proposition or makes a wish: 'as the skin of this fruit is separate from its kernel, so my body is separate from my soul'; 'this light is for knowledge; as the Tirthankar got perfect knowledge, may I too get knowledge.' And worshippers should not only recall those meanings, they should mean them. They should imaginatively experience the qualities or attainments they hold their acts to refer to. In the *puja*, the meanings people assign to actions, the internal act of actually meaning those meanings, and the attitude of devotion which gives those meanings emotional force, are all referred to as *bhav*: the essence of their act of worship.[25] For *samayik* too, pretty well everyone says that for it to work, your *bhav* must be right, but instead of meaning by this an imaginative experience of particular propositions, they seem to mean, by contrast, using religious text to blot out specific thoughts completely. The *bhav* here should be 'pure'. Some people do perhaps dwell on favourite religious images or sayings in something like the way they do in *bhav puja*, but most people talk about *samayik*, and describe what they do in it, in a different way. '*Samayik* is *mala pherana*, *jap*, *nokar*, *dhyan* (telling a rosary, repeating a text, reciting a *mantra*, concentration). We do no bad deeds, and think no bad thoughts. We should have completely clean thoughts (*shuddh bhavana*) and in this way clean our souls.'

About the overall point of the *samayik* ritual there is near unanimity. For a short time, by performing *samayik*, a Jain householder can become like a Jain renouncer. This interpretation was volunteered by almost

---

[24] Typically, after the *paccakkhan*, they proceed through a *pratikraman* for faults committed while preparing to begin the rite, praise of the Tirthankars, veneration of the guru, periods of *kaussagg*, and end with another *pratikraman*, this time in repentance for any faults committed during the course of the rite itself.

[25] See Humphrey and Laidlaw, *Archetypal Actions*, ch. 9.

everyone I spoke to on the matter.[26] But while everyone is agreed on this, the great majority of people have pretty well nothing else to say about the rite. This again is in contrast to *puja*, for which elaborate symbolic meanings and contrasting overall theories and explanations abound. Nothing in *samayik* is thought to have any symbolic meaning, and indeed there is little to read meaning into.

Only lay Jains, not renouncers, perform the *samayik* ritual. Renouncers make an almost identical vow at their first initiation ceremony, and count as being 'in *samayik*' for the remainder of their lives. When they die their bodies are committed (they used to be buried but these days they are cremated[27]) in a seated posture, to show that they died while performing *samayik*. The first difference then, between the *samayik* vow for renouncers and householders is that while the former is for life (*javajjivae*), the latter is temporary. This fact necessitates a number of differences in how the vow is interpreted and in what counts as an infraction of it. Thus while householders must remain perfectly still during *samayik*, renouncers will need to move about. Renouncers say that they should keep all bodily movements to a minimum, just as a householder does during the ritual, but that they are permitted to move (although it remains unavoidably a sin to do so) for four reasons: to obtain food (*ahar*); to move residence regularly (*vihar*); to find a suitable place to do their toilet (*nihar*); and to visit a temple to pay respects to the Jinas (*mandir darshan*).[28]

The second difference between these *samayik* vows is of special interest because it points to the categorical difference, recognized even at the heart of ascetic Jainism, between householder and renouncer. The renouncers' vow prohibits three sorts of sinful activities in any of three modes (*tiviham tivihenam*). The three sorts of sinful activities are those which one does, those which one causes others to do, and those which one approves of others doing. The three modes are with mind, speech, and body. The householder's vow retains the second three-fold formula but for the first, where renouncers say *tiviham*, householders substitute the word *duviham*, indicating abstention from only two kinds of sinful activities. That is, householders vow not to commit any sins, and not to cause anyone else to do so, but they quite specifically do not vow to abstain from praising or

---

[26] Renouncers reiterate it constantly in their sermons and their writings, and it is reported in historical accounts and in the ethnography on Jains elsewhere. See Cort, 'Liberation and Wellbeing', 246–8; Jaini, *Jaina Path*, 221–3; Williams, *Jaina Yoga*, 133–4.

[27] See Stevenson, *Notes on Modern Jainism*, for a description of the burial of a Jain nun early this century.

[28] This last reason obviously does not apply to Sthanakvasis or Terapanthis.

approving the commission of sins by others. So the full *paccakkhan* which
householders recite in Jaipur goes as follows.

I undertake, venerable one, the *samayik*, renouncing for as long as I worship under
this rule, all harmful activities, those which I might do myself and those which I
might cause others to do. I will not engage in such activities with either mind,
speech, or body, nor will I cause others to engage in them with either mind,
speech, or body. I confess, venerable one, all my blameworthy acts; I accept
censure and repent of every one of them, and I cast aside my former self (which
committed those deeds).[29]

Why should it be permitted for people to approve of others committing
sin? Well, it depends on what counts as a sin, and the sins which the
householder is permitted to praise in this context are actually, in terms of
everyday as opposed to renunciatory judgement, 'good deeds'. There is a
vast array of actions which are duties for householders but which, just
because they are active interventions in the world, renouncers must not
do. This includes all kinds of religious acts which earn good *karma* or
punya, such as making religious donations, saving a life, running a business, getting married, or caring for your parents. During *samayik*, of
course, lay Jains should leave such concerns behind, but they cannot be
expected to repudiate one minute what they will be called upon to do the
next. And normally, to praise and approve the good deeds of another,
which is called *anumodan*, is itself considered an important act of merit.
Even though they are not free of the effects of past *punya*, renouncers
must seek not to cause any *punya*, which means not approving of any done
by someone else (for even this is an action). As one nun explained: 'If in
a previous life we have done some act of *punya*, then due to that we may
get reputation and fame in our life as a *sadhu*, but in this life we don't want
to gain any *punya*, or any *pap* (sin).' *Punya* is essential for social order, for
prosperity, good health, and wellbeing in general. But from the point of
view of freeing one's soul from *karma*, the good deeds which lead to it are
sins. They are, as one Khartar Gacch renouncer writes, chains of gold
instead of chains of iron.[30] Another renouncer once explained to me why
householders take only the two-fold vow.

Householders must do many worldly actions, like *puja*, building a temple, giving
a donation, helping the poor. They get merit (*punya*) from these actions, and they

---

[29] I have adapted the translation given by Jaini (*Jaina Path*, 222) in line with the different
text popularly used in Jaipur today, and the comments on meaning I received from
renouncers.

[30] Maniprabha Shri-ji, *Pravacan Prabha*, 35.

also get merit if they appreciate (*anumodan karna*) the good works of others. *Punya* is necessary for everyone, for everything. Without *punya*, there would be nothing. What is the fruit of *punya*? You take birth in a rich family, have good clothes, food, drink, ornaments, servants. Everyone will do what you say. For householders *punya* is necessary but we (renouncers) don't need *punya* because we don't need anything. *Punya* is for the comforts of the body and we don't need this, we only need to do something for the good of our soul.

What the omission of *anumodan* from the *samayik* vow does, is to allow it to be an act of *punya*: to leave open the possibility that although it is concerted non-action, it might also be a good action.

Pratikraman—*A Rite of Self-Coercion*

Pratikraman is a more elaborate ritual than *samayik*. It is longer, and more tightly 'scripted': that is, individuals feel themselves to have much less choice about what they do and the order in which they do it. Almost everyone follows a printed text which has been compiled, or at least validated, by a senior renouncer; or joins a group which is led by a renouncer or an experienced and learned lay person. In addition, *pratikraman* makes much more elaborate demands on the body. The *Candravedhyaka Sutra* gives as one of the great qualities of an *acarya* that he is, 'The one who, thanks to his body with all twelve limbs, has collected the senses, has held the senses.'[31] Another ancient Jain text announces, 'Discipline is the root of religious practice'[32] and in Jainism the key form of discipline is immediate control of the body. The body is used in *pratikraman* as an instrument for controlling the mind and so bringing about the purification of the soul. It is easier to monitor and control one's body than to hold one's mind at rest, so physical austerity is a way of coercing this most recalcitrant of the body's organs. Thus the body is used to coerce the mind into non-action.

For a while I joined a group in Jaipur which met daily to perform the evening *pratikraman*. This decision met with enormous approval from almost all my Jain friends. This way, they declared, I would find out what real Jainism is like. The group met in the preaching-hall of a large *upashraya* in the walled city, under the guidance of a local savant. There were three men in their thirties, but the remaining fifteen or so were probably all grandfathers. Men usually wear a long white cotton loin-cloth and a shawl—an outfit not dissimilar to that worn by renouncers—and

---

[31] Caillat, *Candavejjhaya*, 60, 82.   [32] Lalwani, *Dashavaikalika Sutra*, 9. 2. 2.

carry a brush and mouth-covering.[33] Some changed their clothes at home and made their way through the streets already reciting prayers to themselves, while others, more discreetly, changed on arrival.[34] On average, it took about an hour and a quarter to complete the rite, after which we stayed on for an informal class, in which the man leading the group used a line from the text we had just recited as the starting-point for a disquisition on some important point of Jain philosophy.

The text we used was recently compiled by a Khartar Gacch nun and dedicated to her guru. Most *acaryas* and many of the more learned senior renouncers compose manuals setting out the traditional texts used in *pratikraman*, providing some advice on preparation and performance of the rites, and including prayers which they themselves have composed. The most ambitious of such books, those called *Panc Pratikraman Sutra*, set out five forms of the rite.

1. *raiy-pratikraman*—to cover sins committed during a night
2. *devsiy-pratikraman*—to cover sins committed during a day
3. *pakkiy-pratikraman*—to cover sins committed during a fortnight
4. *caumasik-pratikraman*—to cover sins committed during a four-month period
5. *samvatsarik-pratikraman*—to cover sins committed during a year.

Renouncers perform *pratikraman* twice each day, first thing in the morning and at sunset. These rites apply respectively to faults committed during the preceding night (*raiy-pratikraman*) and day (*devsiy-pratikraman*), and with only tiny adjustments, they are identical. Except when attending *updhan*, almost no lay Jains perform *pratikraman* in the morning. The group I joined was performing evening *pratikraman* daily, and the fortnightly, quarterly, and annual rites are also performed in the evening. The versions which cover longer periods of time are extended by the repetition of elements and the insertion of more prayers and hymns. *Samvatsarik pratikraman*, held once each year (see Chapter 12), is by far the longest.

The neat scheme of five *pratikramans* gives a misleading impression of regularity. In practice, only a very few lay people perform the rite daily, and there are many who only ever perform the annual rite. Between these

---

[33] Women wear a normal sari. One male renouncer I met said that women ought to wear white clothes, but this seemed only to be his own idea. One manual in use in Jaipur instructed women to wear a *dhoti*, along with a petticoat and blouse, but no one did this.

[34] One is not expected to bathe before *pratikraman*. Indeed, as this is an ascetic exercise, it is thought to be a sin to bathe (and so commit violence) especially in preparation for it.

two extremes, things depend very much on local circumstance. In Jaipur, groups of women meet often in the *upashraya*s, especially on regular fast days or if female renouncers are in residence. There are many pious women, especially those in their forties or older, who fast and perform *pratikraman* daily (fasting, as I have mentioned, includes regulated forms of eating—see also Chapter 11), and many more who perform it two, three, or four times each month. A group of men such as the one I belonged to is rarer and exists only on the initiative of particular individuals. This group about doubled in size for the fortnightly rite, but did not increase much more than that for the quarterly one. During Caturmas, especially if renouncers are staying locally and leading group performance, more people will join in *pratikraman*, just as they will fast and attend sermons more often. And although they are believed to be more orthodox, collective performances are in any case only part of the picture. Especially for those who live outside the walled city, it is not always easy to join a group regularly, and women in many families are required to remain at home after dark, so a large number of the most orthodox women who perform *pratikraman* daily, or when they are fasting, do so alone at home.

Pratikraman is arranged so that the sun sets while the rite is in progress, and in winter this is around five o'clock. An integral part of the rite is a vow to fast until forty-eight minutes after sunrise next morning (*paccakkhan naukarsi*). Thus the ritual is not just a self-contained interlude in normal life, but reaches out and shapes conduct beyond its own boundaries. For this reason, and also because it contains ritual acts of each of the six *avashyaka*s, it more or less stands for lay ascetic practice as a whole, for the notion of 'cleansing the soul' through sustained, repeated, and cumulative effort.

The importance of discipline in Jain ascetic rites is emphasized by the fact that you must take the permission of a guru before performing them. This does not mean that any particular person's permission must actually be sought, as lay Jains are taught to regard all renouncers, and renouncers are taught to regard all more senior renouncers, as their gurus. But even this does not go far enough, because the chain of pupilage always goes further, and the guru too needs a guru. So the rites are always performed, whether a renouncer is present or not, before a symbol, called a *sthapanacarya*, which represents the presence of a guru and so a whole chain of higher religious authority stretching back to the Jinas themselves.[35] Our

---

[35] This consists of a small cloth bundle which is placed on four sticks, crossed to form a stand. Inside the bundle, depending on lineage and sect, are five cowry shells, or carved stone

pratikraman always began after a *sthapan-acarya* had been inspected to see that it harboured no insects, and then placed in the middle of the floor, whereupon we all took our places, standing on woollen mats in a wide arc around it.

One does see innovations and variations on this arrangement. In 1990 I was invited to join a family I knew for the evening before Samvatsari. There would be a meal to sustain us through the fast next day, and after the meal, *pratikraman*. Perhaps because they lived in the suburbs, they performed the rite at home. Normally, the sexes are kept strictly apart, not only in separate rooms, but usually even in separate buildings, but this group was mixed. The head of the household was there, as was his mother, his wife, his sister, one son, two daughters-in-law (the other son was out of town), and a cousin who lived nearby. We sat in a circle around a *sthapan-acarya*, men and women opposite each other. Interestingly, it was decided that the most appropriate way to deal with the ends of the two rows, where of necessity a man and woman would have to be next to each other, was to place the two married couples there, with large gaps between the partners (larger in the case of the younger than the older couple).[36] Throughout the ritual the elderly woman kept her face entirely covered with the end of her sari and the other women were partially veiled. There was virtually no eye contact between men and women, and in passing the text between them they observed the avoidance rules followed by renouncers: one person dropped the book on the ground before the other picked it up so that there was no point at which a man and a woman were touching it at the same time. The recitation was led by the older wife, who knew considerable portions of the text by heart (she fasts and performs *pratikraman* regularly), with others joining in for portions they knew (which were few) and by reading along.

The rite consists of sets of quickly repeated physical movements, co-ordinated with rapid recitation of a long Prakrit text. There are three main bodily operations which are repeated time and again at varying intervals. These actions, *padilehan*, *vandan*, and *kaussagg*, are interspersed with a few other postures and movements which are required from time to time. The men in the regular group I attended could all perform these actions. *Padilehan* is a process of examining one's body and accoutrements in such

objects, representing the Jina, the liberated soul, the *acarya*, the learned preceptor, and the renouncer.

[36] Whether it was thought that, being married, they were less likely to have impure thoughts, or that if they did it would matter less, is difficult to say. Either way, the solution seemed thoroughly bourgeois in spirit. I cannot be sure, but I bet that a rural family, faced with the same situation, would have split the married couples up.

a way as gently to remove insects and unseen creatures. Each time *padilehan* was called for, we each unfolded the handkerchief we were using as a mouth covering, and then, holding it by the corner, flipped it over three times in front of us. We used it to brush our forearms and shoulders, then we stood up and brushed the mats we were sitting on. *Vandan* involves three full prostrations, from a standing position to one in which the head touches the floor. Between each prostration we had to place our folded mouth-coverings in front of us on the floor, then place our brushes, head away from us, neatly on top of them. Then each time we rose to our feet again, we again took up our brush and mouth-covering and clasped them in front of us. *Kaussagg* (one of the two standard postures for Jina idols—see Chapter 11) involves standing bolt upright with hands held out a little from one's thighs. Each of the many occasions during the rite where the text involves confession and repentance of sins, penance is called for, so we adopted this position for meditation/concentration (*dhyan*). The man who was reciting the text would call out 'four' or 'eight' or 'sixteen *nokar*' and we would each silently rehearse the *nokar mantra* the prescribed number of times. The idea is to hold body, speech, and mind together, under complete restraint.

As with *samayik*, none of this is in the least symbolic. Nothing is being represented or communicated. Instead, it is work—work on the self—requiring for accomplished performance the mastery of skills which include bodily control, memorization, and accurate recitation. It is these, and not familiarity with any more or less esoteric meaning, that is acquired through performance. There are easier versions of many of the required actions, so that it is possible to remain seated for almost the whole rite, and these, although felt to be less effective, are often adopted by the aged or inexperienced. The easier version of *kaussagg*, for instance, is to sit with your legs crossed in front of you and your hands, palms turned upwards, on your knees. Some people would resort to these easier versions if they became too tired or were beginning to have difficulty maintaining balance and bodily control, and one or two of the oldest employed them all the time. To stumble and fall over is a fault (*ashatana, aticar*), partly because, as an uncontrolled bodily movement, it is *himsa*. The more accomplished could fall forwards in their prostrations smoothly, without losing control and without having to extend their arms in order to keep their balance. One's hands and arms should be held in close to the body throughout.

One of the elderly men had vowed to memorize the whole text, and spent much of his free time trying to do so. He recited from memory as much as he could, and read when necessary. The rest of us were silent for most of the time, but those who knew passages joined in occasionally. Two or three people could remember some of the central passages, consisting of lists of sins and joined in with these. Almost everyone knew one or two of the prayers, like the *shanti*, a sung prayer for peace which comes near the end. We all had texts to follow, and we could tell which major section we were in at any particular time, but no one could translate more than a few fragments of the whole, or even follow it in detail for it was delivered, as is customary, in an utterly regular, monotonous chant—just as quickly as is physically possible.

The relationship between recitation and bodily movement in this rite is a complex one. There are a few passages with a brief sing-song rhythm, almost the beginnings of a melody, but they are fleeting, and soon give way to another staccato list or uninflected chant. There is a certain co-ordination of text and action, so that some passages always call for the same physical movement. In that sense one might be tempted to say that it is like dance, but I think it would be more accurate to call it anti-dance. One times one's movements to coincide with sound, and one strives to achieve smooth and controlled motion. Ideally, one recites (rather than just listening to) the text as one executes these actions. But the recitation does not guide or govern action. It is more like those tests in which you try to perform two different kinds of motion (patting your head and rubbing your stomach in a circle) simultaneously. The chanting does not carry people along, and proficiency in bodily movement, where it is achieved, is achieved against the effect of the sound. And being able actually to do the recitation is yet a further extension of the kind of mastery this requires.

The effect is the very opposite of mental dissociation. One does not relinquish conscious bodily control and follow a rhythm, a beat, or a melody which one receives, already formed and ordered, from outside oneself. Each person performs each action as carefully and completely as they can, but the co-ordination of the participants is not very close. Every few minutes the recitation would stop so that we could all come to rest and then start the next section together. For each period of *kaussagg* we all rehearsed the *mantras* at our own speed, and called out when we had finished. When everyone in the group had done this, the recitation would begin again. So although the ritual is collective, it aims at and achieves no union between participants. The anthropological tradition, running from Durkheim through Mary Douglas and beyond, which sees dance as an organ of social control through the imposition of social categories, sentiments, and codes, seems quite without application here.[37] Bodily control has to be consciously maintained by each individual participant, and it is an entirely inwardly directed, inwardly focused form of control. In this sense it certainly has an element of drill: one is, as Foucault says, among other bodies but not quite with them. But this does not make the rite a form of 'disciplinary coercion'. Although it is a training for everyday action and not an antidote to it—one is supposed to learn greater control in everyday life—this is not training in order to do anything. The forms of bodily control developed do not result in efficiency, agility, or dexterity as applied in the everyday world of practical activity. They provide no purchase of the sort that Foucault traces in penal discipline, for the application of power between persons.[38] The control that one learns through performance of this ritual is centripetal.[39] It is not a form of control which enables the body to act on anything but itself.

What, Foucault asks elsewhere, must one know about oneself in order to be willing to engage in renunciation and self-denial?[40] *Pratikraman* is, after all, a confessional practice. What does it enable one to know about oneself? What one learns, and is enjoined to apply elsewhere, is how to move and control one's body in the light of the truth that the space one moves in is already inhabited. This knowledge, it is true, might be asserted at any time. But here is a way, in both senses, to assume it: in the repeated, apparently obsessive searching and brushing and sweeping of *padilehan* and the firm and always self-monitoring bodily control which the anti-dance element in the ritual promotes. And the mirror of a developing sense of space is the constitution of a comprehended 'inside'.[41] Nothing could be more effective in charting for the penitent the boundaries of the body and in giving conviction, more certain than doctrinal

[37] That tradition includes Durkheim, *Elementary Forms*; Radcliffe-Brown, *Andaman Islanders*; Douglas, *Natural Symbols*; Bloch, 'Symbol, Song, Dance'.

[38] Foucault, *Discipline and Punish*. Elsewhere ('Subject and Power') Foucault clearly distinguishes 'dividing practices', such as those involved in the objectification of the mad, the sick, and the criminal, from techniques of the self, which are the ways in which 'a human being turns him- or herself into a subject'.

[39] This image, from the *Sutrakritanga Sutra* (Jacobi, *Jaina Sutras*, ii. 299), seems apposite: 'A wise man should conquer his greed, and enter upon the noble path, which contains all virtues and is not blamed . . . As a tortoise draws its limbs into its own body, so a wise man should cover, as it were, his sins with his own meditation. He should draw in, as it were, his hands and feet, his mind and five organs of sense, the effect of his bad *karma*, and every bad use of language.'

[40] Foucault, 'Technologies of Self', 17.

[41] Merleau-Ponty, *Phenomenology of Perception*.

assertion or even symbolic recognition could achieve (because, as Bourdieu says, it is not simply a state of mind, but a state of the body as mediator of self and world[42]), to the practical belief which informs the Jain conception of *ahimsa* and the aesthetic which it sustains. Thus one of the central doctrines of Jainism is remembered most eloquently not in words but in bodily practice.[43] And conversely, the reforming of the self which this confession aims at is achieved through what, using the Comaroffs' memorable pun, we can refer to as 'remembering' the body.[44]

Partial Reparation and Infinite Regress

At the heart of *pratikraman*, punctuated and interspersed with *padilehan*, *vandan*, and *kaussagg*, are three long lists of sins. Together, these lists give a good summary of Jain moral psychology, and also an illustration of the characteristic tone of Jain religious ethical discourse. The first covers the range of possible *himsa*, the second is a list of eighteen sins which includes *himsa*, and the third covers infractions of the twelve restraints (one of which, it will be recalled, is *ahimsa*). The first list is in many ways the most terrifying. It declares there to be 8,400,000 forms of life (*jiva-gatis*) in the world.[45] No moving, living being can avoid injuring and destroying some of these. We have no idea how many we have harmed, so in this confession, the Jains list them all.

700,000 kinds of earth beings, 700,000 kinds of water bodies, 700,000 kinds of fire bodies, 700,000 kinds of air bodies, 1,000,000 kinds of individual plant bodies, 1,400,000 kinds of collective plant bodies, 200,000 kinds of two-sensed beings, 200,000 kinds of three-sensed beings, 200,000 kinds of four-sensed beings, 400,000 kinds of gods, 400,000 kinds of hell-beings, 400,000 kinds of five-sensed animals, 1,400,000 kinds of humans.

The second list of confessions is the eighteen kinds of sin (*atharah pap*).[46] This begins with violence, and continues with lying, stealing,

---

[42] Bourdieu, *Logic of Practice*, 68–9. See also Connerton on 'incorporating practices' (*How Societies Remember*, ch. 3), and Godelier, *Great Men*, 232–3.

[43] On cultural knowledge being 'stored' in forms which are not linguistic or language-like, see Bloch, 'Language, Anthropology, and Cognitive Science'; 'What Goes Without Saying'.

[44] Comaroff and Comaroff, *Ethnography and the Historical Imagination*, 70. See also n. 39 above.

[45] This figure is also used in traditional Hindu cosmological writings. I do not know, however, of popular religious practices in Hinduism which dramatize the idea, or attempt in the way the Jains do here to shape everyday conduct in accordance with it.

[46] For renouncers too there are eighteen forms of sin, but the list is different.

sexual intercourse, and possessiveness (*mrishavad, adattadan, maithun,* and *parigraha*), thus covering violations of the five *anuvrat*s (Chapter 8). The remainder of the list covers the passions (*kashay*). Jainism ubiquitously uses two formulas for talking about these, and both are here. The first is the opposed pair, attachment and revulsion (*rag* and *dvesh*). One should be indifferent to pleasure and pain, love and hatred, beauty and ugliness. Attachment or revulsion of any kind leads to one or more of the specific passions, and this is the second formula. First come anger, pride, delusion, and greed (*krodh, man, maya, lobh*); then the subsidiary passions (*no-kashay*): quarrelling, false accusation, back-biting, speaking ill of others, elation or depression, deceitful speech, and heterodoxy (*kalaha, abhyakhyan, paishunya, parparivad, rati-arati, maya-mrishavad, mithyatva*).[47]

The third and longest list of sins is an enumeration of all the many ways in which one might infringe any of the twelve lay restraints (Chapter 8). This section is called *vandittu*. To perform it you crouch on your left leg, with your right knee raised in front of you, and your weight on the toes of the left foot. You hold your hands up, palms together, just in front of your forehead. The posture is that in which Mahavir attained omniscience. It is, as one nun explained to me, the posture of fighting enemies: 'soldiers adopt it [when firing a gun?], and so do we in fighting the enemies of the soul.'

Thus the lists move from the general fact of the already inhabited world, a fact which has implications for every possible action, through the passions which are the general motivations for all sin, to concrete errors and omissions: from cosmology through psychology to cultural practice. Obviously, the three lists are overlapping. We have seen something similar before in the vows for the twelve restraints, and much didactic literature and ethical teaching in Jainism aims at a similar effect. In general, Jainism has what looks like an addiction to lists: the thirteen categories of *jiva* (soul), each of which is further subdivided; the nine kinds of *punya*; the forty-two fruits of *punya*; the eighty-two results of sin; the fifty-seven means of impeding *karma* (*samvara*); the four hundred and thirty-two types of *himsa*. But the apparently analytical format should not blind us to how they work. Typical is the twenty-two kinds of 'inedibles'.[48] Among

---

[47] For variations in the content of the list, compare Williams, *Jaina Yoga*, 207, who gives *ratri bhojan* instead of *rati-arati*; and the *Uttaradhyayana Sutra* (Jacobi, *Jaina Sutras*, ii. 109): 'Anger, pride, deceit, greed; disgust, aversion to self-control and delight in sensual things [*rati-arati*]; mirth, fear, sorrow, carnal desire for women, men, or both.'

[48] Both Williams and Cort cite a list of 22 forbidden foods, although their lists do not

Jains I talked to the idea that there are 'twenty-two *abhaksh*' was fairly familiar. However, almost no one had any very comprehensive idea how of such a list would be composed. Occasionally, my questions provoked people to suggest we look for a list in one of the religious books or manuals they had in the house. The lists we found were often very mysterious. They contained some terms that no one seemed to recognize. In so far as we were able to work them out, it was clear that they aimed at comprehensiveness more than coherence, including as they did things which people are hardly likely to be tempted to eat (poison, clay), things which are not items of food at all ('food eaten at night'), things which encompass other items on the same list ('fruits with many seeds' and also 'aubergines'[49]). Sometimes these lists of forbidden foods contain more that twenty-two items, and in these cases they tend to trail off, having given *zamikand* as a prohibited category, into a dispiriting list of what looks like all the root plants the author can think of: 'tubers, green turmeric, garlic, ginger, carrot, radish, potato, raw potato, yam . . .' I think the real point of such lists, which can hardly be classificatory, is precisely to suggest that, strictly speaking, this list could go on and on. The list not only helps one to avoid prohibited foods, it also intimates how impossible it would be fully to do so. Both the content of the lists of sins in *pratikraman*, and the way they are used, conduces to a similar effect.

The penitent in *pratikraman* is not required, as a result of introspection, to report on the sins he or she is aware of having committed. This 'confession' does not require a review of the things one has done that day, an examination of one's conscience, or an account of how one has spent one's time. Indeed, the opportunity for such imaginative or evaluative thinking is systematically excluded. The ethics and the psychology of both shame and guilt are bypassed as an exhaustive enumeration is attempted of all the possible sins there are. After each list everyone declares that they 'cast off' the self which committed them. One repents of any sins one has done, caused to be done, or approved of anyone else's doing (*kiya, karaya, anumodan kiya*); whether knowingly or unknowingly (*jane-*

exactly match. Where Williams (*Jaina Yoga*, 110) has 'buttermilk with tiny lumps (*gholavataka*)', Cort ('Liberation and Wellbeing', 270) has '*dvidal*', which he glosses as 'articles which cannot produce oil, i.e. pulses'. In lists I saw in Jaipur, both these terms appeared, though people were very unsure about what they meant. And as everyone thinks of pulses as about the only food which Jains are always allowed, this is not surprising.

[49] More or less all lists of '*abhaksh*' contain the item '*anantakay*', that is, foods containing an unlimited number of souls; but I remember one book had a list of '*anantakay*', one of whose items was '*abhaksh*'.

ajane); by thought, word, or deed (*man, vacan, kaya*). Thus in this form of 'confession' one does not decipher, as Foucault has argued is the case with Christian confession, a unique self which is the subject of particular desires and misdeeds.[50] On the contrary those desires and misdeeds are located outside the soul that is discovered here. They are an omnipresent and unalterable fact about the world. Just who and what you are makes no difference to the passions and transgressions you recognize and 'confess'. Instead of an unique self, the penitent here discovers, negatively, that potentially pure, monadic soul, which is exactly like every other and which is progressively uncovered as the self is cleaned away.

The words actually used to cast off all these sins are, '*tassa miccha mi dukkadam*'. This is a Prakrit phrase, found in the earliest Jain texts, and difficult to construe.[51] Although few of them know the language, all lay Jains know some meaning or other which they assign to the phrase: 'May my sin be forgiven', 'I give up all these bad things', or 'I wish to renounce (*tyag*) my sins (*pap*)', and so on. Saying '*micca mi dukkadam*' is in some respects the Jain equivalent of the way Roman Catholics cross themselves. I have heard people say it if they drop a religious book on the ground, if they shoo away an insect, miss a regular visit to the temple, and so on. A none too pious friend of mine made this declaration once on finishing a meal containing onions. The people I spoke to (mostly renouncers) who had detailed ideas about the meaning of the phrase divided into two schools. Some said it means, 'My bad actions arose from error', that is, I know I must have committed sin, but I did not mean to, it was not from malice, and I am sorry. The second school went further. *Pratikraman* is also effective for sins you do mean to commit. Even if you did commit a sin knowingly, *pratikraman* makes you now see it as an error. Thus *miccha mi dukkadam* means just, 'The wrong thing I did was wrong'.

One does not say this to anyone in particular. Curiously, for a confession, there is no addressee.[52] Even if one's guru is present, the rite is addressed to a *sthapan-acarya*, the absent guru. And the *sthapan-acarya*, because it always points back in time and up the chain of pupilary suc-

---

[50] Foucault, *History of Sexuality*, i. 58–67.

[51] Scholars disagree quite fundamentally about what it means. I am extremely grateful to K. R. Norman and to Paul Dundas for explaining the difficulties. Shântâ (*La Voie Jaina*) and Williams (*Jaina Yoga*) take it to mean, 'May all that, done by me, be in vain (i.e. have no bad effect)'; whereas Caillat (*Atonements*) and most of the Jain renouncers I spoke to in Jaipur thought that the phrase made a statement rather than expressing a wish; a declaration that one has committed sin and now recognizes that it is a sin.

[52] Compare Foucault, *History of Sexuality*, i. 61–3.

cession, always points to the Tirthankars, who are not only dead, but entirely removed from worldly affairs. They could not grant absolution even if they could want to. If confession is effective in the Jain tradition, it is because it is itself an austerity, a contribution to removing *karma*. The 'heat' (*tap*) of ascetic practice is, as many of my Jain friends said, like an acid which burns past *karma* off the soul. This is why *pratikraman* should always contain periods of *kaussagg* and should be followed by a fast: to show that the *pratikraman* was not just an empty ritual, and in order to do the work of which the *kaussagg* is only a token. It is also why more *pratikraman* is required, with more *vandan* and more *kaussagg*, to cover a longer period in the fortnightly, quarterly, and annual rites. One does not list more sins, for in every performance all possible sins are confessed. But there is more to counteract. Longer and more regular scrubbing cleans proportionally more from the soul. In a sense *pratikraman* is not so much a confession, as the Christian tradition knows it, as a reparation, and it is always partial.

A kind of infinite regress lies just in the background. *Pratikraman* is after all an action (*karma*), and although its purpose is to remove matter (*karma*) from the soul, it always risks being self-defeating and causing the accumulation of more. It is punctuated with the precautions of *padilehan*. Penitents check as best they can that in performing penance they are not simultaneously committing more sin. In addition to repeated *padilehan*, there are repeated requests for permission from the absent guru before proceeding to the next stage; repeated penance; repeated veneration of the Jinas, the great saints, the sacred texts; and at the beginning of the rite there is confession and repentance of any sins committed in the attempt to confess and repent.

10

Fasting: Scorched Earth
and Fertile Soil

THE words Jains use for fasting are the same as those for asceticism in general—*tap, tapas, tapasya*—all derived from the Sanskrit root for 'heat': the heat that burns *karma* from the soul. Fasting is not the only form of austerity that lay Jains engage in (there are vows of silence, for instance), but it stands for self-mortification in general because it is easily the most widely practised. In this chapter I shall first survey the general forms of Jain fasting and discuss why they have to be governed by a vow; then I shall look at some elaborate magical fasts.

Elective Determinism

There are six basic kinds of fast: *naukarsi, porisi, upvas, ekasan, ayambil*, and *nivi*. *Naukarsi* is an overnight fast lasting from sunset until forty-eight minutes after sunrise. *Porisi* (or *praharsi*) is similar but lasts longer: for one quarter of the time from sunrise to sunset.[1] Both these fasts require total abstinence from food and drink. The remaining four kinds of fast differ according to the foods they permit (in Jainism fasting is often a form of eating, another reason why simply not eating does not count). Each lasts for a whole day; or rather, since one should not eat after dark in any case, they all begin at nightfall, continue through the night, the whole of the next day, and the following night, so last for somewhat more than thirty-six hours.

There are two forms of *upvas*: a four-fold fast (*cauviar upvas*) involves renouncing all food and drink, whereas the three-fold fast (*tiviar upvas*) permits drinking (*panam*).[2] One cannot drink just anything. Boiled water is allowed, and so is something the Jains call *triphala* water. There are, the

---

[1] There are, in theory, other fasts of this kind, which extend to other points in the day, determined by astrological calculation, but I have never known anyone practise such a fast.

[2] Four kinds of food may be renounced: 1. *asanam* (a meal or other solid food); 2. *panam* (water or any other drink); 3. *khaimam* (fruits or dried fruits); 4. *saimam* (things to chew such as areca nut, cardamom, or paan).

reader will by now be unsurprised to learn, lengthy classifications of different kinds of *triphala* water (twenty-one is the usual number), but the basic idea is that this water has been used to rinse a pot or plate so that the last scraps of food dissolve in it. Actually, only renouncers seem to drink this during fasts, and this is what enables some of them to fast for what would otherwise be fatally long periods of time. Most lay people who perform *upvas* take the four-fold vow, and most of those who take the three-fold vow drink only boiled water.[3]

In any event, *upvas* is the most common Jain austerity, and the building-block for extended fasting. There are a number of named targets to aim at. Almost every woman who considers herself seriously religious will try, at least once in her life, to fast for eight consecutive days (*athai*). Real virtuosi aim at a whole month (*mas kaman*).

Ekasan is a fast which allows one meal each day. From one point of view this is a compromise on *upvas*, which enables the old and the ill to participate in important religious occasions. The meal should of course be very frugal, consisting of a restricted range of foods, and I think in every case I have observed this was adhered to. In addition, it is firmly marked at the beginning and end by short periods of prayer so that no opportunity is left for extraneous nibbling to be craftily classified as part of the meal. To mark this boundedness, many people go to a religious eating-house (*bhojan shala*) for a specially prepared meal.

Obviously, it is possible to live indefinitely eating one meal each day, so it would be possible in this way to fast for the rest of one's natural life. Very few people do this, but there is a form of extended fast, of the very highest provenance, which exploits the possibility. In a previous life the first Tirthankar of our era, Rishabh Dev, had tied a bullock's mouth closed for six hours to prevent it from eating. This act attracted *karma* to his soul and before he could achieve omniscience he had to suffer in some way as that *karma* came to fruition. This happened when, as an austerity, he took a vow of silence. No one knew how to offer food to a Jain monk. People offered him jewels and all kinds of treasure, and all manner of delicious food, but every day he had to go without. It was only after six months, when a man named Shreyam miraculously remembered having seen Jain renouncers in a previous life, a very long time before in a previous cosmic cycle, that Rishabh was able to break his fast on some

---

[3] However, several devout laypeople I know do drink *triphala* water regularly, that is to say, when not fasting. To end your meal by rinsing the plate and drinking the water you have used combines a legitimately Jain ascetic practice with frugality, and is also an act of *ahimsa*, because it prevents bacteria from growing and insects from being attracted.

sugar-cane juice. In *varshi tap*, lay Jains emulate this, by alternating a day of *upvas* with a day of *ekasan* for over a year (*varsh* means 'year'). In this way they can perform the full six months of *upvas*, replicating the Jina's penance, and because the intervening days are *ekasan* they need not cease to be under a *paccakkhan* vow during the whole time it takes to achieve this. The fast begins in March, and those who complete it break their fast, as Rishabh did, around the end of April, on the festival of Akshay Tritiya. They all gather at an *upashraya* where they take *paccakkhan* for the last day and other lay Jains take turns in offering them small quantities of the juice.[4] So people of our degenerate times can participate in the asceticism of a better cosmic era, and replicate the super-human feats of great heroes of the past.

The fifth kind of fast is *ayambil*. This too allows one meal during the day, but specifies more precisely what kind of food it should be: one should avoid all the *vighai* (sugar, salt, oil, ghee, curd, and milk). Usually this means eating just a little boiled rice and roasted or boiled pulses, all without seasoning, and often just one kind of grain is used each day. The sixth fast, *nivi*, is a variation on *ayambil*, differing from the latter only in allowing salt. One eats only what people call *rukhi-sukhi* food: food which is plain, dry, and tasteless. There is a handful of occasions throughout the year when *ayambil* or *nivi* is specified, for one or more days, and on these occasions the prescribed food is provided at a *bhojan shala* for all those taking the fast. Partly because these fasts are also meals, they can be turned into social events, with all those undertaking them eating together every day, in a gathering which, although its purpose may be austere, brings people together in a way which can be almost festive. Many groups of renouncers, as a form of corporate *tapasya*, try to ensure that each day at least one of their number is on an *ayambil* fast and this, as we shall see in Part IV, can establish links between them and lay households.

I mentioned above how all fasts are performed under a vow, a

---

[4] The fast runs from the eighth day of the dark half of Chait to the third day of the bright half of Vaishakh the following year. Cort ('Liberation and Wellbeing', 294–5) gives a slightly different account of this fast. He says that Rishabh went without food for a year. This is also what Hemacandra says (Johnson, *Trishashti-shalaka-purusha-caritra*, i. 177). I have been told the story in that form once or twice, but mostly people in Jaipur preferred to say that they were completing the same *upvas* as Rishabh Dev, but taking twice as long to do it. Cort mentions that days of *upvas* alternate with *biasan* (like *ekasan*, but allowing two meals), whereas all but one of the people I met in Jaipur who were doing or claimed to have done this fast, did *ekasan*. I suspect these are just two of several ways in which local traditions vary, with renouncers teaching slightly different ways for practice to reproduce the mythical charter. See also Banks, *Organizing Jainism*, 86–8.

paccakkhan. Without this vow, not eating is simply not eating.[5] Every single person I ever talked to about this was crystal clear: if you break a *paccakkhan* your fast will not be effective, and in addition you should do some penance (*prayschitt*) to make up. You might go to a renouncer privately to take your vow, or join a larger group all doing the same fast. You can take the vow yourself, perhaps in front of a photograph of a renouncer, an idol of one of the Jinas, or a *sthapan-acarya.* You cannot fast by mistake or force of circumstance. It depends upon your intention, but the intention must be enacted in a specific ritual way before it works.

What is the point of the vow? If everything depends on *karma,* how does vowing alter the religious significance of what you do? There are I think three points to make. The first is to recall the theme we encountered in Chapter 2, of the religious importance of realizing and declaring that 'everything depends upon *karma*'. A vow detaches the identity of an action from the intention with which it is actually performed. Having taken the vow, whatever you subsequently think, your action can only be either success or failure in the particular act or acts you have vowed to do. There are no other possibilities (you have, so to speak, done all your intending in advance). In taking a vow to fast, a lay Jain deliberately elects to enter a domain of action in which spiritual victory (or defeat and sin) follows in a straightforward, mechanical, and determinist manner from the physical acts which he or she performs. And in the light of the importance in Jainism of acknowledging the determinism of *karma,* one can see that this is in itself a religious act. In some cases, as we have seen with *varshi dan,* the vow not only specifies the acts you will perform, but also connects what one does, via a narrative, to particular exemplary acts which others have performed in the past.[6]

Secondly, a vow to fast turns not eating into a religious action. One is doing something positive in not eating, because the vow makes this the realization of an intention, and so an act of will. And yet it is a non-action. Nothing will be done, and this, as we have seen, is the only certain way to abide by the principle of non-violence. The intention does a kind of disappearing act on the factors which normally make all action perilous. What it leaves, is an act without activity.

[5] There is a list of exceptions (*agar*), conditions under which one might break one's vow: 1. *annatthanabhogenam*—by mistake, without thinking. 2. *sahasagarenam*—because of rain or other splashing. 3. *mahataragarenam*—with special reason, having taken the permission of one's guru. 4. *savvasamahivattiyagarenam*—for reason of illness or great pain. This looks like a fairly liberal set of exceptions, but is not interpreted that way.

[6] See also Carrithers, *Why Humans Have Cultures,* 109.

And thirdly, having taken the vow, the meaning of what you do no longer depends on your thoughts as you actually do it: every fast of a given type, successfully completed, is treated as equivalent to every other. Undoubtedly, you should spend the duration of your fast thinking pure thoughts, but no-one would deny that you have still completed the fast if you fall from this ideal. The question of whether or not you have completed the fast is settled only by whether or not you carried out the formalized intention expressed in the vow. The determinism of a ritual fast governed by a vow is, so to speak, a refuge from the tyranny of intention, and the point of this becomes clear when we recall the view of the mind and its wanderings discussed in Chapter 9.

However, this effect, which one might call elective determinism, is actually evaded in the circumstances where one is most likely to fall foul of it. People who embark on a long series of *upvas* will take a separate vow each morning to cover the day ahead, and only take the vow for the whole fast on the last morning, when they are sure they will be able to succeed. Because they have been under a series of daily vows, the retrospective reclassification of each single day as being covered by, and an execution of, a single vow to cover the whole period is considered legitimate. Everyone admits there is an element of cheating in this. It would be better to take the whole vow in advance. But no one wants to break a vow, and if you have never tried before to fast, say, for eight days continuously, you might never take the risk. This practice also has the virtue of turning the point at which the vow is taken into a celebration of a successfully completed fast. Successful *tapasis/tapasvi*s arrive in procession at an *upashraya*. They hear their vow recited by a renouncer and receive her blessing (Plate V), before spending the remainder of the day there, perhaps performing *dhyan* and *samayik* (though often, in fact, asleep).

Fruitful Ambiguity

The *varshi-tap* is one of a whole range of formal, named ascetic practices, consisting of scripted sequences of fasting, usually with a mythological charter and tied into the calendrical cycle. In these, the ambiguity which is always present as to whether an action will bring worldly well-being or spiritual purification appears in a highlighted form, because the kind of well-being the actions might give rise to is actually specified. They are, one could say, more precise and specialist tools for acting on the unseen condition of the soul and this raises more sharply the question of the use to which they are put. I shall discuss two more scripted fasts, *naupad oli-*

ji, which is probably the most popular, and *rohini tap*, which is interesting because it is performed only by women.

Naupad oli-ji is a series of *ayambil* fasts. *Oli* means a string or line, and this refers to the fact that this fast, like several others, involves a sequence of days spent fasting and this sequence is repeated, at intervals, several times.[7] *Naupad* means 'nine positions' and this refers to the fact that the fast is associated with a particular magical diagram (*yantra*), the *siddha-cakra yantra*, which is divided into nine sections (Figure 1; see also Plate IV above). The nine positions on the diagram provide the framework for the fast. At two points during the year, once in the spring and once at the end of the rainy season, those who undertake this *oli-ji* perform nine *ayambil*s in a row. The full sequence laid down for the fast requires nine such strings of nine days, so lasts for four and a half years.

An *ayambil* excludes from the diet just those foods which, in the absence of meat, become the main sources of protein, fat, and vitamins. While this is obviously in the narrow sense ascetic, it is also a matter of self-cultivation. The fasts end on the full-moon nights (*purnima*) associated with two important Hindu festivals: Holi, in spring, in the month of Chait (March–April); and Dashehra, during Asoj (September–October), at the end of the rainy season. In both cases it coincides with a change in the seasons. Lots of people explained to me that at these times people become susceptible to illness, especially colds and fever, and that an oil-free diet was the best way to avoid this. The *vighai*, I was often told, cause idleness (*pramad, alasya*) as well as desire (*vasana*). As an austerity, performing the fast removes *karma*, but it also brings well-being and promotes health; the difference between these two unseen processes being always and essentially unclear. This fruitful ambiguity can be sustained only so long as the fast remains an action which is also a non-action, one not motivated by desire, or, to use a popular idiom, action 'only for purifying the soul'.

Like others which are tied to a magical diagram, this fast requires various forms of formal worship, or *aradhana*, including that of the *yantra* itself. Just what this consists of varies from place to place and according to the particular fast, but in all cases the people in a local community who are performing a scripted fast meet frequently together to perform a *puja*, sing hymns, recite prayers, and to attend sermons or religious classes. In

---

[7] Other *oli-ji*s include that for the *bis sthanak yantra*. This is a magical drawing with twenty different positions on it, and the fast requires twenty *upvas* within a six-month period, this to be repeated twenty times, once for each position on the *yantra*: four hundred fasts in all spread over ten years.

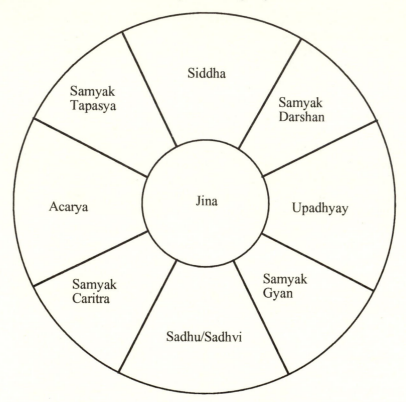

F IG. 1. *Siddha-cakra yantra*. This is the best-known and most commonly used magical diagram in Jainism. Two sets of ideas are represented: a hierarchy of renouncer statuses, and elements of the path to liberation, the *moksh-marg*. The Jina, liberated souls, leaders of renouncer orders, religious teachers, and monks and nuns are the same five categories as are enumerated in the *nokar mantra* as the five 'highest divinities' (Chapter 3). The elements of the *moksh-marg* are the perfected forms of insight or understanding, knowledge, conduct, and asceticism. In addition to its use in the *naupad oli-ji* fast, this diagram is used in many ways. Etched on a metal plate, it is used as an object of worship during *puja* (Chapter 4, Plate IV). It is a common theme of Jain painting, and many Jain families still possess images of the *siddha-cakra* which were used by merchants as mobile shrines in the days when travel was slower. A *siddha-cakra* was painted on paper or cloth, with the Jina, *siddha, acarya, upadhyay*, and *sadhu* all rendered as human figures in the appropriate colours, and this was fixed, perhaps under glass, on the inside of a saucer-shaped piece of metal (silver, brass, or whatever). A similar saucer was then fixed over the painting as a lid. From the outside, the whole object looks quite discreet, and is pocket-sized, but the travelling merchant could perform *puja* to it.

Jaipur, for instance, *naupad oli-ji* is celebrated slightly differently in the Dadabari and in the temples in the walled city. In the former, those on the fast perform *snatra puja* each morning before the *yantra* and an idol of Parshvanath (the twenty-third Tirthankar). In the latter, a *yantra* is placed in a specially constructed shrine to Shantinath (the sixteenth Tirthankar) in one of the preaching-halls, and those performing the fast worship here after visiting all the nearby temples in turn. Some people spend the whole day in an *upashraya*, and between formal rites they sit turning their rosary and chatting among themselves or with renouncers. Especially for women, a collective fast of this kind provides a rare relief from housework, and offers the chance to spend time outside the home, to socialize and relax in an irreproachably respectable pursuit. The day will end with an evening *pratikraman*.

The *ayambil* meal for *naupad oli-ji* in Jaipur consists of one type of grain, chosen each day to correspond to the colour in which the positions on the diagram are traditionally painted.[8] Boiled white rice is eaten on the first day, which is devoted to the Tirthankars, and also on days six to nine inclusive, when the qualities of perfect insight, knowledge, conduct, and asceticism are the objects of worship. The intervening days are devoted to the perfected soul (*siddha*), to *acaryas*, learned preceptors (*upadhyay*), and renouncers, and on these days the grains are red, yellow, green, and black, respectively. For the *puja*, people actively try to introduce symbolic order. Many bring offerings (sweets, flowers, fruits, and so on) of the colour assigned to that day, although not everyone manages to think of something. Men wear white clothes, as they always do for *puja*, but women try to wear saris which also fit into the colour scheme. However, there remains a certain tension between austerity and well-being: white is usually worn only by widows, and black is not an auspicious colour either, so many just approximate, wearing a light-coloured sari, or one with patches of white, and others prefer to wear a bright red one regardless, because that is more auspicious.

In these scripted fasts austere Jain ascetic practices—daily *samayik*, *pratikraman*, and the fast itself—are juxtaposed with the most gorgeous auspicious symbolism. In temple rituals a host of conventionally lucky things are used: coconuts, fruits, almonds, full water pots, fresh flowers, green leaves, unbroken rice grains, milk (but not honey), sweets, including big round sweets with flags stuck in. These things are assigned

---

[8] Banks (*Organizing Jainism*, 92–3) reports that this is not the case in southern Gujarat, where the same grain is eaten on each of the nine days.

meanings which refer to renunciation, self-denial, and asceticism. So when sweets are offered, for instance, this might be said to represent the transcendence of bodily appetites and pleasures. But then the same things are used in triumphal parades, where they represent the enjoyment of success, plenty, good health, and good fortune, and many of the same kinds of things are then actually consumed, when the families of those who have performed the fast host sumptuous dinners where these same kinds of fruits, sweets, and rice dishes are offered to guests in celebration of the successful austerity.

Rohini-tap is the only fast which is performed exclusively by women. There is a three-fold *upvas* once each lunar month, for seven years and seven months. *Rohini* is the name of one of twenty-seven heavenly bodies (a *nakshatra*). According to astrological views which are not exclusive to Jains, but are also common currency among Hindus, a different heavenly body comes into prominence each day, and this fast always takes place under *rohini*. The twelfth Tirthankar, Vasupujya, was born under *rohini* and one element of the *aradhana* prescribed for this fast is twenty rosary cycles using his name as a *mantra*. Rohini is also the name of the first of the sixteen great tantric goddesses (*maha-vidyadevis*) who control magical forms of esoteric knowledge (*vidya*) which they use to bestow favours on faithful followers of the Tirthankars.[9] Concentrated meditation, such as these women are supposed to perform, subdues these goddesses and persuades them to use their power for the women's benefit. Finally, Rohini is the name of a mythical queen, who features in the story associated with the fast.

Throughout each fast day the women are not supposed to show any sorrow or unhappiness. Even if they do feel unhappy for some reason, they must conceal this. The story tells why.

As the result of austerities in a previous birth, Rohini was an extremely fortunate woman.[10] She never had any kind of unhappiness. One day she looked down from the wall of her palace and saw a woman weeping, beating her breast, and pulling her hair. Rohini could not understand this extraordinary behaviour. What is this funny dance she is doing? She asked her husband, Candrasen, to explain. Candrasen, when he saw the woman weeping so bitterly, and saw his wife unmoved, became angry. He tried to make her understand. He explained that her son

---

[9] Shah, 'Iconography of the Maha-Vidyas'.

[10] There are several stories about the deeds which led to this. See Jain, 'Faithful Wife' for one of these. There is another famous Jain story about a girl called Rohini which is associated with the *diksha* ceremony and the five *mahavrat*s. This story does not feature, so far as I know, in the procedure for the *rohini tap*.

had died, but still his wife looked puzzled. In a fury he seized their own youngest son from his wife's arms and cast him down over the ramparts. 'Now you will understand!'

Some gods (*devi-devta*s) came at once and formed a cushioned throne to catch the child, so when the king took his wife down to find his body, they found him playing happily on this throne.

Rohini was also fortunate to live in the time of a Jina, and once, when the Lord came to their country, Candrasen asked him why nothing ever brought unhappiness to his wife. The Lord revealed that in her previous life she had performed a particular fast, and that this was its effect. So the fast is now named after her.

One of the many people who told me this story was a renouncer, who added the following gloss.

Someone who performs this fast will not feel any mental distress. Even if sorrowful things happen, they won't get upset, there won't be a deep effect on their mind . . . If we have done wrong then we have to bear the fruit of that, something bad will happen to us, but the effect of this fast is that we won't feel it so much. Some people cannot tolerate any difficulties, and some can bear them easily. My mother was like that, but I was not, so I am happy that I have entered the life of a saint because if I have to live with someone and they die, I could not bear it. Now I am free from all that. Perhaps in a previous life my mother has done this *rohini tap* and gained *punya* in this way, so she can tolerate unhappiness [we had been talking before about the death of the speaker's father]. If we get some bad luck or some difficulty and we complain about it, we get more *karma*s. If we bear it there will be no new *karma* to bind us.

So she is explicit that the fast brings *punya*: good fortune which here takes a worldly form. For each scripted fast there is some particular form of good fortune that is believed to be its fruit, a result of the merit (*punya*) or good *karma* that comes from it. But how can it be that worldly good fortune is the outcome of world-rejection?

Fortuitous Harvest

I have already mentioned that young unmarried women perform fasts in the hope of securing a good husband. *Naupad oli-ji* is not performed exclusively by women, but in Jaipur the women who perform it outnumber the men by on average about seven to one. Both times during the year when this fast occurs it overlaps with a Hindu fast performed by women, in both cases for the explicit purpose of ensuring the health and well-being of their husbands and families. As usual in Jainism, this worldly object is present, acknowledged, admired, and aimed at, but at the same time subtly hedged around: and the issue is whether or not, or in what ways, the desirable outcome is intended.

Each day after the morning *puja*, everyone performing the fast, and many who are not, gather in the *upashraya* to hear the story associated with it. It is a long story, with many sub-plots, and is told in instalments in renouncers' sermons during the nine days of the fast. Here is a summary of the story, as it was told to me by a Khartar Gacch nun.

This story takes place 200,000 years ago, at the time of the twentieth Jina, Ananthanath.

Ajitsen, king of Champapuri, was murdered by his brother, who usurped his throne. Queen Kamalprabha and her son Shripal fled to the jungle, where they encountered a colony of seven hundred lepers. At first the lepers were unwilling to let them join them, as theirs was not a happy life, but when the queen explained they would be murdered if they were found, the lepers agreed. Shripal contracted leprosy, and was elected by the other lepers to be their king.

One day King Prajapal of Ujjain organized a *swayamvara* for each of his daughters. [This is a ceremony in which a princess chooses the man she will marry from among a gathering of princes, assembled for the purpose.] Sur Sundari, who had been brought up as a Hindu, chose a husband; but Mena Sundari, who had been brought up as a Jain, refused to choose. Mena Sundari said that she had faith only in *karma* and *bhagya*—the results of former deeds and the fate which these lay down for you. The king became angry and said, 'There is no such thing as *karma* and *bhagya*. Whatever I say, that is what will happen.' He vowed to choose a husband to show her that he, and not *karma*, controlled her destiny.

Shortly after this the group of lepers arrived at Ujjain. When he heard, Prajapal immediately called Shripal to his palace and that very day gave his daughter to him in marriage. Shripal tried to persuade his new bride to remain at court, rather than accompany him to the jungle. Mena Sundari replied, 'If the ocean wants to exceed its shores, if the moon wants to leave its orbit, if the sun wants to rise in the west, then these things can happen. But I cannot leave the limits my *karma* has laid down for me. You are my husband and I should live with you.' This she did.

The people of Ujjain started criticizing the Jain religion, because of what Mena Sundari had done. She went to a Jain renouncer and asked him how she could make them have faith in Jainism. He made her a *siddha-cakra yantra* and explained the *naupad oli-ji* fast. Shripal and Menasundari did the *oli-ji* together.

As a result, Shripal was cured of leprosy, and revealed to be a prince. So Prajapal was proved wrong. And with the water in which the *yantra* had been bathed [the *prakshal*, see ch. 4], the seven hundred lepers were cured too. Shripal and Mena Sundari lived together happily, for a further eight births, all the time with wealth, good health, and happiness, but always remembering religion, until together they achieved final release (*moksh*).[11]

---

[11] This story is a distinctively Jain variant of a widespread genre, popular in Hinduism and throughout India, in which a wife's unswerving virtue and her religious devotion

Here we have not just a general hope of well-being, but a recipe for specific forms it can take, and it is easy to see how it can be read as a charter for women to fast for the health of their husbands and families. Although husband and wife both perform the fast, Shripal recovers from leprosy essentially through his wife's devotion and loyalty and her strict adherence to Jainism. And the cure is actually effected through performing the fast.

We should notice that what sets the story in motion is Mena Sundari's uncompromising affirmation that 'everything depends upon *karma*'. This is why she is married to the leper in the first place, and she remains with him because of her determination not to try to duck her fate. The whole story is a demonstration, not so much that she is right in this belief (that is taken for granted), as of the enormous efficacy the conviction gives to the religious actions of those who do believe it. The declaration, like a vow, makes everything she does into an action, 'only for purifying the soul'.

And we should notice too the relation between the intention which leads the couple to perform the fast, and its effects. The reason Mena Sundari gives to the Jain renouncer for wanting to undertake the fast is to glorify the Jain religion. This is *prabhavana*, one of the religious actions which lead to *moksh*. They do not undertake the fast in order to cure Shripal. Similarly, many Jain women who perform *naupad oli-ji* are very uncomfortable talking about the curative powers of the fast. People who are not actually performing the fast are often happy enough to discuss it in these terms. It is common knowledge that it has these effects: the Hindu *karva caut* fast does and why should the Jain fast be any less good? But if you talk to women who are actually engaged in it, or to any reasonably strict lay Jain in the right kind of mood, and certainly if you talk to a renouncer, they are likely to be very cagey indeed.

This might happen, but we cannot ever know.
People do say this.
Benefit can come in many ways, maybe this way too.

And sometimes people will flatly deny it.

How can someone benefit from another person's *karma*? Whose soul is in this body?
No. In Jainism *tapasya* is only for purifying the soul
No. This is not possible. That is just superstition

(usually to a goddess) save her husband's life and preserve her from the curse of widowhood. See, for example, the story of Gangala Gauri, from rural Karnataka, retold in Hanchett, *Coloured Rice*, 83–112.

At issue, again, is whether the same religious practices are understood in terms of the removal of all *karma* from the soul, or in terms of an ambition to accumulate good *karma*. Asserting that the purification of the soul is the higher path, and what Jainism is really about, is uncontroversial. But actually seeing things in those terms is not so simple, and acting in the light of that ideal is not simple at all. As an exclusive goal, the removal of all *karma* involves repudiating family ties and affections, not taking pleasure in the good fortune of others, abjuring the possibility of compassionate intervention in the world around you, and embracing a vision of the world you live in that makes all action of any kind sinful. Declaring all this to be true is one thing, engaging in sustained ascetic practice which embodies and mobilizes that vision is quite another.

But there are ways of massaging the difference between the higher and lower goal. I remember an occasion in 1985 when Caroline Humphrey, Marcus Banks, and I were on fieldwork together in Jaipur. We were staying in a university hostel and living almost entirely on oily institutional food. We joined a group of people who were doing an *ayambil* fast and taking their meal in the *bhojan shala*, which that day was red *channa*. Now, this was not all we had to eat that day, unlike those who were on the fast, but even so, when a plate of plain, unseasoned, roasted grains was put before us we found ourselves nibbling away with some relish, enjoying for a change a natural and simple taste. I forget which one of us first remarked out loud how nice this was, but we were all agreeing on the point when our host protested. 'No, no!', he said. 'This is tasteless, horrible food.' He treated us to a lengthy pantomime of hardly being able to swallow anything so unpalatable and soon had those around him doing the same. As the same man later explained,

The important thing is, we have only to control this [he points to his tongue], we have to control taste. [Laughs] Yesterday you said the food at the *ayambil* was tasty—but it was not! We must not think it was delicious. My mouth is like a letter-box—any parcel, letter, maybe a card—like this we should not taste it. This is action for the purification of the heart. If we are saying a *mantra* or eating at a fast and *bhav* is not there, we are thinking about other things, we are tasting, then rag (desire) and *dvesh* (aversion) will be there. That is useless.

This meal was going to bring good health, and beyond that general good fortune—but only because and in so far as the meal itself was an austerity.
  Here again is the renouncer I quoted above on the *rohini* fast.

The amount of fruit you get depends on the concentration (*dhyan*) you have in doing the *tap*. 'If all you plant is acacia seeds, how will you get to eat mangoes?'

Nowadays when people do this ritual (*kriya*) they get the effects in a small way. In Jainism *bhav* is always important.

So far she is insisting that the rites involved in the fast should be performed with conviction. They should not be done mechanically. You should have *bhav* and give some meaning to your fast. But not just any meaning will do. She continues.

If your *bhavana* (wish) is that you want this happiness, and you think this while you are doing the fast, in our view this is a big mistake. If we do any kind of fast or *tyag* (renunciation, including making gifts), we should not think that we will get this or that happiness out of it. We should do the fast only thinking that 'My *karma* should be cut', and 'My soul should become pure'. But if we do *rohini tap* thinking that we will get happiness, good luck, a husband, or children, whatever kind of wish we have, the fruit of the fast will be destroyed. If we do it without any wish, then naturally some benefit will come. The natural fruit of the *rohini tap* is to get the happiness that Rohini had, but if we do it for that reason, and with that in mind, then we won't get it. It is the message of Mahavir Swami that all our fasting, religious giving, and worship should be without any desire (*nishkam*), only for purity of soul. It is just like when a farmer grows grain, all he is thinking of is growing grain, he does not think that grass should grow, but grass will also grow.

In the light of this view of well-being as a fortuitous harvest, the women I quoted above being cagily agnostic about the likely effects of their fasting, and disinclined to think about worldly motivations and effects, seem to be hitting about the right note. It seems more or less essential for the distinction this renouncer is trying to draw that to purify one's soul is not something that can really be called a 'desire' (*kam*) and it is indeed such a blank and austere idea that desiring it is difficult to imagine. Perhaps the thought is that the purification is intrinsic to the act and not a separate wish. In any case, the hope she holds out is that if you concentrate only on this, good fortune may arise anyway—so long as you don't look. The way to pursue either or both these ends is the same. The action—whether it is fasting, worship, reciting prayers or *mantra*s, or telling a rosary—must be performed with *bhav*, where in this case, as in *puja*, this means that you should mean it. But unlike *puja* what you should mean is that you do not mean anything. The idea which we saw put forward in the *Uttaradhyayana Sutra* in its image of dry and sticky mud, the idea that to avoid sin you should act without pleasure or desire, turns out to be the key not only to making non-action possible in a world where sin is inevitable, but also to finding a religiously sanctioned place for good action and its just rewards.

11

Embodied Ontologies

ENOUGH has been said, I hope, to indicate how much Jain religiosity consists of acts performed on and through the body, and to illustrate the armoury of ascetic practice Jainism has developed for its lay followers. All these forms of austerity—fasting, repentance, observing silence, and so on—are ways of using the body in order to effect some kind of inner transformation. I have suggested that this involves using the body as the soul's ally against the mind, which is at once the most wayward and difficult to control of the sense organs, and, because it is where the passions arise, the front line, so to speak, in the defence against sin. The control of the mind enables you to act with the right *bhav*, which in the case of ascetic practice involves acting without any specific intention or meaning at all. *Bhav* comes to stand in this context not for symbolic or propositional meanings, but for the blotting out of desires, attachments, and purposes. I have tried to show how this way of thinking about ascetic practice, in which religious action comes to be seen as effective in so far as it is performed without desire, allows for an ambiguity, or plurality, in the purposes of ascetic practice so that ascetic renunciation and material good fortune may come to seem compossible. But this is not the only form that ascetic practice can take.

The Body of a Dualist

Just a few lay Jains, though remaining in their home and among their family, use these weapons of ascetic practice on a crusade which far exceeds in severity the rigours of institutionalized Jain renunciation, and they do so in pursuit of a construction of spiritual perfection and conquest which is different from those we have been examining so far. For them the body is not an instrument of religious progress, but an obstacle, and the main target of the attack. Such figures, although they are few in number, have a powerful impact on the Jain religious imagination, so it is worth looking carefully at what they represent.

One of the most celebrated such figures in Jaipur in recent years was the late Shriman Amarcand-ji Nahar. Although he died in 1976, some years before I first went to Jaipur, I often heard him spoken of and described as a 'real Jain'. His daughter became a Jain *sadhvi*. This is how she described him.

It was my father who allowed me to become a renouncer. Initially my husband's family all opposed it, but my father supported me . . . He wasn't a renouncer himself, but he was a very religious man. He kept a vow of silence for twenty years. For ten years he ate no salt, and for years he did *ekasan*, and he observed many limits (*napke*). Sometimes he ate only five raisins, and sometimes all he would have was *triphala* water. He fasted to death, for 36 days. For the first 12 days he drank water, after that, nothing at all. At the end he said, 'Now I will die' and sat in the *samadhi* position and he died sitting like that. When he died people said there was rain of saffron outside, and inside there was a sound of cracking and a wound appeared in his head.[1]

The details varied when others told me about him. Some said he was silent for twenty-seven years, or that he ate only a tiny, carefully weighed quantity of flour each day. But the facts chosen were always immediately apprehensible emblems of a distinctively Jain asceticism: he never ate green vegetables; he gave up salt, spices and oil; when he ate bread he always broke it into little pieces and mixed it with boiled water. No such details are ever explained. My informants would simply state them, because the conclusion to be drawn from them is self-evident: here is a very religious man, a real Jain. It is clear that he became something of an institution even while he was alive. Anyone who completed a long fast would go to him to receive their fast-breaking meal (*parana*) from his hands. Breaking a fast can be dangerous, but he could tell you what kind of food to take. He also had a more general influence, and one still meets people in Jaipur who gave up salt, pickles, or some other sinful food having vowed in his presence to do so.

Amarcand-ji belonged to one of Jaipur's prominent Khartar Gacch jeweller families, and earlier in his life he too had been a successful emerald merchant. His son now presides over the family's large, hand-

---

[1] This last remark draws on cultural tropes which Jains share with Hindus. A good life leads to a good death, one in which the body remains, to the last, under control. The soul can leave the body through several orifices. That of a sinner will leave an already decaying, incontinent body through the anus. The suture at the top of the skull is the purest point of exit. When a body is cremated, the eldest son helps the soul on its way by cracking the skull. In general, renunciation and the saintly life include the idea that one performs one's own funeral rites. An ascetic's death is voluntary, and here, the soul of a dead ascetic makes its own escape from the body at its most pure point. See Parry, 'Death and Cosmogony'; 'Sacrificial Death'; 'Death and Digestion'; 'End of the Body'.

some *haveli*. Like those of many affluent Jain families, this house has been extensively renovated. From outside it looks unchanged, but the old shutters and fly-screens on the inner courtyards have been replaced by large modern glass windows. There are fans, air-coolers, and in the main room an enormous divan, several modern sofas, and an imported colour television and video recorder. As in most such renovations, the elaborate painted pilasters, dadoes, and arches have been removed and now large expanses of plain, clean, whitewashed walls are relieved only by religious prints and the odd poster of an Alpine landscape or a group of cuddly animals. In this house the walls are also covered with scores of little printed stickers with short verses, prayers, and sayings. The family distributes these stickers, whose messages are those penned or favoured by Amarcand-ji, at *puja*s and other religious gatherings and generally works to keep his memory alive. Many of the sayings are rather gnomic, but his son was happy to give lengthy commentaries on them, and on his father's religious life in general. Perhaps the most common saying is, 'Liberation comes only through forgiveness' (*kshama hi se moksha hai*), and it seems he often used this as a *mantra*, repeating it silently to himself for hours on end. The obvious meaning is that to gain liberation one must practise non-violence. But it also means that freedom in this life comes from detachment, from not caring if others harm you. Another favourite is this one.

We have come [into the world] with closed fists, but will leave with open hands.
All luxury will remain behind, both body and wealth are mud,
The true guru teaches his pupils how to take gold from this mud.

Thus my body is no more part of 'me'—the pure gold that is my soul— than are my house, car, and share certificates. This draws together two prominent themes. The soul is imprisoned in its body by *karma*, in the same way that gold is imprisoned in natural ore. To be extracted in their pure form, both must be burned out, their worthless casings destroyed. Asceticism (*tapasya*) provides the heat (*tap*) which is needed to do this: to effect the numbing extraction of the soul from matter. An important prerequisite for this is that the soul must relinquish its own attachment to the body, and to the pleasures derived from it. The attachment is very great. We come into the world grasping ('with closed fists'), and at the mercy of our body's urgent appetites. Constantly we say 'I am feeling tired', or 'I enjoyed that food'. We confuse the body with 'I'. But only the soul is 'I'. Thus a number of *mantra*s and prayers concentrate on the theme that although all embodied souls are coloured by their association with *karmik* matter, the real, underlying, or natural condition of the soul remains present, although hidden and distorted. The soul is pure, and has nothing to do with this body it happens to inhabit. The truth that the body is not part of one is conveyed by Amarcand-ji in the saying,

> If it is mine, then it will not leave me,
> If it leaves me, it is not mine.

Jains call this 'knowledge of the difference' (*bhed gyan*)—the irreducible difference between body and soul. Fully to realize the truth of this is a prerequisite for spiritual advance and liberation.

Another of Amarcand-ji's sayings seems at first sight to go against this, and to signal a slightly more conciliatory attitude to the body. 'The body is well, the soul is glad.' This suggests that spiritual contentment might be reflected in bodily health, or that physical well-being might be necessary for inner happiness. But then, by the body being 'well' Amarcand-ji did mean something very particular. I was shown to the room in which he spent the last years of his life: a tiny cell with a thin mattress taking up one whole side, and apart from this only a small low table in the corner where the old man took his single daily meal. A glass-fronted cupboard set into the wall contained the shrine where he said his daily prayers. There was the usual array of small idols and pictures of the Tirthankars and other saints and divinities, which one finds in the domestic shrines of many Jain homes. The room remained as it had been in the old man's last days, except that it too had now become a shrine. On the mattress where he sat in meditation there was now a large, almost life-size portrait of him, and beside this another similar portrait, this time of the man he took as his immediate exemplar: the celebrated Jain layman from Gujarat, Shrimad Rajcandra (also called Rajcandra Mehta, or Raycandbhai). Both are shown in what would normally be described as an appalling state of emaciation (Plate XI). And in both cases this condition was deliberately self-imposed, slowly, carefully, and by degrees, by a successful and wealthy business-man. The point that Amarcand-ji is making in his saying is that the body is well because it has no desires. Though he slept very little, he did not feel tired; though he ate almost nothing, he was never hungry. He felt no pain, suffered no illness, and died contented. He had defeated his desires and attained equanimity. When the body is well in this way, the soul is glad. Vigorous asceticism subdues, defeats, and destroys the body. Neglected, and unable to make any calls on the soul's attention, it withers away.

Amarcand-ji modelled himself closely on Rajcandra, who also

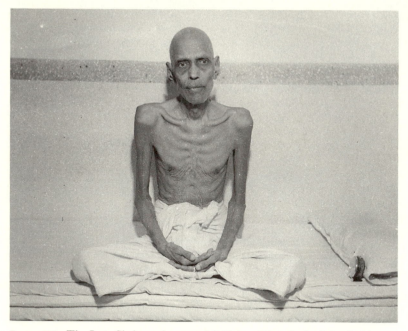

PLATE XI. The Late Shriman Amarcand-ji Nahar. Here, he is sitting in his room at home, where now a painting of him stands on his bed, propped up against the wall.

embarked on a path of rigorous asceticism without leaving his home or joining an order of renouncers. Rajcandra is known outside India because Mahatma Gandhi named him, together with Tolstoy and Ruskin, as the 'modern' people who influenced him most deeply.[2] He grew up in Saurashtra, Gujarat, the son of a Vaishnava Hindu father and a Jain mother. In later life he declared himself a Jain, but also, rather in the manner of Gandhi, a follower of the universal truths which are contained in all religions. He moved to Bombay where he became a successful gem merchant, or, as the Mahatma preferred to put it, 'a connoisseur of pearls and diamonds'.[3] He also became renowned as an astrologer-mystic who performed supernatural memory feats in public (a *shatavdhani*), and as a poet. Since his death, in 1901 when he was thirty-two years old, he has become the centre of a cult, almost exclusively of Jains, who hold variously that he was the greatest saint of our age, that he attained om-

[2] Gandhi, *Autobiography*, 73–5; Iyer, *Writings of Mahatma Gandhi*, i. 139–54.
[3] Gandhi, *Autobiography*, 74.

niscience, that he has been reborn in Mahavideha where there is a Jina now preaching (see Chapter 2), or that he was himself a twenty-fifth Tirthankar. The cult is based in Ahmedabad, in Bombay, and at an *ashram* in Agas, near Cambay in Gujarat, where the first of what are now many temples dedicated to Rajcandra was built. And the neo-Digambar Kanji Swami Panth (which as we saw in Chapter 9 is equivocal about ritualized asceticism) has adopted Rajcandra as a favoured object of devotion.[4] On the ground floor of the Nahar *haveli* a large room has been set aside for use as a temple. In all other respects this is a Khartar Gacch temple, but in 1990 an idol of Rajcandra had been installed, and was awaiting a ceremony to consecrate it.

Rajcandra is certainly the most prominent, and possibly the most un-compromising recent representative of a line of thought that rejects insti-tutionalized renunciation, and what he called the religion of the mouth-covering (*muh-patti*) rather than the soul. He is even reported to have induced one Shvetambar monk to break his monastic vows and become his follower. His best-known work, *Atma Siddhi*, opens with an attack on the outer renunciation (*bahya-tyag*) of those who have pride in their vows (*vrat-abhiman*), who are in thrall to the idol of the Jina or the glorious appearance of the *samosaran*, and goes on to prove the eternity of the soul, and that all souls are equal and capable of liberation through their complete separation from the body. Liberation is achieved when you realize fully that you are only your soul, that only the operations of the soul are truly 'your' actions. This form of realization, experience of one-self as pure consciousness, was declared by Rajcandra to be the real essence of omniscience and liberation.

Now although Rajcandra's claims for his own spiritual status do seem to have gone beyond what Jainism conventionally holds possible in our times, it is unlikely that he actually claimed explicitly that he was a Tirthankar, as many of his followers now do. And although both his reformulation of omniscience and liberation as states of consciousness, and even more his claim actually to have attained these states, were radical and unorthodox, it is also true that he exploited a possibility of contrasting inner spiritual with merely outer bodily religiosity which has deep roots in Jain tradition. In the *Uttaradhyayana Sutra*, for instance, Gautam Swami, who is Lord Mahavir's chief disciple, has this to say when asked whether a Jain renouncer should wear clothes or not.

---

[4] Lay Jain rejection of the spiritual authority of renouncers is much more prominent among the Digambars, largely through the various mystical interpretations which have been given to the writings of the early Digambar *acarya*, Kunda Kunda.

Deciding the matter by their superior knowledge, (the Tirthankars) have fixed what is necessary for carrying out the Law. The various outward marks (of religious men). Now the opinion (of the Jinas) is that knowledge, faith, and right conduct are the true causes of liberation, (and not the outward marks).[5]

The idea that a householder can practise renunciation while remaining in his household is one which today's Khartar Gacch renouncers also endorse. Here is an excerpt from a sermon I attended in Jaipur in 1990. The speaker uses the distinction between *dravya* and *bhav* (Chapters 4 and 9), which here we can take to be opposing contingent and essential qualities, to make the point that it is possible to retain a household and material possessions, without being attached to them. The essence, the *bhav*, of being in the world, is attachment.

Just as a lotus (*kamal*) sits in the dirty water, but sits above it and doesn't sink into it, so we can live in the world. We may live in a family, but we can choose to be like a lotus.[6]

> If I am in the world
> Then danger is far away.
> If the world is in me
> Then I'll surely sink.

This is like the difference between being a boat in the water and water being in the boat . . . living in the world we must do our own religious duty (*dharma*) but we must ignore the senses. We should stay away from the *bhav* of the world.

Another image of detachment, one of which Rajcandra is said to have been fond, is that a lay Jain can be like a nursemaid (*dhay*) to his family. The idea was explained to me by a Khartar Gacch Jain in Jaipur, a venerable emerald merchant who had given up business after his wife died.

A householder can be like a nursemaid to his family, he can provide for them and look after them. He can even cry when they are unhappy. But a nurse knows that really they are not her children. One day they will be taken away. And a householder knows that his family-members are not really his. He has only been given the duty of looking after them. That is a different thing. We should fulfil that duty, but we should also think of our soul, and we should not feel attachments. There is a famous story of Panna Dhay of Chitor. She allowed her own child to die to save

---

[5] Jacobi, *Jaina Sutras*, ii. 123.

[6] This image is a common one in India, not only among Jains. It is popular in renouncers' sermons, and occurs in the canonical *Uttaradhyayana Sutra* (Jacobi, *Jaina Sutras*, ii. 139), although there it describes a renouncer.

the child she was looking after. She had no attachment. Like this: for a house-holder to get *keval gyan* is very difficult, but it can happen.[7]

Rajcandra is said, through contemplating bodies being burned at a cremation ground, to have gained knowledge of his previous lives (*jati smaran gyan*), so he knew that in a previous life he had incurred a debt to his wife. He had to repay this debt by remaining married to her. However, like Amarcand-ji's idea of a well body, Rajcandra's idea of looking after his family comes as a bit of a surprise. I quote from an anthology of his works and sayings published by the *ashram* at Agas.

Educate the wife to high moral conduct. Consider her as one of the party devoted to Sat Sangh (the true religion) . . . True it is that out of delusion caused by *mohaniya karma* [the *karma* which produces delusion], some portion of her body is used for (imaginary) pleasurable experience, but keeping yoga constantly in the mind, forget this idea: 'What amazing pleasure I experience if she is there' . . . Fix conscious attention on the ideal even while in the act of experiencing physically the unclean deeds.

To help achieve this mental dissociation, 'after deep, serene and mature thinking', Rajcandra formulated his 'Views about Woman'.

It is only out of indiscriminate and faulty thinking that a woman has been ima-gined and taken as a source of worldly happiness, but surely that is not so. That part of the body used for the enjoyment of conjugal bliss, when looked at through the piercing eyes of discrimination, does not stand fit even for a worthy receptacle for vomiting. All the substances that are contemptible—all of them have a resi-dence in her body, and for them it is also the place of origin. In addition, the happiness derived therefrom is only momentary and a cause of exhaustion and repeated excitements.[8]

Two years before his death Rajcandra gave up his business and took a vow of complete sexual abstinence. He had other ways of developing detach-ment from the body. He would go out at night to places where he knew there would be many mosquitoes and there he would meditate while the insects bit his whole body, 'The more the bites, the more he engrossed himself in deep meditation'.[9] All the accounts of his life mention that he suffered from illness, but that he continued to practise meditation and to

---

[7] A version of this story is told by Rajputs in the region. The child Panna Dhay nursed was the king's son, and the story serves for them as an illustration of the virtue of devotion to one's ruler.

[8] Mehta and Sheth, *Shrimad Rajchandra*, 20–2; I have altered the English slightly.

[9] Ibid. 107.

fast. In the photographs which survive of him he sits in the same posture as Jina idols. This image has become an icon of strict asceticism for many followers, and one on which Amarcand-ji modelled himself.

Like Rajcandra, Amarcand-ji disclaimed affiliation to any Jain order. His daughter showed me a picture she carried which combines three photographs in one collage. This is a common device, used for showing 'spiritual influence' passing from guru to follower. Thus renouncers often have pictures of themselves superimposed onto one of their recently deceased guru (see Plate XIV), or onto a painting of one of the Guru Devs, with a ray of light shown flowing between them. This one showed her father receiving influence from two sources, from Rajcandra and from Shanti Vijay Suri-ji. The latter is an interesting choice because although he began as a Jain renouncer, he effectively left the order (Chapter 3). Amarcand-ji's life did more resemble that of a hermit such as Shanti Vijay than it did a normal Jain renouncer, because even though he remained in his house, he also withdrew, by remaining in his room and never speaking to anyone (renouncers, by contrast, have a religious duty to teach). I do not know whether Amarcand-ji too gave up rites such as *pratikraman*. His help to his daughter in joining the order suggests that his estrangement from institutional Jainism may not have been as deep as Rajcandra's, but his conviction that he possessed *samyak darshan*, and his commitment to a dualistic view of the body as simply the hated prison of the soul might well have suggested to him that his fasting was a more direct and effective way to break down its bars.

For lay asceticism to be enacted in the particular way exemplified by Shrimad Rajcandra and Amarcand-ji Nahar is very rare indeed (although they are not unique). The neo-Digambar Kanji Swami sect also teaches a radically dualist doctrine—the self, they say, just is the soul, and has nothing to do with the body—but in their case this leads away from asceticism (Chapter 9). Lay fasting in the Khartar Gacch is certainly dauntingly impressive, but it does not generally lead to self-destruction, and is combined in the ways I have already described with life-affirming celebration of the good effects that are expected to flow from it. For fasting to be turned into a concerted attack on the body is a departure from normal Jain practice, a subtle but decisive modulation of the themes I have been sketching in previous chapters. Here, the body becomes the target of a religiosity which conceives it as fundamentally alien—an ontologically distinct other, rather than a part of the self to be properly organized.

This kind of concerted self-emaciation can be distinguished too from the 'normal' practice in Jainism of fasting to death. Such a death (*samadhi maran*) is valid for both renouncers and lay Jains, but it is insistently distinguished both in teaching and in practice from 'religious suicide'. In the final stages of a fatal illness, or, in the case of the very old, at the natural end of life, people sometimes vow to accept no more food or water and thus end their life in a fast. This is an expression not of individual will, but of discipline. They must have permission for their fast from a senior renouncer, and this will be granted only if it is believed that death is anyway imminent (widely held beliefs about longevity being fixed by one's *karma* are relevant here). As with other fasts, the fruit of this—a good rebirth—might take many forms: wealth, heaven, the life of a renouncer, to live in the time of a Tirthankar. And the proper attitude arises from correct performance of the fast itself. Thus those taking this fast do not bring about their death, instead they accept it in an act of disciplined restraint.

Both Rajcandra and Amarcand-ji claimed already to have transcended their body's demands and desires. Their fasting was no longer a struggle against desire and hunger (for they no longer experienced these), and they were no longer concerned with training the body into sinlessness. So for them the body ceased to be an instrument of religious action. And absorbed in the perception that their souls were already pure, their concern was not to discipline the body and use it for religious ends, but to destroy it.

This then is a decisively different way of imagining the self, and the body appears differently too. Familiar ideas appear revalued and rearranged. Dumont has reminded us that it is not enough to speak of such cases in terms of different 'contexts'—an approach which artificially splits the life of concepts, images, and values into scenarios which have no dynamic relation to one another—but neither does it do to explain such revaluations by the supposedly 'bidimensional' character of hierarchy: reversals of value, he says, are 'foreseen, inscribed or implied in the ideology itself'.[10] Without Dumont's faith in systematic holism, it is easy to see that the innovations which occur far exceed 'bidimensionality' and that ideologies do not 'foresee' anything.

Gender and Self-Destruction

The echoes and parallels between this case and the medieval Christian female ascetics whom Rudolf Bell has described (evocatively, if also

---

[10] Dumont, 'On Value', 253.

controversially) as 'holy anorexics', are so strong that they call out for comment. I have found the recent literature on Christian female asceticism very helpful in thinking about Jain practice, but the parallels and inversions between the Christian and Jain cases are very complex, and I shall not attempt a systematic comparison here.[11] Two comments are perhaps worth making. Both are concerned, in different ways, with gender.

All the cases I have come across which realize or approximate to this saintly self-destruction among lay Jains are men, whereas both Bell and Bynum make clear that by far the majority of the Christian cases were women. And both these authors, in their different ways, interpret radical female asceticism as a subversive strategy against male-dominated religious institutions and the patriarchal culture which stood behind this. Obviously the Jain case is not simply an inversion of that—Jain society and culture are unquestionably male-dominated (in so far, which isn't very far, as that phrase picks out anything specific). But Jain renouncer orders are not. Despite the formal deference which nuns are expected to show to monks, they are in practice separate organizations and the nuns essentially run their own affairs. The dominance of nuns among the Khartar Gacch is not merely numerical these days, and in so far as renouncers wield power in Jain society, nuns do this quite as effectively as monks. Unfortunately, I have no evidence to suggest either way whether Amarcand-ji's rejection of institutionalized renunciation was a rejection of something he saw as female-dominated (the remarks I quote above from Rajcandra are certainly misogynistic, but they are also much more besides). Rather than dominance, it may be better to look to the coherence which institutionalized ascetic practice has with other aspects of everyday moral duties for men and women. It is worth noting that women's lives are substantially taken up with acquiring, cleaning, preparing, and distributing food, whereas men are hardly concerned with this at all. They have to decide whether to eat it or not, a decision which, when they make it, is a matter of their own religiosity and nothing more, and of course they are concerned with the questions of status which turn on when they eat and with whom, and these, on the other hand, have nothing to do with real Jainism as such. As I suggested in the previous chapter, women routinely fast as part of the general project of nurturing their family. Perhaps because women practise fasting so much more than men, the mythology

---

[11] See especially Bell, *Holy Anorexia*; Brown, *The Body and Society*; Bynum, *Jesus as Mother*; *Holy Feast*; *Fragmentation and Redemption*.

and symbolism which have come to surround elaborate scripted fasts refer much more extensively to women's lives (and if we recall the active attempts to invent symbolic correspondences which I mentioned in the case of the *naupad* fast, we can see *how* this might happen). This means that the scope for women to pursue Jain asceticism, yet still find value and success in their lay lives as women, and to see these things as congruent and mutually supporting, exceeds such possibilities for men. The point at which, in practice, asceticism becomes intolerant of life-in-the-world, and combining them becomes intolerable, may therefore come sooner for men than it does for women.

This brings us to the other remark I wish to make, which concerns the reasons people have for entering an ascetic order. This is a very thorny topic, and although I have lots of material on it, it is very difficult to interpret, not least because for a renouncer to talk about the subject at all except in certain very stereotyped ways is a sin. But if we consider first the case of a married person, it is clear that the choices open to men and women are different. Rajcandra's course of personal seclusion, sexual abstinence, and increasingly prolonged fasting would scarcely ever be available to a married woman within a household, as neither her labour nor her sexuality are hers to renounce. In one case I know of a woman in this situation was actively encouraged to seek initiation, so that her husband, as a 'widower', would be free to re-marry; and the woman was happy to express her flight from 'this world of suffering' as a triumphant escape from an unhappy marriage.

And in general, unlike the Christian cases, in Jainism men are much more heavily discouraged than women from entering an order. Dowry among Jains is high, and subject to a constant inflationary pull from the richer sections of the community. I know of cases where young women from impoverished Jain families chose renunciation in a situation in which finding a respectable husband was proving very difficult. By contrast, the loss of a son is a financial, organizational, and emotional calamity for the typical Jain family. They would expect their son to 'earn' a dowry at his marriage, to join the family business (and of course there are no problems about dividing the business resources of an entrepreneurial trading family), and to look after his parents in their old age.

There is a very great deal more to consider here: the extent to which images of renunciation chime with broader gender typifications, the extent to which renunciation can stand for women and men for forms of achievement that are closed to lay members of their sex, issues of sexual orientation in mono-sexual environments, and so on. So I would not wish to assign any unqualified causal role to economic considerations of this kind. But still, institutionalized renunciation, with its well-charted limits on self-mortification, its discipline, and its positive duties of teaching and pastoral care, is arguably both more attractive and more readily available to women than to men, and one can see why Jain men occasionally find, when they answer the ascetic imperative, that they undergo the passive loss of appetite for all life's values which William James saw as a feature of 'the sick soul',[12] but which can be read in this Jain idiom as spiritual victory.

Perfect Body, Perfect Soul

Although it is obviously and thoroughly ascetic, it would be a mistake to see Jainism as working around an absolute and antagonistic dualism of the soul and the body. The body may be a prison for the soul, but we have already encountered the view that it is the mind (one might even say the self) that is the enemy who keeps it locked up there. We have already encountered, in *pratikraman*, the idea of the body as an instrument of religious action—a body which is strong and well-controlled. Only the human body (not even that of a god) is capable of doing religious work and achieving liberation. Because the body and the mind are causally connected, bodily discipline and careful comportment are indexical signs of mental equanimity. This theme lies behind the use of pictures of Rajcandra and Amarcand-ji as objects of veneration. Their emaciated bodies are indexical signs of their inner state because their detachment from the body causes them to fast, and because successfully overcoming bodily desire causes in turn further purification of the soul. It is doubtful that Rajcandra would have approved the veneration of images of himself, as he explicitly repudiated idol worship, but he was proud enough of his wizened frame to pose for the rather staged photographs which are in circulation among his followers.[13]

I want now to look at a third topography of the self. Here, the body becomes much more than an index; more, that is, than a clue to something

---

[12] James, *Varieties of Religious Experience*, 127–65.

[13] One should raise the possibility that some of these photographs might be fabricated (they are certainly studio photographs, and in some the head and body do look somewhat disjoined), although actually it would not much matter even if all of them were, for the point would remain that they are the way it has seemed appropriate to his followers to show him. Indeed, if he did not actually look like this, the pictures become all the more eloquent. And if the photographs of Rajcandra are artificial, then Amarcand-ji certainly saw to it that life (or rather death) fairly exactly imitated art.

hidden. The severe dualism we have just been considering strains directly against some of the central symbolic resources of the Shvetambar tradition, in which the presence of divinity in the world is imagined very largely as the presence of a certain body, and in which religious experience consists of an encounter with the appearance of that body.[14] The stone and marble statues of the Tirthankars which are worshipped in Jain temples could hardly look more different from the photographs of Rajcandra and Amarcand-ji Nahar. The reason for this is that they exemplify yet another conception of how the religious subject is constituted and so of the relation between the body and the soul.

The body you are born with is, like your station in life and the length of time you are destined to live, a consequence of your former actions. It is a gross, outer, visible form of the subtle body (the *karmik sharir*), composed of *karma* matter, which clothes and engulfs the soul. One implication of this idea is that the perfect soul, that of an enlightened Tirthankar, resides in a perfect body. His spiritual qualities can be represented in iconic form because they are directly inscribed on his body, which can thus be seen as a catalogue of spiritual perfections—qualities and virtues rendered in bodily form. This notion has been taken very seriously in Jainism, and when the Digambar and Shvetambar traditions have disagreed about a whole range of fundamental religious matters— What is omniscience? What is the unique divinity of the Jina? Who can achieve liberation and how?—they have done so in the form of debates about the body of the Jina and the extent to which persons of different classes may come to resemble it. The most fierce and prolonged debates, which continue to be pursued today, concern whether or not the omniscient Jina continues to feel hunger and to eat; and whether or not it is possible for women to achieve omniscience and liberation. The growth and crystallization of these two debates, and the polemical contributions to them in medieval Sanskrit and Prakrit literature, have recently been surveyed by Paul Dundas and P. S. Jaini and I draw here freely on their accounts.[15] Early Jain texts do not seem to show a great concern with

[14] Michael Williams notes a similar ambiguity in Gnosticism: 'Odd as it may seem, Gnostics who called their bodies prisons were at the same time making a more positive claim . . . according to many Gnostic sources, precisely in the human body is to be found the best visible trace of the divine in the material world' ('Divine Image', 130). However, it does not seem that in Gnosticism there was a vivid and elaborate iconography of this latter thought, as there is in Jainism.

[15] On the debate about food, see Dundas, 'Food and Freedom'. This excellent discussion deals with disagreements between Digambars and Shvetambars on the question of whether or not a person who has attained omniscience continues to experience hunger and consume

the Tirthankar's body, and it may be that sectarian debate has been the main impetus in both traditions for the elaboration of specific views on just how divinity is physically embodied. In any case, the ferocity with which their views are expressed indicates how serious the question has become.

The body in which the Tirthankar is born is already unique, and as he advances towards enlightenment and the destruction of his *karma*, more perfections continue to appear. His body is infinitely strong, with adamantine bones and skin that cannot be cut, and is supremely beautiful and fragrant. It never becomes dirty, never sweats, and his hair and nails do not grow (so in this respect too his body does not produce impurities). His blood is as white as cow's milk,[16] his breath is perpetually fresh with the fragrance of lotuses, and his voice is always sweet and melodious. Although he eats and evacuates, these processes are invisible. (This is the Shvetambar tradition. The Digambars deny that they happen at all.) When he achieves omniscience, and is free of the four *ghatiya* (destructive) *karma*s, a halo appears around his head. Diseases, natural calamities, enmities, and even political unrest are all banished from around him. Signs appear on his body. The *shrivatsa*, a star-shaped sign which is said to represent a beautiful curl of hair, appears in the centre of his chest.[17] A *dharma-cakra*, a wheel representing both religious doctrine and universal temporal sovereignty, appears on the base of his foot. With unmediated knowledge of all things (*keval gyan*), he transcends the senses. The gods also arrange for magical flags, divine parasols, and a flying *dharma-cakra* to accompany him wherever he goes, for heavenly maidens to fan him, and so on. He realizes the innate qualities of the soul: perfect and unalloyed knowledge, insight, energy, and bliss. Yet he still has human form, so that form embodies and makes manifest those qualities.

food. The Shvetambars held that he does, the Digambars that he does not. On the debate about the spiritual liberation of women, see Jaini, *Gender and Salvation*. Jaini, in a book which is a model of how Sanskrit scholars can make difficult and inaccessible texts available to a wider readership, gives translations and detailed commentaries on some of the main sectarian polemics on both sides of this argument.

[16] It is sometimes said that his body too is this colour. But it is also often said of a few of the Tirthankars that their bodies are specific colours. Padmaprabhu and Vasupujya are red and Parshvanath and Malli are blue.

[17] The *shrivatsa* is also the emblem of Shitalanath, the tenth Jina, and is one of the *ashta-mangal*, a standard set of eight auspicious signs found in a number of early representations of preaching Jinas (such as the *ayagapata*s from Mathura) and used still as decoration for temples or for the cover of sacred books. For discussion, see Coomaraswamy, 'Indian Coins and Symbols', and Smith, *Jaina Stupa*.

The Digambars have gone further than the Shvetambars in etherealizing the Tirthankar's body, arguing that it becomes fundamentally unlike a normal human one, ceasing to require food or water.[18] The Shvetambars argue instead that his body is the perfect realization of the human one. It is refined and purified as it approaches enlightenment, but continues to have essentially the same structure, and to be sustained by food, water, and warmth.

The way Jains have represented the Tirthankars, especially in temple idols, directly reflects this deep theological concern with the body as an icon of the soul, and the differences between the Digambars and Shvetambars on these issues are reflected directly in the kinds of idols they fashion and how they behave towards them (Plates III and XII). Considerable stress is placed on the fact that an idol's body must be perfect. All idols show the Jina as strong and youthful. The stone or marble must be unblemished and the figure complete. The way perfection is conveyed is through a remarkably abstract treatment of both surface and volume in Jain statues. Although they are usually bulky in a way which conveys strength, with thick, trunk-like arms and legs, there is never any hint of musculature. Symbolic features, such as the *shrivatsa* are simply applied to an otherwise unrelieved surface and they never have any more integrated relation to the figure as a whole. Each idol is an assemblage of excellences, in which abstract ideas are given bodily form. As is the case with Hindu and Buddhist sacred images there are elaborate rules set out in Sanskrit treatises about the exact proportions of the idols, and prescribing features such as elongated ears and three creases on the stomach. As with similar texts which deal with sacred architecture, little art-historical work has been done to try to determine how and to what extent these texts have actually governed the production of images. The apparently absolute prescriptions of the *shilpa-shastra*s notwithstanding, sacred images in India clearly have a number of regional stylistic histories which cross the religious divisions of the patrons who commissioned them. None the less, the cardinal fact for my purposes here is that unlike the representation of the gods of the Hindu pantheon, each of the twenty-four Jinas is represented as looking exactly like all the others. Of course, sacred images are never quite portraits, but the formalization of Jina images goes beyond any other anthropomorphic tradition I know of. They manage somehow to be at the same time iconic images and abstract symbols—and to combine these in the human form.

---

[18] See Bhattacharyya, *Divinity in Jainism*, 40.

PLATE XII. A Shvetambar Jina idol. This bronze statue, of the sixteenth Jina Shantinath, dates from the early thirteenth century, although the elaborate backplate with flanking animals and attendant deities is later, possibly fifteenth century. The statue has lost the glass eyes which would have been in place when it was in a temple. The auspicious *shrivatsa* is prominent on the figure's chest, and the folds of his loin cloth can just be seen under his right ankle. The statue is now in the Victoria and Albert Museum in London, by whose kind permission the image is reproduced here.

The immediately striking thing about the idols in a Jain temple is that there is such a large number of them. If the temple is more than a few decades old, the idols will probably run into dozens, crowded in every corner of the building. The next thing you notice is that they are nearly identical. They may have emblems on the bases which enable you to tell which is which,[19] but from the figures themselves it is impossible to tell. Of course the style of Jina idols has varied over time and from place to place, and individual workshops and craftsmen produce recognizably different statues, but in each case they will produce idols of each Tirthankar which are exactly like those they produce of all the others.

There is a partial exception.[20] Parshvanath, the twenty-third Tirthankar, is easily recognizable because he almost always has a canopy of cobras over his head, like that on statues of the reclining Vishnu.[21] The reason for this is as follows.

Before he renounces the world and becomes a Jina, Parshva is a prince. He is in the forest one day and comes upon a yogi, practising penances by sitting in the heat of the sun, between four blazing fires. By means of his supernatural insight (*avadhi-gyan*), Parshva can tell that there are two snakes inside one of the burning logs, so he orders his attendants to extinguish the fire and release them. The snakes die, and are reborn immediately as Dharanendra, the king of the Nagas (snake spirits), and his queen, Padmavati.

Remembering Parshva's act of kindness, they become his devotees. The yogi on the other hand vows revenge. He is the latest rebirth of Kamatha, who has been an enemy of Parshva over many previous rebirths. He is now reborn as a demon and comes back to attack Parshva, who has become a renouncer and is deep in meditation. The demon attacks him in all the ways he can think of, finally sending a great thunder storm to drown him. Dharanendra transforms himself into a many-headed serpent and forms a protective umbrella over the Jina, by opening his multiple cobra hoods; and Padmavati, taking the form of a lotus, bears him up on the waters.[22]

---

[19] These emblems (*lanchana*s) include a bull for Rishabhdev, a water-pot for Malli, and a lion for Mahavir. These symbols are not found on the very earliest Jain statues, and appear to have been introduced first in post-Kushan images at Mathura, the full lists (which differ between Digambars and Shvetambars) being finalized in 8–9th c. Their use has never been universal, being preferred more by the Digambars than the Shvetambars.

[20] It could be argued that there are two: in some old statues, Rishabh is shown with long hair, and although the style of hair on Jina idols varies quite a lot, generally in line with local sculptural styles, this does seem to have been particular to him. But this is by no means universal. Indeed, I think it is now a dead tradition.

[21] Statues of Parshvanath with this snake hood have been dated to as early as 1st c. BC (Shah, *Jaina Art*, 8–9; Tiwari, *Ambika*, 3–7). Interestingly, the same motif appears in Islamic mythology in south India and in Buddhist iconography. Pir Nathar Walis is given water by a magical many-headed cobra and Shah Alimullah Qadiriyya is shaded by a cobra while asleep (Bayly, *Saints, Goddesses and Kings*, 130–2). The story of the tree-spirit Mucalinda protecting the meditating Buddha from a storm is rarely represented in Indian art, though it is common in South-East Asia (Zwalf, *Buddhism*, 30–1). But Zimmer (*Art of Indian Asia*, i. 60–6, ii. 71) detects a suggestion of a snake canopy in the halo of Buddha statues found at Mathura (which was also a Jain centre).

[22] Versions of this, as of most such mythological tales, vary. The one I give here is a digest

From the vast body of stories about the lives and former lives of the Tirthankars, this is the only one which is incorporated into the iconography of Jina idols. This is not because Jains are averse to representing these stories. Temples, preaching-halls, and renouncers' rest-houses often contain large relief panels showing several events from the lives of one Jina, usually arranged as small vignettes around a central picture of the Jina in meditation.[23] In all these biographical paintings, in idols, and in manuscript illustrations, all Jinas are represented as looking exactly like each other. Even Parshvanath's snake hood, though it is part of the structure of an idol, is added to a face and a body which is not distinguished from those of the others. So the multitudes of idols in a Jain temple are, essentially, the replication of the same image.[24]

Even more than Buddha statues, Jina ones are extemely standardized. They occur in only two postures: standing in *kaussagg* (on this posture in lay ascetic practice, see Chapter 9), and sitting in the lotus position with their hands placed palms-up, right over left, behind the feet and covering the genitals. The sitting position is that in which the Jina preaches from the *samosaran*, and although the earliest Jina statues are standing, and

of those told me in Jaipur. The following is to give some idea of the variations there are. In Bhavadevasuri's *Parshvanatha Caritra*, there is only one snake in the fire, Dharanendra, and the yogi knows it is there (Bloomfield, *Life and Stories*). Padmavati seems not to be mentioned; Bloomfield says that Dharanendra, 'went there with his divine wives, and placed lotuses at the feet of the Lord'. Burgess ('Papers on Shatrunjaya', II. 279) tells another version, which has only one snake, but Padmavati plays her full eponymous role in saving the Jina from the deluge. Hemacandra has one serpant (Johnson, *Trishashti-shalaka-purusha-caritra*, v), and Padmavati makes no appearance. The idea that there were two snakes in the fire is nowadays common currency, and in more than one Shvetambar temple in Jaipur there are wall paintings depicting this. It is not restricted to just the Khartar Gacch, as both a Kanji Swami Pandit (Bharill, *Veetrag-vigyan pathmala*, 47–9) and a Shvetambar Terapanth leader (Mahaprajna, *Jain parampara ka itihas*, 19) tell versions close to mine. Even local tradition, however, is not unanimous and one booklet of stories recently published by the Khartar Gacch in Jaipur gives a shortened version of Hemacandra's account (Shah, *Jain katha samgraha*, 47–51).

[23] These have much in common with popular Hindu devotional representations, including *par* paintings used in performances of oral epics (Smith, *Epic of Pabuji*) and mass-produced oleographs, on which see Pinney ('Iconography of Hindu Oleographs'). Pinney rightly insists that there is nothing especially Hindu about the narrative conventions these employ.

[24] A striking form of this replication is found in *caumukh* or four-faced idols, which are found in some temples in Western India, temples which recreate, in plan, the *samosaran*. The most striking example is at Ranakpur. There are also (Tiwari, *Ambika*, 9–10) four-faced idols which ante-date the first mention of the idea that the gods set up images of the Jinas at the *samosaran*. In these, four different Jains are shown back to back in the same statue.

these are still popular with the Digambars, sitting Jinas are overwhelmingly preponderant in Shvetambar temples. That objects of worship are so standardized is not perhaps very surprising, but the point applies also to narrative painting of the Jinas' lives. I am sure it would be possible to find exceptions (although I cannot recall having seen any), but in temple wall-panels, didactic pamphlets, children's books, and manuscript illustrations, from the point where he achieves omniscience the Jina is always represented in these same restricted ways. There are stories, which figure in the earliest texts, of dramatic events in the life of Mahavir after his omniscience (the dispute with Makkhali Gosala, founder of the Ajivikas, is one), but even when these are represented, Mahavir is not represented as doing anything. The events happen around him while he stands or sits motionless in meditation. There is in general a great reluctance, and one that I think has over time grown stronger in Jain tradition, to think of the Jina as doing anything in the period between his omniscience and his death, except that combination of meditation and magical preaching which he does from the *samosaran*.[25]

The physical form of the idols is a matter of direct religious concern because, especially in the Shvetambar tradition, temple worship is focused on it. In *puja*, worshippers brush, bathe, scrub, and dry the idol. They decorate it with flowers, rub it with oil, and coat it with sheets of silver foil. In one part of the rite, worshippers daub the body of the Jina with sandalwood paste. This is done in a number of ways. Sometimes the idol becomes covered with neat rows of dots, sometimes they are formed into a necklace or wrist bands, sometimes circles are formed around his nipples or his navel. However, the model which many worshippers have in mind as they do this is the *nav anga puja*, the 'nine limbs *puja*'. In this the following nine parts of the body are anointed in turn: toes, knees, forearms, shoulders, the crown of the head, the forehead, the throat, the centre of the chest, and the navel. This rite is discussed at some length elsewhere.[26] The aspect I want to point to here—the way this daily practice reads spiritual qualities directly onto physical form—is illustrated by this description by a Khartar Gacch nun.

---

[25] While the idol itself represents the omniscient Jain in the *samosaran*, ritual practice recreates all five stages of his life (see ch. 2). When an idol is consecrated, these are enacted in a series of ritual tableaux, with lay Jains taking the parts of the dramatis personae, and quite routinely there are rites in which five series of offerings are made, one for each of the five stages.

[26] Babb, 'Giving and Giving Up'; Cort, 'Liberation and Wellbeing'; Humphrey and Laidlaw, *Archetypal Actions*.

1. When we put sandalwood paste on the feet, we think that this big toe of God is so pure and holy. May its holiness come to me.
2. When the knees are worshipped we remember that it was with the help of these knees that the Jinas walked from country to country and preached for the protection of living beings. So, Praise the knees!
3. It was with these hands that the Jina gave gifts. For a year, giving away a lot of food, clothes, money, everything. The Tirthankar was usually from a kingly family. Not only did he give money from his state to the people, but the gods gave their coffers, they gave thousands every day.
4. When we worship the shoulders we think: these arms have so much strength that they can swim across the sea of worldly life. They have infinite strength. Give me also the strength to get across the world sea and become free from the cycle of rebirths.
5. We put sandalwood on the top of the head. The flowering of the lotus on the top of the head is true spiritual insight (*samyak darshan*).
6. We do an auspicious mark (*tilak*) on the forehead which signifies that the Jina is like an ornament on the forehead of the world. The entire glory of the person is centred in this auspicious mark. He is like a *tilak* of the three worlds. In spite of having a body, he was not attached. There is no deformity or anything wrong about him. So, praise be to you, Lord, that I have come into your shelter!
7. Because it is with this throat that he preached to the world: 'Remove all your sins from your soul, know your soul, where you have come from, who you are. Return to your nature, show the infinite knowledge and insight that your soul has.'
8. It is here in the heart that all evil is. So that heart [the Jina's], which does not contain any evil, desire, pride, anger, or lust, which has thought only of everyone's good, that heart alone is worthy of worship.
9. The navel is considered the origin of creation. Brahma [a Hindu deity] came from here. If the navel is pure, every cell of our being is pure. As is the seed, so is the plant. So the point of origin is responsible for evil as well as good.

There are two important differences between Shvetambar and Digambar Jina idols, and one remarkable similarity. First, the differences: Shvetambar idols have bright glassy eyes while Digambar eyes are carved; and Shvetambar idols wear clothes while Digambar ones are naked. These differences confirm that what is represented in the idols is the iconic qualities of the Jina's body, or rather, that his divinity is embodied.

The different eyes on Digambar and Shvetambar idols reflect the difference in the way the two traditions conceive of the preaching of the Tirthankar. Whereas the former denies that it consists of an act of ordinary speech, and imagines instead a divine sound (*divyadhvani*) emanating from the body of a Jina who is deep in meditation, the latter envisages normal human speech delivered in the vernacular of the day but which, with the intervention of the gods, becomes miraculously comprehensible to all. Moreover, Shvetambar tradition also presents what happens at the *samosaran* as a visual as well as a verbal interaction (Chapter 2 and Plate II). The listeners should see the Jina preaching and see him looking at them. This is why the deities place magical replicas of him (the original Jina idols) facing in all directions. Therefore the bright and arresting eyes of Shvetambar idols are supposed to hold the attention of the worshipper and provide a focus for a visual interaction between worshipper and idol which has much in common with Hindu, especially Vaishnava, *bhakti* worship.[27]

The second difference between Jina idols in the two traditions is that Digambar idols are naked while Shvetambar ones are clothed. The clothing is often very minimal. On seated statues some pleated cloth is shown sticking out in front of the figure, underneath his legs and feet (Plate XII). Sometimes a line on the body of the idol indicates the edge of a loin cloth, but often the idol's being 'clothed' consists simply of the fact that genitals have not been carved, and the place where they would be is left as blank stone behind the feet. This difference in the idols is not at all obvious on seated idols, as is shown by the number of ancient idols claimed by both traditions; although the Digambar insistence that the idols should be naked, and the fact that this means, essentially, that their male genitals should be uncovered, doubtless explains this tradition's marked preference for standing idols.

In her analysis of stories of the lives of female Christian saints, Bynum has shown how, where shedding all one's clothes served as symbolic authentication of the completeness of a saint's renunciation (of wealth, power, and sexuality), the fact that this was socially unacceptable for women prevented the biographies of female saints from realizing the same

---

[27] Toomey ('Krishna's Consuming Passions', 164) reports that Vaishnavite images of Krishna are said to consume food offerings. Worshippers receive his blessing (*prasad*) when they eat returned offerings, but he is also said to transmit his blessing to the food with his eyes.

degree of symbolic reversal and liminality as those of their male counter-parts. Judged by these lights, women's saintly lives were condemned always to be incomplete.[28] Jaini shows in his account of the debates between the Shvetambars and Digambars that the fact that women could not go naked was used by the Digambars as evidence that they remained attached to material possessions and subject to emotional attachments such as shame and vanity. Thus the Digambars defined saintly reversal in such a way that women, without seeming merely immoral, could not attain it. But the Digambars have also argued that the reason women's bodies should be covered is that they are inherently impure. To be born as a woman is the consequence of past sin,[29] and the Digambars argued that this made correct insight (*samyak darshan*), which is a prerequisite for omniscience and liberation, impossible. As the spiritual perfection of the Jina is evident in his body, the former sins of a woman are inscribed on hers.

As Kundakunda pointed out, her genital organs and the area between her breasts are a breeding ground for minute forms of life . . . Menstruation is seen as a source of himsa . . . preventing her from focusing her mind firmly on the holy path . . . The flow of menstrual blood is . . . the result of sexual volition. This begets shame . . . It also makes her subject to the constant fear of being sexually assaulted by males. For all these reasons the Digambars believe that the body of a woman is itself enough to render a woman incapable of attaining moksa.[30]

The Shvetambars have vehemently denied this. They have claimed that women are capable of achieving liberation and indeed that countless women have done so, including many nuns during the lives of the Tirthankars and at least one lay woman, Maru Devi, mother of the Jina Rishabh. They have even argued that the nineteenth of the twenty-four Tirthankars of our age, Malli, was a woman.

---

[28] Bynum (*Fragmentation and Redemption*, 34–41) argues that male hagiographers presented the lives of female saints in these terms, but that in women's accounts of their own or other women's lives, the focus is on how much resistance the woman has to overcome to achieve any such reversal. 'The message is almost, "be grateful for the little liminality permitted to you".'

[29] The Shvetambars too have thought this, but they have maintained that the handicap it represents is not decisive.

[30] Jaini, *Gender and Salvation*, 13–14. Dundas (*The Jains*, 242) writes that the attribution of these views to Kunda Kunda is incorrect. They, 'derive from apocryphal works and should be regarded as indicative of somewhat later attitudes'. Nevertheless, he also mentions other Digambar sources expressing similar views and it is clear that this has become Digambar orthodoxy, as indeed the attribution of the view to Kunda Kunda indicates.

This brings us to the remarkable similarity between Digambar and Shvetambar idols which I mentioned above. Regardless of which Jina is being embodied, even in the case of Shvetambar idols of Malli, and even though genitals are not actually shown, the body of the Jina looks un-equivocally male, bearing as it does all the other diacritical marks of male gender in Indian sculpture: broad shoulders, shallow navel, and squarish hips (not to speak of the conspicuous absence of breasts).[31] This is strik-ingly obvious in sets of statues of all twenty-four Jinas, where Malli is always shown as exactly the same as all the male Jinas. When one consid-ers what an important rhetorical point it has been for the Shvetambars that Malli was a woman, it seems astonishing that they do not give her a feminine body. On one level I take this as confirmation that the emphasis on replication and substitutability is a resilient feature of Jain religious culture. At a deeper level, I think it points to the fact that the gender of the Tirthankar is remarkably underdetermined by the doctrinal identification of his or her sex: and it is also, one should say, not in all respects unam-biguous. In fact, the representation of Jain saints in sacred images and in narrative employs conventions in which body parts and virtuous acts which are gendered male, female, or both at once, are attributed to per-sons regardless of whether they are identified as men or women.

There is a well-known story from the life of Mahavir, which I men-tioned above, when he is bitten by a snake (see also p. 163). This is a popular story which is often represented in narrative panels, books, and the billboards Jains use on their processions. The Jina is shown standing still, allowing the snake to bite him,[32] with the same impassive smile he always wears. He is bleeding, but the blood is white. A Jain friend ex-plained the significance of this.

You see Mahavir had no anger for this snake. He did not care about pleasure or pain. And because of his asceticism (*tapasya*) and chastity (*brahmacarya*), his blood was not blood but *amrit*. Like mother's milk his kindness is flowing out onto the snake, just as it flows onto the whole world.

---

[31] There may be exceptions. Alan Babb has found a photograph in a paraphernalia shop in Ahmedabad, which he was kind enough to copy for me, and which appears to be of a Malli idol with breasts. Neither of us has any idea where, if anywhere, this idol might be. The Lucknow Museum has a headless figure of a female ascetic, dated circa 9th c., which is probably Jain and could be Malli. See Jaini, *Jaina Path*, 72; Pal, *Peaceful Liberators*, 139; Shah, 'Rare Sculpture of Mallinath'.

[32] This is how people I spoke to reconciled this story with the fact that the Jina's skin is supposed to be so strong that it resists being torn or cut. Mahavir had such compassion for the snake and was so indifferent to pain that he allowed the snake to bite him.

There are two points to note about this comment. The first, and more obvious, is that the Jina is represented as having a body which is in one respect like that of a woman.[33] His compassionate role as saviour is equated with the loving kindness and nurturance of a mother. He spills his blood/milk so that the snake will be 'saved' by seeing the value of *ahimsa*. The same theme is taken in a slightly different direction in the notion, which I was often told, that the baby Jina does not take his mother's milk. Instead, he sucks his thumb and derives all the sustenance he needs from the ambrosia (*amrit*) he can obtain from there. This might be seen as distancing his physicality from his mother's biological processes, and from the pollution the Digambars see in a woman's breasts, but this is not how the point was made to me (and I have never heard it suggested, as is claimed for the Buddha, that he is born 'purely' through his mother's side). The emphasis instead is on nurturance, and here that the Jina is self-sustaining and self-sufficient, and this is rendered in the idea that he can be, in this respect, his own mother.

The second thing to note is that in attributing Mahavir's white blood to his asceticism and sexual continence, my friend is drawing on quite a different theme, one which, by contrast, relies on the Jina's being male. Chastity (*brahmacarya*) is an important Jain virtue for both men and women, but it is represented in different ways. As Josephine Reynell has shown, Jain women believe that they can neutralize sexual desire through fasting so that it is 'cooled' and transformed into a 'benign asexual force'.[34] Male chastity is seen, first of all, as a great deal more difficult than it is for women, and, because it requires the retention of semen within the body, as a process of accumulation rather than a stilling, cessation, and controlled flow. For a Jain renouncer, of either sex, to be found to have had sexual relations would be a scandal of astronomical proportions. It is expected that they will not, and their living arrangements would certainly make covert heterosexual relations very difficult to arrange.[35] But while I have

---

[33] There is an interesting near-parallel to this in medieval representations of Christ. Bynum (*Holy Feast*, 269–73; *Fragmentation and Redemption*, 79–117) has shown that Jesus was often represented in words as a mother, and that blood flowing from the wound in His side, though red, was visually equated with lactation. A parallel is often drawn between the milk Christ received from Mary's breast, and the blood and flesh He gives in the Eucharist. In the Jain case, although the blood is shown as white and is said sometimes to be milk, the wound inflicted by a snake, is usually shown as being on the Jina's leg.

[34] Reynell, 'Honour, Nurture and Festivity', 188–90.

[35] Homosexual desire plays an interesting role in the sectarian debates about whether women can attain enlightenment. An ancient text, whose authority is accepted by the Digambars, refers to liberated souls which are 'female' and 'hermaphrodite'. Rather than

never heard nuns described as such, certain monks are specifically praised and renowned as especially *brahmacari*. That is, beyond the fact that none of them actually engages in sexual relations, monks are none the less described as more or less celibate. Monks who were initiated before puberty are sometimes referred to as *bal-brahmacari* (child-celibates), emphasizing that they have never engaged in sexual activity. Shanti Vijay Suri-ji is popularly described as having been 'so chaste' that the *tez* (energy/heat) could be seen shining in his eyes, and another renouncer from Bikaner (a *yati*, whom I never met) was described to me as 'very chaste' so that sometimes you could see light shining around his head like a halo.

The background to statements like this is a set of ideas about the effect of retaining semen in the body, ideas which are certainly very ancient (they are found in the Upanishads[36]) and very widespread (they are reported from Chinese Taoism[37] and from the classical world before the rise of Christianity[38]), but which have been developed in India—in tantric and yogic thought and practice especially—to a degree that is positively Rococo. Dozens of texts announce that retaining semen leads to strength, knowledge, and immortality, and tantric texts describe rites in which adepts even learn to retract semen after ejaculation. Nor is this all esoteric and specialist stuff. Such ideas are widespread and pervasive in South Asia today, although of course they are expressed and evaluated in various ways.[39] The main point to note is that this is an understanding of chastity which is not focused on a direct inquisition of desire, but rather on the training of the body: unintentional night-emission is just as damaging as lust-driven intercourse, and so is a bad diet, which would impair the production of semen in the first place.

---

accept that this is evidence that women have attained release, Digambar teachers prefer to interpret the passage as referring instead to men who in their youth experienced forms of sexual desire which are 'proper' to women and hermaphrodites. See Jaini, *Gender and Salvation*, 10–12. However, Jain rules about celibacy for renouncers show no concern for the possibility of homosexual relations between them. I heard about no rules designed to prevent them. Male renouncers are, for instance, allowed to live and travel in pairs.

[36] Eliade, *Yoga*, 129–30; 255–6.   [37] Ibid. 59; 412–13.

[38] Brown, *Body and Society*, 19; Foucault *History of Sexuality*, ii. 15–17, 117–20, 130–3.

[39] Alter, 'Celibacy and Nationalism'; Cantlie, 'Hindu Asceticism'; Caplan, 'Celibacy'; Daniel, *Fluid Signs*, chs. 3–4; Edwards, 'Semen Anxiety'; Fruzzetti, *et al.* 'Cultural Construction', 13; Hershman, 'Hair, Sex, and Dirt', 288; Kumar, *Friends, Brothers, and Informants*, ch. 19; O'Flaherty, *Siva*; Parry, 'End of the Body'; Rudolph and Rudolph, *Modernity of Tradition*, 192–216; Srivastava, 'Religion and Renunciation', 177–9; Trawick, *Notes on Love*.

Carstairs reports the following from a Rajasthan village (where a great many of his informants were Jain).

Semen of good quality is rich and viscous, like the cream of unadulterated milk. A man who possesses a store of such good semen becomes a super-man. 'He glows with radiant health', said Shankar Lal. He excels all normal men in strength and stamina, both moral and physical. As an example, I was always told of idealised holy men, unlike those imperfect exemplars we had actually seen, whose life of celibacy and piety had brought them to this peak of condition.[40]

The blood which produces semen in men is released from women at menstruation, and in contrast to the purifying and enlivening effect of a man's stored semen, this blood is polluting. Menstruating women are prohibited from Jain temples, and forbidden to cook or to sit on soft furniture (lest they transmit pollution to others). Josephine Reynell describes how they feel themselves to be vulnerable to black magic and possession by spirits, as a result of the weakness that overcomes them as they lose this blood. This pollution affects even renouncers.

This impurity is so great that even to look upon religious articles is polluting. This was demonstrated to me particularly clearly whilst interviewing a nun during her menses. A second nun showed me a picture of the *naupad oli siddha-cakra* [*yantra*]. I turned this picture towards the menstruating nun for further explanation but she abruptly turned her face away from the picture in horror, saying that she would pollute it if she looked at it.[41]

Insofar as this discourse about sex and power recognizes women, it does so only negatively, and for the most part only as the occasion for semen loss by males.[42]

Thus, curiously, the white liquid which runs in Mahavir's veins, although it is 'milk' and represents motherly love, is produced through ascetic sexual continence by the retention of semen in the body: it thus relies on a way of figuring asceticism as male. This somatic understanding of chasity is another reason why even when it is female, the body of

[40] Carstairs, *Twice-Born*, 84.

[41] Reynell, 'Honour, Nurture and Festivity', 178.

[42] Van der Veer ('Power of Detachment', 462–4) reports a similarly asymmetrical interest in chastity among Ramanandis, who figure it almost exclusively in terms of semen retention. Although there are Ramanandi nuns they are, in this respect, 'quite marginal'. Alter ('Celibacy and Nationalism') describes the use of this imagery of semen retention in Hindu nationalist propaganda, which produces 'an unambiguously male ideology'; one which is, 'so fantastically skewed that gender—what it means to be a man in modern India—becomes a purely self-referential question'.

a perfected ascetic renouncer has to be, from another point of view, male.[43]

Of course, one should expect there to be, so to speak, counter-traditions, ways in which female chastity is positively imagined. And it should be said that in a Jain context cooling, stilling, and extinguishing are positive images, and not only for women. That lay women perform fasting and *pratikraman* more than men do, and that more Jain renouncers are women than men, is routinely explained, by both men and women, by the fact that they are more resilient and have more strength (*shakti*) than men. Women's subordination is also widely recognized, as it is among Hindus, in the proverbial observation that a woman's life is itself an austerity—a *tapasya*. And likewise the idea that asceticism gives women power, especially for the benefit and protection of their families, is clearly inscribed in the culture and mythology of fasting.[44] But in the classical Jain iconographic tradition sexual asceticism and the physical strength and vigour which results from it have been imagined and represented as attributes which are gendered male.

This last point recalls the Hindu paradox in which Shiva, the great ascetic, is also the god of the phallus.[45] But the Jains render this in their own, puritanically polite way. The Jina is never shown as ithyphallic. Shvetambars tend not to represent the penis at all, and even in paintings of Mahavir, who is clearly stated in authoritative scripture to have lost his only robe, a convenient branch always supervenes in just the right place to hide his genitals. And even in Digambar tradition, although the genitals, especially on standing idols, are prominently displayed, they are also always rendered (as Leach once observed is the case with Jesus in much of the Western Christian tradition[46]) as being rather small and childish. Thus if it is a male body which practises and displays sexual continence in the most effective way, and if the results include an increase in strength and potency, it is clear that this is not therefore figured as specifically *sexual* potency or virility.

---

[43] For discussion of other cases of the gendering of body parts, attributes, or acts, in ways which are not grounded in a pre-existing biological sex, see Bynum, *Holy Feast*, 247, who illustrates how Christ was at times imagined simultaneously as nursing mother and sensual male lover, and also essays in Collier and Yanagisako, *Gender and Kinship* and Sanday and Goodenough, *Beyond the Second Sex*.

[44] Compare, in Hindu contexts, Egnor, 'Meaning of Sakti'; Mitter, *Dharma's Daughters*, ch. 10; Tapper, 'Widows and Goddesses'.

[45] O'Flaherty, *Siva*.

[46] Leach, 'Pulleyar and Lord Buddha'.

I should say immediately that despite the vividness of these ideas about sexual continence and spiritual power, sexuality has never been elevated in Jainism, as Peter Brown argues it was in early Christianity, to be 'the magnetic pole to which all reflection on the extent of mankind's frailty must turn'.[47] As I have argued above, if there is an overwhelming and pervasively dominant idiom in which Jains talk of virtue, vice, and human frailty, it is *himsa*. While sustained sexual continence is practically possible, prolonged total abstention from food and complete physical immobility are not. Focusing on sex gave early Christian asceticism a tremendous dynamism and inventiveness, enabling it to formulate entirely new kinds of knowledge about the self, and to constitute a secret, underlying self to which sex gave particularly piercing insight.[48] I hope that my description of *pratikraman* makes clear that this kind of inquisitorial dynamic is for the most part very weak in Jainism. If you happen to have been tempted by sexual desire, this does not reveal anything particularly portentous about your soul. It is the fruition of *karma*, and a sin, but if you did not act upon it then its effect is past. The Jain focus on *himsa* as the 'magnetic pole' of human frailty switches attention onto constant monitoring of physical action. This gives rise to a dynamic which is just as relentless as the Christian one, but what it constitutes in terms of the understanding of the self is not a secret sexual self, but a pure soul embodied in a medium of sin; and what it develops, in terms of ethical practice, is an aesthetics of bodily discipline. Uncovering the soul does not require an interrogating search for a unique inner truth, but stilling the mind and body through discipline, so as to prevent the action which reproduces the soul's embodiment.

A Hierarchy of Embodiment

The body of the Jina is represented as a window on, and a material image of, his perfected soul. This is in contrast to a concern with indexical causality linking body and mind by which the body may be used as a tool for purifying the soul. It is also in contrast to a dualistic revulsion for the body and concerted destruction of it. The Jina does not need to destroy his body in order to free his soul. Indeed, his body is a fitting vehicle for

---

[47] Brown, 'Bodies and Minds', 483. Foucault ('Genealogy of Ethics', 340–1) came to a different view about early Christianity, but see also his earlier comments (*History of Sexuality*, i) on the importance of the confession as the prehistory of the achievement, by psychoanalysis, of constituting sex as a 'problem of truth'.

[48] Brown, *Body and Society*; Foucault, *History of Sexuality*, i.

that soul, and the means by which he propagates his doctrines and makes them available to others. I have described how this making available is replicated in the worship of Jina images. Jain temples contain other sacred images: those of powerful protector deities (Chapters 4 and 5) and also idols of Jain renouncer saints who have lived since the time of Mahavir. This latter set of images also employs iconic principles of representation, and we can see in these terms how the qualities they make manifest are systematically inferior to those of the Jina.

Mahavir had eleven principal disciples, each of whom founded a group of Jain renouncers, a *gana*. These leaders, or Ganadharas, are held in very high esteem by all Jains, located as they are before any of the schisms which divide the religious community today. Two are picked out for special veneration: Sudharman Swami, who survived his master and turned a new religious movement into a coherent and continuing organization; and Gautam Swami, the benevolent forerunner of the Guru Devs. Many Shvetambar temples contain idols of these two figures. They are shown preaching, and like the Jinas they sit cross-legged to do this. But unlike the Jinas, and like modern-day renouncers, they also hold a cloth mouth-covering up before their face as they preach.[49] And at their feet can be seen a renouncer's broom. These two objects, the *muh-patti* and the *ogha*, are emblems of the renouncer tradition and identify these saints as transmitting rather than founding the religion. But more than that, they signal that the differences between the Jinas and even their closest disciples are bodily differences. The Jina's breath is pure and cool, and would not harm the *jiv*s which Sudharman and Gautam's *muh-patti*s are there to protect. And the Jina likewise does not need an *ogha* in order to save insects on the ground. From the moment he attained enlightenment his body was raised above the ground and floated there. So, as exemplary Jain saints, these disciples are scarcely less naked than the Jinas. Their mouth covering and their broom, though beyond the boundaries of what we generally think of as the body, are no more external to their person than the Jina's broad shoulders or curl of chest hair, for they are required in order to complete their saintly selves.

Moving down in status, we come to the Dada Guru Devs (Plate XIII). These saints, as mentioned above, were all *acarya*s of the Khartar Gacch

---

[49] Sometimes Gautam has his right hand raised in *abhay mudra*—a position which is first found in the Buddhist sculpture of Gandhara. The term means 'do not fear' and the gesture is a popular one in the iconography of the Buddha. This strengthens the intriguing connection between Gautam and the Buddha which their names suggest, and which several of my Jain informants took for granted, referring to the Jain saint simply as 'Buddha'.

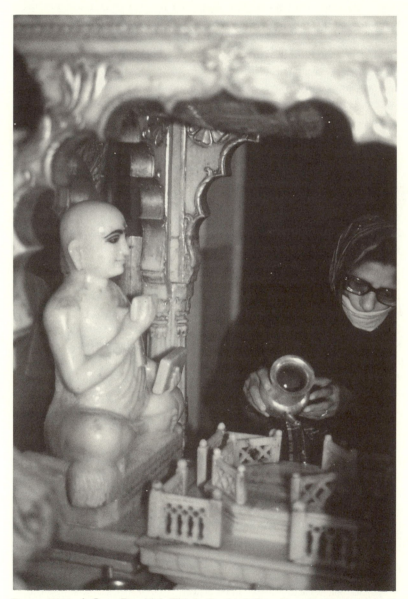

PLATE XIII. A Guru Dev idol. This is the third Guru Dev, Jin Kushal Suri-ji. He is carrying a book in his left hand and a mouth-covering in his right, and his brush (*ogha*) is lying by his right knee. The photograph was taken during *puja*. Blotches of sandalwood paste, left by earlier worshippers, are still on the Guru Dev's body. A lay woman, wearing a mouth-covering, is bathing representations of the Guru Dev's footprints.

and propagated the Jain religion not only through preaching and ascetic example but also by their miraculous deeds. Although the four Dada Gurus lived over a period of more than six centuries, and although they are each known for particular miracles they performed, places they went to, and people they converted or impressed, iconographically, like the Jinas, they have something of a corporate identity. There are not very many idols of the Guru Devs because until earlier this century they were worshipped at shrines which represented only their footprints. But now full idols are worshipped, and are spreading all over India from the centre of their cult in eastern Rajasthan. Even a footprint shrine is decorated with paintings, depicting the great deeds of all four saints, and in these too the four saints are indistinguishable. If one already knows the stories about their lives, it is of course easy to say which is which from the actions which are portrayed, but the figures themselves are identical. As with idols from the same workshop, in paintings by the same artist the faces of the four Guru Devs are rendered in exactly the same way.

Each Guru sits cross-legged, and like the Ganadharas he has an *ogha* at his feet, and a *muh-patti* in his right hand, held up before his face to show that he is preaching. But unlike the Ganadharas, his left hand does not sit on his lap as the Jina's does. It is holding a sacred text, a *shastra*. Having heard the doctrine from the Jina himself, the Ganadharas had no need of a written text. It was they who interpreted the Jina's words to his other followers, and helped to establish the oral tradition that only much later was written down. The Guru Devs, coming later, had to rely on texts. Indeed some of the miracles for which they are remembered involve recovering lost texts, and although they achieved great spiritual feats, they did not attain omniscience.

Only two recent renouncers have become the focus of cult worship in the Khartar Gacch. One is Shanti Vijay Suri-ji, whom we have met before (Chapter 3), and who, as we have seen, was the monk with whom Amarchand-ji preferred to be associated. His idols are much more individualized, showing as they do his beard and his features in ways which are recognizably similar to photographs of him. The other is a nun, and consideration of how she is represented brings us back, I think, to that tension between a dualist attack on the body and an iconography in which it represents spiritual perfection; and also to a line of thought which has led, despite the somatic model of sexual asceticism mentioned above, to a representation of spiritual perfection as female.

A Consecration of Suffering

Vicakshan Shri-ji (1912–80) was one of the *pravartinis*, or most senior nuns, of the Khartar Gacch. Almost immediately after her death the community in Jaipur began to canonize her. An idol was established in the Moti Doongri Dadabari, where she died, and others have since been established elsewhere.[50] The gathering I mentioned in Chapter 6, which brought tens of thousands of Jains from all over India, was for the consecration of a new idol of Vicakshan Shri-ji. She was a highly respected religious leader, and there is much that one could say about her teachings, but what concerns us here is the manner of her death.

When diagnosed as having breast cancer she refused an operation which might have saved her life, and through the whole period in which the disease developed she refused all medicine, so she must have had to bear the most terrible pain. She spent her last years in Jaipur, mostly at the Dadabari, and continued to preach and to encourage her followers to lead a more religious life. According to the accounts of her teachings which I have had from many lay followers in Jaipur, she turned the pain of her disease into an emblem of religious fortitude and ascetic endurance.

Unlike Amarcand-ji, who claimed not to feel hunger, Vicakshan Shri-ji felt pain. Rather than transcending the body's needs and feelings, she reinterpreted them as part of the process of laboriously cleaning the soul. Pain and suffering (*kasht* and *dukkh*), she said, are to be welcomed. Only a fool would try to avert them using medicines. Even if medicine works, it can only delay the suffering that is the inevitable fruit of *karma*. Pain is the *karma* from a past misdeed coming to fruition, and must be endured so that the *karma* becomes disentangled from the soul. Bodily pain is a form of *tapasya*, a purification just like fasting or performing *pratikraman*. Thus, declared Vicakshan Sri-ji, with this disease my whole life has become a *tapasya*. Accordingly she spent all her time telling a rosary as lay Jains do when they perform *samayik*. Conventionally, Jainism has distinguished between deliberate, vowed austerities, and endurances, which you do not bring about, but which you can bear more or less well.[51]

---

[50] There are others in Pipad in Rajasthan, in Duhol in Gujarat, and in Meharauli in the southerm suburbs of New Delhi.

[51] Removing *karma* from the soul is called *nirjara*, and this word is used as a synonym for *tapasya*. One way this distinction between endurance and active asceticism is expressed is by distinguishing the involuntary (*abuddhi-purvak nirjara*) from skilled destruction of *karma* (*kushalmul nirjara*). Vicakshan Shri-ji embraced pain and the experience of pain, rather than death itself. This fixes an important difference between her death and the mythos surrounding *sati* in contemporary Rajasthan. There are important similarities. The *sati*'s virtue is said

Vicakshan here transcends that distinction. By embracing her suffering actively, by welcoming it, by refusing the possibility of relieving it, and by performing the bodily actions of ascetic exercise, she appropriated and redefined her involuntary pain as voluntary asceticism. This consecration of suffering, and Vichakshan Shri-ji's message of forbearance as religious work, obviously had a tremendous resonance, especially among Jain women. She attracted many recruits to the order, and built a large and devoted following. People I knew still talked of Vicakshan Shri-ji as their guru, kept photographs of her, and observed fasts in remembrance of her.

The idols which have been established of Vicakshan Shri-ji are por-traits: realistic representations of a specific individual (Plates XIV and XV). The statues are eerily lifelike. She has red-tinted cheeks, wears spectacles, and is telling her rosary. She is represented as she is remem-bered by her followers: as a kindly, elderly woman with a smile that shows the combination of joy and pain that was her distinctive way of practising Jainism. I have explained how the associations of sexual continence in men make *brahmacarya* a potential source of spiritual authority in a way that it scarcely is for women, but that is only one of several ways in which a renouncer may be thought of as a 'real', 'strict', or 'proper' renouncer. Undoubtedly the quiet, patient, self-deprecating endurance which Vicakshan showed seemed to her followers, both men and women, to be a paradigmatically female virtue. But Vicakshan made it also a specifically Jain one. When she insisted that her disease was the fruition of *karma* she was making the same religious repudiation of common sense as Mena Sundari did in the story which is told during the *naupad oli-ji* fast (Chapter 10).

Vicakshan Shri-ji is, to my knowledge, the first female Jain renouncer to become a fully canonized saint. On the one hand, as a saint so recently deceased, in representing her in a realist (almost hyper-realist) way, the Khartar Gacch is simply extending the logic of the hierarchical scheme of

to produce heat, and this, in recent accounts, lights the funeral pyre spontaneously (see Courtright' 'Iconographies of Sati', 33; Vaid and Sangari, 'Widow Immolation in Rajasthan'). And this heat is popularly compared to the heat (*tapas*) produced by fasting (see Harlan, 'Perfection and Devotion', 81). In *sati*, however, the widow is said to embrace death, under the impetus of religious virtue and inspiration, but she is said not to experience pain. As Sunder Rajan ('Subject of Sati') has pointed out, this denial of pain, which relies on a dualist devaluation of body as distinct from spirit, is part of the discourse by which defenders of the practice represent the *sati* as wholly other and put her 'outside the circuit of sympa-thy'. The religious discourse on Vicakshan, by contrast, foregrounds her pain and engages admirers' sympathy. And it is not her death but the manner in which she bore it that is celebrated by Jains.

PLATE XIV. The late *pravartini* Vicakshan Shri-ji and a disciple. Two photographs have been superimposed here, to represent the relationship and ranking of the celebrated nun and her disciple, who is now also a leading figure in the Khartar Gacch.

PLATE XV. An idol of Vicakshan Shri-ji. This was the first idol of this nun to be consecrated. It is in the Dadabari temple in Jaipur.

representation I sketched in the previous section. They have also, as they always have, been borrowing selectively from the current representational practices of their Hindu neighbours, among whom realist and individual- ized religious images are currently the norm. But in another way these statues of Vicakshan are quite a radical departure, because she in not in these images returned to her physical prime, and shown as she is in some of the photographs I have seen of her, as a young dark-haired woman with a big, beaming smile. She differs from the strong, handsome youths who represent the Jinas not only in being portrayed as a recognizable indi- vidual, and not only because she is shown as a woman, but because she is an old, suffering woman. Like those of the Jina, her idols display her spiritual excellence through the way they represent her body and face, but the qualities thus represented are different.

Vicakshan is not exclusively a women's saint. There are in Jaipur still many women who were close to her in a personal way that men could not be; but although it is as a woman that she represents suffering as a religious virtue, it is not only women who experience suffering. It is not even only women who are constrained to bear it patiently. At the cere- mony in 1986, when her idol was consecrated, only women renouncers were present, but tens of thousands of lay Jains attended. There were more women than men, as there are at every religious event, but not in a greater proportion than normal. Some of the most moving accounts I have heard of her life and death were told to me by men, and when the moment came, just after the final rites had been completed, when her idol was for the first time officially 'enlivened' (*pran-pratishthit*), the frenzied crowd that filled the new building, trying to be among the first to touch and worship the new statue, had men and women jostling pretty equally. For a woman to be the focus of religious thinking about suffering does not imply that it is specifically women's suffering, but rather, as Kapferer has pointed out in the context of Sinhalese possession cults, that the women involved are 'central symbolic figures for the manifestation and projection of suffering and misfortune which Sinhalese, regardless of gender, period- ically experience'.[52] In the case of the cults described by Kapferer, this means women are thought of as the 'foci where the forces of disorder can manifest their greatest effect'. Women blame themselves for men's mis- fortunes, and men project onto women the misfortunes they experience, so that female subordination creates a role for women as a site for the resolution of conflicts which belong to both men and women. Something

---

[52] Kapferer, *A Celebration of Demons*, 142.

essentially similar happens in spirit possession throughout South Asia, including at the Jain temple of Padampura just outside Jaipur. But Vicakshan took the same gender stereotypes and worked them in a different direction. She took the symbolic salience of women's endurance of suffering, and passed it through the distinctive filter of Jain discourse about *karma*. In so doing she transformed that suffering into holy asceticism: a phenomenon that correct middle-class Jains find much more palatable than ecstatic spirit possession. It is too early to say whether Vicakshan Shri-ji's achievement will gain a permanent place in Jain religious culture, whether, like the Ok ritualists described by Barth or the possession priests in Sri Lanka so vividly brought to life by Obeyesekere, she will turn out to have 'made culture' from personal psychological materials, but the signs, I think, are good.[53]

Living Icons

I stressed above how temple worship in Jainism substantially involves a spiritual engagement with the bodily form of the Jina. Temple images are not the only way in which the absent Jina is made present in the world, for living renouncers, in their sermons, are identified in an iconic manner with him.[54] To begin with, the setting replicates that of a temple idol. Before the preacher there is a lamp like the one which burns permanently in a temple, and near it a pattern of rice grains, like that which worshippers lay out during *puja* (Fig. 2). The renouncer sits on the dais, cross-legged in the lotus position, her *ogha* at her feet. Before her is a *sthapan-acarya*, which invokes the line of religious authority stretching back to Mahavir. Her right hand holds her *muh-patti* up before her face, as do those of idols of the Ganadharas and Guru Devs; her left hand rests on her knee, palm upwards with the tips of her thumb and third finger touching, in a gesture which indicates that she is doing *kaussagg*, abandoning the body. This means that her preaching is a form of *dhyan* (meditation). And a good proportion of the audience are also performing *dhyan*. Women especially come to sermons and spend the time in *samayik*, sitting on their woollen mats, their eyes closed, telling their rosaries.

The content of these sermons is often formulaic. Well-known stories are retold and lists of categories in Jain philosophy expounded. At certain times of the year, the sermons are elementary, being aimed at a wide

[53] Barth, *Cosmologies in the Making*; Obeyesekere, *Medusa's Hair*.

[54] Indeed, in the traditions which reject the use of idols, this mode seems to be correspondingly increased in importance.

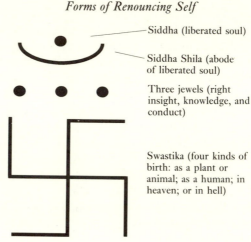

FIG. 2. Rice pattern used in temple-worship and at sermons. The pattern consists of a swastika nearest the worshipper or listener, then three dots, and above this, nearest the Jina/renouncer, another dot just above a curved line (like a crescent-moon lying 'on its back'). The most common interpretation of this would be as follows. The swastika represents the cycle of rebirth (*samsar*), and hence the state of bondage of the unenlightened. Each one of the four arms of the swastika represents one possible type of rebirth: as a deity, a human, an animal or plant, and a hell-being. The left-hand arm, pointing up, represents a human birth, the only one that can lead to liberation. The three dots represent the three jewels (*tri ratna*) of Jainism: right insight (*samyak darshan*), right knowledge (*samyak gyan*), and right conduct (*samyak caritra*). The curved line is the place (*siddha shila*) at the top of the universe to which a liberated soul, represented by the dot, will rise.

audience, so of little interest to the more devoutly religious who attend regularly. The conflict between the religious duty to attend sermons and the boredom of actually being there is one that arises, no doubt, in every religion that makes much of the practice. Innovative and excellent sermons are highly valued in Jainism. A few renouncers are renowned for good sermons, and tape recordings of some of these are circulated for people to listen to at home. But Jain renouncers preach a lot. A group is expected to provide sermons for at least an hour every day it is in residence in a town, and for longer during Caturmas. It would be a fine achievement if these sermons were always worth listening to. But as in many other religious traditions, they are constructed in such a way that they are felt to be worth hearing, even if not much worth listening to.

Tambiah has discussed this at length in the case of Theravada

Buddhism. In his view, in Buddhist sermons and *paritta* chanting, the merit of the Buddha's deeds is transferred to the audience, metaphorically through the utterance of his own words (even though the audience cannot always understand them) and metonymically through actions using sacred chords, lustral water, and other material objects. Like those who attend Jain sermons, Buddhist audiences arrive and leave when they like without having to wait for the whole of the sermon. 'Thus all considered, it is not a distortion to say that more important than the understanding is the hearing, in the proper context and setting, of chants and sermons delivered by the appropriate person'.[55]

This formulation is true of Jain sermons, at least of not very good ones, but it is not quite all there is to say. I put the idea once to a Jain friend of mine, and he began by rejecting it out of hand, before coming back to his own formulation.

If you load a donkey with many books, will it be wise? Will it have knowledge? We can learn from the teachings of a guru. But we can even learn from a sermon by a *sadhu* who has no knowledge, and even by looking. There are many examples. I can give good advice, even if my own thoughts are bad. I can be telling you about religion, but thinking about that friend of yours; what is her name? (laughs) And you would still become wise. Seeing a *sadhu* too can give us knowledge. We look at them preaching and think, 'Ah, he walks on bare feet, he has no clothes of his own, he goes begging for all his food.' Just as they have given up everything, so too should we. This is what Lord Mahavir did. They are doing as Mahavir did. So we can come to know what Jainism is.

The last of this man's comments, about deriving knowledge of Jain doctrine from looking at renouncers, is exactly what people say about looking at Jina idols in a temple. The interaction in a Jain sermon is as much visual as verbal, in a combination which is well expressed in the *Candravedhyaka Sutra*,

What is more ravishing, more marvellous and more magnificent?
As they look at the moon, so everyone contemplates the face of teachers.
As light comes from the moon, from the face of teachers comes the speech of the
   Jina.
Hearing this, people cross the jungle of rebirth.[56]

---

[55] Tambiah, *Buddhism and the Spirit Cults*, 196. On Buddhist sermons in Sri Lanka, compare Gombrich, *Precept and Practice*, 201–6. See also below (ch. 12), the section on 'The Archetypal Sermon'.

[56] Caillat, *Candavejjhaya*, 81–2.

The ceremony in which one pays respect to a living renouncer is *guru vandan* (see Chapter 9), and although this can be done in an abbreviated form—in the case of regular daily encounters it can consist of just a single full prostration and a short salutation—it is thought of as being essentially continuous with worship of Jina images, specifically that part of temple worship which is called *caitya vandan*. A different continuity with temple worship can be seen in practices of reverence directed at the feet of living renouncers. Touching someone's feet, especially the right toe, as a mark of respect is common currency in Indic culture, and it is especially prevalent in guru-cults in contemporary Hinduism (see also Chapters 2 and 4 above). The Dada Guru Devs are most commonly worshipped in the form of stone or marble footprint shrines, which are bathed, and anointed with flowers and sandalwood paste. Jain devotees also anoint the toes of living renouncers with sandalwood—usually powder, or *vasakshep*, rather than paste—and this practice is commonly referred to as *guru puja*.

When a statue of a Guru Dev is worshipped, then instead of just the feet, the whole body is bathed and anointed in the nine-limbs (*nav-anga*) *puja*, just as with Jina statues. And John Cort has described how in the mid-1980s one group of lay Jains in Gujarat made the controversial decision to extend the *guru puja* which they performed to their guru—the Tapa Gacch monk, Acarya Ramcandra Suri—in a similar way. They proposed to anoint nine parts of his body with sandalwood powder. The idea caused instant controversy, because the elevation of Ramcandra Suri's status which was implicit in the proposal was immediately apprehended by rival renouncers and their followers. Debate raged in the newspapers about whether scripture permitted such a practice, and Ramcandra Suri was accused of setting himself up as a twenty-fifth Tirthankar. In the end his followers compromised just a little. They went ahead with the *puja*, and even performed it in a temple, but they drew a curtain in front of the presiding Jina statue so that it would not be offended.[57]

The line that was crossed here is a thin one. The idols of deceased renouncers such as Gautam Swami, the Guru Devs, Shanti Suri, and Vicakshan Shri-ji are all worshipped in this way, and Cort describes worshippers at the funeral ceremonies for one recently deceased renouncer being prevented only by the constant vigilance of lay officials from extending their devotions from the corpse's toes to other parts of the body.[58]

---

[57] Cort, 'Liberation and Wellbeing', 331–2.   [58] Ibid. 332–3.

Reverence for Jain renouncers thus uses the same modes as worship of Jina idols: similar gestures and texts, the same emphasis on visual interaction, the same concern with bodily contact. Like the Jina idol, the renouncer then is a presence, though attenuated and partial, of the perfect soul. But if idols and renouncers are both in their ways icons of the living Jina, the relations between these two icons are curiously complex.

Paradoxical Purities

Lay Jains have remarkably direct and unmediated access to the idols they worship. For morning *puja*, no congregation or quorum is needed. Anyone may come to a temple and worship, and how they do this is to a considerable degree a matter of individual choice. There are no fixed rules and there is no priest to order and orchestrate the worshipper's acts or to impose an official interpretation on them. But householders must ensure that their bodies are pure for *puja*. There are a number of restrictions to observe, but the most important is that immediately before *puja*, they must bathe. As described above, *puja* is an intimate ritual involving bodily service to the idol and purity is required as an expression of reverence and respect.[59]

Renouncers, by contrast, may not touch consecrated temple idols. It is a senior renouncer (always, I suspect, male) who performs the crucial act of the consecration ceremony, by painting its eyes with kohl and, as people say, 'giving the idol omniscience'.[60] But once the idol has been consecrated, new rules apply. Lay Jains, if they have not prepared properly for *puja*, may come to the temple in their normal clothes, worship the idols, and take *darshan* from them, so long as they do not enter the sanctum or touch the idols. Renouncers are in just this position. They may come into the temples and worship, but they may not perform the intimate rites of *puja*. While the lay worshipper climbs up to join the idol on its marble plinth, crouching there the better to scrub and decorate it, the renouncer may only meditate on the idol from the main temple hall. Why is this? One nun explained.

---

[59] And a clean and fragrant body is more fit too for the ritual mirroring of the Jina in worship (Humphrey and Laidlaw, *Archetypal Actions*, 249–50).

[60] This in itself is paradoxical, because the renouncer, of course, does not himself possess omniscience. The rite (*anjan shalaka*) has close parallels in Theravada Buddhism (Gombrich, 'Consecration of a Buddhist Image'; Tambiah, *Saints of the Forest*, ch. 17) and in Hindu practice (Fuller, *Camphor Flame*, 60).

First, it is necessary to take a bath for *puja*, to make the body pure. Second, flowers are used in *puja*, and we cannot touch flowers because there might be insects in them and also they [the flowers] will die. And also, we cannot use *dravya* (things) for we have given up everything, so we cannot do *dravya puja* (those parts of the rite which involve bathing, decorating, and making offerings before the idol).

So there are a number of reasons, which apply to different parts of the rite. Flowers are not necessary for *puja*, so that in itself would not be decisive. I would like to consider here in more detail the reason which the nun gave first, that the renouncer is impure because she does not bathe.[61]

Now of course no one thinks that the Jina himself would be polluted if a renouncer were to touch the idol, but the idol would be. One prominent lay Jain in Jaipur, who sits on a temple committee, told me that the reconsecration rites which would be necessary if this were to occur would be very elaborate and would involve eighteen different ritual bathings (*abhishek*) of the statue.[62] Strikingly, the reasons for the renouncer's impurity in this context are just those actions (the ascetic and 'non-violent' avoidance of fresh water) which are important elements in the purification of his or her soul. The preparations which lay Jains go through to purify themselves would be pollutions to a renouncer. I quoted above (Chapter 7) a Jain renouncer saying that to take a bath in the modern way, which is what everyone does before performing *puja*, is a sin. It is certainly not necessary, and many people told me it is a sin, to bathe before *pratikraman*. It is clear that 'purity' is very different in these two contexts. *Puja* in the Shvetambar tradition requires the use of fresh, clean, unboiled well-water, which Jains are taught by ascetic practice to regard as

---

[61] She mentions also that, as renouncers have no possessions, they have no offerings to make, although there seems no reason, in principle, why they could not have use of (without owning) the materials needed for *puja*, as they do of their clothes and other requisites. The offerings made in *puja* are generally thought of as symbolic renunciations because everyone is clear that the Jina does not receive them. Renouncers make these offerings in non-material form when they perform *bhav puja*. But this exists to some degree in tension with another idea, namely that they are gifts (*dan*) (see ch. 13.) Clearly, the restriction on renouncers' participation in *puja* is (ostentatiously?) over-determined, but none the less I shall pursue the bathing theme here.

[62] I am bound to say that I have no particular confidence that if a renouncer were to touch a Jina idol, the matter would not be dealt with with much less fuss and expense than this. The Jains I knew in Jaipur had a generally rather relaxed attitude to ritual niceties. The man who told me this was, at the time, emphasizing how pure a Jina idol should be. Had I thought to put the question to him again when he had been extolling the virtues of renunciation, I guess he might not have thought such an elaborate rite would be required. Nevertheless, his remark is worth repeating just to emphasize that he had a fairly clear idea of what would be required officially.

a filthy mass of birth, reproduction, and death. It would be a great mistake, I think, to try to separate out how purity works in these different contexts and to identify clear and bounded different concepts, to try, so to speak, to read through the imagery that is used, to a 'real' non-metaphorical subject-matter somehow underlying the different forms of thought and talk.[63] It is easy to see how such an analysis would go. One would say that in one case people are really talking about spiritual excellence and in the other they are really talking about hierarchy and respect, as if it were of no moment that they do so as purity. But this approach, in thus making the situation seem unparadoxical, would I think be misleading.

The incongruence between purity in *puja* and purity in asceticism is not invisible to Jains, even if, in the absence of a troublesome anthropologist, it scarcely requires a second thought. When I asked why renouncers could not touch a Jina idol, many people preferred at first to avoid giving an answer, because they did not want to appear to be criticizing renouncers (the nun I quoted above was confident enough about the virtues of the path she had chosen not to feel embarrassed by the problem). One monk I talked to was evasive in a particularly instructive way. I was asking him about *puja* and came to the point where I asked if he himself performed it. He said, as I expected, that he did not. I hinted at the fact that renouncers do not wash, intending to pass quickly on to other matters, but he contradicted me with some vehemence. 'The *sadhu* is pure', he said, 'absolutely pure. Our *tapasya* and *ahimsa* make us pure. We do not do *puja*, but we can touch a *murti* (idol). I do this, I do this all the time.' This last rhetorical flourish is, I am sure, untrue. I never saw him or any other renouncer do so. Everyone else I talked to agreed that it is forbidden. I recounted his response to a number of lay Jains, who felt the need to explain why he had said this. The way they did so was telling: 'He was talking about *bhav*,' they said. 'In *bhav* a *sadhu* is pure, his impurity is only *dravya*.' This distinction between *dravya* and *bhav* cuts across that which Shrimad Rajcandra used when he saw adherence to renouncers' rules as an external matter (*dravya*), as opposed to considerations of internal states (*bhav*). In this view, by contrast, it is permanent sexual abstinence and the observance of formal rules and ritual observances which are the real essence (*bhav*) of purity, and this introduces a categorical difference between the purity which householders and renouncers can attain. In this view the fact that renouncers' rules are concerned with the body does not make them superficial.

<hr>

[63] Soskice, *Metaphor and Religious Language.*

Both the monk, and the lay people who interpreted his response for me, would then firmly resist the reduction of his inner purity to merely an idiom to talk about something else. The transformations brought about by sexual abstinence are, as we have seen, bodily; and the effects of the practice of *ahimsa*, to a considerable degree, take place on the body's surface, where unseen creatures are either destroyed or saved, and they are no less important for that. But at the same time commitment to the reality of either of these two forms of purity does not preclude commitment to the other.

I have been distinguishing three ways in which Jain religious practice constructs a moral topography of the self. The body is a weapon to use against the unruly mind and a tool with which to clean the soul; it is a filthy prison in which the soul is trapped and the mud with which it is stained; and it is a mirror of the soul, so that in temple images it is an icon of spiritual perfection. Stated thus, none of these ideas is unique to Jainism, which is why I have approached them through the concrete religious practices, where their undoubted distinctiveness can, I hope, be seen. My point has been that while religious practice commits and constructs the subject in a certain way, which is certainly an operation of power in the widest sense, it does not always do so in the same way. Put differently, while it is true that ritual gestures can, as Bourdieu puts it, contain a whole political philosophy,[64] there is nothing to prevent the succeeding gesture from expounding a rival one. Even within the apparently narrow ambit of lay asceticism, there are contrasting and conflicting positions for the religious subject to take.

[64] Bourdieu, *Outline*, 94; *Logic of Practice*, 69.

12

Paryushan: Austerity and Increase in Counterpoint

A T many points in our consideration of Jain religious self-fashioning, we have seen the affirmation of worldly life and good fortune interwoven with asceticism and world-renunciation. We saw this in fasting, where the very substances which are renounced in ascetic practice are displayed and consumed, in celebration of the feat of not consuming them. In the Paryushan festival asceticism and auspiciousness are again combined, and here each occurs in such a heightened form that their co-occurrence presents itself as an almost surreal aesthetic contrast.[1] This occurs in the Jains' own celebrations, but to see its full force, we need to notice that the Jains also participate in a Hindu festival which is celebrated at the same time. As I described in Chapter 5, you can be a Jain without ceasing to be, in the broad sense, a Hindu; and this is essential, I think, to understanding how lay Jain religious identity works. But this is not an easy syncretism, and nor does it quite capture what is going on to say that certain Jain practices have a higher status than do 'popular' Hindu ones. In so far as Jainism is conceived as an ascetic renunciation of worldly life, it needs a conception and experience of what that worldly life is. And in so far as lay Jains are partial, conditional, imperfect, or intermittent practitioners of ascetic renunciation—in so far that is, as they are only occasionally 'real Jains'—that worldly life is more than just a rhetorical background for them. It is their real life, and it is fully and richly conceived in the moral and religious imagination. Paryushan, though itself the epitome of real Jainism, exists in dramatic aesthetic counterpoint to a valued manifestation of real life.

[1] Banks (*Organizing Jainism*, 176–84) describes this festival, as it is celebrated in Leicester. A description of Paryushan in Gujarat can be found in Cort, 'Liberation and Wellbeing', 157–85, 444–9, and notes on it in Folkert, *Scripture and Community*, 189–211. The Digambars have a ten-day festival called Dash Lakshan-ji, which begins just as the Shvetambar equivalent is ending.

Remembering the Jinas

Every Jain family, no matter what the level of religiosity it normally sustains—and it cannot be stressed enough, this varies enormously—intensifies its religious observance during Paryushan. This means both increased attendance at formal religious functions and further restriction of the diet at home. In microcosmic imitation of the ban which some observe on eating green vegetables for the whole rainy season, almost everyone gives them up for just these days. Morning *puja* is more elaborate, and the temples are crammed with people. Large groups gather in the evening for *pratikraman*, and in pretty well every spare moment there are sermons.

Leisured, corpulent gentlemen dressed in crisp, white, hand-loom cotton (adorned with diamond buttons) cluster round the dais, nodding and murmuring contented approval, while their younger colleagues, who arrive in ordinary clothes and wearing a harassed look after the sermon has begun, take their places at the back for an hour or so before going off to work. Everyone is expected to attend, so mothers come with small children, one of whom inevitably starts howling in the increasingly hot and humid atmosphere. But things are very good-humoured. The women all dress up, and even young unmarried girls who normally wear Punjabi suits dress in fine saris: auspicious reds, oranges, and yellows for young and married women, blues and white for widows. All the women wear the end of the sari looped over their head as a veil. The older women sit telling a rosary, swaying backwards and forwards in time with their recitations, and every few minutes a jerk at the sari brings it a few inches further over the face. Towards the back of the hall little huddles of women are sitting chatting; here and there one or two are asleep.

On the evening of the second day a Prakrit text of the *Kalpa Sutra* is taken in procession (*julus*) from each temple to the home or office of one of the wealthy lay families. The whole community is invited to see it garlanded and anointed, and long into the night the crowd holds a vigil (*ratri jagaran*), with enthusiastic singing of devotional songs led by a group of professional musicians. A young girl gives an occasional display of rather folksy classical dancing. Next morning the *sutra* is taken in another procession to an *upashraya*, and formally presented to the renouncers. The sermons from now on are 'translations' of the *Kalpa Sutra* (Chapter 2), in which the sometimes dry enumeration of names, dates, and places in the text is greatly expanded with stories, from some of the many commentaries which are for this purpose scarcely distinguished from the text itself, of the *karmik* consequences of actions and the miraculous deeds of the Jinas.

Mahavir arrived at a village. In this village there was a *yaksha* who in his previous life had been a bullock belonging to a merchant.

The bullock was old and carrying five hundred boxes of gold. It couldn't cross the river so the merchant bought a new bullock from the village. He left some money with the villagers, and asked them to feed it, but they stole the money, and the bullock died of starvation.

As you sow, so shall you reap.

A disease spread through the village. So many people died that there were bones everywhere. People got scared, and started worshipping. The *yaksha* appeared and told them to make an idol of him and worship it. Then after some time Mahavir arrived in the village and went to the temple. The priest at the temple said: don't stay here, there is a bad spirit (*bhut*). Mahavir wasn't scared though, and stayed there to do his concentration. The *yaksha* appeared and tried to frighten him. He appeared first as a raging elephant, then as a fierce devil with a knife in his hand, then as a snake and he even bit Mahavir, but the Lord didn't move. The *yaksha* caused pain in Mahavir Swami's eyes, his teeth, his hands, and his body but still he didn't move. Finally the *yaksha* fell down before Mahavir and worshipped him.

Beneficent Birth

On the fourth evening there is another procession and vigil—but this time with a baby's cradle (*palana* or *jhula*) rather than a sacred book. Just like the text, the cradle is taken next morning to the preaching-hall, where Lord Mahavir's birth is re-enacted. Mahavir Janam (not to be confused with Mahavir Jayanti, which marks what is held to be his birthday) is something of a carnival, and at the same time a properly Jain religious event, and everyone attends. The cradle, when it arrives, is suspended from the ceiling and a young boy chosen to sit in it to play the part of the infant Lord. The hall is brightly decorated and the mood festive. When a Tirthankar's soul enters his mother's womb, she has fourteen visions (Chapter 2), and silver models representing these are presented to the presiding renouncers by lay families who have paid for this privilege. This takes some hours (Chapter 16), after which a renouncer gets up and reads the sections of the *Kalpa Sutra* which describe the dreams and the birth of Mahavir. As she begins her reading everyone starts gathering in an increasingly boisterous and jostling crowd around her. She reaches the birth itself. 'All planets were exalted. The moon was in its best conjunction. The skies were tranquil, pure, and bright. All omens augured success. A pleasant south-wind swept the earth. Fields were green with corn. People rejoiced and made merry.'[2] At this point, to a deafening accompaniment of shouts and cries, she is pelted with rice, as everyone in the crowd, none more vigorously than the young men, lets fly with what should be exactly 108 perfectly whole, white grains. (These they have been nurturing all morning, spending dull moments in the ceremony checking and counting them over and over again.) Instantly this is done they wheel round looking for a sharp edge—a stair or a banister—and try their best to smash a coconut they have each brought with them. The crowd disperses almost at once as people head off towards the corners of the hall, and out into the street. Pieces of coconut are distributed immediately as *prasad* to all those present, friends swap pieces, and the remainder is taken home to be given to visitors.

This ceremony is not the only festive moment in the midst of all the fasting, confessing, and grim sermonizing of Paryushan, but it is the only sustained one. The birth of a Jina is always described as unambiguously auspicious, but here this idea is brought very close to people's own experience, for it is dramatized in ways which employ auspicious symbolism that is also used in Rajasthan by families hoping for children. Ann Gold describes how possessed priests at rural shrines place a coconut in a pouch formed in a woman's clothes, in an 'obvious gesture of impregnation'.[3] On a different occasion, a man breaks a coconut and puts pieces into a possessed woman's pouch.[4] Gold writes that the coconuts, 'seem to stand for the fully developed and safely birthed baby', and she mentions that pilgrims who are blessed with a healthy child after ceremonies of this kind return to the shrines to hang baskets containing coconuts, which they refer to as cradles (*palana*), from trees and rooftops.

In this Jain context, however, the symbolism is interpreted in a more general and less goal-directed way. No one I spoke to said they brought coconuts to this birth celebration in order that they might have children themselves. Easily the most vigorous participants were men, but they distributed the coconut indiscriminately to women and other men, to their sisters as well as their wives. I spent one of these ceremonies with a group of young, mostly unmarried man, and there was no hint of sexual innuendo. Intrigued by the rushing and rice-throwing, I suggested to some people that this might be a good thing to do if you wanted to get married or have children. They granted this was a good idea, because

---

[2] Vinaya Sagar, *Kalpa Sutra*, 143; see also Jacobi, *Jaina Sutras*, i. 251.
[3] Gold, *Fruitful Journeys*, 149–53.   [4] Ibid. 96.

Mahavir was a very healthy baby and gave his mother no trouble in pregnancy or childbirth, but doubted that it would in fact work.[5] 'No, it is just for *mangal* (auspiciousness)—for success in everything.'

Ascetic Success

Through the sixth and seventh mornings of Paryushan, sermons based on the *Kalpa Sutra* continue. The last day is Samvatsari or, more colloquially, Chamcheri. Almost nothing in this generally individualist religion is regarded as compulsory, but fasting and attending the annual *pratikraman* on this day does come close. Things begin the previous evening with a meal to sustain people through the day ahead.[6] After eating, there is *pratikraman*. The first task on the morning of Samvatsari itself is to boil large quantities of water, for those, such as children and the elderly, who will drink during the day. People take the vow for their fast, and then make a short trip to one of the temples for *darshan*. Already, well before eight o'clock, there is the sound of the occasional procession in the streets outside. Those who have been fasting for a number of days—and many unmarried girls do an eight-day *upvas* over the period of Paryushan—are being taken through the streets, in many cases in a horse-drawn buggy. The girls themselves can hardly walk, and scarcely manage a weak smile, but they are accompanied by a little cheering crowd of family and friends and, in the case of the better-off, by a blaring local band hired for the occasion.

The processions go to each of the temples, where the *tapasvi* makes an offering of a large sweet topped with a silver flag, to signify her victory over the senses. The processions converge on the assembly-hall where the renouncers are waiting to conduct the day's ceremonies. Each *tapasvi* is presented to the renouncers who anoint her with sandalwood powder (*vasakshep*) and administer her final *paccakkhan* (Chapter 10; Plate V above). An older woman who has performed a thirty-day fast is fêted with especially great ceremony and presented with gifts and a certificate.

---

[5] Folkert (*Scripture and Community*, 200) reports one Jain monk, in an aside, ascribing the focus on the cradle in these ceremonies to people's belief that it would bring them children. Folkert's notes give no indication of whether any lay celebrants confirmed this to him, or whether the monk made any reference to the coconut when he made the point.

[6] There is of course a wealth of local lore on what the best foods are for this pre-fast meal (*dharana*). People tend to use heavier, less refined grains than the staple wheat, and opt for one of a number of dishes made from millet (*bajra*) or gram flour (*besan*). Certain vegetables, spices, and sweets are recommended. Some people, on the other hand, just eat a lot.

These people are all garlanded, but never with fresh flowers. These would have to be picked for the purpose, which would be *himsa*, and their wilting during the day would represent exactly the morbidity of natural processes the defeat of which is being celebrated. In contrast to Mahavir Janam just a few days before, celebration has become more uneasy. It is hemmed in by a combination of *ahimsa* and the ascetic ethos. Artificial flowers are sometimes used, but a more popular solution is to make a garland of currency notes, as it is customary in any case that a small amount of cash is always given along with a flower garland. That success should be celebrated with money, even during this most earnest affirmation of renunciatory values, is a point to which we shall return below (Chapter 17).

The Archetypal Sermon

The main business of the morning on Samvatsari is a reading of the *Kalpa Sutra*. The extra fans which were installed for the celebration of Mahavir Janam have all been removed, and even the permanent fans are turned off. The crowd is almost as large as for the previous ceremony and the reading will not finish until well after twelve. It is going to be very uncomfortable.

After performing a short prayer and *puja* over the text, one of the renouncers addresses the assembly, warning them sternly that no one must sneeze during the reading (for sneezing is inauspicious and would diminish its effectiveness). The whole text must be read in the original Prakrit, and the renouncers take turns in reading. The *Kalpa Sutra* is also called the *Barasa Sutra*, *barasa* meaning 'around about twelve [hundred]'. This is because the Prakrit original, as distinct from the commentaries on which the sermons of the preceding days have been substantially based, consists of one thousand two hundred and forty-nine couplets. For a Jain religious text, this is pretty short, but even at a fast trot, the reading takes a good three hours. They read so fast that it would be impossible to follow, even if you understood the language, which, with the exception of one or two of the renouncers themselves, no one does.

Every ten minutes or so there is a brief pause. The reader tells us in Hindi where we have reached in the story, takes a deep breath, and starts again. The manuscript is illustrated with scenes from the lives of the Jinas, and while the reading is going on lay helpers hold up pages of the manuscript, turning slowly so that everyone in the hall can see them. The page moves round the room and a ripple passes through the congregation as everyone lifts their hands and bows slowly when their eyes meet the picture. While this is going on other helpers pass among the crowd carrying trays, each with a small pile of sandalwood powder and a page of manuscript. This is *gyan puja*, the worship of knowledge, and everyone takes a little of the powder and respectfully sprinkles it on the manuscript, before adding a note to the accumulating pile of money on the tray. The discursive aspects of a normal sermon are completely absent here. There is almost no sense in which this assembly could be described as listening to the text. They are certainly hearing it, and paying homage to a series of material embodiments of the knowledge it contains: the pages of the text, the illustrations, the renouncer herself. And interaction with these is primarily visual, in a recreation of the *samosaran* archetype.[7]

Universal Forgiveness and Sectarian Celebration

As the Jain congregation sits in the increasingly close room, with children beginning to squeal from heat and hunger, the sound of the *Kalpa Sutra* rattling away is intruded on from time to time by excited voices, celebratory volleys on car horns, and other boisterous sounds from the streets outside. Samvatsari falls on the fourth day of the bright half of Bhadra, which is also Ganesh Caturthi, the principal day in the year for Hindus to worship the god Ganesh-ji. The relationship the Jains have to this ceremony shows again their social strategy of selective and asymmetrical involvement with the non-Jain world (Chapter 5), and also the play of world-affirming and ascetic values which we have seen throughout this part of the book.

Ganesh Caturthi is a big celebration in Jaipur, and for two days and nights much of the city is given over to festival. It culminates, on the day after Samvatsari, in an evening procession of a Ganesh-ji idol through the main streets of the city and on to a fortified temple in the hills. This parade used to be a royal affair. Around 1870, when Louis Rousselet visited Jaipur, the festivities were largely the same as they are now. The main streets were all decorated with flags and coloured poles and there was a similarly grand parade, but the fair, to judge from his description,

[7] The nearest major town to the west of Jaipur is Ajmer. In 1990 there were no Khartar Gacch renouncers in Ajmer for Paryushan and the local leaders appealed for help to their colleagues in Jaipur. Arrangements were made for a young man, knowledgeable in religious matters, to go there to organize the processions, lead *pratikraman* for the men, and stand in for the missing renouncers by giving lectures on the *Kalpa Sutra*. For the recitation on Samvatsari, however, it was considered out of the question that he should do this. Instead, an idol of the Tirthankar preaching in the *samosaran* was placed at the front of the hall, and a tape recording was played of one of the renouncers in Jaipur reciting the text.

was of rather more economic importance. Then, it was centred on the royal palace and the Maharaja led the procession.[8] People told me that in the years after Independence the Ganesh celebrations declined somewhat. Royal patronage became a lot less lavish and the fair became less important. But in recent years the festival has been revived, with different sponsors and a different political significance.

The background to this is as follows. In Bombay for most of the nineteenth century there was no public celebration for Ganesh Caturthi, although Ganesh-ji is particularly popular in that part of Western India (the area that is now Maharashtra) and the festival was marked by domestic ceremonies in Hindu homes and as a modest neighbourhood festival. But in the 1890s the nationalist politician Lokamanya Tilak transformed the Ganesh festival by adding a public and political dimension. His followers formed groups to hold sponsored song sessions, dramas, political speeches, and lectures. They also organized greatly enlarged processions in towns throughout the region. Crucially, this was an all-Hindu affair, bridging the gap between Brahmins and non-Brahmins. Tilak called on Hindus to boycott the Muslim Moharram festival which occurs at this time of year and to organize cow-protection demonstrations against both the British (who ate beef) and the Muslims (who did the butchering for them). For a brief period, until about 1910, the new Ganesh festival was the most potent focus for neo-traditionalist nationalism in the region.[9]

Though not now so explicitly political, the festival has continued to grow in importance, to spread to rural villages in Maharashtra, and to other Indian cities such as Jaipur, where various details of Tilak's format, especially the participation of specially formed voluntary associations in the parades, have been adopted. Since Tilak's time, Muslims have not participated in the festival in Maharashtra, and the same is true today in Jaipur. It has become a pan-Hindu ceremony drawing support from all castes, from Hindu business leaders, and from political groups such as the Hindu nationalist organization, the RSS.[10] The main sponsors in Jaipur now are Hindu merchants: the Oswal, Agarwal, and Khandelwal competitors of the Jains. It is they who occupy a huge dais in the Johari Bazaar and award prizes to the best floats in the procession. The Jains do not take a prominent or an organizing role in these celebrations; but they do quietly make donations towards the cost.

[8] Rousselet, *India and its Native Princes*, 232–3.
[9] Courtright, *Ganesa*, 226–47   [10] Ibid. 188–201.

In today's celebrations in Jaipur, the Ganesh temple close to the Moti Doongri Dadabari is transformed into the centre of an enormous fair. The nearby streets are cordoned off. Buses arrive from villages all round the city, while the police languidly fail to control the traffic. Loudspeakers play deafening pop music day and night around stalls selling food, flowers for *puja*, toys, and a whole kaleidoscope of brightly-coloured trinkets. All the way from the city gate to the temple the road is decorated with canopies and banners and a constant stream of devotees plies back and forth.

As these celebrations increase in noise and intensity, devout Jains move from seeing and hearing 'real Jainism' in the *Kalpa Sutra* reading, to acting it out bodily in the annual *pratikraman*. Only a small proportion of those who attend will have performed this rite regularly during the year, or will be anywhere near proficient. Some know a little and keep up as best they can. Others copy, more or less, what they see others doing. Many remain seated for most of it, going through the hand movements and prostrations, and reciting the *nokar mantra* each time this is called for. This goes on for about four hours. By the time it is finished most people are exhausted, and they still must not eat until morning, so they tend to go straight to bed.

But before this, as they leave the assembly, there remains the last religiously significant act of Paryushan. It is simple, informal, and rather beautiful. There is a Prakrit verse in the *pratikraman* (it occurs in the *Vandittu Sutra*) which expresses a sentiment quite different from the idea I explained above (Chapter 9) of a rigorous and comprehensive repudiation and penance. One is tempted to call the sentiment 'humanist', but of course, because this is Jainism, its application is much wider than merely to other humans.

khamemi savva jive,	I ask pardon from all creatures,
savve jive khamantu me.	may all creatures pardon me
metti me savva-bhuesu,	May I have friendship with all beings,
veram majjha na kenavi.	and enmity with none

As they pour out of the *pratikraman* into the alleyway or street, ready to stagger off home, members of the local Jain community recite this verse to each other, or exchange a shorter greeting, *khamate hai*. Thus they apologize for any offence they may have caused in the previous year, with the same comprehensive formula as is used in the *pratikraman*: for intended and unintended thoughts, words, and actions; for things they have done, instigated, or approved. In this way, as one woman said to me, 'Doing *pratikraman* and *khamate*, we clean both our bodies and our souls.'[11] Thus from the individualizing drill of the *pratikraman* penance, Jains move to an expression, perhaps lay Jainism's most potent expression, of solidarity: a response perhaps to an experience which is, almost in spite of itself, shared.

Next day, which is called Kshamapana Divas, cards and letters are sent to friends and family who were not present at the ceremony, bearing the formula from the *Vandittu Sutra* and, usually, a modern Hindi rhyme expressing a similar or related idea. Thus Samvatsari is extended to renew links between members of the dispersed Jain community, right across India. Paryushan is over now, and breakfast is a fast-breaking feast.[12] Everyone makes sure they meet all the members of their family and other close connections (employers or employees, landlords or tenants) as soon as possible to exchange *khamate* greetings. Gifts of sweets are taken on visits to other branches of the family. And, in a turn which illustrates nicely the ambiguous separateness and belonging of the Jains to the Hindu world around them, people distribute *prasad* from a *puja* to Lord Ganesh.

Ganesh Puja: The Hindu Counterpoint

Jain houses, shops, and offices, like those of their Hindu neighbours, all have a small idol of Ganesh-ji above the door. Ganesh is the elephant-headed son of the goddess Parvati and, though in various ambiguous ways of Lord Shiva, and he is the god of obstacles and beginnings. He is very definitely not part of the Jain pantheon: he has no connection with the Tirthankars, is not a follower or protector of the Jain religion, and his idol is not found in Jain temples (although there is a Jain *yaksha* whose *murti* looks like Ganesh, and some Jains do think of it as him). But almost every Jain home, like every Hindu one, has him posted at the entrance, and Jains invoke this deity, just as Hindus do, before auspicious life-cycle rites such as marriage. As he appears in popular Hinduism today, Ganesh-ji is about

[11] Mrs Stevenson, in a moment of generosity (*Heart of Jainism*, 260), was moved by this practice to the following (still proselytizing) conjecture: 'One cannot help feeling that this beautiful custom of the Jaina is one of the many precious things they will bring as their special tribute to that City of God into which at last shall be gathered all the glory and wealth of devotion of the nations.'

[12] As with the meal they take before a fast, people are influenced by beliefs about what is the safest and healthiest food to break a fast with. Curd is almost always part of such a meal, and for this occasion many families make a sweet dish, a halwa made from sugar and a yellow lentil (*mungh*), or, for the better off, from almonds. And there are several varieties of hot drink made from aromatic spices and almonds or from wild berries.

as far as it is possible to get from Jain asceticism. He is probably the most popular deity in the Hindu pantheon, rather an amoral god who removes obstacles and brings happiness in return for devotion, offerings, and proper worship. He is invoked to help with all the things Jainism says you should renounce: marriage, childbirth, a new job, a new house, or a business deal. A mostly benign and helpful deity to whom you appeal for all kinds of worldly benefits, he is believed, when slighted, to be vengeful and obstructive. All idols of Ganesh are given *puja* on Ganesh Caturthi. Jain households as well as Hindu ones manage this, mostly in the gap between the *Kalpa Sutra* and the confession, where lunch should have been.

A range of offerings is made: incense, flowers, lamps. Sweets are offered and later distributed as *prasad*. Red turmeric paste is dabbed on the idol, and used to form auspicious swastikas on the wall. To the left people write *Shri Labh*, to the right, *Shri Shubh*. *Shri* is a general auspicious epithet, used in so many contexts that it has almost no meaning at all, but it is, among other things, one of the names of Lakshmi, goddess of wealth. *Labh* means increase and profit, and *shubh* means auspicious. For Hindus devoted to Ganesh-ji, this *puja* is no doubt more nuanced and complex, but for Jains, it is a frankly supplicatory devotion and plea for wealth, good health, and good fortune. The equivocations and hedging that surround worship of the Jinas, Jain saints, and even protector deities in a Jain temple are absent here. The scruples that saw flowers replaced by bank notes for garlanding those who had completed a fast, and saw the fans removed from the assembly-hall, are absent too. The Ganesh celebrations are not 'real Jainism', indeed they are in rather effective counterpoint to it. But real Jainism could not ever be all there is.

Next day, on what for Jains is Kshamapana Divas, the Ganesh celebrations continue. But having spent the previous day secluded in their austere meeting-halls, the Jains are now free to rejoin the Hindu world and what for them is a worldly, though still none the less a religious celebration. There is much leisurely eating and chatting, and to-ing and fro-ing between households with gifts of sweets; there are feasts, held by the families of those who completed lengthy fasts; and in the evening, there is the carnival and procession as it makes its way through the Johari Bazaar.

In general, unlike Jain houses, the doorways of Jain temples do not have an idol of Ganesh-ji above them, and they are protected instead by deities such as *bhairu-ji*. However, there are two temples in Jaipur which do have Ganesh idols above the door. For a while I was puzzled by these, and

I finally learned the reason for them from an old caretaker in one of the temples. I have already described how discreet Jain temples are in Jaipur, and how they blend in with the façades of the surrounding houses. These two temples, it turns out, were actually built as houses. As such they of course had the usual idol of Ganesh above the door. When the buildings were consecrated as a temple no one wanted to incur the wrath of the Lord of Obstacles by removing them. That would be a very inauspicious beginning for the new temple. So they remain there and are worshipped by the temple servants, who are, as is usual, Hindu. If asked, most devout Jains will say they do not 'believe' in Ganesh-ji (*Ham nahim mante*). But this means they do not follow him, not that they doubt his existence. The subtle accommodation and discreet interweaving of Jains into the Hindu world is well illustrated by the decision to leave these Ganesh idols where they were, and by the pious Jains who go daily to the temples either without noticing or with only a passing bow to the god above the door, secure in the knowledge both that the job of actually worshipping him is being undertaken by someone else, and that their own compact with this paradigmatic arbiter of worldly fortunes has been made at home.

PART IV

Matters for Negotiation

13

The Values and Perils of Exchange

SHVETAMBAR renouncers obtain their food as alms, under a very elaborate set of rules and restrictions. Dressed in full habit and carrying their staffs, they go out in pairs or alone, just before meal-times when food will be ready in Jain homes. At each of a number of households they are shown to the kitchen and given a little of the family meal. When they have collected enough to feed the whole group, they return to the *upashraya* where it is shared out and eaten.

This part of the book revolves around this apparently simple procedure, and I shall spend some considerable time discussing just what is going on when a small amount of simple food is handed over. I shall suggest that a great deal is happening: that the relationship between Jain renouncers and lay families, both collectively and in individual cases, is re-negotiated in this encounter and that normally conflicting lay identities are reconciled. The import of the argument as a whole will be that the renouncer's alms-round figures equally in the pursuit of personal piety and social status, and so stands at the heart of Jainism as a lived religion.[1] The subject is quite complex, and I shall have to clear the ground somewhat in this chapter with some general discussion about food exchange, and Jain religious gifts.

Religious Giving and the Politics of Hospitality

Alms-giving is a food transaction: members of a lay family receive a renouncer as a guest in their home, and give him or her cooked food to eat.

---

[1] For this reason it is perhaps worth mentioning the quite striking contrast between the way renouncers receive their food in the Digambar and Shvetambar traditions. Digambar renouncers go out individually to seek alms, accompanied usually by a retinue of lay followers. They may not present themselves unannounced at a house, but must wait for a householder to come out and invite them in. They take all the food for a single meal from one family, which they eat at their house and in their presence. Ideally, they eat standing up, with the donors placing food directly into their hands. See Carrithers, 'Naked Ascetics'; Cort, 'Liberation and Wellbeing', 319–22; Fischer and Jain, *Art and Rituals*, 19; Mahias, *Délivrance et convivialité*, 246–51; Shântâ, *La Voie Jaina*, 506–8. Thus, as will be seen, in all of its main particulars the Digambar practice is a direct inversion of the Shvetambar one.

Nowhere in the world, so far as I know, are food transactions socially or morally neutral; but it may be that nowhere in the world are the social consequences so frankly political or the moral implications so powerful as they are in South Asia. The phenomenon is so general and pervasive, yet occurs in so many local permutations, that it is hazardous to generalize. The status ranking of castes in a village can be charted by observing who will accept different kinds of food from whom.[2] The relative status of different categories of kin brought together in a marriage is negotiated through and dramatized by who eats what with whom and in what order at the ceremony.[3] The relations of status and authority within a household can be seen in who cooks for whom under whose direction, who serves whom, who eats with whom, and in what order.[4]

Across a wide range of social relations, from broad socio–political ones to intimate domestic ones, and throughout the subcontinent, similar ideas are in play in practices relating to food transactions. None of these ideas is unique to India, but their conjunction is certainly distinctive. The concerns which are exhibited, the moves and minor strategies which people employ, justify us in saying that a recognizably similar game is being played, though the earnestness with which it is played varies from place to place. The rules of this game are as follows. One's status, indeed one's moral constitution, is precarious. In interaction with others it is constantly at stake, because in a range of interactions, certain substances can transmit moral qualities from one person to another. The world being what it is, this game is generally the concern of those whose status at present is high, so attention is focused on the danger of bad qualities, generally sin, impurity, and/or misfortune,[5] being transferred. However, in certain religious contexts people do hope to have good qualities transferred to them from holy persons or objects.[6]

Food, especially certain kinds of cooked food, is one such transforming substance, which is why cooks tend to come from the same castes as

---

[2] Davis, *Rank and Rivalry*, 74–7; Eichinger Ferro-Luzzi, 'Ritual as Language'; Marriott, 'Caste Ranking and Food Transactions'; Mayer, *Caste and Kinship*; Selwyn, 'Order of Men'.

[3] Appadurai, 'Gastro-Politics'; Inden and Nicholas, *Kinship in Bengali Culture*.

[4] Cantlie, 'Moral Significance of Food'; Khare, *Hindu Hearth and Home*.

[5] Raheja (*Poison in the Gift*) has argued that the impure (*ashuddh*) and the inauspicious (*ashubh*) are completely separate concepts, and that sin (*pap*) is wholly subsumed in the latter. Such an argument would be unsustainable if applied to the Jain case (ch. 11), and Parry ('Hindu Lexicographer') has put forward cogent arguments against it for Hinduism too.

[6] Babb, *Redemptive Encounters*; Gold, *Lord as Guru*.

priests, and why proverbs and sayings such as, 'Your mind will be as your food is', are more or less ubiquitous. Sexual fluids are the same, which is why intercourse with inappropriate sexual partners can lead to weakness, disease, and death;[7] and why marriage with a social inferior lowers the status of an entire local descent group. Cloth is another, which is why a gift of cloth to a woman can constitute, as opposed to merely symbolize, a marriage.[8] Food is particularly important, of course, because it requires that these ideas be acted upon each day.

All exchanges of these substances are therefore potentially dangerous; but—and this is the second major characteristic of the game—gifts are much more dangerous than commercial transactions.[9] The more or less universal potential of gifts to create relations of debt and dependency is employed using a range of non-returnable gifts to encode patron-client relations, such as those between dominant landowners and service castes. The dominant caste gives its sin-bearing substance to its social inferiors in payment for their services, thus simultaneously acting out economic dominance and symbolically constructing cultural superiority.[10]

Two quite different sets of transactions, which will be particularly pertinent in the discussion that follows, are substantially shaped by these considerations. One is payments to priests, who often live entirely on what they receive as gifts from worshippers.

The Brahmin priests of Benares see themselves as endlessly accumulating the sin they accept with the gifts of the pilgrims and mourners who visit the city . . . they liken themselves to a sewer through which the moral filth of their patrons is passed. Theoretically they should be able to 'digest' the sin by dint of various ritual procedures of expiation, and by donating the gifts they receive to another Brahmin with increment. But quite apart from the fact that this is plainly an economic impossibility, they sadly admit ignorance of the correct ritual procedures. The sewer becomes a cess-pit, with the result that the priest contracts leprosy and rots; he dies a terrible and premature death and then faces the torments of hell.[11]

Nor are the dangers entirely on the side of the recipients. Parry describes how, in clear assertions in Brahminical theory and inchoate fears among pious donors, sins committed by wicked priests are shared by those who

---

[7] Daniel, *Fluid Signs*, ch. 4.
[8] Bayly, 'Origins of Swadeshi', 288. See also Cohn, 'Cloth, Clothes, and Colonialism'.
[9] Parry, 'Moral Perils'.
[10] Raheja, *Poison in the Gift*.
[11] Parry, 'The Gift', 460. See also Parry, 'Ghosts'.

give them gifts. So, for instance, donors are responsible for the sins committed with money they give to priests, even though they cannot possibly know the recipients' evil intentions or proclivities. 'It is as if', writes Parry, 'from a moral point of view the donor and recipient are metamorphosed by the gift into Siamese twins.'[12]

The second kind of transaction where these considerations apply is everyday hospitality, which can take on many of the characteristics of guerrilla warfare. Offering food is a way of giving pleasure, but also of transmitting pollution, poison, and moral corruption. It also puts the recipient in debt. If you accept food, you admit that the host is not inferior to you, for you accept his or her moral substance with it. To give, and to refuse to accept in return, is an assertion of superiority. To give more than your guests are able to return puts them in your debt and incrementally increases your prestige. Among the Sherpas of Nepal, hospitably giving beer and food to a neighbour is used, exploiting the status superiority of the host, to press all kinds of requests in a frankly coercive way. As Sherry Ortner remarks, 'Hospitality, then, is an almost unremitting play upon the theme of status'; and this is substantially true throughout the subcontinent.[13]

Jains, in common with other Baniyas, take on the whole a rather conservative and unplayful part in this game. While they engage in commercial exchanges and make charitable gifts with considerable enthusiasm, when it comes to hospitality and morally perilous exchanges of cooked food, they are very reticent indeed.[14] They regard almost anyone else as likely to pollute them, because everyone else's food is the result of a massacre of unseen creatures. Strict Jains never eat in restaurants and hardly ever accept invitations to dine in the homes of non-Jains. Outside their own homes, or those of kinsmen or trusted friends, they will eat food provided in the precincts of Jain temples, but hardly anywhere else. The more pious Jain families buy no prepared foods such as biscuits, savoury snacks, sweets, and cordials, and even the average family buys only such things as are called *pukka* ('complete'), and which are believed to be poor transmitters of impurity. Instead, all potentially dangerous foods are made at home by the women of the family. The family takes in food substances in their most neutral possible state—fresh vegetables, whole wheat, unhusked rice—and organizes for itself as many

---

[12] Parry, 'Moral Perils', 69.

[13] Ortner, *Sherpas*, 84.

[14] Raheja (*Poison in the Gift*, 206–7) comments that the only people in Pahansu to whom the dominant Gujars do not make gifts are Jain Baniyas.

as possible of the processes by which these things are turned into food.[15]

Between Jains themselves, the situation combines a continuation of this general reserve with what is in many ways a less grim version of that described by Ortner for the Sherpas. There is no system of ascriptive status ranking of Jain families, and no categorical rules which prevent commensality between them. In the Jaipur business community, families are for the most part economically independent. Differences in wealth are very great indeed at the margins, but there are large numbers of families who are at roughly the same level: affluent but not rich. So in status terms there is everything to play for. Thus Jain families are, on the one hand, extremely circumspect in accepting food, and on the other they are aggressively hospitable themselves when they have guests to entertain. The cultural paradigm which Appadurai, in an apposite and memorable if unlovely neologism calls 'gastro-politics',[16] covers a considerable amount of everyday etiquette among Jains. Particularly in the domain of inter-household hospitality, the ability to play these politics is a local form of practical good sense or *savoir-faire*.[17] It is what Jains generally expect to happen, instinctively look for, and do their best to manage when food changes hands.[18]

---

[15] This varies considerably according to the wealth of a family. The richer they are the more unprocessed the food they buy will be. Rich families can afford to buy whole sacks of rice or grain at a time, and have servants prepare them under their eyes, but this is not possible for the less well-off. Nevertheless, the ambition to do things this way is, I think, widely shared.

[16] Appadurai, 'Gastro-Politics'.

[17] Although what I am talking about here is very close to what Geertz (*Local Knowledge*, 73–93) calls common sense, there is some reason to distinguish this, which consists of culturally shaped forms of practical judgement, from any species-specific cognitive dispositions which might be identified, and reserving the term 'common sense' for those. See Atran, *Cognitive Foundations*, 212–17.

[18] It is worth noting that while this 'game', as I have called it, is absolutely routine, it is not beyond reflective consciousness. People are perfectly aware that coercive hospitality— forcing more food on people than they really want to eat; refusing food in someone else's house even when it is offered in good faith and when you, in truth, are hungry—that all this is behaviour that is not universal, that they engage in among themselves with some enthusiasm, and of which, when they come to think about it, they do not much approve. I can think of one housewife in particular who would regularly raise the matter for discussion, and just as regularly (though not on the same occasions) launched some of the most effective gastro-political offensives that I ever saw. I think of this as a cultural trait, rather like British reserve, which one can be sadly aware of having, without this awareness reducing much the extent to which one exhibits it. There is no reason to suppose that even such a pervasive form of conduct is evidence of Marriott and Inden's 'South Asian mind'.

Intention and Value in the Gift

After a long absence, gift-giving in India has recently made an appearance in the anthropology of exchange. Parry has drawn to anthropologists' attention again the role played in Mauss's thinking by brahmanical texts on gifts, and Marriott's dictum that in South Asia, 'What goes on *between* actors are the same connected processes of mixing and separation that go on *within* actors', has struck a chord with anthropologists in Melanesia.[19] *The Poison in the Gift*, by Gloria Goodwin Raheja, has been of decisive importance. It is the first full ethnography—of the village of Pahansu in Uttar Pradesh—to focus on religious and ritual gifts (*dan*), and the part these play in constructing and legitimating the superiority of the dominant caste. Together with the writings of Dirks and others, Raheja has reminded us that competing understandings of social superiority are employed and invoked in South Asia, including those related to kingship, and that these are not all reducible to a single hierarchical ideology of purity and pollution.[20] But Raheja's book has been read by several readers (to my mind, not unreasonably) as suggesting that a single logic is at work in almost every prestation made in Pahansu,[21] and the thought has been canvassed that this provides a model for kinship, caste, and kingship for the whole of Indian society.[22] Such ambitions depend on the thought that there is such a thing as 'the Indian gift', grounded in a hegemonic ideology, which is shared by all participants and which structures relations in determinate ways, a thought which Raheja herself has subsequently rejected, in what is, at least, a clarification of the earlier ethnographic account.[23] However, she cleaves still to the view that *dan* is always believed by both donors and recipients to involve a transfer of 'inauspiciousness'. As I have said before (Chapter 2), I doubt that talk of the auspicious and the inauspicious in South Asia can reliably be read in this way, as necessarily implying an ontological commitment to the existence of a special kind of substance. A look at Jainism provides further double inoculation against this line of thought. As we shall see, the alms-round can only be understood as a *dan* which is constructed contrastively, as deeply different

---

[19] Parry, 'The Gift'; Marriott, 'Hindu Transactions', 109; Strathern, *Gender of the Gift*, 348–9.

[20] Dirks, *Hollow Crown*; Haynes and Prakash, *Contesting Power*; Raheja, 'India'.

[21] See for instance Gellner, *Monk, Householder, Priest* 119–24; Gregory, 'Poison in Raheja's Gift'; Madan, 'Auspiciousness and Purity', 293; Östör and Fruzzetti, 'Concepts of Person'.

[22] Quigley, *Interpretation of Caste*.

[23] Raheja, 'Caste Ideologies'.

from other instances of *dan*, and it is routinely understood by different participants in crucially different ways. And, as I shall now discuss, Jain understandings of the metaphysics of gift-giving are contested, and posed against other non-Jain views.

As renouncers cannot obtain food for themselves, alms-giving is essential in Jainism. When this is set beside the symbolic importance of generous giving as a dramatization of sacrifice, as in the *varshi dan* of the Tirthankar (Chapter 2), and against the background of the rather perilous moral nature of gift-giving and food exchange in general, it will perhaps seem almost inevitable that Jain religious teachers have been much exercised over the years with attempts to analyse, classify, and tabulate various types of gift, and to establish the moral and religious importance of the transaction in which they themselves receive alms.[24]

A sample of the classifications which have been developed is given in Williams's discussion of the medieval *shravakacar* literature.[25] Authors identify the five characteristics of a gift as the recipient (*patra*), the giver (*datri*), the thing or substance given (*dravya*), the manner of giving (*vidhi*), and the fruit or result of the gift (*phal*). The first four, which together determine what the last will be, are listed in the *Tattvartha Sutra*, and the texts surveyed by Williams offer various analyses and sub-divisions of each of these primary characteristics. Another popular canonical list holds that a gift must conform in respect of the place (*desh*) and time (*kal*) when it is given, the faith (*shraddha*) and respect (*satkara*) with which it is given, and its being given in the correct manner and order (*krama*).

It is well to note the rhetorical and argumentative purposes which can lie beneath the dispassionately analytical format of these texts. When Hemacandra gives a list of undesirable gifts (*ku-dan*), he begins with ascetic concerns—gold inflames the passions, and so on—but proceeds with a list which, although Williams does not comment on the fact, makes sense only when it is seen as a point-by-point denunciation of popular Hindu religious practice. Thus, in Williams's paraphrase,

Nor can there be any merit in the gift of a cow which destroys living creatures with its hooves, eats unclean things (even though its dung is esteemed holy), and is the cause of suffering to its calf each time it is milked; *go-dana* is therefore a form of *mudhata*, of foolish superstition. Similarly *kanya dana* the gift of a daughter in marriage cannot be regarded as meritorious: whatever fools may think, even the

---

[24] Characteristically, these relentlessly technical exercises are enlivened with edifying didactic stories illustrating the rewards which come to those who give generously. See Balbir, *Danastakakatha*; 'Micro-Genre'.

[25] Williams, *Jaina Yoga*, 149–61.

dowry given at a wedding is no more than an oblation that falls in the dust, for a woman is the key to the door that leads to an evil destiny and bars the way of salvation, it is she who steals away the treasure of the religious life. Offerings to the spirits of the ancestors are equally vain: those who seek to nourish the dead are in effect watering a wooden club in the belief that it will sprout into growth. It is absurd to imagine that the ancestors will derive sustenance from food given to brahmins. Offerings made or ascetic practices pursued by a son cannot absolve a parent from sin.[26]

The list of gifts I heard most often in Jaipur, and the one I shall discuss here as a prelude to consideration of renouncers' alms-rounds, does not appear in Williams's discussion. It is at first sight rather a puzzling one.

1. *abhay-dan*   a gift of fearlessness
2. *supatra-dan*   a gift to a worthy recipient
3. *anukampa-dan*   a gift given out of compassion
4. *ucit-dan*   a gift given out of duty
5. *kirti-dan*   a gift given to earn fame

I have no idea who first compiled this list, or in what circumstances, but it nowadays appears prominently in renouncers' sermons. The individual terms in it are widely used, and when I asked renouncers and learned lay people what Jainism has to say about the subject of gifts (*dan*) this was often among the first things I was told and its elucidation was a prominent feature of the discussions which followed.

Abhay-dan, people explained, is teaching Jain religion, for Jainism brings fearlessness. It does this in two ways. The stress on *ahimsa* means that the more people who follow the religion, the less violence and suffering there will be in the world. Further, what everyone really fears is death, and Jain religion removes that fear by teaching how to conquer death. 'So *abhay-dan* is what we call the Jina (preaching) in the *samosaran* and *sadhu-sadhvi* giving a sermon.' *Supatra-dan* is a gift to religion. *Patra* means vessel, and *supatra* means good vessel. There are two kinds of *supatra*, Jina idols and living renouncers. So *puja* is a form of *supatra-dan*, but the word most often and most naturally refers to gifts of food, clothes, and alms-bowls to renouncers. *Anukampa-dan* is charity, given out of feelings of compassion, mercy, or pity (*anukampa, daya, karuna*). *Ucit-dan* covers a range of conventional payments: gifts to dependents on religious holidays, to members of one's family, and the gift of one's daughter in marriage (*kanya-dan*). *Kirti-dan* is well-publicized charity given with an eye to who

---

[26] Williams, *Jaina Yoga*, 156.

will think well of it. It is 'advertisement', it is 'not really *dan* at all', it is 'just business', it is 'almost sin (*pap*)'.

These are not by any means the only terms used by Jains to describe and evaluate gifts. For instance, a renouncer's sermon is also *gyan-dan*, a gift of knowledge. A gift given on impulse is thought to be especially productive of merit: you see a beggar and you give, without stopping to think. Another highly valued gift is one which is given in secret—*gupta-dan*. Giving in secret avoids the immediate reward of an increase in the donor's public status, and people say that because of this the unseen reward which comes as merit or good *karma* will be greater.[27] If someone benefits from windfall profits, people joke that they must have done *gupta-dan*, perhaps in a previous life. Now, all the gifts in the list, with the obvious exception of *kirti-dan*, can be given either in secret or not. *Gupta-dan*, which does not appear as a type on our list, cuts across the classification given there, although the low evaluation of *kirti-dan* clearly expresses a similar thought. One should also add the apparently paradoxical idea, which we will meet again in the next chapter, that *supatra-dan* is not a form of *dan* at all. Many people will say that because they respect renouncers so much, it would be wrong to describe anything given to them as *dan*, for that, they assert, is only given to inferiors in status, most typically the poor.

It has been common anthropological practice to look at systems of classification to find expressed the 'taken for granted' categories of a culture. In such an exercise it is usually considered a virtue to find a single underlying logic, to show that it is consistently applied, and to be able to harmonize different schemes. This is not what I propose to do here. In formulating and propounding the various schemes of classification which are on offer in this and other domains, I doubt that Jain intellectuals have been codifying their unspoken assumptions for the convenience of visiting anthropologists. Rather, I imagine, they have typically been attempting to change, or at least nudge, their audience's perceptions in a particular way. I take the proliferation of explicit schemes on a topic such as the gift as an indication of the contentiousness of that domain, of the likelihood that attempts are being made to persuade people of things which they may not find in the least intuitive or 'taken for granted'. Given, in this case, that

---

[27] Compare Parry, 'The Gift', 462. It is a general theme in the Hindu *dharmashastra*s that a gift, if boasted about, loses its power to earn merit. See Kane (*History of Dharmashastra*, ii. 849). Intriguingly, many people, when they explained the point of *gupta-dan*, offered the thought that 'The left hand should not know what the right hand is doing', cf. Matt. 6: 3.

there are so many other ways of labelling, talking about, and evaluating gifts, we need to ask what is the point of this one.

The first thing to strike one is that this classification does not look like a classification at all. Like Borges's celebrated Chinese encyclopaedia, the categories seem to overlap and to encompass one another. Yet renouncers insist that any particular act is properly described by one and only one of its terms. Every gift is really one or other of these kinds. We can begin to make sense of this claim if we notice that the first two terms are not concepts, but names. Although they are descriptive expressions ('of fearlessness', 'to a worthy recipient'), the content of the descriptions does not fix the reference of the terms: for an action to conform to the description is neither necessary nor sufficient to guarantee that the name will properly apply to it. Rather, *abhay-dan* and *supatra-dan* are names for practices which also have other names. *Abhay-dan* is also *pravacan*, *vyakhyan*, *samosaran*, *gyan-dan*. *Supatra-dan* is also *puja*, *atithi-samvibhag*, *ahar-dan*, and, as we shall see, *baharana*. The names can be extended metaphorically. I was told that while only renouncers can really perform *abhay-dan*, lay people can perform a lower version of it. Renouncers' teachings are the *bhav* form of *abhay-dan*, and to save the life of some creature is the *dravya* form (see Chapter 4). Lay Jains can do the latter, but obviously it is not 'really' *abhay-dan*. Similarly, and rather more insistently, I was told that a gift to just any recipient who happens to be worthy is not a case of *supatra-dan*. 'We call things we offer to Maharaj Sahab *supatra-dan* because they are the only true *supatra*.' So our classification offers the two names (*abhay* and *supatra*) as the correct descriptions of these practices, because they point to the appropriate evaluation of them. The names offer a characterization and a judgement of the things named.

The other three categories are different. They are not names but concepts, which express criteria for counting as a token of the type. They have paradigm cases, so everyone has a clear idea of a typical *kirti-dan*, but unlike the names for the first two types, which properly refer only to certain specific practices, these paradigm cases are just good examples and the number of possible different members of the class is infinite. Any gift, if it meets the criterion, will count as a token of one of these types. The criteria all concern the thoughts and motivations of the donor. If, on Diwali, you were to think, 'Just look, the sweeper has such ragged clothes, and her little son is in school now, so I think I'll give her much more than usual', then this would be a case of *anukampa-dan*. If on the other hand you thought, 'My neighbour is watching. I'll give her more so he will be impressed', then it would be *kirti-dan*. Thus the trio of terms urges us to attend to the giver's motivation, and to decide what the constitutive intention behind the gift is. We will know what to call it when we know the thought behind it. By contrast, a gift of alms to a renouncer is a *supatra-dan* irrespective of whether the donor makes the gift thinking that the recipient is worthy. That this is the appropriate term for this gift is due just to the identity of the recipient. In this case, for the donor not to think that the recipient is worthy would certainly be a sin, but that is not the point. The gift would still be *supatra-dan*.

As some of the terms are not concepts but names, we should not be looking, in an attempt to grasp the point of the classification as a whole, for a classificatory *principle* underlying distinctions between concepts, but for a rhetorical intention or purpose, motivating the names used. So what could be the point of putting together a pair of names for definite social practices with a trio of terms which distinguish between acts on the basis on the intention with which they are performed? What the list is about, I think, is how exchange between renouncers and lay people differs from the 'give and take' of society at large. The highest kind of gift is that which renouncers (or Tirthankars) give to the laity, and the next highest, the best that householders can do, is gifts from them to renouncers (or to Tirthankar idols). This exchange is in a sense the very constitution of Jain religion. And, according to this classification, it does not need to have been performed with any particular intention to count.[28]

Let me be clear. It will take no trouble at all to find Jains, renouncer and lay, who will say that a person performing *supatra-dan* certainly should do so with a pure heart, with joy, with respect, or thinking this or that. What I do not think will be said is that the absence of such a thought would mean that what they do is not a *supatra-dan*, but some other action. And it is exactly a claim of this sort which our classification does make about all the give and take (*len-den*) of worldly life. The three lower categories between them cover all the various kinds of giving and taking which occur in lay society and assert that they all, however well motivated, rank below

---

[28] Gombrich's discussion of *dan* in Sinhalese Buddhism (*Precept and Practice*, 247–53) suggests that the issues of intention of giver and virtue of recipient are important there too, but the configuration is different. The intrinsic merit of gifts to monks, or, more exactly, to the Sangha, is only a partial violation of a very pervasive ethic of intention. The balance of judgement still comes down on the side of intention. The monks Gombrich talked with agreed that the virtue of a recipient affects the merit of a gift only in so far as this is known to the giver.

the exchange which constitutes and reproduces Jain religion. The hidden distinction which the classification draws is precisely about whether or not motivation is constitutive of the type of action performed. The first two names point to the objective characteristics of the act—the fact of the matter about what is given, the fact of the matter about who receives it—whereas the last three each point to the intention of the donor.[29]

I have suggested that this should be understood against the background of the idiom of transfer of moral qualities which characterizes everyday understandings of *dan* and indeed of other kinds of gift and payment (*upahar*). If we see this list against the background of the common *savoir-faire* of gift-giving which I sketched above, the main point to emerge is that *supatra-dan* is picked out as the only gift which lay people can give whose moral status does not depend on their own moral standing. Thus the danger described by Parry, that gifts to priests might drag donors down into their recipients' cess-pit, are declared not to apply.

If this is indeed what our classification says, it is an attractive, but also an extravagant and contentious claim. In the next chapter we shall see how well it fares in practice. It is worth noting now, however, that this solution can lead to problems of its own. As I hope is clear from Part III of this book, the question of when and to what degree the intention behind an action is morally decisive is a fraught and difficult one in Jainism. One of the consequences of Terapanthi doctrines on compassion, non-violence, and intervening in worldly affairs (Chapter 7) is that in that sect *supatra-dan* is the only kind of gift which has any religious sanction. The Terapanth does not co-ordinate and organize charitable projects, animal homes, and the like, as other Jain traditions do. Its arguments carry weight even with people from other traditions, despite its troubling conse-

---

[29] It may be worth saying a few words to avoid a possible misunderstanding. The thought here is that the quality and identity of a gift depend on the intention with which it is given, not that an intention to give can stand instead of the act; not, that is, that 'it's the thought that counts'. The intention that is at issue here is an intention 'in acting' not a possibly unfulfilled intention 'to act' (on this distinction see Skinner, 'Meaning and Understanding', 60). Authors of the Hindu *dharmashastra*s seem to have been much exercised by this point, and Gonda '*Change and Continuity*, 221' records, 'the conviction, expressed by authorities on dharma that, if a gift is sent to a person, but is stolen or lost and never reaches the donee, the donor cannot reap the "unseen reward" in such a case because there is no acceptance and so no complete dana. This conviction is in perfect harmony with the belief in the autonomous appearance of symptoms or results of sinful or meritorious deeds, the facts, deeds, committal or omission as such leading to definite effects, whatever the intention or grade of consciousness of the person who acts, commits an incorrect deed or is in default.'

quences. Once when I was asking a Khartar Gacch friend about *dan*, he brought up the Terapanth doctrine.

They say the *patra* must be *supatra*. Acarya Tulsi's people, that's what they say. If I give to a poor man, he may do some bad thing and they say the sin will come to me. They say it is not *dharma* to give to the poor. Of course it is good to give to someone who is worthy, and it is best to give to *sadhu-sadhvi*s. But how much do they need? And if I see a beggar in the street and I feel something, it is my duty (*kartavya*) to give. And how can I know what is in his heart? It is not my duty to ask, 'What will he buy?' or 'What will he do?' It is my duty to help, because I feel compassion (*karuna bhav*). Didn't Mahavir Swami feel compassion for everyone? And we should do what we can.

This reflection touches glancingly on most of the issues raised by the classification above, and raises one or two which will become important as we proceed. The speaker acknowledges the superiority of *supatra-dan*, that the dangers envisaged by the Terapanthis of supporting a person who goes on to commit evil deeds do not arise in that context. But this hardly fulfils all a man's duties, and it hardly answers his feelings when he sees suffering about him. We have finer feelings—good intentions—to which it is our duty to respond. They are not to be confused or equated with our properly religious duty, but if we do not recognize them, then what is there to distinguish charity from self-aggrandizement? This, I have suggested, is more or less the point of view for which the gift classification above is arguing. As we have found before, a rigorously determinist position threatens to drag Jainism into an extremely paradoxical and literally anti-social stance. Our classification of gifts finesses the problem, avoiding the nihilism of the Terapanthi position.

However, my friend also alluded to the point that just because renouncers are renouncers, there is not very much a generous man can give them. As we shall see, the opportunity for lay Jains to make this highest gift is rigorously limited in a number of important ways. But it also happens frequently. As renouncers may not store food, each group is obliged to arrange at least one alms-round daily. The responsibility for collecting food is shared among the members of the travelling-group, so that apart for elderly renouncers who rarely go, and those young renouncers who have not yet been confirmed by the *acarya*, most undertake an alms-round at least once every two or three days. It therefore forms a regular, intimate, and, as we shall see, a delicately balanced form of interaction between Jain renouncers and their most pious and devoted followers.

14

The Gift That Doesn't Really Happen

IN the previous chapter I described, first, the cultural context which makes the alms-round, as a food transaction, a charged and morally perilous encounter, and I then described one Jain doctrinal solution to the problem this presents, a quasi-classification whose point is to assert that gifts to Jain renouncers are axiomatically virtuous, and immune from these 'gastro-political' considerations. Both these ideas are enacted in the alms-round as it occurs in Jain communities today, but they do not appear, in practice, as 'problem' and 'solution', so that the latter supersedes and erases the former. For reasons I shall explain, they remain at best in a delicate balance, which both donor and recipient must work, in each encounter, to achieve; and from which both are tempted, for their own reasons, to depart.

Poisonous Alms

If a monk should eat forbidden food which a pious (layman) has prepared for some guest, and which food has been mixed up with even a thousand (times more pure food),[1] he would be neither monk nor layman. [Renouncers] who do not comprehend this and do not know what is dangerous, who care for the pleasures of the moment only, will suffer death an endless number of times, like big fishes who when the water rises are by the water (deposited) on dry land and are killed (there), poor things, by hungry dhankas and herons.[2]

The considerations I described above as the 'gastro–politics' of hospitality are the essential background against which the alms-round must be seen. They are, as I said there, practical good sense, what is 'only to be expected' when cooked food changes hands in domestic contexts and what is always to be feared in the context of religious gifts. Jains, by any standards, and renouncers as much as any others, are very concerned about the purity (*shuddhita*) of the food they eat, and of course (because the ubiquitous

---

[1] Jacobi notes that this passage might be translated as 'though the food passes through the hands of a thousand men before he accepts it'.

[2] Jacobi, *Jaina Sutras*, ii. 243–4.

presence of living things makes food impure) these concerns are also expressed in terms of *ahimsa*.

All cooking and preparation of food involves violence. This is accepted as inevitable, and even the most pious lay women do not, I think, actually feel guilty about cooking. Nevertheless, that it is a sin is culturally recognized. Jain housewives do not talk of cutting or chopping vegetables, but, using the verb *sudharna*, of repairing or amending them. There are some everyday rules about the preparation of food which refer directly to *ahimsa*. Mostly, this is to do with not using a range of spices and other substances which are thought to harbour life-forms. There are other rules, such as the following:

At the end of the day, after the last meal has been eaten, the women have to prepare *kakras* out of the left over *fulka* (a type of wheat bread which is thin, flat and round like a pancake). This involves heating the *fulkas* on a flat pan and at the same time applying pressure, so that all the water is extracted and the *fulka* becomes a wafer thin biscuit. This is an essential task as cooked food containing moisture cannot be left overnight, due to possible bacterial growth.[3]

Renouncers and lay Jains, men and women alike, all agree that the sin involved in breaking or being lax in any of these regulations will fall on all those who consume the food.

But renouncers must also judge the purity of the household from which they take food more broadly than merely in terms of the particular techniques they use in cooking. Lay Jains say that the reason modern renouncers are less rigorous than the great saints of the past is that they receive food from lax modern householders. If a man cheats in business, and buys food with the proceeds, which a renouncer then eats, how will she be able to live strictly? If a woman flirts with her brother-in-law and then cooks food which a renouncer eats, how will the latter be able to observe all the elaborate rules of chastity? Her mind will wander, her concentration will fail, and in the end she will commit some sin. The following story is one of the most popular staples of renouncers' sermons, and indicates, I think, the danger of moral and spiritual poison being transmitted by cooked food. It concerns a lay couple of Mahavir's time, Puniya Shravak and his wife, who have taken the *anuvrat*s.

There was a very religious Jain couple who had both taken a vow of *varshi tap*, that is, to fast on each alternate day for a year (Chapter 10). On a day on which the husband fasted, the wife did not, and vice versa. One day, while her husband was out in the bazaar and the wife was at home fasting, the time came to cook her

[3] Reynell, 'Honour, Nurture and Festivity', 123–4.

husband's meal. She discovered that the fire had gone out but when she called at the house of a neighbour to ask for some lighted wood for kindling, that house was empty. She became very anxious. At nightfall, her husband's fast was to begin. Concerned that he should be able to eat before then, she took a small ember from her absent neighbour's fire and returned to cook the meal.

Next day her husband was unable to perform *samayik*. His mind wandered, and he fell asleep. When he complained of this to his wife she remembered her misdeed. Under the *anuvrat* vow, theft includes taking anything which is not freely offered by its owner, so that in taking the lighted wood in the owner's absence she had broken this rule. The food she had cooked had therefore been impure, and from having ingested this impurity her husband's mind was disturbed. Only when she had performed a penance did his peace of mind return.

The purity of food depends perhaps most of all on that of the person who cooks it. In general, women are held responsible for the health and well-being of their family. It is well known that in most north Indian communities women shoulder much of the blame if their husband dies prematurely, and the Jains are no exception here (the fasts I described in Chapter 10, which women perform for their husband's health, are the other side of this coin). This is only the most extreme manifestation of the way women's moral probity is held to affect their families. A loose or impious woman puts her family in moral peril, in part through the food she feeds them. Therefore it is particularly to the moral and religious standards of the women in the household that renouncers look. Do they fast on the auspicious days of each month? Do they attend sermons? Does the household in general, and the women in particular, follow restrictions on what they will eat, and when, that at least come close to those they follow themselves? Renouncers must not eat or drink after sunset; so only families in which at least one member of the family eats before then can offer the evening meal. In very few households does everyone eat so early, especially in the winter, but many women do. They will have to prepare their husband's meal later, and quite apart from the extra labour this involves, it means that they do not avoid committing *himsa*. But it does enable them to make this gift.

Though a renouncer does not have social status, as normally understood, which she needs to defend or try to advance, her *karmik* status is conceived as being at stake in exactly the same way, through exactly the same exchanges.[4] The dangers of food exchange are common to re-

---

[4] Thus it makes sense that the *Acaranga Sutra* advises renouncers to attend to the ethics, social status, lineage, caste, and occupation of potential donors (Jacobi, *Jaina Sutras*, i. 92).

nouncers and householders, as are the ways to avoid them.[5] Thus renouncers have good reason to monitor the general probity of the families
they accept food from; and this means that the best donors are lay ascetics
(*shramanas*), people who like themselves are progressing, albeit more
slowly, on the path to purification.

Thus far, then, the ethics of renouncers and pious lay Jains are congruent. There are however a number of rules and restrictions in the alms-
round which presume a very different relation between renouncers and
householders: rules which make sense only for the renouncer as Jina icon,
standing already outside the world, and the categorical moral opposite of
the householder. As a consequence, it is very unlike a normal event of
social hospitality.

Grazing

> Like bees from flowers
> Shall we derive subsistence from alms
> Out of what is ready-made
> Without burden to anyone.[6]

If, as I have suggested, the renouncers' alms-round is enmeshed in the
game of gastro-politics, renouncers are constrained to adopt a very unusual strategy in it: a strategy which, as we shall see, amounts in effect to
refusing to play. The alms-round is called *gocari*, which means 'grazing',
literally 'eating like a cow'.[7] As the cow eats only the top of the grass,
leaving the plant to grow, the renouncer takes only a little from each
household, leaving it unaffected. As the cow wanders about eating a little
here and there, no one knows where the renouncer will go. As the cow eats
whatever is available, so the renouncer mixes different kinds of food from
different households, regardless of the taste. And just as the cow is sometimes beaten and chased away, the renouncer risks refusal and abuse by
calling unexpectedly and unannounced at both Jain and non-Jain households. She should not follow a fixed route each day, and should not collect
food regularly from the same households. At each house, she should take

---

[5] Like anyone else, renouncers avoid taking food from families where a death has occurred in the last few days. However, they also observe the same avoidance after a marriage,
to avoid contact through food with sexuality, fertility, and reproduction.

[6] Lalwani, *Dashavaikalika Sutra*, 3. A large portion of this text is concerned with rules
governing renouncers' alms-rounds and it is regarded by renouncers today as the basic
authority on the matter.

[7] This image is also in the *Dashavaikalika Sutra* (Lalwani, 59).

only a little food, so little that its absence will not be noticed. So she must call at a number of houses, collecting a little at each one, until she has enough for the whole group.

In fact, routes followed on *gocari* do not exactly resemble those of a cow, for although they are not formally prescribed, neither are they exactly wandering. Even in the alleys and inter-connecting courtyards of Jaipur city, most renouncers know their way around. Those who are new to the city are directed to Shvetambar households, if not actually accompanied to them, by local lay Jains, sect employees, or officials. So in so far as renouncers' routes do resemble the wanderings of a cow, this is because they go to some trouble to make them so: consciously changing their route from day to day.

The preparation of food involves sin, and a renouncer, as sacred teacher and advocate of world-renunciation, must not be the occasion for this. Here, the danger is not just that the renouncer will be infected by the sins of her donors, a fear any recipient of food might have, but rather that in being the occasion for the preparation of food (and, by extension, any worldly activity), the renouncer might cause householders to commit sin. Not only would this be a perversion of her role as sacred teacher and icon of the Tirthankar, and not only would it wipe out the merit of the gift from the householders' point of view, but in so far as the renouncer were to be the occasion for sinful action, she would share with the householder the bad *karma* issuing from that act. It follows that the food which householders donate, though it must be prepared to very exacting standards of purity, should not be intended especially for them. That is to say, lay householders may only donate food which they have prepared for their own consumption, and which they would have eaten themselves, had not the renouncers come by. In addition, the renouncers should ensure that the householder, having given food, will not then cook more, for the sin of this cooking would fall to them. They should take only a small amount from each household, so little that no one will take the trouble to replace it.

Rules of lay conduct are often expressed negatively: 'Do not eat after nightfall.' Virtues are 'non-violence' and 'non-attachment'. Reflective Jains are quite conscious of this. One young man I knew had a forceful sense of the reason for it.

It is not because Jainism is negative in outlook, but because the Jina and the *acarya*s never tell people to do things which are sinful. If they were to preach that we should eat before nightfall, this would be saying that we should eat, and eating is sin. If they said, 'have sex with your wife', this would also be very bad. They should not even say that you must boil water before you drink it, because really, to boil water is a sin. But it is better to drink boiled water than unboiled water, so they say 'Do not drink water which has not been boiled'.

Let us consider, again, the case of boiled water (though the reader may doubt that there can possibly be more to say). I explained in Chapter 7 that renouncers may drink only boiled water, and that a few householders follow the same rule. I mentioned that most of the boiled water which renouncers actually do drink has been prepared by non-Jain temple servants. This is admitted to be less than satisfactory, but it does get everyone out of a difficult situation. The problem is how to deal morally with the inescapable fact that renouncers can only avoid a whole range of sinful activities because their followers perform them regularly and routinely. The images of cows and bees express the sense in which renouncers' virtue is parasitic on conduct, on the part of householders, which from the renouncers' own perspective is sinful. It is crucial, then, that when householders perform these actions, such as boiling water, they do not do so in order that they may benefit renouncers. The balance is a delicate one.

It is fairly widespread in Hinduism for an ascetic, a priest, or a deity to be thought of as accepting and consuming the impurities and sins of followers, clients, and devotees.[8] Here, in the Shvetambar case, this possibility is acknowledged, but given a vigorous and at the same time punctilious repudiation. It is only because the householder sins that the renouncer does not need to, but the renouncer refuses to allow the householder to sin on her behalf. If householders must sin, Jain renouncers will have none of it.

Conflicting Ideals

There are, I think, two important points to be brought out of these images of cows and bees and the rules which relate to them. The first is that the

---

[8] Babb (*Redemptive Encounters*, 66) mentions that the Radhasoamis share, 'the ubiquitous belief that a sant satguru can actually assume the load of karmic effects carried by devotees. Babuji Maharaj, for example, suffered from a mild case of leukoderma, which he is said to have taken onto himself from a female devotee. In accord with this general idea, an offering to a guru would appear to be, among other things, a possible vehicle through which the offerer can deliver up impurities, his or her 'sins', which are taken by the guru into or onto himself.' Babb concludes (212): 'Devotees are purified by assimilating, and being assimilated by, objects of worship; they are perfected by blending with the perfect.' Gold (*Fruitful Journeys*, 179) describes how snake-bites and mad-dog bites are cured at a Devji shrine in Rajasthan by having the sick worshippers 'swept' with neem leaves which are then offered to the deity: 'The deity, without harm to himself, is able to receive the poison transmitted to him by the sweeping.' See also Parry, 'Sacrificial Death'; 'Death and Digestion'; 'Moral Perils'.

renouncer is *atithi*, an uninvited and unexpected guest. It is very important that the food she eats should never have been prepared especially for
her. Here is a senior male renouncer of the Khartar Gacch, talking on this
theme.

Suppose we were to go for *gocari* and bring it back. There is a rule that we
can't take food that has been prepared specially for us. But suppose we come to
know that this food has been made for us. It is our duty not to eat it, and so we
must throw it away. But it is also a rule (*niyam*) that we cannot throw food away.
We have to dig a small hole in the ground (even though there is some *himsa*
in that), put the food in there, and cover it. This is a *vivekarya pap* (a sin resulting
from lack of carefulness) and we must do *pratikraman* and some *tapasya* as
penance.

Not only does this requirement apply regardless of the piety of the households involved, but the notion that the food one eats should in fact have
been prepared for someone else brings it dangerously close to the possibility of depriving someone else of their sustenance; something which, for
a householder, would be a sin.

The second point to bring out of the *gocari* image then, is that it would
be wrong for a renouncer too, and the danger is spotted and avoided, but
in a very particular way. I cannot say that I have seen the following rule
obeyed, for I have not seen the situation arise, but I was told it often
enough to be sure that it is an important clue to how renouncers see their
position.

If, while a renouncer is receiving food from a household, a beggar should happen
to call, the renouncer may not take and eat the food. She must not accept food
which the beggar needs and asks for. She can fast, so she does not need the food.
However, she cannot give the food to the beggar. She does not own it, she does not
own anything, so she cannot give it. She cannot intervene in the affairs of the
world, so just as she must not deprive the beggar of food, she cannot be a donor of
food either. All she can do is to preach to the beggar, to explain to him that *karma*
is the cause of his suffering, and that attachment is the cause of his *karma*. If only
he will follow Jain religion he too will not mind if he does not eat. The renouncer
must then fast. The food must be thrown away.

For a renouncer, the uncompromising rigour implied here is becoming,
and the resort to preaching is fitting; but how unthinkable that a rich lay
merchant should behave in this way!

So it should be apparent that there is a distinct lack of fit between this
ideal of more or less random grazing, and the rather careful and punctili-

ous concerns about the purity of food which I outlined above. A cow, wandering the streets of an Indian city picking banana-skins and rotting tomatoes out of the gutter, would not do well in gastro-politics. It might be thought that drawing food from many sources is a sort of insurance policy (like agricultural diversification), an attempt to avoid massive pollution from one source by drawing from many, but this is not so. Jainism puts too much stress on scrupulousness, watchfulness, and vigilance, for this ever to seem like a virtuous strategy. And it is too ready to imagine overwhelming calamity resulting from one small slip for it ever to seem a rational one. The two sets of considerations which the renouncer brings to the alms-round are to some degree in tension. This point needs some emphasis. The most obvious solution to the problem of how to collect only pure food, replicating that which householders themselves adopt, would be to call on just a few respectable and religious families on whose general conduct and religious care they could rely, and take food only from them. But this solution, which is the way lay Jains typically play at gastro-politics, is blocked by the requirements encapsulated in the *gocari* image, which have no counterpart in lay ethics. So in practice the renouncers' grazing strategy exists in complex juxtaposition with matters of hospitality and generosity.

If renouncers are spotted approaching the house, a family will launch into a flurry of preparation, but their manner becomes instantly formal and elaborately graceful as soon as the renouncers actually appear (see Plates XVI–XVIII). They perform *vandan*, and then invite them in as they would any honoured guests, 'Come Maharaj Sahab, Come'. And the renouncers are as curt and perfunctory as their hosts are ingratiating. Typically, they march straight to the kitchen without acknowledging the family's bows and greetings. At the door of the kitchen they first look to see that it is clean. To the Jain renouncer, 'clean' means among other things that it must be dry; for any unboiled water (*kacca-pani*) which is lying on the floor or on work surfaces will harbour *jivs*, and is therefore just as 'dirty' as muddy footprints or scraps of food. Similarly, they will not accept food from anyone with wet hands. I have never seen a renouncer turn away from a Jain kitchen, having found it inadequate on this account, but judging by the hurried wiping of the floor and last-minute tidying away I did see, the possibility that she may is at least entertained. The renouncers check that no prohibited food (such as onions or potatoes) is lying around. They will not take food from anyone who has just been cutting green vegetables, or, in many cases, anyone they see near cut vegetables. They check that the gas on the cooker has been switched off.

PLATES XVI–XVIII. NUNS ON THEIR ALMS-ROUND IN JAIPUR.

PLATE XVI. A Khartar Gacch nun prepares to leave the Dadabari temple, carrying her alms bowls and her staff. The colours painted on these indicate which *gacch* she belongs to.

PLATE XVII (above) and
XVIII (left). Alms being
given in the kitchens of
Jain homes.

This is a sign that the housewife will not cook more to replace what the renouncer is given.

When satisfied, they come into the kitchen and produce their alms bowls (*patra*s or *kamandal*s).⁹ Members of the family gather to take part in the offering. The women answer renouncers' sometimes sharp and repeated questions about whether a dish is acceptable for them. They also co-ordinate the offering by members of the family, for they generally know the rules much better than the men, and they show the children how to do it properly. Nevertheless, the male head of the household, if he is present, is usually first actually to present food. His wife passes food first to him, and then to the other members of the household, and each takes turns to place the food in the alms bowls. She must be careful not to touch the *tava* (the flat plate on which chapatis are prepared), and she must not take food from the refrigerator, or touch any electrical switch.

If the renouncers who have come are women, men must be careful to drop the food so that it does not touch the bowl before they have let go. If it does, the nuns will be unable, for at least one *ghanta* (forty-eight minutes), even to touch the food.¹⁰ Renouncers must be careful that nothing which they should not eat is placed in their bowls; for once there, it cannot be taken out. During the whole proceedings, the renouncers keep up a constant refrain, 'Enough! Finish! No, we won't take that! No more of that! Enough!' The householders counter with assurances of the purity and quality of the food, that it has all been prepared in the home, that this dish cannot possibly be eaten without that accompaniment, that they have taken so very little and they must take more. When they have decided they really do have enough, the renouncers wrap up their bowls and go, with the family continuing their appeals and complaints about how little they have taken, even as they leave. On leaving the house,

---

⁹ In his brief description of the Shvetambar alms-round (*Jaina Path*, 219), Jaini writes, 'They are received at the door with respect, brought into the house (but not the kitchen), and offered suitable food and water.' This is an interesting matter, partly because of the considerations about the bodily purity of renouncers which I discussed in ch. 11. I have seen *gocari* performed outside the kitchen, but it is more common for renouncers to come straight into the kitchen. When I asked a friend in Jaipur about this she said, 'We Jains are not so particular about this as many Hindus are. Some people will even go into the kitchen in the morning before taking a bath. Remember, for us, taking a bath is a sin.'

¹⁰ This is a requirement of the renouncers' *brahma-vrat*, which forbids them from any physical contact with the opposite sex, even mediated by other physical objects. Of course, the same rule applies *mutatis mutandis* in the case of monks.

renouncers say the words *dharma labh* as a blessing; but on most occasions when I have been present they had already turned away from their hosts and were on their way into the street by the time they called this out behind them.

These patterns of behaviour are generally adhered to regardless of how well the renouncers and family members actually know each other, re-gardless of how relaxed and informal their intercourse at other times might be. For it is not principally as the individuals who know each other that they meet each other in this encounter. Renouncers are enjoined to call as readily at the houses of those they do not know as of those they do. Householders are forbidden to favour some renouncers over others when they offer food. When they meet in this encounter, it is impersonally, as worthy recipients and qualified donors.

When they have visited a number of households, and collected as much as they need, the renouncers take the food back to the *upashraya*.[11] It is still a matter of concern that renouncers' need for food should not cause anyone else to cook or eat. If someone were to become hungry while watching renouncers eat, or take a fancy to some dish they were eating and go home to eat the same thing, then part of the sin of that act would fall on the renouncer who inspired the action. So they always eat and drink out of public view. The idea that the Jina could not be seen eating is also, I am sure, relevant. One renouncer added a further reason. It would be wrong to give any lay persons who were in the *upashraya* an opportunity to see the food they had collected, for they might gossip about the kind of food they had been given at specific houses, making remarks about the quality of the food. It would be a great sin for the renouncers, she said, to allow someone's reputation to suffer as a result of giving them alms. So Shvetambar renouncers always retire to an inner room or behind a screen. Among the Terapanthis no one, not even other renouncers, may see the *acarya* eat. Sometimes the concealment does seem rather half-hearted. I was once in a group of people talking to a nun when one of her disciples brought her a glass of water. She simply lifted the end of her robe in front of her and drank behind it; but as she later explained, even though people see that she is drinking, they are simultaneously reminded by her

---

[11] They should not eat at a house where they receive food except in special circumstances. If it starts to rain after they have accepted food, but before they leave with it, they should stay and eat at the house, but not in the presence of the family. If they are staying at a lay household rather than an *upashraya*, they may accept food from that family, but not every day.

'concealment' that drinking involves some sin, so they will not be moved to drink too.[12]

We can see, then, how these considerations close off the otherwise attractive solution for renouncers of relying regularly on the same small number of households to provide food, for these households would inevitably prepare enough to accommodate the renouncer, so the food would have been prepared with the intention of some of it being for her. The renouncer would in effect be incorporated into these households and thus no longer outside the world. If this were the case, then among other things the categorical merit of the *supatra-dan* would be lost. It would then be just another transaction in the world, dependent for its virtue on the intentions, and the particular and necessarily imperfect qualities, of the participants.

Divergent Interests

So, renouncers and householders approach the encounter with a set of shared understandings and concerns about the purity of food, its effects on one's inner state, and how to manage transactions where these things are at stake. The householders are keen to be hospitable: in the genuinely double-edged sense of wanting to be disinterestedly generous to their guests, and at the same time seeking to forge a personalized link with them. Yet, on the other hand, the two parties have other, quite different and contrasting projects and ambitions. The character and the religious importance of this practice can only be explained when one sees that different representations of what is most crucially at stake inform the conduct of the two participating sides.[13]

If a family follows the appropriate dietary restrictions, attends religious functions, and refrains from wicked conduct, if, in short, they believe the food they offer to be pure, and so fit for a renouncer, then there is no reason, which could be a reason for them, not to offer as much as they can. In a host of popular Jain stories a householder receives immense rewards as a result of a generous donation of food to a renouncer. This

[12] Yalman ('Meaning of Food Offerings', 85) describes how Buddhist monks in Ceylon, during *katina pinkama*, eat in formal privacy behind a white sheet marking a special area of purity. Yalman sees this as an extreme form of the privacy of food consumption which he notes among lay villagers, but I wonder if considerations similar to the Jain ones are at work.

[13] For an excellent analysis of initiation ritual which hangs on a similar situation, see Houseman 'Interactive Basis of Ritual'.

is one of my favourites, because it also points to the pitfalls of generosity.[14]

There was a very poor widow who had a little son. The neighbours were well-off, and their children used to tell the boy about all the sweets they had at home, but he never got to taste any. His mother cleaned utensils in other people's kitchens. Whatever money she got would only buy plain chapatis, and even then they were always hungry. One day the boy said he wanted to eat kheer (a sweet dish made from rice and milk). Everyone else was eating kheer (there are some Jain religious festivals when it is traditional to do so), but he had never even tasted it. He began to cry, but his mother said, 'How can I make it? From where will I bring the rice, milk, and sugar?' She had great affection for the boy, so although she was a proud woman she went begging to some of the neighbours, and asked for just a little of these things to make kheer for the boy. She got the things, prepared the kheer, covered it, and went out, saying to her son, 'You sit there till I come back. I'm going to fetch water.'

While she was gone, two monks came by. Every day the boy saw people giving food to Jain monks, and had always wanted to give too. But because they never even had enough to eat themselves, they never had. The boy thought, 'How good it is that the monks have come today, when we have kheer to offer.' There was only a very small pot, but he gave it all to the monks, and still he wished he could give more. Seeing this strong wish (*bhavana*) of his, the monks didn't say anything (that is, did not refuse the food). They took the kheer and went.

What a great merit he earned! He had never had this sweet and still he gave it to Maharaj Sahab. There were just scraps left round the pot and he licked at them. His mother came back then and thought he had just eaten it all himself. She gave him the evil eye (*nazar lag gai*[15]). She didn't know what he had done. That night he died. But because he had such pure thoughts, there was no problem in his soul or his mind, only with his body, and he died as if in meditation. Three births later he was born as Mahavir Swami.

Now the point of this story (or the point, at any rate, which it was always told to me to illustrate) is the great reward of a generous gift (how even *keval gyan* can result from it), but we should also notice that one of the reasons for the boy's death is that the monks, moved by the boy's strong feelings, relax their adherence to one aspect of their rules, and accept the

[14] This is the story as it was told to me by a Jain lady in Jaipur. It is clearly a version of one which Balbir ('Stories from Commentaries', 26) translates from a commentary on the *Avashyaka Sutra*. There, it is not a pre-birth story of Mahavir, but the point is still how presenting alms to renouncers can lead to enlightenment.

[15] The story-teller later explained that she didn't think this was deliberate. The evil eye can work unintentionally, and indeed it often does. The mother's gaze, she added, is the most powerful and potentially the most dangerous. Compare Trawick, *Notes on Love*, 93, 269–70. Cf. also Maloney, 'Don't Say "Pretty Baby"'; Pocock, *Mind, Body and Wealth*.

whole bowl of kheer. The attempt by the householder fully to perform his or her duty as a patron and provider, conflicts with the attempts of the renouncer to remain detached from the world and avoid causing action (*karma*) within it. So while the householder presses food in pursuit of a generous gift, the renouncer must resist. The logic whereby the best gift is a munificent gift, which logic applies to the householder performing *dan*, runs counter to a logic by which the renouncer seeks to escape the entanglements of *karmik* causality and to be, like the omniscient Jina, in the world and yet outside it.

Lay Jains never say that they have 'given' something to a renouncer. They avoid the usual verb *dena*, and use instead *baharana*, a word which, so far as I know, is used only by Jains, and only in the context of giving to renouncers.[16] *Supatra-dan*, it will be recalled, is the only form of gift in the classification above which is always given by definition to a superior (this is what lies behind the apparently paradoxical, but actually rather common statement, that *supatra-dan* is not *dan*) and one of the effects of this convention is quite firmly to displace any implication that the recipient might be demeaned or dependent by being in receipt of this gift. The image of the alms-round as grazing in the end implies that although it is a gift, indeed, the best gift, it is not a gift at all.

If the householder does not give, neither does the renouncer exactly receive food. All the food collected from different households is taken back to the *upashraya*, where it is mixed with any brought by other renouncers, and where the leader of the travelling group then redistributes it among all the members of the group. There are always several different foods already in each bowl, and strict renouncers go further and mix all the different foods together in one mass. This makes the food taste less good, so that eating it becomes an austerity, but it also makes each individual's donation indistinguishable from any other. From the moment it is placed in a renouncer's bowl, moreover, it is no longer referred to as food (*khana*). It is called, after the alms-round itself, *gocari*. Renouncers are never spoken of as 'eating food', but always as 'taking *gocari*'. The food

---

[16] Unusually, people I spoke to in Jaipur did not have folk-derivations to offer for this word, and it is difficult to trace. From John D. Smith I learn that the Rajasthani *bairanau* means 'to give alms to a Jain monk', 'to give a meal', and 'to split'; and K. R. Norman has suggested that a possible, though by no means certain derivation might be from the Sanskrit *viphalati*, 'to burst or split', which also has the meaning 'to become fruitful'. The causative of this would mean 'to make fruitful, prosper', and it is just possible that this idea could be used of 'making a donation'. But neither *baharana* nor *viphalati* (used in this sense) seems to occur in ancient Jain texts, and the origins of the word *baharana* as used today remain something of a mystery.

is received by the group, transformed into *gocari*, and shared among its members. In this sense the householder does not give anything which the renouncer receives.[17]

This is not the only occasion in Jainism when something of this sort occurs. When Jains perform *puja* to a Tirthankar idol, they make a number of offerings, including rice, fruits, and sweets. Rather as Hindus do when they perform *puja*, Jains take these offerings and place them before the idol; but unlike in a Hindu temple, they never receive any of these offerings back as *prasad* (blessing) from the deity. As Babb has argued, this is because one of the points of making the offering in the Jain case, reflecting the general concern with sacrifice and renunciation, is to relinquish or give up what is offered. And it is also because the Jina, to whom the offering is made, is absolutely removed from worldly affairs, and does not receive it.[18] Now it is significant, I think, that offerings to Tirthankar idols are the other class of gifts which are named *supatra-dan*. For what is needed in order for a generous gift to count also as an ascetic renunciation (*tyag*) or a giving up, is a recipient who will not receive it.

So the householder makes a generous gift which is utterly unreciprocated, to a recipient who is very unwilling to receive it. The renouncer, on the other hand, obtains food without anyone really having given her any. Now this situation would remain quite incomprehensible if we had to think there was one underlying theory about some supposedly real movement of substances, some ethno-metaphysics of the gift of which practice is an enactment. I have suggested that we see this transaction rather as a ritualized practice which is both constructed and understood by participants with reference to two rather different figurative schemes, the game of gastro-politics and the image of grazing without consequences. I have stressed how, while both these ideas certainly inform the understandings of both sides of the transaction, they inform the *interests* of those participants in rather different ways. To householders, gastro-politics presents the opportunity to forge links with particular renouncers (a point to which we shall return); whereas for renouncers it represents a rather potent danger. For renouncers, grazing is an ideal which condenses much of their world-renouncing project; whereas for householders it represents a set of obstacles to their making a generous gift. All this is reflected in the fact that the two sides refer to the encounter

[17] Van der Veer (*Gods on Earth*, 265) reports that Brahmin *panda*s in Ayodhya claim, less persuasively, that the river Sarayu, not they, receives the gifts of their visitors.

[18] Babb, 'Giving and Giving Up'.

in different ways: to renouncers it is *gocari*; to householders, *baharana*. More importantly, the different ways participants learn to conduct themselves during the encounter enact the contrasting rather than the shared understandings.

The way the two sides behave seems quite fiercely competitive, and the idiom of coercive hospitality again suggests the gastro-politics of competitive giving, in which accepting food creates status inferiority. Yet it would, I am certain, be a mistake to interpret the householder as trying to belittle or subordinate the renouncer by making her indebted. They are, rather, offering tribute. That is what they say they are doing, and while it isn't the whole truth, no interpretation which denied the claim could, I think, be valid. They might well be proud of the food they offer: they know it contains only permitted substances; they know it has been prepared carefully without undue *himsa*; they know it is made with fine quality ghee and good rice; and so on. They might even be proud of their wealth and worldly accomplishments, which make all this possible. None of this in incompatible with also placing extremely high, perhaps one should even say ultimate value on renunciation, and according renouncers commensurate respect. It is just because gifts of alms are ordinarily seen as demeaning that so much trouble must be gone to with this one, but the important point is that lay Jains do routinely go to quite a lot of trouble.

Negotiations of Regard

The impression one gets from watching the *baharana* is that it is like haggling in the bazaar. But a better model for this aspect of what is going on, I think, is barter. Now this might seem very far-fetched, because patently only one type of goods changes hands, and it passes in only one direction; but if we remember that the characteristic context for barter is across social and cultural frontiers,[19] then it might be less surprising to find something like it on the border between in-the-world and out of it. And it seems to me that the social relation which this transaction creates between participants can best be explicated with reference to this form of exchange. Caroline Humphrey and Stephen Hugh-Jones have argued that barter is 'a mode of exchange in its own right', to be set alongside those which have more often been given attention by anthropologists: gift exchange, sharing, redistribution, and commodity transactions.

[19] Thomas, *Entangled Objects*.

Essentially the exchange in barter is determined by the interest which each side has in the object of the other, an interest which is satisfied by the transaction. The objects exchanged have direct consumption values for the participants. Monetary exchange is different: here the value of one exchange object (money) has no direct use, but is merely a claim on other definite values.[20]

Now there are occasions when currency objects can become objects of direct consumption, and in these circumstances money does have a direct use,[21] but as an observation about the difference between distinct forms of exchange, this seems absolutely right. Humphrey and Hugh-Jones go on to argue that barter exchange creates distinctive forms of social relations, 'in its own mode'. They pick out four aspects of such relations. The first, that a barter exchange can be complete in itself, requiring no further transaction (as monetary and gift exchange both do), clearly holds in the case of *baharana*. Indeed, that the transaction is complete in itself, leaving no debt, is perhaps the renouncer's central concern. The second characteristic, however, is that barter relations can become repeatable, and for this to happen it is essential (unlike monetary exchange) that trust develops between exchange partners. I shall return to this point below. The third characteristic of barter exchange (and here it is distinguished from many forms of competitive gift exchange) is that the objects exchanged are dissimilar. Indeed they are frequently incomparable, so that no abstract standard of value (such as money) can be used to measure and match the consumption values. In this respect too the *baharana* is like barter, for although it is intangible and not even in the usual sense a service, the good which the renouncers have—the limited (and hence in the economic sense scarce) opportunity to perform *baharana*—becomes for the householders an object of direct consumption. So while from one perspective there is only one thing which changes hands in the transaction, this thing constitutes two quite different kinds of object of consumption for the two participants.

This helps us to see what the haggling is about. As Humphrey and Hugh-Jones emphasize, the outcome of a barter transaction (how much of each good changes hands) cannot be understood as a reflection of abstract values which exist separately from the particular circumstances and the particular participants in a given transaction. They directly reflect what Marilyn Strathern calls, 'the regard in which the other is held'.[22]

[20] Humphrey and Hugh-Jones, *Barter*, 7–8.
[21] Parry and Bloch, *Money and Morality*.
[22] Strathern, 'Qualified Value'.

Thus it makes no sense to ask, in the abstract, how many oxen a statue is worth. The 'many extraneous factors' which influence the accident of an exchange ratio actually reached are in fact the sum of economic, political, social and psychological pressures on either side brought to bear in a particular instance. Therefore, the values which bartered objects represent are indicative of the confrontation between ways of life . . . Barter thus uses goods to create a relationship of mutual estimation between the self and a partner who is a representative of an 'other' set of values.[23]

When the renouncers and householders in a particular confrontation reach their bargain on how much food the former will accept, and how great a 'benefit of giving' (*dan ka labh*) the latter will receive, they meet, necessarily, as representatives of quite other ways of life (indeed the rules accentuate this). But in accepting their food, renouncers are according regard not just to householders in general, but to that particular family on that particular day. As I have emphasized, the moral standing of the particular families renouncers accept food from is believed, in spite of all precautions, to be a potential moral peril. Donors try to persuade the renouncers to take more, by stressing both the quality and the purity of the food on offer, that is, by stressing the goodness and material well-being which their household, just because it is in the world, can offer, and also that as pious lay Jains their food conforms, well enough, to the values the renouncers' way of life embodies. In one way the situation is straightforward: the more the renouncer accepts the better the regard she is showing for the family and it is this for which the family campaigns. But in another way it is complex, because the way the renouncers accord regard to that particular family, in addition to accepting the food, is by resolutely conducting the transaction as if it might be any family; that is, by sticking strictly to the rules which make their accepting food a grazing and not the acceptance of a personal gift. And for householders the act of giving, even this haggled and disputed giving, is at the same time an expression of devotion and an act of homage, comparable to the offerings they make in temple worship. So what is being haggled about is the relationship which stands at the centre of Jainism, that between renouncers and householders. In *baharana* that relationship, as it pertains to the particular parties involved, is repeatedly and routinely renegotiated.

A Reconciling Context

Humphrey and Hugh-Jones pick out as the fourth characteristic of barter exchange the fact that it results in 'a perfect balance'. This is in contradis-

---

[23] Humphrey and Hugh-Jones, *Barter*, 10.

tinction to gift exchange, in which any given transaction produces or reproduces an inequality or a debt. In principle, they argue, because the transactors are quits, and both sides having agreed to the transaction, 'the very act of barter exchange creates equality out of dissimilarity'.[24] Now in the case of the Jain *baharana*, it would not be correct to say that what the exchange produces is equality. But it does produce something which we might profitably think of as a parallel achievement, in the context of ways of life where the opposition between them is not just radical but logical. That is, it produces, to adapt Strathern's phrase, a mutuality of regard. The result is that despite the appearance of haggling, and despite the fact that the interests motivating the parties in the encounter are different and to some degree opposed, these interests are played off against one another in a way which is, if and only if both sides barter well, of mutual profit.

Jonathan Parry remarks that the gift from which most merit is earned is that given to the most worthy recipient (*supatra*), 'and who should this be but the one who is most unwilling to receive it'.[25] We have seen that from the renouncers' imperative to avoid causing others to sin, it follows that 'unwilling to receive' is exactly what they must appear to their hosts to be. Thus the conduct which the renouncers follow in order to conform to the ideal of gathering creates for the householder exactly the situation required for the most meritorious *dan*. The gift is free and spontaneous, because the renouncers come unexpectedly. They do not ask for anything. They resist receiving the gift, so that everything they do take has to be urged upon them. They give nothing in return. They show no pleasure in receiving what they accept, and leave without expressing any gratitude. On the contrary it is the householders who express gratitude for the renouncers' having accepted food, and who urgently request them to return. The householders, by insistently offering more than the renouncers can accept, enable the latter to practise restraint, and still obtain the food required for their group; while at the same time the renouncer, by refusing excess food, affirms her fitness to receive what she does, confirms the householder's gift as unambiguously generous, and, by showing restraint, increases the merit which accrues to the householder from his or her gift. But there is more to it than this. As I have said, renouncers are very definitely not immune to the gastro–political considerations which impel householders to wish *their* food accepted (it matters very much to

[24] Ibid. 11.
[25] Parry, 'The Gift', 460.

renouncers who they take their food from); and neither are householders indifferent to the particular religious identity of *this* unwilling recipient (for the latter's status as strict renouncers is also at issue).

Although renouncers receive only a small amount of food from any single household, so that the food actually given, while conforming to the grammar of generosity, can hardly be a serious sacrifice, it does become a sign of a mode of living governed by renunciation. For a renouncer to accept food from a household is to recognize that it follows a comprehensive regime, at least with regard to food, which is comparable to that of renouncers themselves. A renouncer who appears careful and strict about how she accepts food thus imputes much more than simple generosity to the donating family. The considerations of gastro-politics mean that she also declares their food to be in the required Jain sense 'pure': which means that she makes a judgement on their general moral probity (including and especially how close its food regime is to being non-violent), and most particularly on that of the women. The family, then, must be austere as well as generous. In performing *baharana* it is both.

On one level, this can be seen as a distinctively Jain solution to the problem of what to do with 'the poison in the gift'. Transactions which are normally fraught with moral peril—in which, in particular, the recipient is usually demeaned, polluted, or rendered inauspicious—are here regarded still as perilous, but the dangers are not of such a form that there have to be losers. This is not at all because the dangers are absent. Indeed, their presence is an essential part of what is going on. For the characteristics of gifts which everyone knows about, which, depending on circumstance, they fear or gleefully exploit, are not obliterated just for this particular act. (How, in any cognitively plausible world, could they be?) The alms-round is constructed out of a complex interplay between general good sense about food gifts, the Jain criteria of *ahimsa* and purity, and a quite different image of grazing. The negotiations I have talked about take place in the space which these different schemes leave open for conflicting interpretations of what, on any particular occasion, is going on.

When food has been given, the renouncer leaves the house and speaks for the first time other than to refuse food. She gives the blessing, *dharma labh*. This simple benediction is condensed and ambiguous. The word *dharma* is notoriously untranslatable, but 'religion' will serve in this context. *Labh* means increase, benefit or profit. The blessing can thus be glossed in two ways. First, as 'May your religiousness increase', that is, may you become more enlightened and detached from the world. Secondly, as 'May you profit from your good (religious) act', in which sense it echoes the popular expression *shubh labh*. This is used by people of almost any religious affiliation as an invocation of good fortune: during Ganesh-*puja* (Chapter 12); on greetings cards and invitations; on buses and taxis as a lucky charm; in shops to help business go well; and, by these same lay Jains, as an inscription to consecrate and open their business account-books (Chapter 17). *Dharma labh* wishes for householders both that they progressively withdraw from worldly attachments, and also that they receive all the worldly good fortune which is the reward of the generous donor. The difference between these two glosses is the difference, for the householder, between being an ascetic striver (*shramana*) as the renouncer axiomatically is, and being on the other hand a rich and generous patron of those who are (like the Indras and other gods). However much of an exaggeration or indeed a fiction this may be in particular instances, for the donating family the identities of lay ascetic and rich lay provider are reconciled.

15

Magnificent Parsimony

IN the previous chapter I explained how it is that the *baharana/gocari* transaction focuses, and to some considerable degree resolves, the tension between conflicting lay Jain religious identities: the ascetic follower and the worldly patron. However, the palpably agonistic atmosphere of the encounter is not an illusion, and the fact that the renouncer and householder must haggle, in order that they both may profit, does not explain why it is that in fact they do. In order to specify fully the form and content of the competition that is involved it is necessary to widen our focus beyond the dynamic of the transaction itself. In this chapter I shall consider first the relations between householders and renouncers over time, then the social context of status competiton between lay Jain families, and finally the contexts where the acts of individual patrons constitute Jain collective life.

Free Gift or Reciprocal Exchange?

From the perspective of anthropology, which has been interested in gift-giving for its role in the creation and reproduction of social relations, the Jain *baharana* is a very peculiar sort of gift, for it is obsessively anti-social. The renouncer comes uninvited, makes no request, and leaves immediately, acknowledging no debt. Donors give, but expect no return. This in itself is not unique. Parry's examination of the 'law of the gift' (*dana-dharma*) in Hindu religious and legal texts suggests that in the religious gift in India, the supposedly universal 'norm of reciprocity', and the obligation to make a return gift, are absent.[1] Yet the Jain gift goes further. Parry points to the Hindu belief that certain categories of religious gift carry with them the sin or inauspiciousness of the donor. He interprets this as an instance of Marcel Mauss's notion of the 'spirit of the gift': the idea that the gift embodies a part of the giver.[2] Instead, if all goes well, the Jain renouncer's alms-round redefines and transforms the substance as it moves, and so de-socializes the transaction.

---

[1] Parry, 'The Gift', 461.
[2] Mauss, *The Gift*, 41.

But do renouncers really give nothing in return? In contrast to some (but not all) Theravada Buddhists, and to Digambar Jain monks,[3] Shvetambar renouncers consider that they have a duty to teach the laity. I often invited them to consider how their duty to teach might conflict with their search for spiritual progress, but their reaction was a mixture of shock and puzzlement. They insisted that teaching the laity is a central part of their *dharma*, a form of religious study (*svadhyay*), and hence one of the internal forms of asceticism. Significantly, they also presented an argument from debt: 'We have to give something in return, we get everything from the householders', and so they do. A renouncer receives everything she uses in the form of a gift from lay supporters: clothes, books, begging-bowls, pens and paper, medicine, and the furniture used in an *upashraya*. The laity in return receive teaching, ascetic example, and various sorts of blessings which include charms and amulets. This image of reciprocity was expressed to me by both lay people and renouncers, although more readily and more forcefully by the latter.

To be seen as a free gift, the act must be taken as a unit in itself. This involves denying at the time of each transaction that it is part of an exchange at all. For an act of giving to be seen as part of an exchange, return gifts must be implied, so that the system to which it belongs is intrinsic to the description of any single act. The semantics of the event turn in a sense on who the participants are there as: whether they are there representing themselves, their household, and their family; or as representatives of estates: the communities of renouncers and lay people (*sadhu-sangh* and *grihasthi log*). It is only under the latter description that either side will admit to the transaction being part of an exchange. So we have two different ideal models with reference to which both gifts and teaching are understood: an isolated, unreciprocated gift and an element in reciprocal exchange. The ambiguity of the *dharma labh* blessing (Chapter 14) draws on both of these models. Interpreted as 'May you become more religious', it is emblematic of the impersonal spiritual example and religious guidance which the renouncer, as icon of the Jina, always gives. Interpreted as referring to the merit which accrues to the donor of a generous gift (and especially if this is seen potentially to include material well-being) *dharma labh* is the expression of the renouncer's approval and good wishes. It is not a gift at all. The effect she approves, the 'fruit' which by the operation of *karma* naturally follows from the act, is not anything which the renouncer can give or withhold.

---

[3] Carrithers, *Forest Monks*; 'Naked Ascetics', 225; Spiro, *Buddhism and Society*, 288.

What lies between these two models, so to speak, is time.[4] The first model, the generous gift, is contained in an instant: the parties who meet in it have no history. The renouncer is an unexpected guest (*atithi*). The householder is a flower which a bee has just happened upon, or a clump of grass a cow has found. The second model, reciprocal exchange, occurs in the collapsed long run of reflection and analysis. It is a feature of an object constituted in thought. The time in which persons interact with each other, and negotiate the relations between them, is excluded from both models. If someone you have met only recently invites you to dinner for the first time, and if you wish this to develop into a friendship, then you invite them back before too long. But you do not invite them back the next day. To do so looks as if you are impatient to discharge the debt, as if you want to close the account at once. It resists the possibility of a developing relationship of reciprocity which the initial invitation was designed to establish. The difference between returning their invitation and, as it were, sending it straight back, lies in the patterning of the actions in time: in the improvisations people make with sequence, delay, and repetition. Both religious models of a gift to a renouncer deny and disguise the existence of all such considerations.

There is evidence of a similar situation in Theravada Buddhism. Tambiah, writing of north-east Thailand, notes how in Buddhist ceremonies monks are first given offerings and then later perform their ritual functions. In spirit-cult ceremonies, when the idea of payment for specialist services becomes explicit, monks do not participate.[5] He adds that the offering to the monks 'is very definitely conceived as a gift'. Ames's discussion of ritual transactions in Sri Lanka gives a similar picture, in which direct reciprocity is seen as acceptable only with the lower deities, not with the Buddha.[6] But I cannot believe that Buddhists are less aware of the long-term reciprocity involved in the systems they approve than are the Jains. Ames completely suppresses, and Tambiah chooses to disregard, the temporal dimension in these transactions. Yet it seems clear that the interpretation of the offerings to monks as a free gift is maintained only through their patterning in time. Tambiah comments simply that the

---

[4] The point made here is adapted from Bourdieu (*Outline*, ch. 1, *Logic of Practice*, i, ch. 6; ii, chs. 1–2). I should perhaps say, however, that I do not accept Bourdieu's finally reductionist notion of 'self-interest', his essentially deterministic rendering of Mauss's *habitus*, or his conception of 'symbolic profits' as quantifiable, such that one could draw up a 'balance sheet'.

[5] Tambiah, *Buddhism and the Spirit Cults*, 346–8.

[6] Ames, 'Ritual Prestations'.

ritual sequence as a whole is 'transactional', thus leaping straight from the instant to the collapsed reversible time of structural analysis. But return in the long run is not the same as return now, and expectation of return covers a variety of possibilities. The difference between immediate return and delayed return is not just that the latter extends the relationship in time, but that it redefines who the relationship is between. A gift given to 'a monk' and a later blessing or service received from 'a monk' maintain the opposition between the world and its renunciation, just as exchange between individual renouncers and householders creates relationships which breach it.

As I have already described, lay Jain families do try to persuade renouncers to come to them for *gocari*. In doing this—in protesting that their food is pure; that today they are not eating salt or oil; that she has not been to their house for some time—they are trying to drag the transaction out of the long run and into real, social time. One of the things they do when they refer to a renouncer as 'our guru' is to claim some measure of success in this. When they do in fact succeed, they create relationships the existence of which, even the possibility of which, is denied both by the semantics of the individual transaction, and by both ideal models of relations between householders and renouncers (and this is why, as we saw in Chapter 4, it is not allowed).

Negotiated Truths

Caturmas, as we saw in Chapter 12, is the period of most heightened activity in the Jain religious year. During this time, more than at any other, familiarity develops between renouncers and the more actively devout lay families. In particular, lay women spend long periods of time with nuns. Because renouncers are in prolonged contact with the same households, special restrictions apply to prevent exclusive patronage of a renouncer by one lay family. The only thing renouncers may accept during Caturmas is food.[7] For the same reason, renouncers are supposed not to call at the same house for *gocari* on consecutive days. This rule is simply not obeyed, but it is at least honoured in that renouncers do avoid calling too regularly at the same house, and reserve the right, unpredictably, not to turn up when expected.

---

[7] This leads to a concentration of gifts of robes just before the beginning of Caturmas, but this has not been elaborated into a public ceremony as have *kathin* presentations at the end of the Buddhist rains retreat. See Gombrich, *Theravada Buddhism*, 99–100; Tambiah *Saints of the Forest*, 278–80.

For those who successfully develop bonds with a renouncer, there are opportunities to perpetuate them beyond Caturmas. Maintaining links with a chosen guru becomes one of a cluster of religious, social, and economic purposes, which combine almost indistinguishably in quite extensive travelling undertaken by lay Jains. Any visit to another town or village, whether undertaken in connection with business, marriage arrangements, or to see family members, always includes a visit to the local Jain shrines and to any renouncers who may be in residence.[8]

I accompanied a family from Jaipur on a four-day visit to Udaipur in 1987, a journey which was typical for the combination of religious and social purposes involved. About thirty miles south of Udaipur is the famous temple of Keseriya-ji. The central idol here is of the first Jina, Rishabh Dev. It is believed to be extremely old and possessed of magical powers. A second grandson had recently been born to the family and the grandmother of the child was particularly keen to return to Keseriya-ji to thank the idol for the safe delivery of the child: a blessing she had asked for on her previous visit. She was accompanied, in addition to a stray anthropologist, by her husband and two of his sisters. To celebrate the birth of the child the family were planning, in the following month, to hold a public *puja* in Jaipur, followed by a large feast. During our time in Udaipur we were staying with some rather distinguished relations whom my companions hoped would return the visit and attend the proposed *puja*. Finally, we hoped to visit a group of renouncers who were resident in the city at the time, led by a particularly charismatic *sadhvi*. The women of the household were especially devoted to this renouncer, who had been in Jaipur for Caturmas the previous year. They felt that an auspicious event such as the birth of this child should be marked by hearing their guru preach, receiving a blessing from her, and taking the opportunity, if possible, to perform *baharana*.

It will be recalled that under normal circumstances renouncers should inspect the kitchens from which they take their food, and return to the *upashraya* to eat it. On this occasion these rules were reinterpreted until they all but disappeared. We arrived early in the morning on the overnight train, and immediately plans were afoot for our trip to see the renouncers. At about eleven we set off for the *upashraya*, which was some three miles from the house, taking food which the women had spent the morning

---

[8] See Sopher, 'Pilgrim Circulation', on the preponderance of Jains among pilgrims in the region.

preparing. When we arrived the men had to wait downstairs while the women went ahead to ask the renouncers to accept the food. When I asked afterwards how they had managed this, I was told that they had explained how far they had come, had reminded the renouncers that they had frequently taken *gocari* from them the year before in Jaipur, and assured them of how confident they could therefore be that the food would be pure. One of the younger renouncers was sent back to where we were waiting, in a covered porchway between two courtyards, where we performed the *baharana*. I discussed above how the apparently contrary purposes which renouncer and lay person bring to the alms-giving are co-operatively reconciled and mutually supportive. The householder can give generously and the renouncer can receive nothing. A background of many successful transactions of this sort can become, in a case such as this one, a source of mutual knowledge and mutual trust, which, unlike a material resource, is augmented rather than depleted as it is used.[9]

During Caturmas the previous year both branches of this family had regularly been included on these renouncers' alms-rounds. The women expected that they would be visited almost every day, and if a few days passed without a renouncer coming for food, one of them would spend the whole of the next morning at the *upashraya* especially to persuade them to come. With this background, it was possible to break the rules, so long as neither party behaved as if this was in fact what they were doing. Put another way, they describe and reframe what is done, until an agreed correct solution is found.[10] In this case there was a lengthy negotiation about whether or not the place we were waiting was sufficiently 'outside' the *upashraya*. Having finally established that it was, the *baharana* procedure described above was enacted there, as if in a household kitchen. The renouncer accepted rather little food as someone from the group had already collected *gocari* earlier, but our attempts to persuade her to accept more were muted, in recognition of the concession they were making in accepting anything at all.

Immediately after *baharana* we all went upstairs to perform *vandan* to the senior renouncer. We found her with a group of perhaps thirty lay persons. She was not giving a sermon but holding an audience: responding to questions, asking for news, and making general comments and

[9] Dasgupta, 'Trust as a Commodity'.
[10] See Elster, *Multiple Self*, 27.

remarks on religious, moral, and social matters. Another devotee arrived shortly after us and was quizzed by the renouncer. Where had he come from? She had been there and remembered a very good *dharma shala*. She turned to the rest of her audience, for she also remembered that food was distributed, at this *dharma shala*, not only to pilgrims but also to the needy of the town. 'This is very good . . .', and so began a disquisition on the merits of charity. More devotees came in, performed *vandan*, and sat for a while. Presently the renouncer's attention returned to our group. Having granted the privilege of performing *baharana* in this unorthodox way, she now set about reprimanding us for travelling all the way from Jaipur to visit her at all. She knew this family to be very religious, so surely we were aware that in Caturmas insects and tiny creatures abound. It is impossible even to walk without treading on an ant or a beetle. Travel during this period is wantonly destructive of life, and just as renouncers are prohibited from travelling at all at this time, the laity should undertake no journey which is not essential. When one of our number suggested that a visit to one's guru was religious (*dharmik*), and therefore essential, an argument which might normally have carried weight, the renouncer replied sternly that no act, if it involved unnecessary violence, could be considered religious.

This was only a few days before the end of the rainy season and the room was filled, as it always would be at this time of year, with devotees who had come to see the nuns before their departure on *vihar*. Many of them, like us, had made special journeys for the purpose. The rebuke was accepted with deference but no one seemed much perturbed. Indeed nods of agreement at the time, and approving comments when we returned to the house, confirmed that they were pleased to have been criticized in this way. The nun had shown that she was well versed in religious knowledge and that her interpretation and application of it were exceptionally strict. On a previous occasion I had seen the same nun stop an elaborate and expensive *puja* which she felt was being badly conducted. This intervention, far from spoiling the occasion, succeeded in rescuing a *puja* which had rather begun to flag. Everyone enjoyed it more as a result. The ability to see sin, most commonly *himsa*, in apparently virtuous actions, is the most powerful form in which religious insight is recognized, so that to be reprimanded by one's guru reinforces her authority and is at the same time a religious experience. The nun's attack was a demonstration of insight and of judgement which contradicted that of the unenlightened, and characteristically was informed not by mystical experience or esoteric analysis, but by strictness in the interpretation and application of well-known rules so that the devotee's experience on being reprimanded and blessed is one of recognition.[11]

Competing to Give

So far I have considered the *gocari/baharana* only from the points of view of the householders and renouncers who face each other across cooking pots and alms-bowls. I have stressed the ideological fact that the renouncers come as uninvited guests (*atithi*), which is of crucial importance in ensuring that nothing which has been done in the acquisition and preparation of the food counts as having been done for them. In practice things are much less clear than this. It is quite common for a group of renouncers to arrange that at any given time at least one of their number is performing an *ayambil* fast. Apart from the two short periods in the year when *naupad oli-ji* is on (Chapter 10), only very few lay Jains perform this fast, so the appropriate food would be very difficult to come by. It is certainly too much to hope that one might just happen on a family which had prepared food of this kind for lunch. So lay families volunteer to prepare *ayambil* food, and to fast, then make this known to the renouncers to induce them to come for *gocari*. And Jain householders can make other kinds of move to persuade renouncers to come to their home. Particularly at times when they have reason to want the auspicious benefit of performing *baharana*—a new business venture about to start, marriage negotiations under way, a job interview coming up—a member of the family might be posted to stay in the *upashraya* all morning, ostensibly attending religious sermons and classes, to bring the renouncers to their house. When the opportunity arises, they might just explain where they live, or comment that the renouncers have not come for some time, and ask to be given the benefit or profit of 'rice-water' (*bhatpani ka labh dena ji*), a euphemistic way of asking them to call for *gocari*.

If a visit from the renouncers is anticipated, special preparations are made to make the gift as generous as possible. The very restricted diet which renouncers are permitted limits the largesse which is possible, but since pious Jains observe substantially similar dietary restrictions, they

---

[11] As Tambiah remarks of Thai Buddhism (*Saints of the Forest*, 321–34), the charisma of a renouncer is not, as Weber imagined, some ever-youthful and inexplicable force which, when organized in rules and institutions, is routinized and exhausted; but actually derives from precise and well-known rules. This is important because the experience of coming from an encounter with a guru with a new piece of religious knowledge, is realized against a background of rules of ascetic conduct which are common knowledge.

have well-practised ways of upgrading a meal.[12] Better quality rice, or more expensive vegetables can be used, and more labour-intensive dishes prepared. In addition to these, which might all be provided for an honoured lay guest, some special measures can be taken to provide for renouncers. There is a range of foods which renouncers can only eat if they have been prepared in particular ways some time in advance. Oranges must be peeled and have the pips removed, nuts can be eaten only if already shelled, and so on.

While *baharana* does not involve direct competition or confrontation between giver and receiver, the palpable feeling of competitiveness derives from the fact that householders are in competition with other households which the renouncers might visit. As I noted above, renouncers are not allowed to store or to throw away any of the food they collect. As they can only accept a limited amount of food, they have only a limited *labh* to distribute. So when family members press food so forcefully on renouncers, this is not with a view to self-aggrandizement at the latter's expense, but in an attempt to outdo, and still more urgently to preempt, these absent competitors. So while the encounter between renouncer and householder, if properly managed, is mutually beneficial, between aspiring donor households there is a fairly straightforward zero-sum game.

To give an idea of how things can go, here are two accounts of alms-rounds in Jaipur, abstracted from my field-notes. The first is fairly typical, and shows the routine *modus operandi*, balanced between competing ideals.

I accompanied two nuns on *gocari*. We headed straight up the neighbouring street for some distance, so I asked if they had decided where to go. They said that one of their group was performing *ayambil*, so they were going to a place where they knew that food would be available. We arrived at Upendra-ji's vast house, one of the grandest I knew in Jaipur, so I asked if it was his wife who was doing the fast (several other families live as tenants in the building). They said no. Nonetheless we went straight to the top floors of the house, where Upendra and his family live, and took *gocari* from them first. Next we went down two floors, and there the woman who was performing *ayambil* was waiting for us. We took food from there, and then a little more from a family at the bottom of the building. Two other women appeared to invite the renouncers in, but were ignored.

---

[12] The reasoning can of course go the other way around. Finding themselves with a particularly fine meal, on account of an auspicious occasion of some sort, a family might regard this as a good time to try to offer food to renouncers.

Going first to the owner's apartments accorded due recognition to his social status and at the same time avoided going straight to the more or less pre-arranged destination. The third call appeared to be genuinely unplanned, and the appearance of the two unsuccessful donors increased the sense that everything was done as it should be.

The second episode is less typical. Here, limits were overstepped in ways that meant that no one really felt the episode had been successful.

I arrived at an *upashraya* to find two young Khartar Gacch monks in conversation with a *yati* who was on a visit to Jaipur from Bikaner . . . All the while we were talking, there were two laymen sitting quietly to one side, listening patiently. One was a middle-aged man, the other a youth who turned out to be his son. After about half an hour one of the monks got up and went into the back room out of sight. While he was gone, another layman, looking slightly out of breath, came in, did *vandan*, and sat down. When the monk reappeared he was carrying his alms-bowls and staff (i.e. was ready to go for *gocari*). The man who had just arrived immediately asked if he would come to his house, whereupon the hitherto silent middle-aged man fairly shrieked in protest. He had been sitting there all morning, he said, and was definitely first in line. Embarrassed, they both looked to the monks, who said nothing, but took up again the subject we had been talking about before. After just a minute or two the second renouncer and the *yati* got up and went to fetch their alms-bowls. They had decided all to go. The first monk asked if I would like to come along.

We went first to the house of the man who arrived last, because it turned out he lived close by (and, I suspect, because the renouncers were a bit irritated at the scene the other had made). His neighbour popped out to ask us in, but the renouncers went on without responding.

It was quite a way to the house where the first pair lived. We had to cross the Johari Bazaar (hazardous at that time of day) and go up a lane I didn't know and which was obviously unfamiliar to the monks too. When we got to the house, a smart and spacious but unmodernized section of a large *haveli*, a woman was waiting by the door. She was got up in a red silk sari and lots of jewellery: evidently not her everyday clothes. There was a very great deal of food, including what she described as a 'special' kedgeree (made from millet flour). While the re-nouncers were producing their bowls the woman asked her son why they had taken so long. When he said we had gone first to another house she shot a withering look at her husband and set about offering food with a vigour I have rarely seen equalled . . .

Just when we thought the deal had been done, she produced some popadams and hurriedly crushed one into a bowl just as the lid was being replaced. The *yati* laughed at this but the younger of the two monks looked pained. They packed up hurriedly, with the woman still complaining bitterly about how little they had taken. The elder monk remarked loudly and somewhat tartly as we left that after all this they would be late in taking their *gocari* (i.e. eating).

Reversing the celebrated case of Gajuku-Gama football, which, as Lévi-Strauss has shown, is a game treated as a ritual,[13] Jains play the *baharana* ritual as a game. Competitors postulated for the purpose as formally equal (and the renouncers are enjoined to treat them as such) strive to outdo each other in competition for a finite set of goods. The competitors do not usually meet face to face (the case I have just described is unusual in this respect). The field of play on which they meet, so to speak, is the person of the renouncers.

Auctioning Austerity

The first time a renouncer receives *baharana* is at the first of her two ordination ceremonies. This, the 'incomplete' or *kacci diksha*, itself consists of two main parts. The initiand renounces her worldly life, her family ties, and her property, and adopts the clothes of a renouncer. For the last time her hair is cut, leaving only a few strands, which are then pulled out by hand in her first performance of *kesh loca*. This part of the ceremony is called *pravragya* (Skt. *pravrajna*), or renunciation. In the second part, the renouncer takes from her new guru the *kharemi bhante* oath under which she remains in a state of *samayik* for the rest of her life (see Chapter 9).[14] The transition between the renunciation and the *samayik* oath is interrupted for a procedure called *ghi boli*. This is an auction, and in this the competitive aspect, which is partially hidden in the everyday *baharana*, comes prominently to the fore.

Ghi boli auctions serve two purposes at once: they raise money to pay for religious functions, and they allocate a ritual role, that of patron of the religion. They are all, therefore, forms of *supatra-dan* (Chapter 13). They occur in four different kinds of religious context. The most common is for the right to perform *puja*. There are several variants of this: certain parts—the *mangal dipak* and *arti*—of a lengthy public *puja*; all parts of the *puja* at a busy pilgrimage site; and the right to be the first to perform *puja* to a newly consecrated idol. The sums raised in the last of these can be very large indeed. The second occasion for *ghi boli* is at the annual re-

---

[13] Lévi-Strauss, *Savage Mind*, 30–3.

[14] Anything between seven days and six months later the 'complete' or *pakki diksha* ceremony is held and her ordination becomes, in theory at any rate, irreversible. At this later ceremony, which is in practice much less grand than the first, the renouncer takes the five *mahavrat* vows (see ch. 8).

enactment of the birth of Mahavir Swami during Paryushan (Chapters 12 and 16). Here, fourteen silver models are auctioned. These represent the visions the Jina's mother had as his soul entered her body (Chapter 2), and those who win them immediately present them to the renouncers who preside over the ceremony, where they contribute to a ritual reconstruction of the Jina's birth. The third auctioned role is that of *sangh-pati* or *sanghvi*, the patron and leader of a pilgrimage. The fourth kind of occasion for *ghi boli*, the rarest and the one which fetches among the highest prices, is for the right to perform *baharana* to a newly ordained renouncer.

A *diksha* ceremony is a vast and extremely expensive affair (along with the consecration of Tirthankar idols, it is the grandest event the Shvetambar Jains hold). People travel from all over the subcontinent to see it, and they must all be fed and lodged. The ceremonies themselves are very expensive, as they include several elaborate *puja*s and a procession on elephants with sweets and money being distributed to all those present. If the initiand's parents are very rich, they will bear these expenses themselves, but otherwise money must be raised.[15] This is done by holding auctions for the right to take roles otherwise held by the parents, such as anointing her forehead, presenting her with clothes and other requisites, and above all performing *baharana*. Since the evening before, the new renouncer will have been fasting and when she breaks this fast, on the day after the ceremony, a lay person will perform *baharana* to her for the first time. From then, until after the second initiation, she can receive food collected by other members of the group, but she does not go for *gocari* herself. The second initiation is preceded by a three-day fast, which is broken when the renouncer visits her parents' house on her first full *gocari*. By tradition, the first time a new renouncer receives *baharana* and the first time she goes for *gocari*, it is her parents who offer the food; but they may give up this right in favour of a winner of a *ghi boli*.

The *ghi boli* is very simple in form, but elaborate and baroque in execution. The expression literally means speaking, or calling out, ghee (clarified butter). This name derives from the fact that bids are not expressed in currency, but in units called a *man*. Notionally, the *man* is a measure of weight, and in shouting their bid, buyers are agreeing to pay the price of that weight of ghee. But in fact the *man* is not in everyday use any more, and at least since the early years of this century it has been

---

[15] Many Jain renouncers come from the less well-off sections of the community and some are not Jains by birth and come from other, much poorer communities.

assigned a fixed value in rupees (one which is much lower than the actual price of the ghee).[16] A layman, usually a member of a Sangh committee, stands up with a microphone and announces the start of the bidding to a huge gathering of lay Jains, dressed in their finest clothes and jewellery. He begins by calling out a starting price and as assistants move among the crowd identifying competitors, encouraging them to bid, and relaying the new bids back to him, he shouts out the new price so everyone can follow. For the most desirable *ghi boli*s scores and even hundreds of thousands of rupees are not unusual bids. It ends with the last opponent dropping out, after being goaded to offer more rather than admit defeat. When his refusals are finally accepted, the auctioneer, in a form which exactly resembles a London auction house, thrice calls the highest bid in case anyone wishes to better it, and declares the contest won.[17]

In the *diksha* ceremony the result of all this, and the privilege for which the winner pays, is to give the new renouncer a little yoghurt, milk, and molasses to drink. This juxtaposition of gregarious festivity and grim asceticism is, as we have seen before (Chapters 10 and 12), Jainism's preferred aesthetic. The striking thing about this particular instance, when one looks for comparisons around the subcontinent, is that privileges of this kind, 'honours' as they are called in the literature, are elsewhere held as the heriditary corporate property of lineages, castes, or professional groups and associations. Especially in south India, these honours have constituted the basic vocabulary of political power and privilege through and beyond the colonial period, ordering relations between major sections of society, whether Hindu, Christian, or Muslim.[18] While the allocation of these honours has changed over time, they have done so as a result of often violent political conflict, and usually

---

[16] Stevenson reported at the beginning of this century (*Heart of Jainism*, 252) that a similar arrangement obtained in Gujarat, in which another unit of weight, a seer, had a conventional equivalent in cash; and Cort ('Two Ideals', 418) indicates that this is still the case. Parry ('Moral Perils', 67) reports that a whole set of such cash equivalents are used for donations to priests in Benares. In the late 1980s in Jaipur a *man* was Rs. 3.5.

[17] Gombrich (*Precept and Practice*, 129) describes a fund-raising auction which occurs during Buddhist ceremonies in Sri Lanka. This is quite different from the situation here, as bidding is not cumulative or really competitive. Donations are called out at random and the honour, in this case of presenting a tray of flowers to the Buddha statue, falls to the last donor, 'in other words, when no more money can be elicited'. Jain auctions are won by the highest bidder, not the last contributor. For an analysis of Jain auctions in Britain, see Banks, 'Competing to Give'.

[18] Appadurai, *Worship and Conflict*; Appadurai and Breckenridge, 'South Indian Temple'; Bayly, *Saints, Goddesses and Kings*; Dirks, *Hollow Crown*; Fuller, *Servants of the Goddess*; Mines, *Public Faces, Private Voices*.

with the intervention and adjudication of the state. Among the Jains they are similarly important status markers, but they are commoditized.

They are commoditized, however, in a very particular way; and, moreover, without ceasing to be gifts. An opposition between gift and commodity exchange hardly begins to capture the complex ways in which value is created, transformed, and appropriated during the 'biography' of this food.[19] Food is bought from the market and transformed according to Jain religious principles by women in the household to make it ready for family consumption. Then, and only then, is it diverted unexpectedly and presented to renouncers in a form which is at the same time a paradigm gift and a barter. If this food is now commoditized, it is, after all, the right to make a gift of it that is sold. We can agree with Simmel that 'we call those objects valuable that resist our desire to possess them',[20] but for the Jains we must add, 'and our desire to give them away'.

In all cases what is won in these auctions, the 'honour', is the role of religious patron. In the case where what is auctioned is the right to perform the *baharana*, one mythological model which is relevant is prince Shreyam, the first person in this world-age to perform *supatra-dan*. When Rishabh Dev, the first Tirthankar, embarked on his renouncer's life there was no one who knew the proper way to offer food to him. As he wandered from place to place, people saw and admired him and tried to offer him alms. But always the way they did so was unacceptable in some respect, and as he was under a vow of silence, he could not tell them why (Chapter 10). This continued until he came to the city where Shreyam was heir to the throne. When he set eyes on the renouncer, Shreyam suddenly gained knowledge of his former births (*jati smaran gyan*), including lives from the previous cycle of cosmic time (this is remarkable, even by the standards of Jain stories). So Shreyam saw how to offer alms to a Jain renouncer, and Rishabh broke his fast on a small offering of sugar-cane juice, whereupon the sky resounded with magical drums and shone with the garments of the gods, a rain of flowers and perfumed water fell on the city, and on Shreyam's house, there fell a rain of precious jewels.[21]

More commonly, the winner is identified with Indra, king of the gods. It will be recalled (Chapter 2) that Indra and his consort Indrani play a large part in the lives of the Tirthankars, celebrating their birth, renunciation, and omniscience in opulent style. They are the paradigm in Jain tradition of the worshipper and devotee who is also a patron. The winner

[19] See Kopytoff, 'Cultural Biography of Things'.

[20] Simmel, *Philosophy of Money*, 67.

[21] Balbir, 'Micro-Genre', 148; Johnson, *Trishashti-shalaka-purusha-caritra*, i. 180–1.

of *ghi boli* and his wife are dressed in robes and crowns (usually rather flimsy things made of cardboard, tinsel, and silver paper) to signify their role as Indra and Indrani, and in the case of some *pujas*, they enact the appropriate episodes in the life of the Jina. Occasionally a single rich patron may sponsor the whole initiation process. In cases such as this, the future renouncer is adopted by the businessman, and he and his wife thereafter take the part of the initiand's parents in the ceremonies which follow. They will provide and present the robes, alms-bowls, and other requisites, and they will probably perform the *baharana* too. Here is an excerpt from a renouncer's sermon about Mahavir's renunciation.

His *diksha* was celebrated by the gods with all the same ceremony as his birth. There were two palanquins waiting to take him, one was provided by Mahavir Swami's brother [his parents were dead], and the other by Indra. Which one should he go in? But by the power of the gods, the two palanquins combined and were turned into one. Men carried the palanquin, while women carried the umbrellas that covered his head and the jars of Ganges water.

The combination of the roles of family member and sponsoring Indra (though not, perhaps, the usurpation of one by the other) thus has some mythological charter.

On the one hand the commoditization involved here allows élite lay Jains to control and appropriate the *baharana* process in a more exclusive way than is normally possible, to do so publicly and in a way which elevates them to the status of representative of the whole lay assembly; but the process by which this happens is a long way indeed from the 'free' operation of a market. And if the same process is also, from a slightly different point of view, an instituted mechanism for raising funds to finance the ceremonial in which the auction itself is contained, it is clearly a long way too from the anthropological paradigm of a gift economy.

Tournaments of Value

It is not unusual for objects (such as paintings) which are normally re-garded as barely suitable for exchange, to have what Appadurai calls their 'commodity dimension' accentuated by their being placed in an auction.[22] Charles Smith, in his book on auctions, has highlighted how they can 'define and resolve' three kinds of inherent ambiguity: questions of value and price, questions of ownership, and those to do with how a good is to

---

[22] Appadurai, 'Commodities', 15.

be categorized or graded. He sees auctions as arenas in which collective definitions of value can be produced and reproduced, as distinct from one in which an imagined underlying value is merely 'revealed'.[23] The *baharana*, which is of decisive practical and symbolic importance in structuring relations between Jain renouncers and their followers, yet which occurs in tiny segmented portions in a series of private and domestic spaces, presents exactly the sort of ambiguities—of value, ownership, and definition—which Smith sees auctions as answering.

So what is actually for sale in the auction? At the most obvious level what the winner gets is the opportunity to give something away. I think it is most helpful to think of this as a form of consumption. Now obviously it is the renouncer who is going to eat the food, and so 'consume' its most obvious use-value. But noting that in many ceremonial feasts in New Guinea, the food is not actually eaten by the participants, Alfred Gell remarks,

What distinguishes consumption from exchange is not that consumption has a physiological dimension that exchange lacks, but that consumption involves the incorporation of the consumed item into the personal and social identity of the consumer. For instance, Lord Rothschild has a Cezanne on the wall of his sitting room. That makes him a member of the elite group of consumers of works by Cezanne, a category from which I am permanently excluded even though I had the pleasure of looking at this painting in the past. I think of consumption as the appropriation of objects as part of one's *personalia*—food eaten at a feast, clothes worn, houses lived in.[24]

I think it is clear that although the winners of a *ghi boli* do not consume in a physiological sense, the purchase they make touches the most intimate aspects of their moral and religious identity, and it is, as consumption goes, about as conspicuous as anyone could wish. At the same time, as in Gell's example, the fact that it is commoditized and sold to the highest bidder does not exhaust the meaning of this form of consumption. If membership of Lord Rothschild's élite group depended only on wealth, it would not be nearly so élite. This painting adds what it does to his personalia because it is also valued by others, whose judgement cannot simply be bought. The National Gallery contributes to maintaining the value of Lord Rothschild's Cézanne, quite as much as he contributes to holding up the price of theirs. For a form of élite consumption to be open

---

[23] Smith, *Auctions*. Smith also argues that these features fit auctions especially for what he calls 'modern' societies, but I shall leave this thought aside.

[24] Gell, 'Newcomers', 112.

and yet closed in complex ways is the best guarantee that it will not come to be seen as merely expensive, in that sense which is substantially synonymous with vulgar. Both the fact that Jain religious honours are commoditized by means of an auction, and the particular relation of the commoditized to the everyday gift-and-non-gift version, are ways in which this particular instance of élite consumption is in the required sense open and yet closed.

I noted above how potential donors in the daily alms-round are formally equal competitors in a zero-sum game. Baudrillard's analysis of art auctions points, if a mite hyperbolically, to a rather important way in which *ghi boli* differs from this.

Contrary to commercial operations, which institute a relation of economic *rivalry* between individuals on a footing of formal *equality* . . . the auction . . . institutes a concrete community of exchange among peers. Whoever the vanquisher in the challenge, the essential function of the auction is the institution of a community of the privileged who define themselves as such by agonistic speculation upon a restricted corpus of signs. Competition of the aristocratic sort seals their *parity* (which has nothing to do with the formal equality of economic competition), and thus their collective caste privilege with respect to all others, from whom they are no longer separated merely by their purchasing power, but by the sumptuary and collective act of the production and exchange of sign values.[25]

Baudrillard writes here as if membership of the 'community of the privileged', which this process institutes, were a clear-cut and unambiguous matter ('aristocratic parity'). But in the Jain *ghi boli*, at least, 'community' is instituted on several different levels. There is a very definite sense in which community is instituted between all those who are present. Partly this is achieved through religious symbolism, partly through the kind of dynamic of participation which Baudrillard is pointing to, as the Jain assembly defines itself as all those who joyfully approve (*anumodan*) the glorification of renunciation. But it is presupposed that this community is sectarian. It would be unthinkable for any religious outsider who was present (a Sthanakvasi, a Digambar, or a non-Jain) to win one of these auctions, whose practical purpose, after all, is to raise funds for Jain religious events. So that the kind of community of participation which is achieved is to some degree fixed in content. And the same process also emphasizes the distinction between those who are really serious participants and those whose insider status consists more of being a knowing

[25] Baudrillard, *Political Economy of the Sign*, 117.

spectator. One element of this partition of the community is gender. Men are direct participants in a way that women, except very occasionally, are not. The other, of course, is wealth and a reputation for wealth. Though not picked out from the congregation, the notables of the community are identified within it. Everyone looks to them to see what they will bid. People joke about who has a measure of rivalry with whom, and whether they will bid against each other, so that the distinction between patrons and mere participants is mapped as a distinction between the looked-at and the looking.

The element of public contest between notables makes this event one of what Appadurai has called 'tournaments of value'.[26] The rich do not need actually to deploy the funds they have in order to assert their status. Those who are only moderately well-off know how to challenge the community leaders and force the price up; but they also know when to stop. These auctions rarely spring surprises on the assembly, and if winning them is a way of both prosecuting and announcing social mobility, this is done only by degrees. You cannot become a notable overnight. No one would gain in status by overstretching himself. Besides, the richer families can well afford to spend beyond their normal levels to put down an upstart if necessary. So although these honours are commoditized, the result is not a free-for-all.

Having said all this, I think it is important not to write off the sense in which this euergetism creates community, in the way Baudrillard seems to be suggesting, between all those who are present. It is manifestly a matter of pride to all that the sums raised should be large. Community funds will be good, and the honour and collective success of the community is affirmed. Most importantly, a spectacular value is created and declared, in terms of more or less hard cash, for a practice which is at the heart of the religion in which everyone is a full participant, and which each of those present, at some trouble but very little expense, can perform in other ways. If, as I have suggested, the daily *baharana* means that lay Jains compete in a zero-sum game, the genuinely collective experience of these auctions creates the possibility of benefit, if not equally, then at any rate for all. As in Buddhism, rejoicing in another's good deeds (*anumodan*[27]) itself brings merit.[28] And if one dimension of the religious meaning of the *baharana* offering is as a token of the patronage and support provided by

---

[26] Appadurai, 'Commodities', 21.

[27] Although the thought is problematic. See also ch. 9, n. 10, and the section on *samayik*.

[28] See Gellner, *Monk, Householder, Priest*, 123–4.

the laity to the community of Jain renouncers, then the sense of the grandeur and opulence of that support—its value—is created on these occasions.

Conversely, it is the fact that everyday *baharana* is difficult (indeed, in a sense it shares with much Jain religious practice, impossible) that explains the ascetic and thus properly religious value of what is on offer in the auction. *Baharana* cannot really be bought with money. It takes labour, care, and knowledge on the women's part to prepare the food correctly. It takes a reputation for religious piety (or at the very least conformity) to qualify as an acceptable donor. To persuade renouncers to call at the house requires participation in religious events, even if it does also occasionally mean bending the rules somewhat. It takes detailed knowledge of the foods that are acceptable to renouncers, and of the many apparently trivial faults which would cause the gift to be aborted. The *ghi boli* is a rumbustious affair, but part of what is being celebrated there is the punctilious care and strictness represented in *gocari*. Smith is correct, I think, in saying that the value assigned in the auction is created right there in the arena. The auction does not just uncover or reveal a price which until then has been merely hidden. But on the other hand, the arena does not exist in a cultural vacuum. And the value of the 'élite consumption' that is won in the *diksha* auction is derived from, and dependent on, the intricacies of meaning which I have sketched out above for the everyday *baharana*.

It is worth pointing up the sexual division of labour in *baharana* and *ghi boli*, to help explain how a single family can tack between the two. *Baharana*, as I have said, is largely women's work. It is they who prepare the food, and it is their religious activities on which the qualifications of the family to participate most directly rest. The everyday *baharana* is a definite and focused instance of the way a woman's individual religious conduct can be converted into a family asset; a way in which a woman, by her religious labours, can purchase merit for the other members of her family. We have seen this already in women's participation in lengthy fasts, such as the *naupad oli-ji*, and in the public processions and ceremonies which dramatize these achievements (Chapters 10 and 12). By contrast, *ghi boli* is a way in which men's business wealth (including more or less black money, as is widely recognized among Jains themselves) can be used in distinctively religious and socially prestigious consumption. Both components, the ascetic and the extravagant, are formally open to everyone, although their combination is very difficult to achieve for anyone apart from the élite. It requires, in Baudrillard's terms, a specific kind of social labour whose product, domination, is not to be confused with economic privilege and profit.[29] The religious division of labour (both physical and symbolic), which weaves together scrupulous asceticism and bountiful good fortune, forms an authoritative pattern of élite consumption and symbolic domination.

The result is the construction of a social identity for the family which speaks simultaneously of riches and renunciation; which, indeed, makes them look like the same thing. There are moments in the *diksha* ceremony when they look very much indeed as if they are the same thing. In the days before the ceremony, there is a whole series of rites which exactly parallel marriage. Women gather for collective singing (*sangeet*) and for the initiand's hands and feet to be decorated with henna (*mehandi*). Neighbouring families invite the girl to their houses to eat. Just as before marriage, there are too many such invitations, so she spends just a little time at each house and eats just a little; and just as at marriage the visits are called *bindauri*. The day before the initiation a ceremony called *varshi dan* (year gift) is held. This ceremony, which replaces the *varghora* procession before a wedding (in fact it is often casually referred to as *varghora*), is a procession in which the initiand rides through the town, usually on an elephant, throwing gifts into the crowd. It re-enacts the year in the life of the Tirthankar in which, having decided to renounce the world, he travelled around his kingdom, giving away all of his vast riches (Chapter 2). As a nun once explained in a sermon, 'When a tree is heavy with fruits, it bends so people can easily pick them. Mahavir gave *dan* every day for a year. Gold coins, from morning to evening— 10,800,000 gold coins. Also he gave horses, elephants, and beautiful jewels. Whatever people wanted would come into their hands.' Just how close modern ceremonies can come to this mythological archetype is illustrated by a *diksha* ceremony held in Ahmedabad in June 1991. Mr Atul Kumar Shah, a twenty-nine year-old bachelor and a diamond merchant based in Bombay, renounced his very considerable fortune to become a Tapa Gacch monk. According to newspaper reports of this event, Mr Shah rode in a chariot in a procession of seven elephants, fifty horses, forty camels, and hundreds of dancers and acrobats, and threw handfuls of silver coins, diamonds, and pearls into the crowd.[30]

The splendour and opulence surrounding the initiand immediately

[29] Baudrillard, *Political Economy of the Sign*, 115.
[30] *The Times of India*, 2 June 1991.

before renunciation recall the princely origins of the Tirthankar and display lay life at its most magnificent. The generosity of the Tirthankar, re-enacted by the initiand, is the ultimate in lay virtue: generosity without bounds, intimately related, indeed leading directly, to renunciation and enlightenment. The rich lay patrons who so publicly provide for all this are thus able to support actions which are certainly worldly, but which are associated really quite as closely as it is possible to conceive with the ascetic renouncer's life, although the latter seems at first sight to be their opposite. The very fact that Jainism stresses and emphasizes the dramatic reversal of life conditions that renunciation implies provides a perfect slot for the rich lay patron to fit into: the greater the wealth the greater the virtue of renouncing it. And a further renunciation is possible. It is not unknown for the rich Jains who win these rights—to offer *baharana*, to give clothes, and so on—instead of resting content with giving generously to the renouncer (*supatra-dan*) and to the assembled religious community (*prabhavana*), to give back those rights to the family of the new renouncer, thus finally turning giving into giving-up.

And Then?

Before we proceed, and as a sort of coda to this discussion, I should like to follow the cultural biography of this food just a little further, even though it takes us, thematically, back to earlier parts of the book. Middle-class India has been largely converted in recent decades to lavatories closely modelled on British ones, but for Jain renouncers, the characteristically Britannic strategy of subduing dirt under oceanic torrents of water is hardly suitable. The canonical texts enjoin renouncers to urinate in sand, so that the liquid will instantly dry up, and, when they defecate, to cover the faeces with dry earth. This should be done in a quiet, secluded spot, where animals are unlikely to come and uncover it, and using only a little boiled water for washing.[31] Those convinced by my account of Jain non-violence in Part III will be unsurprised to learn that the idea is to prevent

[31] Most Jain *upashraya*s in urban areas are provided with small compounds, behind high barbed walls, to provide privacy for this. I commented above that in many respects the way a Digambar *muni* receives his food is a symmetrical inversion of Shvetambar practice. Notably, while Shvetambar renouncers eat in private, a Digambar *muni*'s meal is something of a public spectacle. So it is interesting to learn that Digambar laymen on two separate occasions invited Michael Carrithers ('Naked Ascetics', 233) to join them in observing 'the lavatorial activities' of a Digambar monk.

either of these substances from becoming home or food or otherwise giving rise to new life-forms. As nearly as possible Jain practice ensures that the life of food substance comes, when it reaches Jain renouncers, to a full stop.

PART V

Riches and Redemption

16

Family Enterprise and Religious Community

THE renouncer's alms-round has brought us from the details of food preparation, to the symbolic dominance which élite Jain families are able to assert even in moments when the heights of ascetic renunciation are celebrated. This is not the only way in which religious life and the pursuit of social and economic success for Jain families are mutually constitutive, and so scarcely really separable, domains.

A Community of Competition

I described in Chapter 6 how local Jain communities, because they are not closed or bounded groups, are best seen as the medium and outcome of social clustering around corporate religious property. Families tend to drift out of the community if their membership is not sustained and renewed through some combination of religious observance, economic participation, kinship and marriage links, residential proximity, and day-to-day interaction. The auctioning of silver 'visions' during the annual celebrations on Mahavir Janam (Chapter 12) is a crucial moment in the reproduction of local Jain communities. It is here that funds are raised to maintain their key centripetal institutions: temples, meeting-halls, and *upashraya*s, and to run the religious and public functions which are housed in them. And this is done through a festival in which the whole community comes together to witness competition between its leading members for the honour of supporting those institutions. Thus when a Jain local community comes into being each year, it does so already differentiated. Men and women sit in separate spaces, and in general (there are exceptions) only the former take part in the bidding. And a further distinction, which is inscribed anew among the men as the bidding proceeds and registered immediately among the women, is between households which are agents and those which are spectators, led, respectively, by notables and citizens.

As this is the occasion when most of its working funds are raised, each temple management committee organizes its own function. So in Jaipur, the Khartar Gacch and Tapa Gacch hold separate sets of auctions. And the Shrimals hold their own function, separate from the rest of the Khartar Gacch, to raise money for their temples. But the semi-detached nature of the Shrimals is expressed by the fact that their ceremony is held after the Khartar Gacch auctions are over, so that it is possible to attend both. And the richest and most well-known Shrimal families are careful to win auctions at both venues.

It would have been quite beyond my resources to organize a survey to try to determine what proportion of the Shvetambar Jains in Jaipur, or even in the walled city, are involved in the gem trade. But if I am right about the nature of community membership it would not really have made much sense anyway, for it is not an all-or-nothing matter which is amenable to quantification. That this is a community of jewellers is much better expressed in the straightforward observation that all the people who won in the auctions I attended were gem traders, and that everyone present took it for granted that this would be so.

At no point, I think, during my fieldwork was the help I received from people around me, even those I had never met before, so spontaneously useful as it was at these auctions. I sat in the crowd noting down who won each auction and how much was paid for each of the fourteen visions. People sitting around me started making their own tally of the total so far, to check that I would get the arithmetic right, and for each person who won I was given a careful explanation of who they were, who they were related to, how big their business was, and whether or not the amount they had paid was a lot of money for them. 'Next is the goddess Lakshmi. This will be a lot of money. Ah yes. See, Kothari-ji is going to bid.'

The men who represented the leading families were not just left to decide for themselves whether or not to bid. The Secretary of the Sangh committee, himself a leading jeweller, moved among the crowd, spotting those whose business and social position required that they take part, and those of slightly more modest but still substantial means who ought at least to be invited to do so. 'Ah Dhadda Sahab! It is the throne now. Indra sits here. Do you want to call? Has the feeling (*bhavana*) come? Ah yes, I can see it has.' This recalls again Veyne's account of euergetism. From the first century AD the price of *ob honorem* payments in Greek cities became fixed, partly through the instinctively codifying reforms of Roman authorities. But, as Veyne remarks, because of this they immediately fell out of the realm of euergetism. Notables no longer deigned even to mention these payments in their epitaphs, and soon, because euergetism requires the combination of spontaneity and constraint, these correct payments were regularly exceeded, and became little more than a legal minimum.[1] The Jain auction combines spontaneity and constraint in dramatic and dynamic form. It would be meaningless to think in terms of getting a bargain. As the proceedings are broadcast to the streets outside, the honour of the Jain community is at stake. The Sangh committee, and the audience at large, give voice to their expectation that well-known notables will all give generously, yet because there is always the form of competition—the notables are seen to strive to give, however much they are at the same time induced to do so—their giving is always voluntary. Because some other winner has always been vanquished, the donations are always generous.[2]

The leading notables among the Jaipur Jains are so rich that they might be thought to exist in a completely separate social sphere from the majority of the community they preside over. One of the most wealthy of the big gem-trading families, which also has interests in construction, entertainment, general retailing, and probably much else besides, maintains a vast nineteenth-century *haveli* in the Johari Bazaar area and no less than three modern mansions in a walled and guarded compound in the suburbs, with immaculately kept lawns and a fleet of cars outside. At the other end of the market, I knew a family of six whose bread-winner had died suddenly of an unexpected illness, and they were living in just two small ground-floor rooms on a very meagre budget. But even though quite poor, this family was still unequivocally respectable, and inside the business community. Connected by kinship to some affluent merchant households, the sons had secured promising positions in the market. One was apprenticed to a big merchant and the other was a partner in a very small

---

[1] Veyne, *Bread and Circuses*, 140.

[2] Nearly always. It is possible to get it wrong. In 1990 one of the richest jeweller families was represented for the first time by the eldest son of the grand old *seth*, who was too ill to attend. It was a subject of great interest what he would do. 'He is very miserly,' I was told. 'He can't bear to part with his money. His father always makes a big donation, but I think probably he will not.' The Secretary kept returning to this young man for each new auction, prodding and cajoling him. Initially he seemed to be enjoying the attention, but the prodding became more insistent and more mocking, to the delight of those around me. 'He'll have to bid now.' The merchants at the head of leading families do not actually shout out their bids themselves, but delegate the task to one of their subordinates. Twice this man's deputy joined in the bidding but dropped out before the end. My neighbours were having great fun, 'His reputation (*nam*) will go down if he doesn't win something, and his father will be angry. His honour (*izzat*) will be reduced.' He did win one of the auctions in the end, although there was some confusion about whether or not he had authorized the final bid. One of my neighbours thought it likely that the old man's trusted assistant (*munim*) had made the bid off his own bat to save the honour of the family firm. It was impossible for me to tell if this was true or not. 'But it doesn't matter,' he added. 'He will pay'.

manufacturing operation, dealing mostly, for the present, only in semi-precious stones.

And the difference in what we now call 'life-style', even between families of radically unequal wealth, is largely quantitative. The consumption patterns of the rich consist basically of more, and more expensive versions, of the same things. The interiors of the richer families' homes are of course much smarter, with marble floors, whitewashed walls, and western furniture, but *styles* of decoration are not, so far as I could tell, distinct. The religious community is not partitioned into what Bourdieu calls class fractions, but differentiated on a remarkably shared scale of achievement. The rich have much more expensive clothes, and more of them, but although they are made from better quality cloth, the colours and designs are basically the same. This is clear in the case of women's saris, for which there is a well-known scale of differently priced types and weights of fabric, different prints and brocades, and special weaves from Benares or Patan. Not everyone can afford to buy even one of the most expensive varieties, but they all know exactly what they would buy, if they could. On special occasions, old men dress in a *dhoti* (long loin-cloth) and *kurta* (pyjama shirt) of starched white *khadi*, the hand-spun and hand-woven cloth promoted by Gandhi. The associations this dress has with the Independence movement and Gandhian personal austerity are still surprisingly intact, despite their continued use by the post-Independence Congress Party. On the other hand it admits of subtle differentation between more and less costly versions. To starch and press it properly takes a long time, and so to be able to appear regularly looking clean and smart implies significant laundry bills. The shirt can be of cotton or of raw silk. And the buttons on the collar can be anything from plastic, through bone, to diamonds, so that men's clothes too admit of wide, but continuous, grading.

For their everyday needs the richer and poorer members of this community do not shop in different places, nor do they spend their working time or their leisure time in radically different ways. Family relations and the conduct of domestic life are not significantly different. Given suddenly more money, poorer families could and almost certainly would replicate richer families' spending patterns more or less exactly. They share the same aspirations, the same indices of success, and this is to some considerable degree what makes them a community.[3] This is not true of all

---

[3] This account combines, in a thoroughly unsystematic way, a reading of Barth (*Sohar*, see esp. 62–3) and Bourdieu (*Distinction*, especially the notion of 'integrative struggle').

Jains, even in Jaipur—there are those, for instance, in the University who move in a completely different social world—and so it is not to be explained by reference to religious doctrine. It is a matter rather of a social space—one with both moral and aesthetic dimensions—which is highly differentiated, but not discontinuous.

Credit and Merit

The Jaipur emerald market is firmly oriented to international trade and connected, partly through diaspora Jain communities abroad, to markets overseas. Almost all the raw materials are imported, and only a tiny fraction of the cut and polished stones remains in India. The Jaipur market is affected deeply by changes in terms of trade, by world-wide cycles of boom and recession, and by events such as the war in the Persian Gulf in 1990–1, which deprived it for a while of some of its major markets. It is also highly competitive. Some of the richest merchants come from families which have been prominent in the gem market for generations, but others have risen through the ranks in their own lifetimes, and equally, there are many families who cherish memories of wealth and greatness now very definitely past. This is a market where everyone is acutely conscious that there are fortunes to be made and lost. A rumour that someone has a foreign buyer visiting brings brokers scurrying to his *gaddi*, and traders have a horror of missing opportunities of this sort. This can get rather paranoiac and there is something of a mythology of rumour and gossip: one trader (not as it happens a Jain) told me that in order to keep his business private, and prevent others from poaching his customers, he has all his business mail sent to a numbered box at the central Post Office. Fantasies of a just-vanishing *Gemeinschaft*, though they are subscribed to by many of the traders themselves, are probably just that. However, this is not an abstract free market either, and competitiveness takes forms which are culturally specific. One place where religion and business meet is the very extensive informal credit system which the market sustains.

Speculative trading of stones within the market is very extensive, and there is an elaborate and active brokerage system. Emeralds are traded not only so that exporters can meet deadlines for large consignments of cut stones, but also in anticipation of the price fluctuations within the market which result from such highly time-dependent demands. The liquidity of the market depends on a system of informal banking, in which all the major gem firms participate, and which uses a version of the *hundi*, a type of promissory note used in India at least since Mughal times. Unsecured cash advances, which might have to be arranged at very short notice, are to be repaid after a fixed period of time, and this might in some cases be a matter of hours.[4] The price at which a business can obtain money depends directly on its reputation for wealth, honesty, and prudent business practice and it depends beyond that on the public perception of its creditworthiness, which is informed in complex ways by all the factors we have identified above (Chapters 6, 8, and 15) as constituting membership and leadership of the local Jain community.

Gossip within the market is perennially concerned with the financial standing of others, especially the richer merchants. The amount of money which rich traders are able to offer on credit affects how rich they are perceived to be, and while there is always the suspicion that they might be overstretched, it none the less enhances the reputation of a merchant when people can say, 'You can go to him if you need an advance.' Yet in the context of this particular market, in which many transactions are secret, in which stones are held by people who have not yet paid for them, and in which the value of assets can be judged only by knowledgeable insiders, the management of public perceptions and the determination of reputation are complex processes which depend on factors other than narrowly business ones; for credit (*udhar, sakh*) is at once an economic and an ethical notion.

Everyone in the Jaipur market insists that bankruptcy is almost unknown. To begin with, people are very reluctant indeed to take creditors to court. This brings the prying eyes of the state into places from which they are normally, with some time, trouble, and expense, deflected. Litigation in India can easily take decades, and in any case few deals are supported by documents which could be presented before a court. Perhaps most important, however, is the fact that the ethics on which the market rests resist absolutely the notion that liability can be limited. What people say is, if you wait you will get your money. The debtor's family, his in-laws and his brothers, will have to make him pay. They will advance him money, check his expenditure, or whatever is necessary to repair the damage done to their own credit.

Fox comments that in 'Tezibazar', among the Baniyas, 'there are "business families", not "family businesses"', meaning by this to point to the

---

[4] This type of note, a *maddati hundi*, differs from the *darshanik hundi*, which must be paid on demand. The latter is hardly ever used in the Jaipur market. For evidence of the scale and importance of informal credit markets in the Indian economy, see Rudner 'Banker's Trust'; Timberg and Aiyer, 'Informal Credit Markets'.

inseparability of family and business identity.[5] A family's credit, that on which it is assessed for business purposes, is its stock in the broadest sense, which includes its social position, its reputation, and the moral and religious as well as the business conduct of all its members. There are two important elements to this: there is the way family connections constitute business assets and responsibilities, and there is a set of deeply held beliefs about the kind of conduct which brings good fortune. These are, to some degree, different sides of the same coin, and both can be viewed through more or less religiously tinted lenses.

When a family contracts a good marriage, its credit increases, and as Reynell's study of marriage negotiations in Jain families makes clear, the potential impact on business confidence of particular potential alliances are explicit factors for consideration.[6] And this assessment does not rest merely on particular anticipated business opportunities or advantages, but on an assessment of whether, in a world where being connected to a failed family brings both dishonour and the expectation that you too are liable, the family in question will be in the longer term an asset or a liability. The notion of reputation (*izzat, nam*) is a broad notion of creditworthiness which applies indistinguishably to the businessman and to his family, to the family and the family firm. Sharp practice in business, and failure in business, equally rule out a family as desirable marriage partners; and recklessness among the men, or immodesty among the women, damages the credit of the family, and hence the business standing of the family firm.

Because people look at families as potential marriage partners, marriages being always also family alliances, and because business practice depends in this market so much on trust, moral conduct and financial standing are interdependent. This means that a family's credit lies not only in the hands of the men who actually engage in business, but in that of its women too. When sons succeed automatically to their father's position in the family firm, the future of the business enterprise is, quite literally, in the women's hands. Women's religious activity is seen as a contribution to the honour and general social standing of their families: ascetic practice is a demonstration, because it is also a cause, of the moral integrity, sexual restraint, and nurturing capacity of women. Thus the distinctive religious division of labour in wealthy Jain families—with men

---

[5] Fox, *Zamindar to Ballot Box*, 143. See also Rudner, *Caste and Capitalism*, and the analysis by Jones ('Jain Shopkeepers') of the way Jain money-lenders' interest rates are affected by considerations of caste, religion, and personal links.

[6] Reynell, 'Honour, Nurture and Festivity'.

making generous religious donations and women undertaking periodic extended fasts—has an economic dimension. It is common, as I have said, for these two characteristic forms of religiosity to be linked very closely: a rich merchant will make a religious or charitable donation specifically in recognition of a fast which his wife or daughter has performed. Male generosity and female fasting have reciprocal effects on how the other is seen. A woman's asceticism guarantees that her husband's generosity is an expression of piety rather than profligacy; and a man's generosity is testimony to the auspicious effects of his wife's fasting: that, to use again the idiom chosen by the renouncer I quoted in Chapter 10, the grass of prosperity and worldly success is growing around the corn of spiritual progress.

Female fasting is also a more or less explicit idiom for discussing sexual purity and control. In pious Jain families it is virtually required for young unmarried women to undertake fasts, one object of which is to secure a good marriage. The young woman demonstrates that she has mastery over her appetites, and so prospective in-laws are assured that neither through profligacy nor through sexual misconduct will their credit be dissipated. Men make a point of boasting of their wife's religiosity—how much she fasts, that she never eats after nightfall—and they make an equal point of boasting that they themselves cannot match their wife's achievements. Eating after nightfall is the usual diacritic: they would dearly love to abide by this rule; when they are older and have retired from business they may; but for now their business keeps them so busy that they cannot get home and eat in time. Thus the family's credit is bolstered both by the impressive austerity of its women and by the fact that its men, occupied with the more narrowly business side of the family's portfolio, can manage less in this domain. Instead of fasting, the men make big donations and hold generous feasts to celebrate that done by their wives. In a few cases this linking of kingly generosity and fasting, of giving and giving up, is underwritten by the participation of renouncers who are cited as the 'inspiration' or 'instigator' (*prerak*) of both acts, as in the following case.

There is a girls' school in the Johari Bazaar which was set up about twenty-five years ago by one of the local emerald merchants. Since then his son has taken his place as head of the trustees, along with some other prominent *seth*s. In 1987 I attended the annual founder's day ceremony. As India is a secular state, and only non-sectarian schools receive recognition and support from the government, the curriculum at the school is not strongly marked with Jain influence. But the principal is the wife of a locally prominent Jain savant, the walls of the assembly-hall are covered with pictures of the Jinas, and the school always takes part in Jain public holidays, marching in procession at Mahavir Jayanti and *diksha* ceremonies. So the school is recognizably a Jain institution. For the commemoration ceremony the teaching staff and pupils were assembled in the central hall. Two groups of dignitaries were seated before them on a dais. On the left sat a group of wealthy benefactors, and on the right female renouncers. Two of the renouncers and a number of the benefactors addressed the assembly in turn. The renouncers lectured on the importance of study and of obedience to one's parents; the benefactors about how pleased they were to be benefactors. One of them then took up another theme. He described how his daughter had just completed a lengthy and elaborate fast, lasting for a whole year, and conducted under the guidance of a particular renouncer whom he referred to as 'our guru'. He wished to mark this in some way and to perform some religious act himself, so had consulted their guru as to what best to do. The narrative was now taken up by the school principal, who informed the assembly that the renouncer in question had recommended a donation to this school. She then announced the amount given, and this was met with applause. The 'guru' was not present, but the renouncers who were had been her disciples. They completed the proceedings with short speeches, and a Jain devotional hymn.

Thus the family displays its moral rectitude, and in particular it shows that its women will protect and save its credit, rather than squandering it either through extravagant tastes and unrestrained appetites or through impious conduct or sexual misdemeanours. Writing of the ethics of nineteenth-century north Indian merchants, C. A. Bayly remarks that with this notion of credit, 'the distinction between bad moral and bad economic conduct disappears altogether'.[7]

A rich businessman who is easily successful, for whom all risks turn out to be good risks and all ventures to be profitable, is called a *punyashali*—one who has much merit. He does well by doing good, and his doing well is both outcome and indication of his good actions. The support for this notion from religious teaching is very strong indeed. Scores of religious stories, told again and again in renouncers' sermons, illustrate the good fortune which comes from good actions. As one renouncer explained,

If we do some violence then either in this or in some other life, that soul will trouble us back. Suppose someone is very rich, we think that in his previous birth he has given *dan*. Suppose someone gets a lot of money from a lottery or in some

---

[7] Bayly, *Rulers, Townsmen and Bazaars*, 385.

unexpected way, we think that in his previous birth he has given *gupta dan* (i.e. has made an anonymous gift). From a particular *karma*, there is a particular fruit. Suppose someone is very beautiful, this means that he or she has performed some fast (*tap*) in a previous birth. If someone is very brave and mighty this also means that they have done some fast. If we help someone, we will get good things.

It should be said at once that the *punya* to which success is attributed is not necessarily or even most naturally thought of as itself being flawless religious piety or general saintly austerity. When she wants to account for a person's being rich, or receiving money unexpectedly, the renouncer says they must have made some gift, some *dan*. This is in keeping with the general logic whereby the *karma* one has accumulated comes to fruition in a way which bears a poetic similarity to the action which initially brought it about.

In addition, while the term *punya* (merit) can be used to refer to any good, moral, or religious action, in general it is not used for fasting, which is described as *tapasya* or *dharma*, or for good conduct within the family sphere, which is duty (*kartavya*). This is partly due to the rather delicate ambiguities between acquiring good *karma* and removing all *karma*, whether good or bad, which I discussed in Chapters 2 and 10. In any case, the paradigm of an *act* of merit, and that for which the word is most naturally used in everyday discourse, is a generous public donation. And of course, as everyone knows, people make donations of this kind with a range of different motivations and intentions, which might in some cases be no more than the desire to earn good *karma*. When I suggested to people that the evident and well-recognized fact that people do profit by sinful actions, including by sharp business practice, should undermine one's confidence that success in business is a sign of *punya*, I got two reactions. One was to declare confidently that the effect of bad conduct is temporary—such people will suffer in the end. And one man who said this explicitly compared *punya* itself to business reputation. If you cheat on business partners or go back on your word you might gain short-term benefit, but your credit will go down and you will lose in the end. The other line of thought is more cynical: 'That is because the rich can afford to do *punya*. They can give to any beggar they see without thinking. They have no need to worry about this.' This kind of good conduct costs money. Either way, the idea that a good man is a safe bet does tend to be self-confirming if enough people act upon it, and there can be no doubt that it is current enough in Jain communities to make at least an outward show of religious piety a necessary qualification for participation in a trading milieu which is dominated by them.

The Virtues of Wealth

At the famous Jain temple of Ranakpur, in south-central Rajasthan, there is a statue of an elephant. In a light-hearted game, Jains take turns in trying to crawl between the animal's legs and under its pendulous belly. If they manage to get through, they are said to have plenty of religious merit, or *punya*. They are on course for a good rebirth. If not, they have accumulated sin (*pap*) and must mend their ways to avoid a rebirth in hell.[8]

If the underbelly of an elephant is not quite the eye of a needle, the thought is unmistakably that wealth, and worldly good living, make it hard to live a good religious life. The immense respect accorded to those, such as the wealthy merchant Amarcand-ji Nahar (Chapter 11), who achieve complete emaciation by religious fasting, is another expression of the same concern. But almost nowhere in Jainism have I found the thought expressed that being rich is necessarily a sign of vice or is sinful in itself. On the contrary, the general thought, in line with the central imagery of *karma*, is that wealth is the reward for past and present good deeds. Similarly, poverty is generally seen as the wages of sin and indolence. Only voluntary poverty is virtuous—and you cannot renounce what you never had any prospect of possessing. Moreover, throughout Jain history it seems, and certainly today, the paradigm of the virtuous lay family is a trading family. Some traders doubtless behave badly—adulterating goods, telling lies, and so on—but commerce is not intrinsically evil.

All activity in the world, even moving and breathing, is sinful: commerce and wealth are not picked out for special condemnation. But if commerce when practised virtuously is no worse, indeed better, than most ways of living in the world, it does none the less have its own particular forms of temptation and danger. As Bayly's discussion of popular nineteenth-century stories about Jain and Hindu merchants makes clear, one of the greatest dangers then was being drawn, as a consequence of mercantile success, into owning and managing land, for that was thought to carry the greatest moral peril.[9] Today the equivalent is probably foreign travel, and every pious gem-dealer who travels to North America, Europe, and the Far East comes back with an edifying catalogue of tales of how difficult it was to find pure vegetarian food, and how they solved the

---

[8] Tod (*Travels*, 283) tells of a similar practice at Palitana in the early 19th c. I have heard that this still happens today, although I do not remember seeing it.

[9] Bayly, *Rulers, Townsmen and Bazaars*, 384.

problem; how generally spendthrift everyone is, and how little they themselves managed to spend; with lamentations on sexual immorality, the lack
of family duty, and in general on the miseries of Western materialism, to
set beside stories of how successful the business trip was.

Parry has noted that in Hindu culture in general there is little evidence
for religious condemnation of trade, or of the notion of money as the root
of all evil, and he has contrasted the moral peril in religious gifts with what
he calls 'the innocence of commerce'. Parry considers a number of reasons
why condemnation of commerce and usury, which is certainly a recurrent
theme in moralizing in both Christian and Islamic traditions, should have
had such a limited place in Hindu life. He notes the frequent connection
(in thinkers as far apart as Aristotle and Marx) between mistrust of money
and market exchange and the ideal of autarky—a supposedly natural
economy of self-sufficient households or communities.

The argument which I would like to propose here is that by contrast with the
self-image of autarky and of production for use of the producer which we
encounter in all these cases, the caste order is founded on the fundamentally
different premise of a division of labour between castes and their interdependence.
Production is not for direct use; and neither the household, nor the caste nor
even the local community is an ideally self-sufficient entity. Despite the best
endeavours of nineteenth-century British administrators to discover it, the village
as a 'little republic' sufficient unto itself does not, and did not, exist—either in
practice or in ideology. . . . My contention, then, is that the absence of any
outright antipathy to money and commerce has to be understood in the context of
the absence of an ideology of autarky from which this antipathy has so often drawn
its force.[10]

I quote this at length because I think that at the broad-brush level on
which it is intended, it is true. I want to add, however, that popular ethics
almost everywhere in India does have an ideology and a practice aiming at
autarky—ascetic renunciation.

The renouncer withdraws from the 'give and take' (*len-den*), the everyday interdependencies of commerce and caste, and lives either on what he
can gather from the forest, or in the Jain case (because the other solution
is blocked by considerations of *ahimsa*), on what can be gathered from lay
families without incurring any debts or reciprocities. From this point of
view the rules governing the Jain (and, less rigorously, the Buddhist)

---

[10] Parry, 'Moral Perils', 85. I would add to this that except in circles influenced heavily by
Gandhi (who got the idea from Tolstoy) the view of cities as the home of immorality, and
romantic idealization of the countryside, which in Europe goes back at least as far as Virgil,
is not common in India.

renouncer can be seen as replicating the autarky of the forest renouncer as nearly as is compatible with the religious duties of teaching and ascetic example. In the Jain case we see this in the insistence that the renouncer does not have to eat. If the conditions which preserve her social independence do not obtain, she should fast. The essential difference between these ideals of the autarky of the renouncer and the European ideals to which Parry refers (Christian monasteries are a good example), is that they cannot be a model for a whole community or society. It is necessarily a rejection of society (in a way which presupposes its continuing existence) and not a model for it.[11] It therefore does not provide the basis for moralist condemnation of commerce (in terms of social divisiveness, selfishness, or injustice), which is Parry's point. What it does provide, at least in the Jain case, is a set of reasons nevertheless to be concerned about what the effect of engaging in commerce, as a rather promiscuous form of worldly activity and interaction, might be on the fate of one's own soul.

Among Jain gem-traders in Jaipur (to return to a level which is quite generalizing enough for this kind of subject-matter), the market is not regarded as an isolated, amoral sphere of activity, and nor is the peaceful pursuit of wealth justified, as it has been in Europe, only because it subsumes or tames more destructive vices.[12] The successful merchant is seen as a social good, the wealthy merchant family as the embodiment of moral rectitude: religion, charity, and public life all depend upon them. But this is not the end of the story: the renouncer's critique, so to speak, has not so little purchase as the narodnik's. Many times I have sat listening to a Jain renouncer berating a room-full of ample lay Jains in smart clothes and expensive jewellery about how all their most treasured possessions are really their worst enemies; that their beautiful homes, their furniture, and their prized Western consumer goods are the cause of all their worries and tensions and will bring them sorrow and suffering in the end. But ten minutes later we might be hearing a story about a wealthy merchant who performs a fast or makes a generous gift and earns rebirth in heaven. As I have mentioned before, the role of a wealthy and generous patron is often modelled in Jainism on Indra and Indrani: carefree gods who stage opulent rituals for the worship of the Jina and provide a sumptuous setting for his sermons. Birth as a god is the reward for past good deeds, but life as a god is finite, and obtaining *moksh* from that life is impossible,

---

[11] See also discussion of the *samosaran* (ch. 2), caste (ch. 5), and non-violence (ch. 7). For further discussion with regard to Buddhism, see Collins, 'Monasticism', Silber, 'Opting Out'.

[12] Hirschman, *Passions and Interests*.

because renunciation and asceticism are possible only in the world of suffering and choice.

Jainism figures in Max Weber's *The Religion of India* as a case of this-worldly asceticism, of a quasi-Protestant ethic which could have developed bourgeois capitalism endogenously, had it not been constrained by ritualistic prohibitions, and swamped by the caste traditionalism of the surrounding Hindu world.[13] In this sense Jainism showed, for Weber, that a this-worldly ascetic spirit was not a sufficient explanation for the emergence of bourgeois capitalism.[14] In view of the pivotal place it therefore occupies in the overall project of his historical sociology, it is a pity that Weber's discussion of Jainism is limited to just fifteen pages. But perhaps he was aware of how incomplete his sources were. Jain asceticism, as it is institutionalized and enacted in Jaipur, is in many ways exactly the opposite of how Weber portrayed Puritanism (and assumed Jainism itself to be[15]) in *The Protestant Ethic*. Private, individual uncertainty about the fate of one's soul in Jainism points away from diligent work in the world and the accumulation of riches, even though public and family duty, and the religious good of supporting monks and nuns, all point towards it.

We may doubt, of course, that Weber was right about Puritanism (and I have been presuming all along that it is a mistake to try to specify doctrines in a decontextualized way so that their social and psychological consequences might be identified in the abstract). Simon Schama has argued that in seventeenth-century Holland wealth acted not as a reassur-

[13] 'The compulsory "saving" of asceticism familiar from the economic history of Puritanism worked also among them toward the use of accumulated possessions, as investment capital rather than as funds for consumption or rent. That they remained confined to commercial capitalism and failed to create an industrial organization was again due to their ritualistically determined exclusion from industry and as with the Jews their ritualistic isolation in general. This must have been added to the by now familiar barriers which their Hindu surroundings with its traditionalism put in their way besides the patrimonial character of kingship' (Weber, *Religion of India*, 200). That Jains have not been isolated in Indian society is, I hope, amply demonstrated in ch. 5. The supposed 'ritualistic exclusion from industry', like the 'rule for the laity against travel' (197), is imaginary (see ch. 8, n. 12).

[14] See Gellner, 'Weber and Religion of India', 529. In this sense Weber seems to have regarded Jainism as, potentially at least, an exception to his general observation that it would occur to no Hindu to perceive economic success in his vocation as a sign of grace, as Puritans did in their calling (*Religion of India*, 326). This seems to have been connected to his appreciation of the psychological indeterminacy of *karma* (see ch. 2, above), at least in Jainism and Buddhism (*Protestant Ethic*, 227–8). Munshi ('Max Weber on India', 16–18), has argued that his negative conclusion about Hinduism was based on a misinterpretation of how *karma* has been understood in Hindu tradition.

[15] Weber, *Protestant Ethic*, 196–7.

ing symptom of election, but as a moral agitator—necessary to the survival of the Republic, and no doubt also the result of certain virtues, but also an ever-present danger of surfeit and corruption.[16] Far from endorsing capitalism, Dutch religious leaders did their best to proclaim their disapproval. But theirs was not the only voice around, and in so far as religion generated moral discomfort, this tended to encourage expenditure rather than to dissuade people from making money. Schama describes a negotiation between Puritan and Humanist voices, between the ethics of privation and those of self-cultivation.

This picture is certainly nearer than Weber's to the Jain case as I have been presenting it here. The Jain ascetic imperative just does say something different from other ethical standards such as family duty, caste loyalty, and social leadership. All these different world-affirming ideals can be and are expressed in a religious idiom, but that is not sufficient to make any of them *consistent* with renunciation. Thus the negotiation in the Jain case seems more hard fought that in the Dutch as Schama presents it, for the result is not a compromise (what Schama calls a 'golden mean'— 'the control of overloed through the dam of pious manners'[17]), but more like 'the constant motion of the pendulum', which Doniger finds resolves the conflict between erotic and ascetic values in the mythology of Shiva.[18] In Jainism one finds a range of patterns of accommodation between differently virtuous positions—the different patterns of religious practice adopted by men and women, at different stages in the life-cycle, at different distances from the centre of the religious community, and at different points on the scale of wealth. Accumulation can be related dynamically to renunciation in a single life (for the renunciation or even retirement to be heroic, wealth is to some extent a pre-condition), and it can be related contrapuntally within the family, as when a male gift marks a female fast. When, and in so far as lay Jain businessmen respond to the ascetic injunctions of their religion, they will put down their pens and account-books. In so far, which is quite far, as the Jains have been one of India's major cadres of entrepreneurs, there is no compelling reason to attribute this to the asceticism of their monks and nuns, or to the laity's respect for and emulation of this.

---

[16] Schama, *Embarrassment of Riches*, 124.   [17] Ibid. 158.
[18] O'Flaherty, *Siva*, 318.

17

Diwali: Renunciation Humanized and Riches Redeemed

I ENDED Part III by describing how the asceticism of Samvatsari and the well-being and increase celebrated at the Ganesh festival are dramatically counterposed, in a way that is emblematic both of the location of Jain communities in Indian society, and the ethical and aesthetic contrasts between renunciation and riches as lay religious values. I should like to end this part of the book with a consideration of the other major festival in the Jain religious year, Diwali (see Plates XIX–XXII). On the surface, Diwali could not be more different from Samvatsari, but the two festivals exhibit a different aspect of the same Jain ethos; mixing the same elements to produce a complementary effect.

The ceremonies at Diwali include commemoration of Mahavir's ascent to *moksh*, the attainment of omniscience by his closest disciple, Gautam Swami, and pious remembrance of a host of exemplary renouncers and ascetics from Jain mytho-history. But if Diwali thus celebrates the heights of world-renunciation, it is also and more prominently a comprehensive affirmation of this-worldly values: a vivid celebration of wealth, family, and success. How are these related and combined? There are two main rites of worship, or *puja*s, at Diwali. The disciple Gautam Swami is worshipped at both, although, crucially, he is not the sole object of either. The first rite is a *puja* to Lakshmi: goddess of wealth, personification of good fortune, and, as consort of the great Hindu god Vishnu, paradigm of the perfect wife.[1] I shall argue that in this ceremony the general notions of increase and credit are given a plausibly and specifically Jain content. The second rite is *nirvanpuja*, celebration of Mahavir's attainment of *moksh* (or *nirvan*). Here, conversely, I shall suggest that transcendence and release can be seen as being possible even for those who are burdened and blessed by attachment.

---

[1] Kinsey, *Hindu Goddesses*; Narayanan, 'Goddess Sri'.

Lakshmi-Puja: An Invocation of Riches

Diwali is one of the most important religious festivals for both Jains and Hindus. It is also called *Dipavali*, 'a row of lamps', because it is celebrated in the evening with lights and fireworks. Diwali takes place in late October or early November, on the new-moon night of the lunar month of Karttik, and marks both the official end of the rainy season and the traditional Indian New Year. The celebrations last for several days. Dhan Teras ('Wealth Thirteenth') is followed by Little Diwali (which is also called Rup Caudas, 'Beauty Fourteenth'); and then on the new-moon night comes Big Diwali itself. This festival marks the end of the rainy season, the passage from an inauspicious to an auspicious time of year. Once it is over, for the first time since before the rains began, marriages and Jain *diksha* ceremonies may be held. In the week or so leading up to Diwali many houses are thoroughly cleaned, and perhaps even whitewashed. Other families settle only for a general tidy-up and buying some new cooking pots. But everyone ought to have a new set of clothes, and shopping for these is an integral part of celebrating Diwali.

In the last few days before Diwali shopkeepers decorate the fronts of their shops with coloured lights. Sweet-sellers set up tables in the already crowded lanes in the walled city, and set out mountainous displays of sweets under brightly coloured canopies. Stalls appear selling fireworks of more or less dubious manufacture, and hundreds of the lamps used in the festival. These are mostly little earthenware cups filled with candlewax or oil, but there are also factory-made plastic ones on sale. On the evening of Dhan Teras, some families place one of these lamps outside the house or in the window. This lamp, *yam dipak*, is to encourage Yam Raj (Death) to stay away from the house this year. For Little Diwali, I was told, fourteen lamps should be put out, but I never saw anyone actually do this. The idea that it is 'Beauty Fourteenth', on the other hand, is taken seriously, with young women trying on clothes and jewellery in preparation for the next day, and decorating each other's hands and feet with elaborate designs in henna. Diwali on the whole is a family festival, and at all stages men and women are involved, typically in differentiated ways. On Diwali proper, as we shall see, men take a leading role, but on the preceding days (which are, on the other hand, encompassed by the senior element of the festival) the dominant tone is struck by women's activities. As I have mentioned before (Chapter 7), the fourteenth day of each fortnight is always one for increased religious activity by devout lay Jains. A few people fast on Little Diwali, and others join in elaborate public *puja*s.

PLATES XIX–XXII. DIWALI IN JAIPUR.

PLATE XIX. Last-minute sweet-buying from a street-stall.

PLATE XX. A young Jain woman carries a tray of lamps which will be placed throughout the house.

PLATE XXI. Jain businessmen prepare new family account-books for Lakshmi-*puja*.

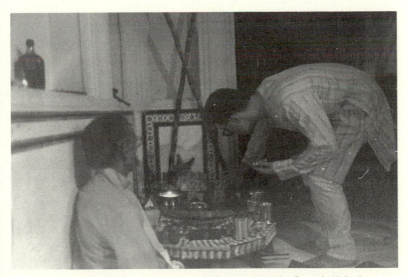

PLATE XXII. The author is instructed on how to worship Ganesh-ji during Lakshmi-*puja*.

The Lakshmi-*puja* is in the evening of Diwali itself, and most of the daytime is spent in final preparations. This is the one festival in the whole religious year when Jains are not called upon to fast, and the most serious and concerted preparations are culinary.[2] A range of special pastries is made, and the women of large extended families take over a courtyard or a big room for hours at a time, sitting in a ring on the floor in a production line of kneading and mixing, and stuffing little pastry parcels with nuts, dried fruits, and spices. The following things are required for the *puja*, in addition to a stock of good quality fruits and sweets: lamps, garlands of flowers, coloured string (*moli*), vermilion paste (*roli*), camphor, and betel leaf, and these are sold wrapped up in packets from stalls in the market. Also needed are two long stalks of sugar cane and throughout the day smartly dressed families can be seen zooming about mounted on a scooter: him driving, with an older child standing between his legs; her sitting on the back, managing her sari, a younger child, and two eight-foot lengths of cane.

Celebrating Diwali is not unique to Baniyas or to the business community: in a business centre such as Jaipur, and I imagine in most towns and cities, it is a public festival in which the whole of the Hindu population takes part. But as a private family festival it is probably most important for Baniyas,[3] and the public celebrations are strongly identified with and led by the business community.[4] Normally, all the businesses in the Johari Bazaar pay jointly for the street to be illuminated with coloured lights, and this is said to be one of the glories of Diwali in Jaipur, but on both the occasions when I was there this did not happen. In both cases local Jain and Hindu business leaders had political reasons for preventing it. In 1987 the whole of western India, and Rajasthan in particular, was in the grip of

---

[2] Perhaps inevitably, a few renouncers have suggested that great merit would be obtained from fasting on Diwali. See Cort, 'Liberation and Wellbeing', 223; Dundas, *The Jains*, 186. I met no one who did this, or even thought they should, and I should be surprised if the idea were to catch on. Cort ('Liberation and Wellbeing', 435–43) also reports attempts to 'reform' the rites which are performed at home during Diwali, and describes celebrations in Patan according to two prescriptive pamphlets, one of which he himself brought to the town. No family I knew in Jaipur celebrated Diwali according to the instructions of a printed text, but rather aimed (more or less successfully) to reproduce what was done the previous year.

[3] Kayasths, for instance, perform some rites which are similar to those described below (those which Jains perform using their family account-books and tools used in business) but they do so at Dashehra, twenty days before Diwali. Hazelhurst (*Entrepreneurship*, 65) implies that some Baniya merchants in the Punjab start their accounts at Dashehra.

[4] Chauhan (*Rajasthan Village*, 199) explains that Diwali is not celebrated at all in the Rajasthan village where he studied because there is only one Baniya family there.

a very serious drought. So although (or perhaps especially because) the urban economy was largely unaffected, and Jaipur was enjoying something of a consumer boom, it was felt that public illuminations would be insensitive, impolitic, and inauspicious. As I indicated in Chapter 5, the idea of Baniyas profiting from famine is an explosive one, and it is an idea the Jaipur business community was keen not to encourage. In 1990 there had been persistent political unrest since the spring. The government, which had already made itself very unpopular with the business community, announced its intention to extend quotas for government jobs to a range of middle-ranking, largely agricultural castes from which it drew electoral support. This would have taken the number of government jobs for which members of the upper castes such as the Baniyas would have been ineligible to over 50 per cent and opposition to the proposals was fierce—including grisly self-immolations by disaffected students. In addition, there had been communal (Hindu–Muslim) violence and the Government of India was seen by Jain and Hindu Baniyas as having taken a pro-Muslim line (the Rajasthan Government, by contrast, took a much more congenial militantly Hindu line). Out of 'respect for those who have died' in these conflicts, and so to protest at government policy and increase the general air of political crisis, the business leaders decided that year that the Bazaar would be left undecorated.

All Jains perform Lakshmi-*puja*, even those, such as the Shvetambar Terapanthis and Sthanakvasis, who do not perform *puja* to the Tirthankars. And of course this is a Hindu festival too, but it is not celebrated with the same enthusiasm by all Hindus. It is more of a Vaishnava than a Shaivite festival, and is especially popular in this part of India with devotees of Rama, and those of Krishna such as the Vallabhacaryas and Satsangis. Most Jain families who live in the walled city, and whose home and place of business are in one building, perform just one Lakshmi-*puja*, but for some who have moved their residence to the suburbs two *puja*s are needed: a brief one in the house and a longer and more elaborate rite, held at the most auspicious time, at the *gaddi*.

Close and trusted business subordinates are included in the family for this festival, and throughout the celebrations enterprise and family are insistently indentified. Extended families which co-operate in business come together for Lakshi-*puja*, even if they maintain separate households. The rite also extends beyond the family, narrowly defined. Rich families with large businesses employ a chief clerk (*munim* or *mantri*) who is often not Jain or a member of their own caste, and these, together with apprentices and other high-ranking employees (but not the labourers who cut and polish stones) attend. Diwali is traditionally the beginning of the accounting year, and notwithstanding the fact that the tax year begins in April, old business account-books (*bahi*) are tied closed on Diwali and replaced by a new set which are opened during Lakshmi-*puja*. Indeed, the greater part of the *puja* is taken up with preparing these account-books.

Lakshmi-*puja* consists of several different procedures, but all are forms of beautification and decoration. A considerable range of objects is used in the ritual, and at first sight it looks as if some complex symbolic scheme might be in operation. But this is not so. My attempts to enquire about possible meanings got absolutely nowhere. The answer was always the same: this is *shubh* or *mangal*. That is, the things used in the *puja* are there to have auspicious effects, and they are the same objects as are used by both Hindus and Jains on a whole range of occasions to connote the very general notion of well-being: lights, fruits, sweets, flowers, leaves, and certain geometrical and floral designs. As I have said before, as a putative referent of a sign, the notion of 'auspiciousness' is almost without content: what these symbols do is to give it form. As Tambiah has shown to be the case in Trobriand canoe magic, this ceremony uses general sensory qualities and paradigmatic 'good things' to construct an anticipatory display of what the general auspicious effects of the rite are supposed to be.[5] The most important point about this, and the reason this rite can occupy the place it does in Jainism, is that the vehicles used in this display are radically underdetermined as regards their meaning.

The house is decorated with auspicious drawings and with lamps. The former is exclusively women's work, and it is generally held that the latter is a male preserve, although it did not seem to be one that was policed very carefully, and I saw several women taking part in this. The drawings vary a lot, from simple leaf patterns to complex geometrical diagrams. Women use either whitewash (in which case the designs are called *mandana*) or coloured wood powder (*rangoli*) to make drawings in various parts of the house, including on the wall where the *puja* will be performed, and some people said these, whatever design they are, are considered to be idols of Lakshmi.[6] This is the only specific meaning assigned to the drawings. Like the fruits, lamps, and other things used in the *puja*, they are otherwise said simply to be good: 'We do them because we are happy and we want to be happy.' A large tray of earthenware lamps is sprinkled with water and vermilion paste and the lamps are then distributed around the

---

[5] Tambiah, 'Form and Meaning'.

[6] This use of geometric drawings is common in India both in high religious art (Zimmer, *Artistic Form and Yoga*) and in folk art (Jayakar, *Earthen Drum*).

house. Then the electric lights are turned off because this looks nicer and Lakshmi will be more likely to come into the house. One of the men is sent out into the street to place a lamp or two in the lane outside, at the nearest crossing, and beside any nearby shrines.

The sugar-cane sticks are set up against a wall so they form a tall arch, leaves are hung round about, and the shrine is set up underneath. Some families have little statues of Lakshmi, Ganesh, or Gautam Swami in their household shrines and if so these are placed in the shrine for the Lakshmi-*puja*. Otherwise, a simple paper print is bought from the market, with Lakshmi and Ganesh portrayed together on it, along usually with Saraswati (goddess of learning, culture, and the arts). These pictures are replaced each year. Lakshmi is always at the centre of the shrine along with Ganesh-ji. This much is true of all these shrines, whether in Jain or Hindu households. Often, but not always, Jain shrines also have an idol or a picture of Gautam Swami, Mahavir's first and most devoted disciple.

The arrangement of the shrine varies greatly from family to family. As Suzanne Hanchett notes, in a study based in southern India, families develop their own styles for celebrating regular festivals, their own preferred offerings for particular occasions and particular deities, their own ideas about the colours to use and the clothes to wear. Thus people combine a concern for getting the details right from year to year with an inventiveness over time that makes such festivals, as Hanchett says, 'India's greatest folk art'.[7] In some households the Diwali shrines are beautifully arranged, with carefully chosen fruits of different colours, each the most perfect example that can be found. This is, among other things, a 'first fruits' festival for the summer crop, and the shrines also contain bowls of baked or roasted grains, a box of sweets, and bowls of food such as boiled rice and curd. There are flowers, and sometimes a lotus sitting in a water pot, which is itself another auspicious symbol. Bowls of silver coins are also common, with commemorative religious coins such as those given out at *updhan* (Chapter 8) mixed up with antique money, and many families buy packets of freshly minted coins from the bank. There will always be a lamp, lighted incense sticks, and a bowl of betel leaves. In well-off families there will be one of each of the cardinal nine jewels (*nau ratna*): emerald, diamond, pearl, sapphire, ruby, coral, cat's eye, blue sapphire, and zircon. Finally, one or two of the family's oldest account-books might be placed in the shrine.

[7] Hanchett, *Coloured Rice*, 49.

This might all look very unorthodox, with Jain idols mixed up with Hindu ones and amulets commemorating rigorous ascetic exercise mixed up with money. Two things are worth pointing out. One is that the inclusion of specifically Jain sacred images is sanctioned by renouncers, who entrust their own idols to devout lay households to be included in the ceremony. The *sthapan-acarya*, which is used as the focal point for renouncers' twice-daily *pratikraman* (Chapter 9), contains tiny idols or sacred symbols. Renouncers, for reasons mentioned in Chapter 11, do not perform *puja* to such idols, but it is believed that the idols should have *puja* performed for them at least once each year, so they are given to a lay family to be included in their Lakshmi-*puja*. The second point is that even as these religious objects are all put together in what looks like a flagrantly syncretistic way, the distinctions between them are carefully marked. The idols and the coins are all bathed in milk and water and dabbed with paste, but while Lakshmi, Ganesh, and the money are dabbed with 'hot' auspicious vermilion paste, the Jina and Gautam Swami idols, the *updhan* medals, and the renouncers' sacred objects are dabbed with the same 'cool' sandalwood paste as is used in Jain temples. Thus 'real Jainism' is marked out within the *puja*, but none of the people I talked to suggested that this marked any difference in the meaning or the purpose of the rite so far as these objects were concerned. The *puja* is auspicious and it brings good fortune. You need good fortune to practise real Jainism as you do for anything else.

The final part of assembling the shrine involves the tools of one's trade. This takes quite some time. For Jain jewellers this means their account-books, but also a collection of other things: tweezers, pens, a magnifying glass, a scoop, and a tiny set of scales and weights for use with gemstones. The first page of each account-book is set out in the same way, copied directly from one of last year's books. In the top left-hand corner a nominal sum such as Rs. 1.25 or 1.50 is entered to put the book in credit. There are longish sections of text written in pen, and several of the men take a hand in this, each filling out one or more books before passing it to the head of the household who adds to it using vermilion paste. He draws a swastika and then writes on either side of this: on the left he writes *Shri Subh* and on the right, *Shri Labh*. These are the same words as are written on either side of the Ganesh-ji idol at Ganesh Caturthi (Chapter 12), but their order is reversed. I asked people why this should be, but no one said anything except that this is the right way to do things. Maybe, I suggested, Lakshmi-*puja* is less materialistic than Ganesh-*puja*, so auspiciousness comes before profit. It could be, I was told. Maybe Lakshmi-*puja* is more materialistic, saving profit till last. That could be too. Anyway, this is how it is done.

Everyone in turn dots a little vermilion paste on the idols of Ganesh and Lakshmi. Then, just as the scales, pens, and other things which are used in business have each had a *moli* cord tied round them and been anointed with paste, each member of the family has a cord tied round their right wrist, and a mark of sandalwood paste and rice grains placed on their forehead. This is a standard procedure both to signify that you have taken part in a *puja*, and, for a collective *puja* such as this one, to designate all those who are to receive the profit (*labh*) or fruit (*phal*) of it. In this *puja* the way this is done directly reflects rank within the family. The male head of the household ties his own, and then everyone receives their *moli* cord from someone who is their senior.

After much waiting while all this writing and tying and so on is done, the *puja* itself is very simple. A camphor lamp is lit and everyone in turn (roughly in order of seniority, men followed by women) waves it in front of the shrine. The flame burns brightly and burns out quickly, so there is a rush to ensure that everyone gets a chance to do this. What people say about the *puja* is equally simple. Luck (*saubhagya*) and auspiciousness (*mangal*) should come into everything. Everything should be good.

The male head of the household is the central agent in this *puja*, the purpose of which is to ensure the success which will enable him to continue to provide for his family and other dependents. Here, however modest the family wealth, he is *punyashali*, the patron and the centre from which wealth is redistributed. At the end of the ceremony he gives small gifts of cash to each member of the family, from his wife to small children and non-kin dependents. The gifts are referred to casually as *dhok*, but this word actually signifies the respect which the recipient shows for the donor. On receiving the money, which is always a crisp, new note, he or she 'does *dhok*' by touching the *punyashali*'s feet. Gifts are also given at Diwali (usually the next morning) to servants, employees, washermen, drivers, postmen, and any others who come regularly to the house to provide a service of some kind, but who would not be invited for Lakshmi-*puja*. To most of these people the gift will be sweets, or, if the patron family is very well-off and generous, cloth. Money is given only to the lowest in status, sweepers and probably the postman. Neither the money given within the family, not the gifts given outside it, are usually referred to as *dan*. People I asked thought that the gifts of money to low-status people might be *dan*. 'But we do not say that', said one man, 'because we think it is something bad'. Thus a range of relationships, of quite different moral qualities, are expressed and reproduced in gifts at this time, and it is interesting that while money is used for the most distant and condescending of these gifts, it is used also to symbolize the closest, most personal, and most moral relationships of all. As Parry and Bloch predict,

Where it [the economy] is not seen as a separate and amoral domain, where the economy is 'embedded' in society and subject to its moral laws, monetary relations are rather unlikely to be represented as the antithesis of bonds of kinship and friendship, and there is consequently nothing inappropriate about making gifts of money to cement such bonds.[8]

This picks out an important truth, and in the Jain case a gift of cash is used to symbolize loving provision and moral authority. Yet simultaneously, a completely different pattern is in play, and this does involve the notion of money as the medium of more distant and morally thin relations. The disjunction, I take it, reflects the division between the realm of trade, trust, and credit; on the one hand, and that, on the other hand, of employment and wages. At the farther reaches of what Sahlins called 'social distance',[9] money rather than food signifies radical hierarchy and is only given to those who are at or beyond the social and moral pale. The difference between these two sorts of money gifts is marked, but could hardly be constituted, by the difference between new notes and loose change.

A Catalogue of Virtues

The family account-books are the most important part of Lakshmi-*puja*. Both the new books and the oldest ones in the family's possession are included, not in an orgy of materialism, but as icons of the continuity, credit, and honour of the family. That honour depends upon financial well-being is obvious, but although narrowly commercial interests are part of what is sought and celebrated, they come nowhere close to exhausting it.

Most families keep sets of old account-books and many do not even know how far back their collection goes. When they need to be disposed of they are reverently burned and would never be merely thrown away—questions of prudence and privacy reinforcing those of reverence and respect. The books are regarded with reverence in part because they

[8] Parry and Bloch, *Money and Morality*, 9.
[9] Sahlins, 'Sociology of Primitive Exchange'.

contain the truth about the family's fortunes: a truth which is wider than, although it does include, profit-and-loss accounts, narrowly conceived. It is a truth which is intensely private: among the various classes of ledger which a family keeps there are some which are, and some which are not, for the eyes of the tax-man. The idea which the members of the Anoop Mandal had (Chapter 5), that the magical power of the Baniyas was somehow cryptically encoded in their account-books, and which has made these books one of the targets when Jains have been attacked,[10] is one which, from a different point of view, the Jains well understand. When so much of business is about persuasion and reputation, about managing other people's perceptions, the family's own view of its true finances is itself a jealously guarded business asset. Thus even with the intrusion of the modern state into business practice, and the need to keep quite separate public accounts, some at least of the features which Bayly has noticed in the attitudes and practices of north-Indian merchants in the eighteenth century are still very strong today. Bayly comments on the reluctance of these merchants to show their account-books to outsiders,

Their opening is always attended by a feeling of ceremony. When a man agrees to show 'my books' (never 'the firm's books,) he is, as it were, discovering the credit of his ancestors. The most reluctant of all to do this were the Jains who maintained strong sanctions against the release of any information about ancestry, commercial or sexual practices, even to Brahmin families which had been associated with them for generations. When merchants claimed that their credit would suffer by showing their books in the ruler's court, they were not simply making a statement about commercial morality, but about the honour of the family. Hence it followed that the production of books in open court was considered superior evidence in a suit even to oaths made on Ganges water. The witness was making a solemn statement equivalent to a Muslim oath over the tombs of ancestors.[11]

The first page of each account-book has the swastika and words already mentioned, and above this, in ink, the syllable *Shri*, one of the names of Lakshmi, is written forty-five times to form a triangle. All this is to be found on both Jain and Hindu account-books, but there are also some important differences. At the top of the page is a short invocation to one or more gods, and as would be expected, Jains and Hindus differ somewhat here. Hindu books are headed with a simple invocation to

[10] For instance, in the famous Deccan riots (late 19th c.), when indebted peasant cultivatiors attacked Jain and Hindu Baniyas and destroyed their account-books. See also Hardiman 'Bhils and Sahukars'.

[11] Bayly, *Rulers, Townsment and Bazaars*, 380. See also Haynes, 'From Avoidance to Confrontation', 272.

Ganesh-ji: *Sri Ganesh Namah*, or something of that sort. Jain ones always begin with the Tirthankar and with Gautam Swami. This is important, as I shall suggest that Gautam Swami is so prominent in the Jain celebration of Diwali because he can stand in as a Jain equivalent of Ganesh-ji. Several of my informants equated them explicitly, saying that Gautam helps Jains the way Ganesh helps Hindus. People said things like, 'The Hindus have Ganesh-ji to help them in their difficulties. We have Gautam Swami, although there is also Ganesh-ji and we also worship him too'.[12] If the two are from some points of view equated, they are certainly not confused. One woman picked out the difference by saying, 'Ganesh-ji is worshipped only for *labdhi*, but our Gautam Swami is worshipped for other things also', meaning that he is also venerated as a Jain saint.

Labdhi is one of a cluster of words which refer to magical powers. There are many kinds of *labdhi*, possessed by different deities, spirits, and yogis. Ganesh and Gautam Swami are both noted for their *labdhi*, and also for their *riddhi* and *siddhi*: powers which are often said to be the 'wives' of Ganesh-ji, just as his 'sons' are *shubh* and *labh*. Gautam Swami already had magical powers before he became a Jain renouncer. As one Jain woman said to me, 'He was not really a Jain'. By this she meant that he was not a Baniya, but a Brahmin.[13] The story goes that when Mahavir was preaching in his *samosaran* and people and gods were converging from all directions to listen, Gautam Swami, who was holding a Vedic sacrifice, at first assumed they were all coming to see him. When he learned that they were not, he marched up to Mahavir, intending to use his perfect knowledge of the Vedas to confound what he assumed to be an unlearned imposter. Mahavir greeted him by name, although they had never met before, and anticipated and answered his learned questions.[14] Gautam thereupon became a follower of Mahavir, and lost what the Jains describe as his Brahmin's arrogance, but he retained his magical powers.

The stories about Gautam's life as a follower of Mahavir stress the help he gave to his own disciples, every single one of whom, it is said, attained *moksh*. His *labdhi*s include the ability to fly through the air, and to appear

---

[12] Similar equations are also drawn between Ganesh-ji and the Dada Guru Devs, but as the latter do not feature much in the Diwali celebrations, I shall not pursue this aspect of things here.

[13] Although Jains insist that all the Tirthankars are Kshatriyas, members of kingly and warrior castes, Mahavir's eleven immediate disciples were all Brahmins.

[14] Comic deprecation of scriptural learning, in comparison with spiritual insight, is a common theme in Jain hagiographies, even those which deal with the most compendiously learned Jain saints. See Granoff, 'Biographies of Haribhadra'; Dundas, *The Jains*, 111–17.

in two places at once, but the most celebrated is the miraculous power to make things increase: *mahanasa labdhi*. This is most famously represented in a Jain 'feeding the five thousand' story.

Gautam Swami was on his way to worship at Ashtapad Parvat—a mythical mountain where Rishabh attained *moksh*. He was followed by many yogis.[15] It is impossible to climb to the top of Ashtapad, there are eight steps and each one is eight miles high, but Gautam Swami took hold of the sun's rays and flew up. The yogis, though they were doing all kinds of *tapasya*, got stuck on the first step. Gautam Swami saw that none of them would manage to get to the top, so he came down to where they were, and preached to them there. When they saw and heard him, they willingly became Jain renouncers and started a Jain fast. On the day when they were to break their fast Gautam Swami asked them what they would like for their *parana* meal. They said they wanted kheer [a sweet rice pudding which also features in a story in Chapter 14].[16] Gautam Swami brought some kheer in his almsbowl from a lay Jain household. His *labdhi* and *prabhavana* were such that all the yogis ate from that one small bowl. He put his thumb in the bowl before passing it round so it didn't run out. Everyone was able to eat their fill.

Gautam Swami is a devout Jain, indeed he is Mahavir's first and most devoted disciple. He performs magical feats, in pursuit of religion and to help others. He is a teacher, and he comes down to meet his followers, although they are on a level far below him. Probably because of this story, resourceful housewives are said today to have *labdhi*. One Khartar Gacch *sadhu* said, 'We believe this story because of Gautam Swami's *labdhi*, and for this reason he is worshipped at Diwali—so we may get the same *labdhi* as Gautam had—that is, that our stock should last forever. This is our wish.' Nor is Gautam Swami's help only worldly. After they had eaten, Gautam took his new disciples to meet Mahavir, and when he got there he found they had already attained omniscience (*keral gyan*).

What are we to make of the identification between Gautam Swami and Ganesh? In a classic paper, Edmund Leach argued that Ganesh-ji is a typical Janus-like deity, a 'man in the middle' who mediates a contradiction

[15] The numbers vary in the story as I have been told it, sometimes five hundred, sometimes fifteen hundred: anyway, 'a lot'. That they are 'yogis' means that they are ascetic renouncers, practising penances, but not Jains. In Jain depictions of the story, they always look like Shaivite ascetics: they have long hair, carry tridents, are covered in ashes, and perform penances in contorted yogic poses.

[16] No one who has told me this story has ever seemed bothered by the fact that renouncers are not supposed to have preferences about what food they eat. It is obviously not essential to the story that they wanted kheer in particular (although it is always specified), but the theme that Gautam Swami fulfils desires does seem to require, from a narrative point of view, that they get the chance to express a preference.

between important principles and values in a religious system. He is identified with, but also in certain crucial respects opposed to, the highest deities of the religions in which he is found, the cases considered by Leach being Hinduism in south India (where his counterpart is Shiva), and Sinhalese Buddhism (where of course it is the Buddha).[17] Leach also pointed out that the characteristics attributed to Ganesh are not consistent across traditions, but vary so as to remain in constant opposition to certain salient features of the high deities with whom he is paired.[18] Leach was interested in the sexual nature of the deities, but in the Jain case once again food seems to be a more prominent theme, and the values which the Jain Ganesh–Gautam seems to mediate—asceticism and beneficence—are seen in terms of fasting, food, and fat.

One of the many characteristics that Gautam has in common with Ganesh is that he is plump: not obese, but definitely healthily plump. All the stories stress this and modern paintings give him a cherubic face, a buttery complexion, and a beneficent grin quite different from the aloof, detached smile of the Tirthankars. As one Jain monk has it, 'his body lustrous like polished gold, and it was fat'.[19] This might be thought unseemly for a Jain renouncer, and indeed there is a story that Kubera, king of the *yaksha*s, and fairly rotund himself, thought so.[20] Gautam Swami had attained *manahparyaya gyan* (clairvoyance), so he knew what Kubera was thinking. He puts the latter's doubts to rest with the following story.

There were two princes, Pundarika and Kundarika. Their father became a renouncer and handed over his throne to Pundarika. After hearing a sermon by a Jain monk Pundarika too decided to become a renouncer and to hand over the throne in turn to his brother. However, Kundarika refused, and immediately

---

[17] We have already seen Ganesh in such a role in Jain religious practice, for he appears in Paryushan (see ch. 12) as the focus of an auspicious counterpoint to Jain lay asceticism.

[18] Leach, 'Pulleyar and Lord Buddha'.   [19] Ratna Prabha Vijay, *Sthaviravali*, 64.

[20] Kubera, depicted as a pot-bellied dwarf with a club and a bag of jewels, figures in both Jain and Hindu mythologies. In the *Ramayana* he is Ravana's half-brother, but fights on the side of Lord Rama. In Shaivite mythology he is Lord Shiva's treasurer. According to the Jains he does the same job for Indra, king of the gods, keeping his vast store of precious metals and jewels somewhere in the Himalayas. He is Dhanapati, 'Lord of Riches', is associated with Lakshmi, and is often worshipped by Hindus at Diwali. The associations between Kubera and Ganesh are close. They are, respectively, keepers (*lokapalas*) of the northern and southern regions and are virtually merged in much Hindu mythology and iconography. See Bhattacharya, *Jaina Iconography*, 113–14; Zimmer, *Art of Indian Asia*, 276–7; Courtright, *Ganesa*, 130–1. Hemacandra makes frequent reference to Kubera, using his patronym, Vaishravana.

became a renouncer himself. Pundarika was then persuaded by his ministers that he could not leave his kingdom ungoverned.

Kundarika lived as a renouncer, practising fierce austerities, and after some time reduced his body to skin and bone. But he tired of the renouncer's life and returned at length to the palace. Pundarika in his turn now took the opportunity to become a renouncer, leaving his brother on the throne.

Both died immediately afterwards. Pundarika died in meditation after his first walking-fast, his body still plump, as befitted a wealthy king. Kundarika died angry. He was furious because the palace servants laughed at him for abandoning his vows. 'Just like a beggar', they said. He vowed that next day he would kill them, and before going to bed he ate an enormous meal. His body was of course unused to this, so he died vomiting and in agonizing pain.

The still plump Pundarika was born again in a high heaven occupied by those who will attain release in their next life. Kundarika in contrast, was reborn in the seventh hell.

Kundarika was a fine and fierce ascetic, but he reneged on his responsibilities to state and family, and refused to accept the proper order of precedence and authority. This element in the story should be understood against the background of a very widespread theme in Indian myths and folk-tales, of the terrible disasters which may ensue when kings renounce their thrones to become ascetics. As we saw above (Chapters 2 and 5) Jain foundation myths insistently highlight the beneficial consequences of kingly conversion and renunciation, but, as here, Jain tradition also recognizes the dangers to state and society and distinguishes between timely and untimely, and well and badly motivated acts of renunciation. Kundarika gave up the worldly life too hastily, and without seeking his elder brother's permission. He was proud of his austerities, but they did him no good in the end. The condition of the mind, says Gautam Swami, is more important in determining your *karmik* fate than how much fat is on your body, and carelessly casting aside your worldly duties is not the path of religion. The comfortable life of a king, and fulfilling your worldly duties are, says Gautam Swami, not necessarily incompatible with progress towards release. It is fitting that Diwali, when Gautam Swami is worshipped, is the one Jain holy day when people are not supposed to fast, indeed they are supposed to eat well. It is inauspicious to feel hungry on Diwali, or to eat plain, simple, or tasteless food. If you eat well and are satisfied then if all goes well, as the *sadhu* said, your stock should last forever.

So the inclusion of Gautam Swami on Jain account-books adds, in a distinctively Jain idiom, some of the characteristics of Ganesh, and as I have said, he is explicitly referred to by Jains as 'our' Ganesh; although, as is common in Jainism, he joins the Hindu god in the ritual rather than replacing him.

But the Jain account-books also differ from Hindu ones in that they contain a list of specific characteristics under the more general headings of auspiciousness and increase (*shubh* and *labh*): a shopping list, as it were, of worldly virtues. The list takes up the lower half of the page (it should, for luck, take up five, seven, or nine lines) and ends with a note of the date and time at which the Lakshmi-*puja* was performed. The lists vary a little from family to family, but every single one begins with 'Gautam Swami's *labdhi*'. There are usually about six or so others, and they too are the qualities for which some figure in Jain mytho-history is especially noted. Here are the most frequently cited.

1. The *labdhi* of Gautam Swami
2. The *padvi* (office or status) of Bharat
3. The *riddhi* (prosperity) of Dhanna and Shalibhadra
4. The *buddhi* (intelligence) of Abhaykumar
5. The *bal* (strength) of Bahubali
6. The *dan-vritti* ('prowess of giving') of Shreyam

What this list does is to break down the auspicious effects of Lakshmi-*puja*, but it does this in a different way from the sensory display of the *puja* shrine where good things heaped together have qualities which are metonymically evocative of well-being. Here, well-being is identified as the specific remarkable qualities of specific named individuals, and these individuals are all, in different ways, not only representatives of worldly excellence and good fortune, but also exemplars of Jain asceticism. They are also all men, which is unsurprising in view of the clear affirmation of male authority within the family which occurs during the *puja* and the business context; and also, perhaps, in view of the fact that one object of the exercise is the seduction of Lakshmi. Initially, each of the exemplars mentioned uses their various excellences in the service of Jainism, as the present-day *seth*'s wealth and business acumen can be. But if they are all patrons of Jainism, they are also ascetic achievers. So the general notion of auspiciousness is not only given a specific content, it is given a specifically Jain content. It should be said at once that as a list of hopes and desires, both worldly and spiritual, it is not a modest one. Let us look at what they are, and the great figures who exemplify them.

The *padhvi* of Bharat

Bharat's office was that of a *cakravartin*, a universal emperor or ruler of the four quarters. Bharat is also (Chapter 2) one of the celebrated people who have attained omniscience and release, the ultimate goal of ascetic renunciation, although they lived as householders and never became Jain renouncers. So he is both a supreme kingly patron of Jainism, and the most fortunate of listeners (*shravak*), who received magical redemption without undergoing the rigours of the monk's life.

The *riddhi* of Dhanna and Shalibhadra

The tale of the two friends Dhanna (or Dhanya) and Shalibhadra is one of the best known Jain didactic religious stories. It is one of a number in which a seemingly insignificant event is the catalyst, the *nimitt*, of renunciation; but the two men are also remembered as extremely wealthy and generous merchants and it is their immense wealth that is invoked here.[21] *Riddhi* means prosperity, success, and good fortune (one of the 'sons' of Ganesh), and the story always begins with a highly coloured description of how rich the two men were, for it depends on the idea (which we have met above in the story of Rohini) that it is possible to be so rich and happy that you are untroubled even by the thought that others are not so fortunate. Dhanna enjoyed every sort of worldly happiness: fabulous wealth, innumerable wives, inexhaustible supplies of food, and the finest imaginable clothing. The story is both an evocation of what *riddhi* can bring in worldly life and another indication that such luxury does not preclude eventual spiritual success. This, with the eulogy on his stupendous wealth omitted, is the version I heard many times in Jaipur.

Dhanna was the scion of a merchant family of unparalleled wealth. His first experience of discomfort or unhappiness occurred as he was taking a bath one day. One of his wives was unhappy because her brother, Shalibhadra, was to become a renouncer. Shalibhadra's family, including his many wives, had protested about

[21] The story, which is retold in different forms by many Jain writers, first appears in the *Avashyaka* commentaries and is a popular subject of manuscript illustration. See Bender, 'Dramatis Personae'; Bloomfield, 'Salibhadra Carita'; Coomaraswamy, *Catalogue of Indian Collections*, iv; Johnson, *Trishashti-shalaka-purusha-caritra*, vi. 254–62; Nahar, 'Illustrated Salibhadra MS'; Winternitz, *History of Indian Literature*, ii. 497. The focus of the story as I heard it in Jaipur and as I tell it here, differs from Hemacandra's version in that the focus of narrative attention (and also of wealth and virtue) is concentrated more on Dhanna than on Shalibhadra.

this, and as a concession he had decided to leave the world gradually, renouncing one of his wives each day and giving away all his fabulous wealth bit by bit. But now the time of his final renunciation was approaching. His sister was thinking of this as she was rubbing cool scented oil into her husband's skin. A hot tear fell on Dhanna's flesh. Dhanna, recoiling at the unprecedented discomfort, tried in vain to comprehend his wife's emotion. The experience was so traumatic that he himself renounced the world there and then. He joined his brother-in-law, and they retired to the mountains to practise austerities together. Dhanna attains *moksh* and Shalibhadra, who is interrupted in his meditations in the crucial moments before death, is reborn in the highest heaven.

The *buddhi* of Abhaykumar

At the time of Lord Mahavir, the area in north India which is now Bihar was the kingdom of Magadha. Both the Buddha and Mahavir lived there when it was ruled by King Shrenik.[22] One of Shrenik's sons was Abhaykumar. Abhay wanted to become a renouncer and follow Mahavir, but his father refused to give permission. So Abhay remained a prince until after his father's death and used his remarkable intelligence (*buddhi*) to play clever tricks on the enemies of both his father's kingdom and the Jain religion. He tricked thieves into giving themselves away and enemy armies into giving in; he prevented a fire from destroying the city and an epidemic from ravaging it; he escaped captivity and captured his captor before finally becoming a Jain renouncer.

The *bal* of Bahubali

Bahubali was the second son of Rishabh Dev, and Bharat's younger brother. As his name implies, he was remarkable for his physical strength (*bal*). This he used most notably in two ways: in a duel with his brother, and in performing Jain austerities. When the two brothers wrestled, the whole earth shook and Bahubali, who had already become a renouncer, defeated Bharat who had temporarily become somewhat arrogant and forgotten that the world renouncer finally stands above the world conqueror.[23] The importance of Bahubali's physical strength in his pursuit of religion is even more well-known. In statues of Bahubali, of which the

[22] The Buddhists call him Bimbisara, and both Jains and Buddhists claim him as a follower of their religion, although even Jains admit that his son and successor, Ajatashatru, was a Buddhist. Jains say that Shrenik was related to Mahavir. Barnett (*Antagada-dasao*, p. vii) prints a genealogy showing Shrenik (Senie) married to Cellana, a daughter of Cetaka, who is sister to Mahavir's mother Trishala. Shrenik, it is believed, will return to earth as the first Tirthankar in the next world era, although he is presently in hell.

[23] Hemacandra gives a characteristicallly magnificent description of the duel. See Johnson, *Trishashti-shalaka-purusha-caritra*, ii. 308–22.

Digambars are particularly fond, he is shown engaged in asceticism, standing upright in the *kaussagg* position, with creepers growing up his arms and legs. The creepers have grown because the strength he used to defeat his brother is now turned to holding his body stock-still for months and years of continuous ascetic penance.

The *dan-vritti* of Shreyam

The story of Shreyam has been told above (Chapters 10 and 15). When Shreyam presented alms to Rishabh Dev he became the first person in the present era to perform *supatra-dan*, so that his *dan-vritti*, his power of giving gifts, is the greatest there has ever been. He became the leader of the whole lay Jain community.

Thus Jain account-books not only embody the honour and continuity, of the family, but also its most extravagant aspirations. This is a catalogue of what auspiciousness would ideally bring, of the qualities the perfect *punyashali* would possess. What otherwise remains a rather general desideratum—'all good things'—is specified in terms which hardly make it more attainable, but do give it a fairly clear semantic content: a content, moreover, which is tied at every point, though in diverse ways, to ascetic renunciation. Now I do not think this list conceals a secret about just how worldly wealth and good fortune should be connected to renunciation: it does not propose a model for reconciling the different forms of lay religious identity. Should one, like Bharat, be a kingly patron of renouncers and hope for chance enlightenment at the end of one's life? Should one, like Shalibhadra, slowly give away material possessions and make a gradual withdrawal from one's family, or, like Dhanna, a flick-of-the-switch decision to renounce? Should one, like Abhaykumar, delay renunciation in obedience to family duty, and serve both family and religion by the application of the same worldly skill? Should one, like Bahubali, fight for the honour of renouncers and practise fierce asceticism? Or is Shreyam's more conventionally lay life preferable, combining gifts to renouncers with observance of lay vows?

When completed, the front page of the new account-books is an object of *puja* in the same way as the idols on the shrine are. A betel leaf is placed on the page, along with a coin, some betel nut, and some powdered turmeric and coriander. The lamp from the shrine is waved over the books, and left to burn until morning.

After the *puja*, many people will eat some of the special foods prepared earlier in the day, but it is dark by now, so stricter Jains will not. Most people climb to the roofs of their houses to set off fireworks, but that too is *himsa*. If Lakshmi-*puja* expresses worldliness in a distinctively Jain idiom, not everyone is beguiled. I had one stern friend (and he was the only one) who insisted that he only worshipped Saraswati and Gautam Swami on Diwali, and not Lakshmi or Ganesh. 'Saraswati represents knowledge (*gyan*), so we can worship her, but it is the duty of Jains to worship only the Jinas, liberated souls, and renouncers.' But then he added, 'I will do Lakshmi-*puja*—for my family, although I will not really be worshipping her.' The great pastime after Lakshmi-*puja* is playing cards. Of course, this is something else which is not allowed in Jainism, but with so much luck around, almost everyone makes an exception.

Nirvan-Puja: Final Renunciation

His magic, his benevolence, his similarities to Ganesh-ji, and even his girth notwithstanding, Gautam Swami is, after all, a Jain renouncer. In two major texts of the Shvetambar canon, the *Bhagavati Sutra* and the *Jivajivabhigama Sutra*, he is Mahavir's chief interlocutor, and these texts consist largely of Gautam's penetrating questions on Jain doctrine and Mahavir's responses. The *Uttaradhyayana Sutra* describes Gautam's pivotal role in founding the Jain order. When Mahavir attained enlightenment there was already a body of renouncers following the Jain path. Led by Keshi Kumar, they were followers of the order founded centuries before by the twenty-third Tirthankar, Parshvanath. The rules followed by the two orders were slightly different but Gautam effects a union between them, showing the differences in their vows and habits to be merely external matters, and persuading Keshi's followers that Mahavir is the new Tirthankar. The renouncers in Parshvanath's order took vows for only four 'great restraints' (*mahavrats*) whereas Mahavir's followers took five. Gautam explained to Keshi that in the time since Parshvanath was alive the condition of the world had deteriorated. Men were more sinful and more easily led from the path. For this reason more rules and regulations were required.[24] So in this as in other ways Gautam is shown as an agent of compromise and reconciliation: a magical, but at the same time rather human foil to Mahavir.

The morning after Lakshmi-*puja*, the celebration of Diwali continues. Hindus commemorate Lord Ram's return from exile, after his defeat of

---

[24] Jacobi, *Jaina Sutras*, ii. 119–29. Jaini (*Jaina Path*, 17) insists that the texts do not say that Parshva's order had 'four vows', but rather that it expressed its views in 'four modalities'. The distinction is not one that my friends in Jaipur are familiar with.

Ravana and his retrieval, albeit temporary, of his consort Sita. This day is also 'Gobardhan', the day on which Lord Krishna lifted a mountain of that name to protect the people of Mathura from a rain storm. Agarwals in Jaipur, both Hindus and Digambar Jains, perform *puja* with cakes of cow dung (*gobar*), which again is said to bring wealth (*dhan*). At the Shvetambar rite Gautam Swami is present once again, but instead of being in the company of Lakshmi, Ganesh-ji, and other representatives of worldly happiness, he is with his guru, Mahavir.

The Jains hold that it was during the night of Diwali that Mahavir extinguished the last of his *karma* and attained final liberation. The *puja* to celebrate this is held early, at the very first light of dawn. Unlike Lakshmi-*puja*, which is domestic, this is a public ceremony. People come to the temple with large round sweets made from molasses, called *nirvan ka laddu*. The sweets are said to represent victory, or to be the best sweet for the best thing, or it is said that 'it represents *nirvan* because it is round and complete'. The *puja* is very simple. Everyone gathers in a big crowd around the idol of Mahavir and sings a song from booklets which are available in the temple. The song is the *Nirvan Stavan*, said to have been composed by Vinay Pravbha Upadhyay (a disciple of the third Guru Dev, Jin Kushal Suri-ji) and it tells the story of Mahavir's attaining *moksh*. When the song reaches this point, the sweets are offered. As always with worship of the Tirthankars, these sweets are offered and left in the temple: a renunciation or giving up.

Gautam Swami figures in the story of Mahavir's release, and in the *puja* to celebrate it, in the following way: although he was a marvellous guru, and all his disciples attained enlightenment, he himself did not at first, because he was so devoted and attached to Mahavir. As Mahavir explained,

Gautam! Forever you have been attached to me with affection. Forever, you have been singing in praise of me. Forever, you have served me. Forever, you have followed my instructions. In your previous lives as a god in heaven, or as a human being on this earth, you have had a link with me, and what [is] more, even after we die from here, when this body will be no more, we will be equals, with a common purpose, without difference.[25]

Mahavir devotes part of his last sermon to trying persuade Gautam to give up his attachment so that he will attain release.[26] But when he knows that

[25] Quoted in Lalwani, *Sramana Bhagavan Mahavira*, 59. The passage comes from the *Bhagavati Sutra* (14. 7).

[26] Jacobi, *Jaina Sutras*, ii. 41–6. See the discussion of this by Jaini, *Jaina Path*, 45–6.

his death is approaching, Mahavir sends Gautam on an errand. As one woman in Jaipur told me the story,

When Mahavir Swami knew he was going to *moksh*, he sent Gautam Prabhu away, because he thought, 'He has too much love for me, and when he sees that I have gone he will not be able to bear it.' When Gautam was coming back, the gods (*devtas*) were flying through the air and told him that Mahavir Swami had gone to *moksh*. Gautam was very upset and started to weep, 'Why did you send me away', he said, 'I wasn't asking you to give me *moksh* too.'

The *Kalpa Sutra* tells us that this is the origin of Diwali, and of the use of lamps to celebrate it. To mark Mahavir's passing to *moksh*, the rulers of the time set up public illuminations, declaring that 'The lamp of inner light is extinguished; let us now burn lamps of ordinary clay.'[27] In addition, my friends in Jaipur told me, the lamps at Diwali also symbolize knowledge—the fact that on that day Gautam Swami finally did become omniscient, and thus ensured that when he died he too would attain *moksh*.

The gathering in the temple moves from the idol of Mahavir to that of Gautam Swami, to continue the song. In the style of Hindu *bhakti* (devotional) poems it describes Gautam Swami's sorrow as like that of a child who has lost his mother. But then Gautam realizes that Mahavir has not really abandoned him. He has left behind Jain texts and the Jain religion so that he, and indeed everyone, can follow him. With this realization, he overcomes his attachment, and attains omniscience. Three of Mahavir's eleven original disciples survive him and set about building the Jain order. As Jains tell it, this is a story of charisma and routinization working together, with Gautam working miracles to give help to the followers of Jainism, and Sudharman organizing groups of renouncers and laying down rules and regulations. Sudharman's organizational mantle is passed to Jambu, the last person in this world-age to achieve omniscience and liberation.

It is unsurprising that it should be Diwali rather than Holi, the other great carnival of popular Hinduism, that the Jains should have developed so fully. Holi is of no religious significance to Jains. Most Jains play Holi, some with great enthusiasm, although quite a few do scorn it. But unlike Diwali it is given no specifically Jain significance, and those who participate do not do so as Jains. Holi is a rite of rebellion, with systematic status reversal, breaking of taboos, sexual innuendo, and riotous behaviour, and like all such rites it is a period when the everyday structure of social life is

[27] Vinay Sagar, *Kalpa Sutra*, 193–5. See also Jacobi, *Jaina Sutras*, i. 266.

to some degree dissolved, reversed, or transcended. When Jains take part in Holi they do so on its own terms. Some find irreverent status reversal congenial, others do not. They choose to take part or not in something which has nothing whatever to do with Jainism. Diwali is a different matter. Diwali, while it is certainly festive enough, remains firmly within hierarchical social categories. Indeed if it is about anything, it is about them: ties of family, neighbourhood, and economic patronage are enacted, and in the process distinctions of age, gender, wealth, and status are clearly set out. The festival celebrates and seeks success within a world which is divided and structured along these lines.[28]

In scripted fasts, world-renouncing ascetic practice can be seen as conducive of family welfare, but the connection is hedged around, and believed to be effective just to the extent that it is not, in fact, in view. At Samvatsari—or rather in the co-occurrence of that festival with the Ganesh celebrations—austere and auspicious themes are both given clear and dramatic articulation. Hymns to riches and renunciation are played together, but the effect, although it may be satisfying, is undoubtedly something of a cacophany. Things are different again at Diwali, which only makes the sense it does against the background of ascetic practice which is, uniquely, suspended for it. Even people who hardly ever fast themselves all know that this is the one occasion in the year when they are not even really enjoined to do so. Various connections are made during Diwali between riches and redemption, but for once Jains allow themselves actually to say, with St Augustine, 'but not yet', and certainly not today.

Two things happen in the Diwali celebrations which happen, I think, nowhere else. This-worldly well-being—wealth, family continuity, auspiciousness, and good fortune—is explicitly catalogued in a specifically Jain idiom, and placed beside ascetic renunciation in so many slightly different ways that one is almost forced to see a connection. And the highest goals of Jain ascetic renunciation are made available, if not quite yet, to those who not only retain bonds of attachment, but who are fat.

---

[28] It might be thought odd that the two festivals which are, on my account, crucial to an understanding of Jainism are also, though in different ways, Hindu festivals. This is not because I think Jainism is part of Hinduism. Far from it. The reason is rather that Jainism is contrastively constituted against Hinduism—even as the world-renouncing parts of Jainism are constituted against conceptions of worldly flourishing. Doubtless Jainism could be constructed in this contrastive way against other others. It was, against Buddhism and pre-Hindu Brahmanism in the past, and it may come to be so now outside India. And if this all makes Jainism dependent on Hinduism, it means that this dependence is of a strikingly dynamic, and not altogether passive, variety.

18

Conclusion

THIS book has attempted to show how, unlikely as it seems at first sight, those who profess the Jain religion can live by its strikingly austere ideal of world-renunciation. On the one hand Jainism can appear to be a simple and wholly consistent system. And some of its leading contemporary teachers insist that it is not, properly speaking, anything so jumbled and incoherent as a religion. They argue that it is a philosophy for escaping earthly life—a soteriology and nothing more. On the other hand it is clear that no one could live a whole life, and no self-reproducing communities could be sustained, on the basis of such a system. The more Jainism is defined as a single and complete theory, the more the lives of those who do claim to live by it come to seem incomprehensible, for these lives are, necessarily, also informed by other quite contrasting values. I do not mean to deny these teachers' claims that there is a soteriology, and a set of rules and regulations which follow from it. But I have tried to show that that is not the Jainism people live by. It is not that the impressively austere ideals of Jain renunciation are ignored. Jains do, definitively, both revere and emulate their heroic renouncer-saints. But they do not do so as the application of a theory, as the execution of a programme.

I have tried to show how values and ideals which are, in themselves, unrealizable, can nevertheless inform a life which answers also to other, conflicting values. The situation becomes more comprehensible, not less, to the extent that one recognizes the conflicts of values, the incompatibility of ideals, and the multiplicity of forms of ethical thought that make it up. There is a sense, then, in which the problem we have addressed is rather a venerable one for anthropology, even though the discipline has been concerned hardly at all with Jainism. In his early essay, 'Baloma', Malinowski wrote what is in effect a meditation on the fact that the notion of a 'culture' fails to deal with the evident variation in individual belief.[1] If his solution—distinguishing between cultural idea and individual opinion, between 'rules and regulations' and actual behaviour—is not one I have found very useful, he nevertheless saw clearly enough that the

---

[1] Malonowski, 'Baloma'. I am indebted to Stocking's interesting discussion in 'The Ethnographer's Magic'.

problem for anthropology is how to make sense of, 'a seething mixture of conflicting principles'.[2]

An important theme in this book has been that values and ideals can exist in counterpoint: a relation which is not logical or semantic, but aesthetic. Incompatible ideals can remain compelling, and indeed, in so far as ideals can be attractive just because they are unrealizable,[3] each can contribute to the vividness and authority of the other. I noted in Chapter 1 that anthropologists have increasingly come to recognize that for cultural values to be logically integrated in a consistent scheme is not a necessary, or even a normal or natural state of affairs. It has perhaps not quite been appreciated that in situations of ethical complexity—and I am inclined to think that this means all situations—cultural integration as anthroplogy has traditionally conceived it would have to be at the expense of vividly imagined ethical life.

I do not want to try to summarize an account of which the point, so often, has lain precisely in the details. But it may be worth reviewing briefly the theme of ethical complexity, and to do this I want to return to Foucault's writings on ethics, which I mentioned in Chapter 1. As I said there, Foucault saw ethics as a matter of self-formation, of the relationship one has with oneself. He understood that relationship to consist of four elements, so that an ethical tradition may be characterized according to how it answers four generic questions. I have claimed that it is only if we see that Jainism is an ethics, and not just a moral code, that we shall understand how it is that people live by it. Let me, in summary, review the ethical dimensions of Jainism which I have discussed above, using Foucault's four questions.[4]

First, there is the question of the part of ourselves, or the part of our behaviour, which is relevant for ethical judgement. The answer to this question tells us about what Foucault called the 'ethical substance': the part of oneself which is the object of ethical thought and work. This is the matter I treated in Part III, as the moral topography of the self. I tried to show how different ethical projects in Jainism—different religious styles, as we might say—rely on, and construct, different conceptions of the 'inside' and 'outside' of the self; how they operate on and through a different ethical substance.

---

[2] Malinowski, *Crime and Custom*, 121.

[3] This is the phenomenon which Elster (*Sour Grapes*, 111 ff.) has analysed as 'counteradaptive preferences': the principle that 'forbidden fruit is sweet', which is, as he notes, the opposite of 'sour grapes'.

[4] See Foucault, 'Genealogy of Ethics', 352–6; *History of Sexuality*, ii. 25–8.

The first of these topographies sees the direct object of ethical attention as the body, because it is an instrument through which to work on the soul, and this is because the latter is the always-precarious product— always being re-formed and re-constituted—of all one's actions. One could say that this conception is basically triadic, as soul, mind, and body are equally important terms within it, but only so long as it is understood that this does not mean these terms are posed as wholly separate or autonomous. The essence (if I may) of this conception, is that these parts of the self are causally, dynamically, and also in both senses of the word 'substantially' linked. One of the things I have tried to bring out in the course of this book, is the way this topography of the self allows action to be simultaneously directed towards contrasting ends and values. The space it creates for a conception of bodily action in which the soul is engaged, but which is performed without intention or desire, is crucial to the way ascetic exercises (Chapter 9), fasting (Chapter 10), and gifts to renouncers (Part IV) can all serve both world-renouncing and also world-affirming ends. This is why it is so central to understanding how pursuit of the goal of *moksh* can be part of lay Jains' lives.

But it takes only a shift of stance to imagine the self in a different way, and although I cannot show it, I suspect that a radical dualism which posits the soul as eternally pure, and the body as that soul's wholly alien other, has always been a possibility in Jain thought and practice. Certainly those who take this path can plausibly appeal to ancient and venerable texts. Although it would be artificial to assign different topographies of the self exclusively to different groups or persons, I think this one can be seen, in different ways, informing whole ethical projects in the case of the Kanji Swami Panth, and the exceptional lay individuals I discussed in Chapter 11. It is worth noting that Jain dualism seems to be largely a lay project, although it resembles somewhat the standard portrait of Jain doctrine which emerged in Western Oriental scholarship towards the end of the nineteenth century, and therefore would be expected, in Weberian terms, to be the preserve of the 'cultured professional monks' and more or less revised or compromised upon, by the laity. That this is not the case gives the measure, I think, of the extent to which that standard portrait misrepresented the Jain tradition.

I suggested that in iconic images of Jinas and Jain saints, and in practices relating to them, we can see a third topography of the self. This time the body's surface is seen as a locus of its inner qualities. Spiritual qualities are written on the body, in features which are not just causes or consequences but direct expressions of those qualities. In such an icon, the self is imagined holistically, and although the particular virtues which the saint exhibits—generosity, strength, compassion, insight—are certainly distinguished, when the devotee comes to mirror the icon imaginatively in worship, he or she does this, ideally, with the whole self. Whereas in our first topography, the body is the medium through which the self—a substantial, socially located, and particular person—is the object of incremental ethical work; and whereas in the dualistic version it is the 'mud' surrounding the eternal and unchanging soul, in this iconic version a perfect body—though that of a God rather than one's own—is the means by which one imagines one's self—soul and body at once—transformed. In this case then the ethical substance includes parts that we would not normally think of as part of the self at all.

This is also true in quite a different way. When Foucault wrote of ethics as the relationship we have with ourselves, he seemed to take it for granted (as perhaps the texts he was dealing with do) that the self is always conceived as an individual human being. It seems to me that in the Jain case this is not always so, and much of the religious self-fashioning we have looked at has been fashioning of the family as an ethical subject. Its topography is, as we have seen, a matter of gender, age, and status.

Foucault's second question concerns what he calls the 'mode of subjection'. What are the ways in which people are invited or incited to recognize moral obligation? We have seen a number of ways this happens in Jainism: in the thoroughly widespread procedures—employed by what Barth calls 'the reflective many'[5]—of questioning their own practices in relation to conceptions of religious authenticity; in narratives which present exemplars of good conduct and give archetypal reference-points to lengthy scripted fasts; in the play of individual decision and constraint involved in taking vows; and in the way the aesthetic of non-violence sets a standard of personal fastidiousness and bodily discipline. These are all ways in which Jains are invited to fashion themselves as, in the broad as well as in the narrow sense, ascetic subjects. There are certainly socially sanctioned rules, instances of morality taking a law-like form, but few of these are specifically Jain, and it would be a mistake to interpret in this way the many instances we have seen of one further mode of subjection in Jainism, namely tabulation.

Time and again we have seen apparently paradigmatic and logical schemes which I have had to read round, or place in some kind of pragmatic context: the 'theory' and classifications of *karma* (Chapters 2 and 4);

---

[5] Barth, *Balinese Worlds*, 218.

lists of prohibited foods (Chapter 7); schemes of numbered lay vows (Chapter 8); the six 'necessary duties' (Chapter 9); types of fast (Chapter 10); and ways of classifying gifts (Chapter 13). There is a general point to make with regard to these wayward schemes, to the effect that social thought is often rather less tamed than anthropology is wont to suppose (a point made forcefully by Jack Goody[6]); and that when such thought does take apparently logical forms this may be a rhetorical expression of hope, desire, or imagination, and not always a recognition of fact, on the part of the people who draw them up (something we learn from Quentin Skinner[7]). There is also a more specific point, that these schemes could be taken in practice as moral codes, but as it happens they are not. In terms of Foucault's distinction between moral codes and ethics, which I outlined in Chapter 1, Jain asceticism is developed in lay life as an ethics, much more than it is as a socially sanctioned code of rules. Where these schemes are used to frame compulsions, this is generally done by means of a vow, so it becomes a matter of the individual *adopting* certain restrictions, as part of an ethical project. Were this not the case, were Jain ideals of renunciation taken as quasi-legislative moral codes, and universal claims issuing from nature, they would not be compossible with values of auspiciousness and this-worldly well-being, and a life lived by the light of them would indeed be impossible.

Ascetics—'self-forming activity'—is Foucault's third aspect of ethics. We have looked at forms of meditation, confession, fasting, and so on. But it is also a matter of ascetics, in the broad sense, when Jains seek the mirroring transformation of the self through worship. And if we follow the point made above, that the self can be conceived as a collective self, partly constituted by certain relationships, then we can see that we have often been in the presence of practices of self-fashioning by the family, conceived as a moral personality:[8] where fasting is concerned with future good fortune; where pious generosity and prudent business practice are concerned with a family's credit, especially where these are combined in a gender-ordered tacking between fasting and philanthropy; and in so far also as the combination of austerity and generosity in *baharana* forges relationships with renouncers. This is where Carrithers' distinction between *moi* and *personne* moral theories (Chapter 1) seems to break down; or rather, it is where ideas and practices are polyvalent enough to find a place on both sides of the distinction. We saw this also, in Part II, in the

---

[6] Goody, *Domestication of the Savage Mind*.

[7] Skinner, 'Meaning and Understanding'; 'Motives and Intentions'.

[8] See Mauss, 'Category of the Human Mind'.

ways in which Jain social distinctiveness is figured, and Jain local communities are constituted. Ideas and practices which must have been formed in the context of speculation about the individual soul in a cosmic, natural, and spiritual context, and which continue to be treated as such in explicit philosophical reflection and religious teaching, plainly figure prominently when one looks at what it is for a Jain to be a member of a social collectivity. Thus imagery and practice which looks at first sight—and also is—resolutely world-renouncing, plays a central part in living a life in a socially complex, status-divided, and in many ways intensely competitive world.

The fourth of Foucault's questions is, 'What is the kind of being to which we aspire? For instance, shall we become pure, or immortal, or free, or masters of ourselves, and so on?'[9] What is the telos of forms of ethical self-fashioning? What is the mode of being which they commit one to?[10] We saw in Chapter 11 that while the ideal of self-purification is a prominent one, it involves crucial ambiguities. The goal of *moksh*, the pure, perfect, and self-less soul, is clear enough in conception—brilliantly simple, vivid, and I think compelling for many of the Jains I knew—and the idea that 'we should become like them' is very common currency indeed. But it is not at all clear that it provides a conception of what one should live as. When Amarcand-ji Nahar (Chapter 11) decided to spend almost his whole time sitting alone in his room, in silent, motionless contemplation, he may have had in mind some notion of liberation while alive (*jivan-mukti*). I do not know. But if he did, it remains the case that for almost all Jains, that ideal is necessarily unrealizable. Imaginatively experiencing in worship the excellences of the omniscient Jina is probably the closest one could reasonably hope to get to 'becoming like them'. But Jain imagery also provides a whole catalogue of exemplars to which, in Foucault's terms, one might aspire. At the opposite pole from our dualist anorexics lie the benevolent, grace-dispensing gurus such as Gautam Swami and the Guru Devs, and it is an important part of contemporary Jainism to be the special devotees of such figures. The sectarian identity of the Khartar Gacch is overwhelmingly focused on this. We saw in Chapter 2 that the figure of the Tirthankar implies a range of religious others, a range of different subject positions, and therefore a range of different religious stances. As we have seen, these are not just theoretical possibilities, but identities that are inscribed in everyday social practice. The

---

[9] Foucault, 'Genealogy of Ethics', 355.
[10] Foucault, *History of Sexuality*, ii. 27–8.

ascetic striver is the representative of what is called 'real Jainism', and in that sense always the discursively dominant figure, but often combined, as we saw for instance in the case of fasting, with that of humble recipient of auspicious beneficence. The role of generous patron—the paradigm here is Indra—is one we have seen replayed in many different ways, and aligned in various ways with ascetic striving, and I have suggested that it is pivotal to the construction of Jain social collectivities.

In summing up here, I have stressed the fact of ethical conflict and complexity because there is a paradoxical way in which Jainism is uniquely good to think with in this respect. Precisely because it can be so easily formulated as a total system of prescriptions, inexorably derived from a set of metaphysical postulates, and because it is actually formulated that way so readily by practising Jains, it is inescapably striking that this is not how it works in people's lives. The problem then has been to describe the social arrangements whereby people live in the light of ideals they do not meet, and to describe how values which cannot be realized are none the less given motivational force. That understanding a cultural tradition rests on these problematics is not, I think, a fact only about Jainism, but a general fact about cultural life which Jainism helps us see.

GLOSSARY

ācārya spiritual teacher; senior male renouncer; leader of a renouncer lineage

ahiṃsā 'non-harming'; an all-encompassing ethical principle in Janism which enjoins avoidance of harm to all living beings

aṇuvrats five lay vows, which parallel those taken by renouncers at *dīkshā* (q.v.); they number among the *bāravrat*s (q.v.)

arādhanā formal worship, especially during a fast and relating to a *yantra* (q.v.)

baharānā presenting alms to Jain renouncers

Baniyā trader or merchant; member of a caste traditionally associated with trade or money-lending

bāravrats twelve vows or restraints taken by some lay Jains

Bhagwān 'God'; word most commonly used to address a Jina in prayer

bhairu a fierce male deity, widely believed to be a form of Shiva

bhakti devotion; fervent emotion of loving supplication and worship; tradition of religious practice which emphasizes such emotion, and of poetic writing which evokes and celebrates it

bhāv meaning, essence, sincerity, emotion, internal; logically opposed to *dravya* (q.v.)

bhojan-shālā a room or building where special food is served, especially during a fast

bhūmiya male deity, usually guardian of a particular village, temple, or place

caitya-vāsi 'temple dweller'; medieval Shvetāmbar renouncers who lived in temple compounds; opponents of founders of the Khartar Gacch

Dādābāṛī garden or complex housing a shrine to a *Dādā-gūrū-dev* (q.v.), usually built outside a town or village and often marking the place where he was cremated or has appeared miraculously after death

Dādā-Gūrū-Dev (also Gūrū-Dev) patron saint of the Khartar Gacch

dān charity, alms-giving, religious or ritual gift

darshan 'beholding' an idol, a saint, or a renouncer; worship by seeing and being seen; also insight and system of philosophy

devtā/devī male/female deity

dharma '*Dharma* can be and has been translated in a thousand ways "righteousness", "truth", "the Way", etc. It is best not translated at all' (Gombrich, *Precept and Practice*, 60).

Dharma-shala 'House of Religion'; a hall used for housing and sometimes feeding pilgrims and other visitors; for congregational gatherings; and for other religious and community purposes

dhyān concentration/meditation

Digambar 'sky-clad'; the branch of Jain tradition whose most advanced male renouncers go about naked

dīkshā the rites of renunciation, and initiation into a renouncer lineage

Dīwālī major Hindu and Jain festival. Ceremonies are performed at home for wealth and good fortune in the year ahead. Jains celebrate the *moksh* (q.v.) of Lord Mahāvīr (q.v.), and the *keval gyān* (q.v.) of Gautam Swāmī (q.v.)

dravya substance, material, appearance, outer; opposed to *bhāv* (q.v.)

gaḍḍi soft cushion or bolster; throne; 'seat' of a religious leader; place where the owner of a business sits, and, by extension, office.

gacch a renouncer lineage; the term is commonly used only of those Shvetambar traditions which build temples and worship idols

Gaṇesh Hindu deity, the 'Lord of Obstacles and Beginnings'. Worshipped or invoked on many auspicious occasions, including Dīwālī (q.v.)

Gaṇesh Caturthi The most important day in the year for worshipping Lord Gaṇesh (q.v.); coincides with Saṃvatsarī (q.v.)

Gautam Swāmī One of Lord Mahāvīr's (q.v.) chief disciples. A popular Jain saint worshipped at Dīwālī (q.v.)

ghī boli auction, usually for the right to perform honoured roles in ritual

gocari the alms which are presented to Jain renouncers; the act of collecting such alms

guṇasthāna fourteen stages of spiritual purification

Gūrū-Dev see Dādā-Gūrū-Dev

gūrū-vandan ritualized obeisance to living renouncer or to the shrine of deceased saint

gyān knowledge

hiṃsā violence; aggression; any infringment of the principle of *ahiṃsā* (q.v.)

jāp repeated recitation of a prayer or *mantra* (q.v.); telling a rosary while reciting prayers

jīva soul; sentient being

Jina 'Conqueror'; one who has overcome all spiritual obstacles, subdued all desires, and will attain the state of *moksh* (q.v.); a synonym of Tīrthaṇkar (q.v.)

Kānji Swāmī Panth A Neo-Digambar Jain sect

karma action; the particles of matter that adhere to the soul as a consequence of action; the moral trace of action; the law which brings to one the just fruit of one's former actions; hence, loosely, one's fate

karmik adjective from *karma* (q.v.)

keval-gyān omniscience

Khartar Gacch a Shvetambar renouncer lineage and the lay followers thereof

kshetrapāl 'guardian of the place'; a kind of male protector deity whose idols are often found by the door of Jain temples

Mahāvīr 'Great Hero'; the twenty-fourth and last Jina of our era; an elder contemporary of the Buddha

Mallināth the nineteenth Jina, held by the Shvetambars to have been a woman

mandala a magical diagram

mantra sacred chant; formulaic contraction of a prayer; sacred syllable; magical spell

moksh liberation; salvation; permanent release from earthly life and suffering

muh-patti mouth-covering worn or carried by renouncers, and by lay Jains during worship, and rites such as *sāmāyik* (q.v.) and *pratikraman* (q.v)

mūrti sacred statue or picture; idol

nokār mantra/namaskār-mantra nine-line prayer, the most sacred and most frequently used sacred formula in Jainism

oghā brush carried by Jain renouncers, which they use to sweep insects harmlessly from their way

paccakkhān temporary vow, taken during fasting, and also *pratikraman* (q.v) and *sāmāyik* (q.v.)

pañc-kalyānak the five 'beneficent moments' in the life of a Jina: conception, birth, renunciation, omniscience, and death and final release; the ritual re-enactment of these five events in *pūjā* (q.v.)

Pārshvanāth the twenty-third Jina of our era

Paryūshan eight-day festival, held during the rainy season

prakshāl liquid in which an idol or sacred image has been bathed

pratikraman ritualized confession

pravārtinī leading female renouncer

pūjā rite of worship, of a deity, renouncer, or saint, often involving offerings before a *mūrti* (q.v.)

pūjārī ritual officiant; temple servant. A *pūjarī* in a Hindu temple would be a priest, but this is not a sacred office in Jainism

sādhu/sādhvī male/female renouncer of any Jain order, who has taken the five 'great vows': non-violence, truth, not taking anything which is not given, sexual restraint, and non-possession or non-attachment

samavasarana assembly of gods, men, and animals to hear a Jina preach; model replica of this event; synonym of *samosaran*

sāmāyik 'equanimity'; lay ritual of meditation and prayer

samosaran synonym of *samavasarana* (q.v.)

samsār the world of death and rebirth; the ocean of suffering

Samvatsarī important Jain festival; one of the eight days of Paryūshan (q.v.); coincides with Ganesh Caturthi (q.v.)

samyak-darshan perfect insight; correct view of reality; faith in Jain teaching

sangh religious community, that is, male and female renouncers together with their lay following

seth honorific title and form of address for wealthy and respected merchant

shasan-devtā/shasan-devī male/female guardian deities associated with the Jinas; often referred to as *yakshas/yakshīs* (q.v.)

shramana/shramanī 'striver'; term for variety of non-Vedic renouncer movements which include the Jains and Buddhists

shrāvak/shrāvikā 'listener'; man/woman who accepts Jain teaching; a lay Jain, especially a pious and devout lay Jain

shrāvakācār text prescribing righteous conduct for lay Jains; the whole body of such literature written in Sanskrit between the fifth and thirteenth centuries

Shvetāmbar 'white-clad'; the branch of the Jain tradition whose renouncers all wear white robes. This tradition includes the Khartar Gacch, the Tapā Gacch, the Sthānakvāsis, and one of the groups called the Terāpanth

siddha 'perfected', liberated soul; soul in the state of *moksh* (q.v.).

siddha cakra magical diagram used in *pūjā* and as an amulet; represents the Jina, the *siddha* (q.v.), the levels of the monastic hierarchy among renouncers, together with the qualities of spiritual insight, knowledge, good conduct, and asceticism

snātra pūjā daily morning ritual which re-enacts the bathing of the infant Jina by deities

Sthānakvāsi 'hall-dweller'; a Shvetāmbar renouncer order that does not keep temples or practise *pūjā*

Tapā Gacch a Shvetambar renouncer lineage and the lay followers thereof

tapas/tapasyā 'heat'; austerity; ascetic practice

tapasī/tapasvī 'ascetic'; term used for someone who undertakes a fast

Terāpanth (1) a Shvetāmbar sect, under the leadership of a single *ācārya* (q.v.) which does not keep temples or practise *pūjā*

Terāpanth (2) a tradition within Digambar Jainism

tilak forehead mark; identifies members of particular Hindu sects; (when red) identifies women as married; (when formed of a paste used during worship) identifies those who have attended and taken part in a religious ritual that day

Tīrthankar 'ford-builder'; one who founds or refounds the Jain tradition; a synonym for Jina (q.v.)

tyāg renunciation; relinquishing or giving something up

upāshraya dwelling-hall for Jain renouncers; used also for renouncers' sermons and for the laity to undertake fasts and religious rituals

vandan obeisance; ritualized form of respectful salutation

varshī dān 'year gift', the act of giving away all his or her possessions, performed by a Jina (q.v); re-enactment of this by person taking *dīkshā* (q.v.)

vidhi ritual, and also law, method, and system; rules for performing a ritual correctly; manual containing instructions on ritual performance

vihar monastery, and, in Jain tradition, the 'houseless' journeying of renouncers

vrat restraint; a vow to observe some set of religious prohibitions

yaksha/yakshī male/female spirit or demon, associated especially with tree-cult and found in the mythology of Jainism, Hinduism, and Buddhism; another name for *shasan devtās/shasan devī*s (q.v)

yantra magical diagram

yati male Shvetambar cleric who differs from a Jain *sādhu* in having a permanent home, keeping personal property, and travelling in vehicles, and who tends to work as a ritual officiant and to practise esoteric and magical arts; present-day representative of *caitya-vāsi* (q.v.) tradition

REFERENCES

AGARWAL, BINOD C., 'Diksa Ceremony in Jainism: An Analysis of its Socio-Political Ramifications', *Eastern Anthropologist*, 25 (1972).
——'Changing Patterns of Jati Among Jains of Madhya Pradesh', in K. S. Mathur and B. C. Agarwal (eds.), *Tribe, Caste and Peasantry* (Ethnographic and Folk Culture Society, Lucknow, 1974).

AHUJA, D. R., *Folklore of Rajasthan* (National Book Trust, Delhi, 1980).

ALMOND, PHILIP C., *The British Discovery of Buddhism* (Cambridge University Press, Cambridge, 1988).

ALSDORF, LUDWIG, 'Niksepa—A Jaina Contribution to Scholastic Methodology', *Journal of the Oriental Institute of Baroda*, 22 (1973).
——'Jaina Exegetical Literature and the History of the Jaina Canon', in A. N. Upadhye, Nathmal Tatia, and Dalsukh Malvania (eds.), *Mahavira and his Teachings* (Bhagavan Mahavira 2500th Nirvan Mahotsava Samiti, Bombay, 1977).

ALTER, JOSEPH S., 'Celibacy, Sexuality, and the Transformation of Gender into Nationalism in North India', *Journal of Asian Studies*, 53 (1994).

AMES, MICHAEL M., 'Ritual Prestations and the Structure of the Sinhalese Pantheon', in Manning Nash (ed.), *Anthropological Studies in Theravada Buddhism* (Yale University Press, New Haven, Conn., 1966).

APPADURAI, ARJUN, *Worship and Conflict under Colonial Rule: A South Indian Case* (Cambridge University Press, Cambridge, 1981).
——'Gastro-Politics in Hindu South Asia', *American Ethnologist*, 8 (1981).
——'Commodities and the Politics of Value', in Arjun Appadurai (ed.), *The Social Life of Things: Commodities in Cultural Perspective* (Cambridge University Press, Cambridge, 1986).
——'Is Homo Hierarchicus?', *American Ethnologist*, 13 (1986).
——'Topographies of the Self: Praise and Emotion in Hindu India', in Catherine A. Lutz and Lila Abu-Lughod (eds.), *Language and the Politics of Emotion* (Cambridge University Press, Cambridge, 1990).
——and BRECKENRIDGE, CAROL A., 'The South Indian Temple: Authority, Honour and Redistribution', *Contributions to Indian Sociology*, NS, 10 (1976).

ASAD, TALAL, *Genealogies of Religion: Discipline and Reasons of Power in Christianity and Islam* (John Hopkins University Press, Baltimore, 1993).

ATAL, YOGESH, 'The Cult of Bheru in a Mewar Village and its Vicinage', in L. P. Vidyarthi (ed.), *Aspects of Religion in Indian Society* (Kedar Nath Ram Nath, Meerut, 1961).

ATRAN, SCOTT, *Cognitive Foundations of Natural History: Towards an Anthropology of Science* (Cambridge University Press, Cambridge, 1990).

AXELROD, PAUL MARK, 'A Social and Demographic Comparison of Parsis, Saraswat Brahmins and Jains in Bombay', Ph.D. thesis (University of North Carolina at Chapel Hill, 1974).

BABB, LAWRENCE A., 'Glancing: Visual Interaction in Hinduism', *Journal of Anthropological Research*, 37 (1981).

—— 'Destiny and Responsibility: Karma in Popular Hinduism', in Charles F. Keyes and E. Valentine Daniel (eds.), *Karma: An Anthropological Enquiry* (University of California Press, Berkeley, 1983).

—— *Redemptive Encounters: Three Modern Styles in the Hindu Tradition* (University of California Press, Berkeley, 1987).

—— 'Giving and Giving Up: The Eightfold Puja among Svetambar Murtipujak Jains', *Journal of Anthropological Research*, 44 (1988).

—— 'Monks and Miracles: Religious Symbols and Images of Origin among Osval Jains', *Journal of Asian Studies*, 52 (1993).

—— 'The Great Choice: Worldly Values in a Jain Ritual Culture', *History of Religions*, 23 (1994).

BAJEKAL, MADHAVI, 'The State and the Rural Grain Market in Eighteenth-Century Eastern Rajasthan', in Sanjay Subrahmanyam (ed.), *Merchants, Markets and the State in Early Modern India* (Oxford University Press, Delhi, 1990).

BALBIR, NALINI, *Danastakakatha: Recueil Jaina de huit histoires sur le don. Introduction, edition critique, traduction, notes* (Collège de France, Paris, 1982).

—— 'The Micro-Genre of Dana-Stories in Jaina Literature: Problems of Interrelation and Diffusion', *Indologica Taurinensia*, 11 (1983).

—— 'The Monkey and the Weaver Bird: Jaina Versions of a Pan-Indian Tale', *Journal of the American Oriental Society*, 105 (1985).

—— 'Stories from the Avasyaka Commentaries', in Phyllis Granoff (ed.), *The Clever Adultress and Other Stories: A Treasury of Jaina Literature* (Mosaic Press, Oakville, Ont., 1990).

BANKS, MARCUS, 'Competing to Give, Competing to Get: Gujarati Jains in Britain', in P. Werbner and M. Anwar (eds.), *Black and Ethnic Leaderships in Britain: The Cultural Dimensions of Political Action* (Routledge, London, 1991).

—— *Organizing Jainism in India and England* (Clarendon Press, Oxford, 1992).

BARNETT, L. D., *The Antagada-dasao and Anuttarovavaiya-dasao*, Oriental Translation Fund, NS, vol. 17 (The Royal Asiatic Society, London, 1907).

BARTH, FREDRIK, *Sohar: Culture and Society in an Omani Town* (Johns Hopkins University Press, Baltimore, 1983).

—— *Cosmologies in the Making: A Generative Approach to Cultural Variation in Inner New Guinea* (Cambridge University Press, Cambridge, 1987).

—— 'Towards Greater Naturalism in Conceptualizing Societies', in Adam Kuper (ed.), *Conceptualizing Society* (Routledge, London, 1992).

—— *Balinese Worlds* (University of Chicago Press, Chicago, 1993).

BAUDRILLARD, JEAN, *For a Critique of the Political Economy of the Sign* (Telos Press, St Louis, 1981).

BAYLAY, C. A., 'Gazeteer of Jaipur', in *The Rajputana Gazeteer*, ii (Office of the Superintendant of Government Printing, Calcutta, 1879).

BAYLY, C. A., 'Local Control in Indian Towns—The Case of Allahabad, 1880–1920', *Modern Asian Studies*, 5 (1971).

——*Rulers, Townsmen and Bazaars: North Indian Society in the Age of British Expansion, 1770–1870* (Cambridge University Press, Cambridge, 1983).

——'The Origins of Swadeshi (Home Industry): Cloth and Indian Society, 1700–1930', in Arjun Appadurai (ed.), *The Social Life of Things: Commodities in Cultural Perspective* (Cambridge University Press, Cambridge, 1986).

——*Indian Society and the Making of the British Empire* (Cambridge University Press, Cambridge, 1988).

BAYLY, SUSAN, *Saints, Goddesses and Kings: Muslims and Christians in South Indian Society, 1700–1900* (Cambridge University Press, Cambridge, 1989).

BECK, BRENDA E. F., 'Colour and Heat in South Indian Ritual', *Man: The Journal of the Royal Anthropological Institute*, NS, 4 (1969).

BELL, RUDOLPH M., *Holy Anorexia* (University of Chicago Press, Chicago, 1985).

BENDER, ERNEST, 'The Dramatis Personae of a Jain Old Gujarati Presentation', *Journal of the American Oriental Society*, 106 (1986).

BENNETT, PETER, 'In Nanda Baba's House: The Devotional Experience in Pushti Marg Temples', in Owen M. Lynch (ed.), *Divine Passions: The Social Construction of Emotion in India* (University of California Press, Berkeley, 1990).

BÉTEILLE, ANDRE, 'Race, Caste and Gender', *Man: The Journal of the Royal Anthropological Institute*, NS, 25 (1990).

——'Caste and Family in Representations of Indian Society', *Anthropology Today*, 8 (1992).

BEVERIDGE, ANNETTE SUSANNAH (trans.), *Babur-Nama: Translated from the Original Turki Text of Zahiru'd-din Muhammad Babur Padshah Ghazi* (Oriental Reprint, New Delhi, 1979; 1st pub. by the translator, 1922).

BHANDARKAR, D. R., 'Jaina Iconography', *The Indian Antiquary*, 40 (1911).

BHARATI, AGEHANANDA, 'The Denial of Caste in Modern Urban Parlance', in Paul Hockings (ed.), *Dimensions of Social Life: Essays in Honour of David G. Mandelbaum* (Mouton de Gruyter, Berlin, 1987).

BHARGAVA, BRAJKISHORE, *Indigenous Banking in Ancient and Medieval India* (Taraporevala and Sons, Bombay, 1934).

BHARILL, HUKAMCHAND, *Veetrag-vigyan pathmala*, pt. 2 (Pandit Todarmal Smarak, Jaipur, 1985).

BHATT, BANSIDHAR, *The Canonical Niksepa: Studies in Jaina Dialectics* (Brill, Leiden, 1978).

BHATTACHARYA, B. C., *The Jaina Iconography*, rev. 2nd edn. (Motilal Banarsidass, Delhi, 1974).

BHATTACHARYYA, HARISATYA, *Divinity in Jainism* (Devendra Printing, Madras, 1925).

BHAYANI, H. C., 'The Narrative of Rama in the Jain Tradition', *Bharatiya Vidya*, 25 (1965).

BLOCH, MAURICE, 'Symbol, Song, Dance, and Features of Articulation: Is Religion an Extreme Form of Traditional Authority?', *Archives Européenes de Sociologie*, 15 (1974).

——'Language, Anthropology, and Cognitive Science', *Man: The Journal of the Royal Anthropological Institute*, NS, 26 (1991).

——'What Goes Without Saying: The Conceptualization of Zafimaniry Society', in Adam Kuper (ed.), *Conceptualizing Society* (Routledge, London, 1992).

BLOOMFIELD, MAURICE, *The Life and Stories of the Jain Savior Parcvanatha* (Johns Hopkins Press, Baltimore, 1919).

——'The Salibhadra Carita: A Story of Conversion to Jaina Monkhood', *Journal of the American Oriental Society*, 43 (1923).

BOURDIEU, PIERRE, *Outline of a Theory of Practice* (Cambridge University Press, Cambridge, 1977).

——*Distinction: A Social Critique of the Judgement of Taste* (Routledge, London, 1984).

——*The Logic of Practice* (Polity Press, Cambridge, 1992).

BOYER, PASCAL, 'Causal Thinking and its Anthropological Misrepresentation', *Philosophy of the Social Sciences*, 22 (1991).

——'Cognitive Aspects of Religious Symbolism', in Pascal Boyer (ed.), *Cognitive Aspects of Religious Symbolism* (Cambridge University Press, Cambridge, 1993).

BRADFORD, (Capt.) E. R. C., *Jeypore Agency Reports*, India Office Library and Records, London (17 May 1870; 1870–1; 1871–2).

BRADFORD, NICHOLAS, 'The Indian Renouncer: Structure and Transformation in a Lingayat Community', in Richard Burghart and Audrey Cantlie (eds.), *Indian Religion* (Curzon, London, 1985).

BROWN, PETER, *The Cult of the Saints: Its Rise and Function in Latin Christianity* (SCM Press, London, 1981).

——*The Body and Society: Men, Women and Sexual Renunciation in Early Christianity* (Faber, London, 1989).

——'Bodies and Minds: Sexuality and Renunciation in Early Christianity', in David M. Halperin, John J. Winkler, and Froma I. Zeitlin (eds.), *Before Christianity: The Construction of Erotic Experience in the Ancient Greek World* (Princeton University Press, Princeton, 1990).

BROWN, W. NORMAN, *A Descriptive and Illustrated Catalogue of Miniature Paintings of the Jaina Kalpa Sutra as Executed in the Early Western Indian Style* (Freer Gallery of Art, Washington, 1934).

BRUHN, KLAUS, 'Avasyaka Studies 1', in Klaus Bruhn and Albrecht Wezler (eds.), *Studien zum Jainismus und Buddhismus: gedenkschrift fur Ludwig Alsdorf* (Franz Steiner Verlag, Weisbaden, 1981).

——'Repetition in Jaina Narrative Literature', *Indologica Taurinensia*, 11 (1983).

BUHLER, J. G., *Life of Hemacandracarya*, trans. M. Patel (Singhi Jaina Jnanapitha, Santiniketan, 1936).

BULTMANN, RUDOLF, *The History of the Synoptic Tradition*, rev. edn. (Basil Blackwell, Oxford, 1972).

——*New Testament and Mythology and Other Basic Writings*, selected, ed., and trans. Schubert M. Ogden (SCM Press, London, 1985).

BUNNAG, JANE, *Buddhist Monk, Buddhist Layman: A Study of Urban Buddhist Monastic Organisation in Central Thailand* (Cambridge University Press, Cambridge, 1973).

BURGESS, JAMES, *The Temples of Satrunjaya, The Celebrated Jaina Place of Pilgrimage Near Palitana in Kathiawad* (Sykes and Dwyer, Bombay, 1869).

——'Papers on Satrunjaya and the Jainas, I–Kathiawad and the Jainas; II–The Tirthankaras or Jinas; V–Satrunjaya Hill', *The Indian Antiquary*, 2, (1873).

——'Papers on Satrunjaya and the Jainas, VI–The Jaina Ritual; VII–Gachchhas, Sripujyas, Yatis, Nuns, &c; Jaina Marriage', *The Indian Antiquary*, 13 (1884).

BURGESS, JAMES (ed.), 'The Satrunjaya Mahatmyam: A Contribution to the History of the Jainas by Professor Albert Weber', *The Indian Antiquary*, 30 (1901).

BURGHART, RICHARD, 'Hierarchical Models of the Hindu Social System', *Man: The Journal of the Royal Anthropological Institute*, NS, 13 (1978).

——'Wandering Ascetics of the Ramanandi Sect', *History of Religions*, 22 (1983).

——'Renunciation in the Religious Traditions of South Asia', *Man: The Journal of the Royal Anthropological Institute*, NS, 18 (1983).

BUTLER, JUDITH, *Gender Trouble: Feminism and the Subversion of Identity* (Routledge, London, 1990).

BYNUM, CAROLINE WALKER, *Jesus as Mother: Studies in the Spirituality of the High Middle Ages* (University of California Press, Berkeley, 1982).

——*Holy Feast and Holy Fast: The Religious Significance of Food to Medieval Women* (University of California Press, Berkeley, 1987).

——*Fragmentation and Redemption: Essays on Gender and the Human Body in Medieval Christianity* (Zone Books, New York, 1991).

CAILLAT, COLETTE, *Candavejjhaya: introduction, édition critique, traduction, commentaire* (Institut de Civilisation Indienne, Paris, 1971).

——*Atonements in the Ancient Ritual of the Jaina Monks* (L. D. Institute of Indology, Ahmedabad, 1975).

——and KUMAR, RAVI, *The Jain Cosmology* (Harmony Books, New York, 1981).

CANTLIE, AUDREY, 'Aspects of Hindu Asceticism', in Ioan Lewis (ed.), *Symbols and Sentiments: Cross-Cultural Studies in Symbolism* (Academic Press, London, 1977).

——'The Moral Significance of Food among Assamese Hindus', in Adrian C. Mayer (ed.), *Culture and Morality* (Oxford University Press, Delhi, 1981).

CAPLAN, PAT, 'Celibacy as a Solution? Mahatma Gandhi and *Brahmacharya*', in Pat Caplan (ed.), *The Cultural Construction of Sexuality* (Routledge, London, 1987).

CARMAN, JOHN B., and MARGLIN, FRÉDÉRIQUE APFFEL (eds.), *Purity and Auspiciousness in Indian Society* (Brill, Leiden, 1985).

CARRITHERS, MICHAEL, 'The Modern Ascetics of Lanka and the Pattern of Change in Buddhism', *Man: The Journal of the Royal Anthropological Institute*, NS, 14 (1979).

—— *The Buddha* (Oxford University Press, Oxford, 1983).

—— *The Forest Monks of Sri Lanka: An Anthropological and Historical Study* (Oxford University Press, Delhi, 1983).

—— 'An Alternative Social History of the Self', in Michael Carrithers, Steven Collins, and Steven Luke (eds.), *The Category of the Person: Anthropology, Philosophy, History* (Cambridge University Press, Cambridge, 1985).

—— 'Passions of Nation and Community in the Bahubali Affair', *Modern Asian Studies*, 22 (1988).

—— 'Naked Ascetics in Southern Digambar Jainism', *Man: The Journal of the Royal Anthropological Institute*, NS, 24 (1989).

—— 'Jainism and Buddhism as Enduring Historical Streams', *Journal of the Anthropological Society of Oxford*, 21 (1990).

—— 'The Foundations of Community Among Southern Digambar Jains', in Michael Carrithers and Caroline Humphrey (eds.), *The Assembly of Listeners: Jains in Society* (Cambridge University Press, Cambridge, 1991).

—— *Why Humans Have Cultures: Explaining Anthropology and Social Diversity* (Oxford University Press, Oxford, 1992).

—— and HUMPHREY, CAROLINE, *The Assembly of Listeners: Jains in Society* (Cambridge University Press, Cambridge, 1991).

—— 'Jains as a Community: A Position Paper', in Michael Carrithers and Caroline Humphrey (eds.), *The Assembly of Listeners: Jains in Society* (Cambridge University Press, Cambridge, 1991).

CARSTAIRS, G. MORRIS, *The Twice-Born: A Study of a Community of High-Caste Hindus* (Hogarth Press, London, 1957).

—— 'A Village in Rajasthan: A Study in Rapid Social Change', in M. N. Srinivas (ed.), *India's Villages*, 2nd edn. (Asia Publishing House, Bombay, 1960).

—— *Death of a Witch: A Village in North India 1950–1981* (Hutchinson, London, 1983).

CHAKRAVARTI, ANAND, *Contradiction and Change: Emerging Patterns of Authority in a Rajasthan Village* (Oxford University Press, Delhi, 1975).

(MUNI SHRI) CHANDRASHEKHAR VIJAY-JI, *Call for Vigilance*, trans. S. R. Falniker (Kamal Prakashan, Ahmedabad, 1977).

CHAUDHRY, P. S., *Rajasthan between the Two World Wars* (Sri Ran Mehra, Agra, 1968).

CHAUDHURI, K. N., *Trade and Civilization in the Indian Ocean: An Economic History from the Rise of Islam to 1750* (Cambridge University Press, Cambridge, 1985).

—— *Asia before Europe: Economy and Civilization of the Indian Ocean from the Rise of Islam to 1750* (Cambridge University Press, Cambridge, 1990).

CHAUHAN, BRIJ RAJ, *A Rajasthan Village* (Associated Publishing House, Delhi, 1967).

CHEESMAN, DAVID, '"The Omnipresent Bania": Rural Money Lenders in Nineteenth-Century Sind', *Modern Asian Studies*, 16 (1982).

COHN, BERNARD S., 'Political Systems in Eighteenth-Century India: The Banaras Region', *Journal of the American Oriental Society*, 82 (1962).

——'Cloth, Clothes, and Colonialism: India in the Nineteenth Century', in Annette B. Weiner and Jane Schneider (eds.), *Cloth and Human Experience* (Smithsonian Institute Press, Washington, DC, 1989).

COLLIER, JANE FISHBURNE, and YANAGISAKO, SYLVIA JUNKO (eds.), *Gender and Kinship: Essays Toward a Unified Analysis* (Stanford University Press, Stanford, 1987).

COLLINS, STEVEN, *Selfless Persons: Imagery and Thought in Theravada Buddhism* (Cambridge University Press, Cambridge, 1982).

——'Monasticism, Utopias and Comparative Social Theory', *Religion*, 18 (1988).

COMAROFF, JOHN, and COMAROFF, JEAN, *Ethnography and the Historical Imagination* (Westview Press, Boulder, Colo., 1992).

CONNERTON, PAUL, *How Societies Remember* (Cambridge University Press, Cambridge, 1989).

COOMARASWAMY, ANANDA K., *Catalogue of the Indian Collections in the Museum of Fine Arts, Boston*, iv (Museum of Fine Arts, Boston, 1924).

——'Notes on Indian Coins and Symbols', *Ostasiatische Zeitschrift*, 4 (1927).

COOPER, ILAY, 'The Painted Walls of Churu, Jhunjhunu, and Sikar Districts of Rajasthan', *South Asian Studies*, 2 (1986).

CORT, JOHN E., 'Liberation and Wellbeing: A Study of the Svetambar Murtipujak Jains of North Gujarat', Ph.D. thesis (Harvard, 1989).

——'Models of and for the Study of the Jains', *Method and Theory in the Study of Religion*, 2 (1990).

——'Two Ideals of the Svetambar Murtipujak Jain Layman', *Journal of Indian Philosophy*, 19 (1991).

——'The Svetambar Murtipujak Jain Mendicant', *Man: The Journal of the Royal Anthropological Institute*, NS, 26 (1991).

——'Svetambar Murtipujak Jain Scripture in a Performative Context', in Jeffrey R. Timm (ed.), *Texts in Context: Traditional Hermeneutics in South Asia* (State University of New York Press, Albany, 1992).

——'An Overview of the Jaina Puranas', in Wendy Doniger (ed.), *Purana Perennis: Reciprocity and Transformation in Hindu and Jaina Texts* (State University of New York Press, Albany, 1993).

——'Jains, Caste, and Hierarchy in North Gujarat', in Arjun Appadurai (ed.), *Caste In Practice: Essays in Honor of Thomas Zwicker* (University of Pennsylvania Department of South Asian Studies, Philadelphia, forthcoming).

COTTAM, CHRISTINE, 'The Merchant Castes of a Small Town in Rajasthan: A Study of Business Organization and Ideology', Ph.D. thesis (School of Oriental and African Studies, London, 1983).

COTTAM ELLIS, CHRISTINE M., 'The Jain Merchant Castes of Rajasthan: Some Aspects of the Management of Social Identity in a Market Town', in Michael Carrithers and Caroline Humphrey (eds.), *The Assembly of Listeners: Jains in Society* (Cambridge University Press, Cambridge, 1991).

COURTRIGHT, PAUL B., *Ganesa: Lord of Obstacles, Lord of Beginnings* (Oxford University Press, New York, 1985).

—— 'The Iconographies of Sati', in John Stratton Hawley (ed.), *Sati, The Blessing and the Curse: The Burning of Wives in India* (Oxford University Press, New York, 1994).

CROOKE, W., *The Tribes and Castes of the North-Western Provinces and Oudh*, 4 vols. (Office of the Superintendent of Government Printing, Calcutta, 1896).

CURTIN, PHILIP D., *Cross-Cultural Trade in World History* (Cambridge University Press, Cambridge, 1984).

DANIEL, E. VALENTINE, *Fluid Signs: Being a Person the Tamil Way* (University of California Press, Berkeley, 1984).

DARLING, MALCOLM, *The Punjab Peasant in Prosperity and Debt* (Oxford University Press, London, 1925).

DAS, VEENA, *Structure and Cognition: Aspects of Hindu Caste and Ritual*, 2nd edn. (Oxford University Press, Delhi, 1982).

—— 'Paradigms of Body Symbolism: An Analysis of Selected Themes in Hindu Culture', in Richard Burghart and Audrey Cantlie (eds.), *Indian Religion* (Curzon, London, 1985).

DAS GUPTA, ASHIN, *Indian Merchants and the Decline of Surat, c. 1700–1750* (Franz Steiner Verlag, Wiesbaden, 1979).

—— 'Indian Merchants in the Age of Partnership, 1500–1800', in Dwijendra Tripathi (ed.), *Business Communities in India: A Historical Perspective* (Manohar, Delhi, 1984).

DASGUPTA, PARTHA, 'Trust as a Commodity', in Diego Gambetta (ed.), *Trust: Making and Breaking Cooperative Relations* (Basil Blackwell, Oxford, 1988).

DAVIS, MARVIN, *Rank and Rivalry: The Politics of Inequality in Rural West Bengal* (Cambridge University Press, Cambridge, 1983).

DENTON, LYNN TESKEY, 'Varieties of Hindu Female Asceticism', in Julia Leslie (ed.), *Roles and Rituals for Hindu Women* (Pinter, London, 1991).

DIRKS, NICHOLAS B., *The Hollow Crown: Ethnohistory of an Indian Kingdom* (Cambridge University Press, Cambridge, 1987).

DIXIT, K. K., *Jaina Ontology* (L. D. Institute, Ahmedabad, 1971).

DOSHI, SARYU, *Masterpieces of Jain Painting* (Marg Publications, Bombay, 1985).

DOUGLAS, MARY, *Natural Symbols: Explorations in Cosmology* (Barrie & Rockliff: The Cresset Press, London, 1970).

DUMONT, LOUIS, 'World Renunciation in Indian Religions', *Contributions to Indian Sociology*, 4 (1960).

—— *Homo Hierarchicus: The Caste System and its Implications*, rev. edn. (University of Chicago Press, Chicago, 1980).

——'A Modified View of Our Origins: The Christian Beginnings of Modern Individualism', in Michael Carrithers, Steven Collins, and Steven Lukes (eds.), *The Category of the Person: Anthropology, Philosophy, History* (Cambridge University Press, Cambridge, 1985).

——'On Value, Modern and Nonmodern', in *Essays on Individualism: Modern Ideology in Anthropological Perspective* (University of Chicago Press, Chicago, 1986).

DUNDAS, PAUL, 'Food and Freedom: The Jaina Sectarian Debate on the Nature of the Kevalin', *Religion*, 15 (1985).

——'The Tenth Wonder: Domestication and Reform in Medieval Svetambara Jainism', *Indologica Taurinensia*, 14 (1987).

——'The Digambara Jain Warrior', in Michael Carrithers and Caroline Humphrey (eds.), *The Assembly of Listeners: Jains in Society* (Cambridge University Press, Cambridge, 1991).

——*The Jains* (Routledge, London, 1992).

DURKHEIM, EMILE, *The Elementary Forms of the Religious Life*, trans. Joseph Ward Swain (George Allen & Unwin, London, 1915).

ECK, DIANA L., 'India's Tirthas: "Crossings" in Sacred Geography', *History of Religions*, 20 (1981).

——*Darsan: Seeing the Divine Image in India* (Anima Books, Chambersburg, Pa., 1981).

EDWARDS, JAMES W., 'Semen Anxiety in South Asian Cultures: Cultural and Transcultural Significance', *Medical Anthropology*, 7 (1983).

EGNOR, MARGARET, 'On the Meaning of Sakti to Women in Tamil Nadu', in Susan S. Wadley (ed.), *The Powers of Tamil Women* (Manohar, Delhi, 1980).

EICHINGER FERRO-LUZZI, GABRIELLA, 'Ritual as Language: The Case of South Indian Food Offerings', *Current Anthropology*, 18 (1977).

——*The Self-Milking Cow and the Bleeding Lingam: Criss-Cross of Motifs in Tamil Temple Legends* (Harrassowitz, Wiesbaden, 1987).

ELIADE, MIRCEA, *Yoga: Immortality and Freedom*, 2nd edn. (Princeton University Press, Princeton, 1969).

ELIAS, NORBERT, *The Court Society* (Basil Blackwell, Oxford, 1983).

ELSTER, JON, *Sour Grapes: Studies in the Subversion of Rationality* (Cambridge University Press, Cambridge, 1983).

——*The Multiple Self* (Cambridge University Press, Cambridge, 1987).

——*Political Psychology* (Cambridge University Press, Cambridge, 1993).

ENDICOTT, KIRK, *Batek Negrito Religion* (Clarendon Press, Oxford, 1979).

ERDMAN, JOAN L., *Patrons and Performers in Rajasthan: The Subtle Tradition* (Chanakya, Delhi, 1985).

ERSKINE, K. D., *Rajputana District Gazeteers: The Mewar Residency* (Scottish Mission Industries, Ajmer, 1908).

——*Rajputana District Gazeteers: The Western Rajputana States Residency and the Bikaner Agency* (Pioneer Press, Ahmedabad, 1909).

FEUCHTWANG, STEPHAN, *The Imperial Metaphor: Popular Religion in China* (Routledge, London, 1992).

FINDLY, ELLISON B., 'Jahangir's Vow of Non-Violence', *Journal of the American Oriental Society*, 107 (1987).

FISCHER, EBERHARD, and JAIN, JYOTINDRA, *Art and Rituals: 2500 Years of Jainism in India* (Sterling Publishers, Delhi, 1977).

FOLKERT, KENDALL W., *Scripture and Community: Collected Essays on the Jains*, ed. John E. Cort (Scholars Press, Atlanta, 1993).

FORBES, A. K., *Ras Mala: Hindu Annals of the Province of Goozerat in Western India*, 2 vols. (Oxford University Press, London, 1924 [1856]).

FOUCAULT, MICHEL, *Discipline and Punish: The Birth of the Prison* (Allen Lane, London, 1977).

—— *The History of Sexuality, i. Introduction* (Penguin, Harmondsworth, 1981).

—— 'The Subject and Power', in Hubert L. Dreyfus and Paul Rabinow (eds.), *Michel Foucault: Beyond Structuralism and Hermeneutics* (Harvester, Hemel Hempstead, 1982).

—— 'On the Genealogy of Ethics: An Overview of Work in Progress', in Paul Rabinow (ed.), *The Foucault Reader* (Pantheon, New York, 1984).

—— *The History of Sexuality, ii. The Use of Pleasure* (Penguin, Harmondsworth, 1984).

—— 'Technologies of the Self', in Luther H. Martin, Huck Gutman, and Patrick H. Mutton (eds.), *Technologies of the Self: A Seminar with Michel Foucault* (Tavistock, London, 1988).

FOX, RICHARD G., *From Zamindar to Ballot Box: Community Change in a North Indian Market Town* (Cornell University Press, Ithaca, 1969).

FRASER, NANCY, *Unruly Practices: Power, Discourse, and Gender in Contemporary Social Theory* (University of Minnesota Press, Minneapolis, 1989).

FRUZZETTI, LINA, ÖSTÖR, ÁKOS, and BARNETT, STEVE, 'The Cultural Construction of the Person in Bengal and Tamilnadu', in Ákos Östör, Lina Fruzzetti, and Steve Barnett (eds.), *Concepts of Person: Kinship, Caste, and Marriage in India*, new edn. (Oxford University Press, Delhi, 1992).

FULLER, C. J., *Servants of the Goddess: The Priests of a South Indian Temple* (Cambridge University Press, Cambridge, 1984).

—— *The Camphor Flame: Popular Hinduism and Society in India* (Princeton University Press, Princeton, 1992).

FUSTEL DE COULANGES, NUMA DENIS, *The Ancient City* (Johns Hopkins University Press, Baltimore, 1980).

GANDHI, M. K., *An Autobiography: Or the Story of my Experiments with Truth* (Navajivan Publishing House, Ahmedabad, 1927).

GEERTZ, CLIFFORD, *Negara: The Theatre State in Nineteenth-Century Bali* (Princeton University Press, Princeton, 1980).

—— *Local Knowledge: Further Essays in Interpretive Anthropology* (Basic Books, New York, 1983).

GELL, ALFRED, 'Newcomers to the World of Goods: Consumption Among the Muria Gonds', in Arjun Appadurai (ed.), *The Social Life of Things: Commodities in Cultural Perspective* (Cambridge University Press, Cambridge, 1986).

GELLNER, DAVID N., 'Max Weber, Capitalism and the Religion of India', *Sociology*, 16 (1982).

——'Monastic Initiation in Newar Buddhism', in Richard F. Gombrich (ed.), *Indian Ritual and its Exegesis*, Oxford University Papers on India. vol. 2, pt. 1 (Oxford University Press, Delhi, 1988).

——'What is the Anthropology of Buddhism About?', *Journal of the Anthropological Society of Oxford*, 21 (1990).

——*Monk, Householder and Tantric Priest: Newar Buddhism and its Hierarchy of Ritual* (Cambridge University Press, Cambridge, 1992).

GHOSH, AMITAV, *In an Antique Land* (Granta Books, London, 1992).

GILLION, KENNETH, *Ahmedabad: A Study in Indian Urban History* (University of California Press, Berkeley, 1988).

GODELIER, MAURICE, *The Making of Great Men: Male Domination and Power among the New Guinea Baruya* (Cambridge University Press, Cambridge, 1986).

GOLD, ANN GRODZINS, *Fruitful Journeys: The Ways of Rajasthani Pilgrims* (University of California Press, Berkeley, 1988).

——'Spirit Possession Perceived and Performed in Rural Rajasthan', *Contributions to Indian Sociology*, NS, 22 (1988).

GOLD, DANIEL, *The Lord as Guru: Hindi Sants in the Northern Indian Tradition* (Oxford University Press, New York, 1987).

GOMBRICH, RICHARD F., 'The Consecration of a Buddhist Image', *Journal of Asian Studies*, 26 (1966).

——*Precept and Practice: Traditional Buddhism in the Rural Highlands of Ceylon* (Clarendon Press, Oxford, 1971).

——'From Monastery to Meditation Centre: Lay Meditation in Modern Sri Lanka', in Philip Denwood and Alexander Piatigorsky (eds.), *Buddhist Studies: Ancient and Modern* (Curzon, London, 1983).

——*Theravada Buddhism: A Social History from Ancient Benares to Modern Colombo* (Routledge, London, 1988).

GOMBRICH, RICHARD, and OBEYESEKERE, GANANATH, *Buddhism Transformed: Religious Change in Sri Lanka* (Princeton University Press, Princeton, 1988).

GONDA, JAN, *Change and Continuity in Indian Religion* (Mouton, The Hague, 1965).

GOODY, JACK, *The Domestication of the Savage Mind* (Cambridge University Press, Cambridge, 1977).

GOONASEKERA, RATNA SUNILSANTHA ABHAYAWARDENA, 'Renunciation and Monasticism Among the Jains of India', Ph.D. thesis (University of California, San Diego, 1986).

GOPAL, SURENDRA, 'Jainas in Bihar in the Seventeenth Century', *Proceedings of the Indian Historical Congress*, Muzaffarpur Session (1972).

——*Commerce and Crafts in Gujarat, 16th and 17th Centuries: A Study of the Impact of European Expansion on Precapitalist Economy* (People's Publishing House, Delhi, 1975).

——'Jain Merchants in Eastern India under the Great Mughals', in Dwijendra Tripathi (ed.), *Business Communities in India* (Manohar, Delhi, 1984).

GORDON, A. D. D., *Businessmen and Politics: Rising Nationalism and a Modernising Economy in Bombay, 1918–1933* (Manohar, Delhi, 1978).

GRANOFF, PHYLLIS, 'Religious Biography and Clan History among Svetambara Jains in North India', *East and West*, 39 (1989).

——'The Jain Biographies of Haribhadra: An Enquiry into the Logic of the Legends', *Journal of Indian Philosophy*, 17 (1989).

——'Jain Biographies', in Phyllis Granoff (ed.), *The Clever Adultress and Other Stories: A Treasury of Jain Literature* (Mosaic Press, Oakville, Ont., 1990).

GREGORY, C. A., 'The Poison in Raheja's Gift: A Review Article', *Social Analysis*, 32 (1992).

GUPTA, B. L., 'The Migration of Traders to Rajasthan in the Eighteenth Century'. *Proceedings of the Indian Historical Congress*, Goa Session (1987).

GUPTA, SATYA PRAKASH, *The Agrarian System of Eastern Rajasthan (c. 1650–1750)*. (Manohar, Delhi, 1986).

HABIB, IRFAN, 'Usury in Medieval India', *Comparative Studies in Society and History*, 6 (1964).

—— 'The System of Bills of Exchange (Hundis) in the Mughal Empire', *Proceedings of the Indian Historical Congress*, Muzaffarpur Session (1972).

HAMPSHIRE, STUART, *Morality and Conflict* (Basil Blackwell, Oxford, 1983).

HANCHETT, SUZANNE, *Coloured Rice: Symbolic Structure in Hindu Family Festivals* (Hindustan Publishing, Delhi, 1988).

HANNERZ, ULF, *Cultural Complexity: Studies in the Social Organization of Meaning* (Columbia University Press, New York, 1992).

HARDIMAN, DAVID, *The Coming of the Devi: Adivasi Assertion in Western India* (Oxford University Press, Delhi, 1987).

——'The Bhils and Shahukars of Eastern Gujarat', in Ranajit Guha (ed.), *Subaltern Studies*, v (Oxford University Press, Delhi, 1987).

HARLAN, LINDSEY, 'Perfection and Devotion: Sati Tradition in Rajasthan', in John Stratton Hawley (ed.), *Sati, The Blessing and the Curse: The Burning of Wives in India* (Oxford University Press, New York, 1994).

HASAN, S. NURUL, HASAN, K. N., and GUPTA, S. P., 'The Pattern of Agricultural Production in the Territories of Amber (c. 1650–1750)', *Proceedings of the Indian Historical Congress*, Mysore Session (1966).

HAYNES, DOUGLAS E., 'From Tribute to Philanthropy: The Politics of Gift Giving in a Western Indian City', *Journal of Asian Studies*, 46 (1987).

——'From Avoidance to Confrontation? A Contestatory History of Merchant–State Relations in Surat, 1600–1924', in Douglas Haynes and Gyan Prakash (eds.), *Contesting Power: Resistance and Everyday Social Relations in South Asia* (Oxford University Press, Delhi, 1991).

——*Rhetoric and Ritual in Colonial India: The Shaping of a Public Culture in Surat City, 1852–1928* (University of California Press, Berkeley, 1991).

HAYNES, DOUGLAS, and PRAKASH GYAN, (eds.), *Contesting Power: Resistance and Everyday Social Relations in South Asia* (Oxford University Press, Delhi, 1991).

HAZELHURST, LEIGHTON W., *Entrepreneurship and the Merchant Castes in a Punjab City* (Duke University Press, Durham, NC, 1966).

——'Caste and Merchant Communities', in Milton Singer and Bernard S. Cohn (eds.), *Structure and Change in Indian Society* (Aldine, Chicago, 1966).

HEESTERMAN, J. C., 'Householder and Wanderer', in T. N. Madan (ed.), *Way of Life: King, Householder, Renouncer* (Vikas, Delhi, 1982).

——*The Inner Conflict of Tradition: Essays in Indian Ritual, Kingship and Society* (University of Chicago Press, Chicago, 1985).

HERSHMAN, PAUL, 'Hair, Sex and Dirt', *Man: The Journal of the Royal Anthropological Institute*, NS, 9 (1974).

HIRSCHMAN, ALBERT O., *The Passions and the Interests: Political Arguments for Capitalism before its Triumph* (Princeton University Press, Princeton, 1977).

HOERNLE, A. F. RUDOLF, *Uvasagadasao, Or the Religious Profession of an Uvasaga, Expounded in Ten Lectures, Being the Seventh Anga of the Jains* (Bibliotheca Indica, Calcutta, 1888).

HOUSEMAN, MICHAEL, 'The Interactive Basis of Ritual Effectiveness in a Male Initiation Rite', in Pascal Boyer (ed.), *Cognitive Aspects of Religious Symbolism* (Cambridge University Press, Cambridge, 1993).

HUME, DAVID, *The Natural History of Religion*, ed. A. Wayne Colver, and *Dialogues Concerning Natural Religion*, ed. John Valdimir Price (Clarendon Press, Oxford, 1976).

HUMPHREY, CAROLINE, 'Fairs and Miracles: At the Boundaries of the Jain Community in Rajasthan', in Michael Carrithers and Caroline Humphrey (eds.), *The Assembly of Listeners: Jains in Society* (Cambridge University Press, Cambridge, 1991).

——and HUGH-JONES, STEPHEN (eds.), *Barter, Exchange and Value* (Cambridge University Press, Cambridge, 1992).

——and LAIDLAW, JAMES, *The Archetypal Actions of Ritual: A Theory of Ritual Illustrated with the Jain Rite of Worship* (Clarendon Press, Oxford, 1994).

INDEN, RONALD B., and NICHOLAS, RALPH, *Kinship in Bengali Culture* (University of Chicago Press, Chicago, 1977).

IYER, RAGHAVAN (ed.), *The Moral and Political Writings of Mahatma Gandhi, i. Civilization, Politics, and Religion* (Clarendon Press, Oxford, 1986).

JACOBI, HERMANN, *Jaina Sutras*. pt. 1, Sacred Books of the East, xxii (Clarendon Press, Oxford, 1884).

——*Jaina Sutras*, pt. 2, Sacred Books of the East, xlv (Clarendon Press, Oxford, 1895).

JAIN, K. V., *Trade and Traders in Western India (AD 1000–1300)* (Munshiram Manoharlal, New Delhi, 1990).

Jain, Kamal Kishor, *Digambar Jain atishay kshetra Shri Mahavir-ji: Vikas aur vistar* (Prabandhakarini Committee, Digambar Jain Atishay Kshetra, Shri Mahavir ji, Jaipur, 1987).

Jain, L. C., *Indigenous Banking in India* (Macmillan, London, 1929).

Jain, Prem Suman, 'The Faithful Wife Rohini from the Akhyanakamanikosa', in Phyllis Granoff (ed.), *The Clever Adultress and Other Stories: A Treasury of Jaina Literature* (Mosaic Press, Oakville, Ontario, 1990).

Jain, Ranu, ' "Jain Oswal" of Calcutta as an "Ethnic Group": A Socio-Historical Perspective', *Man in India*, 67 (1987).

Jain, Shobita, 'A Social Anthropological Study of Jainism in North India', B.Litt. thesis (Oxford, 1971).

Jaini, Padmanabh S., 'Jina Rsabha as an Avatara of Visnu', *Bulletin of the School of Oriental and African Studies*, 40 (1977).

——'Bhavyatva and Abhavyatva: A Jaina Doctrine of "Predestination" ', in A. N. Upadhye, Nathmal Tatia, and Dalsukh Malvania (eds.), *Mahavira and his Teachings* (Bhagwan Mahavira 2500 Nirvana Mahotsava Samiti, Bombay, 1977).

——*The Jaina Path of Purification* (University of California Press, Berkeley, 1979).

——'Karma and the Problem of Rebirth in Jainism', in Wendy Doniger O'Flaherty (ed.), *Karma and Rebirth in Classical Indian Traditions* (University of California Press, Berkeley, 1980).

——'The Disappearance of Buddhism and the Survival of Jainism: A Study in Contrast', in A. K. Narain (ed.), *Studies in the History of Buddhism* (B. R. Publishing Corporation, Delhi, 1980).

——*Gender and Salvation: Jaina Sectarian Debates on the Spiritual Liberation of Women* (University of California Press, Berkeley, 1991).

——'Jaina Puranas: A Puranic Counter Tradition', in Wendy Doniger (ed.), *Purana Perennis: Reciprocity and Transformation in Hindu and Jaina Texts* (State University of New York Press, Albany, 1993).

James, Henry, *The Portrait of a Lady* (Penguin, Harmondsworth, 1984).

James, William, *The Varieties of Religious Experience* (Longmans, Green and Co., London, 1902).

Jayakar, Pupul, *The Earthen Drum* (National Museum, New Delhi, 1980).

Johnson, Helen M. (trans.), *Trishashti-shalaka-purusha-caritra, or The Lives of Sixty-Three Illustrious Persons, by Acarya Shri Hemacandra* (Oriental Institute, Baroda); i (1931), ii (1937), iii (1949), iv (1954), v and vi (1962).

Jones, J. Howard M., 'Jain Shopkeepers and Moneylenders: Rural Informal Credit Networks in South Rajasthan', in Michael Carrithers and Caroline Humphrey (eds.), *The Assembly of Listeners: Jains in Society* (Cambridge University Press, Cambridge, 1991).

Kaelber, Walter O., 'Tapas and Purification in Early Hinduism', *Numen*, 26 (1979).

Kakar, Sudhir, *Shamans, Mystics and Doctors: A Psychological Inquiry into India and its Healing Traditions* (Unwin, London, 1984).

KAMAL, K. L., and STERN, ROBERT W., 'Jaipur's Freedom Struggle and the Bourgeois Revolution', *Journal of Commonwealth Political Studies*, 11 (1973).

KANE, PANDURANG VAMAN, *History of Dharmashastra*, 5 vols. (Bhandarkar Oriental Research Institute, Poona, 1930–62).

KAPFERER, BRUCE, *A Celebration of Demons: Exorcism and the Aesthetics of Healing in Sri Lanka*, 2nd edn. (Berg, Oxford, 1991).

KEESING, ROGER M., 'Conventional Metaphors and Anthropological Metaphysics: The Problematic of Cultural Translation', *Journal of Anthropological Research*, 41 (1986).

KESSINGER, TOM G., 'Regional Economy (1757–1857): North India', in Dharma Kumar and Meghnad Desai (eds.), *The Cambridge Economic History of India*, ii (Cambridge University Press, Cambridge, 1983).

KEYES, CHARLES F., 'Ambiguous Gender: Male Initiation in a Northern Thai Buddhist Society', in Caroline Walker Bynum, Stevan Harrell, and Paula Richman (eds.), *Gender and Religion: On the Complexity of Symbols* (Beacon Press, Boston, 1986).

—— and DANIEL, E. VALENTINE (eds.), *Karma: An Anthropological Enquiry* (University of California Press, Berkeley, 1983).

KHARE, R. S., *The Hindu Hearth and Home* (Vikas, Delhi, 1976).

——*The Untouchable as Himself: Ideology, Identity and Pragmatism among the Lucknow Chamars* (Cambridge University Press, Cambridge, 1984).

KINSEY, DAVID, *Hindu Goddesses: Visions of the Divine Feminine in the Hindu Religious Tradition* (University of California Press, Berkeley, 1986).

KLATT, JOHANNES, 'Extracts from the Historical Records of the Jainas', *The Indian Antiquary*, 11 (1882).

KOLENDA, PAULINE M., 'Religious Anxiety and Hindu Fate', *Journal of Asian Studies*, 23 (1964).

KOPYTOFF, IGOR, 'The Cultural Biography of Things: Commoditization as Process', in Arjun Appadurai (ed.), *The Social Life of Things: Commodities in Cultural Perspective* (Cambridge University Press, Cambridge, 1986).

KRAMRISCH, STELLA, 'Jaina Painting of Western India', in U. P. Shah and M. A. Dhaky (eds.), *Aspects of Jaina Art and Architecture* (Gujarat State Committee for the Celebration of 2500th Anniversary of Bhagavan Mahavira Nirvana, L. D. Institute of Indology, Ahmedabad, 1975).

KULKE, HERMANN, 'Max Weber's Contribution to the Study of "Hinduization" in India and "Indianization" in Southeast Asia', in Detlef Kantowsky (ed.), *Recent Research on Max Weber's Studies of Hinduism* (Weltforum Verlag, Munich, 1986).

KUMAR, NITA, *Friends, Brothers, and Informants: Fieldwork Memoirs of Banaras* (University of California Press, Berkeley, 1992).

LAIDLAW, JAMES, 'Profit, Salvation, and Profitable Saints', *Cambridge Anthropology*, 9 (1985).

LALWANI, K. C., *Arya Sayyambhava's Dasavaikalika Sutra* (Motilal Banarsidass, Delhi, 1973).

——*Sramana Bhagavan Mahavira* (Minerva Associates, Calcutta, 1975).

LATH, MUKUND, *Ardhakathanaka: Half a Tale. A Study in the Interrelationship Between Autobiography and History* (Rajasthan Prakrit Bharati Sansthan, Jaipur, 1981).

——'Somadeva Suri and the Question of Jain Identity', in Michael Carrithers and Caroline Humphrey (eds.), *The Assembly of Listeners: Jains in Society* (Cambridge University Press, Cambridge, 1991).

LEACH, EDMUND, 'Pulleyar and the Lord Buddha: An Aspect of Religious Syncretism in Ceylon', *Psychoanalysis and the Psychoanalytic Review*, 49 (1962).

LÉVI-STRAUSS, CLAUDE, *The Savage Mind* (Weidenfeld and Nicolson, London, 1966).

LEWANDOWSKI, SUSAN, 'Merchants and Kingship: An Interpretation of Indian Urban History', *Journal of Urban History*, 11 (1985).

LITTLE, J. H., *House of Jagatseth* (Calcutta Historical Society, Calcutta, 1967).

LODRICK, DERYCK O., *Sacred Cows, Sacred Places: The Origin and Survival of Animal Homes in India* (University of California Press, Berkeley, 1981).

——'Rajasthan as a Region: Myth or Reality?', in Karine Schomer, Joan L. Erdman, Deryck O. Lodrick, and Lloyd I. Rudolph (eds.), *The Idea of Rajasthan: Explorations in Regional Identity i. Constructions* (Manohar, Delhi, 1994).

LUHRMANN, T. M., 'The Good Parsi: The Postcolonial "Feminization" of a Colonial Elite', *Man: The Journal of the Royal Anthropological Institute*, 29 (1994).

MACINTYRE, ALASDAIR, *After Virtue: A Study in Moral Theory*, 2nd edn. (Duckworth, London, 1985).

MADAN, T. N., *Non-Renunciation: Themes and Interpretations of Hindu Culture* (Oxford University Press, Delhi, 1987).

——'Auspiciousness and Purity: Some Reconsiderations', *Contributions to Indian Sociology*, NS, 25 (1991).

——'The Ideology of the Householder Among Kashmiri Pandits', in Ákos Östör, Lina Fruzzetti, and Steve Barnett (eds.), *Concepts of Person: Kinship, Caste, and Marriage in India*, new edn. (Oxford University Press, Delhi, 1992).

MAHAPRAJNA (YUVACARYA), *Jain parampara ka itihas* (Jain Vishva Bharati Prakashan, Ladnun, 1988).

MAHIAS, MARIE-CLAUDE, *Délivrance et convivialité: Le Système culinaire des Jaina* (La Maison des Sciences de l'Homme, Paris, 1985).

MALINOWSKI, BRONISLAW, 'Baloma: The Spirits of the Dead in the Trobriand Islands', in *Magic, Science and Religion and Other Essays* (Free Press, New York, 1948).

——*Crime and Custom in Savage Society* (Routledge, London, 1926).

MALONEY, C., 'Don't Say "Pretty Baby" Lest You Zap It with Your Eye—The Evil Eye in South Asia', in C. Maloney (ed.), *The Evil Eye* (Columbia University Press, New York, 1976).

MALVANIA, DALSUKH, 'Jaina Theory and Practice of Non-Violence', in *Jainism: Some Essays* (Prakrit Bharati Academy, Jaipur, 1986).

(GANI) MANIPRABH SAGAR, *Nakora tirth ka itihas* (Kanti Prakashan Pratishthan, Palitana, 1988).

(SADHVI) MANIPRABHASHRI, *Pravacan Prabha: A Series of Discourses*, trans. Gyan Jain (Shri Vichakshan Prakashan, Indore, 1988).

MARGLIN, FRÉDÉRIQUE APFFEL, *Wives of the God-King: The Rituals of the Devadasis of Puri* (Oxford University Press, Delhi, 1985).

MARRIOTT, McKIM, 'Caste Ranking and Food Transactions: A Matrix Analysis', in Milton Singer and Bernard S. Cohn (eds.), *Structure and Change in Indian Society* (Aldine, Chicago, 1968).

——'Hindu Transactions: Diversity Without Dualism', in Bruce Kapferer (ed.), *Transaction and Meaning: Directions in the Anthropology of Exchange and Symbolic Behaviour* (Institute for the Study of Human Issues, Philadelphia, 1976).

——and INDEN, RONALD B., 'Towards an Ethnosociology of South Asian Caste Systems', in Kenneth David (ed.), *The New Wind: Changing Identities in South Asia* (Mouton, The Hague, 1977).

MAUSS, MARCEL, 'Body Techniques', in *Sociology and Psychology: Essays by Marcel Mauss.* trans. Ben Brewster (Routledge & Kegan Paul, London, 1979).

——'A Category of the Human Mind: The Notion of Person; The Notion of Self', in Michael Carrithers, Steven Collins, and Steven Lukes (eds.), *The Category of the Person: Anthropology, Philosophy, History* (Cambridge University Press, Cambridge, 1985).

——*The Gift: The Form and Reason for Exchange in Archaic Societies.* trans. W. D. Halls (Routledge, London, 1990).

MAYER, ADRIAN C., *Caste and Kinship in Central India: A Village and its Region* (University of California Press, Berkeley, 1970).

——'Public Service and Individual Merit in a Town in Central India', in Adrian C. Mayer (ed.), *Culture and Morality* (Oxford University Press, Delhi, 1981).

MEHTA, MAKRAND, *Indian Merchants and Entrepreneurs in Historical Perspective* (Academic Foundation, Delhi, 1991).

MEHTA, RASHMI, 'Community, Consciousness, and Identity: A Study of Jains in a Village', M.A. thesis (Rajasthan, 1986).

MEHTA, SARYU R., and SHETH, BHOGILAL G., *Shrimad Rajchandra: A Great Seer* (Raojibhai C. Desai, Shrimad Rajchandra Ashram, Agas, 1971).

MERLEAU-PONTY, M., *Phenomenology of Perception* (Routledge, London, 1962).

METTE, ADELHEID, 'The Tales of the Namaskara-Vyakhya in the Avasyaka-Curni: A Survey', *Indologica Taurinensia*, 11 (1983).

MICHIE, BARRIE H., 'Baniyas in the Indian Agrarian Economy: A Case of Stagnant Entrepreneurship', *Journal of Asian Studies*, 37 (1978).

MINES, MATTISON, *Public Faces, Private Voices: Community and Individuality in South India* (University of California Press, Berkeley, 1994).

MINES, MATTISON, and GOURISHANKAR, VIJAYALAKSHMI, 'Leadership and Individuality in South Asia: The Case of the South Indian Big-Man', *Journal of Asian Studies*, 49 (1990).

MITTER, SARA S., *Dharma's Daughters: Contemporary Indian Women and Hindu Culture* (Rutgers University Press, New Brunswick, 1991).

MUNSHI, SURENDRA, 'Tribal Absorption and Sanskritization in Hindu Society', *Contributions to Indian Sociology*, NS, 13 (1979).

——'Max Weber on India: An Introductory Critique', *Contributions to Indian Sociology*, NS, 22 (1988).

NAHAR, PRITWISINGH, 'An Illustrated Salibhadra MS', *Journal of the Indian Society of Oriental Art*, 1 (1933).

NARASIMHACHAR, D. L., 'The Jaina Ramayanas', *Indian Historical Quarterly*, 15 (1939).

NARAYANAN, VASUDHA, 'The Goddess Sri: Blossoming Lotus and Breast Jewel of Visnu', in John Stratton Hawley and Donna Marie Wulff (eds.), *The Divine Consort: Radha and the Goddesses of India* (Graduate Theological Union, Berkeley, 1982).

NEEDHAM, RODNEY, 'Skulls and Causality', *Man: The Journal of the Royal Anthropological Institute*, NS, 11 (1976).

NEVASKAR, BALWANT, *Capitalists without Capitalism: The Jains of India and the Quakers of the West* (Greenwood Publishing, Westport, Conn., 1971).

NIETZSCHE, FRIEDRICH, *On the Genealogy of Morals: A Polemic*, trans. Walter Kaufmann, in *Basic Writings of Nietzsche* (Modern Library, New York, 1969).

NORMAN, K. R., 'The Role of the Layman According to the Jain Canon', in Michael Carrithers and Caroline Humphrey (eds.), *The Assembly of Listeners: Jains in Society* (Cambridge University Press, Cambridge, 1991).

NUSSBAUM, MARTHA C., *The Fragility of Goodness: Luck and Ethics in Greek Tragedy and Philosophy* (Cambridge University Press, Cambridge, 1986).

OBEYESEKERE, GANANATH, 'Theodicy, Sin and Salvation in a Sociology of Buddhism', in E. R. Leach (ed.), *Dialectic in Practical Religion* (Cambridge University Press, Cambridge, 1968).

——*Medusa's Hair: An Essay on Personal Symbols and Religious Experience* (University of Chicago Press, Chicago, 1981).

—— *The Cult of the Goddess Pattini* (University of Chicago Press, Chicago, 1984).

O'FLAHERTY, WENDY DONIGER, *Siva: The Erotic Ascetic*, 1st pub. in 1973 as *Asceticism and Eroticism in the Mythology of Siva* (Oxford University Press, Oxford, 1981).

——(ed.), *Karma and Rebirth in Classical Indian Traditions* (University of California Press, Berkeley, 1980).

OJHA, CATHERINE, 'Feminine Asceticism in Hinduism: Its Tradition and Present Condition', *Man in India*, 61 (1981).

OLIVELLE, PATRICK, *Renunciation in Hinduism: A Medieval Debate*, 2 vols. (Institute of Indology, Vienna, 1986/7).

ORTNER, SHERRY B., *Sherpas through their Rituals* (Cambridge University Press,

Cambridge, 1978).

——*High Religion: A Cultural and Political History of Sherpa Buddhism* (Princeton University Press, Princeton, 1989).

Östör, Ákos and Fruzzetti, Lina, 'Concepts of Person: Fifteen Years Later', in Ákos Östör, Lina Fruzzetti, and Steve Barnett (eds.), *Concepts of Person: Kinship, Caste, and Marriage in India*, new edn. (Oxford University Press, Delhi, 1992).

Pal, Pratapaditya (ed.), *The Peaceful Liberators: Jain Art from India* (Thames and Hudson, London, 1994).

Pappu, S. S. Rama Rao (ed.), *The Dimensions of Karma* (Chanakya Publishing, Delhi, 1987).

Parfit, Derek, *Reasons and Persons* (Oxford University Press, Oxford, 1986).

Parkin, David, 'Reason, Emotion, and the Embodiment of Power', in Joanna Overing (ed.), *Reason and Morality* (Tavistock, London, 1985).

Parry, Jonathan, *Caste and Kinship in Kangra* (Routledge & Kegan Paul, London, 1979).

——'Ghosts, Greed and Sin: The Occupational Identity of Benares Funeral Priests', *Man: The Journal of the Royal Anthropological Institute*, NS, 15 (1980).

——'Death and Cosmogony in Kashi', *Contributions to Indian Sociology*, NS, 15 (1981).

——'Sacrificial Death and the Necrophagous Ascetic', in Maurice Bloch and Jonathan Parry (eds.), *Death and the Regeneration of Life* (Cambridge University Press, Cambridge, 1982).

——'Death and Digestion: The Symbolism of Food and Eating in North Indian Mortuary Rites', *Man: The Journal of the Royal Anthropological Institute*, NS, 20 (1985).

——'*The Gift*, the Indian Gift and the "Indian Gift"', *Man: The Journal of the Royal Anthropological Institute* NS, 21 (1986).

——'The End of the Body', in Michel Feher with Ramona Naddoff, and Nadia Tazi (eds.), *Fragments for a History of the Human Body*, pt. 3 (Zone, New York, 1989).

——'On the Moral Perils of Exchange', in Jonathan Parry and Maurice Bloch (eds.), *Money and the Morality of Exchange* (Cambridge University Press, Cambridge, 1989).

——'The Hindu Lexicographer? A Note on Inauspiciousness and Purity', *Contributions to Indian Sociology*, NS, 25 (1991).

——and Bloch, Maurice (eds.), *Money and the Morality of Exchange* (Cambridge University Press, Cambridge, 1989).

Peabody, Norbert, 'In Whose Turban Does the Lord Reside?: The Objectification of Charisma and the Fetishism of Objects in the Hindu Kingdom of Kota', *Comparative Studies in Society and History*, 33 (1991).

Pearson, Michael N., *Merchants and Rulers in Gujarat: The Response to the Portuguese in the Sixteenth Century* (University of California Press, Berkeley, 1976).

PEIRCE, CHARLES SANDERS, *The Collected Papers of Charles Sanders Peirce*, ii. *Elements of Logic*, ed. Charles Hartshorne and Paul Weiss (Harvard University Press, Cambridge, Mass., 1932).

PERLIN, FRANK, 'Proto-Industrialization and Precolonial South Asia', *Past and Present*, 98 (1983).

PHILLIPS, D. Z., *Religion without Explanation* (Basil Blackwell, Oxford, 1976).

PINNEY, CHRISTOPHER, 'The Iconology of Hindu Oleographs: Linear and Mythic Narrative in Popular Indian Art', *Res*, 22 (1992).

PLUNKETT, HUGH SHERIDAN, *Weaving the Web of Power: Middlemen and Social Change in Rajasthan* (Bahri Publishing, Delhi, 1984).

POCOCK, DAVID, *Kanbi and Patidar: A Study of the Patidar Community of Gujarat* (Oxford University Press, London, 1972).

——*Mind, Body and Wealth: A Study of Belief and Practice in an Indian Village* (Basil Blackwell, Oxford, 1973).

——'The Ethnography of Morals', *International Journal of Moral and Social Studies*, 1 (1986).

PUTNAM, HILARY, *Reason, Truth and History* (Cambridge University Press, Cambridge, 1981).

PYE, MICHAEL, *The Cardinal Meaning: Essays in Comparative Hermeneutics: Buddhism and Christianity* (Mouton, The Hague, 1973).

QUANUNGO, KALIKA RANJAN, *Studies in Rajput History*, 2nd edn. (S. Chand, Delhi, 1971).

QUIGLEY, DECLAN, *The Interpretation of Caste* (Clarendon Press, Oxford, 1993).

RADCLIFFE-BROWN, A. R., *The Andaman Islanders*, (Cambridge University Press, Cambridge, 1922).

RAHEJA, GLORIA GOODWIN, *The Poison in the Gift: Ritual, Prestation, and the Dominant Caste in a North Indian Village* (University of Chicago Press, Chicago, 1988).

——'India: Caste, Kingship and Dominance Reconsidered', *Annual Review of Anthropology*, 17 (1988).

——'Caste Ideologies, Protest and the Power of the Dominant Caste: A Reply to Gregory and Heesterman', *Social Analysis*, 34 (1993).

RAM, PREMA, *Agrarian Movement in Rajasthan: 1913–47* (Panchsheel Prakashan, Jaipur, 1986).

(MUNI SHRI) RATNA PRABHA VIJAY, *Sthaviravali* (Shri Jaina Siddhanta Society, Ahmedabad, 1948).

REICHENBACH, BRUCE R., *The Law of Karma: A Philosophical Study* (Macmillan, London, 1990).

REYNELL, JOSEPHINE, 'Honour, Nurture and Festivity: Aspects of Female Religiosity among Jain Women in Jaipur', Ph.D. thesis (Cambridge, 1985).

——'Women and the Reproduction of the Jain Community', in Michael Carrithers and Caroline Humphrey (eds.), *The Assembly of Listeners: Jains in Society* (Cambridge University Press, Cambridge, 1991).

Rosaldo, Michelle Z., *Knowledge and Passion: Ilongot Notions of Self and Social Life* (Cambridge University Press, Cambridge, 1980).

Rose, H. A., *A Glossary of the Tribes and Castes of the Punjab and North-West Frontier Province Based on the 1883 and 1892 Census Reports*, 3 vols. (Government of the Punjab, Lahore, 1919).

Rousselet, Louis, *India and its Native Princes: Travels in Central India in the Presidencies of Bombay and Bengal*, rev. and ed. Lieut.-Col. Buckle (Chapman & Hall, London, 1876).

Roy, Ashim Kumar, *History of the Jaipur City* (Manohar, Delhi, 1978).

Rudolph, Susanne Hoeber, and Rudolph, Lloyd I., *The Modernity of Tradition: Political Development in India* (University of Chicago Press, Chicago, 1967).

——*Essays on Rajputana* (Concept Publishing, Delhi, 1984).

Rudner, David West, 'Religious Gifting and Inland Commerce in Seventeenth-Century South India', *Journal of Asian Studies*, 46 (1987).

——'Banker's Trust and the Culture of Banking among the Nattukottai Chettiars of Colonial South India', *Modern Asian Studies*, 23 (1989).

——*Caste and Capitalism in Colonial India: The Nattukottai Chettiars* (University of California Press, Berkeley, 1994).

Rungta, Radhe Shyam, *The Rise of Business Corporations in India* (Cambridge University Press, Cambridge, 1970).

Russell, R. V., *The Tribes and Castes of the Central Provinces of India* (Macmillan, London, 1916).

Sahlins, Marshall, 'On the Sociology of Primitive Exchange', in Michael Banton (ed.), *The Relevance of Models for Social Anthropology* (Tavistock, London, 1965).

Sanday, Peggy Reeves, and Goodenough, Ruth (eds.), *Beyond the Second Sex: New Directions in the Anthropology of Gender* (University of Pennsylvania Press, Philadelphia, 1990).

Sangave, Vilas Adinath, *Jaina Community: A Social Survey*, 2nd rev. edn. (Popular Prakashan, Bombay, 1980).

——'Reform Movements among Jains in Modern India', in Michael Carrithers and Caroline Humphrey (eds.), *The Assembly of Listeners: Jains in Society* (Cambridge University Press, Cambridge, 1991).

Sarkar, Jadunath, *A History of Jaipur* (Orient Longman, Hyderabad, 1984).

Sarkar, Sumit, *Modern India 1885–1947* (Macmillan, Delhi, 1983).

Schama, Simon, *The Embarrassment of Riches: An Interpretation of Dutch Culture in the Golden Age* (Collins, London, 1987).

Schneider, David M., *American Kinship: A Cultural Account* (Prentice-Hall, Englewood Cliffs, NJ, 1968).

Schwab, Raymond, *The Oriental Renaissance: Europe's Rediscovery of India and the East 1680–1880* (Columbia University Press, New York, 1984).

Schubring, Walther, *The Doctrine of the Jainas: Described after the Old Sources* (Motilal Banarsidass, Delhi, 1962).

SELWYN, T., 'The Order of Men and the Order of Things: An Examination of Food Transactions in an Indian Village', *International Journal of the Sociology of Law*, 8 (1980).

SHAH, A. M., 'Division and Hierarchy: An Overview of Caste in Gujarat', *Contributions to Indian Sociology*, NS, 16 (1982).

SHAH, (SHATAVDHANI PANDIT) DHIRJALAL TOKARSI, *Jain katha sangraha* pt. 1 (Punya Svarna Gyanpith, Jaipur (V.S. 2033)).

SHAH, UMAKANT PREMANAND, 'Iconography of the Sixteen Jaina Maha-Vidyas', *Journal of the Indian Society of Oriental Art*, 9 (1942).

——*Studies in Jaina Art* (Benares, 1955).

——'A Rare Sculpture of Mallinath', in *Acarya Vijayvallabhasuri Commemoration Volume* (Mahavira Jaina Vidyalaya, Bombay, 1956).

SHÂNTÂ, N., *La Voie Jaina* (OEIL, Paris, 1985).

SHARMA, BRIJ KISHORE, *Peasant Movements in Rajasthan (1920–49)* (Pointer Publishers, Jaipur, 1990).

SHARMA, G. D., 'Indigenous Banking and the State in Eastern Rajasthan during the Seventeenth Century', *Proceedings of the Indian Historical Congress*, Waltair Session (1979).

——'Vyaparis and Mahajans in Western Rajasthan during the Eighteenth Century', *Proceedings of the Indian Historical Congress*, Bombay Session (1980).

——'The Marwaris: Economic Foundations of an Indian Capitalist Class', in Dwijendra Tripathi (ed.), *Business Communities in India* (Manohar, Delhi, 1984).

SHARMA, J. P., 'Hemacandra: Life and Scholarship of a Jaina Monk', *Asian Profile*, 3 (1975).

SHARMA, URSULA, 'Theodicy and the Doctrine of Karma', *Man: The Journal of the Royal Anthropological Institute*, NS, 8 (1973).

SHULMAN, DAVID, *Tamil Temple Myths: Sacrifice and Divine Marriage in the South Indian Saiva Tradition* (Princeton University Press, Princeton, 1980).

SHRISHRIMAL, SAUBHAGYAMAL, SAMPADAK, PRADHAN, BHANAVAT, NARENDRA, BARLA, C. S., and BHANAVAT, SARJIV (eds.), *Jaypur Jain Shvetambar Samaj dayrektri* (Samyojak Prakashan Samiti, Jaipur, 1984).

——*Jaypur Jain Shvetambar Samaj dayrektri, purak suci* (Samyojak Prakashan Samiti, Jaipur, 1987).

SILBER, ILANA FRIEDRICH, ' "Opting Out" in Theravada Buddhism and Medieval Christianity: A Comparative Study of Monasticism as Alternative Structure', *Religion*, 15 (1985).

SIMMEL, GEORG, *The Philosophy of Money* (Routledge, London, 1978).

SINGH, DILBAGH, 'Nature and Incidence of Taxes Levied in the Inland Trade of Eastern Rajasthan during the Seventeenth and Eighteenth Centuries', *Proceedings of the Indian Historical Congress*, Bhubaneswar Session (1977).

——*The State, Landlords and Peasants: Rajasthan in the 18th Century* (Manohar, Delhi, 1990).

SINGHI, N. K., 'A Study of Jains in a Rajasthan Town', in Michael Carrithers and

Caroline Humphrey (eds.), *The Assembly of Listeners: Jains in Society* (Cambridge University Press, Cambridge, 1991).

SINHA, SURAJIT, 'State Formation and Rajput Myth in Tribal Central India', *Man in India*, 42 (1962).

SISSON, RICHARD, *The Congress Party in Rajasthan: Political Integration and Institution-Building in an Indian State* (University of California Press, Berkeley, 1972).

SKINNER, QUENTIN, 'Meaning and Understanding in the History of Ideas' (1969) and 'Motives, Intentions and the Interpretation of Texts' (1976), in James Tully (ed.), *Meaning and Context: Quentin Skinner and his Critics* (Polity Press, Cambridge, 1988).

SMITH, CHARLES W., *Auctions: The Social Construction of Value* (Harvester Wheatsheaf, Hemel Hempstead, 1989).

SMITH, JOHN D., *The Epic of Pabuji: A Study, Transcription and Translation* (Cambridge University Press, Cambridge, 1991).

SMITH, VINCENT A., *The Jain Stupa and Other Antiquities of Mathura* (Archaeological Survey of India, Allahabad, 1901).

——'The Jain Teachers of Akbar', in *Commemorative Essays Presented to Sir Ramkrishna Gopal Bhandarkar* (Bhandarkar Oriental Research Institute, Poona, 1917).

SOPHER, DAVID E., 'Pilgrim Circulation in Gujarat', *The Geographical Review*, 58 (1968).

SOSKICE, JANET MARTIN, *Metaphor and Religious Language* (Clarendon Press, Oxford, 1985).

SOUTHWOLD, MARTIN, *Buddhism in Life: The Anthropological Study of Religion and the Sinhalese Practice of Buddhism* (Manchester University Press, Manchester, 1983).

SPENCER, JONATHAN, 'Tradition and Transformation: Recent Writing on the Anthropology of Buddhism in Sri Lanka', *Journal of the Anthropological Society of Oxford*, 21 (1990).

SPERBER, DAN, *Rethinking Symbolism* (Cambridge University Press, Cambridge, 1975).

SPIRO, MELFORD E., *Buddhism and Society: A Great Tradition and its Burmese Vicissitudes* 2nd edn. (University of California Press, Berkeley, 1982).

SPODEK, HOWARD, 'Rulers, Merchants and Other Groups in the City-States of Saurashtra, India, around 1800', *Comparative Studies in Society and History*, 16 (1974).

SRIVASTAVA, VINAYA KUMAR, 'On Renunciation: A Caritra Account of Shri Shanti Suri-ji Maharaj, A Svetambara Jain Ascetic', unpublished paper (1991).

——'Notes on Women and Renunciation', unpublished paper (1992).

——'On Religion and Renunciation: The Case of the Raikas of Western Rajasthan', Ph.D. thesis (Cambridge, 1993).

STERN, HENRI, 'L'Edification d'un secteur economique moderne: L'Example d'une caste marchande du Rajasthan', *Purusartha*, 6 (1982).

STERN, ROBERT W., *The Cat and the Lion: Jaipur State and the British Raj* (Brill, Leiden, 1988).

STEVENSON, MRS SINCLAIR, *Notes on Modern Jainism: With Special Reference to the Svetambara, Digambara and Sthanakavasi Sects* (Basil Blackwell, Oxford, 1910).

—— *The Heart of Jainism* (Oxford University Press, Oxford, 1915).

STOCKING, GEORGE W., 'The Ethnographer's Magic: Fieldwork in British Anthropology from Tylor to Malinowski', in George W. Stocking Jr. (ed.), *Observers Observed: Essays on Ethnographic Fieldwork* (University of Wisconsin Press, Madison, 1983).

STRATHERN, MARILYN, *The Gender of the Gift: Problems with Women and Problems with Society in Melanesia* (University of California Press, Berkeley, 1988).

—— 'Qualified Value: The Perspective of Gift Exchange', in Caroline Humphrey and Stephen Hugh-Jones (eds.), *Barter, Exchange and Value* (Cambridge University Press, Cambridge, 1992).

—— 'Parts and Wholes: Refiguring Relationships in a Post-Plural World', in Adam Kuper (ed.), *Conceptualizing Society* (Routledge, London, 1992).

SUBRAHMANYAM, SANJAY, and BAYLY, C. A., 'Portfolio Capitalists and the Political Economy of Early Modern India', in Sanjay Subrahmanyam (ed.), *Merchants, Markets and the State in Early Modern India* (Oxford University Press, Delhi, 1990).

SUNDER RAJAN, RAJESWARI, 'The Subject of Sati: Pain and Death in the Contemporary Discourse on Sati', *Yale Journal of Criticism*, 3 (1990).

SWALLOW, D. A., 'Ashes and Powers: Myth, Rite and Miracle in an Indian God-Man's Cult', *Modern Asian Studies*, 16 (1982).

TÄHTINSEN, UNTO, *Ahimsa: Non-Violence in Indian Tradition* (Rider, London, 1976).

TAMBIAH, S. J., *Buddhism and the Spirit Cults in North-East Thailand* (Cambridge University Press, Cambridge, 1970).

—— 'Form and Meaning of Magical Acts', in Robin Horton and Ruth Finnegan (eds.), *Modes of Thought* (Faber, London, 1973).

—— *World Conqueror and World Renouncer: A Study of Buddhism and Polity in Thailand Against a Historical Background* (Cambridge University Press, Cambridge, 1976).

—— 'The Renouncer: His Individuality and His Community', in T. N. Madan (ed.), *Way of Life: King, Householder, Renouncer* (Vikas, Delhi, 1982).

—— *The Buddhist Saints of the Forest and the Cult of Amulets: A Study in Charisma, Hagiography, Sectarianism, and Millennial Buddhism* (Cambridge University Press, Cambridge, 1984).

—— *Buddhism Betrayed? Religion, Politics, and Violence in Sri Lanka* (University of Chicago Press, Chicago, 1992).

TANK, UMRAO SINGH, *Jaina Historical Studies* (Printing and Publishing Company, Delhi, 1914).

TAPPER, BRUCE ELLIOT, 'Widows and Goddesses: Female Roles in Deity Symbolism in a South Indian Village', *Contributions to Indian Sociology*, NS, 13 (1979).

TATIA, NATHMAL, *Studies in Jain Philosophy* (Jain Cultural Research Society, Benares, 1951).

TAWNEY, C. H. (trans.), *Prabanddhacintamani, Or The Wishing-Stone of Narratives* (The Asiatic Society, Calcutta, 1901).

TAYLOR, CHARLES, 'The Moral Topography of the Self', in Stanley Messer, Louis Sass, and Robert Woolyolk (eds.), *Hermeneutics and Psychological Theory* (Rutgers University Press, New Brunswick, 1988).

——*Sources of the Self: The Making of Modern Identity* (Cambridge University Press, Cambridge, 1989).

THAPAR, ROMILA, *Ancient Indian Social History: Some Interpretations* (Orient Longman, Hyderabad, 1978).

——*Cultural Transaction and Early India: Tradition and Patronage* (Oxford University Press, Delhi, 1987).

——'Imagined Religious Communities? Ancient History and the Modern Search for a Hindu Identity', *Modern Asian Studies*, 23 (1989).

THOMAS, NICHOLAS, *Entangled Objects: Exchange, Material Culture, and Colonialism in the Pacific* (Harvard University Press, Cambridge, Mass., 1991).

THORNTON, ROBERT, 'The Rhetoric of Ethnographic Holism', *Cultural Anthropology*, 3 (1988).

TILLOTSON, G. H. R., *The Rajput Palaces: The Development of an Architectural Style, 1450–1750* (Yale University Press, New Haven, Conn., 1987).

TIMBERG, THOMAS A., 'A North Indian Firm as Seen through its Business Records, 1860–1914: Tarachand Ghanshyamdas, A "Great" Marwari Firm', *Indian Economic and Social History Review*, 8 (1971).

——*The Marwaris: From Traders to Industrialists* (Vikas, Delhi, 1978).

——and AIYAR, C. V., 'Informal Credit Markets in India', *Economic Development and Cultural Change*, 33 (1984).

TINDALL, GILLIAN, *City of Gold: The Biography of Bombay* (Temple Smith, London, 1982).

TIWARI, M. N. P., *Ambika in Jaina Art and Literature* (Bharatiya Jnanpith, Delhi, 1989).

TOD, JAMES, *Annals and Antiquities of Rajast'han, or The Central and Western Rajput States of India*, 2 vols. (M. N. Publishers, New Delhi, 1983; 1st pub. 1829–32).

——*Travels in Western India Embracing an Account of the Sacred Mounts of the Jains and the Most Celebrated Shrines of the Hindu Faith between Rajpootana and the Indus with an Account of the Ancient City of Nehrwalla* (Wm. H. Allen, London, 1839).

TOOMEY, PAUL M., 'Krishna's Consuming Passions: Food as Metaphor and Metonym for Emotion at Mount Govardhan', in Owen M. Lynch (ed.), *Divine Passions: The Social Construction of Emotion in India* (University of California Press, Berkeley, 1990).

TRAWICK, MARGARET, *Notes on Love in a Tamil Family* (University of California Press, Berkeley, 1990).

TRIPATHI, DWIJENDRA, *The Dynamics of a Tradition: Kasturbhai Lalbhai and His Entrepreneurship* (Manohar, Delhi, 1981).

——and MEHTA, MAKRAND, *Business Houses in Western India: A Study in Entrepreneurial Response, 1850–1956* (Jaya Books, London, 1990).

UNNITHAN, MAYA, 'Constructing Difference: Social Categories and Girahiya Women, Kinship and Resources in South Rajasthan', Ph.D. thesis (Cambridge, 1990).

VAID, SUDESH, and SANGARI, KUMKUM, 'Institutions, Beliefs, Ideologies: Widow Immolation in Contemporary Rajasthan', *Economic and Political Weekly*, 26/17 (27 Apr. 1991).

VAN DER VEER, PETER, 'Taming the Ascetic: Devotionalism in a Hindu Monastic Order', *Man: The Journal of the Royal Anthropological Institute*, NS, 22 (1987).

——*Gods on Earth: The Management of Religious Experience and Identity in a North Indian Pilgrimage Centre* (Athlone Press, London, 1988).

——'The Power of Detachment: Disciplines of Body and Mind in the Ramanandi Order', *American Ethnologist*, 16 (1989).

VEYNE, PAUL, *Bread and Circuses: Historical Sociology and Political Pluralism* (Allen Lane, London, 1990).

(MAHOPADHYAYA) VINAYA SAGAR (ed.), *Kalpa Sutra: Eighth Chapter of the Dashashrutaskandha of Bhadrabahu with Hindi and English Versions and Coloured Reproductions of Original 16th Century Miniatures*, text edn. and Hindi trans. Mahopadhyaya Vinaya Sagar; English trans. Dr Mukund Lath (D. R. Mehta, Prakrit Bharati, Jaipur, 1977).

WADLEY, SUSAN SNOW, *Shakti: Power in the Conceptual Structure of Karimpur Religion* (Munshiram Manoharlal, Delhi, 1985).

——and DERR, BRUCE W., 'Eating Sins in Karimpur', *Contributions to Indian Sociology*, NS, 23 (1989).

WEBER, MAX, *The Protestant Ethic and the Spirit of Capitalism* (George Allen & Unwin, London, 1930).

——*The Religion of India: The Sociology of Hinduism and Buddhism* (Free Press, New York, 1958).

——*Economy and Society: An Outline of Interpretive Sociology* 2 vols., eds. Guenther Roth and Claus Wittich (University of California Press, Berkeley, 1978).

——'The Social Psychology of the World Religions', in Hans H. Gerth and C. Wright Mills (eds.), *From Max Weber: Essays in Sociology*, new edn. (Routledge, London, 1992).

WHITE, CHARLES S. J., 'Mother Guru: Jnanananda of Madras, India', in Nancy A. Falk and Rita M. Gross (eds.), *Unspoken Worlds: Women's Religious Lives in Non-Western Cultures* (Harper & Row, San Francisco, 1980).

WILLIAMS, BERNARD, 'Persons, Character and Morality', in *Moral Luck: Philosophical Papers 1973–80* (Cambridge University Press, Cambridge, 1981).

——*Ethics and the Limits of Philosophy* (Fontana, London, 1985).

——*Shame and Necessity* (University of California Press, Berkeley, 1993).

WILLIAMS, MICHAEL, 'Divine Image—Prison of Flesh: Perceptions of the Body in Ancient Gnosticism', in Michel Feher, with Ramona Naddaff and Nadia Tazi (eds.), *Fragments For a History of the Human Body*, pt. 1 (Zone, New York, 1989).

WILLIAMS, R., *Jaina Yoga: A Survey of the Mediaeval Sravakacaras* (Oxford University Press, London, 1963).

WILLIAMS, RAYMOND B., *A New Face of Hinduism: The Swaminarayan Religion* (Cambridge University Press, Cambridge, 1984).

WILLS, C. U., BAJPEYI, (PANDIT) PRASAD, and SINGH, (THAKUR) MAHENDRA PAL, *A Collection of Reports of a Committee of Inquiry Regarding (i) the Thikanas of Panchpana-Singhana (ii) the Tahig of Babai (iii) the Thikana of Sikar (iv) the Thikana of Uniar (v) the Thikana of Patan and (vi) the Thikanas of Khandela in the Jaipur State (AD 1934–5)* (Delhi, 1935).

WINTERNITZ, MAURICE, *A History of Indian Literature*, ii., *Buddhist and Jaina Literature*, new edn. trans. V. Srinivasa Sarma (Motilal Banarsidass, Delhi, 1983).

WITTGENSTEIN, LUDWIG, *Philosophical Investigations* (Basil Blackwell, Oxford, 1958).

——*Lectures and Conversations on Aesthetics, Psychology and Religious Belief*, ed. Cyril Barret (Basil Blackwell, Oxford, 1966).

——*Remarks on Frazer's Golden Bough*, ed. and rev. Rush Rhees (Brynmill, Retford, 1979).

WOLFRAM, SYBIL, 'Anthropology and Morality', *Journal of the Anthropological Society of Oxford*, 13 (1982).

YALMAN, NUR, 'On the Meaning of Food Offerings in Ceylon', in R. F. Spenser (ed.), *Forms of Symbolic Action: Proceedings of the American Ethnological Society* (University of Washington Press, Seattle, 1969).

ZIMMER, HEINRICH, *The Art of Indian Asia*, vol. 1: Text. vol. 2: Plates, 2nd edn. (Princeton University Press, Princeton, 1960).

——*Artistic Form and Yoga in the Sacred Images of India* (Princeton University Press, Princeton, 1984).

ZWALF, W., *Buddhism: Art and Faith* (British Museum Publications, London, 1985).

INDEX

Figures in italic refer to illustrations.

abhay-dan 78, 296, 298
Abhaykumar 380, 382
(Mount) Abu 62, 91, 100 n.
Acaranga Sutra 43, 304 n.
account-books 108, 370, 371, 372, 374–84
Adivasis/tribals 100–3, 106
age and religious practice 169, 183–5, 206
ahimsa 1, 28, 54, 153–66, 181, 191–4,
    210–11, 258, 280, 296, 344–5, 360,
    383–4
  as *abhay-dan* 296
  in *anuvrat/baravrat*s 173, 179, 180, 181
  and female body 252, 254
  and food 170, 171–2, 303
  in Hinduism 94
  as non-action 191–4, 219
  in *pratikraman* 210–12
  see also *padilehan*; vegetarianism
Akshay Tritiya 218
alms to Jain renouncers 54, 99, 289–344,
    310, 311
  baharana 298, 316, 318
  barter 318–21
  competition 332–6
  dharma labh blessing 313, 322–3, 325
  Digambars 289 n.
  as élite consumption 336–44
  exchange 324–7, 339
  general description 289, 309–14, 320
  gocari 305–7, 308, 316–17, 318
  laity encouraged to give 180, 295,
    298–301
  and *puja* compared 317, 320
  requirements on donors 54, 99, 113,
    302–3, 304–5, 314, 322
  rules and regulations 171, 301, 306–8,
    309–12
  striving to give 142, 312–13, 318, 320,
    321–2, 327–44
  see also Jain renouncers, diet
Alter, Joseph S. 256 n.
Amber 122–3
Ames, Michael 326
Anand Shravak 37, 187–9
Ananthanath 226

animal homes 143–4 n.
Anoop Mandal 107–8, 375
Antakriddashah Sutra 171, 382 n.
anukampa-dan 296, 298
anumodan 194, 202–4, 213, 340, 341
*anuvrat*s 160, 173–5, 179, 183, 188, 190,
    211–12, 303–4
aparigraha 1, 28, 154 n., 173, 177, 181,
    186
Appadurai, Arjun 13 n., 152 n., 293, 338,
    341
Asad, Talal 152
asceticism:
  as autarky 360–1
  as bathing/cleaning 27, 112–13, 153,
    191, 201, 206, 207–8, 214, 262,
    273–4, 283–4
  Christian 239–42, 243 n., 251–2, 257
  and death 7, 171–2, 233; *see also* fasting
    to death
  discipline 206–7, 238–9
  gendered female 257, 261–7
  gendered male 254–7
  as heat/sacrifice 28, 112–13, 197, 215,
    216, 232, 247, 255, 262–3 n.
  imperative and 'rules' 153, 166–70,
    187–9
  as path 153, 173, 305
  as purification 28, 31–2, 43, 173–4,
    185, 221, 242, 245
  and self 19–21, 43, 47, 151–2, 166–72,
    182–3, 188–9, 214, 255, 389–94
  and semen retention 253–7
  suffering as 257, 262–7
  and vows 190–5, 200–1, 202–3
  as warfare 34, 152–3, 198, 199, 212,
    230
  see also *baravrat*s; fasting; *kaussagg*;
    shramana; *shravak*
asteya vrat 173, 179, 194, 304
atithi 308, 326, 331
atithi-samvibhag 180–1, 298
Atran, Scott 293 n.
attachment 1, 50, 75, 102, 113, 153,
    154 n., 162, 164, 194, 212, 228, 232,
    236–7, 250, 252
auctions 96, 334–45, 349–51

auspiciousness/inauspiciousness 27, 40–1,
    59–60, 76, 168, 180, 223–4, 244 n.,
    278, 285, 290, 294, 365, 370–1, 373,
    380, 383–4
  see also Jinas, as auspicious
Avashyaka Sutra/Niryukti 195–6, 315,
    381 n.
*avashyaka*s 195–8, 210, 206,
ayambil 216, 218, 221, 223, 228, 331

Babb, Lawrence A. 58, 61, 68, 77 n., 90 n.,
    253 n., 307 n., 317
baharana, see alms to Jain renouncers
Bahubali 380, 382–3
Bajekal, Madhavi 125
Baniyas 88–9, 103–4, 107–8, 108,
    115–16, 368–9
Banks, Marcus 97 n., 115 n., 134, 228,
    275 n., 336 n.
*baravrat*s 160, 174–5, 176 n., 179–89, 212
Barth, Fredrik 8, 9, 84, 147, 267, 352 n.,
    391
bathing/cleaning:
  as form of worship 44, 45, 69–70, 249,
    260, 270–1, 271–2, 365
  before *puja* 271–2
  by renouncers 1, 156, 272
  as sin 182, 205 n., 272–3, 312 n.
  see also asceticism, as washing; *snatra
    puja*
Baudrillard, Jean 340–1, 342–3
Bayly, C. A. 124, 357, 359, 375
Bell, Rudolf 239–30
Bennett, Peter 170
Bhagavad Gita 194
Bhagavati Sutra 384, 385 n.
bhagya/saubhagya 27, 226, 373
bhairus 65, 71, 74–5, 80
  see also Nakora Bhairu
Bharat 36–-7, 111 n., 380, 381
Bharatiya Janata Party 104
bhav 78–80, 210, 228–9, 230, 236, 273,
    298
Bhils 106, 107
bhojan shala 131, 139, 217, 218, 228
bhumiya 65
biasan 218 n.
bis sthanak oli-ji 221 n.
Bisa, *see* castes, Bisa and Dasa
body:
  dualistically opposed to soul 152, 230,
    232–9, 242–3, 258, 263 n., 274, 390
  ethical significance 165–6, 273–4

icon of soul 152, 242–71, 274, 390–1
  indexically related to soul 152, 242,
    258, 274, 390
  as instrument of religious action
    151–2, 204, 208, 210 n., 230, 239,
    242, 274, 390; *see also* asceticism;
    fasting
  postures/control in ritual 196, 197 n.,
    202, 204, 207–9, 212
Bourdieu, Pierre 211, 274, 326 n., 352
Boyer, Pascal 8, 74 n.
Brahma Kumaris 58
brahmacarya 74, 112–13, 173, 177–8, 182,
    184, 207, 237, 241, 253–6
  see also Jain renouncers, celibacy
Brahmins 30 n., 40, 52, 111–13, 282, 291,
    376
Brown, Peter 6, 240 n., 258
Buddha 6, 36, 41, 247 n., 254, 259, 377,
    382
Buddhism 3 n., 4 n., 10–12, 16–17, 36,
    55, 87, 176–8, 191, 194 n., 199,
    259 n., 269, 271 n., 326–7, 327 n.,
    336 n., 341, 377, 382 n.
  see also renouncers (Buddhist)
business 92–3, 97–8, 101, 105–6, 241
  and caste 88–9
  and family 354–8
  contrasted with gift-giving 291, 360
  in Jaipur (gem trade) 4, 105, 123,
    125–31, 350, 351–2, 353–8, 361
  and religion 4, 27–8, 72, 83–4, 87–9,
    179, 181 n., 182–3, 184, 222, 342,
    353–4, 355–8, 359–63, 374–5
  and the state 90–1, 124–6, 127, 352,
    268–9,
Bynum, Caroline Walker 240, 251–2,
    254 n., 257 n.

Cakeshvari 65
Caillat, Colette 214 n.
*caitya-vasi*s 50–2
  see also *yati*s
camatkar, see magic/miracles
Candrasen 224–5
Candravedhyaka Sutra 204, 269–70
Carrithers, Michael 9, 16, 147, 344 n.,
    392–3
Carstairs, G. Morris 256
castes 84 n., 88–9, 100–4, 109, 110–11,
    111–16
  Bisa and Dasa 114–16
  origins of 90–1, 111 n., 114, 116

Caturmas 54, 98–9, 141, 206, 268, 327–8, 330
caubis stavan 195–7
  see also *puja*
caudah niyam 181–2
celibacy, see *brahmacarya*; Jain renouncers, celibacy
Christianity 75 n., 239–42, 243 n., 251–2, 254 n., 257, 258, 297 n., 360–1
Comaroff, Jean and John 8, 211
community, *see* Jain community
Cort, John E. 51 n., 56, 103 n., 110 n., 115 n., 143 n., 191, 212 n.–213 n., 218 n., 270–1, 275 n., 336 n., 368 n.
cosmology/cosmography:
  in Hinduism 36, 211 n., 224
  in Jainism 2, 33, 35–8, 72–3, 157–8, 211, 224, 384
  see also *samsar*
Cottam Ellis, Christine M. 88

Dada Guru Devs, *see* Guru Devs
Dadabari temple *2, 66,* 133, 140–1, 262, *265*
darshan 76, 102, 271, 279
Dasa, *see* castes, Bisa and Dasa
Dashavaikalika Sutra 305 n.
daya 28, 164–5, 296
death rites 95, 111–12, 185, 202, 231 n., 305 n.
deities 2, *32,* 33, 41–2, 59, 65–8, *66, 67,* 102–3, 211, 224, 225
  as devotees of Jina 44–5, 47, 65, 69, 246, 247, 251
  Hindu 39, 65, 67, 77 n., 97 n., 250, 257, 281, 364
  not capable of liberation 2, 41–2, 242, 361–2
  see also *bhairu, bhumiya,* Ganesh-ji; Guru Devs; *kshetrapal;* Indra; Nakora Bhairu; Ravana; *yaksha*s
deshavkashik vrat 180, 181–3
Dhanna 380, 381–2
Dharanendra 247, 248 n.
dharma-cakra 244
dhok 373
diet:
  Jains differ from Hindus 156–7, 166, 170
  variations among Jains 153, 166–8, 276
  see also foods
Digambars 1, 48, 55, 56, 84, 85, 104 n., 106, 109–11, 111 n., 113, 117–18, 126–7, 141, 154 n., 235 n., 245, 249, 250–3, 254–5 n., 275 n., 289 n., 325, 344 n.
diksha 334–7, 343–4
Dirks, Nicholas B. 294
Diwali 94, 170, 298, 364–87
Doniger, Wendy 363
Douglas, Mary 209
dravya 78, 80, 182, 236, 272, 273–4, 295, 298
Dumont, Louis 5 n., 115–16, 239
Dundas, Paul 214 n., 243, 252 n.
Durkheim, Émile 19, 209

educational institutions (Jain sponsored) 109, 142, 143–4, 356–7
ekasan 216, 217, 231
Elias, Norbert 14
emotions 153, 211–12
  see also attachment; intention
ethics and morals 17–20, 191, 389, 391–2
  see also asceticism, imperative and 'rules'
euergetism 108, 142–8, 176 n., 186–7, 324, 341–2, 349–51
  in Hellenistic Greece 142–3, 145, 350–1
evil eye 315

fairs 101–3
family:
  as business enterprise 354–8, 369–70, 374–5
  as religious agent 58–9, 139 n., 342–3, 355–8, 373, 391, 392
  renunciation within 233–4, 236–7
fasting 1, 54, *57,* 78, 99, 155–6, 168, 181–2, 185–6, 188, 197, 206, 216–29, 276, 308, 335, 368 n.
  associated rituals 221–2, *223,* 231
  for benefit for others 225–8, 240
  to death 153, 162, 163, 168, 188, 231, 238–9, 379
  different for men and women 240–1, 257, 355–8
  extended 217
  local variations in practice 218 n., 221–3
  mostly by women 224, 225, 240–1, 342, 355–6
  not on Diwali 368 n., 379, 387
  at Samvatsari 279
  scripted 217–18, 220–9, 240–1, 387

fasting (*cont.*):
  as social event 183–4, 185–6, 218, 220,
    223, 276–80
  and well-being 171, 218, 220–9, 238,
    387
  see also asceticism; *paccakkhan*
feasting 108–9, 144–6, 186, 224, 285, 328
feet (as objects of veneration) 51, 63, *260*,
    261, 270
fieldwork 134–8
Folkert, Kendall W. 110n., 275n.
food transactions 289–93
foods:
  eaten and avoided by Jains 153, 156–7,
    166–70, 212–13, 276, 292–3,
  for health and well-being 166, 170, 221,
    231, 279n., 284n.
  used for religious purposes 108–9, 170,
    218, 221, 223–4, 251n., 279, 368,
    383–4, 385
  see also diet; fasting; feasting; Jina,
    eating; *puja*
Foucault, Michel 18–20, 58, 152, 210,
    214, 258n., 389–93
Fox, Richard G. 354–5
funerals, *see* death rites
Fustel de Coulanges, Numa Denis 145

gacch organization 48–57, 60, 138–9, 240
Ganadharas 259
Gandhi, M. K. 154, 352, 360n.
Ganesh Caturthi 95, 281–3, 284–6, 364,
    387
Ganesh-ji 281, 284–6, 371, 372, 373,
    376–80
gastro-politics 289–93, 302, 305, 309,
    317–18, 321–2
Gautam Swami 47, 60, 235–6, 259, 364,
    376–80, 384–7, 393
Geertz, Clifford 293n.
Gell, Alfred 339
gem trade in Jaipur, *see* business
gender and religious practice 56–9, 142,
    168, 169, 174, 176n., 183–5, 200,
    206, 217, 224, 225, 237, 239–2,
    254–7, 261–7, 340–1, 342–3, 349,
    367, 370
Ghantakarn *67*, 72n.
ghi boli, *see* auctions
gift giving 291–2, 324, 337–8, 373–4
  classifications 294–300
  male activity 184–6, 342–3, 355–8
  to renouncers 55–6, 296, 300–1,

    315–16, 317–18, 321–3, 325, 327n.
  see also *supatra-dan*
Girahias 107
Gnosticism 243n.
gocari, *see* alms to Jain renouncers
Gold, Ann Grodzins 4n., 71n., 137n.,
    278, 307n.
Gombrich, Richard 6, 177, 191n., 299n.,
    336n.
Gonda, Jan 300n.
Goody, Jack 392
Goonasekara, Ratna Sunilsantha
    Abhayawardena 49
Goyama 171
Guru Devs 47, 50–1, 60, 71–7, 79–80,
    90, 259–61, *260*, 270, 376n., 385, 393
gupta-dan 297, 358
guru puja 270–1
gyan-dan 297
gyan puja 280–1

Hampshire, Stuart 13–14
Hanchett, Suzanne 371
Hannerz, Ulf 84
Harikesha 112
(Acarya) Hastimal-ji 62–3
Haynes, Douglas E. 143n.
Hemacandra Suri 31, 37n., 44, 69, 91,
    111n., 154, 218n., 248n., 295–6,
    377n., 381n., 382n.
himsa, *see ahimsa*
Hindu deities, *see* deities, Hindu
Hindu festivals 94–5, 275, 387n.
  see also Diwali; Ganesh Caturthi; Holi
Hinduism 3n., 4n., 73n., 360–1, 378
  features shared with Jainism 14–15,
    38–9, 94, 97n., 108, 160n., 198, 250,
    251, 255, 257, 266, 270, 271n., 278,
    281–2, 284–6, 297n., 324, 378–80,
    385, 386
  fundamentalist nationalism 89, 104,
    282, 369
  karma in 30n., 194, 362n.
  as point of contrast for Jains 71, 76, 78,
    105, 197, 226, 227, 275, 278–9, 281,
    283–6, 295–6, 307, 317, 324, 376
  see also renouncers (Hindu); deities
    (Hindu)
Holi 94, 386–7
homosexuality 241, 254n.–255n.
'honours' 336–7
Hugh-Jones, Stephen 318–21
Hume, David 6

Humphrey, Caroline 101 n., 102, 134, 136, 147, 228, 318–21

idols/images 5 n., 65, 71–2
  Buddhist 245, 247 n., 248, 271 n.
  clothes 246, 250, 251
  consecration 249, 266, 271, 272, 334
  controversial 31, 48–9, 102–3, 104 n., 242
  eyes 246, 250–1, 271; see also *darshan*
  of Ganadharas (including Gautam Swami) 60, 259, 270-1, 371
  of Ganesh 281, 284–6, 371
  gender 253
  genitals 104 n., 251, 257
  of Guru Devs 51, 71, 259–61, *260*, 270–1
  Hindu 245, 247, 248 n., 266, 281
  of Jain renouncers/saints 51, 62, 145, 261, 262–3, *264–5*, 270–1, 390–1
  of Jinas 33, 43, *45*, 71, 170, 175, 219, 235, 244 n., 245–52, *246*, 390–1
  of Lakshmi 370, 371
  of laymen 235, 242
  magical 71–2, 100–3, 328
  in *sthapan-acarya* 206 n.–207 n.
  in worship 34, 44, *45*, 170, 249–50
impurity, *see* purity/impurity
Inden, Ronald 15 n., 293 n.
Indra/Indrani/Indras 33, 40, 44, *45*, *46*, 45–7, 69, 73, 90, 111, 323, 337–8, 350, 361, 377 n.
intention 191–5, 199–200, 300 n., 390
  in Buddhism 191, 299 n.
  in fasting 218–20, 225–9
  in making gifts 296, 298–300, 306, 314
  in *pratikraman* 213–15
  in *puja* and *samayik* 201–2
Islam 3 n., 51, 72, 83–4, 88, 90, 104 n., 104–5, 113, 115, 247 n., 282, 360

Jagaccandra Suri 51
Jain community:
  boundaries of 95–6, 100–3, 137–8, 147
  as business community 83, 87–9, 117, 293, 350
  and caste 113–16, 140–1, 147
  and class 105, 116, 139 n., 293, 352
  conceptions of 34, 35, 46–7, 83–4, 131, 135, 137–8, 146–8, 283–4, 340–1, 349
  divisions within 108–11, 116–19, 134
  in Jaipur 3–4, 48, 53, 85, 113–14, 118, 131–2, 138–48, 293, 349–53
  organization of local communities 54–5, 141–8, 349
  outside India 92–3, 97 n., 336 n., 353
  participation 141–2, 185–6, 340–2, 349
  patronage 142–8, 176 n., 186–7, 276, 337–44, 349–51
  regional level 84–7, 126–7, 147
  see also euergetism; sectarianism
Jain renouncers:
  as auspicious 59–60
  celibacy 1, 63, 112–13, 254–5 n., 312 n.; see also *brahmacarya*
  contrasted with *yatis* 52
  clothing 1, 48, 55, 156, 184, 235–6
  defecation 202, 344–5
  diet 99, 113, 167–8, 171, 331, 336; *see also* alms to Jain renouncers
  founding Jain castes 90–1
  gender of 52–3, 53 n., 56–7
  as gurus 59–64, 98–9, 175, 206–7, 219 n., 238, 263, 327–31, 356–7; *see also* Guru Devs; Gautam Swami
  as icons of the Jina 267–71, 280–1, 281 n., 305, 306, 325
  initiation, see *diksha*
  and kings 91, 155, 379
  from non-Jain families 100, 115, 335 n.
  not causing *karma* (action) in others 306–9, 313–14, 315–16, 331
  as objects of veneration 59, 60–3, 195, 201 n., 270–1; *see also* idols, of Jain renouncers/saints
  organization 48–50, 53–5, 56–7, 60, 61, 240, see also *gacch* organization; sectarianism
  preaching 54–5, 57, 99, 226, 236, 267–70, 280–1, 296, 325
  purity 271–4, 312 n.
  reasons for renouncing 157, 187, 241–2
  rules for conduct 1–3, 53–6, 155–6, 158, 195, 202, 203
  and temple ritual 49, 70 n., 93, 202, 372
  see also alms; gifts to renouncers
Jaini, Padmanabh S. 55, 70 n., 87, 97 n., 153–5, 160–2, 173–4, 189, 190, 243, 244 n., 252, 312 n., 384 n.
(Maharaja Sawai) Jai Singh II: 123–4
Jaipur:
  description 122–3, 128–34, 136
  history 120, 123–8
James, Henry 95
James, William 242

jati smaran gyan, see knowledge of former
  lives
Jinabhadra Suri 193–4
Jinas/Tirthankars 3, 30, 38–9,
  as ascetic strivers 30–1, 35, 42
  as auspicious 40–2, 59–60, 277–9,
  bathed by gods 44–5, 69–70
  body 243–5, 250, 252, 253–4, 256, 259
  clothes 42, 251–2, 257
  in cosmology 35–8, 43–4
  eating 243–5, 313
  as ford-builders 34
  former lives 38, 163, 247–8, 315
  gender 56, 251–2, 253–5
  life story 31–5, 38–47, 69, 249
  as objects of veneration 3, 33–4, 34,
    44–7, 69–70, 195, 201 n., 270, 376;
    see also *caubis stavan*; idols; *puja*
  as royalty 31, 34, 40, 42, 44, 90, 247,
    343–4
  as teachers 31–3, 37–8, 42–3, 248–9,
    251, 296
  see also *samosaran*
Jinasena 111 n.
Jineshvar Suri 50
Jivajivabhigama Sutra 384
Johari Bazaar 128–32, 136
Jones, J. Howard M. 106

Kalpa Sutra 39, 276–8, 279, 280–1, 386
Kamatha 247
Kanji Swami Panth 49–50, 154 n., 192–3,
  198, 235, 238, 248 n., 390
Kapferer, Bruce 266
karma 2–3, 26–31, 37, 38, 43, 65–9,
  75–6, 77, 99–100, 162, 191–5, 197,
  199, 203, 212, 215, 217, 219, 225,
  226–9, 239, 243–5, 262–3, 306, 325,
  357–8
kaussagg 195, 201 n., 207–8, 209, 215, 248,
  267, 383
  see also asceticism
Keseriya-ji 101 n., 328
Keshi Kumar 384
keval gyan 42, 237, 244, 315, 377, 386
Khartar Gacch 3–4, 48–9, 50–1, 71–2,
  118, 134, 186, 193 n., 235, 238, 248 n.,
  393
  origins 50
  renouncers 2, 48, 52–3, 56, 141, 236,
    240, 261, 262–8
Khartar Gacch Sangh (Jaipur) 139–1, 350
kingship in Jainism 31, 33–4, 40, 89–92,

379, 382
kirti-dan 296–7, 298–9
knowledge:
  esoteric 224, 247, 376, 378
  of former lives 163, 217–18, 225, 237,
    337
  'of the difference' 233
  see also *keval gyan*
Krishna 39, 170, 369, 385
Kubera 41 n., 378
Kumar, Nita 132 n.
Kumarapala 91, 155
(Acarya) Kunda Kunda 50, 235 n., 252
kshetrapal 65, 66

Lakshmi 40, 285, 350, 364, 371, 372, 373,
  375, 378 n., 380
  puja 365–74, 380, 384–4
*lanchana*s 247 n.
Lath, Mukund 115 n.
lay-ascetic interaction 54–6, 60, 63–4
  distinguished from worldly life 299–
    300
  during alms-round 289, 309, 312–13,
    317–18, 320
  during Caturmas 98–9, 327–8
  during *updhan* 176, 178–9
  at *upashraya* 55, 329–31
lay Jain identities:
  as Baniyas 88–9
  as deities/kings 45, 46, 45–7, 89–92,
    146, 155, 323, 381; *see also* Indra
  as Hindus 94–6, 275, 281–6, 365, 368–
    70
  as *punyashali* 357, 373, 383; *see also* as
    deities; *see also* euergetism; Jain
    community, patronage
  as (formerly) Rajputs/warriors 89–92,
    155
  reconciliation 289, 320–3
  in relation to deities 45–7
  in relation to Jinas 30, 31, 34–5, 38–47
  in relation to renouncers 59–64, 151–2,
    173–5, 201–2, 289, 299, 305, 307–9,
    319–23
  see also *shramana*; *shravak*
Leach, Edmund 257, 377–8
Lévi-Strauss, Claude 334
listener, see *shravak*
Lodrick, Deryck O. 144 n., 145 n.

Madan, T. N. 14–15
magic/miracles 60, 61, 62, 65–80, 234,

247, 261, 376–7
Mahajan 88–9, 142
Mahavideha 37, 235
Mahavir Janam 141, 277–9, 334–5, 349–51
Mahavir Jayanti 110 n., 357
(Jina) Mahavir Swami 36, 39–47, 60, 163, 187, 212, 247 n., 249, 253–4, 257, 277, 301, 315, 338, 343, 364, 382, 384–6
Mahavir-ji temple 101
*mahavrat*s 173, 174
Malinowski, Bronislaw 131, 388–9
(Jina) Mallinath 56, 244 n., 247 n., 252–3
Manibhadra Vir 72 n.
mantras 37, 160 n., 199, 224, 232
    see also *nokar mantra*
marriage ceremonies 98, 139
Marriott, McKim 15 n., 293 n., 294
Maru Devi 36–7, 252
Mauss, Marcel 15–16, 294, 324, 326 n.
medical institutions (Jain sponsored) 142, 143–4
meditation 198, 208, 224, 267
Mena Sundari 70, 226, 263
merchants, *see* business
merit (*punya*), 27–9, 78, 112, 195, 197, 203–4, 212, 225, 297, 315, 321–3, 342, 357–8, 359, 385
migration 84, 89, 92–4, 97–8, 116–17, 126, 132,
mind 193, 199–200, 204
Mines, Mattison 138 n.
moksh 2, 35, 43, 227, 232, 364, 376, 390, 392
    not possible for deities 2, 41–2, 242, 361–2
    possible for householders 36–8, 188
    see also *siddha*
money, used in ritual 280, 371, 373–4, 383
Moore, G. E. 65, 78–9
muh-patti 1, 55, 259, *260*, 261, 267
murti 5 n.
Muslims, *see* Islam

Nahar, Shriman Amarcand-ji 230–43, 393
Nakora Bhairu-ji 71–4
Nakora-ji temple 54, 71–4, 75, 101
narrative, didactic 25–7, 99, 196, 219, 253, 267, 276–7, 295 n., 361, 391
    examples 29 (Gajsukumal), 37 (Bharat), 39–43 (life of Mahavir), 50 (Jineshvar

Suri), 51 (Jagaccandra Suri), 90 (caste origins), 91 (Jains and Rajput kings), 101 (origin of Nakora-ji), 101–2 (statues found underground), 111 n. (origin of *varna*s), 112 (Harikesha), 112–13 (the true Brahmin), 163 (Mahavir as a lion; Mahavir and the snake), 171 (Goyama), 187–8 (Anand Shravak), 194 (the theft of light), 217–18 (Rishabh's fast), 224–5 (Rohini), 226–7 (Shripal and Mena Sundari), 236–7 (Panna Dhay), 247 (Parshvanath, Dharanendra, and Padmavati), 253 (Mahavira and the snake), 277 (Mahavir and the *yaksha*), 303–4 (Puniya Shravak), 315 (giving kheer to renouncers), 376 (Gautam Swami becomes a Jain), 377 (Gautam feeds the yogis), 378–9 (Pundarika and Kundarika), 381–2 (Dhanna and Shalibhadra), 385–6 (Mahavir's *nirvan*)
    see also Jinas (life story of); Jinas (former lives of)
naukarsi 206, 216
naupad oli-ji 99, 220–3, 225–8, 241, 331
nav anga puja 249–50, 270–1
Neminath 171
Nietzsche, Friedrich 7
nirvan-puja 385–6
Nirvan Stavan 385
nivi 216, 218
nokar mantra 59–60, 136, 201, 208, 222, 283
    see also *mantras*
non-action 162, 164, 181, 192–5, 204, 219, 221, 229
non-attachment, see *aparigraha*
    see also attachment; emotions
Norman, K. R. 187–8, 214 n., 316 n.

Obeyesekere, Gananath 177, 267
O'Flaherty, Wendy Doniger, *see* Doniger
ogha 55, 259, 260, 261
Ortner, Sherry 39 n., 292–3
Oswals 88, 90, 91, 93, 97, 107, 110, 114, 117, 118, 140–1

paccakkhan 191, 195, 198, 201 n., 203, 206, 218–19, 279
Padampura temple 101 n., 267
padilehan 207–8, 210, 215
(Jina) Padmaprabhu 244 n.

Padmavati 65, 247, 248 n.
Palitana *96*
Panc Pratikraman Sutra 205
Panna Dhay 236–7
pap, see sin
parana 144
Parry, Jonathan 290 n., 291–2, 294, 300,
    324, 336 n., 360–1
(Jina) Parshvanath 36, 43, 72, 73, 223,
    244 n., 247–8, 384
Parvadas (Digambars) 117–18
Paryushan *57*, 98, 168, 275–86, 335
paushadh 177, 180
Peirce, Charles Sanders 152
persecution/violent attacks on Jains 94,
    104, 106–8
population 84–7, 89 n., 97–8, 120
porisi 216
prakshal 69–70, 71, 226
pratigya 175, 191
pratikraman 151, 180, 192–3, 195–8,
    201 n., 204–15, 223
    anti-dance 209–10
    confession 213–15
    intention and self 211, 213–15, 258
    lists of sins 211–12
    as reparation 215, 308
    at Samvatsari 279–80, 283–4
    variations 207
    when performed 205–6, 276, 279
pritibhoj 144
processions 96–7, 101–2, 109–10, 253,
    276, 277, 279, 281
puja 44–5, *46*, 76, 102, 126–7, 134–5,
    196–7, 201–2, 221, 223–4, 249–50,
    260, 271–3, 276, 284–5, 296, 298,
    317, 328, 330, 334
    see also *guru puja; gyan puja;* Lakshmi
    puja; nirvan-puja; snatra puja
*pujari*s 52
punya, see merit
purity 4, 43, 69–70, 232–3, 239, 244, 250,
    256, 271–4, 290, 291, 294, 302–4,
    307, 393
    see also Jain renouncers, purity of

Raheja, Gloria Goodwin 290 n., 292 n.,
    294
Raikas 62 n., 99, 100, 105
(Shrimad) Rajcandra 37, 233–43
    doctrine 235
Rajputs 89–92, 120–1, 125
Ram 160 n., 369, 384–5

Ramanandis 61
Ramayana (Jain versions) 108, 378 n.
Ranakpur 359
Ravana 108, 378 n., 385
renouncers:
    Buddhist 4–5, 299 n., 314 n., 325,
        326–7, 360–1
    Hindu 4–5, 15 n., 60–2, 360, 377
    see also Jain renouncers
reputation 146, 351 n., 354–8
    see also status
Reynell, Josephine 58, 136, 254, 256, 303,
    355
(Jina) Rishabh Dev 31–4, 36, 44, 56 n.,
    97 n., 111 n., 217–18, 247 n., 328,
    337, 377, 382, 383
ritual:
    associated with fasts 221–2
    clothes for 200, 204–5, 223
    equipment for 139, 200, 204–5, 206–7,
        207–8
    karmik effect of 192
    manuals for 196, 200–1, 204, 205 n.,
        368 n., 385
    and ritual acts 196–7
(Queen) Rohini 224–5, 381
Rohini 224 n.
rohini tap 224–5, 228–9
rosary, use of 197, 200, 201, 262, 267
Rousselet, Louis 281–2

sacred geography 86
Sahlins, Marshall 374
(Sathya) Sai Baba 61
saints, *see* Jain renouncers (as gurus);
    magic/miracles
samadhi maran, see fasting to death
samayik 151, 155, 177, 180, 195, 196,
    197–204, 304
    as act of merit 203–4
    body in 200–1, 202
    different for renouncers and laity
        202–3, 334
    lay Jains become like renouncers 201–3
    as meditation 198–200
    mental states in 200–1
    at renouncers' sermons 267
Samayik Sutra 197, 200–1
samosaran 32, 32–5, 38, 44, 163, 235,
    248–9, 251, 280–1, 296
samsar 2–3, 157, 160, 191–2, 194, 268
    monsoon rain 154, 157–8
Samvatsari 168, 205, 207, 387

samyak darshan 99, 157–8, 163, 238, 250, 252, 268
Saraswati 371, 384
sati 262–3 n.
sattar-bhedi puja 76
satya vrat 173, 179
saugandh, see *pratigya*
Schama, Simon 362–3
sectarianism 48–53, 85, 109–11, 117–18, 140, 238, 243–5, 251, 254–5 n., 340
self 15–21, 43, 151–2, 166–72, 182–3, 208, 210 n., 221, 391, 392
  in asceticism 151–2, 203, 233, 239, 239–42, 258
  moral topography of 152, 230, 239, 242–4, 274, 389–91
  in *pratikraman* 211, 213–15, 258
  in worship 47, 229, 249–50, 391, 392, 393
seth 89, 142, 146
sexuality 237, 241, 252, 254–8, 291, 305 n.
  see also *brahmacarya*; Jain renouncers, celibacy
shakti 62, 74–5, 257
Shalibhadra 380, 381–2
Shântâ, N. 214 n.
Shanti Vijay Suri 61–2, 100, 238, 255, 261
(Jina) Shantinath 223, *246*
(Jina) Shitalanath 244 n.
Shiva 257, 284, 363, 377
shramana/shramani 30–1, 113, 197, 305, 323
shravak/shravika 34–5, 38, 175, 188–9, 381
  as social status 183–7, 188
shravakacars 195 n., 295
Shreyam 217–18, 337, 380, 383
Shrimal Sabha 140–1
Shrimals 88, 90, 93, 110–11, 117, 118, 134, 350
Shripal 226
shrivatsa 244–5
shubh/labh 285, 323, 372–3, 376
Skinner, Quentin 300 n., 392
siddha 34, 59, 222, 223
  see also *moksh*
siddha-cakra:
  puja 46, 222
  yantra 46, 71, 221, *222*, 226, 256
Simandhar Swami 37–8
Simmel, Georg 337
sin (*pap*) 26, 28–9, 59, 164, 211–12, 297,
330, 359–60
renouncers' and householders' 203–4, 306–8
transferred between persons 290–1, 292–3, 303–4, 306–7, 313
Smith, Charles 338–9, 342
Smith, John D. 316 n.
snatra puja 44, 70, 223
soul 2–3, 152, 161, 212, 390–1
  capable of liberation 235
  discovered in confession 214
  and *karma* 17, 26–7, 28, 29, 34–5, 43
  innate qualities of 2–3, 244
  uncovered in asceticism 43, 47, 258
  see also *siddha*
Southwold, Martin 10–12
Sperber, Dan 41
spirit possession 266–7
Srivastava, Vinay Kumar 100, 105,
status:
  competition 144, 290–3, 324, 334–5, 336–44
  and consumption 339–40
  see also reputation
stereotypes of Jains 88, 103–4, 106–8
Stern, Henri 98
Stevenson, Mrs Sinclair 87 n., 161 n., 284 n., 336 n.
Sthanakvasis 48–9, 62, 93, 115, 141, 164, 174, 196 n., 369
sthapan-acarya 206–7, 214–15, 219, 267, 372
Strathern, Marilyn 131 n., 294 n., 319, 321
striver, see *shramana*
Sudharman Swami 60, 259, 386
supatra-dan 296, 298, 300–1, 316–17, 334, 337
Sutrakritanga Sutra 191–2, 210 n.
swamivatsal 144–5

tabulation 25–6, 212, 267, 297–9, 391–2
  examples 43 (types of *karma*), 173 (*anuvrats*), 179–81 (*baravrats*), 182 (14 *niyams*), 195–8 (6 *avashyaka*s), 205 (5 *pratikraman*s), 211 (8,400,000 living things), 211–12 (18 sins), 212–13 (22 inedibles), 216 (6 kinds of fast), 217 (*triphala* water), 295 (characteristics of a gift), 296 (types of gift)
Taiwan, temple funding on 147 n.
Tambiah, S. J. 174, 176, 177–8, 268, 326–7, 331 n., 370

tantrism 70, 106, 198, 224, 255
Taoism 255
Tapa Gacch 4, 48–9, 53, 57 n., 72 n., 118,
    270–1, 343
    origins 51
Tapa Gacch Sangh 139–41, 350
tapas/tapasya, *see* asceticism as heat;
    fasting
Taranapanth (Digambar) 118
Tattvartha Sutra 295
Taylor, Charles 152
temples (Jain) 55, 96–7, 100–3, 134, 138,
    246, 248 n.
    in Jaipur 96–7, 131, 133, 139–41, 145,
    285–6
Terapanthis (Shvetambar) 48–9, 93, 113,
    115, 141, 199, 248 n., 313, 369
    on *ahimsa* 164–5
    on gifts 300–1
Thapar, Romila 147
Tillotson, G. H. R. 123 n.
tithi 145
(Pandit) Todarmal 50
trade, *see* business
(Acarya) Tulsi 49, 164

ucit-dan 296
Upasakadasha Sutra 187–9
*upashraya*s 55, 138–40, 185, 198, 220,
    313, 344 n.
updhan 175–8, 205
upvas 216–17, 224
Uttaradhyayana Sutra 194, 212 n., 229,
    235, 384

Van der Veer, Peter 61, 256 n.
vandan 195–7, 207–8, 270, 309, 329–30
varshi dan 42, 45, 250, 295, 343
varshi tap 217–18, 220, 303–4
vasakshep 57, 270
(Jina) Vasupujya 224, 244 n.
vegetarianism 89, 94, 99–100, 153, 166

Jain and Western compared 162 n., 167
Veyne, Paul 142–3, 145, 146, 350–1
Vicakshan Shri-ji 54, 262–7, 270–1
vighai 168–9, 182, 218, 221
Vinay Prabha 385
vows 190–1, 218–20, 231, 235, 391
    see also *anuvrats*; *baravrats*; *mahavrats*;
    paccakkhan; *pratigya*; *pratikraman*;
    samayik

water:
    boiled and unboiled 154–9, 165–6,
    216–17, 306–7, 309
    filtered 158–9, 179
    triphala 216–17, 231
Weber, Max 6, 68, 83–4, 87 n., 126, 142,
    181 n., 331 n., 362–3
will/volition:
    in Jain vows 190–1
    in morality and ethics 18
Williams, Bernard 17–19, 162 n.
Williams, Michael 243 n.
Williams, R. 212 n., 212 n.–213 n., 295–6
Wittgenstein, Ludwig 9
women:
    capable of liberation 252–3
    morally responsible for family 304, 322,
    342, 355–7
    temptation to men 58, 237, 296
    see also asceticism gendered; gender and
    religious practice; idols, gender; Jain
    renouncers, gender; Jinas, gender

*yakshas/yakshi*s 41 n., 65, 112, 277, 284,
    378
Yalman, Nur 314 n.
*yantra*s 46, 70–1, 198, 221, 256
*yati*s 52, 70 n., 101, 139–40 n., 140, 255,
    333

zamikand 156–7, 213